# The
# WESTMINSTER
# CIRCLE

First published 2006
by Historical Publications Ltd
32 Ellington Street, London N7 8PL
Tel: 020 7607 1628

**ISBN 1-905286-15-5**
British Library Cataloguing-in-Publication Data
A catalogue record for this book is available from the British Library


Typeset in Palatino
Production by Liz Morell
Colour reproduction by Gilderson's, Pitfield Street N1
Printed by Edelvives, Zaragoza, Spain

# The
# WESTMINSTER
# CIRCLE

*The people who lived and worked*
*in the early town of Westminster, 1066-1307*

## David Sullivan

HISTORICAL PUBLICATIONS

# Contents

# List of Plates and Acknowledgments

# General Acknowledgments

My indebtedness to others – historians, creators or owners of illustrations and maps, library staff, my publisher, and my wife – for the knowledge and energy needed to create and complete this book is immense. Of living historians, the learned works of Barbara Harvey, Emma Mason, Gervase Rosser, and Richard Mortimer – and their example – have taught me most about Westminster (abbey and town), and the histories of both, and the period; and Emma Mason's *Westminster Abbey and its People, 1050-1216* has been particularly valuable for the earlier part of this period. The illustrations and maps have done much to illuminate and revitalize the history, and the maps drawn by Sophie Lamb, of the Museum of London, exactly reflect my wishes. The ever-helpful staffs of the Institute of Historical Research, the Library and Muniment Room at Westminster Abbey, the Westminster Local Studies and Archives Centre, and other libraries, have guided me in the search. John Richardson of my publishers has been kind, constructive and skilful in coping with my eccentricities of purpose and computing; and Ann has been her supportive, patient and understanding self over the years which we have traversed. All thanks to them all. Otherwise the road has largely been a long and lonely one.

While each of the illustrations and maps has been acknowledged individually in the List of Plates, I wish in particular to thank David Gentleman who has generously allowed me to use some of his pictures, showing historical reconstructions of events and scenes both at Westminster Abbey and in connection with the building by King Edward I of the original Eleanor Cross at Charing in 1292-94. Seven centuries later, all travellers on the Northern Line of the London Underground have had, and will continue to have, reason to thank the same artist for brightening their perhaps disheartening journeys or waiting-times, with his two latter pictures (and many others depicting the building of the same Eleanor Cross), in the form of a stimulating pictorial narrative – like a modern Bayeux Tapestry – at Charing Cross underground station. And like the old Tapestry, may the new one last more than nine centuries.

# Abbreviations and References

In the references for printed articles or records cited in footnotes or the bibliography, I have used the usual abbreviations for recognised historical journals or records; and if a reader is not familiar with these, any librarian will be able to help. Otherwise most abbreviations (which are never used in the main text) should either be obvious from the context, or are obviously shortened versions of familiar words: eg. 's. of' = son of; 'w. of' = wife of; 'ww. of' = widow of; 'ref.' = reference; 'Exch.' = Exchequer; kings' names sometimes shortened to H. I, or E. I or Edw. I, etc. Again in footnotes and eg. Index, I have often used WA and WM for the Abbey and Westminster; Bp. and A/Bp. for Bishop and Archbishop; eg. A/(Berking) for Abbot (Berking); Cant. for Canterbury.

A few not-immediately-clear references are:

| | |
|---|---|
| A-NS | = Anglo-Norman Studies |
| CRR | = *Curiae Regis Rotuli*, ie. rolls of the king's court |
| DB | = Domesday Book (always in the Phillimore edition): eg. 'DB. *Mdx* 4/3', means the 3rd holding (=Hampstead) of the 4th landholder (= Westminster Abbey) in the Phillimore volume for Middlesex |
| VCH | = Victoria County History : eg. 'VCH *Mdx* 9/92', means volume 9, page 92 of the VCH for Middlesex |
| WAC | = Westminster Abbey Charters, 1066-*c*.1214, the cartulary created by Dr Emma Mason |
| WAM | = Westminster Abbey Muniments, identified by numbers (for 99% of documents from the abbey's archive): eg 'WAM 17369'. See further Select Bibliography, p. 415 |
| 3/183 | = This format signifies volume [3] and page [183]: see eg. under VCH above |

# Preface

This book – and its predecessor – owe their lives to some words of G. M. Trevelyan which moved me when I was young. He was describing, if I remember it rightly, the satisfactions which he had had from seeking to recreate the lives of real people in the past – when he was not dealing with the more dusty issues of history, but trying to breathe a spark of new life into the men and women who had formed a past society or culture. He even spoke lightly, as I recall, of a historian having to try to peer into illuminated houses, in an effort to see the occupants revealed against the background of the dark outside.

But the occasion when his talk was given was wartime. For me the thread with his thought was soon broken and I had to put his words aside. Now, very many years later when opportunity has arisen, I have come back to them. But this resuscitating of once-living people is more easily dreamed of than achieved. When we are separated from them by a great gulf of centuries, the clear evidence and the familiarities which more modern history can rely on are lacking. So in this search for long-lost lives, there is often only a name, and perhaps an occupation, or a place and a tenuous date to enter into the record of a past life.

However, it is the context of the times – the contemporary history, into which any 'circle' of people are born – that can provide the true setting for the evidence of the way they lived. So my object in this book has been to weave a framework of the relevant national history, with what is known of the circle of people who lived or worked in Westminster and were most closely affected by what went on there, during the two to three centuries after the Norman Conquest. This is particularly important in a place like Westminster which began in the twelfth century to become the very hub of that national history.

I could never claim to have seen into the illuminated house of any resident of Westminster (as the professor might have sought). But to try to identify where any resident may have lived, and from what background he came, and what he did, and for whom, and with what success, and what others he may have met in the street, or worked with – any such questions appear to me to be as important for a better understanding of an early society as other more sophisticated issues of history; and in touch with the temper of our own time.

Quite separately I have two regrets. First, about the abbey's manor of Hendon. I included Hendon in some detail in *The Westminster Corridor*, since it was one of the main estates, lying along the 'corridor' of the old Watling Street, on which the abbey was particularly dependent. The inclusion there of some of its nearby estates seemed to provide a frame for the abbey and its home-ground of Westminster, as I hope the contrasting manors of Eye and Hampstead may do in the present book. But although in this book I have dealt briefly with the later relationship of the abbey with the principal manor of Hendon, there were other 'sub-estates' and many other aspects of Hendon's manorial history with which I have not had the time or space to deal.

Secondly, I had orginally conceived a trilogy of books to deal with the history of Westminster and its abbey during the medieval period. But the learning-process and research for this book has been protracted and my programme has become so retarded that I fear that, with the weight of years, no further sequel to this second book will be possible.

# Introduction

This book is a sequel to the story which *The Westminster Corridor* began, and which ended with the Norman conquest of England.

On the 6th January 1066, even before the Normans had set foot in England, the abbey church of St. Peter in Westminster – by then rebuilt, from wood to shining stone – stood ready to receive the burial of its second builder, King Edward known as 'the Confessor'. So when on Christmas day, at the end of the same dramatic year, the new Norman conqueror of England was crowned in the same church, to the over-loud acclaim of the Normans present, the small village of Westminster had already witnessed – within the space of an eventful twelve months – a royal burial, a foreign invasion and the coronation of an alien king.

That year of 1066 provided the climax of the last century of Anglo-Saxon and Danish rule after the foundation of the abbey church of St. Peter in the previous century. The context of those earlier years both in Westminster and in some of the abbey's nearby lands was the theme of my earlier book.

This book now covers the period in Westminster from the time of the Conquest and of Domesday Book twenty years later, through the reigns of the later Norman kings to a turning point in the turbulent but creative life of the first Angevin king, Henry II, in the twelfth century. From there it leads through the subsequent explosions during the thirteenth century, of population, enterprise, and, finally, monastic temperament.

The main objective of this book is to turn as much light as possible onto the life of early people in Westminster, by rediscovering, in their proper sequences of history and context, many of those who lived and worked in and around the waking town and the abbey, and in two of the abbey's nearby manors in what is now Greater London.

Of course much of the history of this emerging town is also bound up with the lives and actions of the kings themselves, and with the management of an England which they were beginning to administer more and more through reformed organs of government, now based in or around their royal palace in the town of Westminster. Equally, much of this history also reflects the personalities and conduct of the monks, and in particular of their abbots whose power was sovereign over the town and land of Westminster. So both these two themes, of town and church, form major parts of this book, and being contemporaneous, each part has to be interwoven with the other.

My aim has been to enable readers to follow this story in its chronological sequence – after they have initially seen, in the first three chapters, the topographical background of Westminster and the settlements of which it was composed during these early centuries.

The limiting factor in any story relating to such an early but seminal period is, of course, the extent of surviving evidence. But a hundred years after the Conquest, a progressive movement in the re-location of government and its institutions to Westminster was already taking place during and after Henry II's reign (1154-1189). This accelerated even more when shortly afterwards records in England were not only being made more frequently in writing, but by deliberate policy began to be preserved more systematically. The result of this progressive change was that after about the year 1200 the number of surviving records began to increase. At the same time the population and the life of Westminster were rapidly expanding.

So both national and private records were now more likely to survive, and at the abbey itself many hundreds of transactions between private people, and also between individuals and the abbey itself, have been recorded in the form of admirably succinct 'charters' – many of them no more than two to three inches from top to bottom. Within limits, each of them tells or hints at a story of its own, and helps to create brief chronicles of people and the events in their lives and occupations. At the same time the expanding *national* records also enable us to see some of the early features of personal life in Westminster, between the more conventional events of English history such as wars and other major social forces.

Inevitably in the stories which such sources help to recreate there are gaps and problems which are difficult or sometimes impossible to fill or resolve. But these are no more than the ruses that History plays, as I said in the introduction to *The Westminster Corridor*, on those who seek to read the past. So for information about personal and private life and human relationships in the town, I have often had to rely on no more than the bare bones which such charters disclose and the inferences which can be drawn from them.

### Method
As in the previous volume, I have tried to provide a choice for the reader, between a limited or a more extensive participation in this book. The main text contains, I hope, a clear and readable story which can be understood on its own, if the reader wishes. But the footnotes, given on the same page in the text, serve several different purposes: they identify many of the sources, for those who need them; they may add contexts and explanations; and give signposts to other associated passages in the book which relate

to the people or events in question. So for the inquisitive reader, the frequent need to chase further information lost in footnotes somewhere at the end of a book, or to scour the index, can be avoided or at least reduced. Past readers' reactions to this method in *The Westminster Corridor* have confirmed my own thoughts about its effectiveness.

### Some of the points of interest
This may be one of the first times on which the stages of the very early development of such an important medieval town and the identification of so many of its inhabitants and their lives during a period of two and a half centuries has been attempted in detail and in chronological form.

There are clear indications that the town of Westminster initially grew out of a number of identifiable settlements, not solely as one centre developing outwards. Of course there was, and there remained, one centre – the obvious one, where the abbey and the palace stood from before the Conquest. But other topographical and historical factors, such as the existence of a crucial crossing at Charing, where early roads met (with even a much earlier history of an active Saxon settlement nearby), and the other influences of the two ancient main roads leading to and from the city of London, mean that the town grew together from a number of quarters, rather than by expansion solely from one nucleus.

The local descriptions in some of the charters help us to identify much more clearly a rough road system in Westminster *and* its adjoining manor of Eye (now Pimlico and Belgravia, with Hyde Park and half of Mayfair), by at least the thirteenth century. The same sources also enable the location of the old village of Eye beside the boundary stream of the Tyburn, at the site of the present Buckingham Palace, to be authentically established, and they help to show that the date of the creation of this village may have been as late as the mid-thirteenth century.

With the help of the geography disclosed by the charters, new maps can now show graphically and dependably how even early medieval 'traffic' in Westminster could make its way around the central area of our modern St. James's Park, to reach the main routes towards the west, or south-westwards towards Chelsea.  From the earliest years this area of St. James continued to form an agricultural oasis for the abbey's tenants, until many centuries later when an acquisitive Henry VIII was able to snap it up for his hunting – together with his other seizures round the West End – for which ironically all of us, as inheritors, should be humbly grateful.

Some evidence has survived in the charters which I have described, to show the character of the more urban streets of Westminster (such as 'King Street', Longditch, Tothill Street and Charing Street), including the patterns of housing in certain quarters, the course of some early building developments and even the exact measured sizes of sundry plots for individual houses.  Several of these measurements given for plots on the slope between Charing Street (part of our modern Strand) and the river Thames spell out the larger houses which were the forerunners of the later well-known and grander mansions of the magnates, which in later centuries lined that slope and its shoreline.

But above all, the identities, occupations and lives of several groups of the Westminster residents which I have illustrated, and the activities of the abbots, and of resident kings, and the work of their institutions of the financial exchequer, the law courts, the royal councils of magnates and later their emergent parliaments, as described throughout this book, may help to provide an ever-changing picture of what life may have been like for people in an early and unique medieval town.

# CHAPTER 1

# Context and contours of a young town

## The abbey and its town, 971-1307: a summary

Nearly a hundred years before the Norman Conquest, two anglo-saxon royal charters in favour of the new monks of Westminster preserved from oblivion all that we know about the district *at that time.* From about 971 the first abbey was being built in wood, rising above the flat marshes. In favour of these newly-arrived monks, the two charters defined in old English the boundaries and other topographical features of rural Westminster with which the monks were endowed.

The ensuing hundred years after the abbey had been founded saw two spectacular changes in both the physical appearance and the status of Westminster — firstly, the great Romanesque rebuilding and enlargement of the abbey in stone by King Edward the Confessor after about 1045; and secondly, the final establishment of a royal palace on the Westminster bank of the river Thames. Apart from these two major changes, little detail is known about the development of a 'vill' at Westminster itself at that time. But towards the end of this hidden period the invasion of the Normans in 1066 severed the line of the anglo-saxon kings; yet the invaders endorsed the new national status of the stone abbey in Westminster, which they deemed fit even for their first Norman crowning. Twenty years later, in 1086, the Domesday Survey projected for the first time a succinct but informative picture of the rest of Westminster, its population and the manorial activities of the villagers.

Nearly another hundred years were then to elapse before more reliable topographical and social details about the district of Westminster began slowly to emerge in the twelfth century. It is only in the second half of that century, during Henry II's reign (1154 – 1189), that the main features of the embryonic Westminster town and its rural neighbourhood begin to be more visible to us. Selected by the king as the main centre for a reformed administration, Westminster began to acquire a swelling population, a growing importance and an expanding economy.

Then throughout the century after 1200 the physical setting and the development of the various sectors of the town swim more and more into our focus. Conditions in the town were thriving, and in about 1245 the devout King Henry III began and, by the time of his death in 1272, had completed much of his ambitious plan for a second rebuilding of the abbey, this time in the new Gothic style. By the point at which his son Edward I died in 1307, the town of Westminster had reached the peak of its first stage of substantial growth.

But towards the end of the century the abbey, which had flourished during its rebuilding, fell into a trough of embarrassing calamities in the years before and after 1300. Having recently been headed by four capable and enterprising abbots in succession, it eventually became the victim of violent domestic disputes and a concluding explosion between the fourth of these abbots and his prior, created by a clash of intemperance in each of their personalities.

Finally the nearly contemporaneous deaths in July and December of the same year, 1307, of the king Edward I and the abbot Walter of Wenlock left both the nation and the abbey free of their obstinate, though competent, leaders – but each now at the mercy of an incompetent successor at its helm, and full of foreboding as to its immediate future.

## To begin with: the anglo-saxon charters

The details of the two charters for Westminster have already been described, both visually and verbally, in *The Westminster Corridor*.[1] In brief, the geographical scene was that the boundaries of the Westminster estate were defined by rivers on three sides: on the south-east, by the curving and at that time the marshy and wide-flowing Thames; and on the east and west sides of the estate, by the tumbling streams, the Fleet and the Tyburn, whose sources lay on the ridge of Hampstead and Highgate.

Laterally, the manor of Westminster was dominated by the two great Roman roads which ran east and west and gave access to and from the city of London – namely the east-west section of *Watling Street* (our Oxford Street and Holborn); and *Akeman Street* (as our 'Strand' is oddly named in one of the two charters, with an allusion to a *strande* in the other), which after the Charing crossroad, curved up towards the level which is now Piccadilly, leading towards the south-west.[2] It was the former of these two roads which acted as the northern boundary of the Westminster estate.

To the west, beyond the Westminster boundary marked by the Tyburn stream, there lay 'the little manor of Eia', which was given to the abbey within twenty years after the Domesday Survey. Eia (usually called 'Eye' in this book) included the important districts now called Pimlico, Belgravia and Hyde Park and became closely bound up with the development of Westminster and its abbey.

The geology of the Westminster estate was, at its lowest point, the marshy silt in which a gravel island lay, on which the abbey

stood; with further inland from the river Thames, a higher sloping shelf of river gravel where Villiers Street, the Haymarket and St. James's Street now rise upwards (the latter towards the Piccadilly level); and a second, more northern, shelf of gravel, to which Regent Street and Park Lane, with Baker Street beyond, now incline more gently up.[3]

But of the other physical features of the estate at that time, the information is sparse. The hub of the district was, of course, the abbey's gravel island near the Thames bank. There, with royal help, the small wooden church had originally been built in the tenth century; only to be rebuilt in stone by King Edward the Confessor shortly before the Norman Conquest. Meanwhile it had been joined in Westminster by a royal palace, wedged between the site of the abbey and the Thames river bank. So, already in the tenth and eleventh centuries, church and state had uniquely congregated within a circle of a few hundred yards – as they remain to this day, nearly a thousand years later.

Within the boundaries of Westminster, the most significant of the other topographical features of which we know from the two early charters were *'cyrringe'*, *'cuford'* and *'bulunga fen'*. In view of their relevance to later history in Westminster, each of these deserves a re-emphasis : –

**(a)** From *Akeman street* (or *'strande'*), as given in the Westminster charters, one can readily identify the position of *cyrringe* as the settlement of Charing (round the Trafalgar Square area). The name *'cyrringe'* in old English meant a bend, such as there

---

1 For the effect of the two charters: see coloured Maps M and H, after p. 96, in *The Westminster Corridor*; and pp. 79 ff. and 166-7 of that book.  For the later Domesday entry, see *ibid.*, Plate 8 (p. 86) and pp. 136 ff.

2 The Holborn-Oxford Street stretch was known as 'Watling Street', *The Westminster Corridor*, pp. 166-7. 'Akeman Street' was the *older* Roman name for the road from St. Albans to Bath, but this name is also used in the second Westminster charter for our present 'Strand'; see *ibid*, pp. 167, 80 and 82.  At that time the road did run closer to the 'strand' of the marshy Thames which lapped the bottom of the slope up to the road.

3 All these levels are still clearly visible as you walk or drive through the centre of the West End of London.

undoubtedly was, and still is, to carry the extended line of the 'strand' road up the first gravel terrace, which now curves up the slope shown by the present Haymarket and Lower Regent Street to the higher and drier shelf on which the Piccadilly road stands.[4] It is clear that even then the settlement at Charing was a nodal point, since (because of the great bend of the Thames at this point) it was only from there that another road or track could and did diverge southwards from the main road, towards both the abbey and the royal palace at the centre of Westminster itself.

Curiously this road, which was to become the primary road of a busy Westminster, lying in part on the line of the present Whitehall, seems only to have received a formal name two or three centuries later, when (whatever description of it may have earlier been used in ordinary speech) it began to be known officially as 'the king's street', and even later 'King Street'.

So Charing was always an obvious place for a settlement, and both its significance and size were later to grow widely until it became merged with the main community of Westminster, which at first had been centred around the palace and the abbey and then spread up 'King Street' to meet the Charing settlement.[5] In any case, one must remember that Charing had already shared an even earlier and important history, when a settlement lay in its neighbourhood during the period from about 700 to 860. This settlement had arisen at the time when the Saxons had been peacefully active in *Lundenwic* (Aldwych to Westminster), outside the city of London, before the main Viking attacks were directed against the city.[6]

**(b) The name *cuford* ('the cowford')** which appeared in both of the anglo-saxon charters for Westminster, is a name which survived for at least 250 years after those charters, and probably for yet longer – from about 971 until at least the 1240s and after. By that time it had become '*kuford*', still acting presumably as a 'cow-ford' through the Tyburn stream. The Tyburn, on its way southwards towards the Thames from the present Mayfair area, had to cross both the old Roman highway, now Piccadilly, and a lower roughly-parallel road (later to be called *Spitalstrete*), which also ran from the Charing crossroad, roughly along the route of our present Pall Mall in a curving direction towards Knightsbridge. So the ford known as 'cowford' must have run originally through the Tyburn stream, where the stream crossed one or other of these roads.

Probably this crossing by ford was over the lower of the two roads. One reason for this is that since its name *as a ford* was still being used even in the 1240s, this suggests that at that time the road still ran *through* the river instead of over a bridge. In contrast the higher road now known as Piccadilly may already have crossed over the Tyburn by a stone bridge. The middle of the thirteenth century was a period when all the skills and materials for stone bridges were available; when a number of private houses were being built of stone; when population had grown and was continuing to grow; and when the main traffic for London and its neighbourhood, using the upper road, must have greatly increased. It seems reasonable to assume that by then a bridge had already been built to carry the higher road over the stream; but the lower road still had its ford for the cows.[7]

4   See *The Westminster Corridor*, p. 82, note 15, and Honeybourne, 'Charing Cross Riverside' L.T.R. 21 (1958) p. 44. I was wrong in giving a capital 'C' to 'cyrringe' (*cierring*) in the translation of the second charter set out on p. 167 of *The Westminster Corridor* and in the text at p. 55.

5   See at pp. 26-30 below. For Charing and the roads of Westminster, see the double-spread Map A, on Plates 2-3.

6   See *The Westminster Corridor*, pp. 20-1.

7   The later bridge carrying the Piccadilly road over the Tyburn, which was known as 'Stone Bridge' in the C17 (see Gatty, *Mary Davies and Ebury*, Plate 31), and as 'Kingsbridge' at an earlier date, see Prideaux, 'Notes on Salway's Plan', L.*Top.Rec.* iii. (1906) 62-3; and Barton *Lost rivers of London*, pp. 36, 37, 43 n. 2. The 'lower road' (Spitalstrete) must also have acquired a bridge over the Tyburn at some date later than the thirteenth century, or the old bed of the stream may have been culverted beneath the road.

Another factor which confirms that the ford lay on the lower road is that in the 1240s (when the name *'kuford'* was still being used for the purpose of identifying the location of adjoining land) the lower road passed the comparatively new leper Hospital of St. James which stood by that time on the site of the present St. James's Palace. By then the road had already become known as 'Spitalstrete', the hospital road.[8] It was on the side of this lower road that a landowner, Beatrix the heiress of her father Brungar (a duelling 'champion')[9] owned land in the neighbourhood of Spitalstrete, including one acre which she was about to donate to the abbot of Westminster and his monks. That acre lay, we are told, 'at *kuford'*.[10] So the old English name for the ford over the lower road had survived already for at least two to three centuries, and since it was still current in at least the 1240s, it also probably continued to survive for some time thereafter.

**(c) And then there is *bulunga fen*. The** position in which that name appears in the description of the boundaries detailed in the first anglo-saxon charter for the estate of Westminster leaves no doubt that it was the name at that time for the marshy area which later became known as the 'Tothill Fields' (in many different spellings) or the great 'Field (*campus*) of Tothill'. This was an area which remained substantially unbuilt-on for many centuries.[11] Even its bleakness and prevailing

dampness, which in due course required much dyking, and its vulnerability to river flooding contributed to it becoming a good hay and pasture area. The southernmost sector of the Tothill Fields, next door to both the Thames and the western branch of the Tyburn river, became in due course the largest and principal meadow in the manor, and was known, at least in the thirteenth century, as the 'Great meadow of Westminster' – until by the 1290s it became regarded as part of the adjoining manor of Eye, and was called *Markedemede* or Marketmead.[12] It is also no accident that the *'common pasture of the vill of Westminster'* and *'the place where champions are wont to fight'* were located conveniently in the northern part of these Tothill Fields.[13]

**An eye-witness at the abbey, c. 1065**

At least by 1050 these early marsh areas in the southern part of Westminster had been brought under some form of agricultural control. Shortly before the Norman Conquest an unknown eye-witness, the unnamed biographer of King Edward the Confessor, saw them and described the region round the abbey as *'a delightful place, surrounded with fertile lands and green fields, near the main channel of the river which bore abundant merchandise of wares for sale, from the whole world to the town [London] on its banks'.*[14] As the rebuilding of the new stone abbey rose slowly above the flat landscape, one can picture a pattern of water meadows drained by the kind of ditches which

---

8  See *The Westminster Corridor*, p. 82, note 15. St James's Hospital had been founded, probably during Henry II's reign, to house a small group of leprous women (attended by an even smaller group of monks), at a place in the land west of Charing; on the site of the present St James Palace.

9  For Brungar *'Athleta'*, see WAD 555, WAM 17314, and pp. 49 and 393 below. For the use of such a champion in a real 'trial by battle' relating to land in Westminster, and also for the site in Westminster where such battles took place, see pp. 34 and 49 below, and WAMs 17444 and 17392A.

10  WAMs 17415 and 17110. Beatrix's acre also adjoined 'St. Edward's watercourse', for which see both this and next page. The hospital road appears to have begun somewhere near the start of the present Mall at Charing and then veered slightly northwards to the line of Pall Mall, to pass the hospital on its northern side, see *Survey Of London*, vol. 29, p. 322, and then to continue across part of our present Green Park towards Knightsbridge.

11  Even as late as 1807, see the view from south-west of the abbey on Tothill Fields, on Plate 3 on p.57.

12  See chapters 19 and 20 below, at pp. 336 and 356-9.

13  For the Field of Tothill, see also p. 58 below. For the 'common pasture', see *ibid.* and WAMs 17340, 17345, 17519 and 17522. For the place 'where champions are wont to fight', see WAM 17392A, and p. 49.

14  See *The Westminster Corridor*, pp. 136 and 145.

Plate 1. A 'reconstruction' of the first rebuilding of the abbey at Westminster, drawn by David Gentleman. Built originally in wood, the abbey was being rebuilt in stone shortly before the Norman Conquest. King Edward the Confessor had had it redesigned in the new Romanesque style, and as depicted here, he no doubt watched over its reconstruction closely, as its next rebuilder undoubtedly did. The second rebuilding – by King Henry III in the thirteenth century – was effected in the even newer Gothic style. See p. 63, and chapter 15 at p. 241.

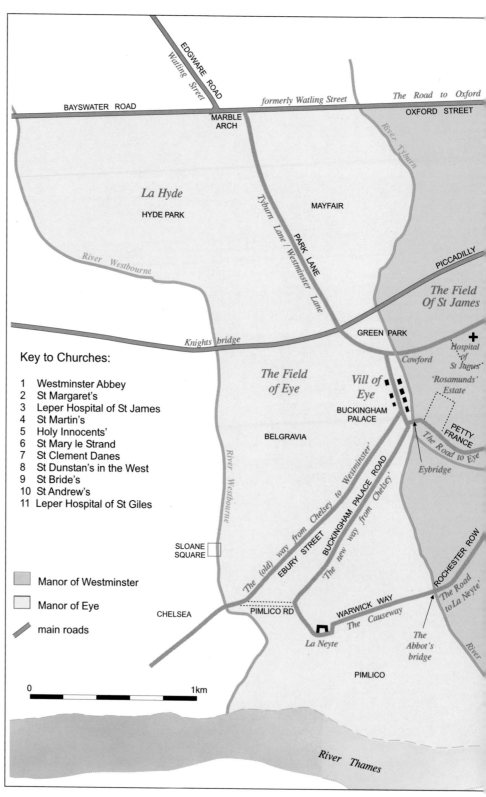

Plates 2-3. Map A.

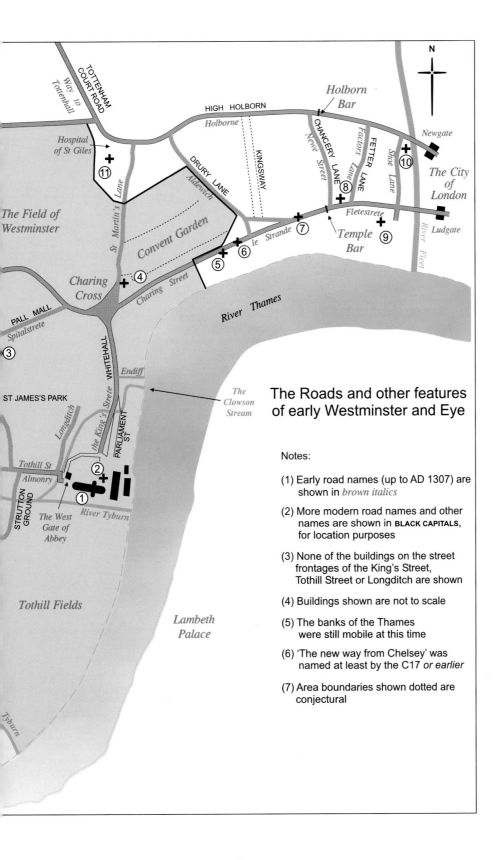

The Roads and other features
of early Westminster and Eye

Notes:

(1) Early road names (up to AD 1307) are
    shown in *brown italics*

(2) More modern road names and other
    names are shown in BLACK CAPITALS,
    for location purposes

(3) None of the buildings on the street
    frontages of the King's Street,
    Tothill Street or Longditch are shown

(4) Buildings shown are not to scale

(5) The banks of the Thames
    were still mobile at this time

(6) 'The new way from Chelsey' was
    named at least by the C17 *or earlier*

(7) Area boundaries shown dotted are
    conjectural

Plate 4. The abbey's late-Norman Chapel of St Katherine, drawn by David Gentleman, was built within the infirmary quarters, as prayer was part of the healing treatment for sick monks brought into the chapel. But it was also used for meetings, of eg. the kings' 'great councils' and even for legal inquiries. See pp. 108, 165 n.55, 192, 221.

later became such a feature of Westminster.[15] The presence of much meadowland and pasture was all the more necessary, since the Domesday survey was to record the existence of at least ten teams of plough oxen in Westminster, needed for the purpose of dealing with the acreage of arable land which Westminster also enjoyed then; with enough spare meadow as well to justify an eleventh team. In theory this could have meant a herd or herds of up to eighty oxen which needed to be fed; even without allowing for any spare animals.

## The watercourse of Edward the Confessor, king and saint

Another feature which may have been visible in Westminster during the first rebuilding of the abbey was a development of the water supply for the abbey. In tune with that rebuilding, the complement of monks was in due course to rise from twelve to eighty, and it would be astonishing if thought had not also been given to the effect of such a change on the water needs of the abbey. There is no direct contemporary evidence in the eleventh century about this, but it is clear that a strong tradition existed in Westminster about the part played in this respect by Edward the Confessor. Nearly 200 years later this tradition (stated as fact, rather than mere conjecture) and the surviving evidence of work attributed to him began to be referred to in a number of different legal records and in different connections. Perhaps the first such occasion was the grant already mentioned above, of one acre *at kuford* which the landowning Beatrix, daughter of Brungar, made to the abbey in about the 1240s. She identified the position

of her acre by stating that it lay next to *'the street, on the east'* (Spitalstrete), and on the west, *'where it descends to the watercourse of St Edward'*.[16]

This 'watercourse' was also used as a landmark to identify the locality of another nearby property, this time a particular house standing on the same street, (now given its name, Spitalstrete), in the neighbourhood of the leper hospital. On several successive occasions this house was subsequently sold and resold during the period between about 1270 and 1306.[17] During this period, for example, John Curteis, the trumpeter of the king, Edward I, was reselling the house in 1299 and described it as lying *'with the watercourse of the Blessed King Edward on its west'*. The last occasion of resale when the same phrase was used was in 1306. But after Edward I's death in 1307 no further reference to 'the watercourse of St. Edward' appears.

There can be no doubt that the 'watercourse' must have carried water from the Tyburn stream, which itself crossed Spitalstrete in the present Green Park, west of the leper Hospital of St. James. But whether it refers to the old bed of the river itself (after improvements attributed to Edward the Confessor), or to some new bed for it, or to a canal fed by the Tyburn, one cannot say with any certainty – although the first of these possibilities seems the more likely. The fact that many of the later mentions of this 'watercourse' occurred during the reign of a new King Edward (Edward I) does suggest that people used the description for a kind of flattery, because in Edward I's reign they had simply become conscious of the eponymous repetition of a royal name, for the first time since Edward the Confessor's reign, about 200 years before?[18]

15 Less than a century after DB, Alexander Neckham wrote in 1178 that on approaching London from the NW., the first he saw of London was the central tower of the abbey at Westminster, Maclean, *Med. Eng. Gardens* 63. For the Westminster ditches, see pp. 52 ff. below.
16 WAM 17415. King Edward had been canonised in 1161, see *The Westminster Corridor*, p. 61, and pp. 84-5 below. Beatrix's grant was made for the benefit of the anniversary of the monk Gregory of Staines, and Harvey, *WA Estates*, 392 attributes the founding of this 'anniversary' to Edward I's reign, but it should be earlier than that. The grant should be dated, in my view, to about the 1240s when Richer of the Cross was reeve, because he was a witness *as reeve* to the charter. Cf. Pearce, *Monks*, p. 52.
17 WAMs 17115, 17116, 17111, 17112, 4835.
18 Edward I had been significantly reminded by his father that he was named after Edward the Confessor.

It so happens that these later mentions of the watercourse were made at a time when another 'water feature' was recorded in Westminster. By 1285, during Edward I's reign, the monks clearly possessed an 'underground aqueduct' for water, running from the northern part of the manor of Eye, in the area of either the present Mayfair or Hyde Park, when they granted a lease of land in 'Cresswellfeld' in that area, with a reservation of their right to repair their own pipe system.[19]  Either this grant might relate to water from the Westbourne river and the springs of water in the Paddington area; or it may be that the small flurry of later charters referring to 'St. Edward's watercourse' (all made by lay donors, not by the abbey) were designed to emphasise that in addition to water from the Westbourne, other water still came to the abbey (and perhaps  to other properties) from the Tyburn as a result of works which the older King Edward had carried out.[20]

## The Domesday Survey, 1086

The next surviving information about 'the vill of Westminster' comes from Domesday Book, twenty years after the Conquest. This too has been detailed in *The Westminster Corridor*.[21]  In the Domesday survey we find the meadowlands large enough to feed eleven ploughs, with ten ploughs actually there. But more important, for the image of a vill, were the *'25 houses of the abbot's men-at-arms and other men'* (the latter, surely, the main lay servants of the enlarged abbey).  Some of these houses no doubt lay within the abbey's precinct, with others perhaps clustered close at hand but outside the precinct wall: made of timber, wattle and daub, and almost certainly with none of them in stone at that early date.[22]

Then there were the Domesday villagers, also accomodated in the area of the vill: one with 100-120 acres for himself, nine with perhaps 15 acres, one with five acres, and 41 small cottagers with 'gardens' (gardens paid-for collectively; almost allotment-style): gardens being a physical feature which became a regular presence in Westminster for the next eight centuries, both for private sustenance and enjoyment and later also to take advantage of the insatiable food demands of the palace, the abbey, the expanding town and inevitably the city of London and its other suburbs nearby.[23]

Nearby too on the bank of the Thames there now stood the palace, but that was unrecorded because such a possession as the king's palace was above the purpose of Domesday Book. The palace's complement of staff was also unspecified - save perhaps for the 30 unfortunate cottager serfs, who in the terms used in the Survey hardly counted as people: human chattels which (as the Book itself makes clear) the king still 'owned' in Middlesex.[24]  The picture is already a neat vignette of an early medieval community, shortly after a violent conquest.

19   *The Westminster Corridor*, pp. 43-4; and p. 282 below; and cf. p. 345 (new 'farms' in that area).

20   If water did still come from the Tyburn, this runs counter to the suggestion, made by Barton *Lost Rivers of London*, 36, 41-2, that probably water from the Tyburn was not then being used for the abbey.  I was inclined to follow this in *The Westminster Corridor,* 41-42 and 43, not then knowing of the details of these later charters.  The Tyburn was even called a 'torrent' (*torrens*) in the present Mayfair area, see p. 282 n.80 below.

21   *The Westminster Corridor*, Plate 8, p. 86, and pp. 136 ff.

22   By contrast, at Bury St. Edmund's, the town surrounding another great abbey, no less than 342 houses were recorded, all of them built since the Conquest on arable land belonging to that abbey, see DB2, *Suffolk* 14/167 (f. 372a). It too had men-at arms quartered at it, but 34 of them, more than the 15 at Westminster.  A comparable survey of the position as to lay houses in Westminster would have been fascinating, but no doubt the scale would have been very different because Bury had clearly been subject to an organised and well-planned development, as its town-plan of streets bordering its 'Norman Tower' still shows to this day.

23   For Westminster gardens, see pp. 27 and 33-34 below.

24   DB *Mdx*. 1/1 and 2.  For discussion about the palace and the part played by these cottagers, and the curious nature of the king's few possessions still held by him in Mdx, see *The Westminster Corridor*, pp. 140-1.

## The next hundred years

After the great Survey, a comparative silence falls as to changes taking place in the physical development of the vill. It was a period when difficult and sometimes brutal adjustments were having to be made in society, as a result of the Normans' subjugation of the English and their imposition of new restraints upon the nation.

However, before the eleventh century was out, the Westminster monks who now had a powerful Norman abbot, Gilbert Crispin, received a useful benefaction from one of the other Norman overlords in Middlesex. Geoffrey de Mandeville, one of William I's barons, had received a vast fief in about ten counties after the Conquest, including a number of sizeable estates in Middlesex. In 1082, four years before the Domesday Survey was complete, he was also given what he called his 'little manor' of Eye (Eia) immediately next door to Westminster.[25] Before 1100 he had already shown other generosity towards the abbey, as well as considerable concern for the spiritual health of his own soul and the souls of his two successive wives and his children, which he hoped to benefit by charitable gifts made by him. And now he gave his little manor of Eye to the abbey.[26]

Eye thereafter became doubly significant to successive abbots, first as the closest source of produce and stock during virtually the whole of the rest of the medieval period, and secondly and later, in and after the 1220s, as the area where they were able to purchase and keep for their own personal and private use a country house, called La Neyte, with its own lands attached, away from the busy work of the monastery. In due course the manor also became intertwined with Westminster socially, with Westminster residents acquiring cultivatable land and houses in Eye, and Eye residents not only acquiring houses or lands in Westminster but also contributing to the social and commercial life of the town.

Another significant factor in the early years of the Norman period in Westminster's history was the 'ruinous vacancy' which occurred in the abbacy after the death of Gilbert Crispin, the Norman abbot who presided over the abbey from shortly before the Domesday Survey until 1117. When Abbot Crispin died towards the end of 1117, it was over three years before his successor, Herbert, was confirmed as the new abbot, and during those years the abbey was administered by officers appointed by the king (now Henry I), who exercised his royal right to take in hand and to manage the abbey's assets and lands in his own interests during such a vacancy.[27]

This brief and obscure interval may have been crucial to the detriment of the abbey's interests in the town of Westminster because – as we will see later – several of the abbey's lands and assets appear to have been alienated to others by the king's officers, or even by the monks themselves, and proved to be difficult for them to recover in later years.

These initial significant events were in turn followed by the more disturbed and even more overcast years of the savage civil war between King Stephen and the Empress Matilda, with its troublesome periods of prelude and aftermath (1135 - 1154). So one reaches the accession of the first Angevin king, Henry II of Anjou, just after mid-century, with

25 DB. *Mdx* 9/1. For the abbey's Norman abbot at this time, Gilbert Crispin, see pp. 70-73 below.
26 WAC 436. The grant was expressed to be '*for my soul and that of my first wife Alice and those of my sons and daughters, and I wish my second wife Lesceline and my son and heir, William, to be associated with this act of charity*'. See pp. 327-8 below for further details; and also *The Westminster Corridor*, p. 84n. and coloured Map L (after p. 96) for Geoffrey's extensive lands in Edmonton, Enfield and Northolt in Middlesex.
27 When an abbot died, his office became vacant until a new abbot had been appointed or elected. The king (by 'regalian' right) became temporarily entitled to act as the manager of the abbey, ie. to appoint his own men to control the administration and finances of the abbey's estates, and to take the profits so long as the vacancy continued. Since the king was often involved in the process of election or appointment of a new abbot, it was within his power to delay a replacement, and meanwhile to benefit in taking the profits.

little clear evidence of what obvious changes may have been taking place within Westminster itself. The comparatively quiet life of the abbey had of course continued even during these periods, and some (but not all) of the actions of the abbots and their monks are known to us. But in particular they or the king's officers do appear to have granted away many significant estates of land within the manor of Westminster itself, as we shall see later.[28] But with the exception of these important transactions, few of the monks' activities during the first half of the eleventh century appear to have had a bearing on any ascertainable configuration of Westminster and its neighbouring areas.

However when Henry II, aged twenty one, came to the throne in 1154, a new era dawned for the nation and for Westminster. For the first time in over a century the succession to the throne, when it happened, was unopposed. Peace reigned in England as a result of the 'love and fear' in which the new heir was held, even when he had to be absent in Normandy or his other continental domains.[29] The innovative reforms of national administration made in England by King Henry were all reflected in geographical changes taking place in Westminster. In particular, during the second half of the century three changes, which affected the topography of Westminster, made their mark on the shape and character of the abbey's estate in the town.

## The three changes
### 1. The early colonisation of the bank of the Thames
Firstly the new king, Henry II, decided to move his centre of government and its necessary staff progressively from Winchester to Westminster, and as a result the area along the bank of the Thames northwards from the royal palace saw a marked increase in residential and official development carried out there. Details of this area of expansion in Westminster and the people involved in it are described later.[30] The erection of houses and other complexes of buildings on this bank, extending up to and beyond a lane called Enedehithe, and on the frontages of 'the king's street' from Charing southwards to the palace, (which began from about 1160 and continued for the next hundred years and more), was one of the first big physical changes in the lay-out of the new Westminster.

### 2. The granting of rewards to abbey servants in Longditch and Tothill Street
A second district in Westminster which also began to be transformed in the second half of the twelfth century was the area of Longditch and Tothill Street. This change owed its origin primarily to the abbey, but there can be little doubt that a new atmosphere of expansion and innovation, induced by the king's policies, contributed to it.

Longditch was the lane which ran northwards from near the abbey's west gate. That gate faced along the westward-extending Tothill Street, the street towards 'Tothill', the ancient look-out eminence on the edge of the Tothill fields west of the abbey, near the site of the common pasture of the vill.[31] Since Longditch ran northwards, also from the abbey's west gate, it therefore formed a near-right angle with the road leading to the settlement at Tothill. At the start of the

---

28   For the abbots' lives and actions in these periods, see pp. 70-84. See also the charters of the abbots, priors and other monks printed or calendared in WACs 234 - c.306. For some of the individual estates in Westminster which had been granted away, see pp. 21-23 below and the list in Appendix A, pp. 391 ff.

29   Mortimer, *Angevin England*, p. 6. Henry already had lands or claims to lands in Normandy, Maine, Anjou, Poitou, Marche and Gascony. Later even the peace in England was disturbed by his own family's disputes.

30   Principally in chapters 6 and 9, see eg. pp. 95 ff. and 154 ff. below.

31   According to the second Westminster charter of about 1002, there had been a 'mound' in this area, see *The Westminster Corridor*, pp. 81 and 166; and Gelling, *Place Names* 171 for the meaning of Tothill. The

Longditch lane, and to its east, there flowed a 'ditch' or branch stream which had diverged from the main arm of the Tyburn on its way towards the Thames at the 'millbank', south of the abbey. This minor channel lying alongside Longditch lane then curved north-eastward in a wide circle (across the modern Whitehall area of government offices) towards the Thames, on its way passing under a bridge in 'the king's street', before turning north again and eventually curving back towards the Thames which it reached south of Enedehithe lane. On this route it became known as the 'Clowson' stream with a sluice on it, east of the road;[32] and the bridge was known as 'Clousenbridge'.

The areas on either side of the Longditch lane, being very close and convenient to the abbey, appear to have been used by the monks in this new era as a source of land to bestow on favoured lay officers who held important posts in different departments within the abbey. The indications are that this process began seriously during Henry II's reign, but in one or two cases it may have predated his accession. It was probably rendered necessary and desirable both by the need, as the abbey became more sophisticated, to make room within the abbey precinct, where perhaps too many of its lay servants had been quartered, and by the wish (no doubt, common to both the monks and their servants) to make use of the wide spaces nearby in Westminster which the monks still had at their command, as a reward for valuable services rendered. Again the details of this expansion and the people involved in it will be described later.[33]

So before 1200 we find a number of the senior lay officers of the abbey in occupation of land and houses in the Longditch and Tothill district. Some of the other houses found there in the period after the turn of the century must have been the product of house-building carried out (still in timber, wattle and daub, but with at least one house built in stone) during the reigns of the first Angevins, Henry II (1154 - 1189) and his two sons, Richard I (1189 - 1199) and John (1199 - 1216), on parcels of land which apparently were vacant when they had been initially granted. By that time these abbey's officers had also been joined in the same neighbourhood of Longditch, or in some cases replaced, by freshly-arrived government officials who were now spreading into areas other than the main Thamesbank district where their invasion had started.[34]

### 3. The alienation by the abbey of some of its lands in Westminster

The third development which affected the character and the shape of Westminster in or before the Angevin period was of a less detectable but much more far-reaching kind.

From a very early date the abbots of Westminster had been prepared to lease some of the abbey's widespread lands, or even whole estates, to lay men or institutions. Although by early ecclesiastical law it had been forbidden that an abbot should seek to alienate any of his abbey's properties, in due course an alienation became acceptable if all the monks consented to it.[35]

In some cases a grant of land was labelled, in the language of the time, a 'fee' (feudum,

mound or hill, probably originally raised by hand against Viking attacks, must have been levelled again over time. See also Barton, *Lost Rivers*, p. 38, ('near Vincent Square'), and p. 47 below.

32  For the sluice, see WAM 17333.
33  See eg. (William of Hurley and Pavia), pp. 96, 147, and 160 below; (Adam of Sunbury and Juliana), pp. 148 and 163 below; (Walkelin I and II), pp. 100 and 148-9 below.
34  The most notable example is the arrival in Longditch of the Mauduit family of royal chamberlains, see pp. 113 ff. and 159 ff. below.
35  See Barbara Harvey, 'Abbot Gervase and Fee-Farms', BIHR 40 (1967) 137 and n. 5. In time the popes saw the problem created by an absolute rule, and reduced its impact by ruling in effect that an abbot who wished to alienate an abbey property could do so if his convent of monks consented; see Harvey *WA Estates*, p. 84; and also see below at pp. 78 and 82, (Abbot Gervase); 131 (Abbot Wm. Postard); 132 (Abbot Ralph of Arundel).

later *feodum*), a term used sometimes without precision but carrying a suggestion that the land might not be recoverable by the abbey. When it was actually intended that land should be irrecoverable, this could be reflected with varying degrees of clarity, or obscurity, in the wording in any charter recording such a grant.[36] In other cases the same effect was sometimes unintentionally produced when looser language used in a grant had the same result, or when an appropriate legal remedy or even a court effective to give recovery at a material time did not exist.

But the practice of letting the abbey's properties as 'fees' for long-term or indefinite periods had at first originally been limited to lands which were physically distant (by medieval standards) from the abbey, eg in the 'western parts' of the country. It had been unusual for the monks to alienate land or houses near the abbey itself. But during the later twelfth century, even that rule went by the board as regards middle-distance and nearby manors, and many such estates in Essex, Middlesex and Buckinghamshire were farmed out by the abbey to lay holders.[37]

However the manor of Westminster itself was surely a special case. It had been the first and principal estate of the monks, on the very doorstep of the abbey, where one would least look for alienations. However, there can be no doubt that in early days many *ostensibly* irrecoverable grants of lands within Westminster itself were being made to lay people and organisations. But a great part of the evidence for this is contained, not in surviving charters which actually granted such lands, but in the form of a number of indirect, fortuitous and subsequent *allusions* to the continuation (or even the past existence) of some of these 'fees'.

These allusions were usually made in later charters, most of them during the thirteenth century; and they name the holders, at *that* time, of all or part of these already established 'fees'. One or two of these subsequent holders were even referred to as if they had actually become 'chief lords' (*domini capitales*) of the land in question – as if they had even supplanted the abbey as 'tenants-in-chief' of the king.[38] In some cases there is no evidence to suggest that such later holders were still obliged to pay even any rent or other service *to the abbey* for their 'fees'.

A detailed list of some of these 'fees' in Westminster, which had been granted earlier by the abbey is set out in Appendix A below.[39] As discussed later, this list cannot be complete,

---

36  See eg. WAC 242 (in about 1116 Abbot Crispin granted land in Bucks *in feudo* to a sheriff *'and his heirs in hereditary right'*; in Latin, of course). Such a grant envisaged at least that the land would be irrecoverable so long as there were successive heirs in the line. If in similar grants, other stronger words such as *'in perpetuo'* (for ever) were used as well, it could be argued and sometimes held that the irrecoverability was not dependent on there being heirs, so that the recipient could transfer the land to whoever he wished. In effect it could be like the grant of a modern fee simple, save that, logically by the feudal notions then current, rents could continue to be payable to the 'chief', and intervening tenants, in theory for ever. Cf. WAC 262 (Abbot Gervase, 1138 x 1157; no *feudo* used). Cf. Reynolds, *Fiefs and Vassals*, pp. 353-4.

37  Harvey, *WA Estates*, 77.

38  See WAM 17401 (1220s ?), in which Laurence, son of William parvus ('the small'), a well-known family with lands in Tothill, Longditch, the area of the present St James's Park, and Eye) is described as *'chief lord of the fee'*, receiving 19d as rent. For Laurence and his father William, see further pp. 201, 330-1, and 393 below. John, son of Edward was also referred to, more correctly, *'tamquam* (as if)' the chief lord, see WAC 447, receiving 2s. 6d. rent for a half-messuage in Tothill Street. In Dr. Mason's note to WAC 327 (1206 x 1214), other 'chief lords' are identified as probably the nuns of Clerkenwell and two named lay men, who are also referred to in WACs 386-7: but this was a case where the houses were on Ludgate hill and outside Westminster.

39  See pp. 391 ff. The result of these early lettings of Westminster lands is described by Dr Rosser in his *Medieval Westminster*, when he says briefly (pp. 44 and 16) that "By 1200, as a result of grants made by the abbot during the last two centuries a considerable part of the area had passed into the hands of lay landholders". But their nature and extent, and the circumstances in which they were made, have not been discussed in any detail, as far as I can see.

but it provides at least a glimpse of the categories of people and institutions who benefitted by receiving 'fees' in Westminster, either as a result of over-generosity, carelessness or enforced disposals on the part of the monks, or by reason of high-handed actions on the part of the king, or of his managers during 'vacancies' when an abbot had died and had not yet been replaced.

The creations of these 'fees' in Westminster must have been grants of land on the monks' own doorstep, subtracted from their ancient and first endowment. And it is as though almost all records (where there were any) of such grants had been deliberately suppressed, save for the few which have survived, and their very absence makes it appear that the grants were disposals about which later monks were sorry, ashamed or angry.

In most cases the 'fees' granted seem to have been regarded as very real in their perceived legal effect. One therefore finds that those who had already received an early 'fee' from the abbey could then, and sometimes did, grant similar sub-tenures to other people, which they also described as 'fees': in effect as 'sub-fees'.[40]

For two reasons, it is certain that this list of fees cannot reflect the total number of the fees so made by the monks (or by royal managers during a vacancy in the abbacy). First, it would be incredible if a chance collection of fortuitous later allusions to a number of 'fees' which had previously been granted happened to coincide with the total number of the actual lettings which the monks or royal managers had actually made. It is fortuitous that such allusions were made; and it is also fortuitous that the charters in which they were made have survived – while others have not survived, as certainly happened with many charters.

Secondly, there is no doubt that in the period of the active land-market in Westminster, which began before 1200, there were other sellers or donors of 'fee' property in the town who have no known connection with the original holders of these earlier 'fees'. Where did such other sellers or donors acquire their properties? The original holders of the 'fees' must themselves have sold them 'in the market', or donated them to others.

The result is that, after such developments, one has to see Westminster not as surviving in the form of one integrated estate of the abbey, but as containing also a number of other much smaller but separate and almost independent 'empires'. In a few of these cases, as old feudal concepts weakened, the abbey may no longer have even been regarded as the ultimate 'chief lord' and received neither rent nor even any former 'feudal service' of labour or other duty.

This third change in Westminster had probably begun even before the two geographical changes on the Thamesbank and the Longditch-Tothill areas – and when those areas were being colonised, it was sometimes in the form of such 'fees' that the lettings there were expressly made.

## Spreading Westminster – the mix of town and country

In spite of this gradual fragmentation of Westminster which took place in the twelfth century, one of its distinguishing features was that, unlike some other urban developments elsewhere, the whole estate remained for long a real mixture of town and country and took many centuries to become a compact urban unit.[41] By the start of the thirteenth century the urban parts were still comparatively small, and all the rest of the manor and the abbey's

---

40  See eg. WAC 449, where John, son of Edward the reeve, who held his father's 'fee' from the abbey, in turn identified Adam of Sunbury, William the Waller, Edric of the Garden, and Martin Smud (incidentally all servants of or connected with the abbey) as holding 'fees' (in effect, sub-fees) from him. All these were on Tothill Street, see also p. 163 below.

41  Westminster did not acquire the status of either a borough or a city until 1585, after the Dissolution, when a statute was passed ratifying a system of local administration for it, rather than the 'arbitrary

adjoining estates of Eye, Knightsbridge, Westbourne and Paddington were intensely rural where agricultural life prevailed and for long continued to prevail almost exclusively. A contrast in the immediate neighbourhood of the abbey has been rightly drawn by Dr. Mason between 'the artistic and scholarly activities' (to say nothing of the religious activities) being conducted within the precinct of the abbey, and the 'haymaking and other agricultural occupations which were in full swing barely a kilometre away'.[42] In fact some of the latter occupations and activities were really much nearer than a kilometre.

Even 300 years later, in 1531, only nine years before the abbey was finally dissolved under Henry VIII, an abbey survey of its farm lands in the area between the old leper hospital of St. James and the Tothill district (ie. the present St. James's Park area) and in other nearby areas reveals the continued existence *even at that time* of at least the following fields and crofts: -

- in *'St James's Field'*, 8 acres and another 8 acres of meadow; 7 acres and 11 acres of arable, and several small lots amounting to 10 or more acres of arable (totalling 44 acres of meadow and arable in all, most of it around or near the present St James's Palace, then the site of the former leper Hospital of St. James);

- in *'Eybury Field'* (one of the great Fields in the manor of Eye, known earlier as 'the Field of Eye', lying on the west and south-west of the present site of Buckingham Palace), various parcels amounting to 36 acres of arable;

- in *'Brokshot'*, (a croft in Eye lying next the Tyburn south of the Mayfair area, and adjoining the crossroads at the present Hyde Park Corner) about 4 acres of arable, alongside a brick field used by the then abbot, John Islip;[43]

- in the sub-'manor' of *'Rosamund's'*, which lay south-east of the present Buckingham Palace, perhaps 20 acres or more;[44]

- another 'great croft' east of *Rosamund's*, (probably part of the grounds of a mansion existing at that time, called 'Petty Calais' (*Pety Caleys*), about 30 acres in extent.[45]

So, even more than three centuries later, over 100 acres of land were still in agricultural use around the old hospital area, some of them quite close to the abbey, and it is impossible to doubt that way back in the twelfth and thirteenth centuries the rural presence in the

government' which the abbot's jurisdiction had originally performed, see Rosser, *Med. Westminster*, 226; Maitland, *London*, ii. 1348; *The Westminster Corridor*, 135, 166. In its physical amenities today, Westminster and the rest of modern London still benefits from the selfish acquisitiveness of Henry VIII, to whom posterity owes the circle of his personal hunting parks: the present St. James's Park, Green Park, Hyde Park and Regent's Park – which had largely survived as open lands, for the king ultimately to grab and convert.

42 Mason, 'A truth universally acknowledged', *S. Ch. Hist.* 16 (1979) 171. See chapters 19 and 20 below, at pp. 327 ff. and 350 ff, for the agricultural occupations in full swing in nearby Eye, a kilometre and less away.

43 For *Eybury Field*, known earlier as the 'Field of Eye', the home *campus* in Eye, see also pp. 59-60 and 400, n. 3, below. *Brokshot* was a smaller field lying south of the field of Ossulton.

44 For Rosamunds, see pp. 50-1 and 285-6; plus another 53 acres, see p. 286, n. 99.

45 WAM 17131 (15 June 1531). This abbey survey was clearly carried out in preparation for the 'compulsory acquisition' of this area which Henry VIII was making in his plan to create a great hunting park or parks in a semi-circle west and north-west of London. In addition to the above abbey lands, there were also 185 acres of the St. James leper Hospital which Henry VIII acquired (*Letters, etc, of H.VIII*, Vol 5, § 406, 606); and the further 80 acres of land on which the great mansion of 'Pety Caleys' or Petty Calais, north of Tothill, had by then been built (*ibid.* § 404, 673 no. 23; and cf. 857). In 1531, when Henry VIII acquired this mansion, it (a) had been occupied by Lord Berners, the 'deputy of Calais' (the probable source of the names Petty Calais and the present street 'Petty France' nearby, first appearing about 1518), and (b) included the garden land (*Mauduitsgarden*) which the Mauduit family had held in the C12, 13 and 14; see also the geography in *Survey of London*, vols. X, p. 7-8 and XIII, p. 257-260. For the Mauduits, see pp. 113 ff. and 159 ff. below.

neighbourhood of the abbey and the main part of the town was far wider still; to say nothing about the rest of the adjoining rural estates of Eye and Knightsbridge.   In tracing the development of the town of Westminster in earlier centuries, we do not have to identify a progressive enlargement of one compact centre, but to discover initially those pockets in different areas of the whole manor where small settlements began and grew (with plenty of agricultural land around or among them), eventually to join up and form a whole. This process of identifying such pockets from which Westminster gradually became consolidated is pursued in the next chapter.

In the more northern districts of the manor of Westminster, there also continued to be other wide swathes of arable and pastoral land in the 'Field of Westminster', eg. eastwards from the Tyburn boundary-stream (in part of the present Mayfair and Soho districts) as far as the St. Giles enclave to the east – where St. Giles, the earlier of the two leper hospitals founded on land originally within Westminster, had stood since Henry I's time – and from there southwards to the convent's 'great garden', the present Covent Garden area.[46]

The same is true of the other great open area on 'Tothill Fields', extending southerly from the place where the 'common pasture of the vill' lay at or near Tothill.[47]   And even in the places where serious urban building was taking place, there are constant reminders in the charters of interspersed farming activities, such as the presence of a grange, a barn, some residual obligations of manual labour in the fields, more than one smithy, and of course the farming qualifications given as the 'occupational' names (whether past or contemporary) of some of the residents themselves and their forebears.[48]

---

46 WAM 17539 and WAC 408. See also pp. 34-5 and 58 below, concerning the area round the St. Giles enclave.  This Westminster swathe, east of the Tyburn stream, was matched *west* of the stream by the fields of *Tyburne, Mabeliscroft, Ossulston, Cressewellefeld, La Redelonde* and others in the manor of Eye (part of the present Mayfair area), see also pp. 345-47 and Plate 23. For the hospital of St. Giles, see p. 35 below.  For the transfer of the 'great garden' to the convent by the abbot, see pp. 33 and 199 below.
47 WAMs 17340, 17345, 17519, 17522. For Tothill Fields, see p. 16 above.
48 eg. WAM 17401 (a grange on Tothill Street, in 1220s); WAM 17155B (a barn at Charing, in 1246/7); WACs 405, 446, 447, 448 (a man to mow hay and reap corn, on one day a a year, from a half messuage 'towards Tothill', late C12 to temp. John); WAM 17155A (a smithy near St. Martin's church, 1225).  For farming occupations, see eg. *vannator, le heyward, vaccarius, porcarius* in the occupations listed in App. E, at pp. 412 ff.

# CHAPTER 2

# People in the dispersed
# settlements of Westminster

Both the sector of the town between the Thames bank and 'the kinge's street', and the district of Longditch and Tothill, were already beginning to grow dramatically before 1200.[1] But other more scattered pockets of residence had also begun to form at an early stage throughout the manor of Westminster, and they too continued to expand during the years before and after 1200, until eventually they blended together to form a fairly continuous band of development, starting from the extended boundary of the city of London and reaching to the abbey and palace in Westminster and beyond.[2] In this process, each pocket of settlement can be identified with some of its own local families, and the identities of these pockets and their residents appear to have survived for a time even after the general merger of the dispersed settlements had begun to take place.

So the following descriptions and plans of these outlying settlements are designed to reveal the main features of their geography within Westminster, rather than to depict the historical sequences of events within each settlement, or their development into a blended town. Inevitably the process of such development was gradual and it would be difficult to chart the individual settlements in great detail.[3] Although it was the two central areas of Thamesbank and Longditch/Tothill which led the way towards the consolidation of Westminster, the outlying settlements also had and partly retained their own identities and family connections.

In this account of the separate 'hamlets' of which the later town came to be composed, some of the resident families, their more prominent members and some main features or buildings are identified, in order to create a link between such personalities or features and the places or events described in the chronological chapters which follow this topographical section.

## 1. Charing and the Charing cross-road

The nearest community was that which stood around the cross-roads at Charing, near which the chapel, and later the first church, of St. Martin 'of Charing' (an early predecessor of the present St. Martin's in the Fields) stood.[4] It was here that the great east-west road along the former anglo-saxon *strande* (now the present Strand roadway) had met 'the kinge's road' which came northwards from the abbey and the palace, while St Martin's lane (still so

---

1  See pp. 20-1 above. For more detail:- on Thames bank and 'King's Street', pp. 109-14 ff., 156-7 and 159 ff. below; on the Longditch/Tothill area, see eg. pp. 47, 96-7, 113-4, 143-5.

2  The secular and ecclesiastical boundaries between the city of London and the abbot's 'liberty' of Westminster had changed, as indicated below on pp. 36-7, and App. B at pp. 396.

3  Equally inevitably – because the evidence is fragmented – such sequences as can be described here in any of these communities cannot follow a continuous path of chronology. See Chapter 4 for the start of chronological history, at pp. 63 ff.

4  WAC 404 (temp. Henry II) to which the chaplain of St. Martin's was a witness, and WAMs 17143B, 17144, and 17155A (1225). St Martin's chapel had probably been founded in the second half of the C12. For the main map of Westminster (and nearby Eye), see Plates 2-3, after p.16.

named) wound northeasterly to the old leper Hospital of St. Giles.[5] Near the crossroads a spring called 'St. Martin's fountain' flowed (apparently breaking through the gravel of the first river terrace), with a stream, which 'ran through Charing to the Thames'.[6] As further signs of the still semi-rural nature of the settlement, there were at least one, if not two, smithies and a barn which, commonplace as they were, even found their way into legal charters which were usually reticent about such mundane things.[7] Numbers of properties were visibly changing hands in Charing from the second half of the twelfth century, as recognisable Charing families moved about. A second cluster of families formed a nearby group living in the nearer stretch of the present Strand, which became known as Charing Street.[8]

St. Martin's church stood a little way up 'St. Martin's lane', not at the corner of an open square as the present church does. But the lane originally began a little further south than it does today, and so the present church stands on or near the site of the old one. Even to this day the rest of the little road is still called a 'lane', and on its way to St. Giles continues to have the characteristics of narrowness and a curving course, like a lane still winding its way between the fields. The church had a churchyard; and at least three gardens belonging to other private holders lay to the east between the churchyard and the abbey's 'great garden' (the present Covent Garden).[9] Probably in the twelfth century the church had originally been a chapel annexed to St. Margaret's the parish church of Westminster, but by the early thirteenth century it had become an independent church with its own parish, which was probably small initially but was later considerably increased.[10]

Some of the early priests of St. Martin's church can be identified, and they incidentally

5  St. Giles's hospital had been founded 'in the fields' by Henry I's first and pious queen, Matilda, in the early C12, with land probably taken by the king from the abbey's estate in Westminster.

6  For the spring and stream, see WAM 17146 (1220s) and 17144 (1230-40s); for the gravel geology of this area, see *The Westminster Corridor*, p. 27 and coloured Map D.  Probably this spring caused the drainage problems and fast-flowing ditches described by Honeybourne, 'Charing Cross Riverside', L.T.Rec, 21 (1958) at pp. 45-7.

7  For the smithy 'of **Richard faber**', see WAM 17155A (1225), and for the barn, see WAM 17155B (1246-7).  There was also another smith, **Henry Blund** 'faber, of Charing' at about the same time as Richard, see WAM 17143B, 17146 and 17147, so maybe there were two smithies, which was quite possible at or near such a nodal crossing of roads.

8  See WAMs 17143A - 17145, 17147-17151B, 17155B, 17157-17159, 17161; post-1300 : 17162, 17164.  It is sometimes difficult to distinguish between the group around the Charing cross-roads and the group in 'Charing Street' (see pp. 33 ff. below), but the impression one gets from the charters is that these groups tended initially to be separate, although they gradually became one whole, as more houses were built before and after the early years of the thirteenth century.  Some of the families around the crossroads were the **Blunds** (the smiths, see note 7 above; although the name was also that of a great London family); the **Berkings** (see WAMs 17147, 17148A and B, 17161, and pp. 177-8 below); the family of **John the Tailor** 'of Charing' (see WAMs 17387 and 17460); the **Huts** 'of Charing', (see WAMs 17155A, 17141, 17142, WACs 440 and 445.

9  WAM 17150 (1240s). Two of the gardens were held at that time by **Henry Pelliparius** (the skinner) and **Walter Ostremonger** (the oyster-seller?); and the third was held by **Ralph 'of the bridge of Eye'**, who donated to the Lady Altar of the abbey the 2s. 4d. rent he got from it. The 'bridge of Eye' was probably the one later named the Eybridge, not far from the southern end of the Eye high street, see p. 49 below, rather than the 'Abbotsbridge' leading to the abbot's country house, La Neyte, see p. 48 below. For the cult of the Lady Altar, see pp. 126 ff. below.

10  Fortunately WAM 17155A, which is unusually and elaborately dated 27th March 1225, speaks of a Charing site (held by one of the **Hut** family of Charing) as lying *'between the smithy of Richard faber and the road which leads from the great royal road to the church of St. Martin of Charing'*, and it is correctly endorsed *'next to the lane of St. Martin'*. For mentions of a parish, see eg. WAMs 17141, 17142 (WACs 398 and 399, temp. John), 17151B, 17157 (1246 x 1258).  But when St Martin's church and its cemetery were referred to in the great arbitration Award of 1222, no mention was made of a *parish*, see below p. 337 and App. B, p. 399.

help to show connections between neigh-bouring areas. In probably the 1180s, the 'chaplain of St. Martin's' was called William; and a 'second' William, the 'vicar' of St. Martin's, emerges later in the first half of the next century. The first of these Williams had two, possibly three, sons: Salamon (also a priest), Alexander and (perhaps) Ralph of Tothill.[11] Properties connected with one or more contemporary Alexanders appear to have been spread around Charing and the area round the leper hospital of St. James, and in Eye.[12] The later vicar of St. Martin's church, William, bought an annual rent of 3s. from one of the Charing smiths, Henry Blund, and shortly afterwards made a donation of it to the abbey.[13] This was a rent for land which lay next to the *stream running through Charing to the Thames'*, which may have flowed from the 'fountain of Charing'.[14] As shown below, this stream and its fountain illustrate well some of the problems met in trying to match members of families with their localities.

In one case, different members of a family who lived in one part or another of the Charing area had separate locative identifications : 'of the spring' (*de fonte*) and 'of the cross' (*de cruce*). In or before the 1190s there were two brothers, Hugh *de fonte* and Geoffrey *de cruce*, whose father had been Richer *de fonte*.[15] Since this was long before the erection of the Eleanor Cross at Charing in 1294 by King Edward I, Geoffrey's 'cross' may have been the 'Stone Cross' in the Strand, which Henry I had erected in the

early years of the twelfth century.[16] If so, Hugh lived near the crossroads of Charing, with the Charing spring nearby, and Geoffrey had gone to live further eastwards in Charing Street towards the Stone Cross, from which he took his name. Or it may be that Hugh's *fons* fed the stream which we know crossed the Strand near the Stone Cross, so that all the family may have come from and lived in that *eastern* part of 'Charing', but later became known by the two different names, of *de fonte* and *de cruce*.

Hugh *de fonte* is also known to have 'given' a customary tenant called 'William son of Herbert' to his daughter, Margaret, together with a one acre tenement in Westminster which was customary land held by the tenant. Hugh had thus granted to his daughter the allegiance and services which the tenant had owed to him, presumably by virtue of some lost grant to him from the abbey.[17] Geoffrey *de cruce*, for his part, was probably a prominent servant of the abbey, since he appeared thirty six times as a witness to extant Westminster charters recorded in the abbot's court, and in the early thirteenth century he also donated a rent of 2s. 8d. pa. to the Lady Altar in the abbey, at the request of his wife and son.[18] At that time it appears that Geoffrey may have become infirm, since his charter giving this charitable donation records that his son (who as an heir had given up his own rights in the rent) had to place the charter, as was the custom, upon the Lady Altar on his father's behalf.

11  WAC 404 (temp. Henry II); Mason, *Beauchamp Cartulary*. Nos. 187, 189, 195.
12  Mason, *ibid.*, Nos. 196, 197-200; WAMs 17111-12, 17115-16, and CP 25(1) 146/5/15A.
13  WAMs 17143B (1220-30s) and 17144 (1230-40s).
14  WAM 17146 (1220s) and 17144 (1220-30s).
15  WAM 17314 (WAC 406, late 12C, before 1197).
16  For the Eleanor Cross, see p. 30 below; and for the Stone Cross, see The *Westminster Corridor*, p. 49 and note 16; and see also p. 39 below. The Stone Cross became the 'Broken Cross' in due course.
17  WAM 17320 (WAC 416, late 12C). Later, Margaret and her husband made a charitable donation of the rent from the land to the Lady Altar at the abbey, see WAMs 17432 and 17413 (WACs 417 and 418). For the Lady Altar, see pp. 126 ff. below. To take the family further, another **Richer *de fonte*** became the Westminster reeve in mid-C13, and a **Richer *de cruce*** had immediately preceded him in that post in the 1240s; WAM 17415; Rosser, *Medieval Westminster*, 328 and 330.
18  WAC 415 (temp. John).

There is little doubt that from the twelfth century there were strong connections between the area of Charing and two of the adjoining districts – of the leper hospital of St. James and the manor of Eye. These connections were both physical, via 'the hospital road' (*Spitalstrete*), which led directly from Charing, past the hospital of St. James, to a junction north of the Eye high street; and social, through families who held lands there.[19] The hospital road was a much closer route for people to use for keeping physical contact in these areas than another much more circular road from Charing to Eye – down 'King Street', along Tothill Street, and from Tothill along the road towards Eye.

Close to where the Charing cross-road merged eastwards into 'Charing Street' (the western end of the modern Strand), there later stood at least one property on the great inner bend of the river Thames, which had already been granted away by the abbey during the twelfth century. It extended from the roadway down to the river itself.[20] Being more than three acres in extent, it had apparently been granted before 1199 by the abbey to the great William Marshal, the marshal and justiciar of King Richard I. His 'fee' there contained a number of houses which the marshal sub-let to Master Jocelin, his deputy-marshal and personal deputy at the court of exchequer, as both a convenient residence near the palace and as an office for the marshal's own 'wardrobe' or personal finance staff, administered by Master Jocelin. In doing so, the marshal reserved for himself the right to lodge there with his staff when he had to attend on the king at his palace in Westminster, and the site seems to have remained known as 'the marshal's' during his lifetime.[21]

However in about 1230 the marshal's eldest son, also named William Marshal, who had succeeded him as Earl of Pembroke, granted the property to an Augustinian priory based in Roncevalles, Navarre in Spain. The Spanish priory acted as a hospice for pilgrims journeying to Compostella, and over the next 150 years its branch house at Charing was now to act in the same way, for the probable purpose of providing shelter and care for pilgrims on their way to the shrine of Edward the Confessor at the abbey at Westminster. It became known as 'the hospital of St. Mary Rounceval', and Chaucer's 'gentil pardoner', with his notorious sale of indulgences, was a product 'of Rouncival', based perhaps on a real Brother 'Lupus' at the hospital in the 1280s.[22]

Towards the end of the thirteenth century, when the Charing settlement had become conjoined with properties along 'King Street' leading south to central Westminster, the site

---

19 For the hospital road, see next settlement, below at p. 30. As to landholding families in these areas, see also pp. 22 n. 38, 201, 330-1 and 393 for William **Parvus** ('the small') and his son **Laurence** of Eye. **Richard Altus** ('the tall', his height a contrast with that of William Parvus) was another.

20 Two other similar sites on or near the same bend, extending from the road to the river, may have been those much later recorded in WAMs 17157 (1246 x 57) and 17159 (?1283 x 90s).

21 Crouch, *William Marshal*, pp. 146 and 168. **Wm Marshal**, starting as an illiterate younger son of a baron and becoming the exemplar of both loyalty and martial chivalry, raised himself to the heights of royal service for three kings, Henry II, Richard and John; and finally as the earl of Pembroke and the regent of England during the first three years of the boy king, Henry III; before dying in 1219. Royal influence may have led to the abbey's grant of this fee to the marshal. For **Master Jocelin**, his deputy in the court of the exchequer, see pp. 178-9 below. For the marshal's land, see also p. 392, and for his 'ditch' as a boundary line with adjoining land , see WAM 17141, and p. 53 below.

22 Rosser, *Medieval Westminster*, pp. 310-2, Honeybourne, 'Charing Cross Riverside' LTR 21 (1958) 48 ff, and Cal. Ch. R. 1226-57, pp. 167-8. The hospital had a chequered history in the C14, after which it finally became lost to the Spanish priory towards the end of that century; and the real legal break came when alien religious houses were suppressed in England by statute in 1414. Chaucer as a resident in Westminster in the later C14 was well placed to know of the old hospice and its practices; but for the benefit of less local readers the Coghill 'translation' of *The Canterbury Tales* renders 'Rouncival' as 'Charing Cross'.

at the crossroads, opposite the Ronceval hospital, was honoured with the erection of an 'Eleanor cross'. This was the final and most important of the successive stone crosses which Edward I caused to be erected in homage to his dead queen Eleanor of Castile, along the winding route which her cortège had followed after her death. The funeral procession had started in Nottinghamshire where she died in 1290, and at last wound its way to London; thence along Fletestrete and Charing Street to the Charing cross-roads, and so southwards to the abbey where her main and most splendid tomb still stands.[23] The stone cross at the cross-roads was completed by 1294, and the property of the Ronceval hospital was described in the following century as standing *'devant la crux de Charryng'*. Queen Eleanor had been Spanish by birth, and appropriately her final cross at Charing faced a Spanish religious house.

## 2.   The hospital road – Spitalstrete

Another group of residents had favoured the road which ran westwards from the cross-roads at Charing in the general direction of Knightsbridge, already a long-standing but small settlement on the road to Bath, with its

bridge over the Westbourne river. When the new leper hospital of St. James had been founded on the edge of this road (probably in the reign of Henry II), the road – as, no doubt, it became more built-up with houses – had inevitably become known as 'the street of the hospital of St. James'. It continued to have that name for another fifty years or more.[24] By that time it was called a *regia via*, a royal road or highway, and was probably paved. It passed the hospital on its north side, and its course then ran through part of the present Green Park towards Knightsbridge. Just before the hospital, probably on its east side, there was a prominent group of elm trees which were a landmark used to identify the location of properties.[25]  By at least 1235, if not before, the road from Charing had inevitably become known as 'the hospital street', ie. 'Spitalstrete'.[26] And as one went westward after passing the hospital on its north side, the road ran through the waters of the Tyburn stream, or 'the blessed King Edward's watercourse', in the Green Park area.[27] This crossing was the ford already discussed, still known in the 1240s as *'kuford'*, which had been *'cuford'* in royal charters in anglo-saxon times, more than 250 years before.[28]

23  Queen Eleanor had three tombs (in Lincoln, Blackfriars in London, and the abbey of Westminster), in which different parts of her body were buried, see Prestwich, *Edward I*, p. 125. The cross was erected where the Hubert le Sueur statue of Charles I now stands at the top of Whitehall. Revered by Edward, the queen was a cultured lady, but greedy for land (which had beneficial effects for the abbey, as we shall see; see pp. 305-7 below). The making of the Charing cross is commemorated by David Gentleman's striking artistic and historical pictures on the down-platform at Charing Cross on the Northern Line of the London Underground. The cross survived until 1647 when the puritans felled it, but it still lives in the Agas map of London in the C16. For its construction, see Plates 5 and 6, pp. 21 and 32.

24  WAMs 17109, 17110 (1240-50s). For the  hospital road, see also p. 17.

25  WAM 17113 (1230-40s).

26  WAM 17109-17113, 17115-6, 17415. For the date 1235 or earlier, see CP 25(1) 146/5/15A, where one of the parties was already known as **'Alexander of Spitalstrete'**: the date was either 1235 or 1219. This Alexander must have been different from the **Alexander** (also known as Alexander of Eye) who was one of the sons of **William the priest of St. Martin's Church at Charing**. Alexander owned land all round the area, including at Charing as well as in the vill of Westminster itself, see Mason *Beauchamp Cartulary*, No. 195, 196; WAC 311-2, 413, 419, 440, 447. The house of **Beatrix**, daughter of **Brungar** the champion, (see above, p. 16 is one other major one of which we know in Spitalstrete, while a third one can be traced down a line of identifiable holders during the later C13, see p. 17, n. 17 above.

27  See p. 17 above. It may be that the original making of a pond or lake in the obvious declivity which can still be seen in Green Park was part of the works which came to be called 'the blessed King Edward's watercourse', see also *The Westminster Corridor*, p. 41 and n. 77 there. Another much later pond in that place also became known as Rosamund's Pond, see p. 50, and cf. pp. 285-6 below.

28  See pp. 15-6 above.

**Plate 5.** Some Purbeck 'marble' used for the Eleanor Cross at Charing came from quarries at Corfe in Dorset, cut by Robert of Corfe. With wedges, the quarriers have here split off the rough block of stone needed, and are prising it away from its base, before squaring it off. Much Purbeck marble had also been used for Henry III's new abbey and its Cosmati pavement, and Ralph of Corfe (a quarry-owner, and Robert's father?) had had a house in the new village of Eye. See pp. 30 n.23, 231 and 338.

**Plate 6.** Crucial stages of a design of an Eleanor Cross were the setting-out of full-scale details on parchment, and the making of three-dimensional models of parts of the final work. David Gentleman's mason is here using a small wooden compass to set out a curve, and a model-maker adds information gained from his model. See p. 30 and n. 23

## 3. Charing Street and Aldewich

Along 'Charing Street', which formed the western section of the modern Strand, there grew up a significant frontage of properties on the north side of the street; with their backs to the southern earth-wall of 'the great garden' belonging to the abbey.[29]

This 'great garden', later known as the Convent Garden and hence, by elision, the modern 'Covent Garden', had originally always been called the garden 'of the abbot', and it continued to have only this name until at least 1227 when it was transferred to the convent.[30] At the western end of the garden, the wall surrounding the garden met the boundary of a group of other private gardens which lay behind St Martin's churchyard, and from there its long southern wall of earth stretched eastwards as far as 'Aldewich' (a street partly on the line of the present Drury Lane).[31] However *north* of St. Martin's churchyard and the private gardens, the 'great garden' appears to have extended even further westwards, up to the very frontage of St. Martin's lane. At the other end, the 'great garden' had an eastern gateway which opened onto Aldewich, facing in the 1240s a line of new houses recently erected on the *east* side of that road.[32]

This whole neighbourhood was home to many gardens. It was part of an area of two square miles to the west and south-west of London which has been called 'the greatest concentration of gardens in the whole of England' and was mainly devoted to producing fruit and vegetables for the city's population.[33]

Later the district included one other large garden called 'Tockesgardin' which, like the abbey's great garden, also fronted onto Aldewich and faced across that road to the frontage of new houses recently erected on the other side by the prominent Westminster clerk, Henry of Belgrave.[34] Stretching (like the northern part of the abbey's 'great garden') from Aldewich to St. Martin's lane, Tockesgardin lay immediately north of the abbey's garden and was 'suburban' land held (with other houses) by the early London family of the Bucuintes, which Sir Henry Bucuinte had won before 1236 in a legal action begun in the king's

---

29 For the frontage of the houses, see WAMs 17136, 17137, 17138, 17149, 17150, 17163, 17449.
30 See eg. WAMs 17136, 17137, 17138. But in 1227 arbitrators decided that Abbot Richard of Berking should hand the great garden over to his convent of monks (see p. 199 below), and a separate administrative office of 'gardener' was created by the convent to manage both it and the funds earmarked for it, and to render accounts. However other charters such as WAMs 17149 and 17449 which are to be dated *after* 1227 refer to it still as 'the abbot's garden'. The great garden was either 40 or 'at least 27' acres in size, see *Survey of London*, 36/p. 19, or Dyer, *Everyday Life in Med. Eng.*, p. 114. The abbot's 'smaller garden' was behind the west side of 'King St.', see WAM 17370 and App. D. at p. 406.
31 WAMs 17150 (1240s), 17086, 18836-7 and 18843, see *Survey of London*, vol. 36, p. 19.
32 WAM 17366 (1250-60s), and 17431 (1240s). For the developer, Henry of Belgrave, see next page and n. 36.
33 Dyer, *Everyday life in Med. England* 122.
34 Gardens: WAMs 17149, 17150, 17351, 17431, 17481; post-1300: 17163, 17164, 17166. Tockesgardin: 17431 (?1240s). A Richard Tocke held a house nearby and was a witness to the charter, but he was not a party to this transfer of the garden, and by 1211 a William Toke had succeeded Master Jocelin as deputy-marshal at the exchequer (see p. 29 above), and the family continued in Aldewich (WAD 623b). Other nearby gardens were the garden 'of Tholy' (Tholus?) and 'the gardens stretching as far as the house of Simon the weaver' (all referred to in 1222 in the 'great arbitration' award between the abbey and the bishop of London, pp. 36 ff. below and App. B, p. 396 ff; and also (much later, in 1354) the garden 'called the garden of the Pied Friars', off Charing Street: WAM 17166. Many other gardens existed elsewhere in Westminster, particularly in the Longditch-Tothill area where, for example, the large garden of the Mauduits ('*Mauduitsgarden*') set a high standard, see p. 160-1 below.

court but then decided 'by battle' between champions at Tothill.[35]

After this legal (and military) success, Sir Henry had then let the garden, at a rent of two and a half marks, to another Henry, Henry of Belgrave a clerk (who was himself a landowner roundabout – in Charing, in the neighbourhood of Spitalstrete and St James's Hospital, and in Eye).[36] But all or part of Tockesgardin then came back into the possession of the abbey, because Henry of Belgrave (who became another *dominus*, 'lord' or 'sir') later made a gift 'in soul alms' of his interest in the garden to the monks, subject to their paying the rent to Sir Henry Bucuinte who was still the 'landlord'.[37]

During the thirteenth century the residents in Aldewich road appear to have become part of the same urban community as the Charing Street group, but at the beginning of the century the area round Aldewich had started as a rural and garden neighbourhood, where a half-acre strip in the 'Fields' (a name sometimes used for the 'Field of Westminster', and sometimes for the adjoining 'Fields of St. Giles' surrounding the enclave of the leper hospital) and closes of

five acres and two acres can be identified.[38] Even the text of the great arbitration award of 1222, which described a reduced boundary between the diocese of London and the abbot's 'liberty' of Westminster, did so by mentioning four different gardens and 'marshland' in the St. Giles and Aldewich areas.[39]

The value of a garden in an area like this on the threshold of London, measured by its produce more than its intrinsic amenity, is well demonstrated by the rent of one garden at Charing in the next century. When this was leased by the abbot in 1341, its rent was 13s. 4d. pa., not much less than the rent of 29 acres of arable land at Ossulston (in the present Mayfair area) which was let at the same time, at 16s. 11d. pa.[40] Although a garden like this might be more valued for its produce than for its amenity, this did not mean that amenity might not also be a matter of concern to its owner or even to the residents nearby. Westminster was full of gardens, and within another area of the town in the early years of the next century we even find an owner letting his garden for seven years, with a careful condition imposed that the lessee

35 WAM 17444 (1236-7), and CP 25(1) 146/8/129 and cf. 100; and for the place, see WAM 17392A and pp. 49 and cf 145, n. 40. The **Bucuinte** family were said to be of Italian origin, see Glyn Williams, *Med. London*, p. 20, but see Reynolds 'Rulers of London in the C12', *History* 57 (1972) 339-40). However the family contributed much to early London life and government. For two pedigrees of Bucuintes, see Williams *Early Holborn*, § 1676 and 693, where they also held much property. For a later legal claim against the abbey by grand-daughters of H. Bucuinte about a rent of two marks arising from their inheritance of this garden, followed by their subsequent grant of it back to the abbey, see WAM 17481 (1296). For the Bucuinte family, see also Glyn Williams, *Med. London*, p. 73; Brooke and Keir, *London*, p. 214. Another good London name in the St Giles and Holborn areas was Andrew Bucherel, whose son became Mayor of London in the 1220-30s.
36 WAM 17444 (1236-7). For **Henry of Belgrave's** holdings :- (in Charing) WAM 17145, 17151A and B; (near the hospital) WAMs 17109, 17110; (in Eye) CP 25(1) 146/8/109 and 146/10/197. After taking the garden, Henry of Belgrave had let part of it, WAM 17431, revealing in his charter that he had been the 'developer' who had built the new houses in Aldewich. Henry of Belgrave may have been a Bucuinte himself.
37 See WAM 17351; and also 17352 and 17355. Later Abbot Ware (1258-83) sought to develop the gardens area near Aldewich, see WAD 621b, 622b and 623b-4 and p. 237 below.
38 WAC 408 (temp. John). See also p. 58 below. For more about the residents of the areas round Charing Street, the church of the Holy Innocents and Aldewich, see the text following.
39 The 'marshland', south of the St. Giles hospital site, was still known by that name in 1585, see the plan of that date in the lawsuit Bristow v. Wilson, recorded in *Survey of London*, Vol. 32, Plate 1 (redrawn clearly in Ldn. Top. Soc. Pubn. no. 54) and in later maps as well. For the arbitration, see text below, under *The parish of the Holy Innocents*, at pp. 36 ff. and App. B. at p. 396. One of the great Cantilupe family (Master Roger) held a garden between St Martin's church and the abbey's garden, which his son restored to the abbey, WAD 620b. For the Cantilupes, see pp. 273-4 below. John *le Convers* (see pp. 283-5) held a house by the east gate of the abbey garden, WAD 621b.
40 WAM 17164.

should not lop the trees or their branches without the owner's permission or (more significantly) without the neighbours being consulted and agreeing.[41]

Most of the identified tenants in the Aldewich area were known at that time by their locative name: for example Alan, Paulinus and Henry, son of Humphrey, were each described as being 'of Aldewich'.[42] But here also William and Walter, each 'of the garden' had lands and houses. Each of them was almost certainly an abbey servant who worked in the abbey's great garden at different times during the thirteenth century, as Eadric 'of the garden' had too, probably as the senior manager in the garden.[43] North of the settlement there stood the enclave of the leper Hospital of St. Giles, for which in the earlier years of the twelfth century King Henry I had probably taken land from the abbot's 'liberty' of Westminster, to enable his wife, Queen Matilda, an independent and strong-minded English lady, to found and endow that first leper hospital 'in the fields', well outside the city of London.[44] The hospital had its own garden too, on its north side.[45]

In contrast, the sloping land which stretched down from the southern frontage of Charing Street to the shoreline of the Thames began to develop a character of its own in the thirteenth century. The whole littoral strip, stretching eastwards from the bend of the river at Charing Cross towards the marshy area which lay round the wide mouth of the Fleet flowing into the Thames, was destined to become and to remain for centuries a zone of large establishments which far exceeded in size and opulence the more ordinary residences in the environs of the London to Westminster road. We have already noticed the large property of the Earl of Pembroke (William Marshal) opposite the crossroads at Charing, which in about 1230 became an Augustinian hospice belonging to a Spanish priory.[46] But, even among the discontinuous collection of abbey charters, we have other evidence that already additional large properties had been formed along this favourable south-facing slope, where the first gravel bank rose up from the silt of the river shore.

In about 1250 William 'le Teuler' sold 'all his land in the parish of St. Martin at Charing', together with one annual rent of 4/1d., to Geoffrey of the Hyde and his wife Isabel, all for the considerable price of 15 marks (£10) and a 'robe of green'.[47] Fortunately the land

---

41 WAM 17560. This garden was in Longditch. See also WAM 17653 and 17636, where a prohibition against cutting down growing trees was imposed when the large and old garden, dating back to the C12, of the Mauduit family, having been restored to the abbey in 1344, was being leased out again in 1350 by the abbot.

42 WAC 408 and 415 (temp. John).

43 For Eadric, who held a 'fee' in this area, see App. A at p, 391 and pp. 149-50 below.

44 Brooke and Keir, *London 800-1216*, p. 319; VCH *Mdx* 1/206. Its foundation signified 'an important epoch in medieval attitudes to social welfare', Brooke and Keir, *ibid*. The C12 and C13 saw a great increase in the incidence of leprosy in Europe, and the creation of 'hospitals' for the victims (later called lazar houses, after the biblical Lazarus) had increased dramatically. There is little doubt that the motive was both to protect the healthy from the contagion as well as to provide homes for the sick: see Clay *Medieval Hospitals*, 35 ff.; Honeybourne, 'Leper Hospitals', TLMAS 21 (1965), 1-61. In the C13 and C14 many royal and civic decrees were directed at detecting and isolating the disease, but the two leper hospitals on former Westminster land (St. Giles's and later St. James's) had already been founded earlier 'in the fields', significantly, well outside London, during the C12.

45 See the reference to it in the 1222 award itself, WAM 12753; also printed in *Acta of A/Bp. S. Langtoni*, No. 54, p. 69. See the award, at p. 36 below, and App B at p. 396. For the hospital, see Plate 8, p. 167.

46 See p. 29 above. For the great houses (eg. Arundel, Suffolk, Durham, Salisbury, Worcester, Somerset) built later along the Thames slope, see Hollar's 7 'unpublished drawings' (London Top. Soc.'s Publn. no. 50).

47 WAM 17157 (1246 x 1257). Geoffrey was also going to have to pay a large annual rent of 40s. to the Templars for this site (see also App.A. at p. 392) , as well as 3s. 4d. to St. Mary's chapel at the abbey. For other Hyde family members, see also pp. 281-3 below.

is described in some detail. In length it extended all the way from the Charing Street down to the river, and in width it measured 105 feet at its frontage on the highway and widened out at the shoreline to 132 feet. These distances were far greater than the usual sizes of ordinary properties in the general neighbourhood.[48] The new purchaser was probably a land-holder in the area of the present Hyde Park, an area which was certainly known as 'the Hyde' later in the same century, as well as 'Hyde Manor' (in effect a sub-manor formed in part of the old manor of Eye) in the next century.[49]

Then towards the end of the thirteenth century another large and similarly-sited property was leased by Abbot Walter of Wenlock to Nicholas *pistor* (baker) and his wife Cecily for their joint and several lives.[50] The property was a 'tenement near La Cherringe', and it too ran from the highway down to the river, but its sizes are not further given. Nicholas had the locative name 'at the cross' (*ad crucem*). By the end of the century, this cross could be either the Eleanor Cross which Edward I had erected in 1294 in memory of his queen, or the older Stone Cross in the Strand.[51] Most likely it was the former, because it would be more difficult to describe the latter as lying near Charing. The site was next door, on both sides, to houses which had 'formerly belonged to John of the Hide', who may perhaps have been the father of Geoffrey of the Hyde, the purchaser of the large property mentioned above.[52]

So already the Thames bank had various substantial establishments to show; and further eastwards along this south-facing slope other similar large sites and their buildings were also becoming visible.[53]

## 4. The parish of the Holy Innocents – and the great Arbitration of 1222

*Preface.* About half way along the Strand roadway, we run into problems about boundaries in medieval times, which have to be mentioned here – and can, I hope, be legitimately by-passed without too much complicated detail.

In 1222 five papal arbitrators, headed by the archbishop of Canterbury Stephen Langton, had to define the line of the eastern ecclesiastical boundary of Westminster, between the parish of St. Margaret's, the parish church of Westminster, and the bishop of London's diocese.[54] The boundary defined by them ran roughly south-eastwards from the enclave of St. Giles on the Holborn road, to the Strand roadway and so down to the river Thames. To the west of this boundary lay the area of Westminster over which the abbot could still exercise his old ecclesiastical jurisdiction. To the east lay the diocese of London over which the bishop of London now had an undisputed jurisdiction.

This boundary line was very different from the earliest boundary line given to the monks for their endowment manor of Westminster by King Edgar, when he founded

---

48　For a discussion of plot-sizes in Westminster and Eye, see App. D at pp. 406 ff.

49　See WAMs 4874 ('La Hyde in the parish of St. Martin's') and 4881 ('La Hyde near Westminster'), 4879 ('La Hyde near Knightsbridge'), 4877 ('La Hyde in Eye'), 4873, 16265 ('manor of La Hyde'), 4878 ('manor of La Hyde')

50　WAM 17159 (probably c.1300)

51　See p. 30 above (Eleanor Cross), and 39 below (Stone Cross); and *The Westminster Corridor*, p. 49.

52　John of the Hyde was also the name of a later holder of the (sub)manor of the Hyde, and in turn his son was yet another John. But the dates and any family relationship are difficult to establish. For Geoffrey, see WAMs 17157 above, and 17420, and pp. 35, 281 n. 76.

53　See also pp. 39-40 below for other large houses above the river shore.

54　For the circumstances in which this arbitration came to be necessary, see App B at p. 396 ff. The issue of the *eastern* boundary was only a part, and not the most important part, of the arbitration. The core issue was whether the abbey was 'exempt' from the ecclesiastical control of the bishop of London, see Appendix B.

the abbey in about 971. The earliest boundary between the abbey's land and the city of London had been the line of the river Fleet, more than a kilometre to the east, on its southwards course between the city and Westminster to join the river Thames.[55] So it is clear that at some later point of time the abbey's area of jurisdiction in Westminster had become significantly reduced – from the river Fleet to the arbitrators' line of 1222.

The question arises whether it was the arbitrators' decision about the boundary in 1222 which was the event which itself *reduced* the abbey's sphere of ecclesiastical power; **or** whether that decision was no more than a restatement or confirmation of a boundary already existing at *that* time, to which the earliest boundary (the river Fleet) had been changed at some time or times in the course of the *previous* 250 years since the foundation of the abbey.

Little of the evidence about this boundary has survived, and some of the difficult issues are considered in Appendix B, below.[56] But after at least 1222 there can be no doubt that, to the gain of the bishop of London, the abbot had no *ecclesiastical* authority in the settlements east of the boundary described by the arbitrators. Secondly the abbey had also lost, in probably the twelfth century, any secular jurisdiction in mainly (but not exactly) the same area, to the city of London.

In these circumstances, only a limited account is given here about the settlements around the churches of the Holy Innocents, St.

Clement Danes, St. Dunstan in the West and St. Bride in and near Fleet Street, and St. Andrew, Holborn, which lay *eastwards* as far as the river Fleet.

At the time when the five papal arbitrators were considering their verdict about the questions put to them, there stood a small church of 'The Holy Innocents' at the point where 'Charing Street' merged into, and became known as, the 'Strand' roadway. The site of the church was on a small part of the ground on which the frontage of the present-day Somerset House stands, the part which is nearest to and facing towards the present 'islanded' church, St. Mary-le-Strand.[57] This more modern church of St. Mary, which now stands alone, in a swirl of modern traffic, is the distant successor of the old church of the Holy Innocents. During the first part of the thirteenth century the church of The Holy Innocents had had its own small parish which is recorded in many Westminster charters,[58] but in effect this parish appears to have been on the London side of the boundary as it was defined in 1222 by the arbitrators, and was therefore *outside* the abbey's ecclesiastical jurisdiction in this part of Westminster.[59]

In 1235 a house standing 'opposite the church of the Holy Innocents' was now described as being 'in the suburbs of London', perhaps reflecting a mistaken view about the effect of the arbitration Award of 1222.[60] So the church and its name were still unchanged thirteen years after the arbitrators' Award, but

55  See *The Westminster Corridor*, pp. 79-80, 166 and coloured Map M.
56  See pp. 396 ff. The Award also deals with the dominant issue about the abbey's 'exemption' from the supervision of the bishop of London.
57  Williams, *Early Holborn* § 1447, referring to the visible foundations of the old church and evidence of burials. The church of the Holy Innocents had been called 'the white monastery' in a charter (WAC 309, which has been dated to 1191-1200); but later it is several times called 'the church', with a 'chapel' nearby. Even the arbitration Award in 1222 refers to this chapel 'next the church of the Innocents'.
58  WAMs 17134 - 17138.
59  But it is clear that there were still some legal arguments about some finer details of the boundary, because the arbitrators expressly reserved certain issues in their definition of it, see p. 398 below.
60  CP 25(1) 146/9/117. The description 'in the suburbs of London' does not assert that it lay within the boundary of London itself, but may reflect some doubts about the status of the ambiguous area between the secular and ecclesiastical boundaries. The secular boundary of the city now lay at Temple & Holborn Bars, pp. 41 and 396-8.

the reference to the city's suburbs seems to have recognised the area's closer connection with London and its bishop. About two years later the church was rebuilt on a site a short distance to the north in the roadway, and it was re-dedicated as 'St. Mary [in] the Strand', as its later islanded building still is; and as such, it soon received royal donations, such as the gift of 150 wax tapers which the ever-religious King Henry III donated to it in April 1240.[61] By 1251-2, another house involved in legal proceedings was identified as now lying in 'the parish of St. Mary le Strand'.[62]

Although by the 1240-50s the church itself of The Holy Innocents had been replaced by a new church of St. Mary the Strand and the abbey no longer held any power over the parish, an existing 'hospice [hospitaria] of the monks of Westminster' still lay somewhere near the new church.[63] We know that there had been a chapel near the church of the Holy Innocents, since the arbitration award of 1222 actually refers to such a chapel, and also that it was called 'the chapel of St. Margaret', perhaps meaning that it was a chapel of the Westminster parish church, St. Margaret's.[64] It is possible that the monks' hospice may have been connected with this chapel, or even housed with it.

It seems that both the church of the Holy Innocents and its successor St. Mary-le-Strand were designed to meet the religious needs of the immediate community, even though there was also the church of St. Martin not far away. The hospice however, and perhaps the chapel as well, were probably for the benefit of abbey

monks who were not well or needed rest.[65] Alternatively they might have been staffed by monks of Westminster, but used for the rest, accomodation and service of pilgrims and travellers on their way to Westminster or beyond.

The fact that a new church was needed at this place does suggest that the resident population along the road and in the vicinity was already strong, and a hospice, if it was for travellers, could indicate that by the mid-thirteenth century the traffic moving on the road was considerable.

Two known chaplains were connected with either the church of the Holy Innocents or the chapel and hospice, or perhaps both. The first was Richard 'chaplain of the Holy Innocents' (as he was called in the charters), who in King John's reign (1200-1216) bought two grants of land which lay in the 'fee' of William of Mohun in the adjoining parish of St. Martin in the area of Charing.[66]

The second chaplain, Robert, who was Richard's son, is known to have been in charge of the hospice, because he was actually named as the *hospitarius* in a charter, with the same title, Robert 'of the Innocents' as his father. He too clearly had finance to run his hospice and authority to deal in relation to property, because in the 1240-50s he purchased a rent of 2d. pa. for the hospice for 12d. Local people apparently contributed to the upkeep of this *hospitaria*, since we find it was a woman, Cristiana, of the nearby Godegrom family who had sold to him this rent of 2d., receivable by her from local land.[67] Later Robert himself

61 See *Cal. Lib. R.*, 1226-40, p. 462, and Williams, *Early Holborn*, § 1449.
62 CP 25(1) 147/17/320.
63 WAM 17542 (1240-50s).
64 WAM 17135 (1240-50s) refers to a chapel by this name, 'in the parish of the Holy Innocents', and this is likely to be the same chapel as that referred to by the arbitration Award. The abbot and monks of course had control over, and were the rector of, the parish church, St. Margaret's, lying by the abbey.
65 See WAM 17445, where Robert the *hospitarius* in making a transaction evinces a concern for sick monks.
66 WAMs 17141 and 17142. One of these lands adjoined 'the ditch of the marshal', and must have lain next to William Marshal's property at Charing crossroads, see p. 29 above. Of the Mohun 'fee', see App. A, p. 392 and 215.
67 WAM 17542 (probably 1240-50s). Although this grant was made ostensibly as a charitable gift 'in soul alms', it was nevertheless a sale. But the price was favourable to the hospice (a purchase rate of only

sold a rent of 3s., receivable from a tenement in the local 'fee of Mohun', to the convent of monks at the abbey for the sum of 24s.[68]

Also near the Holy Innocent community there stood, in the Strand road itself, the old 'Stone Cross' (erected perhaps by King Henry I) where the royal circuit justices 'in eyre' had begun to hold their Middlesex sittings from early in the twelfth century.[69] As one instance we can see Richard Russell the son of Gervase Cocus 'of Westminster' (maybe the head cook at the abbey?), recording with what sounds like a note of triumph that the house, which in the 1240s he was charitably donating to St. Mary's Altar at the abbey, had been previously won by him *by the law of the land before the justices in eyre at the Strand*, in a family dispute with Hawise, his own sister, probably arising from the death of their father.[70]

South of the Strand, where the slope ran down to the edge of the Thames, the old river shore-line slightly further west is still marked to this day by the later Buckingham Water-Gate near the bottom of Villiers Street. It was on this gravel 'strand-bank' of the Thames that the future pattern of great houses, stretching west and east along the river in later centuries, was foreshadowed by early land transactions

of which we have already seen something in the twelfth and thirteenth centuries. The history-to-be of the large properties along this favoured south-facing slope had been forecast earlier, by the 'sale' by the abbot in 1198 of a large area of land there to two lay people, Stephen of Turnham and his wife Edelina.[71] Their new site, described as 'next to the church of the Holy Innocents', had a wide frontage on the street itself of 93 feet (nearly 30 yards) and was even wider nearer the river; and it extended for at least 306 feet if not more (over 102 yards), from its frontage on the street right down to the Thames shore.

About fifty years later a comparable site on the same slope above the river, but slightly further to the west in Charing, was also sold, this time solely between laymen. As we have already seen, it too stretched from Charing Street down to the river shore, and also had rather bigger frontages than Stephen's property, both on the roadside and on the river.[72]

And yet another similar sale of a substantial property on this slope above the river took place twenty or more years later still, again solely between laymen. Roger Chese 'of Westminster' and his wife Elen were the new purchasers in about the 1270s of a messuage and land on the

---

six, rather than the average market rate of ten), so some element of charity was perhaps sufficient to justify the style of the sale. For the Godegrom family in the Charing Street set, see p. 40 below.

68 WAM 17445. For the 'fee of Mohun' which was an early Charing estate, see n. 66 above. The charter also reveals the father/son relationship of Richard and Robert. The figures suggest a large property.

69 See WAMs 16251, 17419 and 17104 and fuller detail in *The Westminster Corridor*, p. 49 and note 16. The Strand Bridge, over a small stream, also stood near here. The Stone Cross still remained the venue of the court in 1354 (WAM 16251). The added presence of the Eleanor cross at Charing by 1294 creates difficulties for the identification of residents' locative names referring to a cross (like Geoffrey '*de cruce*', see p. 28 above). The adjective 'stone' does not help much, because both crosses were made of stone. But the cross in the Strand also became known as the 'Broken Cross' when it fell into disrepair.

70 For his donation, see WAM 17419. The legal action may have been started by the fairly new writ of *mort d'ancestor*, which had been introduced by Henry II about seventy years before; cf. the new remedies referred to at pp. 67, n. 20.

71 WAC 314 (11th November 1198). Shortly before, this site had been recovered by the abbey from Henry fitz Reiner (of a great family in the city of London), when it accepted the site in exchange for a release of a 3s. annual rent; WAC 309 (in which the full measurements are given; with the *length* of the site being greater than 102 yards. The subsequent 're-sale' of the site to Stephen and Edelina was recorded in a court compromise between them and the abbey in the king's court, when in exchange for the Thames site the abbey received from the couple a considerable prize, two hides of land (about 250 acres), plus another one and a half virgates, all in Battersea across the river from Westminster.

72 WAM 17157 (1246 x 1257). See also above, p. 35-6. The price there was a premium of 15 marks (£10) and 'a robe of green'.

river slope where 'King Street' met Charing Street, for the large sum of thirty marks (£20); with considerable rents to pay as well. Roger also owned lands in Eye, from where his forebears may have come. But this large property south of the Strand which had a street-frontage and at the back ran right down to the river shore was probably bought as their main home in Westminster.[73] Its exact measurements are not given, but its size must have been at least comparable with the other great plots, if not much larger still because of the higher price and the rents still to pay.

Finally one should remember the other large property further to the west near Charing which became the subject of a lease for lives granted by the abbey towards the end of the thirteenth century, by Abbot Walter of Wenlock. It too stretched all the way from the road down to the Thames.[74]

The main families living or landholding in or around Charing Street, the Strand or near the successive churches of the Holy Innocents and St. Mary-le-Strand were the Godegroms, the Belgraves, the Hospinelles, the Rockinghams, the Huts, all or some of the *de Fonte* and *de Cruce* family, Stephen de Stranda and family, the Cordwainers and the Parmenters. They appear well established as a continuing 'set', and in the charters relating to the area they become wholly identified with it, in their different capacities as buyers, sellers, donors or witnesses.[75] At least part of this area belonged to the 'fees' of William of Rockingham and the Mohun family.[76]

There were other topographical features in the neighbourhood of which we know a little. A plot, later named 'the Eldehaghe' or 'Elderhawe' (the elder hedge?), is identified to the north of Charing Street, backing onto the 'abbot's garden'.[77] On the south side of the street, 'Coliareswe' or 'Coliereshagh' (? the colliers' way, or hedge) was probably a lane running down to the Thames, and may possibly have been used for the carriage of coal or charcoal landed from the river.[78]

73 WAM 17378. No less than five different tiers of rents were payable for this house. For the Cheses, see also WAMs 17160, 4778 and 4835. They may have been, or had family connections with, the Cheses and Chesemans, who also figure in the early C14 in Knightsbridge and Westbourne and have first names in common, see WAMs 16230, 16171, 16224, 16266, 16273, etc. Their known lands in Eye at that time were 'one plot, with houses built upon it' in the vill of Eye, one acre of arable and two half-acre strips near the vill, one of which lay between 'the watercourse of King Edward' and 'the road to Ossulton' (the Hundred meeting place in present Mayfair, see *The Westminster Corridor*, pp. 52-3. This 'road to Ossulston', leading to the present Hyde Park Corner, and thence to Westminster Lane (later Tyburn Lane, now Park Lane, see *The Westminster Corridor*, p. 82), ran not far from the line of the present Constitution Hill. No measurements are given for the Cheses' new Thames-side property, but cf. the length of 102 yards or more for a similar property, as given in note 71 above, which also ran from the street down to the river. For the vendor, Laurence II of the castle, see p. 269 below.

74 WAM 17159 (c. 1290-1300). Unfortunately its measurements are not given. See also p. 36 above.

75 WAM 17143B, 17145, 17146, 17152, 17153, 17153*, 17154, 17155A, 17156. *Post-1300*: 17163, 17165, 17166, 17167. For Stephen de Stranda, probably an early *professional* attorney, see pp. 289 ff. and 374 below.

76 For William of Rockingham and his father Robert, see pp. 393 and 174-5 below. Half of one house in that fee had belonged to Matilda, wife of Richard Hospinelle, while the other half of the house was held by Matilda's sister, Avice; see also WAMs 17152, 17153, 17153*, 17154 and 17156. The house 'Hoppindehalle' (WAMs 17476 and 17692) on the west side of 'King Street' (see *Survey of London*, vol xiv/3-4) is probably different, in spite of the similar-sounding name. For the Mohun family, see p. 392 and 215 below.

77 WAMs 17163 (dated 1336) and 17641 (1346). The 'Skynner' family, involved in these, were definitely 'of Charing', at that time. Therefore the 'abbot's garden' referred to in these charters is probably again 'the great garden' (now Covent Garden) north of Charing Street, although it had been handed over to the convent more than a century before, see p. 33 above. But the abbot had also had his own 'smaller garden', probably more personal to him, behind the west side of 'King Street', see WAM 17370 (1220s).

78 WAM 17357 (1253), 17424 (1240-50s). Both coal and charcoal were commodities in use at this time. Much later a similar naming took place, when Temple Lane, in the Temple area, became known as the landing lane for the oranges and lemons by which St. Clement Danes was known in song.

## 5. The church and parish of St. Clement Danes

Still further eastwards along the Strand from the church of the Holy Innocents lay the parish of St. Clement 'of the Danes', centred on the site of the present church which like St. Mary-le-Strand stands closely islanded in the Strand in the midst of modern traffic. As had happened with the parish of the Holy Innocents, any entitlement in law on the part of the abbey to the church and parish of St. Clement's could not have survived the decision of the papal arbitrators in 1222 – if it had not been lost many years before.[79]

Both the early history of St. Clement's and its connection with the Danes are largely legendary, although the very survival of such a name does give credibility to the tradition that it was an area where the Danes had once congregated, for whatever reason.[80] St Clement was honoured with dedications among the Danes and other northern peoples, and there is evidence that the nearby parish of St Bride may also have been a similar place of settlement for other northern invaders, namely Norse Vikings coming via Ireland.[81] This suggests that the area outside the walls of London may well have been settled (or resettled) by various groups of Danes and other northerners, perhaps towards the end of the tenth century, or during the eleventh century when a Danish king, Cnut, had become king of England.[82] But details of any history and topography of the St. Clement's parish are limited, although the abbey still has a small group of charters relating to it.[83]

Most significantly the church stood 'outside the bar', ie. beyond (to a person travelling *from* London) the tollgate at the New Temple which had been established by the city of London in the twelfth century, to denote a new *secular* boundary between the city of London and the 'liberty' of Westminster, long before the papal arbitrators of 1222 had recorded the ecclesiastical boundary of Westminster.[84]

Unlike the present church, the old church did not stand on quite such a narrow 'island', directly surrounded by thundering traffic. It lay between the southern end of the Aldewich ('Wic' or 'Wych Street') and the street of the Strand, and it certainly had a number of properties lying 'behind' it (*retro ecclesiam*), with their occupants named.[85] Even as late as 1677, in Ogilby and Morgan's map of London,

79 See p. 36 above and App. B, pp. 396 ff. below.
80 One can mistakenly see the Danes in London as always hostile. But there is no doubt that they had 'settled' in the south in the same way as in the Danelaw, though far less pervasively. But they were foreigners, with prejudice and hostility to overcome, and so a settlement outside the city makes sense; cf. the next note and text.
81 Brooke and Keir, *London 800-1216,* 139-140 and 141-142 made a strong case that the nearby St. Bride's was rebuilt and rededicated by other men from the north, Irish Norse settlers, in the C11. This appears similar to the ostensible link between St. Clement's, a nearby parish also established outside the walls of London, and a Danish origin. The existence of a settlement and/or the church at the site of St. Clement's, and at the adjoining site of St. Dunstan in the West, at an even earlier date (in or after the C10) is suggested in *The Westminster Corridor,* p. 55 (where the issue concerns an even earlier foundation for such churches, in the high anglo-saxon era). Another indication of a genuine ancient origin for the original St. Clement's church is the fact, according to Brooke and Keir, *ibid.,* 134, that apparently it stood near the site of an old cross.
82 See *The Westminster Corridor,* p. 67-8
83 WACs 393-397.
84 WAC 395 (1197 x 1198). 'Ansegod de Barra' (of the bar), a witness to WAC 397 (another St. Clement's charter, to be dated 'late C12') clearly lived near the barrier. Did he perhaps operate its opening and shutting? It looks as though the bar probably stood where the present boundary of the city of London's ward of 'Farringdon Without' stands, at 'Temple Bar'. Williams, *Early Holborn* §§9 and 816 also refers to the erection of a similar bar or bars in High Holborn before 1183 (nearly forty years before the arbitration), and suggests that the creation of that bar may have taken place when the Templars established their English headquarters there in 1128.
85 The holdings 'behind the church' are named in WAC 395 (c. 1198).

there were still properties shown standing on an island behind the church, in a row which that map, perhaps mischievously, called 'the backside of St. Clement's'. Among the holders of properties in this group in 1198, we can see 'Simon of the gaol' (who has been named as an abbey servant, ie. the gaoler of the Westminster prison, housed in the abbey gateway leading onto Tothill Street).[86] We can see also a resident member of the Rockingham family, Robert of Rockingham;[87] as well as 'Robert of the Temple', perhaps an official or member of the adjoining New Temple which had been established in about 1161.[88]

John, the 'parson' of the parish, and William, his brother the chaplain, are also named (as witnesses), together with some of the other local residents.[89]

Although the parish of St. Clement's lay outside the 'bar' marking the *secular* boundary of the city of London, there can be little doubt that the parish must have enjoyed a considerable stimulus which proximity to a commercial city can give to an outlying suburb. Whether or not the parish had already been subject to the *ecclesiastical* hand of the bishop of London in his nearby seat of power

in the city, it certainly became so after 1222 and (from whatever date) it may have also benefitted in the secular field from the closer connections with power which a relationship with a nearby bishop could give.

In 1161 the Knights Templar had moved from their quarters at the Old Temple, a site at the top of the present Chancery Lane, having acquired land south of Fleet Street, presumably from Robert of Beaumont, the second Earl of Leicester, one of Henry II's justiciars who had strong affiliations to the Templars and was the lord of that fee.[90] Although this site, unlike St. Clement's, was marginally *within* the city of London's 'bar' at the top of Fleet Street and therefore was (and still is) part of the city, it lay immediately adjacent to the parish of St. Clement's, and the Templars with all their business activities clearly brought a different neighbourhood and milieu for that parish. They built their new quarters at the New Temple, with a notable gateway and a second round church which was dedicated in 1185 by the visiting Patriarch of Jerusalem, probably in the presence of King Henry himself.[91] St. Clement's next-door must have felt these vibrations of both secular and ecclesiastical power.

86  Rosser *Westminster* 17.  But at about the same time Simon sold all his land 'in the vill of Westminster' to the Lady Altar at the abbey (WAM 17323 or WAC 411, 1197 x 1200).  Comparison of WACs 411, 395 and 397 (and the abutments in those charters) suggests that Simon could also have been known under the recorded name 'Simon of Fleet Bridge'; and that the lands sold by him to the abbey were in St. Clement's parish, and that the 'gaol' might even have been the city's Fleet prison (close to the Fleet bridge), rather than the abbey gaol.  But for Simon of the gaol as a servant of the abbey, see p. 100 below.

87  For Robert of Rockingham, a senior clerk of the royal chamberlain, Robert Mauduit who had one of the major establishments in Longditch and Tothill in Westminster, see pp. 174-5 below.

88  For the importance of the New Temple as a 'bank' and treasury for Westminster and government, see also text below and p. 176-7.

89  As witnesses in WAM 17077 (WAC 397, late C12).  Notable residents of the city of London itself did not usually act as witnesses to transactions relating to land outside the walls, see Mason, *Westminster Abbey Charters*, p. 22, and most witnesses were either those who lived locally or those who had interests in the subject-matter of the transaction.

90  Any records of the 'purchase' have eluded me.  Perhaps it was Henry II who simply ordered it in favour of his Templars.  See Lees, *Records of the Templars*, pp. lxxxviii - ix and liii; and see Williams, *Early Holborn*, § 1315.  Before 1185, the Templars had also acquired the advowsons of the church of St. Clement Danes and the chapel of the Holy Innocents, Lees, *ibid*, pp. lxxxv and 13.  Almost certainly Henry II's influence had been at work in these moves.  In 1159, he had already granted or procured the grant to the Templars of not only other land on the bank of the river Fleet (towards its exit to the Thames, below Baynard Castle), for them to make a mill there, but also a messuage near the Fleet bridge, see Williams, *ibid.*, § 1/238 and 245, 2/1316, and WAM 13436 (WAC 354, late C12).   For the Templars' holding as a fee, see pp. 391-2 below. For early 'hard-up' Templars, see Plate 8, p. 167.

91 The gateway is actually noticed in WAM 17139 (temp. John).  The Old Temple church had also been round.

From that new site the Templars continued to exercise their financial activities as both a treasury and, in effect, an international 'bank', with close links with the king and his financial officers, and indeed with all who wished to deposit, borrow or despatch money or treasure.[92] So although still just outside the limits of the city, the adjoining parish of St. Clement was moving into a new world.

## 6. The lost area

But beyond this point (where the city boundary still stands) the scene further eastwards had entirely changed in the three centuries since the abbey was founded. Even the secular writ of the abbot of Westminster, with all its financial benefits for the abbey such as tolls and increasing rents, no longer ran beyond the established roadway 'bar' (shortly to be known as the Temple Bar); nor beyond Holborn Bar on the other great road; nor beyond the boundary which joined those two Bars and then extended down to the Thames. As for the abbot's ecclesiastical jurisdiction, the original limits of that had already been left way behind at *another* jagged boundary-line, as confirmed by the papal arbitrators in 1222, which stretched south from St. Giles to the parish of the Holy Innocents and so down to the Thames.

In these areas of Fleet Street and Holborn, reaching eastwards to the erstwhile boundary formed by the river Fleet, which were now subject to the administrations of both the city of London and the bishop of London in their different spheres of power, the tempo of life appeared to be much more hectic. For along the Thames shoreline, even westwards from St Clement Danes, bishops and secular magnates were already lined up to acquire or develop sites on the slope between the roadway and the Thames, where they could build substantial 'inns' for themselves, for use as their town houses when new parliamentary duties and other increasing royal commands or diocesan obligations required their presence in the capital.

From about 1174 other bishops, such as Richard of Ilchester, now the bishop of Winchester, and after him his two illegitimate sons who in sequence became bishops of Salisbury, were successively esconced in their substantial 'inn' south of Fleet Street.[93] Other ecclesiastical institutions too, such as the Order of Carmelites (the 'White Friars' or 'Carmelites of Fletestrete'), the Canons of St. Osyth's Priory in Essex and Westminster's own leper Hospital of St. James were equipping themselves with sites of their own on Fleet Street and its hinterland.[94] A Dominican house had already been established in Shoe Lane by 1220. Even the abbey of Westminster itself, the former lord of all this block of land, had joined in the growing acquisition and development of property within what had once been part of its own foundation endowment from King Edgar. But now the abbey did so merely as a purchaser, vendor, donor or donee of individual sites.

Meanwhile as property continued to develop in the northern block of land between Fleet Street and Holborn, the linking of these two main roads by one original solitary lane called Scholande (now 'Shoe Lane') lying near the bank of the river Fleet, had been echoed by the creation of the 'Newestrete of the

---

92 For details about the New Temple's function as a treasury, and financial agency, see pp. 176-7 below, where William of the Temple, an official of Robert Mauduit the royal chamberlain, is discussed; and Brooke and Keir, *London*, pp. 231-233. Later in the C13 the New Temple was to contribute to political events, when a hall on the site became the place where 'parliaments' met in 1259 and 1272 during Henry III's dealings with some of his barons.

93 For Richard of Ilchester, see below pp. 87, 111 n.97, 181 and 392.

94 BL. Add. MS. 15664 f. 149 and Williams, *Early Holborn*, 1/775; WAM 13847 (WAC 392, temp. John); WAM 13846 (WAC 390, temp. John); WAM 17459 (1282). The last-mentioned charter was a royal order to the abbot of Westminster to take special care to prevent the escape of a felon, Roger of Hertford, who had been convicted of murder and robbery in the Carmelites' house in Fletestrete and then had (presumably) been apprehended within Westminster and lodged in the gaol in the abbey gatehouse. See also Williams, *ibid.*, § 1/242 and 1309-11.

Templars' (now Chancery Lane) and later by the 'Factors' Lane' (now Fetter Lane); each of these three new nearly-straight roads made access between south and north yet more easy and facilitated the spread of the more tortuous later developments in this area.[95]

But none of this physical and financial 'growth' benefitted the abbey, as it once might have done if the abbey had not lost, to the city, its secular powers over this area in the twelfth century.

Equally there were the old churches and parishes of the lost sector of the abbey's old 'liberty': – St. Dunstan's in the West, at the top of Fleet Street; St. Bride's between Fleet Street and the ancient river marshes of the Thames, each with its early foundation in anglo-saxon times; and the oldest of all, St Andrew's, Holborn, which had already been an 'old wooden church' at the time when the abbey was founded in about 971, and stood near to the crossing by the extended 'Watling Street' over the deep bed of the river Fleet, on the road's passage into the city of London.[96]

Whatever the date when the loss to the abbey of ecclesiastical rights over this sector occurred, it had now been confirmed by the papal arbitrators (as it were, the final court of appeal) that none of the financial and other benefits from these churches and their parishes would ever again accrue to the abbey. And for his part, the bishop of London knew for certain after 1222 that the precise boundary of his rights over the abbey's erstwhile eastern sector was assured without further dispute, even if he did not know it already.[97]

95  See the clear impact of these three north-south roads on subsequent developments in this rectangular block of land, still revealed visually even as late as 1682 in the Morden and Lea map of London and Westminster.

96  For the anglo-saxon charter, see *The Westminster Corridor*, pp. 79-80 and 166.  If it is difficult to imagine now the then form of the oldest church of St. Andrew near what is now the Holborn Viaduct, one can learn from the little not-too-distant part-Saxon church of Greenstead, near Ongar in Essex, which still has at least one side of its nave composed of upright but halved tree trunks on the outside, in part a surviving 'old wooden church'.

97  Apart, that is, from minor issues about small details in the boundary which the arbitrators' Award had expressly reserved, see App. B, at p. 398 (c).

# CHAPTER 3

# Roads, ditches and fields

## A. The roadways and lanes of Westminster[1]

While the principal roads which crossed Westminster were the two east-west Roman 'streets' giving access to the city of London from more distant parts, a network of shorter roads had already developed within the central area of the manor and, as we shall see, most of these played an even more significant role in the expansion and shaping of Westminster than the two great streets did.

### *'King Street'*

One of these shorter roads was the immediate means of access from the crossroads at Charing to the centre of Westminster, where the palace and the abbey stood. This road, or track as it must have been originally, which in part lay on the line of the present Whitehall, was eventually to become the main street of a busy Westminster. But in the early days of the abbey in the tenth century, traffic on the road would have been small, since there was no royal palace yet at the end of the road, and pilgrims and other visitors had little incentive at that time to travel to a small monastery set in a still marshy area, particularly while war and aggressive Danes continued to threaten the London area.

But with the establishment of peace and the accession of the Danish king, Cnut, to the English throne in 1016, it may be that Westminster was beginning to become a more attractive place to visit. King Cnut is said to have favoured Abbot Wulnoth, one of the early anglo–saxon abbots, and on frequent visits to the abbey to have presented valuable relics to

it, which may have enticed future pilgrims.[2] And with the return of an English king in 1042, the whole scene began to change. The rebuilding of a much grander church in stone by King Edward the Confessor and the creation of a palace for himself next door to the church, capped by his own burial in the abbey which resulted in an increase of interest in the abbey's shrines and relics – all of these created an entirely new situation in which a road of access to the centre of Westminster was bound to become far more often used. Then the arrival of the Normans, the Conqueror's choice of the abbey for his crowning and of the palace at Westminster for his Christmas feasting, and the enormous increase, from twelve to eighty, in the number of monks at the new abbey had all served to confirm this new situation.

From then on, the growth in traffic making its way both towards and away from the centre of Westminster must have begun to reach increasing totals. Consider some of the categories of horse-borne or walking travellers and of the ox-drawn or horse-drawn traffic which progressively had to use this principal road – the progresses of the successive Norman and later the Angevin kings, when they set out on their country-wide journeys, or returned from them, with their escorts and equipment-carrying carts; the movements of foot soldiers or mounted men during military excursions; horse-borne, cart-borne or walking visitors to the palace on royal business; deliveries of produce, wood for fuel and other essential supplies, being carried by cart to both the palace and the abbey from outlying

---

1 The sections on 'Ditches' and 'Fields' begin on p. 52 and p. 56 respectively.
2 *Flete* (ed. Robinson), pp. 70 and 81; see further for context, *The Westminster Corridor*, p. 66 and n. 7.

manors; pilgrims and travellers visiting the abbey in fulfilment of religious duties or on business; and as Westminster became more built-up, the movements of the residents themselves on journeys away from the town and back, or within the town on business or pleasure.[3]

And yet the strange thing is that for nearly 200 years after the Conquest this essential road seems to have been virtually nameless, in contrast to other nearby streets. *'The kinge's street'*, as it occasionally came to be called in the early thirteenth century (more as a description than a name), was usually described in the previous century in roundabout expressions in formal documents: eg., *'the road which runs from Charing to the king's palace at Westminster'*; or *'the road which leads from London to the abbey at Westminster'*; or sometimes in reverse direction, during the twelfth century, *'the road which runs from the palace of Westminster to London'*.[4] Before 1250, many houses which can be identified, from other evidence, as standing in this main but narrow street were described in charters without the use of any street name. Very often, all that they received as a description of their location was *'in the vill of Westminster'*, an ambiguous form of identification, which in some charters can be shown to refer to different parts of the town.

By way of contrast, we can see that many streets within the city of London were already being identified by specific name; and even in other parts of Westminster itself the same was true. The names of roads such as Longditch or Tothill Street in Westminster were certainly commonplace before the end of the twelfth century. This may indicate that it was those sections of the Longditch and Tothill roads nearest to the abbey which had become more built-up, and more quickly, than 'King Street', and confirm impressions based on other evidence that 'King Street' was less urban on its frontage in the late twelfth century than one would expect, even if it was already beginning to become the home of new government officials imported by King Henry II.[5]

### The line of 'King Street'

Unlike the modern Whitehall, this medieval main street was no wide thoroughfare. To modern eyes the old street appears, both on later maps and in pictures, to have been a narrow and, for at least half its length, an oblique one, without pretensions; but no more so than most medieval main streets. In its course from Charing, the street began by following the line, but fell far short of the width, of its modern successor, Whitehall. But from the point where Downing Street now lies, the old 'king's street' diverged to the west of the line of the present Parliament Street, and approached the cemetery wall of the abbey precinct nearly opposite the door of the abbey's north transept. It was only much later in the eighteenth century, long after intervening Tudor street-alterations, that the southern end of the former 'king's street' was abandoned as a main thoroughfare and was superseded in a more modern road development, which opened in 1750 on the site of the wider and straighter roadway of the modern Parliament Street.[6]

---

3   The river also remained a common vehicle for all movements and may have drawn off some of the road traffic.

4   To avoid having to use such roundabout descriptions, the name 'King Street' in *inverted commas* will always be used in this book to denote the street, regardless of date.

5   As regards the appearance of the frontages in early 'King Street', and of frontages in Tothill Street and Charing Street, some of the C12 and C13 charters fortunately give actual measurements of the properties involved. It is therefore possible to attempt a few patterns of housing in parts of these streets, but these closer details are relegated to Appendix D, at pp. 405-9 below.

6   *Survey of London*, vols. x, p.1, and xiv, Plate 67. Sir George Scharf's two drawings of King Street, made in 1859, show the street in its C19 condition, ie. updated as regards buildings, but still extremely narrow and 'old' in appearance ; Jackson (ed), *Sir G. S.'s Drawings of Westminster*, pp. 12-15 (London Topog. Soc., Publ. 147, 1994). This part of the King's Street was retained as late as1898 when the wedge of old housing between it and Parliament Street was demolished; Parliament Street was further widened, and larger government offices were built over the sites of the old 'King's Street' and its frontage houses.

### Enedehithe lane (Endiff)

Running towards the Thames, at right angles from the Charing-to-palace or 'king's' street, there lay a lane which became progressively more important after the first major development of the Thamesbank area took place in the late twelfth century. Known as *Enedehithe lane* or, more commonly, Endiff lane or just *'Endiff'*, it afforded an ancient access to a river wharf, which must have been used for personal access and residents' provisions.[7] But its history was older than even the palace, since its name was an old English one, meaning apparently *'wharf frequented by ducks'*.[8] The lane became an important artery, both for the prominent residents who came to live nearby and for the transport of people and goods carried by the extensive river traffic between London and Westminster, and it gave its name to the area immediately surrounding it.[9]

### The Longditch and Tothill Streets

By way of contrast with 'King Street', Tothill Street and Longditch (a lane or a street) were already known precisely by those names in the years before 1200.[10] The outlying and separate site of the settlement of Tothill itself, the point towards which Tothill Street was directed, was of great antiquity, a place on the edge of the marshy area known later as Tothill Field(s). There is no doubt that in its early years Tothill was regarded as a settlement on its own, named even as a 'vill', which later was still being referred to as distinct from the 'street' which ran towards it. It was the place where in the tenth century a small hill or mound had been recorded in the second Westminster charter. At that time it had probably been used as a lookout against the Danes, but was later eroded by natural or human forces until it disappeared.[11] From an early date, the road which ran towards Tothill from the abbey and was known as Tothill Street had been the site of the extensive abbey almonry, a separate building complex on the south side of the road outside the abbey's west gate.

As already indicated, the area lying in the angle between the two roadways of Longditch and Tothill Street was used extensively by the abbey, at least in the second half of the twelfth century, for the bestowal of land on favoured servants, as need arose, and a number of buildings in those roads had been built. In turn these senior servants had also tended to grant sub-lettings to other colleagues, sometimes more junior ones.[12]

Apart from such piecemeal developments, Tothill Street was used later in the period both before and after 1230 as the site of at least two new housing developments. One was the building of fourteen houses or more on the north side of the street opposite the abbey's almonry.[13] The other was called the 'Virgin Mary's new rent': about a dozen houses, designed apparently by or for the abbey, to provide homes for twelve workmen (including at least four masons who were employed on abbey business), and thereby to raise money, in the form of rents, for the building of a new chapel for the Virgin Mary on which the monks were engaged at that time.[14]

---

7   The palace apparently soon had its own quay. The name Enedehithe is spelt in several different forms. The vulgar but easiest form, 'Endiff', is usually employed hereafter.

8   Rosser, *Med. Westminster* 18. The marshes no doubt remained along the shorelines of the Thames and wild ducks still swam and flew around the wharf in the C12 and C13.

9   For some of the earliest known residents of Endiff, see pp. 110-12, 155-7 below.

10  Tothill Street: WAC 446 (1194-97); Longditch: WAM 17312 (WAC 230, 1194 x 1198). The latter ran from the abbey's west gate northward along the Clowson stream.

11  See *The Westminster Corridor*, pp. 81 and 166. A mound stood either at the Broadway (Tanner, TLMAS 1948-51, 16/235), or near the present Vincent Square until after the mid-seventeenth century, (Barton, *Lost Rivers*, p. 38). 'Tothill' indicates a look-out hill (Gelling, *Place-Names*, 171; M.E *toot*).

12  For these stages of development, see p. 23 above, and other references given in note 33 on p. 21.

13  See pp. 270-1 below. This was probably a private development by the Mauduit family, for investment ends.

14  WAD 520-27, Rosser, *Medieval Westminster*, pp. 48 and 152, Colvin, *Building A/cs*, pp. 229, 249, 297 etc. For the new Lady Chapel, see pp. 129, 137-8 and 190 below.

### The La Neyte road

Further westwards along Tothill Street, at the present Broadway where the vill stood, another road branched off left, towards the present Strutton Ground (once *Stretton Ground)* and thereafter Rochester Row, in the direction of the rather bleak and marshy Tothill Fields. This road ran towards the southwest, in the direction of an 'islanded' site in the manor of Eye and a building there, which in the 1220s became the abbot's private country house called 'La Neyte'. 'The island' (as it was called, being apparently moated all round, and perhaps having once been a genuine island in an even more marshy area) was probably held in the early years of the century by a prominent resident of Eye who also held properties in Westminster, and was known as 'William the little *(parvus),* of Eye'.[15]

But it was William's son Laurence, a clerk probably in the employ of the abbey, who after his father's death sold the 'island' in about 1223 to Abbot Richard of Berking.[16] The abbot thereupon began the practice, which his successors followed, of using La Neyte as his personal house, to which he could retire, the better to withstand the pressures of abbey administration. Previously he had already begun to follow a more private routine in his own quarters at the abbey, but could now do so in a place more remote from the business of the abbey itself.

To reach the next-door manor of Eye, the road towards La Neyte had to cross a branch of the river Tyburn (flowing southwards to reach the Thames not far from the present Vauxhall Bridge) by a bridge which lay near the modern junction of the Vauxhall Bridge Road and Warwick Way and understandably became known as the 'Abbotsbridge'. This was one of probably five bridges over the Tyburn which were built at different times on the roads leading from the manor of Westminster to its western neighbour, the manor of Eye.[17] After crossing the bridge, the abbot could reach La Neyte by a causewayed road which was raised above the marshy fields (on the line of the present Warwick Way) and was known as the Willow Walk.[18]

It was probably at the point where the road to La Neyte branched off from Tothill Street that various houses lay *between the two roads,* just after the fork.[19] The effect was that each of these properties fronted and backed onto different roadways. This was certainly the case in the second half of the thirteenth century and afterwards, and it had probably been the same much earlier. On one occasion, a property was even described as lying between the two roads *'as though enclosed with walls'.*[20]

---

15  For William Parvus, see further pp. 22 n. 38 and 330-1 below. The name 'island' *(insula)* was used principally for La Neyte, but of course 'Eia' itself (ie. the whole manor of Eye) had also meant an 'island'. See Map A, on Plates 2-3.

16  WAM 4772, see p. 201 below. 'Island' was still being used later in the C14 to describe the site of La Neyte house, in a/cs kept by the king's bailiff in 1315-27, when Edw. II briefly held La Neyte 'at the will of the abbot and convent'; cf. Harvey, *W. of Wenlok,* p. 57. It had 5 gardens, Mclean, *Med. Eng. Gdns,* 107-8.

17  For 'Eybridge', see p. 49 below. For bridges on the Piccadilly road, and the 'lower road' (ie. Spitalstrete), see pp. 15-6 above. The fifth bridge (or a culvert) was built on the present Oxford Street at the point where the Tyburn had crossed that Street (near the present Stratford Place), *The Westminster Corridor,* pp. 42-44.

18  Rutton, 'Manor of Eia', Archaeologia, vol. 62 (1910), p. 41. There are frequent references, in the Eye farm accounts, to the willow trees in the manor, particularly on the 'abbot's causeway' or 'willow walk' (now Warwick Way) and round the mill ponds, eg. DS, *Eye A/cs,* pp. 81, 94, 109, 115 etc.

19  WAMs 17392A (1280s); 17642 (1346).

20  However each of these roads was said to lead to the 'vill of Eye'. This raises questions as to whether it was the fork of the La Neyte road or some other fork, on another road. But on balance it was probably the former.

## The duelling ground

On the south of the road leading towards La Neyte there lay *'the place where champions are wont to fight'* – where 'trial by battle' in legal 'actions of right' relating to the title of land could still take place in the mid-thirteenth century. Even at this time it was still possible, if not usual, to have such an issue decided by a duel between the parties themselves or their appointed champions. This, in spite of the fact that, nearly a hundred years before, Henry II in the course of his judicial reforms had provided a legal means for deciding issues of proprietary rights to land by a 'jury' of twelve knights of the shire.[21]

One such recorded instance of a trial by duel in Westminster had taken place before about 1236, when Sir (*dominus*) Henry Bucuinte, a citizen of London, had won some valuable land north of the abbey's 'great garden' (the present Covent Garden) in an action decided *'per duellum percussum'*.[22] Towards the end of the previous century there had even been a professional 'champion' resident in Westminster, who had owned a house and lands in the vill. This had been Brungar *Athleta*, 'Brungar the champion'; whose daughter Beatrix later held the property, which adjoined Spitalstrete west of the leper hospital near the river Tyburn, as well as a house and other lands nearer the hospital.[23] To stretch a point, he could well have been Sir Henry's champion.

## The road towards the the village of Eye, and the location of the village itself

The village of Eye lay only just across the Tyburn stream which formed the manor boundary between Westminster and Eye, and it formed a vital link in the circle of the Westminster road system. For that, and other reasons, it should be considered in the context of Westminster.

Its geography and history are dealt with below, but it is clear from various charters that the main street of the village ran in a roughly south-north direction, with the 'ditch' or bed of the Tyburn lying roughly parallel on the east of the road, and with village houses and plots sited between the road and the stream-bed.[24] Its exact location is considered in detail in Appendix C. For the first time, the village can now be proved to have been at the site of the modern Buckingham Palace and its garden.[25]

The road to Eye from Tothill (after leaving the fork to the La Neyte road) had continued westwards along the stretch now called Petty France, before turning north-west along the road now known as Buckingham Gate, leading to the site of Buckingham Palace.[26] South of the site of the later palace, the road crossed the river Tyburn by another bridge, which later became known as *Eybridge*. Having now entered the manor of Eye, the road then approached the village from the south and ran northwards along the Eye 'high street', and after leaving it, then continued into the

---

21  After 1179 this new method of trial was called the 'king's grand assize'. In an action over a proprietary right, a defendant accused of wrongly withholding land could now decline the crude Norman method-of-proof by 'battle' and could choose to be tried by a 'jury' of twelve knights in the royal court: see Warren, *Henry II*, 348-354; Sutherland, *Novel Disseisin*, 35-6. The 'jury' formed their own view, from local knowledge and inquiry. But the option still lay with the defendant to have a trial by battle. That method of trial naturally fell into disuse, but survived in theory. Finally when, as late as 1819, a defendant (accused of murder in a private prosecution) sought to have the issue tried by battle, that form of procedure had to be abolished rapidly by statute, as 'a mode of Trial unfit to be used'.

22  Bucuinte's 'battle': WAM 17444 (1236-7), and see pp. 33-4. Resonantly, *'percussum'* echoes the clash of battle.

23  Brungar and daughter: WAD 555 and WAMs 17314 (WAC 406, late 12C), 17415, 17109, 17110, 17427; and see also pp. 16 and 393. Another trial by combat in Westminster is also recorded, see p. 146 n. 40.

24  See WAMs 4787, 4788, 4789, 4790, 4792, 4793, 4819, 4830, 4835.

25  For App. C, see pp. 400 ff. Rutton, 'Manor of Eia', *Archaeologia* 62. (1910) p. 42 asserts, with no reasoning, that the present Palace 'nearly occupies' the situation of the vill, but had already said (incorrectly, I believe) that the Eycross, near the old *cuford*, was the position of the vill, again without giving reasons.

26  'Petty France' was a later name, derived probably from the name in or before 1531 of a mansion in this area called 'Pety Cales', occupied by Lord Berners, the custodian in charge of Calais. It lay on the site

southern part of the present Green Park. There at a junction, marked later with a cross which became known as *Eycross*, this road from the 'vill of Eye' met *Spitalstrete*, which was coming from St. James's leper hospital and Charing. The two conjoined roads then continued, as one, north-westwards in the direction of a simple crossroad (at the present highly complicated Hyde Park Corner), and from there heading on the main road towards the village of Knightsbridge, clustered round its bridge over the Westbourne river. So a circle of roads joining these parts of Westminster and Eye had been completed; with its final exit to the westbound main road.[27]

### 'Rosamund Manor'

Between Tothill and Eye, a small private estate known as 'Rosamund's Manor' was created as a sub-'manor' of Westminster, at some point of time in the late twelfth or the thirteenth century. It is included here because it fronted towards the Tothill to Eye road (just described), and it had a toll-gate on that road. The site itself lay partly under the present Birdcage Walk and the adjoining Wellington Barracks, in the south-west corner of the present St James's Park, adjoining the road from Tothill to Eye (now 'Buckingham Gate'). The house and garden probably contained up to twenty acres, and the 'ditch' which served it became the boundary of an adjoining meadow. Part of the estate was later turned into a large pond, but this was apparently filled in in the late eighteenth century.

The reason why this sub-estate was created is obscure, nor is the original recipient of it known. Presumably it was granted by the abbey either for its own purposes or at the request or direction of the king. The first we know of the estate authentically is that in the years around 1300 it was occupied by John Benstead, Edward I's closest clerk and confidant.[28] Where the estate faced towards the Tothill to Eye road, one of the seven tollgates for entry to the Westminster fairs was positioned in the mid-thirteenth century.[29] The right to hold two fairs each year had been granted to the abbey by Henry III in 1245, and the tolls were one of the means whereby the abbey benefitted from the grant, as the king in his enthusiasm for the abbey had intended.[30] It is doubtful that the sub-manor of Rosamund's was created as some adjunct to a toll-gathering exercise, but that possibility cannot be ruled out entirely.

A more sensational explanation for the origin of Rosamunds links it with King Henry II personally. That king's strong connections with Westminster, in choosing to bring his main government offices close to his palace in Westminster,[31] and his periodical presence at the palace, has made it tempting to link the creation and naming of the sub-manor with Rosamund Clifford, the king's beloved mistress with whom he lived openly for a time before 1176. Certainly the position of the sub-manor, so close to the palace, would have been convenient for a liaison. Moreover there were suspicions of an apt and very recent precedent

---

of the old 'Mauduitsgarden', which from there stretched as far eastwards as Longditch, see also pp. 24 n. 45 and 160-1. 'Buckingham Gate', the modern name for the old road from Tothill to Eye at this point, took the place of an intervening name for the same street, St. James's Street (as shown on the 1755 map at Westminster Archives).

27 For this, see the relevant Eye and Westminster charters, the later Private Act by which Henry VIII acquired the abbey's lands in the St. James's area in 1531, and a map of the manor of Eye in 1614. For the Act, see 23 H. VIII, c. 33, and *Survey of London* vol. xiv / 257 ff.; and for the 1614 map, see Appendix C at p. 401 below.

28 *Cal. P. R.*, 1307-10, p. 58. For John Benstead, who also held much land in Eye, see pp. 285-7 below.

29 Rosser, *Medieval Westminster*, p. 105.

30 See pp. 204 and 212 below. For the tollgate, see also p. 285 below. In 1298 the two fairs were reduced to just the one in October, but the length of that one (in October) had been progressively extended to 15 days in 1248 and finally to 32 days in 1298, see pp. 212 and 308 below.

31 See pp. 67-8 and 117-8 below.

for a local royal intrigue, in the much-criticised grant of the manor of Chelsea by the illegitimate Abbot Gervase to Dameta, his mother who was the mistress of his father King Stephen.[32] But intriguing as such a story about the 'Fair Rosamund' is, no reliable evidence (other than the name itself) has been found to link the sub-manor with King Henry's mistress.[33] However, rather appropriately, numerous legends about the site and name of the 'manor' grew up later, and in the seventeenth and eighteenth centuries Rosamund's estate and its pond became a favourite meeting place for lovers.[34]

Another more hopeful explanation for the name is that in the second half of the thirteenth century (presumably before John Benstead was granted the estate) a clerk called Master John Rosamund, who was certainly alive at that time, may have occupied land there – after whom the sub-'manor' could have been named. But the hope is faint.[35]

The name of the estate reappeared in a charter later in the fourteenth century, when *'a ditch leading to the manor of Rosamund'* was described as the boundary of some land in the meadow of 'Lousmede' in what is now St. James's Park.[36] And in the troubled decade after the Black Death (1349), when many empty properties were being put up for sale,

we find that between 1355 and 1361 the estate (now more openly called a 'manor') successively passed through the hands of each of three other citizens of the City of London, each described as a goldsmith (John of Chichester, Thomas Baldeswell and Richard of Weston), before being bought back in 1361 by nominees acting for the abbey.[37]

### The road from Tothill to the leper Hospital of St. James

Yet another road, possibly a smaller lane or track, is described as running from Tothill Street to the leper Hospital of St. James.[38] We cannot be certain whether this road ran straight across the present St. James's Park area to the hospital, or whether the description refers to the circular route which ran via the road from Tothill to the vill of Eye and beyond (as just described), and thereafter joined up with Spitalstrete – but then, *eastwards*, towards the hospital. This latter circuit of roads would have afforded an extremely roundabout route *to* the hospital *from* Tothill Street. For their part, the agricultural lands in what is now St. James's Park were known to be marshy in places, but all the evidence shows that old fields in that area were used extensively and must have been 'fed' by at least footpaths or agricultural tracks. So on balance it sems more

---

32  WAC 262 (1138 x 1157). See further pp. 78 and 82 below.

33  Rosamund had been a nun at Godstow Abbey near Oxford, and returned there after her liaison with the king, to live a virtuous life and to be buried there in front of the high altar. But that did not stop her being disinterred in 1191 at the order of the saintly bishop Hugh of Lincoln and reburied *outside* the church itself. About her there are unbelievable stories told by the chroniclers, and conflicts among later historians, see Weir, *Eleanor of Acquitaine*, pp. 171-3 and 225-6.

34  Barton, *Lost Rivers*, pp. 36, 41-2; Morden and Lea's map of London and Westm., 1682 (L. Top. Soc. pub. 15); Norman, 'Rosamund Ponds', LTR xiv (1928) p. 54. The name 'Rosamund's pond' was also used later in the C18 & 19 for a more modern pond in Green Park on the line of the river Tyburn: see above p. 30 n. 27, and Norman, *supra*, and a drawing of the pond in a collection made by Kingsford, L. Top. Soc., publ. 56.

35  If the coincidence of his existence and his name at this time is surprising, the only evidence suggests he was a citizen of London: see Cal. Letter Bk. C. (Ldn) pp. 45 and 46; Cal. Anc. Deeds, A 1705, 1785, 1786.

36  WAM 17610 (1333). 'Lowismede', near the Hospital, survived in its name at least until the Dissolution.

37  WAMs 17660, 17664, 17666, 17667 and 17681. These dates, starting a few years after the Black Death of 1349-50, suggest strongly that this 'manor' may have been disposed of to such individuals at that time because of the deaths of previous holders, caused by the plague. The name survived for various purposes until just before the Dissolution, WAMs 18000 and 18900. But we are still in the dark about the original history.

38  WAMs 17318 (WAC 427, temp. John); 17610 (1333).

likely that the road 'to the hospital' ran directly across the present park area from Tothill.

There is even, to this day, what could be the relic of a former track or right of way running from Tothill Street across the present Park in the direction of the old St. James's Hospital: ie. (using modern names) from the present Broadway, via Queen Anne's Gate and through the old, but still existing, right of access into and across the newer Bird Cage Walk (then part of the rural area), and so along the path in the park towards the place where there is now a modern bridge over the later lake, and so directly to the nearby Palace of St. James (the site of the old hospital). This public access into the Park and out of it is still shown in later maps, eg. Kip's 'Prospect of London & Westminster', 1720, sheet 8; and the paths in the Park, in The Society of Antiquaries' map of 1835.[39]

### Other roads

Other significant streets in Westminster such as Spitalstrete, St. Martin's lane, Charing Street and Aldewich have been described above, in relation to the dispersed communities which resided in them.[40]

## B.   The ditches of Westminster

Fresh water and waste-drainage are opposites, but in some historical periods they have been inseparables too. The stream which carries water for drinking and washing does so in a channel or ditch, and in any early or unsophisticated community, whether urban or rural, such a ditch was, and still is, easy to convert to an additional use, as a vehicle for the discharge of waste for the purpose of primitive sanitation. In modern terms, this had, and still has, fearsome consequences for hygiene and health.[41] Few medieval histories bother with such a commonplace but vital feature of early everyday life; but one illuminating book *The Common Stream* rightly makes it the very core of a medieval community.[42]

Apart from this use, or misuse, of natural stream-beds, ditches which had been excavated by spade also played another function, namely the deliberate marking of boundaries between properties. Westminster had been at first an almost completely rural locality, parts of which were slowly to become semi-urban, and finally fully urban. It is hardly surprising that even in the short formal charters produced in and after the twelfth century for legal transfers of property in Westminster, one of the most repeated features which is recorded and recurs time and again to mark a boundary is 'the ditch' — eg. the ditch of the palace; the ditch of the (abbey's) almonry; the 'common ditch of the vill of Westminster'; the ditch of Master Odo the carpenter; the ditch 'next to the common pasture'; the ditch of Master Odo the goldsmith; the 'new ditch where our vines are planted'; the ditch 'which leads to the manor

---

39  Of course none of these named modern features then existed, but the still demonstrable 'way' could well have done so, and it is consistent with the C12 charter. For the Kip's map of 1720, see the London Topog. Soc's publ. No 161 (2003), Sheet 8.  For the Soc. of Antiq.s' map of 1835, see Saunders, 'The Extent of Westminster', *Archaeologia*. vol. xxvi (1836) 223, Plate XXVI and p. 226.  No bridge is shown in that map, but it is noticeable that the paths shown at that time (on *both* sides of the present lake) led towards the place where the modern bridge now is, and then their lines each divert (oddly) in a different direction, as they would have had to do, since a formal lake had by then been made *without a bridge*.  In the 1733 map of Westminster, the old access to the park area from the Broadway is also shown, but no available paths are shown *within the park* — at a time when royal ownership was more assertive than it has since become.

40  See pp. 30 above (*Spitalstrete*); 33 (*Charing Street and Aldewich*); 27 (*St. Martin's lane*).

41  In this present television age, the spectacle of mixed water and sewage in communities in some developing countries can teach one a good deal about early medieval situations.

42  By Rowland Parker, Collins 1975 and Paladin 1976. Cf. *The Westminster Corridor*, p. 41, and n. 81.

of Rosamund'; the marshal's ditch; the ditch of the Archbishop of York; the ditch of Sir John of Stonor; the ditch of William *le rous* (the red); the ditch of the warden of St. Mary's Chapel; and so on. One gets the impression of a landscape riddled by a network of ditches; and there must have been countless other ditches which never found their way into any legal document, particularly those which acted as serious dykes in the wetter and more rural areas such as the Tothill Fields ('the *campus* of Tothill').[43]

Most of such ditches were wholly artificial, having been dug either for the definition of boundaries (with or without an additional function as soakaways for human waste, leading to cesspits), or for draining land; others were clearly lengths of the natural streams themselves, or channels dug to carry water away from the streams. Often the same word, *fossatum*, was used to describe both what was clearly a natural stream-bed, dug out by nature, and the artificial ditch, dug out by human hand. Sometimes the former may have combined both functions, where running water in the stream was employed to help to disperse human waste. Only rarely was the natural character of a stream recognised by the lawyers, and then a word such as *rivulus* was sometimes used to describe it, or in one rare instance, *torrens*, which was once used to give a (too vivid?) picture of the Tyburn stream in the present Mayfair area.[44]

### The 'common ditch'

But one of the unexpected features in Westminster to be found in the charters is 'the common ditch'. It is clear that in the second half of the thirteenth century when either a planned development was being built, or when the frontage of a road had become substantially built-up, a *shared* ditch at the very back of the frontage properties was constructed, to run parallel to the road, with the houses and their curtilages between the ditch and the road.[45] Sometimes this was called 'the common ditch' or 'the common ditch of the vill of Westminster'; the latter title being reserved, it seems, for the ditch behind the properties lying in the northern half of 'King Street', on its western side, while the former title was accepted as sufficient for the ditch lying behind the properties on Tothill Street.

Before the 'common ditch' is first mentioned in the second half of the thirteenth century, ditches had usually been named as 'belonging' to individual owners; in effect, as though in the earlier days of the century the ditch were a personal piece of property, constructed on the land of the individual involved or designed to constitute the boundary of his land. The days of 'public' or even 'cooperative' designing of a boundary or a sanitary service had not yet been reached, it seems. Thus when Alexander, a clerk of the Exchequer, donated a house and its curtilage in 'King Street' to the Lady Altar at the abbey in the early 1200s, he described the curtilage as extending to *'my ditch in front of'* another adjoining house (which he also owned, and indeed called *'my capital messuage'*).[46] Even in the 1250s, when Felicia, a widow who was the daughter and heiress of an early resident, Laurence Muschat, was selling her house on the *east* side of 'King Street', she described it as

---

43 For a dyke on Tothill Fields still in the early C19, see Plate 7, p. 57 below. The edge of the Fields also held the 'common pasture', and private property in the late C13 and the C14 centuries, generally in the form of small plots of one acre in extent, see WAMs 17522, 17523, 17524, 17389, 17488, and p. 62 below.
44 WAM 4875 (1285). See also p. 283, n.82.
45 'Built-up' here does not mean built-up in terrace-fashion, but built-up with all or nearly all the houses having appurtenant lands on the frontage, ie. houses with curtilages.
46 WAM 17416 (WAC 414, temp. John). For this Alexander, see also p. 171.

extending to *'the ditch of Master Odo the Carpenter and William Plantefolie and Matilda'* (the latter being the couple who were actually purchasing Felicia's house, and were therefore already her neighbours).[47] So the ditch on that side of the road was still being regarded as being a 'private' affair, albeit with at least two separate 'owners'. But by the second half of the thirteenth century we have 'common ditches' being named, both behind the north-west section of 'King Street' and also a little later behind the backs of houses north of Tothill Street.[48]

The 'common ditch' lying behind these properties on the west side of 'King Street' must have acted as a convenient common boundary line for the row of houses, as well as a method presumably of disposing of human waste. It may also have been devised as a slow soakaway for marsh-waters in the swampy parts of the present St James's Park. There may be some significance in the fact that it is sometimes called, not just the 'common ditch', but the 'common ditch of the vill of Westminster', as though it had some greater importance than the common ditch of a small number of buildings on the street. It is never referred to as a 'stream', but one has to remember that, so far as water was concerned, not very far away to the north-west there was *'the watercourse of the blessed King Edward'*, and that certainly a *'marsh'* lay behind one or more of these 'King Street' properties, and another *'marsh'* in the Longditch area.[49]

In contrast there is no mention of a 'common ditch' on the *east* side of 'King Street', and the reason for this is understandable. Some of the properties on the *west* side were, it seems, houses or plots of much the same size (fitting as they did between the road and the common ditch) and may have been first developed in sections along the road. But the 'back area' on the *eastern* side (between the 'King Street' houses and the bank of the Thames) was, as we shall see, first developed at an earlier date and in a much more unsystematic manner, containing larger spaces, and indeed groups of buildings 'as they came'; several of which were described eventually as a 'capital *curia*': a courtyard or complex of buildings held by a single owner.[50]

So on the one hand, the geography and later timing of development on the *west* side of the road lent itself to the construction of a common back boundary and a joint sanitation system. On the other hand, on the *east* side of 'King Street' the construction of a common system of ditch or ditches for the houses on the frontage of the street was forestalled by the earlier piecemeal manner of development of disjointed properties.

This did not mean that there were no ditches at all on the *east* side of 'King Street'. But instead of a 'common' system, there were individual ditches, such as that 'belonging' to Master Odo the goldsmith in the 1230s, and another, later belonging to Master Odo the carpenter and William Plantefolie and Matilda in the 1250s, as mentioned above. Another much later charter used the ditch of the great establishment of the Archbishop of York at *Endiff* to describe the back boundary of

---

47  WAM 17511 (1250s).

48  For 'King Street', see WAMs 17482, 17499. For Tothill Street, see WAMs 17569 (1316) and 17589 (1325).

49  For the watercourse, see p. 17 above. For the marshes, see WAD 562b (WAC 432, temp. John), and WAMs 17317 (1220s?), 17368 (1250s) 17600 (1327) and 17647 (1348). The presence of water in and around the present St. James's Park area is amply evidenced, even to this day; and this in spite of other evidence that there was also much agricultural land there. Barton *Lost Rivers of London* 34 ff. reviews some of the conflicting evidence about the Tyburn, and suggests only a stagnant swamp in St. James's Park. But what about 'the watercourse of St. Edward' and the 'stream' of Longditch (the *Clowson* stream, with a bridge and even a sluice in the C13)?

50  For this early development of the 'Thames bank' area, see pp. 20, 110 ff. For examples of a 'capital *curia*' in this area, see WAMs 17505, 17454, 17372 (in the years 1230-50s)

someone else's property.[51]   Even before it had been purchased by the Archbishop, this large complex of buildings had grown to become 'a noble palace', in the words of the monk-historian Matthew Paris;[52] but it still had to have its own ditch – which brings it down to earth.

### Ditches in Longditch

In contrast to Tothill Street and the north-west section of 'King Street', Longditch lane or street appears to have been developed irregularly, with individual ditches but no 'common ditch'.  In this respect Longditch seems to have resembled the 'east bank' area between 'King Street' and the Thames.  It can be no coincidence that in the second half of the twelfth century it was in this sector between Longditch and Tothill Street that another large complex of buildings began to grow up under the control of the Mauduit family, the royal chamberlains, just as Richard fitz Nigel the first royal treasurer of the revived exchequer had begun to acquire his 'curia' of buildings on the Thames bank *east* of 'King Street' at about the same time.[53] Longditch was clearly an old and thriving residential area, which the monks had created by bestowing land there on favoured servants. In addition those properties in Longditch for which we have actual physical measurements suggest irregular forms of holdings and unsymmetrical development in that area.[54] This accords with the picture which the area west of the *southern* end of 'King Street' presented even as late as the Tudor, Stuart and early Georgian periods, with its 'courts, alleys and yards', before its redevelopment and the construction of Great George Street in the eighteenth century.[55]

### Ditches in the vill of Eye

In the adjoining vill of Eye (on the present site of Buckingham Palace), it is clear that it was the Tyburn stream itself which performed the function of a 'common ditch'. The road through the vill appears to have run north-south, with most recorded houses or plots on the east side.[56] Behind the houses and plots on the east of the road, the Tyburn stream acted at their rear in three capacities – as a boundary for the whole line of properties, and as a manor boundary, dividing Eye from Westminster, and as a 'ditch', probably carrying away some of the waste matter from the houses.[57]   As such, the stream was variously called a 'ditch', and a 'brook', and even 'the blessed King Edward's water-course'.[58] There is no surviving evidence of other ditches in the vill.

### Dykes

It is difficult to identify which ditches (or 'dykes') had been made purely for the purpose of the natural draining of land. Westminster, particularly in its southern alluvial parts of the Tothill Fields nearest the river Thames, had had its fair share of what almost certainly had once been water-logged land, and the manor of Eye next door shared the same condition near the Thames. But these parts must have been drained successfully to produce the *'fertile lands and green fields'* which surrounded the abbey at the time of the Norman invasion, and later the good hay crops of *'the great meadow of Westminster'*, renamed Marketmead and Westmead.[59] The 'common pasture' of the vill of Westminster lay on the nearer part of the Tothill Fields, and it seems more than likely that the ditch which (according to two charters) lay *'alongside the common pasture of*

---

51  WAM 17625 (1337).
52  Paris, *Chronica Majora*, (ed. Luard), iv, pp. 243-4.
53  For Richard fitz Nigel, Henry II's first treasurer in Westminster, see pp. 110-13 and 155-6.
54  See Appendix D, at p. 409.
55  The higgedly-piggledy character of this area at that time is well illustrated in the map in the *Survey of London*, Vol. X, Plate 13 (plates positioned towards the end).
56  For the location of the vill, see p. 49 above and Appendix C, at pp. 400 ff. below.
57  WAMs 4787, 4788, 4789, 4790, 4792, 4793, 4819, 4771, 4821, 4791, 4761, 4830.
58  WAMs 4793 and 4789 (ditch); 4792 (brook); and 4835 (K. Edw.'s watercourse).
59  *Life of K. Edward*, (2nd), ed. Barlow, p. 66-9, see above pp. 16-17. For hay crops, see pp. 336 and 356-9.

*the vill'* in and before the 1260s was one of the dykes which had been excavated in a previous era for drainage purposes.[60] It may be that the very deep drainage ditch which centuries later was recorded in a picture of Tothill Fields in 1807 gives some idea of both such a ditch and the surrounding wet land which may have been used as common pasture in the twelfth and thirteenth centuries by the men of Westminster.[61]

### An abbey vineyard, and its ditches

South of the site of the abbey almonry, itself on the southern side of Tothill Street, the abbey had planted a vineyard in or adjacent to a meadow which had been assigned to the precentor's office, and in about the 1280s the monks surrounded their vineyard with a new ditch.[62] This may just have been for its protection because, let us assume, thefts of grapes had taken place; or perhaps the new ditch was designed to assist the irrigation of the vines. Twenty to thirty years later the vineyard appears to have needed replanting, and in 1302, for no doubt the better carrying out of this purpose, the abbot and convent arranged for the meadow to be assigned to the Inner Cellarer, who (as the monk in charge of food and drink, the most pragmatic and organisational department of the abbey) was probably more suited to such a down-to-earth task than the Precentor.[63] At that time the vineyard was described as *'surrounded with hedges and ditches'*.

### The 'shire ditch'

Uniquely but much later, in 1531, the 'ditch' or bed of the Tyburn stream, in the present Green Park area, was actually called the 'shire ditch'. If accurate, this name would have had implications for earlier cnturies. The name appears in the survey of the nearer St. James's fields carried out before Henry VIII acquired the abbey's lands there.[64] The place in question was at the point where the stream was crossed by the road called Spitalstrete (west of St. James's hospital – near 'Eycross', where Spitalstrete met the road leading northwards from the village of Eye). Although the Tyburn had certainly once been the boundary between two manors, it was never a boundary relevant to the 'shire' of Middlesex. This unusual name for it either must have been a simple mistake, or may indicate that the old *manor* boundaries were regarded at that time as part of a common network shared in some way by the *shire,* and so deserving of this title. The river bed had often been called just a 'ditch' in the earlier centuries with which this book deals, but never (so far as I know) the 'shire ditch' at those times.

## C. The fields of Westminster

Our knowledge of the fields of Westminster itself and their locations within the manor is comparatively limited. But it is still possible to obtain some picture of those parts of the manor which were, and continued to be, rural during the twelfth and thirteenth centuries, while the rest were being converted to an urban or at least a semi-urban scene. Unfortunately none of the monks' own 'farm accounts' for the demesne lands retained by them in Westminster have survived. And so, such names of the fields in Westminster, and details about their location and character, as are still known to us are derived principally from the many fortuitous particulars mentioned in private charters among the abbey's records.

---

60  WAMs 17522 (1260s) and 17340 (1260-70s).

61  See Plate 7, next page.

62  WAM 17461.  The vineyard was probably just off the present Abbey Orchard Street, where it is commemorated. From time immemorial the practice had been to plant a hedge along the mound of soil dug from a boundary ditch; cf the A-S hedge on the Hampstead boundary, *The Westminster Corridor,* Map O & pp. 105, 169.

63  WAM 17489.

64  WAM 17131; see p. 24 above.  Presumably by that time there was a bridge or culvert where Spitalstrete crossed the Tyburn and did not have to go *through* the old ford ('*kuford*'), see p. 15 above.  More accurately the river Fleet was also called 'the shire ditch of Middlesex' in 1498, WAM 16004.

**Plate 7.** The Field *(campus)* of Tothill combined marshland, rough pastureland and fields of rich meadowland, broken by ditches and larger dykes. In this view, looking north-eastwards towards the abbey in 1807, more than 700 years after the Norman Conquest, the bleakness and wetness of even the nearer parts of the *campus* were still evident. Seen here in the foreground, there is a short length of a track which is now the built-up Rochester Row, with (in 1807) a deep dyke and bare waterlogged land lying beyond the dyke. This track was once a length of the old 'abbot's way', leading south-westwards towards the abbot's private house 'La Neyte'. In the middle distance, the horse and cart are taking the 'horse ferry' road down to the Thames, across the southern reaches of the *campus*. See Map A (Plates 2 and 3) and pp. 48, 55-6, 58 and 356-57.

The early history of the demesne lands in Westminster is probably only to be seen, reflected obliquely, in three 'great Fields' (the *campi*) which continued to be so named even into the thirteenth and fourteenth centuries. By that time the great fields had, it seems, largely been divided up into smaller pockets of rent-paying land, with few or no remaining obligations of physical service to the abbey.[65]

The three known *campi* in Westminster were, firstly, the *campus* of Tothill; secondly, the field which at least by the late twelfth century had become known as the *campus* of 'St. James', because the leper hospital of St. James had been built in the area; and thirdly, the *campus* of Westminster.

The *campus* of Tothill was the wide, once very wet, sector south-west from the abbey, which can more or less be identified as the area south of Tothill which now includes Horseferry Road and extends as far as Vauxhall Bridge Road. It started where the 'common pasture' of the town lay, near the road junction where the road to La Neyte and the road to the vill of Eye divided.[66] There were certainly a number of one acre plots of arable land in the nearer part of the field in the second half of the thirteenth century, and some evidence that slightly larger plots had also been held there.[67] Because of its very nature, as something between dyked water-meadows and waste land, the *campus* (however sub-divided) was probably kept mainly as pasture and fallow. The big exception was that part of it which was originally called 'the Great Meadow of Westminster', stretching down to the very bank of the Thames. This demesne meadow contained $36\frac{1}{2}$ acres and was the largest source of hay, at first for Westminster but later for the adjoining manor of Eye, into which it became incorporated in or before 1290 under the new name, *Markedemede* or 'Market-mead'.[68]

The *campus* of St. James was the land round the leper hospital, covering all or some of the present St. James's Park and the now wholly built-up district between Pall Mall and the present Piccadilly road).[69] The name *campus* for this area may have been a late one, but there always had been much agricultural land, including arable, round the hospital.

The *campus* of Westminster apparently was in the northern part of Westminster and covered most of the land which lies between the line of Tyburn stream where it runs through Mayfair, eastwards towards the present Soho area and beyond, to the enclave of the leper hospital of St Giles. By at least the thirteenth century its identity was largely that of a sub-divided market garden area, adjacent to a hungry city. For example, in the 1250-60s, an expensive four acres of arable, south of the St. Giles land, within the 'field of Westminster' was sold for 24 marks (£16). This land appears to have been close to the convent's 'great garden', and its large price no doubt reflects its value as land for commercial small-holding or orchard purposes for the market to feed the city of London.[70]

65 One of the only identifications of servile condition (with services no longer owed to the abbey, but to a lay man, who had probably received the right to such services when obtaining a 'fee' from the abbey at some unknown date) is to be found in WAM 17320 (WAC 416) in which Hugh *de Fonte* in late C12 'assigned' a serf, William son of Herbert, to his daughter, Margaret, together with an acre of land held by William from Hugh (plus another free acre). For other refs. to William, see WAMs 17432 (WAC 417) and 17413 (WAC 418). Since the *de Fonte* family lived in the Charing Street area (see p. 28 above), it may be that William son of Herbert lived and worked in the fields between the 'great garden' (still the abbot's garden at that time) and St. Giles. for the three great Fields, see Map A at Plates 2-3.

66 WAM 17392A, and see p. 48 above.

67 WAMs 4822, 17522, 17523, 17524; 17389.

68 See further pp. 336 and 356-9 below.

69 For a C18 representation of the still-open land *north* of the hospital site, see *The Westminster Corridor*, Plate 17, page 148. The hospital was probably built during Henry II's reign in the second half of the twelfth century, and I do not know what had been the previous name of this *campus* before that time.

70 WAM 17440 (copied in WAM 17551). The land lay *south* of other land held by the Master and Brethren of St. Giles. For gardens in this area, see pp. 33-4 above.

By way of contrast, the adjoining manor of Eye presents a clearer picture of an agricultural estate. There, four distinct areas can be recognised. First a district where a *campus*, the 'Field of Eye', lay on the west side of the vill of Eye, extending northwards, through the modern Belgrave Square and Grosvenor Place areas towards the main road at Knightsbridge and a road junction at the present-day Hyde Park Corner.[71] This *campus* appears to have survived in part as a large subdivided 'Crowfield' *(Crooe feilde)* in the later 1614 map of the manor of Eye.[72] A second identifiable district, the whole of which may originally have been known simply as *Ossolston* (ie. Ossulston, the name of the old 'Hundred') comprised the western half of modern Mayfair (ie. west of the river Tyburn, including the place where the Hundred court used to sit) and it too was called a *campus*.[73] This area had been mainly customary land for the manor tenants; and later at the end of the thirteenth century it became known as a number of fields which were being leased out by the abbey to a new and often 'free' tenantry, some of them 'foreign' incomers from Westminster. The names of the fields often betrayed their origin or their location: *Mabeliscroft , Martineslande, Tyburne, La Redelonde, Ossulston, Brookshot, Cresswellfeld.*[74]

A third distinctive part of the old manor of Eye was the house La Neyte and extensive lands which Abbot Richard of Berking in about 1223 bought as his and future abbots' private estate, running down to the river Thames, with fields whose names became familiar and identifiable: *Tameshote, Twenty Acres, Westmede, Marflete, Abbot's Croft, Neytemede, Cowlese.*[75]

A fourth district of Eye can also be clearly defined, namely the La Hyde area in approximately the modern Hyde Park, which became the perquisite of large independent families to whom the abbey progressively sublet the area, ultimately as a 'sub-manor'. But precisely because they were independent, few records about them and their lands in this area survive.[76]

It is impossible to be sure about exactly where in plan the great Fields began and ended. It is likely that their boundaries, which once may have been more definite, became blurred in the course of time, and that they subsequently remained generic 'areas' rather than demarcated units. But their earlier historical existence as precise entities is confirmed by the rather unreal survival, in some places, of their names in later descriptions of 'fields within Fields'. These referred to the existence of smaller fields or 'cultures' lying within the great Fields. The 'fields within Fields' concept is visible much more often in the adjoining estates of Eye and Knightsbridge than in Westminster. Thus, for example, one finds the following description of certain areas of land which were being restored at that time to the abbey: –

'Of the 48 acres of land, 18 acres lie in the *campus* of Knightsbridge in the 'culture' called La Doune ...; 4½ acres lie in the said *campus* in the 'culture' called Brokeshot ...; 13½ acres lie in the *campus* of Eye in the 'culture' called Carswellsfield ... .'[77]

71 Yet another nearby *campus* existed, it seems, in the convent's adjoining manor of Knightsbridge, probably on the north-west of the village settlement there. The village itself was clustered round the eponymous 'knight's bridge', where the main road crossed the Westbourne river.
72 For the 1614 map. see City of Westminster Archives 1049/12/115 and Gatty, *Mary Davies and Ebury*, Plate 31, vol 2/238 and pp. 20-3.
73 eg. WAMs 4835 (*campus* of Eye); 16212 (*campus* of Knightsbridge); 4776, 4786 and 4834 (*Campus* of Ossulston). For the Hundred and its court, see *The Westminster Corridor*, p. 53 and Map M.; **but note**: - in Map M there, the *symbol* (as shown on the Map itself: a green circle with a green cross in it) for the two sites of the hundred court was omitted in error from the explanatory Note (4) to the Map.
74 See pp. 345-7 below, and Plate 23 (Map B) after p. 288.
75 See p. 356 and Plate 24 (Map C) after p. 288. For Abbot Berking's purchase, see p. 201 above.
76 See pp. 281-3 below.
77 WAM 16212 (1354) and 4834 (1308). In the latter charter, unusually the word *campus* had a capital C.

Since both Eye and Knightsbridge had a large number of named 'cultures' and other similar smaller fields, there are a number of cases where we find in those estates similar 'tiered' locative descriptions of 'fields within Fields'. But the smaller fields were sometimes regarded as sufficient locative units on their own, and accordingly one sometimes finds properties simply described as lying 'in Le Brocforlang', or 'in the field called La Brache', or 'in Withibedde', without any reference to the great Fields. All these three smaller fields mentioned were parts of the original Field of Eye, together with 'Wodlond', and 'Shortespottes'.

In Westminster the names of the great Fields themselves continued to be used often to identify the location of specific plots (eg. '1½ acres in the Field of Tothill'),[78] without indication of a smaller *named* field lying within the greater. But we do know that in Westminster there were a few named fields or closes of a smaller size than the *campi*, which must have lain within the generic areas of these greater Fields. For example within the general area of the fields around the hospital of St James there was a well-known smaller meadow called 'Lousmede' (or Lusmede, and other spellings), which is named on several occasions as an individual field, but not specifically as lying within a larger field.[79] 'Lousmede' probably lay between the leper hospital and the Mauduit complex in the Longditch/Tothill area, and therefore within the original *campus*. It actually adjoined the 'road which leads from Tothill to the hospital',

ie. the one leading across the present Park, as suggested above.[80] Immediately to the west of a plot of one acre *within* Lousmede lay a feature named 'Le Southagh', possibly a prominent hedge marking the southern limits of the field.[81] Although named as a meadow, Lousmede contained at least one acre of arable one year.

A few other named fields of a smaller kind were also to be found in Westminster, as follows: -

1. A small meadow, lying apparently on the western edge of Tothill near where the road running towards the vill of Eye curved northwesterly, had also received a specific name, 'Liversunmede'.[82]

2. The location of another pasture field, named 'Chisellepettes', is not revealed. Nicholas 'the Frenchman' *(le Fraunceys)*, who held the hereditary office of the abbey 'summonser', was divesting himself (perhaps on his deathbed) in 1302 of his office, his house and all his lands in the 'fields of Eye, Paddington and Tothill', including 'the pasture of Chisellepettes', in favour of his son, Walter.[83] From the way in which this charter is worded, it looks as if this pasture field may have been at Tothill. But the prefix 'c(h)isel-' can be associated with 'gravel' in old English, a rather unlikely connection with the area of Tothill. While it is true that the abbey itself stood on its own island of gravel, the main Westminster gravel only began higher up the slope above the Thames, at and beyond

---

78  WAM 17389 (1250 x 60s)

79  WAMs 17143A (1230s); ? 17407 (1250 x 1260s); 17546 (1272 x 1307; le Southagh to the west); 17610 (1333; adjoining the road from Tothill to St. James); 17636 (1344; the Mauduit property); 17653 (1350, the Mauduit property).

80  See p. 52 above. The name Lousmede survived into at least the C16.

81  WAM 17546. 'Hagh' usually denoted a hedge; or an enclosure.

82  WAMs 17404 (1250 x 60s); 17344 (1270s). Nearby there was an unidentified feature called La Brodewall, which was probably an earth wall, acting as the boundary of the one acre plot of land being transferred by the first of these charters. As regards the whole district of Tothill, one must remember that apart from Tothill Street itself, there was also a settlement at what is named as 'the vill of Tothill' in at least one charter, WAM 17518 (1300?), lying, I think, towards the end of the 'street' at the present 'Broadway', where the road to the abbot's house at La Neyte branched off to the left, and the road to the leper Hospital branched off to the right, (see pp. 48 and 51-2 above). The area of 'Tothill' became a wide and probably rather imprecise area, just as the area of any modern suburb can be, even when it contains within itself an established older village.

83  WAM 17488 (1302).

Charing. So the location of this pasture land, with its interesting name, remains uncertain.

3. A field (of unknown character) was called 'the Bromfeld' and lay some way *south* of the almonry, with a small road or track leading to it from Tothill Street.[84] 'Brom', as a place name, can be associated with the plant 'broom', which is usually to be found on heath or waste land. There may well have been broom on parts of the area towards Tothill Field, but in any case the location is clear in this instance.

4. Further to the south-west, lying along the Tyburn boundary between Westminster and Eye, a familiar feature was a long narrow field which had its own appropriate identity and name, as 'Longemore' (the long marsh), containing apparently some one-acre plots and meadow land.[85] But confusingly another 'Longemore' also appears in the area of the northern Field of Westminster, near the leper hospital of St. Giles. There too, land at 'Haggehegge' is shown *south* of the main road, but another 'Haggehegge' is also named as lying in the fields of Kentish Town (and therefore outside Westminster).[86]

But compared with the adjoining manors of Eye and Knightsbridge, it is remarkable how few *names* of fields were still retained in Westminster, particularly in the areas round Tothill and the Hospital of St. James, in spite of the considerable amount of agricultural land which is referred to in that area. The *'common pasture'* of Westminster (probably poorer open land) which lay near the great Field of Tothill and may have formed part of it, apparently needed no other more specific name. And we do not know whether *'the place where champions are wont to fight'* (presumably a separate field or piece of open ground) near Tothill had a proper name of its own.[87] The comparative lack of rural field names in Westminster was clearly due to the greater urbanisation which was taking place within the vill, at least from the second half of the twelfth century.[88]

On the other hand we can see that some fields were retained in the areas round Tothill and Longditch, without being given specific names, so long as they were kept within the abbey fold. In general, abbey lands in these areas had been used by the monks from early times as a source from which to endow deserving abbey servants with places to live.[89] But even more importantly, other rural lands in these areas (in addition to new urban plots and houses) had been used for specific allotment to different abbey departments, as sources of income for those departments in the administration of the abbey.[90] As a result we know of a number of fields in and around the Tothill area which were known, not by any proper names, but simply in the form (eg.) 'the meadow of the sacrist'. Even though the sources for our knowledge of these holdings are limited, the following can be identified as lying in the neighbourhood of Tothill and Longditch: –

84 WAM 17461 (1260s)

85 WAMs 17446, 17447, 17450, 17455, 17456, 4819. Longemore also appears frequently as a demesne meadow of c. 20 acres in the Eye accounts, see DS, *Eye A/cs*, pp. eg. vol 1/42, 50; vol 4/191, 206; vol 5/256.

86 17556. The former Haggehegge (WAM 17332) is also shown bordering on St. Martin's lane; another was in Kentish Town (see p. 318 n. 30 below).

87 WAMs 17340, 17345, 17519, 17522 (common pasture; it was also called the common pasture 'of Tothill'). For the place 'where champions fight', see WAMs 17392A and 17444, and p. 49 above,

88 i.e. the urbanisation in Longditch, the Thames bank area north of the palace, and in 'King Street'. For the significance of this early period for Westminster, see pp. 20-21.

89 For the rewarding of deserving abbey servants, see *ibid*, and the references given there.

90 An accurate dating of all original allotments of assets to specific departments of the abbey would be extremely difficult. The *large-scale* division of assets between the abbot and the convent began initially in 1225, with a chequered history thereafter, see pp. 196 ff below; but the allocation of assets for specific convent purposes had begun much earlier, see pp. 123-6 below.

- the abbot's 'great meadow': this lay in Tothill, north of the street;
- the meadow of the precentor: this also lay north of Tothill Street, alongside an unnamed track leading to the abbot's 'great meadow';
- the meadow of the sacrist: this lay in Longditch;
- the meadow of the convent: this lay south of the almonry on Tothill Street;
- the cellarer's meadow and other 'land': this lay some distance from Tothill or Tothill Street, from which a separate road led to it.[91]

Reliable proof of the existence of earlier 'strip-holdings' in any of the great *campi* is outside the limits of surviving evidence. But many crofts or 'one-acre' holdings of land were changing hands during the thirteenth century. Even from limited sources, one can identify about twelve transfers of one-acre holdings in the *campus* of Tothill or at Tothill; some of meadow, others of arable;[92] and there are many others elsewhere in Westminster. Comparable sales were also taking place nearby in the manor of Eye, including there a number of half-acre holdings, in a field aptly named 'Shortespottes'. These half-acre holdings even survived in that form and were later referred to individually, as small ancillary lands included in greater transfers of land in the fourteenth century, at a time when a number of estates in Westminster and its neighbourhood were consolidating into larger and larger units.[93]

But transactions about agricultural lands or rents within the more urban parts of Westminster had not been limited to such small holdings as one-acre or half-acre plots. Larger acreages or their rents were also being assigned or traded. Thus we can see the rents of separate small-holdings of three or four arable acres at Tothill being donated to the abbey in the first half of the thirteenth century; while in the middle of that century we have already seen another valuable holding of four arable acres being sold privately (for the large price of 24 marks, = £16) in the 'garden area' of the Field of Westminster, near the land of the leper hospital of St. Giles.[94]

91 WAMs, as follows:  **Abbot**, 17401 (1220s) and 17350 (1260s).  **Precentor**, 17462 (1258 x 1283), 17489 (1302) and 17350 (1260s).  **Sacrist**, 17485 (1299).  **Convent**, 17461 (1258 x 1283).  **Cellarer**, 17404 (1250-60s); and for two acres of the 'cellarer', much later in St. James's Field, see 17131 (1531)
92 WAMs 17462, 1739, 17523, 17524, 17389, 17340, 17344, 17345, 17350, 17404, 17463; and see also 17318, 17401, 17319 for mixed holdings round Tothill.
93 WAMs 17560 (1309), 4826 (1323); 17589, 17590, 17591A and 17592 (last four, each of 1325/1326). For the consolidation of estates, see pp. 285 n. 77, p. 346 n. 80 below, and Appendix F , at pp. 412 ff.
94 WAMs 17318 and 17319 (1210 x 1230?, at Tothill); the transaction also included one of the one acre holdings).  WAMs 17440 & 17551 (1250-60s, near St. Giles); see pp. 58 and 34-35 above for this small-holding of probably market-garden land, in the garden district near Aldwych and St Giles.

# CHAPTER 4

# Early people and powers in Westminster

## The start of a thousand years

For at least three generations before the Norman Conquest the lives of lay people in Westminster had already been subject to the forces of national history. Even in that anglo-saxon era the people of the small rural settlement west of London had lived under the constant influence of both the king and the church. And after the Conquest these two national forces became even further visible; and ever since then, their presence in the evolving town has continued to grow for nearly a thousand years.

To begin with, it had been the king himself and the church, in the persons of King Edgar and St. Dunstan the archbishop, who had originally joined forces in about 971 to found a small abbey of Benedictine monks, on an island of gravel, in the marshes on the northern bank of the Thames – amongst whatever rural community may have lived there already.[1] The time proved hardly auspicious. Created in a short and sheltered period of peace, within ten years the abbey had to witness a further outbreak of attacks along the river by the Danes against London,

lying only one mile to the east of Westminster. But by 1016 London had at last become free again from aggression, when for the first time a Danish king, Cnut, was accepted as also king in England. So, on Westminster's very doorstep, London was once again able to grow uninterruptedly as an international port, and no doubt Westminster began to benefit too.[2]

In 1042 it was again the turn of an Englishman, Edward the son of King Ethelred – one day to be called 'the Confessor' – to become king; and in or before 1050 he not only began to build a new stone abbey at Westminster in place of the wooden one, but also moved his palace from London to a site on the Thamesbank next to the abbey itself. In this way the combined royal and religious presence in the small settlement of Westminster became more pervading.[3] About sixteen years later the completion of the essential parts of the abbey, and the inauguration of Westminster as the joint seat of a royal palace and a new national shrine, occurred in the same year as the invasion of England by Duke William and his Normans.[4]

---

1  See *The Westminster Corridor*, pp. 56-60. In view of an *earlier* existence of a minster-church at Westminster (staffed not by monks, but by priests; see *ibid*. pp. 23-4, note 56), it is probable that even before the C10 there was already a small settlement of lay people living near the site later chosen for the abbey. In any case the new abbey, small as it was, would have quickly drawn lay helpers to itself.
2  *Ibid*, p. 67.
3  *Ibid*, p. 68. It is a neat coincidence that these simultaneous building works upon both abbey and palace in Westminster were to be mirrored in those carried out by Henry III 200 years later in the C13, with dramatic results upon the environment and the population of the town at that time, see pp. 247 ff. below. Dr Mason, in her W*A and its People* at pp. 11-2 & 14, showed that the removal of the royal palace from London to Westminster in the C11 may have taken place even earlier, during the reign of King Cnut or his son Harold Harefoot. For this rebuilding of the abbey, see coloured Plate 1, after p. 16.
4  For the consecration of the abbey, and the great ones who attended it on the 28th January 1066, see Barlow, *Edward the Confessor*, p. 244 ff.

## The first population grows

So it was that when Domesday Book came to be compiled twenty years after the Norman Conquest, the existing rural population of Westminster was already being supplemented by four other important presences, each of which was to contribute to the future growth of the population in the emerging town : -

(1) The number of the monks in the 'Church of Saint Peter', as the abbey was called, had increased dramatically from twelve (as it had been before Edward the Confessor began to rebuild the church) to eighty. This greatly enlarged complement of monks in their new stone abbey was now to live alongside, and in various capacities to be served by, increasing numbers of lay people, including some of the 19 villeins and 42 cottagers (with their families) who were recorded in 1086 in the Domesday Survey as the other residents of the 'vill' of Westminster.[5] In their turn the monks themselves often drew other lay people to Westminster. Not only did more monks draw more lay people to perform services for them, but it is also clear that in the course of time those monks who came from different parts of the country were themselves often joined in Westminster by members of their own families or by other inhabitants of the home communities from which the monks themselves had come.[6]

(2) Another lay group of about 25 men-at-arms and other 'abbot's men' (ie. men who were feudally pledged to the Abbot as their 'lord') were now also close neighbours, with their families, of the rural residents and the monks. Some of these lived in the 25 houses which were actually mentioned in the Domesday Survey, and which may well have stood either within the large abbey precinct or fairly close to it. There can be little doubt that some, perhaps most, of the 'abbot's men' were employed as senior lay officers of the abbey. A 'civil service' of this kind had already become essential for the management of the enlarged abbey and the expanding countrywide-estate which the abbey had already begun to enjoy under Edward the Confessor.[7] And this need for administrators continued to grow in succeeding years as the abbey's estate grew even further.

(3) The construction of the new stone abbey and the adjoining palace had undoubtedly caused an immigration of craftsmen and building labourers into the small town, to reside or to be billeted there while the building works continued, and in some cases to stay on afterwards. Since some of them may have had to live in Westminster for up to twenty years, they and their progeny must have significantly increased the population, even if others had been migrant workers and later moved on to other jobs elsewhere. We have little contemporary evidence of the actual course of the works necessary for these enterprises.[8] But one has only to contemplate the scale of the surviving

---

5  For the DB. record, see *The Westminster Corridor*, Plate 8 on p. 86, and for discussion there of the indigenous residents themselves, see *ibid*, pp. 138-141. For the number of monks, see *ibid*, pp. 56 and 140.

6  For example, during his abbacy the Abbot Gervase (1138-57) had two of his brothers with him in Westminster, see WAC 258 & 269. The next Abbot, Laurence, had one brother and one nephew, WAC 280 & 284. But this practice was not limited to the abbots or senior monks: other monks too, and no doubt their lay-servants also, were followed to Westminster by relatives or neighbours. Later as a centre of power, the town itself could attract other residents from places as far away as a hundred miles distant: Rosser, *Medieval Westminster*, pp. 182-90; Mortimer, *Angevin England*, p. 176, or indeed from places even more distant.

7  See *The Westminster Corridor*, pp. 142-4. The abbey's civil service is also well illustrated *after* Domesday (and before 1100) by Hugh of Colham, the abbey's first *dapifer* or steward of whom we know, see pp. 98-99 below.

8  The most we know is from the anonymous 'biography', *Vita Aedwardi Regis (The Life of King Edward)*, ed. Barlow, pp. 45-6; as further discussed in Colvin, *King's Works*, 1 / 14-17, and Gem, 'The Romanesque Rebuilding of WA', A-N S (1980) at 33-60. *The Westminster Corridor*, p. 78, and text at p. 6

ruins of Westminster's sister church, at Jumièges in Normandy, to appreciate the number of workmen needed at Westminster to build the greater part of a church (which actually surpassed Jumièges in size) in so short a space of time as fifteen to twenty years (c. 1050-1066); see Plate 6 in *The Westminster Corridor*.[9]

The names of three masons, two English and one possibly German, who were responsible for much of the work at Westminster, have survived : Leofsi ('of London') and Godwine; with Teinfrith, described as the king's 'churchwright', probably a master-mason.[10] A few of their workmen who subsequently remained in Westminster may be included among the 42 Westminster cottagers recorded in the Domesday Survey. But years passed after the Conquest and indeed after the Domesday Survey before the abbey and its domestic buildings could be finally completed, so that the need for a work force remained. In any case the presence of such comparatively large buildings, even when they were finally completed, meant a continuing need for workers with special skills for repairs and improvements.[11]

(4) The palace built alongside the rising new abbey had also to be administered and supplied. This was the case at all times, but more particularly whenever the king and his court were in residence. In addition to the senior personnel who were needed for this purpose, the palace appears to have been provided with a ready supply of labourers and suppliers in the form of another group of 30 cottagers, and their families, whom (in the strict tenor of Norman feudalism) the king 'owned'. These cottagers were servile and were listed collectively in Domesday Book as just another royal 'possession'.[12] Here too was another source for the future growth of a lay service-population within Westminster. Of the more senior personnel of the palace, we do know something specific, as indicated below.[13]

## The mists begin to rise
### (Domesday to the reign of Henry II, 1086-1189)

During the next period of about a hundred years, the small window which the Domesday Survey had opened upon Westminster society swings slightly more ajar and the view from it widens a little. In the concluding years of the twelfth century the position changes and the mists outside begin to rise.

It was a period which had had remarkable contrasts within it. Covering the unsettled decades immediately after the Conquest and, later, the anarchic civil war between King

9   Unfortunately no part of Edward's abbey has survived,  except in traces, see eg. Plate 13 in Barlow *Edward the Confessor*, opp. p. 232. Even if one disregards its surviving *later* additions, the ruins of Jumièges reveal a spectacular construction architecturally; and Westminster apparently was even bigger. The connection between Westminster and Jumièges is underlined by the fact that Robert the abbot of Jumièges had come to England at an early stage in King Edward's reign, to become not only the Bishop of London (and later Archbishop of Canterbury) but also the chief adviser to the king and the rebuilder of the abbey at Westminster.

10  The sources are given and discussed by Gem, *'Romanesque Rebuilding of WA'*, A-NS 3 (1981), 39 & 204.

11  Comparably, the *second* rebuilding of the abbey and other building works on the palace undertaken in the C13 by Henry III caused a further large inflow of new workers into Westminster, see p. 260 below. Some of these inevitably stayed on afterwards and became residents, pursuing their particular occupations and skills there in the necessary maintenance of the new abbey and its domestic buildings.

12  For discussion of these cottagers' connection with the palace site, see *The Westminster Corridor*, p. 141. As a group, they were one of the very few royal 'possessions' left in Middlesex in 1086, see DB. *Mdx.* 1/1. When the church at Westminster had been founded in the early 970s, most of the few remaining royal estates in Mdx had been bestowed upon it, some of them forming 'the Westminster corridor' along Watling Street, see *The Westminster Corridor*, pp. 69-70;  and see discussion in Mason, *People of WA*, pp. 9-10.

13  See pp. 106 ff. below.

Stephen and the Empress Matilda (with both a prelude and an aftermath to that war, from 1135-1154), it was a century in which the lesser folk of Westminster initially figure dimly, having survived only faintly in the records. So the manner in which the lay population of Westminster developed during the period up to about 1160 remains largely hidden, apart from some scattered appearances which are illustrated below. The occasional residents who can initially be identified by name and occupation were mostly officers or servants at the abbey, together with a few royal officers and personnel necessary for the administration of the palace. Later on many more became needed to man the early institutions of national government, when these came to be located within Westminster.

On the other hand there were two periods within the twelfth century when really creative advances were being made in the development of these institutions of government – and these ultimately transformed the character of Westminster. Each of the two periods was the reign of a king Henry, namely Henry I (1100-1135), and his grandson, Henry II (1154-1189). But their two reigns were separated by 'the nineteen years of anarchy', the violent civil strife between Stephen and Matilda, and as a result the advances which had been made in Henry I's reign were nearly lost. Indeed that earlier progress during his reign would probably have been undone altogether, if his grandson had not been an even more enterprising administrator. However the effect of their separate but cumulative efforts was to shape the direction which the whole later history of Westminster was to take. Initially that history was to be closely linked with the principal organ of government known as the 'Exchequer'.

Henry I, a ruthless but intelligent man like his father the Conqueror, had been served by an outstanding minister, Roger of Salisbury, who had progressively advanced from the position of king's chaplain to the national posts of chancellor and then justiciar. It was to Roger and the king that the creation of the pivotal body of English medieval administration, which came to be called the exchequer, was due.[14] The exchequer, with its complement of 'barons of the exchequer',[15] was to become both the central revenue-accounting and auditing body of the king's government and also a court which delivered legal judgments on issues initially relating to the king's fiscal affairs.[16] At that time it was based in Winchester, which was still the focal point of government in Henry I's reign.

But on the death of Henry I in 1135, with his only legitimate male heir long since dead, the new administrative machinery had at once been threatened by the dynastic rivalry of Stephen (Henry's nephew) and Matilda (Henry's daughter) and by the ensuing civil war. But the eventual conclusion in 1154 of the disturbances left over from the civil war saw the start of the Angevin dynasty, with the unopposed coronation of Matilda's son, Henry, Duke of Normandy and Count of Anjou, with his queen, Eleanor of Aquitaine. The crowning was carried out in Westminster Abbey by Theobald, the archbishop of Canterbury, on the 19th December 1154. Henry was still only twenty one years old but two years before, by his marriage to the heiress Eleanor, he had increased his own previously inherited control over a quarter of modern France to nearly a half.

## The effect on Westminster of the creative energies of Henry II

Although much of Henry II's ensuing reign was taken up with war, with family

---

14  Green, *Govt. of England under Henry I*, pp. 40 ff. Roger of Salisbury may also have commissioned the sending of justices on circuit into the provinces, *ibid.*, p. 45-46 and 108.

15  The 'barons of the exchequer' were first mentioned in 1110, although a less formalised financial audit by royal officials belonging to the king's household had evolved earlier, Poole, *DB to Magna Carta*, p. 416.

16  See also p. 112 below.

fights and with the fortunes of his possessions in major parts of modern France,[17] it was his great governmental reforms in England which had direct effects on Westminster. For the next 35 years Henry featured as a powerful force in driving his administrative reforms through, even though his own family relationships were disastrous, while baronial unrest and revolts also weakened his standing.

The first of his administrative initiatives was to revive his grandfather's central instrument of government, the Exchequer. But he quickly made a significant geographical change in its place of operation. For three centuries the main seat of government had been Winchester, ever since the men of Wessex under Alfred and his successors had united England.[18] Henry now moved the exchequer and his treasury to Westminster, so establishing the first permanent connection between Westminster and the government of this country – which has survived for over 800 years. Twice a year the barons of the court of the exchequer now sat in Westminster with all their staff; and a tide of the king's agents, the sheriffs of the counties, and other debtors had to flow periodically with their attendants into the town, to account for and pay over their collected revenues, or to pay other debts owed or seek their postponement.[19]

But like his predecessors the king himself remained itinerant, either regularly travelling the country or, more often, going abroad to the continent for long periods of war or diplomacy. And so although Westminster now became his seat of English financial administration and although governmental decisions could be taken in his absences by competent ministers, his own executive role, when necessary, still had to be performed wherever he and his court might be.

Henry's other main reforms which affected Westminster were legal and judicial ones. These resulted in an extended circuit system of royal justice in the counties and also in the growing prominence of Westminster as the hub of the judicial system for the next 800 years. Up to this point the *curia regis* (the king's own court) had been peripatetic, following him on his travels. Not only were changes made in the court system itself, but also the 'forms of actions' which were available to people seeking justice in the courts were extended and reformed. By this introduction of new remedies in law, litigants were enabled to obtain an easier restoration of injured rights in certain defined situations: where, for example, occupiers of land were ousted from their occupation of it, or heirs were deprived of their inheritance.[20]

With such reforms in place, a section of the justices from the personnel of the king's court began after about 1178 to sit more permanently in Westminster, as a court to hear common pleas of these kinds, even when the king was absent. This became known as the *curia capitalis*, the 'chief court', or the 'Bench' or in more localised terms, *'the king's court at*

---

17 Consequently neither Henry nor Eleanor were later buried in England, still less at Westminster Abbey, but lie at the abbey of Fontevrault in Anjou in France, where their effigies may still be seen, together with the effigies of their son Richard I (Coeur de Lion), and Queen Isabella of Angoulême, second wife of another son, King John.
18 See *The Westminster Corridor*, pp. 22-3.
19 Details of the process and of some of the senior officers who staffed the court are given at pp. 110-12 and 156-9; and of others less exalted, in chapter 10, *passim*, and particularly at pp. 178-181 and 183-5.
20 The new remedies could be sought by starting actions with special 'writs' (bearing complicated names, such as *novel disseisin; mort d'ancestor;* or *darrein presentment).* But each new writ was designed to deal with well-known situations in which legal remedies were particularly needed. Decisions by 'juries' were involved in each. Another major change was the reformed *'writ of right'*, by which after 1179 legal rights to land could (at the choice of the defendant) be decided by a jury of twelve knights of the shire, instead of by 'battle'. But see p. 49 above for one such 'battle' which took place in Westminster in the C13, and p. 146 n. 40 for another slightly earlier one.

*Westminster near the exchequer'*.[21] After a brief interruption in its sittings during King John's reign, this court was in effect reinstated by Magna Carta after 1215, which specifically required that one part of the king's court should not follow the king but be held in some fixed place, which in practice usually meant at Westminster once again.[22] The great benefit to a would-be litigant which the Westminster sittings gave was that he did not have to chase the king in his travels through the provinces or even onto the continent, in order to procure justice.

So the 'chief court' came to sit in the comparatively new Westminster Hall, or in a nearby building in the palace complex.[23] The Hall, built by King William *Rufus* by 1099, had been used both by Henry I in 1102 and by Stephen in 1135 for the first great councils of their reigns. But it also later became the place where (at different points of time) each of the three main historical courts of England – the Courts of Common Pleas, the King's Bench and Chancery – began and thereafter continued to sit.[24] The progressive effect on the town of Westminster was marked. With these legal changes, which flowed from initiatives by Henry II, there came an increasing flow of royal officers, lawyers, litigants and judges into Westminster, some of them both to work and live there, others just to work in the business of the legal courts.[25]

The increased availability of justice, both in Westminster and elsewhere in the country, in turn resulted in a need for more 'paper work' (ie. 'parchment work', then) by the legal secretariat, the chancery scribes in the chancellor's office, who had to make, check and supply the appropriate writs and other legal documents.[26] Some of these members of the chancellor's staff now also began to work more permanently in Westminster, instead of constantly following the king.

So it was a period in which the creation of administrative documents by the king's personal scribes, the exchequer scribes and the chancery scribes had grown threefold.[27] This new government bureaucracy which began to develop under Henry II was the factor which made it possible for the first systematic gathering together and retention of national documentary archives, most of it in Westminster, which evolved during the next two decades after Henry's death in 1189.[28]

---

21  See Warren, *Henry II*, pp. 295-8, 330-1; Mortimer, *Angevin England*, p. 61. Often the justices of the court were also barons of the exchequer, so that they were sitting in Westminster at different times with different hats on (literally as well as figuratively).

22  Magna Carta, cl. 17. But the Charter had to be reissued several times in later years, after the pope had annulled the 1215 version, on the grounds that King John, who had become his vassal after the king's submission under the interdict (see p. 133 below), had been under duress in signing it; its final re-issue was in 1225.

23  The Hall was still less than 100 years old. As the builder of it, William II (*Rufus*) was said to have thought it 'not half large enough'. Apart from short later interruptions of the courts' use of the hall, it was not until 1882 (following the Supreme Court of Judicature Act 1873) that the last remaining civil courts and their lawyers finally left Westminster for their new site in the Strand.

24  The three courts filled two corners of the hall, and a place on the west wall near the entrance; with the two sections of the exchequer housed adjoining to the hall. See also note 29 below.

25  Westminster and Winchester acted like buckets in a well. As the former flourished with the new influx of personnel, so the latter declined as a centre of power, Mortimer, *Angevin England*, p. 183.

26  Mortimer, *ibid.*, pp. 63, 64-5. Paper was not used in England until c. 1307 (the nominal end of this book): Clanchy, *Memory to Written Record*, p. 120.

27  Clanchy, *ibid* (1993) pp. 57-62. It appears that there were no 'union rules' to prevent significant interchange of the various roles between them, when occasion demanded; and the same was also true of the executive officers of the other staffs employed in the bureaucracy.

28  *ibid.* pp. 48-57. See also pp. 121-3 and 164-6 below for the influence of Hubert Walter, the great justiciar in Richard's reign and chancellor in John's reign, in the development of record-making and keeping.

In effect Henry II's reign became a watershed, both in national history and in the local history of Westminster, the future centre of government and law. It is hardly surprising that the year 1189, when Henry died and his son Richard I was crowned, became established, by later statutes, as the legal limit of human memory, the terminal date *'from which memory runneth not to the contrary'*. This meant that a litigant did not have to prove facts *before* that year in order to sustain a claim. The earlier practice had been that, because documents were less frequently made or retained at that time, the legal limit of human memory had successively been taken as the coronation of the previous king. But late in the thirteenth century statutes fixed the coronation of Richard I (3rd September 1189, two months after Henry II his father had died) as the legal limit of memory, which remained fixed for the rest of the Middle Ages. It was a recognition that the proof of claims would in future be able to rest primarily on records rather than the recollection of living witnesses.[29]

---

29 *ibid*. p. 123. For two outstanding illustrations of such medieval courts in session – albeit at a date later than the subject period of this book – see Plates 17 and 18 in the block of coloured plates towards the end of the book, after page 288.

CHAPTER 5

# The constant presence of the abbots

Throughout the time when these national events were making their impact on the Westminster scene, it was the abbey which, in the person of the abbot as the perpetual lord of the manor, remained astride the small town and maintained a constant presence over it. Through his manor courts the abbot had complete jurisdiction within the whole 'liberty' of Westminster, even to the extent of an ultimate power (within the law) of life and death over the residents.[1] And individual monks, when engaged either in the town or elsewhere on occasional business outside the abbey's precinct, must by their physical presence have been a constant reminder to local people of the power of the abbot which they indirectly represented.

In the period from the abbey's foundation until Domesday, six abbots had presided over the abbey, four of them being English, with two Norman abbots between 1071 and 1085.[2] After seventeen years of office during Edward the Confessor's reign, the last English abbot, *Edwin*, had also managed to survive for at least

two more years into the Norman period. But few known events during those six abbacies have much relevance to the development of the town of Westminster or its relationship with the abbey or the 'corridor estates'.[3] Still less is known about other individual monks.

But in the century after Domesday a few of the abbey's monks become well known to us, and principally of course these are the abbots and some of the priors. The five abbots who directed the affairs of the abbey during the period from Domesday until the death of Henry II in 1189 stand out among the visible figures.[4]

## Abbot Gilbert Crispin  *(c. 1085 - 1117)*

The five begin with the impressive Norman, Gilbert Crispin, a well-born and learned leader of men, who remained abbot from just before Domesday for a period of over thirty years and presided over a complement of eighty monks, the largest convent which the abbey was ever to have.[5] Originally he had come from the abbey of Bec in Normandy, but

1  Although at this period there are no surviving court records to prove it, the power (within the law) was absolute.
2  For the names and short mentions of the four English abbots, see *The Westminster Corridor*, p. 159.
3  The best account of the little which is known about the abbots during this period before Domesday is to be found in Mason, *WA People*, pp. 19-24.  It is worth noting that during this period Abbot Vitalis commissioned the first 'history' of the abbey, up to the reign of Edward the Confessor, from the monk Sulcard. He also carried out some building works at the abbey and the palace.
4  The short biographies given here for the abbots are limited to known aspects of the abbots' lives and actions which reflected their relationships with the king, the town of Westminster and their own monks, or revealed the issues which they faced in their administration of the abbey.  In general, the evidence relating to *lesser* residents in Westminster is scarce during this period, but is dealt with in the next chapter, at pp. 95 ff.
5  For his whole life and abbacy, and his writings, see Robinson, *Gilbert Crispin*; Mason, *WA People*, 24-32; Harvey, *WA Estates*, 95.  He was a highly respected writer and teacher, who alone fostered 'a mood of intellectual excitement' at the abbey, Harvey, *ibid*.  'Crispin' apparently was a descriptive name, referring to the inherited style of his family's hair, which stood on end.  Doubtless, in his case, a tonsure partly subdued it.

had been serving at Canterbury before being appointed to Westminster. Once he was installed there, one of his tasks was to carry out the building of those works to the monastic quarters at the abbey which had not been undertaken by King Edward the Confessor before his death in 1066, and which still remained unfinished at the time of Domesday.[6] He also took part in an attempt to promote a cult of King Edward whose tomb lay at the abbey, with a view to procuring that king's ultimate canonisation and the reflected glory which would be added to the abbey from the harbouring of a saint.   As part of this promotion he presided over an official opening of the dead king's tomb in 1102, when the body was said to have been found to be still wholly uncorrupted.[7]

### Grants of local lands by Abbot Crispin

During his abbacy Crispin made at least three important awards of land within the 'corridor' of estates adjoining the abbey. Firstly, within Westminster itself he granted the 'berewick of Totenhala' to a 'knight', William Baynard, as one of the abbey's knights' fees.  It seems from the terms of the abbot's charter that the grant was in return for some benefit or benefits which Baynard had conferred upon the abbey.  This land (which lay either in 'Tottenhall', just north of modern

High Holborn, or in 'Tothill', just west of the abbey itself) had been previously held by an anglo-saxon thegn, no doubt on similar terms to those on which Baynard was now to hold it. One of his obligations was to serve as (or to provide) a man-at-arms to act as one of the abbey's quota of fifteen 'knights', whom the abbey was feudally obliged to provide when called on to do so.[8]

Secondly, the manor of Chelsea, an earlier royal estate which before Domesday had been granted by the Conqueror to one of his barons, Edward of Salisbury, had (in some unrecorded way) been acquired by the abbey during the time when Crispin was abbot.[9]  But in about 1116, shortly before his death, the abbot leased Chelsea (with other lands further afield) to the king's sheriff of Berkshire, William of Buckland.  This grant of Chelsea was at a rent of £4 pa., for the sheriff's life only, with reversion thereafter to the abbey; and as a result of this time-limitation, the manor came back to the abbey before at least 1138; only to be the subject of scandal when it was granted away again by Abbot Gervase, and on that occasion permanently, for the same rent.[10]

Thirdly, before 1102 Crispin also granted another fee, in the manor of Hendon, to 'his man Gunter' and his heir, for an annual food-rent of 'one week's farm', ie. in theory, the amount of food required to feed the abbey for

---

6   Summarised in *The Westminster Corridor*, p. 153, note 21.
7   See Barlow, *Edward the Confessor*, pp. 267-269; Mason, *ibid.*, pp. 27, 295, 298; Robinson, *ibid.*, pp. 23-5. Crispin had to upbraid a bishop who tried to pull out a hair from the king's beard. The king's saint-hood was not achieved until nearly 50 years after Abbot Crispin's death, see below, pp. 76-7 and 84-5.
8   WAC 236 (c. 1086).  There is still uncertainty about the location of the 'berewick': was it either in Tottenhall or Tothill ?; see *The Westminster Corridor*, p. 80-81 and the authorities mentioned there in note 9.  Dr Mason in *WA People*, p. 29, and others stand by Tothill, but I adhere to the view expressed originally by Dr Gelling in 1954 (based on the terms of the Ethelred charter of 1002) and agreed by Dr. Rosser (*Med. Westminster*, 252) that the 'berewick' was in effect the area of St. Giles, which extended into Bloomsbury, until part of it was appropriated, probably by Henry I for his Queen Matilda's foun-dation of the leper hospital there.  This accords with many factors: the terms of the Ethelred charter; the description 'berewick' (a description only used in Westminster in that charter and in the grant to Baynard); the name Totenhala itself; and even the boundaries which survived thereafter.  For the ab-bey's feudal quota of 15 'knights', see *The Westminster Corridor*, p. 142.
9  For Chelsea's importance in A-S times, see *The Westminster Corridor*, pp. 20, 137 and 138.  I do not know how it passed from Edward of Salisbury to the abbey.   Edward was ancestor of the first Earls of Salisbury.
10  For the grant to Wm. of Buckland, see WAC 242 (c. 1116).  For Abbot Gervase's grant, see p. 78.

one week of the year.[11] The value of this food-rent, when assessed about fifteen or more years later, was apparently £8. 10s. Gunter's estate or 'fee' was not a 'knight's fee'. It was expressly labelled a 'fee-farm' and did not carry any obligation to serve as, or to provide, a man-at-arms for the abbey.[12] The relationship between Gunter's family at Hendon and the abbey was to prove a long-standing one, and it is a constantly recurring one in this chapter.[13]

It is worth noting that a fourth nearby fee, actually described as a knight's fee, had been created by the abbey *before* Domesday, in the manor of Battersea (held by the abbey) on the southern shore of the Thames. Domesday Book itself records that four hides were held in that manor by an unnamed knight.[14] This knight's fee too could have been created by Abbot Crispin, since he had become abbot in about 1085 (when the Survey was ordered); though there is no surviving record of the grant; and it may have been made by an earlier abbot.

One other act, a minor one, possibly carried out by the abbot concerning nearby land, was a grant of a 'corrody' (a right to receive food and/or drink from the abbey) which he may have made to a local hermit, named Godwin. His little hermitage existed just off Watling Street (now the Edgware Road), just within the boundary of the abbey's manor of Hampstead in what is now the Kilburn area.[15] The hermitage was one which

under Crispin's successor was to become a small nunnery, which for all its size figured prominently in records and became known later as 'Kilburn Priory', surviving for four centuries until the dissolution of the monasteries in the sixteenth century.[16] But in Abbot Crispin's time the hermitage was far less prominent, even though it was close to the main pilgrim route to St. Albans; perhaps at that time Godwin did not welcome passing travellers, who might have supported him. But later as a nunnery there, its reputation as a place of shelter and alms-giving grew and attracted travellers who passed and repassed along the road.

### Food and rents for the abbey's monks

The manner in which the monks of Westminster were fed and maintained, during and after Crispin's abbacy, is known to us because of the survival of a special accounting record made shortly after the abbot died in about 1117. For the next three to four years after he had died, during a 'ruinous vacancy' in the abbacy while the post was waiting to be filled, the king's managers were in control of the abbey's assets, and during this period a succinct 'render-list' was made, showing the food-renders (ie. rents in the form of farm produce) and other money rents and contributions required by the monks from various estates, and how these were used or spent.

In view of the retrospective clues which this render-list contains as to abbey

---

11　WAC 241. For Hendon, see *The Westm. Corridor*, pp. 87 ff., 156-7 & Map N; and the Introdn. to this book.

12　But apparently a rent-paying tenant could sometimes owe military service, Reynolds, *Fiefs and Vassals*, p. 352.

13　For Gunter and his family at Hendon, see also pp. 75-6, 79-81, 84 below. See also the change from the food-rent, made by Abbot Gervase many years later, on pp. 80-81. Later still the food-rent for the Hendon lands was later re-introduced, and the amount of food which was being paid over 100 years later by an even later descendant in the family was revealed as 36 quarters of wheat, 20 quarters of grout, and 40 quarters of brewing oats, in addition to an even greater money rent of £22 pa., WAD 121b, see p. 202 below.

14　B. *Surrey* 6/1. Battersea had been obtained by the abbey from William the Conqueror, when the king had granted it (and two other manors in Essex) to the abbey in exchange for the abbey's manor of Windsor (which the king wanted for hunting). See also p. 74 below, for a temporary loss of Battersea by the abbey.

15　Hermits were a recognised religious order, subject to their own rules; see eg. Cutts, *Middle Ages*, pp. 93 ff.

16　WAC 264, and Robinson, *Gilbert Crispin*, p. 34. These later nuns had an obligation to pray for Crispin's soul, WAM Bk I, *Liber Niger*, 125, & cf. WAC 264. Harvey, *Living and Dying*, 239-40, interprets 'the

administration in an even earlier period *before* the Norman Conquest, the details of the render-list have already been discussed at length in *The Westminster Corridor*.[17] The main lessons from this vital document are firstly that at the abbey in Westminster the ancient system of 'rent' in the form of food-renders, which was in force from anglo-saxon times, was still partly in existence in the early part of the twelfth century, and secondly that the obligations of the nearby estates to provide food-produce for the monks had not yet been entirely commuted to money rents. For some manors the duty was now a hybrid one: partly produce and partly money.

In summary, the document reveals what the abbey's weekly requirements of produce (in wheat, oats, malt and grout) from its nearer manors and properties in London were during the early twelfth century; on similar lines to the food-renders on which the abbey must have depended during its earlier anglo-saxon existence.[18] But in addition to the food renders, considerable money demands, for specified purposes, were also being made by the abbey upon at least twenty named manors, most of them in its nearby estates in Middlesex, Essex and Hertfordshire.[19] Moreover all the more distant manors, no doubt particularly those in the 'western parts' (Gloucestershire and Worcestershire) of the abbey's estates, had to contribute to a weekly money rent of £8. 10s, a considerable sum representing, it seems, the value of a weekly food-rent for the abbey.

Gilbert Crispin died in c.1117, or possibly 1118.[20] It was to be three or four years before a new abbot was appointed, and so the vacancy in the abbacy arose, with the consequence that royal managers controlled the abbey's assets for three or more years. This meant that such managers, whether acting on the king's orders or on their own account, could sell or let properties of the abbey, without being strictly accountable to the abbey.

## Abbot Herbert *(1121 - 1138)*
### *Recouping the 'disastrous vacancy'*

There is little doubt that the vacancy (1117-1121) before the appointment of Abbot Herbert was grievous for the abbey. The monks suffered serious losses of their properties during a period which must have been anarchic for their abbey while it remained in the hands of the king's managers. Unfortunately most of the losses are difficult to identify, and this presents a problem for us in relation to Westminster, and it certainly presented a problem for Abbot Herbert at that time.

Like his predecessor, Herbert was probably also of Norman birth. But unlike Crispin, he was already a monk of Westminster and had been the abbey's almoner before being elevated to the abbacy.

corrody of Abbot Crispin' in WAC 264, as meaning a double corrody of food as supplied *to* Crispin as abbot, rather than a corrody granted *by* Crispin; but query? For the nunnery later, see pp. 75-6, 79.

17  See pp. 150-7 of that book, and p. 19 above; also Robinson Cri*s*pin, 41. The list is WAM 5670. Since the king could influence the speed at which an abbot's election took place, he or his managers could engineer a longer profit.

18  The major difference between the anglo-saxon and post-Conquest periods was that by 1117 the complement of monks had increased from 12 to 80, so that now the food (and money) needs were more than six times greater.

19  The only manor in the abbey's adjoining 'corridor' which is specifically named (in the document) as required to provide a sum expressed in money terms was Knightsbridge. The sum was 20s., to pay for the annual ceremony of the Maundy. The manor of Knightsbridge, with Westbourne, had probably been added to the abbey's estates during the reign of Edward the Confessor. It had not been part of the abbey's original endowment of Westminster, which was only five hides. The vill of Knightsbridge (among others) was held to be included in St. Margaret's parish, in the great arbitration of 1222, see pp. 36, 336-7 and Appendix B at p. 399.

20  A very worn effigy, said to be Crispin's, can still be seen in the S-E. corner of the abbey cloisters.

In fact he was the first monk *of the house* to be made abbot for more than seventy years.[21] Much of the new abbot's energy throughout his abbacy was spent in trying to recover the abbey's recent losses, by lobbying in the royal court for Henry I's help in effecting this recovery. There is much evidence that he was successful in obtaining royal help – for which the abbey was then liable to pay heavily.[22] But the identities of many of the properties which had been lost and recovered (or not recovered, as the case may be) are unknown. The reason for this is that although the king did in some cases order specific properties in distant parts to be returned or held for the account of the abbey, a number of the wider orders which he made were in general terms, in effect merely commanding all his barons, sheriffs and other officers to ensure that the abbey did recover all lands, unspecified, which had been lost by it.[23]

### Westminster lands during the vacancy

As already shown in chapter 1, before the middle of the thirteenth century many lands within the manor of Westminster had already been granted to 'tenants' and so were held in personal estates which had been called 'fees'; and in some, if not many, of these cases it seems that the abbey did not have any right to recover the properties.[24] The dates when these dispersals of lands within Westminster

had taken place are in issue. So the question arises whether any of them had happened during this vacancy, when clearly some people had been playing fast and loose with the abbey's other possessions before Abbot Herbert took office.

Only one of Henry I's orders to help the abbey appears to relate to any specific property in Westminster. But this one exception seems to concern only the right of the abbot to have certain stalls in an early fair or market at Westminster (an issue about which some dispute had obviously arisen), and does not relate to any substantial alienated property or fee.[25]

Some of the subsequent royal orders relate to unidentified properties in nearby London. Others refer to named properties in London; and there was one other property in the vicinity of the abbey which in 1123 formed the subject of a specific royal order for its recovery by the abbey, namely the manor of Battersea across the Thames, which had been appropriated by Rannulf Flambard, an unscrupulous former minister of William Rufus.[26] Neither these London orders nor the Battersea one support any argument that properties *within* Westminster were improperly alienated from the abbey during this period. All other royal orders for specific lands to be recovered by the abbey relate to places and properties further afield.

21  Robinson, 'Westminster in the Twelfth Century: Osbert of Clare', Ch. Q.R. 68 (1909), p. 337.
22  For royal orders made to assist the abbey, see WACs 73, 75-82, 84-92, 94-96. The abbot found himself being 'billed' in 1130 at the Exchequer for a debt of a thousand marks (£666. 13s. 4d.) for the 'fines' which he was liable to pay for the royal services which he had invoked. In fact only about £100 was paid by, or credited to, him before 900 marks of the debt were cancelled, maybe because it was realised that the abbey's cash flow could never match such a debt, see Mason, *WA. People*, 33-34. Probably the reason why the king was willing to give such assistance to the abbey was contrition. During the period of the vacancy he had himself suffered two crushing personal losses. In 1118 his beloved queen Matilda had died, and in 1120 his only legitimate son had been drowned in the wreck of *The White Ship* in the Channel. As a result he may have been distracted from the task of supervising his agents; and/or recognised he was responsible for any misdeeds committed in his name.
23  eg. probably the widest (but most succinct) order of all was WAC 75 (1121 x 1122), a writ of the king, made very early in the abbacy, which ordered *'his barons, sheriffs and officers that Abbot Herbert is to be given seisin of all lands which were alienated from the abbey, or granted without the assent of the chapter'*. In addition, *'if anyone brings a claim about these lands'*, the abbot was given jurisdiction to deal with him *'in his own court'*. See also Mason, *WA People*, p. 33, for an analysis of all the king's orders.
24  See pp. 21-3, and for a list of the known 'fees', see Appendix A at pp. 391-5.
25  WAC 94 (c. 1129 x 1133). See also Robinson, *Crispin*, p. 157.
26  For London, see WACs 77 - 90. For Battersea, see Harvey, *WA Estates*, 357n and 359n, and WAC 82 (1123); and cf. WAC 83 (probably forged).

As regards the king's 'general' orders to his barons or his royal officers, it would seem extraordinary if undesired alienations had taken place on the abbey's very doorstep and no specific complaint about them had resulted in any royal order directly related to any one of them.

So on the limited evidence relating to the vacancy, there are several possible results:

(a) there had been no known alienations of Westminster lands during this vacancy;

(b) there had been such alienations, but the monks felt they had no ground for complaint about them;

(c) for some other reason, the king was not lobbied about such alienations;

(d) the monks had lobbied the king, but the king had refused to help them.

Of these, the fourth result looks the least likely, since in view of the support given by the king in order to assist the monks to recover properties elsewhere, he was very unlikely to have refused to assist them about lands in their own domestic manor, if complaint was made to him. But again, if there had been *improper* losses in this, the abbey's immediate domain, the new abbot and his monks who had pursued similar complaints about properties elsewhere would have complained about losses so close at hand. So it is possible that no improper transfers of Westminster land took place during these four years – or the monks felt they could make no complaint, or for some other reason made no such complaint.

### The challenge to the abbey by Gilbert, the bishop of London

One quite different issue came to a dramatic head during Herbert's abbacy. There had already been a dispute between the abbey and the bishop of London as to whether the abbey was within the jurisdiction of the bishop and under his supervision. Geographically the abbey certainly lay within the diocese of London, but there had been a strong tradition at Westminster that the abbey (by reason of its special status as the coronation church and the repository of royal regalia) was subject only to the pope and that the bishop had no authority there.

But in 1133, on the 29th June the feast of St. Peter and St. Paul, Bishop Gilbert ('the Universal', as he is known) presented himself at the abbey in his full canonical finery and proceeded not only to celebrate mass there, but even to appropriate the offerings. This was the final straw for the monks: they at once incurred the heavy cost of sending an indignant complaint to Pope Innocent II in Rome, and by the 30th September a papal *bulla* had already been signed and addressed to Henry I, authorising him to take the abbey 'under his protection' and excluding it from the control of the bishop.[27] This was the first surviving genuine document establishing the abbey's exemption from the bishop's general powers of control, which he could exercise only when he had a right to 'visit and correct' the churches and priests in his diocese.[28]

### Gunter of Hendon, and the Kilburn hermitage

Two other known events which took place within the boundaries of Westminster's 'corridor' of estates during Herbert's abbacy concerned, respectively, the Hendon estate of Abbot Crispin's 'man', Gunter; and the little hermitage at Kilburn.

With the death of Abbot Crispin, the rights of Gunter in his estate in Hendon which he had received from that abbot needed to be authenticated by the new abbot, and Gunter

---

27 WAC 155 (30 Sept. 1133). For the earlier tradition and later history, see Mason *WA People*, p. 121-3 and Knowles, 'The Growth of Exemption', *Downside Review* 50 (1932) pp. 417-420.

28 But already the abbey's *scriptorium* under the direction of its prior, Osbert of Clare, had created a whole series of forged 'earlier' charters in an attempt to prove this and other points in support of the abbey, see main text below. For the craft of forgery at the abbey, see *The Westminster Corridor*, pp. 60-63.

succeeded in obtaining from Abbot Herbert a confirmation of his own right and his heir's right to inherit it, in the same terms as Abbot Crispin had granted it.[29]

As already indicated, Abbot Crispin may have been the first Westminster abbot to have become involved personally with Godwin's hermitage established at Kilburn in Hampstead. But now Godwin, who had originally built the hermitage, surrendered it to Abbot Herbert, and in return was appointed for life as the warden, at the same place, of a cell of three nuns, named Emma, Gunilda and Cristina, to whom by 1134 the hermitage was formally granted by Abbot Herbert, his prior Osbert of Clare and the whole convent. For the support of the nuns' cell, which much later became known as a Priory at Kilburn, various endowments (including some wooded or waste land in the manor of Knightsbridge, called the Gore, a name which still exists as 'Kensington Gore') were made to the nunnery.[30]

### The egregious prior, Osbert of Clare

The extraordinary Prior Osbert of Clare, who participated in his abbot's grant to the nunnery, deserves further mention here, in the context of this abbacy.[31] A learned but voluble, if not garrulous, man, Osbert was a restless supporter of causes, who was adept at making himself a nuisance to those who mattered. He had already become the prior of Westminster during the vacancy in the abbacy between 1117 and 1121, and accordingly regarded himself as having been unfairly passed over for the abbacy, when at the end of that vacancy it was the abbey almoner (Herbert) who was made abbot. It seems that the king himself may have interfered with this election, giving his preference for Herbert. And sure enough, the new Abbot Herbert and his prior were soon having differences, which resulted in Osbert being expelled ('proscribed' was his own more vivid word) in or before 1123 and sent off to serve time at the Abbey of Ely, where he remained until 1134. While there, he could not restrain himself from hurling abroad by letter his own high-flown and often barbed self-justifications, sometimes mixed with Heep-like unctuousness.

Restored to Westminster in about 1134, Osbert – now prior again – was instrumental in drafting and creating, in support of the abbey and its refounder King Edward the Confessor, the finest collection of grandiloquent but forged charters to be found in any monastery. But one of his smaller genuine successes was the foundation of the nunnery at Kilburn: his name, specifically mentioned in two charters, shows him to have probably been the moving spirit in relation to the nunnery.[32]

His last and greatest failure was a project to procure the canonisation of Edward the Confessor, which his flowery forgeries and his biography of the king, *The Life of King Edward*, were designed to underpin.[33] Although in 1139

29  WAC 245, and see pp. 71-2 above. Apparently Gunter's son Gilbert then inherited the estate before the death of King Henry I in 1135. See further pp. 79-81, 84, and 305 n. 58 below.

30  WACs 249, 250, and 264 and 265 during the next abbacy; see also p. 72 above. The bishop of London, Gilbert the Universal, gave his assent to the creation of the new nunnery. The land called the Gore was granted to the nuns 'ad sartandum', for assarting; ie. with the task or right to convert the wood or wasteland to cultivation. Some more details of the history of the nunnery are given below in chapter 21 about Hampstead, at pp. 366-8.

31  For his life, see Barlow, *Edward the Confessor*, pp. 267-9, 272-8, 280-1; Robinson, 'Osbert of Clare', p. 336; Williamson (ed), *The Letters of Osbert of Clare*; Mason, *WA People*, pp. 89-91, etc. His confrontations with his own abbots were later mirrored in the even more volcanic disputes which erupted between Abbot Walter of Wenlock and his prior, Reginald of Hadham, at the start of the fourteenth century, see pp. 319-26 below. But by Wenlock's time, a prior's position was much stronger relatively.

32  WACs 249 and 265. Some of the ornate style and content of the founding charter (WAC 249) of the nuns' 'priory' also reveals the hand of Osbert in the drafting of it.

33  For a list of some of his forgeries, see *The Westminster Corridor*, p. 190. His biography of King Edward was a rewrite of the original *Vita Aewardi Regis*, the contemporary biography written at the end of the king's life (see *ibid.*, p. 136, Barlow (ed. & trans.) (1992), but missing out its major theme.

(under the next abbot, Gervase) Osbert made the long journey to Rome to present a petition for canonisation and to argue that theme, he returned without success, for lack of sufficient testimonials of support from bishops and abbots. However to his credit he earned a commendation for himself from the pope and successfully procured another general order, this time a papal one, for the recovery of the abbey's still lost properties.

In his dealings at home, he had fallen out with his new abbot (Gervase), and may have already besmirched his name with the pope. No longer prior, Osbert was again sent away from Westminster for a time, to look after a small church. Later his biography of King Edward (itself a rewrite) had to be rewritten again; Edward's canonisation had to wait for another twenty one years; and the glory of its procurement went elsewhere. Nothing happened by halves with Osbert. But at least he was allowed to return to Westminster, finally to die at the abbey as an unofficed monk.

So Abbot Herbert, having inherited ruinous problems (though not it seems in the town of Westminster) from the earlier vacancy and a disappointed and prickly prior ready to point out every fault, himself received a reputation for the incurring of great expenses and for poor administration. But it is difficult to see what else the poor man could have done to shield and restore his uncomfortable inheritance, particularly if the expense of obtaining the king's help was essential for the attempt to recover the abbey's lost properties.

At Christmas 1135 the new King Stephen was crowned in the abbey at Westminster, in the same month as Henry I had died from eating lampreys against his doctor's advice. The prelude to the civil war with the Empress

Matilda had started.[34] There was no abbot present at the coronation, perhaps because Herbert was already too old or ill, or too politically astute to attend a contentious occasion. The abbot died in September 1136, or perhaps 1138. If it was the former year, another two-year vacancy in the abbacy began in 1136, during the disorderly period before the civil war actually began; and this could only have compounded the abbey's problems about its lost properties, problems which had already been present when Abbot Herbert inherited them fifteen years earlier.

## Abbot Gervase  (c. 1138 - 1157)
### An illegitimate abbot and his reputation

The character and the actions of Abbot Gervase have been a fiercely-fought battleground. His name was blackened by those who came after him, and has more recently been only partially whitewashed. The complex details of these historical battles have tended to obscure the story of his life and times. A measured context for his career has been given by Dr. Emma Mason, and one can see more clearly the objective events during his abbacy, which indicate the reasons why he undeservedly received some of the criticisms from contemporaries and posterity.[35] Here, his actions and the events of his abbacy are of course limited to those which bear upon Westminster and the abbey itself or the abbey's nearby estates.

An illegitimate son of King Stephen, Gervase looks like a strange choice for appointment as an abbot of Westminster. In fact he owed both his appointment, and also his ultimate deposition from the post under Henry II, to the fact that he was Stephen's son, an indication of the greatly changed political situation between 1138 and 1157. In spite of

34 Matilda, H. I's daughter, was 'Empress' because her first marriage was to the 'Holy Roman' Emperor Henry V, who died in 1125, and she then kept her title, although she remarried Geoffrey of Anjou in 1128, & her son by him, Henry of Anjou, in due course became Henry II of England and in 1154 half of modern France.

35 See Mason, *WA People*, 37-51. For Gervase's critics, see Robinson (ed), *Flete, History of WA*, pp. 88-91; Robinson, *Westminster in 12C : Osbert of Clare*, pp. 353-4; *et al*. For his (limited) defenders, see Richardson and Sayles, *Governance of Med. England*, 414-5, 418-21; and Harvey, 'Gervase and Fee-farms of WA', BIHR. 40 (1967) 127-142.

the reputation which he received Gervase, though still young when appointed, appears to have earned the respect both of his monks (apart from Osbert of Clare) and of senior churchmen, including later at least two successive popes.

But even the abbot's defenders have to accept that his grant of the adjoining manor of Chelsea to his mother Dameta, who had been the king's mistress, was indefensible in most respects. The grant was made by him 'in fee and inheritance', without any limitation of time such as Abbot Crispin had imposed when he let the same manor to William Buckland only *for his life*. The rent was still the same as in Crispin's case, £4 pa., but the practical effect of it being a permanent grant was that the rent received by the abbey remained the same for 400 years and the monks derived no benefit from the hugely-changing value of money over that period.[36] It is true that Dameta paid a 'fine' (ie. a premium for obtaining the grant) of 40s. and bestowed a 'pall' worth 100s. on the abbey, but this represented only a fraction of the capital value of the grant even at that time, let alone a recompense for the loss which the abbey was to suffer as a result of the permanency of the grant.[37] With the effects of inflation added, the imbalance is even greater. In addition, in breach of proper practice and papal injunctions, no consent by the convent for the actual grant of Chelsea was recorded; and even if there were in fact any witnesses who attested the charter,

their names were left out of the only surviving record of it, in the abbey's great book of copy-charters.[38] Above all, the circumstances of such a grant by the abbot created great scandal, because of the king's extra-marital relationship with Dameta, and the close accessibility of the manor of Chelsea upstream from the palace over a short length of the Thames.

### Early grants by Abbot Gervase of land in Westminster and Kilburn

Gervase was responsible for one of the earliest abbatial approvals of a transfer, between lay men, of land within Westminster itself of which we know, because he confirmed certain land in *Endiff* (Enedehithe lane, north of the palace) to one Gerin, who was both 'an officer of the king' and also the abbot's own 'man'. It was not a primary grant to Gerin, but in effect a confirmation of a purchase made by Gerin from an existing lay holder, named Walkelin (possibly an officer of the abbey's almonry). It was made with the consent of the prior, named Elias, even though the convent of other monks was not otherwise mentioned.[39]

The occasion was also remarkable for the unusually graphic recording in the charter of the fact that all the witnesses to the transaction were 'standing and listening' there in the abbot's court, when the vendor Walkelin and his brother William and son Robert 'gave seisin' of the land to Gerin; and Gerin in return gave Robert (clearly the heir) 2s. for, in effect, the giving-up of his rights in the land.[40]

---

36  A market rent for the manor of Chelsea in 1367 (on a lease-back by the then tenant to the abbey, for the life of the tenant) was at least £20 pa, with remission of the £4 rent. So the annual value had grown dramatically.

37  The value recorded in 1086 by Domesday Book had been £9, and if the value had still been in that range in, say, the 1140s, the fine and pall were comparatively even less sufficient as a consideration for the grant. But if £4 was an insufficient rent, it had been imposed even earlier by Abbot Crispin's grant, so if blame is to be given, it could be argued that Crispin might have to receive some of it too. But Crispin's grant was limited only to the life of the tenant and the price was therefore justifiably smaller than it should have been for a permanent grant.

38  WAD 114a (WAC 262). In legal terms it was a tricky document, because the convent was in fact mentioned with the abbot, but no record of any assent was made: yet the ambiguous plural 'we' was used for the grant.

39  WAC 261. For *Endiff*, see pp. 47 and 111. For Gerin, see below at pp. 109-111; cf. pp. 107 and 109. For this particular 'Walkelin', see pp. 100 and cf. 148, and 391 below.

40  'Giving seisin' had to be a symbolic act, such as the handing over of a turf or a wooden rod or perhaps relevant charters, to record the actual transfer.

Walkelin had held his interest for himself 'and his heirs', which did not on its face include the right to transfer it to a third party, such as Gerin, and so the abbot must have been asked to confirm the grant himself. The abbot could have refused his approval, but that would not have effected any recovery of the land by the abbey. Indeed an ultimate recovery of the land by the abbey stood a better chance with Gerin holding the land, instead of Robert who was clearly a younger man and likely to live longer, to say nothing of the possibility of claims by later heirs.

Another grant made by Gervase which related to Westminster property was a grant made to William of Wenden and his wife, Adelaide. Adelaide's father, William Stantus, had been the hereditary serjeant of the buttery and vestibule at the abbey, and by reason of his post was entitled to certain 'tenements', some of them inside the abbey's precinct and others outside it in the town. When he died, the 'serjeanty' fell to Adelaide, as his heiress, and her husband, William of Wenden. At some point, Gervase made a grant to William and Adelaide of both the two offices and the annexed tenements, as indeed he was bound to do since they were hereditary entitlements.[41] In the event, the same family survived as holders of these offices for more than another 150 years, before surrendering them back to the abbey.

Gervase also followed in the footsteps of Abbot Herbert in confirming his predecessor's two grants to the nunnery at Kilburn, with the full approval of his monks. In these two acts Gervase also extended the nuns' right to receive certain extensive food corrodies, and also to hold, free of any rent or other service, the once-wooded land in Knightsbridge called the Gore which Abbot Herbert had originally granted.[42]

### Disputes over Hendon

But as regards the Hendon estate, held now by Gunter's son Gilbert, the issue arose as to whether Gilbert's heir would also be entitled to receive the estate in due course, and Gervase's eventual confirmation of the estate to Gilbert, but with the inclusion of his heir, had to be extracted from him under compulsion – by order of the next king Henry II, after an interesting history of claims and complaints during Stephen's reign. It seems that disputes had arisen between the abbey and Gilbert, after Abbot Herbert had died, and from the sequence of the surviving charters one can trace how these disputes developed and were resolved. The story reveals the intermeshed channels of episcopal influence, royal power and papal dominance which could prove so important in medieval times when an issue arose as to family interests in land.[43]

The original grant of Hendon had been to 'Gunter and his heir', without any further stronger words such as '*in hereditate*' or '*in perpetuo*'. Taken at its face, the grant clearly entitled Gunter and his heir to hold the estate in succession, as they then did; but there was doubt as to the position of any *further* generation after them. At that time this was a fruitful ground for claims and disputes, and there were legal decisions then being made in favour of the entitlement of long-standing families. Gilbert, son of Gunter, having now inherited, had clearly requested the abbey in about 1136 to have his title to the Hendon estate confirmed again, with at least *his* heir now included as well. But he apparently had received no satisfaction.[44] Whether this was

---

41 WAC 254. For the meaning of 'serjeanty', see pp. 99-101 below. See also *The Westminster Corridor*, p. 155 and note 30, for these two particular serjeanties. We do not know where the 'outside' tenements were, but they were probably fairly close to the abbey, eg. in the Longditch-Tothill area where other servants were granted land.

42 WACs 264 and 265. For the previous history, see WACs. 249 and 250. It was Gervase's main grant in WAC 264 which referred to 'the corrody of Gilbert Crispin', see pp. 72 and n. 16 .

43 For the earlier story, see pp. 71-2 and 75-6.

44 Gunter had had his, and his heir's, grant from Crispin confirmed by Herbert, when he acceded to the abbacy, see WACs 245 and 241.

because of a vacancy at the abbey in and after 1136, or because of any deliberate policy by the monks, or because the matter was overlooked or shelved during the exigencies of the incipient civil war, we do not know. But a huge web of influence was now spun by Gilbert in order to achieve his aim; and this may be good evidence of the high standing which he had acquired.

On getting no response from the abbey, Gilbert had sought the help of the new King Stephen, who gave it in about 1136-7 by ordering the abbey to confirm Gilbert's Hendon estate on the same terms as his father Gunter had been entitled.[45] Again there was no response from the abbey, and presumably the king, still involved in the prelude to a savage civil war, was too much engaged to worry further about Gilbert. In any case there were conflicting interests at play, because the king was just about to appoint his own son Gervase as the abbot of Westminster.

So in order to protect his family's interests, Gilbert had to resort elsewhere. In about 1138 he requested the help of Henry of Blois, the powerful bishop of Winchester, who was also the king's brother and had been temporarily put in charge by Pope Innocent II of the diocese of London (during yet another vacancy, this time in the bishopric of London). The bishop had then in turn requested the help of the pope himself in favour of Gilbert's claimed rights to the Hendon estate, and the pope had reacted in April 1139 by himself *'confirming and taking the lands which Gilbert of Hendon and his predecessors held of the abbey into his own protection'*.[46]

Abbot Gervase had meanwhile been appointed by his father the king to the abbey at Westminster, and so the pope had at once to notify Gervase that the Hendon estate was now under papal protection.[47] As the abbey was subject only to himself, the pope had assumed the right to control its lands in favour of other claimants, over the head of the unresponding abbey. Presumably the abbot and the monks accepted this result, but did nothing formal for over fifteen years to confirm it themselves!

So the matter rested until after the civil war and its disturbed aftermath, the 'fifteen years of anarchy'. But Gilbert of Hendon was still not satisfied. After the young Henry of Anjou had been crowned Henry II in 1154, the persistent Gilbert must have again sought royal help in his quest for the protection of his family's interests in the Hendon estate. This resulted in yet another royal order, probably in 1157, this time from Henry II, instructing 'the abbot and monks' (preferring not even to name Gervase, the son of the new king's former enemy) to confirm Gilbert's estate in the same terms as his father Gunter had held it.[48]

Then came the twist in the Hendon story. In the spirit of the king's order rather than its letter, Abbot Gervase did a deal with Gilbert – and on better terms for the abbey. He and his monks confirmed the Hendon estate to Gilbert, but in place of the rent of one week's food render (worth £8. 10s.) which Gunter had previously had to pay, they procured a rent in money terms alone, at £20 pa. (more than twice as much), and in exchange enlarged the grant to cover further heirs of Gilbert's family.[49] In view of the barrage of help which Gilbert had obtained, it must have been clear to Gervase that there was no hope of resisting further

---

45   WAC 107 (1135 x 37).
46   WACs 157 and 124
47   WAC 157 (22nd April 1139).
48   WAC 124 (Dec. 1154 x Aug 1157/58)
49   WAC 263 (Dec. 1154 x 57). The 'heir', in the grant to Gunter, now became 'heirs' in the confirmation to Gilbert, but there was still no '*in perpetuo*', or the like, in the charter, so the door was open for further arguments by the abbey in the future. For the effect of such wordings see p. 22, n. 36 above. However it may be that the dispute with Gilbert had only been about financial terms, rather than the principle of a continuation of the family interest. If so, the result was a handsome success for the abbey, even if the monks may have originally demanded better terms than they ultimately got.

retention of the Hendon estate by this family, but the monks nevertheless were able to obtain a greatly enlarged rent, at a time when there was no firm evidence of rising rents, still less of the great inflation which was to follow by the end of that century.[50]

### Was Gervase's poor reputation deserved?

So in the face of all this, why was it that Abbot Gervase incurred such a bad reputation after his death? There is little doubt that at the end of his abbacy the affairs of the abbey were in a parlous state, as indeed they had been for many years. But the question is, Why was this? Was Gervase the original cause of it, or if not, had he added to the damage? The next abbot, Laurence, in turn received an inheritance which must have appeared depressing, and it is certain that the story that the situation was the result of dissipation of the abbey's resources by Gervase emanated from historical sources close to Laurence.[51] Those who were reaching the top of the ladder were keen to pull down those who had reached there before them.

Many of the abbey buildings at Westminster, it is true, were again in ruinous condition. But the abbey, on the evidence of a senior churchman (the abbot of the abbey of St. Edmundsbury, who was no admirer of Gervase and was unlikely to provide his memory with false excuses) had recently suffered a devestating fire, one of a number of such fires which happened throughout the abbey's history.[52] Moreover, even earlier, its buildings and administrative state had already been in a ruinous state from the time of the long vacancy *before* Abbot Herbert was appointed. Back in Abbot Herbert's time, that other antagonist of abbots, Prior Osbert of Clare, had described it in graphic detail (even if with some of his usual hyperbole): '*the dilapidation of the church, the starving of the servants, the ruin of the monastic buildings, roofs out of repair, meals of the seniors cut down, the resources of the treasury diminished, walls and battlements broken and ruined...*'.[53] However unreliable Osbert might have been in his unbridled promotion of his 'causes', it is impossible to believe that so graphic a factual description was wholly imaginary, particularly as it was written (from 'exile') to Abbot Herbert himself who was present at the abbey itself and would know perfectly well what the true state of facts there was.

Further the existing stringency in the finances of the abbey, dating both from the first vacancy and from Herbert's abbacy, had also been compounded by ruinous damage done during the civil war to the abbey's great estates in Gloucestershire, Worcestershire and Oxfordshire by 'the violence of Earl Robert of Gloucester and particularly his advisers', the most powerful supporters of the Empress Matilda.[54] For the abbey these estates were a major source of money (though not so much, of food; the estates being so distant). And even the period *after* Henry II's accession in

50 cf. Harvey, 'Fee Farms of WA', *ibid.*, p. 136. For the inflation, see pp. 118-120 below.
51 See Mason, *WA People*, 50-51. Cf. the interesting discussion at *ibid.*, pp 184-5.
52 See Mason, *ibid.*, 51. Flete, *History of WA*, 92 also records the fire. It is certain that the 'domestic offices and their lead plumbing' were for the most part 'burnt and ruinous', and had to be repaired by Laurence, the next abbot. Another major fire, spreading from the palace, was suffered by the abbey in 1298, see pp. 312-14 below.
53 Cited by Robinson, *WA in 12C: Osbert of Clare*, 340. Osbert had even gone out of his usual way to praise Abbot Herbert for his efforts to repair the physical damage, but there is every indication that, in the difficult periods which followed, it had not proved possible to set the abbey and its finances to right. The debts which Herbert had had to incur, in order to comply with his major obligation to recover lost properties and rights (see text above), had obviously weighed heavily both on the objective financial situation, and subjectively on the minds of the monks and other observers.
54 Flete (ed. Robinson), *History of WA*, 92. The main estates still occupied there by the abbey were the manors of Pershore and its many associated manors in Worcs. The great manor of Deerhurst in Glos., which in the early years of the civil war had legitimately been fee-farmed by Gervase to William of Darnford, with the half-hundred of Deerhurst, for a rent of £30 (in addition to an obligation of hospitality

1154, when the real anarchy was at an end, was not an easy time for the putting to rights of the abbey's problems at home, let alone those in their more distant possessions.

Another factor in the denigration of Gervase was the fitful presence of Osbert of Clare at Westminster during his abbacy. Although these two had initially been at peace and had cooperated with one another, it seems virtually certain that Osbert later had a hand in rewriting (ie. forging) at least part of one of the papal bulls which he brought back from his unsuccessful journey to Rome, so as to cast blame and papal disapproval on the abbot. Relations between them deteriorated and it appears that Osbert was demoted from the priorship and again left Westminster for a period. However he returned once more to the abbey as a simple monk and may even have been present there when, for political reasons but to the obvious humiliation of the monks, their abbot Gervase was deposed by order of the king in late 1157 or early 1158.[55] It is not difficult to infer what tales a disappointed and indignant Osbert could whisper in the ear of the incoming Abbot Laurence about the condition of the dilapidated abbey and its causes.

Gervase's great offence to his fellow monks had been to let Chelsea permanently to his mother in a high-handed manner, and no doubt to great scandal. This must have coloured much else in his reputation. His other grants of properties, which formed the main grounds for later censures by John Flete, the abbey historian in the fifteenth century, have since been exhaustively analysed by both the critics and the defenders, and the censures largely dismissed. One of the major complaints was high-handedness on the abbot's part, in

acting without his convent's consent. One or two of his other grants do raise certain other queries, but none of them can be justified as a proven ground for very serious condemnation. Save in the case of Chelsea, Gervase is not shown to be any worse than the temper and history of his time warranted; and in some respects he may have been better. He had had to steer the abbey through violent times. And who does not feel a little sympathy for an abbot who uniquely, during such violent times, could take advantage of a pause between more significant events, to grant 8s. from the tithes of the parish of White Roding (Essex) to the abbey preceptor, for the repair of books in the library; and during another pause, to procure an exchange of land in Wandsworth to enable fulling mills to be sited on the river Wandle for the benefit of his abbey?[56]

### Events in Westminster before and during the civil war

During the abbacy of Gervase, both the abbey and the town of Westminster played their usual parts in those national events of the kingdom which came their way. They had already witnessed the crowning of Stephen as king just before Christmas 1135, towards the end of Abbot Herbert's time and in his absence; the holding at Easter 1136, of the king's first elaborate and ceremonial court and council in Westminster Hall, attended by three archbishops (one from Rouen) and fifteen bishops; and in December 1138 the consecration of Gervase (albeit a bastard) as abbot by a papal legate, Alberic bishop of Ostia, sent to England by Pope Innocent II.[57]

Even during the ensuing civil war the abbey and town continued to share, at second

---

which the holder owed to the abbot) must also have suffered seriously and may not have been able to pay its dues in later years; see WACs 98 & 136, & a rewritten charter, WAC 271. For its repurchase by the abbey in 1299, see p. 307 below.

55 See Mason, *WA People*, pp. 48-51, 90-1. For Osbert's failed attempt to secure the canonisation of King Edward the Confessor, see pp. 76-7 above.

56 See WACs 251 and 268. 'Robert le bokbyndere', a resident in the C13-14, affords later clues as to books in WM. For later history of the abbey's fulling mills, see Mason, 13 *Bulletin of Wandle Group*, 4, (Dec. 1984).

57 The legate had also opened a great legatine council in Westminster Abbey four days before dealing with Gervase; Wilkins, *Concilia*, i. 413-8; Whitelock, *Councils and Synods*, vol 1, pp. 766-779.

hand, in other scenes of triumph and disaster. In 1141 it was the Empress Matilda's turn. Having won the battle of Lincoln, in which she had captured King Stephen himself, and having secured the treasury at Winchester, she came to celebrate her triumph in Westminster and London. She entered Westminster in procession, and remained at the palace for a few days, transacting urgent business and even beginning already to style herself as 'Queen', but more commonly as 'Lady of the English'.[58] The latter name was in more modest anticipation of a coronation at Westminster which she expected to enjoy shortly, after visiting the city of London.

But her later entry and stay in the city of London (which had earlier sided with Stephen) proved to be short and stormy, and by her behaviour she deprived herself of her own crowning as queen. After demanding heavy taxes from the citizens of London and shouting at them when they proved reluctant, she had to flee the city and its neighbourhood when Stephen's indomitable queen (the real queen, confusingly also named Matilda) surrounded the city with an army, and the citizens rose in rebellion 'like a swarm of bees' against the 'upstart' Empress.[59]

Later in the same year, Stephen was free and back again in Westminster. Released in November on a prisoner-exchange for the Empress's half-brother, Robert of Gloucester (who had been captured by the queen's forces), Stephen was able to attend a council in Westminster held at the abbey, with 18 bishops and about 30 abbots present, to recognise his restoration. There he heard of all the double-dealing which the civil war had been producing during his own imprisonment, including that of his own brother, Henry of Blois, the bishop of Winchester who had remarkably managed to switch sides twice.

The war, and its participants, then swung away from London and Westminster and began again to centre largely in the midlands and the west and south. When the Empress, despairing of success, finally left the country for good in 1148, her son the young Henry of Anjou became the new Angevin leader in England.

After a further five years of war, Westminster came back into its own when at last peace negotiations between Stephen and Henry took place in both Winchester and Westminster in the autumn of 1153. In December an important and formal charter, executed at Westminster by Stephen and witnessed by fourteen bishops and eleven earls, confirmed a final peace treaty drawn up earlier in Winchester. By its terms Stephen was to remain king, recognising Henry (aged only twenty) 'as his son and heir', in place of his own eldest son who had suddenly (and, so far as the national interest was concerned, opportunely) died.[60] But within a year Stephen himself died (equally opportunely, for Henry), and the abbey at Westminster was soon to witness yet another coronation, that of both Duke Henry and his wife Eleanor of Aquitaine at Christmas 1154.[61]

Although Gervase was the son of King Henry's enemy, he survived as abbot for a further three years, but it cannot have been an easy period. Although the king already had

---

58 Bradbury, *Stephen and Matilda*, p. 103. For her title '*Domina Anglorum*', see Poole, *DB to Magna Carta*, p. 143; and also eg. WAC 98 (probably 1141), by which (under that name) she confirmed Abbot Gervase's grant of the manor of Deerhurst in Glos. to William of Darnford, see notes 54 above and 80 below.

59 Much additional damage was done at this time, by the besieging army of the real queen, to the countryside round London, until it became '*a home only for the hedgehog*' (cited by Bradbury, *ibid.*, p. 107), and this must have sigificantly affected Westminster and the abbey's 'corridor' estates.

60 *Regesta Regum A-N*, pp. 97-9, No. 272. See also Poole, *DB to Magna Carta*, p. 165.

61 Osbert of Clare, still serving at the abbey, was never one to miss a good opportunity, particularly one which called for exaggeration. He took it upon himself to fire off two letters of congratulation: one, a sober-ish letter, to the Archbishop of Canterbury for his part in encouraging the negotiations to '*restore order to our distracted country*', and a typical second one, to the king himself, '*a leader given to us by God.....[who] shall found a new Jerusalem*'; Williamson (ed.), *Letters of Osbert of Clare*, pp. 122 and 130.

much else on his mind during the first years of his reign, in January 1156 while waiting at Dover to sail over to France to meet the French king, he found time at Dover to confirm Gervase, by name, as abbot of Westminster, in all his rights over lands, tenants and liberties and to order all to observe those rights.[62] But other orders made by the king during this period in favour of or against the abbey refrain from using Gervase's name and speak anonymously of 'the abbot' or 'the monks', perhaps reflecting a growing dissatisfaction with the abbot of Westminster.

It was during this period, probably in 1157, that Gilbert of Hendon sought Henry II's help in his differences with the abbey over his family estate at Hendon, as described above, and the king (then itinerating at Northampton) peremptorily ordered the (again un-named) 'abbot and monks' of Westminster to confirm the estate to Gilbert.[63] By about the end of 1157 the king's alienation from Gervase was complete, and *'Abbot Gervase of Westminster was disseized of his lands in England by the will of King Henry'.*[64]

## Abbot Laurence   *(1158-1173)*

So, just as his two predecessors had done, the new abbot inherited a sorry scene at the abbey; and it was easy for him and his supporters to regard the most recent incumbent as the responsible party. Like Gervase, Laurence who had been at the abbey of St. Albans had a reigning king's support; having been chosen from there by Henry II for the abbacy at Westminster.[62]   But he differed from Gervase in having one great

advantage, namely he was abbot during a period of comparative stability and active regeneration in England. While there was war and negotiations in plenty on the continent concerning Henry's great possessions there, and baronial rebellions and later family rebellions as well, yet during this period there was only one king in England, both in law and in fact.[66]

### The canonisation of King Edward the Confessor

Laurence, like Gilbert Crispin, was an abbot who brought intellectual achievement to his post. He had studied theology in Paris and was both a good preacher and a fertile writer of sermons 'suitable for different seasons of the year and feasts of the saints'. But in addition he was apparently competent in carrying out practical enterprises: for example, in having restoration work carried out on the ruined domestic quarters in the abbey and their plumbing; in recovering goods and manors of the abbey in the 'western parts' which had been damaged by Robert of Gloucester; and in organising with great care and personal effort the assemblage of new evidence for a renewed campaign to obtain the canonisation of Edward the Confessor, which Osbert of Clare had previously attempted without success.[67]

It is probable that Osbert himself, back again at the abbey, was able to participate for a second time in this renewed venture, at least in collecting evidence and giving advice. John Flete, the later historian of the abbey, records Osbert's name and his earlier embassy to

---

62  WAC 122. The year 1155 had been spent by Henry in dealing with rebellious barons, arranging for the expulsion of Stephen's mercenaries from England and *'rooting out all causes for renewal of warfare'*, as the chronicler Gervase of Canterbury put it.

63  WAC 124. For the earlier history, and the outcome in the 1150s, see pp. 79-81 above.

64   As recorded in a lawsuit 43 years later, CRR. I/464-5; cf. Mason, *WA People*, 50-1. It is not clear exactly why the king became so dissatisfied with Abbot Gervase in that year, when he had earlier been pre-pared to put up with him and even to endorse him.

65  Harvey, *WA Estates*, 95; Flete, *History of WA*, 92.

66  Henry was unwise enough to have his eldest son crowned in 1170 as a joint king with himself, but this created a different situation from that which had obtained during the civil war period.

67  See Barlow, *Edward the Confessor*, pp. 279-280; and pp. 76-7 above. Laurence even visited Paris again in promoting this enterprise.

Rome twice in this connection, and also even asserts that it was Osbert whom Abbot Laurence sent (for a second time) to Rome with the fresh evidence in support of the case for canonisation, to return home successful 'with glory and honour'. But this story that the second embassy to Rome was made by Osbert has no other evidence to support it and has been doubted, and it may be that Flete was relying on some now-lost and no doubt highly coloured document left by the inventive old man.[68] At all events Pope Alexander III was persuaded by the new evidence, which included at least certain extant letters from Henry II, two Cardinal legates, one archbishop, six bishops, one abbot and others, together with a 'book of the miracles' performed by King Edward (which Osbert probably created) and even the unfaded vestment, in which the uncorrupted body of Edward was said to have been wrapped in his tomb in the abbey in 1102 when it had been opened.[69] At last on the 7th February 1161 the pope executed a 'bull' authorising the canonisation.[70] So the abbey had finally succeeded in obtaining a saint of its own. After delays, Edward's tomb was again opened, and the body of the saint was found to be still uncorrupted. Eventually on the 13th October 1163, in the presence of the king and many bishops and nobles, the body was taken and 'translated' to a new tomb prepared for it in front of the high altar in the abbey.[71]

### Royal favour for Abbot Laurence

There is no doubt that Abbot Laurence received great assistance in his ventures from King Henry. The works of abbey repair, the recovery of lost manors, and the canonisation campaign each benefitted from 'royal favour',

as Flete reported. Moreover there may even have been a close personal link between the king and the abbot, illustrated perhaps by the fact that they even shared the services of the same doctor, Master Ralph of Beaumont. The doctor was also a clerk and a *familiaris* of the king, a member of the group of confidential royal advisers, and a man to be cultivated. The abbot took steps to ensure that Master Ralph, 'our beloved doctor', was well taken care of, by presenting him to the church of Bloxham in Oxfordshire.[72] But even here the abbot's pragmatic sense was also shown. Not only did he require a comfortable annual sum, a 'pension', of £3. 6s. 8d, to be paid to the abbey, in effect a rent, by this new incumbent, but he also made it expressly clear that Master Ralph was not to alienate the church and that if he died or became 'a monk or a bishop', the church was to revert to the abbey. Unfortunately however these arrangements did not last long, because in March 1170 Master Ralph was drowned in one of the ships of the king's company when it was wrecked in a great storm while returning from Normandy to Portsmouth.[73]

### Difficult relations with St. Alban's abbey

During his abbacy, Laurence had a chequered relationship with the abbey of St. Alban's. He had previously been a monk at that abbey at the time when the king had chosen him as the royal candidate for the abbacy at Westminster, and he therefore had a close attachment to St Alban's. Indeed after he had arrived at Westminster and had surveyed the precarious state of affairs there, he approached Abbot Robert of his former abbey and pleaded that Westminster was impoverished. Abbot Robert responded

68  For the repairs and the Osbert story, see Flete, *ibid.*, 91-2, Barlow, *ibid.*, p. 280, and Pearce *Monks*, 42.
69  Apart from the extant letters, there were undoubtedly other letters or documents now lost. The extant ones are set out in Barlow, *ibid.*, 309-23. For the first opening of the tomb by Abbot Crispin in 1102, see p. 71 above.
70  Set out in Barlow, *ibid.*, Appendix D, at pp. 323-4.
71  Over a century later the body was again disturbed, for the third time, by Henry III and moved to a grand new shrine in 1269, see pp. 239 and 266 below.
72  WAC 286 (1158 x 1170). See also p. 103 below.
73  Roger of Howden, *Gesta Henrici*, RS vol 1, p. 4.

generously by making valuable gifts to the abbey at Westminster, worth nearly 200 marks (£133. 6. 8d), but fate then muddied the waters between the two abbeys. The prior of St. Alban's, Alquin, had been deposed as a result of certain charges against him, and he fled to Westminster where Laurence admitted him and kept him in the Westminster community, to the great indignation of the monks at St. Alban's.[74] For this and other reasons, there were various other recriminations at St. Alban's against the abbey at Westminster, which reached a point where certain disputes had to be resolved in proceedings before a distinguished group of the 'king's justices', sitting in the restored court of the Exchequer in Westminster at the early date of 1165.[75] The claims by the St. Alban's monks against Westminster were withdrawn, and in return Abbot Laurence, who must have felt at fault, gave 23 marks (£15. 6s. 8d) and the abbey surrendered a right to pasture 20 pigs in Aldenham Wood in autumn each year *'at the time of the acorn harvest'*.

### Abbot Laurence's support for the sacrist, to promote rebuilding

It may have been the original ruinous state of the abbey and the distressed condition of the monks at the time when Laurence became abbot which made him wish to benefit the department of the abbey sacrist thereafter, so far as he could, because that abbey department was charged with the maintenance of the abbey church, the altar lighting and other buildings.[76] So it was that, at the convent's wish, he granted the valuable church of Sawbridgeworth to the sacristy, and also required his own clerk, Maurice, who became the perpetual vicar at the Sawbridgeworth church, to pay the large annual sum of £15 to the sacristy of the abbey, for the benefit of certain 'works' then being carried out, as the price for his receiving the right during his lifetime to take the gifts and offerings made to that church.[77]

Again it was the sacristy which gained another asset when the abbot granted the church at Bloxham (Oxon) to Master Ralph of Beaumont, as described above. The annual payment of £3. 6s. 8d. which the royal doctor had to make was directed specifically to the sacrist's office.

Yet another benefit which Abbot Laurence conferred on the sacristy was another 'pension' (in effect an annual rent) of two marks (£1. 6s. 8d.) pa., which he obtained when he presented a priest called Stephen as the incumbent at the church in the abbey's nearby manor of Hendon. He had earlier presented Stephen's father Ralph to the same office, but Ralph had died and his son was permitted by Laurence to follow him, paying the above pension in each year. After his insitution by the bishop of London, this Stephen then remained in office for at least forty three years.

At the end of that period in the next century, long after the death of Abbot Laurence, Stephen

---

74  See Walsingham, *Gesta Abbatum St. Albani*, (Riley, ed.) RS i. 107-10, 112, 133-4.   The charges against Alquin were based on the fact that he was said to hold a spurious abbey seal which he intended to use without authority. Later Alquin was made the prior at Westminster under Laurence, and was eventually exonerated of the charges which had been made against him at St. Albans. Both Laurence and Alquin had had an earlier common connection at Durham where each had been in his earlier past.

75  WAC 281 (29 Sept. 1165).  The case included claims on behalf of three lay men in Aldenham, who received the benefit of the payment and surrender. See also Mason, *WA People*, pp. 164-5

76  In spite of efforts like these to assist the sacristy, by the last decade of the century the continuing 'poverty of the sacristy' was being used as a reason for its further support by the then bishop of London, WAC 216 (1192 x 6).

77  Grant of church: WAC 283 (1161, or earlier ?). The grant was to pay for the lighting of the abbey altars and relics and also for a pittance of wine and extra food for the whole convent. So the monks themselves also stood to gain by the grant, which may have contributed to their enthusiasm for it, which is obvious in the terms of the charter.  Grant to Maurice: WAC 284 (c. 1161 ?). This grant was presumably a part-variation of the outright grant of the church to the sacrist. No doubt the abbot had himself presented Maurice to the vicarage.  The 'works' were probably works of repair to the ruined buildings of the abbey.

the priest at Hendon was still alive and continuing to act.  To protect themselves the monks were able to obtain from Stephen a record in the form of a charter, establishing their entitlement to the advowson, their right to present the priest.  This was to prevent anyone else seeking to take advantage of the unusually long period since Stephen had been presented, by making a false claim to the post at the *same* pension.  This was particularly significant to the monks because of the effect of a great monetary inflation which had been beginning in the period leading up to about 1200.  Stephen had had the marked advantage of paying only a fixed pension to the sacristy for an extraordinary number of years already, while other prices were escalating; and if that advantage were to continue in favour of someone else in the future after Stephen's death, the sacristy would continue to suffer – to say nothing about future inflation, which was still continuing, albeit at a slower rate.[78]

### The abbot's cultivation of other figures

Quite apart from Laurence's success in his relations with the king, he was also shrewd and adept in his dealings with other powerful figures.  From Pope Alexander III, he succeeded in obtaining the important ecclesiastical right, as an abbot, to wear a mitre and episcopal ring on special occasions, so becoming a 'mitred abbot'; this probably reflected his more important status now that the abbey had

acquired a saint of its own.[79]  From the same pope he sought and obtained in 1171 another confirmation of the abbey's right to be exempt from the authority of the bishop of London, and this move was probably a response to various disputes which he had been having with the bishop.[80]  But even with the bishop, he was sufficiently diplomatic to maintain a reasonable working relationship and did not fall out with him completely, in spite of their differences.

Abbot Laurence also cultivated the ubiquitous and potent figure, Richard of Ilchester, the Archdeacon of Poitiers and an intimate adviser in Henry II's circle.[81]  The abbot (after consulting his brethren) invested the archdeacon with an abbey property in London, and also granted him the rectorship of the church at Datchworth, an abbey manor in Hertfordshire.[82]  Laurence then joined Richard (in his capacity as rector of that church) in procuring the due institution of a new perpetual vicar there, Elias the clerk.[83]

So in addition to his reputation as a great preacher and writer of sermons, Laurence was a diplomatic administrator, with a keen eye for moves which might advantage the abbey.  Indeed it may have been his liaison with Richard the archdeacon, as the king's agent in the exchequer, which helped the abbey to obtain many releases in the exchequer from the exaction of various fines and taxes on abbey properties which the abbey would otherwise have had to pay.[84]

78 WAC 459. This later charter is dated by Dr. Mason 1206 x 1216, long after Abbot Laurence had died in 1173.  But it is introduced here, because the need to get this charter from Stephen (who was still going strong, and for all we know may in fact have continued to be the Hendon priest *after* the charter) only arose because of his original presentation by Laurence and the very long period during which he had continued to hold the position at Hendon church.  As regards the inflation at c. 1200, see pp. 118-121 below.
79 WAC 173 (probably in or shortly after 1161)
80 WAC 172 (3rd Dec. 1171). The bishop was Gilbert Foliot (1163-1187). For the disputes (eg. the bishop's claim to dues from St. Margaret's Westminster; and a dispute over the Darnford family's entitlement to the manor of Deerhurst in Worcs.), see Mason, *WA People*, 55.
81 For Richard of Ilchester, see eg. App. A at p. 392 below, and refs. there.  As a favoured 'king's man', he became a special representative for the king in the exchequer, and finally was promoted to the bishopric of Winchester.
82 WACs 277 and 278 (a house in the Fishmarket, London). The rectorship: Mason *WA People*, 57.
83 WACs 222 and 468 (c. 1164 x 1166). Elias was a clerk of the archdeacon of Huntingdon, whose confirmation of the vicarage had to be obtained, see WAC 468.
84 See Mason, *WA People*, 56. The fines were 'murder-fines' in five counties, and the taxes were 'geld' in twelve counties. The saving amounted to nearly £57. But on the other side of the balance sheet, Laurence

### Great events at the abbey and palace

As had happened during Gervase's abbacy, the palace at Westminster and the abbey witnessed other great events of national history during Laurence's abbacy.

They included the following: –

(i) The fateful church council held on the 23 May 1162 in Westminster, when Thomas Becket, hitherto the king's broad-minded chancellor and his close friend, was formally 'elected' Archbishop of Canterbury. Later the temperamental archbishop, as a defender of 'God's law' (as he perceived it, when it was ranged against claims of royal rights), became rigidly set on a path in opposition to the king's claims, which led ultimately to his own murder. But at this stage all was well between him and the king, and his election as archbishop had been rigged, because all opposition to it had been stifled in advance by the king, who had himself chosen Becket as the candidate, against serious disquiet elsewhere;

(ii) the even more ill-omened royal council held in Westminster Hall on the 1st October 1163, called by the king for a debate on various issues, including the burning one which stood between Becket and himself, whether a priest who had committed a crime could be tried by a secular court after a church court had tried and degraded him.[85] After the debate each of the bishops was cross-examined individually by the king, but each affirmed his support for Becket in denying the right of any secular court to do this. The council ended

with the king angrily asserting that they had all formed a conspiracy and used sophistry in their concerted answer against him; and finally storming out of the meeting;

(iii) only twelve days later, the 'magnificent ceremony' which the archbishop conducted on the 13th October 1163 in the abbey in the presence of the king, carrying out the translation of the body of the now canonised St. Edward from its old tomb to the new shrine prepared for it;[86]

(iv) the coronation (the first of two) of the king's eldest son, 'Henry the younger', as a *joint* king with his father, celebrated at the abbey at Westminster by Roger, Archbishop of York, on the 24th May 1170, in the presence of the king and six supporting bishops but in the absence of Archbishop Becket who was abroad on self-imposed exile. It was followed by an equally magnificent coronation feast held in Westminster Hall, at which the boar's head was brought in *'with trumpets before it according to the custom'*, and to mark the occasion the king himself served his son on bended knee.[87]

### Progress of King Henry II's reforms

When Abbot Laurence died in 1173, Henry II had still another sixteen years to live.[88] But already by 1173 the king had started introducing other administrative reforms, for which his name is famous, including the measures which were destined to make the town of Westminster the centre for government. The restored court of exchequer

---

slipped up in other directions and received a heavy fine of £100 in the exchequer, possibly for showing indirect favour to supporters of Archbishop Thomas Becket in his dispute with King Henry; Mason, *ibid.*, 56 and 59.

85 For this, the real issue, see Warren, *Henry II*, p. 468-9. The issues became muddied by Becket's obstinacy.

86 For the canonisation and translation, see p. 84-5 above.

87 Henry II had what appears to have been a King Lear complex, being determined to divide his dominions among his sons, even if this was only to be fully complete after his own death. The young Henry's coronation as a joint king with his father (based on the practice of the French royal family) was one step in that direction; see Mortimer, *Angevin England*, p. 31-2. The crowning by Archbishop Roger caused great additional offence to Becket who regarded it as his unique prerogative to crown a king; and he excommunicated the Archbishop of York and two of the other bishops who had assisted him in the coronation. Their protests and appeal to the king may have been one of the contributing factors to the king's famous anger and Becket's resulting murder.

88 The worn effigy said to be that of Abbot Laurence, like that of Crispin, can still be seen in the south-east corner of the cloisters.

was already functioning there, to control revenue and to hold the county sheriffs to more accurate account. On the legal front, the town was shortly to become the seat of a 'Bench' of justices, and this would in due course be the first fixed national court in England. Meanwhile the tide of government officials and other royal servants, arriving to live and/or to work in Westminster, had already begun to flow; and indeed since the second half of the twelfth century it has never ceased.[89]

## Abbot Walter of Winchester *(1175-90)*

### *Another vacancy*

Walter's accession to the abbacy did not begin until at least July 1175; or perhaps even a year later still. So there had been yet another vacancy, of two to three years, during which the abbey was once again in the hands of managers appointed by the king, and held for his interest. And inevitably once again it seems that the abbey's possessions, at least those in the 'western parts', were being threatened or actually despoiled or neglected during this period. In fact King Henry had to order all his 'justices, sheriffs and bailiffs' in Gloucestershire and Worcestershire to ensure that the abbey's possessions were treated 'as though they belonged to the king himself', and that all tenants were compelled to render their due services.[90] And again, back in Westminster, the finances and other interests of the abbey were suffering accordingly, and in any event all *profit* (if any) was now accruing to the king, not to the benefit of the abbey.[91] The king spent only a very limited time in England

during this period, and as so often happened, his own agents had obviously been taking advantage of his absence to further their own interests, or to neglect both the king's and the abbey's.[92]

Fortunately, although Abbot Walter may not have had the same influence with the king and other powerful figures in the national administration, as Abbot Laurence appears to have had, he clearly had a careful and competent grasp of abbey interests. He had been the prior at Winchester before being called to Westminster, and so was already familiar with many aspects of administration. He soon followed Laurence's example and successfully petitioned the pope, now Alexander III, for additional ecclesiastical privileges of dress, so obtaining for himself, as abbot, the right to wear the dalmatic tunicle and sandals on specific occasions, and the right to wear gloves during solemn mass at festivals.[93] Such extra privileges added to the abbey's status, which was now growing further since the canonisation of King Edward in 1161.

### *Protection of churches belonging to the abbey*

Walter's main administrative objective during his abbacy seems to have been the protection of the churches which the abbey held and the enlargement of the income which could be derived from them. One of the practical problems which an abbot had to face during this period of both expansion and inflation was the inviting prospect which valuable churches owned by the abbey could

---

89  See pp. 67-9 and 110 ff. below.

90  WAC 137, which was probably executed during the vacancy, at a time when the king was at Droxford in Hampshire, perhaps in 1175.

91  This is the start of one of the periods recorded by Harvey, *WA Estates*, 64, as being a time when the resources of the abbey were particularly strained. This would no doubt account for the strenuous efforts made by Abbot Walter to increase the cash-flow of the abbey, as described in the text below.

92  Henry's stays in England were only April-July 1173, and 8 July-8 Aug. 1174, and after 8/9 May 1175; see Dr. Mason's note to WAC 137. It was probably in 1174 during this vacancy that the king's officers granted a large fee on and behind Fleet Street to the bishop of Winchester, Richard of Ilchester, which became the 'Inn' of his sons the successive bishops of Salisbury, see p. 43 above.

93  WACs 174 and 175. Dr. Mason has shown in *WA People*, 62, how the abbot's men had had to chase the pope around on his itinerary, in order to obtain what they wanted, viz. the 'bulls' WAC 175 and WAC 176 (next note).

hold out for any covetous clerk who wished to obtain a lucrative benefice for himself on favourable terms, particularly when there was political or royal influence or pressure which he might be able to enlist to make the abbey grant him such a benefice. It was this danger which must have induced Walter to obtain from Pope Alexander III another 'bull' which included an express prohibition against the alienation of any of five valuable (and named) churches held by the abbey, a self-sought prohibition which made the abbot less vulnerable to such pressures.[94] Four of these five churches lay in Middlesex and Hertfordshire: it was nearby churches such as these which might be particularly convenient and attractive for ambitious clerks, who were now arriving in Westminster on royal or other government business.

One of his other achievements in relation to the abbey's churches was to procure from the bishop of London, Gilbert Foliot, a confirmation of the abbey's title to each of the churches which it held within the whole diocese of London, identifying each one of them by name. This is the first known document containing a definitive list of the abbey's churches in the diocese, including those in London itself.[95] There were twelve churches so held within the city itself, and one other which was shared equally with Bermondsey Priory. Outside the city there were five other churches held within the diocese, including the church at Hendon.

Other main steps which Abbot Walter took to protect the abbey's churches and other interests were to obtain papal 'bulls' both in 1177 and also in 1189, the last year of his life, confirming the abbey's title to all its possessions and also its right of exemption from the control of the bishop of London.[96] In particular, the 'bull' in 1189 specifically gave protection (no doubt as sought in the abbot's petition to the pope) to all the 'pensions' payable to the abbey from the churches held by it.[97] The fact that the abbot's envoys to Rome stressed or implied the need for such a protection perhaps underlines the difficult financial situation of the abbey in a period of escalating inflation and the abbot's need to secure every part of its income.

### Relations with the bishop of London

Although on two occasions the abbot had to seek confirmation from the pope that the abbey was exempt from the bishop of London's authority, yet his relations with the bishop, Gilbert Foliot, were normally cordial. It is true that the abbot and the bishop may have fallen out about an issue as to which of them held spiritual authority over the cell of nuns at Kilburn; and this may be one of the reasons for the abbot's need for a renewed endorsement of the abbey's right to freedom from the bishop's authority.[98] But on that occasion their differences, however they had arisen, were ended when the bishop, apparently with grace, conceded both the abbot's spiritual powers over

94  WAC 176 (1177). The five churches were Staines (Mdx), Ashwell, Aldenham and Wheathamstead (each in Herts.), and Oakham (Rutland).
95  WAC 211 (c. 1180 x 1187)
96  WACs 176 (1177) and 179 (1189). See also Mason, *WA and People*, pp. 63 and 125.
97  The protection was actually limited to churches held by the abbey before the Third Lateran Council of the Roman church in 1179, ten years before the 'bull' in question. The Lateran Councils were held at the Lateran, the pope's main residence in Rome, and their object was to effect unifying reforms of the whole Roman church.
98  WAC 205 (1163 x 1187). I say 'may be', because it is not clear whether the dispute in question does belong to this period or to an earlier period, between 1128 and 1134 (ie. under Abbot Herbert), when the bishop was also named Gilbert (but known as 'the Universal'), see p. 75 above. The charter here does not specify which Gilbert was involved, nor which abbot, and is undated. It could also have been in Abbot Laurence's time, in or after 1163, because of the coincident years of Walter's and Foliot's periods of office. In any case, whenever it happened, it is part of a now familiar struggle between these two ecclesiastical rivals, this time for control over the nuns of Kilburn during this early part of their history.

the nuns at Kilburn, and his right to administer their cell through agents as well as personally.[99]

In other respects as well, Abbot Walter and Bishop Gilbert appear to have had dealings which reflected no antagonism. On two occasions the bishop, when called upon to arbitrate as papal delegate in disputes which Westminster Abbey had with other churchmen, restored Feering church in Essex and two churches in Lincolnshire to the abbey; and he also as bishop instituted the abbey's candidate for the benefices of the Middlesex churches of Greenford and Hanwell.[100]

### Abbot Walter's attempts to improve abbey income

Apart from his activities to regularise and protect the abbey's churches and its income from them, Abbot Walter undoubtedly was concerned to improve the abbey's whole financial position, if he could, by granting abbey properties at no doubt current rents, reflecting the increasing rate of inflation. A large number of charters have survived to record the grants of property whch he made. Most of these were grants of abbey lands and houses in the city of London. Out of twenty two properties, thirteen were in London; four were in counties round Middlesex (two in Surrey, one in Essex, and one in Buckinghamshire); and five were in distant counties (Lincolnshire, Staffordshire, Worcestershire, and two in Gloucestershire ).[101]

The total income for the abbey from the rents for these properties was over £43 pa., a large sum. This does not however mean that the £43 was all additional income which the abbot was creating for the abbey. But it is probable that a substantial part of this sum (perhaps even up to one half) was additional income and helped the abbey's cash-flow position a little, in what was a difficult period of inflation. Nevertheless in spite of these efforts to increase the abbey's cash-flow, the abbot had to borrow money to meet his obligations and got into debt for £16. 13s. 4d. with Aaron the Jew of Lincoln, a debt which after Walter's death was handed down to his successor and was still unpaid eleven years later.[102]

But what was the price which the abbey was paying for these attempts to raise its income? With only two exceptions, all the grants were clearly designed to be long-term disposals. Most of them were grants to 'X and his heirs' or 'in inheritance' ('X et heredibus suis', or 'in hereditate', or 'iure hereditario'); some had the words 'in fee', or 'in fee-farm', as well; sometimes even 'in perpetuo'. So even if the rents did reflect the state of inflation during that period, there was no chance of increasing them again later during the continuation of the full term, if inflation continued further (as indeed happened, at varying rates of increase). As so often in medieval times, the long-term and the medium-term had to be (or were) sacrificed to the short-term, viz. the immediate need for cash. The two exceptions were grants which were expressly limited in time: a grant of land at Penge, Surrey for a thirty year term (with an express provision for reversion to the abbey after the term); and the grant of the vill of Perton for the life of the tenant (with a similar provision). The grant of land at Penge in 1176 is an early but sophisticated letting for a term of years.[103]

---

99  WAC 205.
100  WACs 207, 208 (1176 x 1180) and 209 (1175 x 1187). WAC 210 (1183 x 1186).
101  For London, see WACs 289-295; and for others, Mason, *WA People*, p. 65.
102  Stenton (ed.) PRS (NS) 3 John (1201), p. 260; Mason, *WA People*, p. 66.
103  WACs 298 (Penge) and 304 (Perton). Simpson, *Intro. to Hist. of Land Law*, pp. 68, and Harvey, *WA Estates*, 82, suggest that a grant for a term of years was unusual in the C12, and particularly unlikely at WA (a conservative body). But the Penge charter is a subtle document, which by its terms even anticipates future negotiation between the abbey and the heir of the tenant at the end of the term for, in effect, some form of renewal of the letting, and also provides expressly, as a precaution, for the heir to take over the present letting if the tenant died before the end of the term of 30 years. Perhaps Master Nicholas and Master Jordan, the abbot's clerks who were the first named witnesses to the charter, had devised the form of it; for other refs. to them see WACs 209, 224, 468.  However, even for

In spite of the depredations suffered by the abbey since the death of Abbot Crispin, and the damage caused by events in the civil war, it has been calculated that the abbey's total net income had actually increased from about £515 at the time of Domesday to about £740 by the year 1200, a rise of nearly 44%.[104] If this is right, at least a small part of the rise may justifiably be attributed to the increase in rents which Abbot Walter probably brought about by the lettings which he and the convent effected. It is significant that even the rise in the abbey's total income over the previous century was insufficient to counteract the effect which (among other factors) inflation must have been having on the abbey's finances. Also it seems that when the abbot and convent, driven by the abbot's need to avoid further borrowings, made other long-term lettings of manors and vills (two of them as late as 1190), they were not following any policy of seeking to *recover* tenanted manors and vills in order either to avoid, or to take advantage themselves of, inflated prices for produce. In fact they were doing the precise opposite.[105]

### Recovery of Paddington

But one of the most important transactions for the abbey's 'corridor' estates during Walter's abbacy was the surrender of an estate in Paddington by two laymen to the abbey.[106] This recovery of an estate by the abbey was negotiated as a compromise in a legal action before the 'Bench' of justices sitting at their new seat in Westminster.

Paddington had not been mentioned specifically in Domesday Book, but had almost certainly been included in the Survey as part of the thirteen and a half hides of the manor of Westminster. Recognised again as a separate estate of the abbey in its own right, it had subsequently been assigned by the abbey to its own almonry, as one of the income-providing assets of that department, which of course needed funds of its own for the supply of charity to the poor on a large scale. By about 1137 the almonry's management of the estate was under the control of a 'monk-warden', and the estate had been freed by King Stephen from certain dues.[107]

But apparently a large area within the estate of Paddington had earlier been granted to a lay family, perhaps during the vacancy of three-four years (c. 1117-21) after Abbot Crispin's death. Before 1185, the surviving members of that family were two brothers known as Richard and William of Paddington, and certainly some issues, if not real disputes, had arisen between them and the abbey about the land and their own future. No doubt the abbey was anxious to re-assert its title and recover the property, particularly since by then serious inflation had begun, and it is likely that with this very object in mind the legal action had been started by the abbot and convent as a contentious one in the king's court.

---

this letting, and other lettings in medieval times, the sophisticated modern concept of a 'review of rent' (by reference to 'reasonable current rents' in the market) at stated intervals during the running of a holding, to enable terms of years to be granted which gave the landlord some protection against inflation, had not yet been devised, and indeed was lacking for many centuries ahead.

104 Harvey, *WA Estates*, p. 56-7. This calculation was based on certain assumptions which Miss Harvey has spelt out, applied to the total figures of income received during the vacancy after Abbot Laurence's death by the king's managers of the abbey's lands in only two counties. An extant account records these figures, and the assumptions made are then used to convert them to a figure of £739 for the whole estate.

105 WACs 300, 301 and 305.

106 For Paddington *before* Domesday, see *The Westminster Corridor,* pp. 112-3.

107 WAC 105 (Dec. 1135 x 1137), apparently a genuine writ of King Stephen, shortly after his coronation. Other similar but more generous writs in favour of Paddington, ostensibly made by Henry I and Henry II, and another one by Stephen, were probably forged by Osbert or other monks: WACs 62-64, 106, 126. One cannot date either the almonry's 'title' to the manor or define the true scale of its 'freedoms' at this time.

At all events a compromise agreement between the brothers and the abbey was then made and enrolled at the court, which sat in Westminster on the 31st May 1185.[108] The brothers were perhaps getting old, and they each had a wife who had to be provided for. So they surrendered their Paddington land, and in return the abbey paid them a large sum, forty marks of silver (£26. 13s. 4d.), and undertook as well to provide four daily 'corrodies' of food and drink for the brothers and their wives. Either it was obviously valuable land, or the monks were prepared to pay over the odds for this nearby estate. The corrodies for the two brothers were to continue for up to twelve years, which may have been intended as a safe estimate of their remaining lives. Those for the two wives were to continue for their full lives, and were to include 'extras and pittances', additional food generally of higher quality and paid for by special donations.[109]

So now the monks had recovered their property in Paddington, but at considerable expense, and for their part the Paddington brothers and their wives were adequately pensioned off. The high cost to the abbey may also have reflected low chances of success which the monks attributed to their own case, so it is likely that the Paddington family had originally been granted even more than a 'hereditary' title, or other rights which appeared difficult to assail.

But before leaving this Paddington action, we should also note the calibre of the justices sitting in Westminster in 1185, no doubt in the king's great Hall, who on that occasion formed the segment of the *curia regis* which now sat regularly in Westminster. Heading the court was **John ('of Oxford'), Bishop of Norwich**, a royal clerk and a trusted *familiaris* who had been nominated by Henry II for the see of Norwich after Becket's murder. Having previously been the *bête-noire* of the archbishop, John of Oxford had been excommunicated by him.[110] Next on the bench was **Ranulf of Glanvill**, the king's justiciar, another royal clerk who had combined both military ability and great judicial authority, and to whom the famous legal treatise on the laws and customs of England, commonly known as *Glanvill,* used to be attributed; here was the man 'whose wisdom established the laws which we call English'.[111] Then followed **Richard fitz Nigel**, the king's treasurer who presided over the court of the exchequer and was one of the first official residents in Westminster, in his house overlooking the Thames.[112] **Godfrey of Lucy**, a royal servant, sheriff, custodian of castles and prestigious justice (who was later to become the bishop of Winchester under Richard I, in succession to Richard of Ilchester), was also present on the bench;[113] and after him **Hubert Walter**, soon to become the most powerful and creative royal servant of all under King Richard I; creator and preserver of public records; in various capacities as Archbishop of Canterbury, papal legate and justiciar in charge of all administration in the king's

---

108  WAM 16194 (WAC 296; in 1185.). Such an action could be begun either as a contentious one, or one started merely for the purpose of having the compromise of 'friendly' issues recorded as a 'fine' by the court, ie. as a permanent legal record; see pp. 121 below for the start of the records system of 'fines'. It is likely that in this case there was initially a real legal dispute about the brothers' title to, in effect, a fee simple, which (as often happened) was then compromised; cf. Harvey, *Living and Dying*, pp. 196-7 and 240.

109   For details of the quantity and quality of food and drink provided, and the effects of such corrodies on the abbey and the poor, whose alms were thereby depleted, see Harvey, *Living and Dying*, pp. 179 ff. and 239 ff.

110   Warren, *Henry II*, pp. 494 and 535. For a coloured picture of a later Bench, see Plate 18, after p. 288.

111   Roger of Howden, *Chronica*, II, 215, cited by Warren, *Henry II*, 295. It is not certain now whether the early treatise was in fact Ranulf of Glanvill's work; rather it may have been composed collectively by justices serving under Ranulf; Clanchy, *From Memory to Record*, 18-19, etc.

112   For Richard fitz Nigel, see also pp. 110-13 and 155-6 below.

113   For Godfrey of Lucy, see Turner, *English Judiciary*, 81-82, 84-85, etc; and WAC 140

absence on crusade; and to round it off, later as chancellor under King John.[114] Penultimate on the bench was **William Basset**, another royal servant chosen from the wide-spread Basset family, himself the descendant of two chief justiciars, a baron of the exchequer, a former sheriff, a regular justice and a ubiquitous agent for the king for use on royal business.[115]

Did such a powerful array on the bench reflect the importance of the abbey's interest in recovering this nearby estate, or the abbot's influence in securing the attendance of such a bench? Or had difficult or interesting issues about the title of the Paddington brothers indicated to the justices the desirable prospect of an important or stimulating decision in law, in which these members of the court wished to join, only to be frustrated (as still so often happens) by a sudden compromise between the parties?

### Death of the abbot

Abbot Walter died on the 27th September, 1190, and another eventful vacancy lasting a year took place at the abbey. In the previous year the old king, Henry II, had also died, and already by December of that year his son, the new King Richard I had left the country, to go on crusade only three months after his coronation. During the ensuing year England lay under the control of William Longchamp, an unprincipled justiciar injudiciously appointed by the king to act in his absence. So when Abbot Walter died, Longchamp also became the king's agent to manage the abbey until a new abbot was appointed, and he grasped the opportunity to try to intrude a brother of his, Robert, as the new abbot of Westminster. Although he managed to extract the convent's reluctant consent to this manoeuvre, the attempt eventually failed because Longchamp was himself ousted in a national power-struggle before November 1191. In place of the proposed intruder, the existing prior William Postard was elected as the new abbot by the monks themselves, but only at the price of a substantial 'fine' which they had to pay to the exchequer for the right to hold a free domestic election of their own, the first since the Conquest.[116]

---

114   For Hubert Walter, see also pp. 121-3 and 164-6 below.
115   Warren, *Henry II,* 310; Richardson & Sayles, *Governance of Med. England,* 203, 211
116   See Mason, *WA People,* pp. 66-7 and 69. During the vacancy the abbey once again suffered violent depredations and intrusions. For the start of Abbot William's abbacy and the 'fine', see pp. 129-130 below.

# CHAPTER 6

# Abbot's men and king's men

Before Domesday, almost all 'ordinary' residents of Westminster are nameless to us. From our standpoint, it was a dark-age for memorials of the ordinary man. But after the signpost of Domesday was passed, the view opened a little. In the early twelfth century, more of the lay people living or working in Westminster begin to emerge, but only to the extent that some extract of their personal histories or fortuitous mention in extant records happens to survive. Certainly the presence of the abbey and the palace within Westminster meant that some of the personnel necessary for managing each of these organisations and their different activities in the town were becoming more visible. In this early period we cannot expect to see a detailed picture of either place or people; but as the century proceeded, further features of the salient people begin to emerge, and there are clues as to the complexion and culture of the town and the character and activities of those who lived there.

Since the evidence is scattered and tends to be episodic, it is featured here in that form. It is from such fortuitous chronicles of time that one can begin to create at first a faint, but progressively more positive, impression of the emerging Westminster. And by 1189, when Henry II died, the town was astir.

In this chapter, the abbey's people come first, and those connected with the king are identified later.[1]

## A. The presence of abbey personnel
### (1) Abbot Crispin's personal 'household' or 'family'

The abbot of Westminster, as a tenant-in-chief in the Domesday Survey, was a magnate holding great estates, and holding them directly from the king. Already he was far removed from the head of a simple monastery such as the rules of St. Benedict had provided for in the sixth century. Like any other magnate, he had to surround himself with laymen who could assist in the management of his own household and the property of his abbey. One of the earliest and most informative lists of some of the personnel (mostly laymen) at the abbey appears in a charter which was made by Abbot Gilbert Crispin in about 1116. This was shortly before the end of the abbot's life, but still only thirty years after Domesday.[2]

On that occasion a group of eleven of his household officers witnessed the making of the charter in question. They are described as his *familia*, his 'household' of personal officers and advisers, and from this we learn that the Abbot had:-

- his own personal chaplain, named William;
- his *dispensator* (his provisioner; or domestic steward), named Herbert;[3]
- a domestic chamberlain, also named William;
- another servant, simply named Picot;[4]

---

1  Details of 'royal' personnel, ie. the king's household staff, and government officials, starts below on p. 106.
2  WAC 242; Robinson, *Gilbert Crispin*, pp. 154-5. The abbot was granting several lands, including Chelsea (on a life tenancy), to the king's sheriff of Berkshire, William of Buckland, see p. 71 above.
3  See Robinson *ibid*, p. 30.
4  Perhaps Paul Picot, see WAC 245. The Picot family later became more prominent in Westminster towards the end of the twelfth century, eg. Geoffrey Picot, seneschal or abbey steward of Abbot Walter in 1190, see p. 139 below.

- and at least seven other servants, named but with functions unidentified.[5]

There is no doubt that each of the successive abbots maintained his own personal *familia* of this kind. For example, some of those who later in this period filled the shoes of William, the above chamberlain of Abbot Crispin, were

- Gerold, chamberlain of the next succeeding abbot, Herbert: (1121-1136)
- Roger, chamberlain of the next-but-one abbot, Laurence (1158-1173);
- Ralph and Adam, chamberlains of the next abbot, Walter (1175-1190).[6]

These chamberlains had probably the closest lay relationship with their abbots, as their duties included the running of the intimate domestic arrangements in the abbots' *camera* or chamber.

Abbot Herbert, Crispin's immediate successor, also had his own chaplain, and later abbots likewise. With the help of such members of the *familia*, the abbots were already in the first part of the twelfth century living fairly independently of the rest of their monks, a departure from the precepts of Saint Benedict.[7] A personal chaplain meant that the abbot sometimes could and would have mass said for him in private, instead of at the abbey in the company of the other monks. About 50-60 years later, Abbot Walter of Winchester in the 1180s was blessed with no less than three personal chaplains, Roger, Matthew and Robert, perhaps emphasising the even greater independence of the abbot by that time.[8] Apart from the holding of the abbot's personal masses, a domestic chaplain's duties included

acting as an intimate priestly counsellor when called on, and even acting as a scribe, when his other clerks were absent.

Although neither an usher (*hostarius*) nor a butler (*pincerna*) were specifically identified in Abbot Crispin's list, it is certain that even at that date the abbot, as a Norman magnate, would have had lay members in his *familia* to perform the functions which these posts described. So perhaps two of the named but unidentified persons in the list acted as his usher and butler; the one, to deal with, escort and announce visitors, and the other nominally to oversee the buttery and the provision and serving of drink for the abbot's table. Later Abbots certainly had their own ushers and butlers.[9]

More than sixty years later, during the 1180s, the usher of Abbot Walter can be identified as William of Hurley, living at that time with his wife Pavia on a small estate in Longditch in Westminster; and it seems that the same William may already have been or later became the abbot's butler, moving from one post to the other.[10] William's significance is that he was one of a group of identifiable abbey servants holding property in Westminster from the abbey, and already by the 1180s a pattern was being established for such senior lay servants of the abbey finally to restore such property to the abbey, by way of gift or sale. William the usher was just such a donor; before he died he restored a group of his 'lands and meadows' (with perhaps a house?) in the Longditch area of Westminster to the abbey, which in the next decade the abbey was able to let to one of the recent and

5   As to the 'unplaced' officer who is called Tovius Ganet, see p. 108 n. 78, and 145 n. 38, below.

6   WACs 269, 404, 298, 297. No chamberlain of Abbot Gervase is evident, but the abbot must have had one. Apart from that chance exception, Stephen and Adam, chamberlains (WACs 319 and 409) of the subsequent abbot, William Postard (1191-1200), and Geoffrey, chamberlain (WAC 402) of Abbot Ralph Arundel (1200-1214) complete a century of the chamberlains' service to their abbots.

7   WAD 124; Harvey, *Estates*, p. 132. For St Benedict, see *The Westminster Corridor*, pp. 56-8 and 158-59.

8   Mason *Beau. Cart.* No. 183 (1182 x 1186). Later abbots also had two or three personal chaplains, Mason *WA People of WA*, pp. 98-9. For Abbot Walter of Winchester, see pp. 89 ff. above.

9   eg. Thomas, the *pincerna* (butler) of Abbot Gervase, WAC 263, or Henry, *pincerna* of Abbot Walter, WAC 291. For the seven principal officers in the abbot's travelling cortege in 1215, 100 years after Crispin, see p. 136 below; and nearly 200 years later at the end of the C13, see pp. 301 ff.

10  Mason, *Beau. Cart,* No 191. And 30-40 years before, another William of Hurley had been Prior of Hurley Priory, a dependent house of WA, but no family relationship appears to be provable: WAC 266.

prominent family-residents of Westminster, the royal chamberlain Robert Mauduit, and his heirs.[11]

It is worth noticing that later, after the death of William the usher, his widow Pavia was also adding to Robert Mauduit's growing complex of houses in that area by selling to him her interest in two further messuages and a meadow in the Longditch area (of which the abbey still owned the 'reversion'). The price for these was (a) ten marks (£6. 13. 4d.) which, as she revealed,, she needed as a dowry for her daughter, Joan, who was getting married; and (b) a further mark (6s. 8d) from her son Thomas who, as her heir, confirmed his mother's grant and so precluded any inheritance claim on the properties. There was also a rent of 4d., which now was to be paid annually by Robert Mauduit to the abbot of Westminster, as the tenant in chief.[12]

Other servants whom the abbot also needed were a marshal, to deal with his stables, the maintenance of his horses and other means of transport, the mobilisation of his *familia* when travelling, and the organisation of lay ceremonies;[13] and a provisioner (*dispensator* or food-store officer), and of course a cook. Again such officers may well have been among those persons named in the listed *familia* of Abbot Crispin, with their roles unidentified.

Each succeeding abbot, for obvious reasons, chose for himself the members of his own 'domestic' family, and there appears to

no evidence that there was any recognised right of 'inheritance' for any of the posts (where held by laymen) in the personal entourages of the abbots. This understandable absence of heritability in such posts contrasts with the status of the more 'public' offices, known as 'serjeanties', which were filled by other lay people who served the general needs of the abbey, rather than those of the abbot personally. Such serjeanties, and the hereditary rights given by them, are described below.

Both at this early date and later the abbots were peripatetic, making journeys near and far, when it became necessary to view the abbey's estates; sometimes as far afield as the west country.[14] On such visits some members of the abbot's *familia* would normally accompany him, together with any other necessary monks or abbey officials. On such journeys the members of the *familia* would perform their respective duties personally for the abbot, both when the abbot exercised a right on his part to receive hospitality from lay tenants at certain abbey estates en route, and also in manors still in the abbot's hands.[15]

There can be little doubt that most of these senior members of the abbot's family, and other abbey servants, were housed close at hand in Westminster, as William of Hurley had been. Some of them may also have had other property in the surrounding countryside or in more distant parts of the town, as Hugh of Colham the abbey's general steward did

11 WAM 17614 (WAC 311, 1194 x 1200). For William and Robert Mauduit, see pp. 113-4 and 159-64 below. The new increased rent for these houses, which the monks now once again controlled, was 11s. pa. from Robert Mauduit, a considerable addition for the coffers of the abbey infirmary to which it was allocated. Thomas, a later butler to the next abbot was probably William of Hurley's son Thomas; perhaps having learnt the secrets of that post from his father ? See Mason *WA People*, p. 252; WAC 315, 319; Mason *Beau. Cart.* No. 192.

12 Mason, *Beau. Cart.* Nos. 191 and 192. These properties were to the *east* of Longditch street, ie. in the present Treasury area. In Mason, *ibid.*, No 193, another half acre of meadow was sold, for one mark.

13 Abbot Gervase had an identified marshal called Robert in perhaps the 1140s, WAC 269.

14 WAC 248A, a letter written by Abbot Herbert, Crispin's successor, in the years after 1124 in which he, almost casually, referred to a forthcoming visit by him to the Worcestershire area (where the largest estates of the abbey lay), implying that it was common practice for him to make the journey.

15 For the abbots' rights of hospitality at selected manors, such as Hendon (Mdx), Denham (Bucks), Deene (Northants) and Deerhurst (Glos.) and for the officers they took with them see pp. 136 and 301 ff. below, and Harvey, *Walter de Wenlock*, p. 8n. For allocations of manors between abbot and convent, see pp. 200-1.

(described immediately below). One or two of them, such as the abbot's chamberlain, may perhaps have had a room or rooms in the abbot's *camera* (his lodgings next to the abbey cloister, which had been completed by Abbot Crispin in the period after Domesday) or elsewhere within the domestic quarters of the abbey itself. Some of them may have had small quarters inside the large abbey precinct or in its close neighbourhood. Other more menial servants may have simply slept on the floor where they could.[16]

### (2)  *The abbey steward*

An even earlier charter, made not later than 1100, reveals that at that time the principal lay officer within the hierarchy of abbey personnel, the abbey steward (known as the *dapifer*, at that time), was named Hugh of Colham.[17] Colham (presumably his birthplace) was a manor and vill in west Middlesex, which did not belong to the abbey. Although Hugh's status as the steward of the abbey lands was that of the premier officer of the abbey, he is also identified as one of the abbot's pledged 'men', similar perhaps to the 'men of the abbot' who had been described in Domesday Book as occupants of some of the 25 houses attached to the abbey; indeed he may himself have been one of those pledged 'men'.[18] Hugh, or an ancestor of his,

had apparently been granted by the abbey a large estate of two hides (200-250 acres) of land in Cowley, constituting in effect the whole of that manor (which did belong to the abbey) on the western borders of Middlesex, next door to Colham.[19] But he continued to be known by the locative name of his birthplace, rather than his newer estate name. We can be sure that, as both the abbey's *dapifer* and the abbot's 'man', Hugh had his own house in Westminster as well, perhaps living in one of the houses within the abbey precinct or nearby.

The way in which important abbey families of this kind were set to ramify through the various estates of both Middlesex and nearby counties is well illustrated by Hugh's son and brother and other later relations, who became progressively named Richard of Cowley (Mdx), William of Northolt (Mdx), Roger of Missenden (Bucks) and Walter of Greenford (Mdx).[20]

Although the post of steward was probably hereditary, Hugh of Colham, as the abbot's first identified *dapifer*, was succeeded in his office by others who were probably not of his family and little is known about them.[21] Under Abbot Herbert, the steward was known as Gregory, while later and better-known holders of the post were Geoffrey Picot in the 1180-90s; Theobald, also in the 1190s; and Richard of Dol before and after 1200.[22] Well

---

16  cf. Harvey *Living and Dying* p. 166.
17  WAC 47, (1085 x 1100), ie. a charter made at about the time of the Domesday Survey itself or not many years thereafter. In origin a *dapifer* was the man who brought meat to his lord's table, in effect a steward.
18  WAC 488 (1095 x 1098); see also DB *Mdx* 4/1, shown in *The Westminster Corridor*, Plate 8, p. 86, and p. 141 in that book.
19  WAC 453. For the position of Colham and Cowley, and any other Mdx estates referred to in the text, see the coloured Map B in *The Westminster Corridor*, after page 96, and pages 69-70 of that text.
20  WAC 453, 454, 455, 201, 306. Three of these estates were abbey estates, but not Missenden. These other relatives of Hugh were not provincial unknowns. William of Northolt, Hugh's great nephew, pursued a career as a priest, became a 'Master'(*magister*), the parson of Hanwell (another Middlesex estate of the abbey) and then the Archdeacon of Gloucester, and ended up as Bishop of Worcester, see WAC 206 & 453. In turn, his nephew Walter of Greenford helped William in land dealings, WAC 454. Before 1225 Walter of Greenford had become a knight and then a 'former knight' (? having retired through age or poverty, see Harvey, *Estates* 115, 116).
21  The evidence for the post being hereditary is that a later relative of Hugh, called Walter son of Thurstan 'of Colham', claimed to be entitled to the post in a legal action against the abbey in 1198, and the abbey had to buy him out, suggesting some entitlement on his part: WAC 310.
22  Possession of the manor of Cowley held by Hugh was never recovered by the abbey, which continued to receive only the fixed rent of £1. 10s until the Dissolution in the C16 (when in any case the manor was valued at only £1); Harvey *Estates*, p. 350. For Gregory, see WAC 250; and for Geoffrey Picot, Theobald and Richard of Dol, see pp. 139 ff. below, and also Mason *WA People*, pp. 248-9.

before the end of the century the steward's Latin title *dapifer* had been changed to *seneschal*, an old French word, so that Gregory was still *dapifer*, while Geoffrey, Theobald and Richard each had the title *seneschal* by his time.

### (3) Other 'serjeants' of the abbey

In about 1120, (during the four-year 'vacancy' in the abbacy after the death of Abbot Gilbert Crispin), there were already recognised posts at the abbey for senior lay servants who carried out work in many of the executive departments serving the needs of the monks: –

in the kitchen
the bakery
the brewery
the garden
the vineyard
the infirmary
and the gatehouse.[23]

We can see from this that the abbey had already developed a regular 'civil service' of laymen to carry out the work of its essential departments, each under the control of the monk 'obedientiary' in charge of his department. It is probable that some, if not all of these posts were already hereditary offices, known as 'serjeanties'. We know of at least one other heritable office in the abbey at this early date – not included in the above list – namely the serjeanty of the 'vestry and the buttery', described below.

Such serjeanties were of considerable value to the holders, enabling them to use their position of power within the abbey to earn a substantial living, to hire and dismiss under-servants, as well as to pass on the post to their heirs. Such offices were assets which could even be bought or sold.[24] Their significance for present purposes is that (as was the case with other forms of serjeanty during the Middle Ages)[25] such posts sometimes carried with them the right to hold specific land or lands annexed to the post.

The serjeanty of 'the vestry and the buttery', as its name reveals, linked two different tasks. The vestry (*vestibulum*) normally meant the room in the church where vestments were kept and put on, and where the church vessels were stored. Its link with the buttery, which obtained and distributed wine for all occasions when it was required, was, perhaps, with the wine served in a silver 'vessel' in the celebration of the mass.[26]

In the period around 1120 the serjeant or current holder of these two posts was a man named Walter Stantus, who also held a number of 'tenements' in the town in right of his office. In addition, and in the same right, he held certain 'corrodies'or pensions [27] receivable from the abbey, and also other customary benefits attached to the offices. Moreover Walter had a daughter, Adelaide, who married a man called William of Wenden and became her father's heiress, because her

---

23 WAM 5670 (WAC 339, 1118 x 1120); Mason *People of WA*, p. 253. For this 'render-list' of food-rents and money-rents payable to the abbey at that time, *and* some of its servants in named departments, see pp. 72-3 above; and also the longer discussion about this significant document in *The Westminster Corridor*, p. 150 ff.

24 There are several recorded instances of later sales or lettings of such posts: see eg. next page, note 30.

25 In a national context, the manor of Lileston (containing the modern Lisson Grove area in London) which lay within the sharp turn of Watling Street at the point of our modern Marble Arch, was annexed to the royal serjeanty of *cuneator*, the king's cutter of the coin 'dies' for the mints, for nearly 200 years, see *The Westminster Corridor*, pp. 73 & 103-4, and Map A, after p. 96 in that book.

26 The vestry was used later for the entertaining of visitors by the sacrist, Harvey, *Living & Dying*, 168.

27 Generally a corrody was in effect a pension in kind, generally in the form of daily food and / or drink or housing, granted by the abbey to those who paid for it or conferred other benefits on the abbey or to whom some other obligation was owed, see Harvey *Living and Dying*, pp. 179 ff. Another early purchaser of a corrody from the abbey was an unnamed abbey janitor (clearly a hungry man, or one with a hungry wife and family), in the time of Abbot Herbert (1121-1136), who was to receive two 'messes' of cooked food per day, in addition to another corrody to which he was entitled *ex officio*; Harvey, *Living and Dying*, 240.

brother Geoffrey renounced his own prior right *'from the time of their marriage unto eternity'*. When her father died, Adelaide and her husband were formally invested with the two offices by Abbot Gervase in the period after 1138, together with the same town properties, corrodies and other customary benefits which went with them.[28]

This does not necessarily mean that William and Adelaide received all these hereditary assets free. The abbot's charter does not indicate whether or what they had to pay as a price ('relief') for the grant, and it was not unusual at that time for the price of a transaction to be omitted from the written record of it. The entitlement was to inherit the post, but at whatever price was demanded or had been earlier agreed when the original office had been granted. The right to have such a post, with or without land or other benefit attached, arose from the terms of its original purchase from the abbey by the same family at an earlier, usually unknown, stage of history.

The value of such an office and the importance attached to it are shown by the fact that the Wenden family still held the two posts and their assets in 1298, more than 150 years later, when 'Master William of Wenden' surrendered them all to the abbey, in return for 'spiritual benefits' (memorials and prayers, etc.) for various members of the family.[29] By that time the monks were anxious to repurchase these offices, whenever they could, in order to keep the abbey's assets more under their own control and to obtain for the convent the benefit of both the posts (for resale) and

the assets which had earlier gone with them.

At the end of the twelfth century other serjeants of the abbey can be identified as landowners in Westminster. For example, there was 'Walkelin serjeant of the almonry' who was already holding 'land' in Longditch street, which he or his forebears had acquired at an earlier date, perhaps as adjuncts to the tenure of the serjeanty. Only 'two doors away' in the same street there was other 'land' which 'Thomas, serjeant of the sacristy' had earlier owned, but had restored to the abbey for the support of one of the sacrist's main obligations, the care of the abbey's high altar (eg. for its lamps, candles, etc). Geoffrey son of Fredesent, the abbey's 'summonser', was another serjeant who held both 'land' annexed to his office and an *ex officio* monk's corrody before the turn of the century.[30] Other abbey servants who held land in Westminster towards the end of the century were Edward the reeve of Westminster who owned substantial property in the Longditch and Tothill area, and Simon 'of the gaol' who was a house-holder near the church of St. Clement Danes.[31]

Since the almonry was a separate department of the abbey's organisation, with its own buildings in Tothill Street starting at the 'square' outside the west gate of the abbey precinct, Walkelin's property close by in Longditch was conveniently situated for the purpose of his duties as almonry serjeant. But it so happens that considerably earlier in about 1157 a man who was also called Walkelin, without other identification at that time,[32] had owned and sold a property nearer the Thames

---

28 WAC 254, & WAM L. Adelaide's brother, Geoffrey, had renounced his prior right as the heir.

29 *Flete* (ed. A. Robinson) 117, Harvey, *WA Estates*, 386, 393-4 and 400. Master William also had his name put in the abbey's 'great book of martyrology', as a benefactor; cf. WAM 17483. For the book, see p. 128, n. 47.

30 WACs 444, 328 (Walkelin, and Thomas), and 402 (Geoffrey,). WACs 402 and 403 also show that in about 1209, after Geoffrey's death, Nicholas, his son, granted to another man his inherited office as 'summonser' and all its perquisites, including the land, on a lease for twelve years for a premium of £2. 10s, and shortly afterwards granted all these rights *in perpetuity* to the same man for the sum of £5 and a 'rent' of 4d. annually. Presumably Nicholas was short of ready money, or found he could not perform or did not like his duties.

31 For Edward the reeve, see p. 142 below; and for Simon of the gaol, see p. 42 above, where the issue is whether the gaol was the Fleet gaol (outside Westminster), not the gaol in the abbey's west gate.

32 This earlier Walkelin is recorded as having some members of his own family in the town: a brother

in Endiff lane, north of the royal palace,[33] and he too has been described as 'a servant of the almonry'.[34]

Other almonry servants as well featured strongly in the second half of the twelfth century. A significant one was Gilbert of Claygate (Surrey) who also became a serjeant in the almonry during Henry II's reign, when he restored land and other rights in the manor of Claygate to the abbey, and in return received a generous price, namely the post of serjeant in perpetuity, two corrodies (for himself and his wife Alice) and two houses within the abbey's precinct. Later when the Third Crusade mustered in 1188, Gilbert joined it and *'took the road to Jerusalem'*, after making a gift to the abbey of at least one of the houses, a gift not to take effect until his wife died.[35]

The abbey's function as distributor of alms to the poor was not only an important one, but also a very early one, dating back into the anglo-saxon period. Before Gilbert's time, further financial provision had been made for the supply of alms to the poor, when the tithes of the new parish of St. Margaret's church (alongside the abbey) had been allocated to the almonry, and thereafter the almoner *ex officio* was the rector of the parish church.[36] It was fitting that the almonry buildings (the *'domus'*

of the almonry) had been sited beyond the abbey's west gate, since the poor could foregather in their hundreds in the open space there to receive their alms.[37] Moreover the almoner, as the monk in charge of his department's charitable obligations, had also been allotted the profits of the estate of Paddington (and other lands in Essex and Surrey, and maybe elsewhere) at some early date, certainly before c. 1137, as further sources of the necessary funds for the performance of his duties. All or part of Paddington had then been let to a lay family, but actual possession of it was restored to the abbey, and so to the almonry, in 1185.[38]

The system and the title of lay 'serjeants' remained with the abbey throughout the next century and beyond. Thus over a hundred years later, in 1293, Richard de Aqua, the serjeant in charge of the abbey's western gate (facing Tothill Street) and the abbot's prison inside the gatehouse, was trying to argue in a legal action with the abbey that he had no obligations as regards the prison and the prisoners, but lost his claim.[39]

### (4) An abbot and his 'armiger'
One officer who held an unusual position with Abbot Gervase (1138 x 1157) was the

---

called William and a son and heir called Robert, who are each named in the same charter, WAC 261, as being also present in the abbot's court, 'standing and listening' there while the charter was actually being executed. One can picture the scene. It was they who 'delivered seisin' to the purchaser, ie. invested him with a physical token of his new interest in the land, such as a rod or turf.

33  WAC 261. For Endiff lane and Walkelin's significant purchaser, Gerin, who was both the king's *minister* and the abbot's 'man', see pp. 109-110 below.

34  Rosser *Med. Westminster,* p. 18. The temporal distance betwen these two Walkelins was nearly 40 years: the earlier one may have been the father of the later one.

35  WAD 465b, WAC 347, Harvey, *Living and Dying,* 240, Mason, *WA People,* 219 and 254. See also pp. 181-2 below, for three brothers 'of Claygate', exchequer officers, probably Gilbert and Alice's sons.

36  Rosser *Westminster* 252-3. For the new parish church, see *The Westminster Corridor,* 83-4. It is virtually certain that the Norman Abbot Herbert was himself the abbey's almoner for some period probably within the second decade of the century, before he became the abbot in 1121, Pearce *Monks* 41. I have not traced records of alms for the poor at the abbey before Edward the Confessor, but it appears that during his reign the royal Hall at the palace was filled each day with the poor and the sick who received food and help, *Vita Aedw. Regis,* ed. Barlow, 41.

37  WACs 236 (c. 1086) and 296 (31 May 1185). The former charter, Abbot Crispin's grant to Wm. Baynard, actually refers to the *domus* and the almonry's existing 'tithes'; and see p. 71 above.

38  For this Paddington estate, see WAC 105 (c. 1135 x 37), and pp. 93-4 above.

39  See p. 304 n. 52 below.

abbot's *armiger* (an 'arms-bearer' or squire), named John.[40] But the charter which tells us this was probably made in the earlier years of Gervase's abbacy at a time when the civil war or its preceding disturbances were in full swing, and this evidence raises the question whether at such a time of trouble the abbot himself was able to keep his own military arms. There is no traced evidence that any other abbot within this century employed an *armiger*. In fact the only other *armiger* in Westminster, so far traced in the twelfth century, appears in the same period of civil war: namely Ralph, the *armiger* of Abbot Gervase's marshal, Robert.[41]

The circumstances were in fact unique, and not only because of the lawlessness of the civil war period, but also because Gervase was a son (albeit illegitimate) of King Stephen, one of the two principal protagonists in that war. As a royal bastard he would have been entitled – in the lay world – to his own heraldic arms, albeit with the appropriate *bend* or *baton sinister*. But although there are many records of civil activity on the part of Gervase in his formal capacity as abbot, there appears to be no record of his having taken even any active civil undertaking *on behalf of* his father (unless his grant of the manor of Chelsea to his mother can be so counted), let alone military action.[42] During Gervase's abbacy, his father was the ostensible maker of many charters at the abbey, often in its favour, and Gervase certainly travelled on occasions with his father, for example to Shrewsbury in 1139, and once in a judicial role attended a meeting with him at the Tower of London.[43] But no military

activity is suggested, and indeed it would be surprising if such family affiliations had prevailed over his religious duties. However it would not have been unique in the abbey's history for a monk to have and even to use military arms,[44] and during the civil war in the twelfth century (which affected London greatly, and Westminster) many things may have happened which would have been unthinkable in better times.[45] An alternative explanation might be that the title *armiger* meant in this context one of the abbey's professional men-at-arms who had become one of the abbot's close *familia*, or simply a squire who had been deputed to act as a personal bodyguard in a wartime situation for an abbot who was related by blood to one of the royal protagonists in the war.

### (5) *The abbot and his doctor : benefices and benefits*

Churches could be sources of much power and wealth, both to those who had the right to present a future incumbent (whether as rector or vicar) to a church, and to those who became the incumbents. So in cases where the abbey at Westminster had the right to present an incumbent to a church, the abbots and their monks could exercise considerable powers of patronage. These powers gave them the ability to advance people known or recommended to them to such livings, and this they did frequently, generally for a price, but sometimes simply as a reward for past benefits received by the abbey. However the corollary of these powers was that covetous clerics, particularly those who could count on support

---

40  John the *armiger* was a witness to WAC 254 (dated by Dr. Mason 1138 x 1157, Abbot Gervase's dates). We also know that the same abbot had a 'marshal', called Robert, WAC 269.

41  WAC 269 (1138 x 1157).

42  For Chelsea and his mother, Dameta, who was his father's mistress: see WAC 262, and p. 78 above. Was this so that she might be near the King when he was at Westminster? See Richardson and Sayles, *Governance of Med. England*, p. 415. The wider propriety of his right to make the grant has been an issue for other historians as well; see Harvey 'Abbot Gervase de Blois and the Fee-Farms of Westminster Abbey' BIHR 40 (1967) 127, and Mason, *WA People*, 42-43.

43  WACs 105-121 (several forged by no doubt Osbert of Clare or his former pupils);  Mason, *WA People*, p. 154.

44  See Pearce, *Monks*, pp. 6 and 107, about John Canterbury, and *ibid*., p. 86, about Abbot Litlington, in 1386.

45  See pp. 81 ff. above.

from other powerful figures, might prove to be a danger or a nuisance in bringing pressures to bear upon the abbey, in order to obtain valuable benefices for themselves.[46]

However there were also additional reasons for Abbot Laurence to present his own physician Master Ralph de Beaumont, 'our beloved doctor' to the church of Bloxham in Oxfordshire.[47] For Ralph was also a close *familiaris* of Henry II, one of the group of royal clerks and other advisers who, in the absence at that time of any formal privy council, had the confidence and the ear of the king and wielded great powers of influence over the royal will.[48] Even more importantly, he was also the king's doctor as well as the abbot's.[49] Abbot Laurence was not just a fine theologian, but also an adept politician who knew the advantage in seeking and maintaining influence at court, and his presentment of Ralph can probably be seen in this light. It is not known whether Ralph held any property in Westminster, but in view of his professional relationships with both the king and the abbot he must have been present there whenever needed, staying perhaps in either the palace or the abbey precinct, if not in some property of his own.

Unfortunately for Abbot Laurence the doctor's influence with the king did not survive for as long as the abbot may have hoped, because Master Ralph was drowned in March 1170 in one of the ships of the king's company, when the king was crossing back from Normandy to Portsmouth.

Ralph of Beaumont was not the only identifiable doctor on the Westminster scene or near at hand within this period. Even in the second decade of the twelfth century a doctor called Clarebald *medicus* was acting as a witness to an important charter of Abbot Crispin; and later in the same century Edmund *physicus*, Master Henry Belet *medicus* and Master Richard *medicus* were appearing as either parties or witnesses in land transactions of various kinds. As one would expect, medical men were (according to the extant evidence) more widely present in the more sophisticated milieu of the City of London nearby than in Westminster. It is there too, in the City, that we also find Stephen *sanitarius*, the 'healer', who had been a London householder and was a practitioner, one assumes, in a form of 'alternative medicine' which may well at that time have been commoner than a more 'professional' practice, even if it is more rarely recorded.[50]

### (6) The reeves of Westminster

As the abbot's 'liberty', Westminster owed no part of its status to any royal charter, as many of the newer boroughs did, for it had no chartered independence. This in no way hindered its flourishing development. [51]

---

46 For instances where the abbey (or the abbot alone) was exercising such rights during this period, see WACs 253, 255, 270, 284, 315, 323.
47 WAC 286 (1158 x 1170). For Master Ralph, see also p. 85 above.
48 To laymen Master Ralph's influence came expensive. It cost one litigant $36\frac{1}{2}$ marks (£24. 4s, an enormous sum) to obtain his influence in a dispute in the king's court. In view of the name 'de Beaumont', Master Ralph may have been a relative of the Earl of Leicester; and also perhaps a Canon of Lincoln: Lally, 'Secular Patronage at the court of H. II', *BIHR* 49 (1976) 173.
49 Henry II was exceptionally active and fit physically, although he wore himself (and his entourage) out by his constant exertions, dying at 57. But a modern doctor has detected in his history distinct signs of a manic depressive condition, which the Plantagenets had in good measure; Brewer *A Medical History*, p. 37. In view of this, perhaps Master Ralph was a good doctor of the mind.
50 WAD 504 (WAC 242, 1115 x 1117); WAD 501b-2 (WAC 196, 1150 x 52); WAD 648a-b (WAC 304, Feb. 1190): WAD 493 (WAC 361, 1183-4). It is not clear whether Clarebald was from Westminster or from Buckinghamshire. The Belet family, of which Master Henry was apparently an early member, had also held a serjeanty of the king's butlery from the early C12, see Harvey *WA Estates*, p. 189; and Master Roger Belet appeared in the fourteenth century as butler to King Edward III's Queen Philippa, see p. 271 n. 22 below.
51 Mortimer, *Angevin England*, 178

But until the physical spread of the town of Westminster developed in full earnest during the thirteenth century, large parts of the manor continued to be a green and agricultural. Indeed even *after* the long process of urban expansion, areas of meadow, arable, garden and market-gardening land still remained in use during the whole of the medieval period. These can still be seen even in some of the first Tudor panoramas or map-views of the London and Westminster areas, more than 350 years after the period presently under discussion.[52]

As in any other manor, the farming of the abbey's 'demesne lands' in Westminster had been carried out mainly through the customary labour services owed by local tenants to their 'lord'. Such services and the working of the land of course had to be organised. And as had been the custom since the Anglo-Saxon period before the Conquest, the man in charge of the local organisation of such services and the carrying out of daily work on the abbey's own farmlands in each manor was the local 'reeve', usually chosen from amongst the more influential customary tenants. In the Latin of the records, the reeve was entitled the *prepositus* (or *praepositus*) – the 'man put in front' of the others.[53]

Westminster as the primary estate of the abbey was in a special category. The whole or substantial parts of some of the abbey's *other* manors had been 'leased out' by the monks, at varying points of time, to long-term tenants, who thereafter paid an annual money-rent or food-rent (sometimes both) to the abbey.[54]  As

a result, those estates or large areas of them were outside the factual control of the monks, until such time as possession of them might be recovered or restored to the abbey.

But it is certain that Westminster itself had never been 'leased out' as a manor, and indeed it would be surprising if the monks had been prepared at any time to lose control of the whole of it to any one tenant, however temporarily, since it was their primary estate, immediately surrounding the abbey itself. Equally no single lease of any substantial part of it had ever been made.

Nevertheless there is no doubt that in the early part of the twelfth century or before, the monks (or perhaps the king's managers during 'vacancies' between abbacies) had granted many separate and comparatively small parts of Westminster to tenants, some certainly as 'fees' by way of 'hereditary' or other forms of long-term or indefinite 'leasing'.[55]  And this meant that a large part of Westminster progressively fell outside the managerial control of the monks – until later recoveries were gradually made in the thirteenth century.

So the demesne lands over which the reeve of Westminster had to perform his duties were being reduced accordingly. But for all those parts of Westminster which the monks retained in their own hands, the earliest reeve identified to us by name is Richard the reeve, who served for a protracted period during the civil war and its aftermath, from at least 1136 to 1154 and maybe longer.[56]  In this capacity he acted frequently as a witness to the abbots' charters, where he was often listed in a senior

---

52  eg. the broad open spaces shown behind the mainly 'ribbon development' in the Wyngaerde drawing of 1543/4, illustrated in *The Westminster Corridor*, Plate 16, page 147. In addition, a long verbal description in June 1531 of the fields of meadow, pasture and arable which still existed in the area of the present St. James's Park and Green Park is set out in WAM 17131; and see pp. 24-5 above.

53  For the functions of reeves, see *The Westminster Corridor*, pp. 130-32 and 142-5.

54  For the 'corridor' estates *before* the Conquest, see *The Westminster Corridor*, passim, and for some of the differing fortunes of each such estate *after* the Conquest, see herein: (Paddington) pp. 92 ff; (Hendon) p. 72 and other refs. given there; (Chelsea) pp. 71 and 78; (Hampstead) pp. 362 ff.  'Leased out' is not an accurate description of the medieval relationship, but conveys the practical effect to the modern mind.

55  For this process see pp. 21-3, and App. A, pp. 391 ff below.  For the monks' campaigns to promote charitable restoration of such lands, or to re-purchase such lands whenever they could, see pp. 120-1 and 126 ff. below.

56  WACs 250, 258, 261, 263, 265, 269.  See also Mason, *WA People*, p. 255.

position ahead of other witnesses, and he was appropriately identified as *prepositus*. Among his other duties, Richard would have been principally responsible for the mustering and overseeing of local tenants who by their conditions of tenure still owed service to the abbey[57] – usually an onerous and invidious task in any community.  However it is possible that, having regard to both the importance which Westminster had as the abbey's closest manor and primary endowment, and the high standing of the reeve with his frequent access to the abbot's courts, part of this duty may have been a task which was delegated to a deputy.

One of the reeve's other main tasks was to present orally each year to an abbey official an annual account for the management of the abbey's demesne land in his manor, with such evidence as he had retained.  In later periods this account was then reduced to writing, and subsequently audited.  Unfortunately it was not until the 1250s that the Westminster monks began the practice of making (or at least retaining) any written records of farm management on their manors.[58]  Even after about 1250, many of the records kept in this way have been lost subsequently.  Moreover even when the practice of making and retaining such records had finally begun at the abbey, none of the farm accounts for the demesne land of Westminster itself (or of its courts before 1364) have survived at all.  So

while the practices and benefits of farming after about 1260 can be illustrated for some other local manors such as Eye and Hampstead, they cannot be shown for Westminster.

After the spotlight thrown on Richard the reeve in and before the mid-century, there is a gap in the list of reeves until in the last decades of the twelfth century we meet 'Edward the reeve', undoubtedly a significant figure in Westminster, holding an estate of land and houses mainly in the area of Longditch-Tothill Street, and known as 'Edward of Westminster', a style of name which not many residents received.[59]  When he died shortly before 1200, his son John, who was always known as 'John, son of Edward', inherited his father's estate, and carried out a number of land dealings in the town during the first and second decades of the new century.[60]

After Edward the reeve, the names of later Westminster reeves become more identifiable.[61]  But in spite of that, the details and profitability of the agricultural work carried out under their control within the bounds of Westminster itself remain unknown, both in this period and in the next century – all because of the lack of records.

So much for some of the earliest lay workers who can be identified as employees at the abbey.  Equally there were other named people, who pursued known occupations but who may or may not have been servants of

57  As described in *The Westminster Corridor*, p. 144.  A few allusions to physical agricultural 'works' still owed to the abbey in Westminster and in Eye by some of not only the customary tenants but also 'free' tenants appear in a number of the charters, eg. WACs 405 (late 12C), 446 (1194 x 1197), 447 and 448 (each temp. John): WAMs 4821 (1260s), 4819 (temp. Ed.I); see further pp. 329-335.  Apart from such descriptions of specific works, there are many generic references to unspecified services owed, both in early charters such as WACs 242 (c.1116) or 406 (before 1197); and in later charters as well, such as WAM 4764 (temp. Ed. II), where the recipient of a grant in Eye had to perform 'due and customary service'.  What this latter service amounted to, we do not know, but in some cases it looks as if the phrase may have been no more than an habitual legal 'formula', empty of precise content and de-signed merely to 'pick up' any forgotten entitlements.
58   Such as those which (in part) are extant for the abbey's demesne-lands in the 'corridor', in the manors of Eye and Hampstead, see chapters 19 and 20, at pp. 333 ff. and 350 ff. (for Eye); & chapter 22 at p. 378 ff. (for Hampstead).
59  For Edward the reeve, see pp. 142 ff. below.
60  For John son of Edward, see pp. 143 ff. below.
61  Later reeves whom we will meet below were **Roger Enganet** (see pp. 108-9), **Richard Testard and Henry Sumer**, jointly (see pp. 145-6), **Odo the goldsmith** (see pp. 151-3), etc.  For other lists, see Rosser, *Med. Westm.* p. 328 ff. (but Richard of Dol should not be there) and Mason, *WA People*, p. 353.

the abbey. We see, for example, a number of 'cooks' – Lambert, Aelwin, Richard, Osmund, Simon – but were they cooks at the abbey?[62] Probably these named ones were, because the charters for which they stood as witnesses were abbey charters, executed by one of the early abbots; but other cooks leave us no such clue. And then there were other named men whose occupations were not even identified, so that it is impossible to place them.

## B.  The presence of royal personnel

### (7)  The keepers of the king's palace: the Levelond family

Apart from the abbey, there was, of course, the palace. For this we have to go back to Domesday. One of the first lay people who can be identified by name as living in Westminster at that time was the keeper of the palace himself. He was a 'knight' known as Richard, otherwise called 'Richard the constable; and he probably was the earliest known resident who was *not* connected with the abbey.[63]

His claim to have been the keeper is not based on direct evidence, but arises indirectly from his undoubted right to hold certain land in Kent. According to the Domesday record Richard held the manor of Leaveland near Faversham in that county.[64] But we know that from at least 1130 (only 44 years after Domesday) that manor was definitely annexed to the office of the keepership of the 'king's

houses of Westminster' (the more usual name by which the palace complex was known at about that time).[65]

So if, at the earlier time of Domesday, the manor of Leaveland had already been annexed to the office of the keeper of the palace in Westminster, it would follow that Richard the constable must have been the keeper of the 'king's houses'. In that event he would probably have had his own house or quarters in the palace complex, as later keepers did.

At all events Richard was succeeded as holder of the Leaveland manor by 'Wimund de Livelande', who (for the same reasoning) was probably the subsequent keeper of the Westminster palace towards the end of the eleventh century. However, even if these early claims cannot be fully substantiated, there is little doubt that from 1130 the family (now usually called 'the Levelond family') were the official keepers of the palace. It has also been claimed that that family, in some of its ramifications and with some interruptions, retained the right to the office of the palace-keepership until 1558, a period of at least 428 years, a remarkable continuity.[66]

The current member of the Levelond family in about 1130 was called Geoffrey *ingeniator* ('the engineer'), who was followed by his son Nathaniel from about 1156, and the latter in turn by his son, Robert in 1201 (after a rather checkered history): and so on down the years. Indeed, during the twelfth century several other men acting as 'deputy-keepers'

---

62  WAC 234 (before DB), 250 (early 1130s), 258, 259 and 269 (c. 1150s). In the charters, from Domesday until 1300, the number of identified cooks is quite remarkable. Rightly it was recognised as an important occupation which called for clear identification of those who professed it.

63  The story of the keepers of the palace is considered in some detail by C.T.Clay, 'The Keepership of the old Palace of Westminster' *EHR* 59 (1944) 1. However that article throws up a lot of unanswered questions. In addition, Williams *Early Holborn* 1/169 ff. also refers to the keepership of the palace in his (perhaps unreliable) history of the office of the custodian of the Fleet gaol (with which the office of the palace keepership subsequently became conjoined, see below at pp. 116), but with wide differences of fact: see Clay's note at page 5 in his article.

64  He held the manor from the Archbishop of Canterbury, whose pledged 'man' he was, as indeed later acknowledged keepers of the palace at Westminster were, see Clay, *ibid.*, p. 3.

65  Pipe Roll 31 H.I p. 143, and Clay, *ibid.*, p. 1. The keeper's office was a heritable serjeanty, a royal one this time, just as abbey servants held serjeanties from the abbey, as described on pp. 99-101 above.

66  Clay, *ibid.*, pp. 10 and 15

were also qualified as 'engineers' to carry out their duties of repair and improvement of the royal buildings.

The expertise of an 'engineer', which often at that time had a military flavour, was broader and less specialised or technical than a modern engineer's skills. Indeed the medieval 'engineer's' job covered many aspects of work which we would now expect from an architect or surveyor or from an experienced builder, rather than from an engineer. The more technical disciplines of the modern engineer or architect, and the qualifications for them, were not differentiated in medieval times; nor indeed, it should be said, in later periods until the nineteenth and twentieth centuries.[67]

### (8) Gerin the knight; and Ailnoth – the deputy keepers of the palace

It is clear that the official palace-keepers (the members of the Levelond family) sometimes preferred to act through deputies. So a person apparently *acting* as the palace-keeper and living in Westminster at any particular time may have been a deputy, rather than a member of the Levelond family itself. There are at least two candidates for this role of deputy: first, a 'knight', named Gerin, in the second quarter of the twelfth century, who was expressly identified by our friend Osbert of Clare, the prior, as 'the keeper of the royal palace of Westminster': but Gerin appears to have had no known blood connection with the Levelond family, and so was probably a deputy.[68]

But it also happens that in the first half of the century there apparently was a man called 'Gerin the engineer' living in Westminster or London.[69] It is not impossible that *Gerin the knight* (the keeper of the king's palace) had other skills as well and was the same man as this *Gerin the engineer*. If so, he was a knight, a deputy-palacekeeper and an engineer, all in one.[70]

There was certainly a strong connection between military skills (such as an experienced knight might have had) and the lay 'engineering' skills employed in building and repair work.[71] The Angevin kings regularly employed groups of skilled men called 'engineers' to oversee the building and repair of their castles and halls throughout the country, in addition to other specialist work carried out by them on military engines designed for both siege and defence. There can also be no doubt that, for the needs of the complex of 'king's houses' on the palace site in Westminster, considerable building abilities were needed, for the purposes of both repair of the old and construction of the new.

A second candidate for the role of deputy palace-keeper during the second half of the twelfth century was Ailnoth. Ailnoth too was an *'ingeniator'*; clearly an Englishman by his name, he was one of Henry II's most expert overseers of royal buildings of every kind. He was working regularly between 1158 and 1189 on the 'king's houses' in Westminster, while also carrying out other works elsewhere, on eg. the Tower of London, on the building of

---

67  A dictionary of medieval 'architects' has been created by J. Harvey in his *English Med. Architects*.

68  Barlow (ed.) *Vita Aedw. Regis*, pp. 158-9. Mason, *WA. People*, p. 150. It is, of course, not impossible that unknown to us Gerin *was* a member of the Levelond family. Osbert, describing miracles said to have been performed by King Edward the Confessor, recorded that the 'knight' Gerin, the keeper of the royal palace, was cured of a fever by Edward's holy influence. For Osbert, see 76-7, 78, 81-4 above. A 'knight' was a man-at-arms, not necessarily one on a horse, as the modern image has it.

69  WAC 255 (1141 x 1150), in which 'Gerin the engineer' was one of the witnesses to the charter in question. The charter related to a church in London, hence the doubt as to where Gerin lived.

70  To make matters even more confusing, there was yet 'another' Gerin, who was called 'the king's *minister'* (or officer) in Westminster at about the same time (referred to below on pp. 109-110). One cannot even rule out the possibility that this *'minister'* too was the same man, appearing now in yet a fourth role.

71  Round, *The Staff of a castle in the Twelfth Century* EHR 35 (1920) at pp. 93-5; and see in particular on this subject Salzman *Building in England*, p. 11.

the Fleet gaol, and on castles such as Windsor and other royal residences.[72] At the same time he was drawing the substantial fee of 7d a day to which the keeper of the palace was entitled, although he was strictly only the deputy for Nathaniel Levelond. He was also receiving or at least handling other large sums for both repairs and new work in the royal quarters in the palace at Westminster (on 'the new hall'; 'the Queen's chamber'; 'the king's chamber'; the 'chapel of St John'; glass windows at Westminster; a new wharf on the Thames and landing stairs).[73] During this period he was almost certainly quartered within the palace complex, when he was not working elsewhere in the country.

Ailnoth was not restricted to the king's employment, but worked also at the abbey. A close relationship with the abbey authorities is shown by the fact that he may have designed the chapel of St. Katherine in the infirmary in about 1160; he also repaired the refectory in 1175 during a 'vacancy', and built a stone arch in 1187 at the abbey.[74]

So significant a man could hardly have refrained from investing as well in property in Westminster or its surrounds, but we do not know a great deal about his assets there. He certainly seems to have had a claim on at least two acres of land in the 'fields of Westminster', described as lying 'within the Long Hedge', which his widow Matilda held after his death in or before 1197; and he may also have held or had some claim on a meadow in Longditch.[75] He retired in about 1189, perhaps because his main employer King Henry had died.

### (9)  Roger Enganet, the engineer

Yet another important engineer was also busy both on royal works and on abbey works in Westminster from about 1177 until 1216.[76] A well-known Westminster resident, he too was employed on the 'king's houses' in the Thames-side palace, and receiving payments for the repairs carried out by him there. Moreover, like his predecessor Ailnoth, he was not limited in his professional work to this Westminster role, but worked later as well on other royal projects elsewhere, eg. in London, on the Tower of London.[77]

This was Roger Enganet, the third (perhaps the fourth) known engineer involved with the 'king's houses' in Westminster in the second half of this century. He was almost certainly the son of Ailnoth himself, who had been in overall charge of the palace complex when Roger first appeared;[78] and the name 'Enganet' looks like a corruption of 'the little engineer', an appropriate name for a son of the prominent man whom he succeeded in the maintenance of palace buildings.

At all events Roger Enganet must have been an engineer himself, although in the extant records the description 'ingeniator' was not used with his names (perhaps because 'Enganet' itself said it all). In addition to his occupational duties on behalf of the king, he also had connections with the abbey, as his father had had. He became a familiar figure among those standing in the abbot's court, and witnessed many charters which have survived. And more importantly, he later became the reeve of Westminster towards the end of the 1190s.[79]

---

72  His competence was such that he may even have been responsible for the state-of-the-art design and building of Orford Castle in Suffolk, Henry II's answer to the rebellious Hugh Bigod, earl of Norfolk.
73  Salzman *ibid.*; Colvin *King's Works* 1/57-8 and 493; J. Harvey, *E. Med. Architects*, pp. 2-3; Saunders *Westminster Hall*, p. 26.
74  J. Harvey, *ibid.*; Tyerman, *Who's Who in early Med. England*, pp. 222-3. For the chapel, see Plate 4.
75  CP 25(1)/146 /1/11 (15/10/1197); Clay, *Keepership of Palace*, p. 7.  See also Roger Enganet, next in text.
76  J. Harvey, *English Medieval Architects*, p. 100.
77  Clay, *ibid.* p. 7.  Much of the work, executed in the 1190s, was strictly just outside the period at present under study, but Enganet was qualified and operating well before that time; since at least 1177.
78  Clay, *ibid.*, p. 7, and see the connection in CP 25 (1) /146/1/11. An earlier forebear of Roger may have been Tovius Ganet, one of Abbot Crispin's household officers, see p. 96 n. 5. See p. 145 n. 38 below for the possibility of family connections between the Enganets, the Testards and the Sumers.
79  WAM 17320 (WAC 416, late 12C).

But it seems that all or most of his work for the king on the palace buildings was not carried out by him as holder of a permanent post as deputy of the Levelonds, but in a free-lance capacity as a skilled man acting on his own account on works ordered piecemeal by the king and his officers.[80]

So, like his father and many others, he bridged the two Westminster worlds, of both the abbey and the palace, and he also bridged the two centuries, working for four kings, for Henry II, his sons Richard and John, and also for young Henry III for a few years.[81]

As one might expect, Roger became a man of some wealth. By at least the first years of the next century he occupied a house in Westminster which, exceptionally in the town at that time, was built of stone, unlike most of the usual timber-frame and daub houses of the period. His stone house was not a 'tied' house for a palace-keeper, ie. within the palace, but probably stood in a prominent place, such as the Longditch area or in 'King Street'.[82] He also seems to have had a house standing within the abbey precinct, and one or two other houses as well, one of which he sold to William of Ely, the king's treasurer.[83] But his estate was not all houses: in a compromised legal action he obtained a tenancy on two acres of land in the 'fields of Westminster', which his mother Matilda, Ailnoth's widow, had

previously held; although in return he had to surrender rights which he had claimed in a meadow in Longditch.[84]

The fact that he was appointed as 'reeve of Westminster' indicates that, in addition to his building works at the palace during the 1190s, Roger had also become sufficently trusted by the abbey to earn that position. However he appears to have stayed only one year in the post, before being replaced by Henry Sumer and Richard Testard (apparently as joint reeves).[85] Since he was also busy on royal tasks in the 1190s, there may have been a clash between the demands of the king and the abbey.

### (10) Gerin, the king's officer ('minister')

While the keepership of the palace, as a royal office, had begun perhaps about the time of the Domesday Survey, it is not until about 1157 that we hear of a quite different kind of royal officer as a resident in Westminister, at the end of the abbacy of Abbot Gervase. In about that year a 'king's *minister*', who was also a 'man' pledged to the abbot and again bore that well-worn name of Gerin, bought 'land' at Endiff in Westminster, from a man called Walkelin (possibly the serjeant of the abbey's almonry?); and Abbot Gervase as the chief lord of the land in question then formalised the purchase by confirming it to

---

80  This may have been because in about 1197 the Levelond family had to re-assert, by legal action against a usurper, their right to be the true keepers of the palace, and thereafter the family members apparently sought to carry out their duties in person, at least for a period.  The usurper, from 1189, had been Robert Longchamp, brother of William Longchamp, Richard I's unprincipled chancellor, justiciar and regent (during Richard's absence abroad), who had advanced his brother to the executive post of keeper of the palace. See p. 94 above.

81  For readers' convenience, his career is exceptionally completed here, not in the next section of the book.

82  WAM 17438 (WAC 435, 1200 x 1214).  In favour of Longditch, this charter which refers to the stone house has both a Mauduit and a Mitcham connection; Mitcham being also a place where the Mauduits had property.

83  WAM 17438 (WAC 435, 1200 x 1214) for the stone house: and next door to his stone house Enganet also held an interest in another messuage, for which he received an annual rent of 4s, *ibid*.  See WAC 347, WAD 465b and Harvey, *Living and Dying,* p. 240 for his precinct house, which stood next to the house which Geoffrey Picot was leased by the abbey, and p. 140 below.  See also Clay, *ibid.,* p.7 and Rosser *Med. Westminster,* p. 20, for Enganet's sale to William of Ely: this house stood within William of Ely's own close off 'King Street'.

84  CP25(1) 146/1/11 and Clay, *ibid.,* p. 7.  The two acres were described as lying within 'the Long Hedge'.

85  For Richard Testard and Henry Sumer, see pp. 145-6 below.

Gerin, at a rent to the abbey of one pound of pepper annually.[86]

There are two possibilities about this Gerin. He may have been the first royal officer to arrive in Westminster, the herald of Henry II's gradual removal of government offices from Winchester.[87] But he was also 'the abbot's man', which suggests that, at least under that hat, he was not a new arrival. By 1157 Henry II had been on the throne for only three years: three very eventful years during which he was much engaged with war and diplomacy on the continent.[88] If the king had been able, as early as 1157, to complete the changes necessary for the move of at least the exchequer to Westminster and which undoubtedly were more fully in place later in his reign, he had certainly moved fast.[89]

Alternatively this Gerin may even have been the same Gerin as the one we have already met: the one who was already performing at this time the differing roles of a 'knight', a deputy-keeper of 'the king's houses' and an engineer as well.[90] If so, it would not have been out of place to describe him as a *minister*, an officer of the king: much less important officers were also called by that name.[91] If he was indeed the deputy palace-keeper, perhaps the reason why he bought this

other 'land' in Endiff in about 1157 was that open space for storage, or perhaps a site for a warehouse, was needed near the loading and unloading area of the wharf on the riverbank.

Already by 1157 the district of Endiff was a recognisable and no doubt partially built-up area. One of the existing residents, 'Herdewinus of Enedehithe', was one of the witnesses to the charter which recorded Gerin's acquisition in that area.[92] No doubt the wharf of Endiff (like others along the river[93]) had considerable importance not only for the river traffic which kept Westminster and the palace supplied with food and goods, but also served some of the transport for residents and workers in Westminster and London on their visits to and fro.[94]

**(11)  *Richard fitz Nigel, the king's treasurer: and the court of the Exchequer***
The next known and significant person to arrive in Westminster was intimately associated with the wider history of the national revenue 'court', the Exchequer. For many years, indeed since the early days of the reign of Henry I (Henry II's grandfather, whose death in 1135 had led to the civil war), the financial administration of the country had been carried on through the court of the

86 WAC 261 (1154 x 1158). 1157 is the only date given in Pearce, *Monks*, p. 44, for Prior Elias who witnessed the charter. For Endiff, see p. 47 above.

87 Rosser, *ibid*, p. 18. A 'Robert son of Gerin' held at least two houses next door to each other in Westminster at about the turn of the C12-13, and granted one of them to Geoffrey the roofer (thatcher) WAC 440.

88 During the first *eight* years of his reign, he was in England for only two periods of about a year each (Warren *Henry II* p. 260), and in those periods he spent much of his time in curbing the still lawless barons of the preceding civil war.

89 HG. Richardson, 'Ric. *fitz* Nigel and the Dialogus' *EHR* 43 (1928) pp 161 ff.

90 Barlow (ed), *Vita Aedw. Regis*, pp. 158-9; Mason *WA People*, p. 150.

91 eg. the king's purveyance officers who at the end of the C13 were sent to requisition corn and stock from the abbey's manors near London and Westminster, under the king's right to take 'prises'; see pp. 348-9 below. These prises appear often in the later farm accounts of Eye, near the end of the thirteenth century, when even the abbey's manors were being raided by such '*ministers*', who sometimes had to be bought off with bribes.

92 WAC 261 (1138 x 1157).

93 Like the king's wharf at the palace; see eg. Chelsea, Lambeth, Putney, *The Westminster Corridor*, p. 59n.

94 For the importance of this river traffic in medieval times, now largely lost, see *ibid*. As one illustration, for the carriage in 1303 of Westminster monks to and from London by boat in suspicious circumstances, see the vivid evidence given to the judicial Inquiry held to investigate the great burglary of the king's treasure from the vault below the abbey's chapter house in that year, pp. 317-8 below.

exchequer. Managed and already running efficiently in that reign under the meticulous Bishop Nigel of Ely, Henry I's treasurer, the workings of the exchequer had then suffered dramatically in the disorganisation caused by the fifteen years of anarchy during the civil war and its aftermath, when 'its expertise had almost perished'.[95] But after Henry II became king in 1154, he was able to recall Bishop Nigel from retirement to advise about the task of restoring the competence of the exchequer, and before 1160 (for the price of £400 said to have paid by the bishop) the king had appointed the bishop's illegitimate son, Richard, in his place as the treasurer, a position which Richard then occupied for nearly forty years.

It was this Richard fitz Nigel who now arrived in Westminster, so that he could be near his place of work in the revived Exchequer. He acquired land and a number of houses in the area north of Endiff lane,[96] and set up an establishment there which became almost an official residence for use by government officers for over half a century. He himself occupied a house facing the river, and it may have been in that house that he later described himself as *'sitting at a turret window overlooking the Thames'* in the year 1176-7, as he began to write the unique book for which he has become famous, the first book to describe the working of a government department in England. *The Dialogue of the Exchequer*, as it is usually known to us, is a detailed account of the personnel and procedures of the exchequer, with which the royal treasurer was by then so familiar both from his father's teaching and his own personal experience of many years. It was written in the form of a conversation between a 'Master' and a 'Scholar', and its expressed purpose was to ensure that the treasurer's specialised knowledge of exchequer practices (described

as 'the holy mysteries') should not die with him but should be passed on to those who should follow him.

The court of the Exchequer (*scaccarium*) sat twice yearly at Easter and Michaelmas round a large table. From now on it sat usually in Westminster. Its main task was to receive and investigate the accounts of all taxes and other monies received and expenses incurred which were produced by the sheriff of each of the counties, and to collect or by grace to defer what was owed by each sheriff and by other debtors to the crown. It was called the exchequer because of the nature of the cloth covering the table, on which counters were placed to represent differing sums of money and were then moved so as to reflect the state of the account between the crown and the sheriff or other debtor. The cloth was checkered, not in black and white squares, but in columns as on an abacus. The findings and decisions made by the court were taken down on parchment rolls by a number of 'clerks' (ie. clerics), including those who wrote the official record of the court on the great roll known as the Pipe Roll for each year.

The king's treasurer received the accounts and oversaw their audit which was carried out by question and answer, the main questions being directed by the treasurer himself and the chancellor's clerk. The rest of the court dignitaries sitting round the table consisted of the king's chief ministers or their appointed deputies: the justiciar as the president of the court, the chancellor, the constable, two chamberlains, the marshal, two 'watchdog' members,[97] and other influential office-holders, to whom the title 'Barons of the Exchequer' was accorded.

The other less exalted but highly professional staff of the court came to have

---

95  *Dialogus de Scaccario*, ed. C. Johnson, p. 50.
96  These houses and other later properties are subsequently referred to in WAM 17313, (WAC 313, 1196); WAD 341b-2 (WAC 219, 1196); WAD 342 (WAC 147, 1200); WAD 342b-3 (WAC 439, 1218 x 21).
97  Richard of Ilchester, later bishop of Winchester, and Master Thomas Brown, both of them introduced by the king, in effect to keep a watch on proceedings in the exchequer, to keep the treasurer awake and to be responsible for the keeping of separate copies of the roll. But the treasurer Richard fitz Nigel preferred in his book to play down suggestions that he was subject to their supervision.

great significance for Westminster, being often residents of the town and sometimes closely associated with the abbey too. They fell into two groups: firstly the various clerks and scribes of the senior barons, engaged in writing the individual records of the court's decisions. At the Michaelmas sitting the roll recorded the final results of the accounts and the various debts for that year. Some of these decisions were in effect decisions of law, which in due course became precedents for later cases. The second group consisted of executive officers of the court, such as the accountant, the weigher, the melter, four tellers, the usher, and various serjeants, who from this period also swelled the ranks of the population of the town of Westminster.[98]

The sittings of the exchequer were usually, but not always, held at Westminster, perhaps at first in the treasurer's own house at Endiff but later within the palace complex, in separate rooms, between the great Hall of Westminster and the king's chamber towards the Thames. This building contained both the 'court' room itself, the Upper Exchequer (with its own withdrawing chamber, where the barons could adjourn to discuss issues), and another room, the office of 'Receipt' or the Lower Exchequer where the money paid by any of the debtors, sheriffs or other accountable persons was received, counted, sampled and, for various purposes placed in sealed chests, wooden bowls or purses.[99]

'Customised' as the concept of this national exchequer was, it did not remain unique to Westminster or to national government. It was quickly adopted by some of the greater magnates who, like the king but on a smaller scale, had large revenues to collect and fiscal issues to determine. For example, as early as the 1180s the Earl of Gloucester was referring to his own *scaccarium* which was held at Bristol, and others followed suit.[100]

In 1189, when Henry II died, his treasurer Richard Fitz Nigel was still hard at work on his Westminster duties and still occupying his Endiff house. Moreover in addition to his exchequer business, the treasurer had been sitting regularly in judicial work in the *curia regis*, the king's court, part of which was now sitting permanently at Westminster, and he was also travelling as a justice in the revived periodical 'eyre' circuits of judges in the south-western counties. Indeed on occasions he had followed the king himself on his royal itinerary when opportunity allowed, and had even been sent abroad to Normandy to help with the reorganisation of the Norman exchequer.[101] Although reasonably educated, he was not a particularly learned man, but his great strength lay in his methodical professionalism and perseverance as a loyal servant of the crown.

He must originally have received dispensation from the pope for his illegitimacy, and his long service with the king was rewarded with many ecclesiastical appointments as well, as a canon of St Paul's, dean of Lincoln, and finally as bishop of London late in 1189. In this, his further elevation is a good illustration of the policies adopted by Henry II to use his own 'new men' in place of members of the families of older magnates. Richard fitz Nigel became one of the 14 active bishops (out of 22) who had formerly been royal clerks, owing all to their position in the royal entourage. But even after his ecclesiastical appointments Richard still continued as the king's treasurer, with both his exchequer and judicial work, and was based still at his Westminster property until 1195-6 when he passed it on to William of Ely, his kinsman and successor as treasurer.[102]

98    For such exchequer staff, see eg. chapter 10 below, at 170 ff.
99    Colvin *King's Works* 1/538-9. Later in the C13 the exchequer was moved but still within the palace site. By then it had already begun to lose some of its unique significance as the central organ of government, to the king's 'chamber' and 'wardrobe'.
100   Stenton, *English Feudalism* 1066-1166, p. 68 and 267
101   Richardson, 'Wm. of Ely' TRHS (4th) 15 (1932) p. 52-3n.
102   For the further history of the treasurer's property and his successors there, see pp. 156-7, 159, 187-8, 193 and 261 below.

When Richard Fitz Nigel died in September 1198, he left remarkable objects as legacies to St. Paul's church, his cathedral seat, but none to the abbey at Westminster.[103]

### (12)  William Mauduit – a royal chamberlain

Another significant arrival in Westminster in the second half of the twelfth century was a family, the Mauduits, whose successive family heads had royal and official duties.[104]  Of these, William Mauduit was the first incomer.  Like Richard fitz Nigel he came to Westminster to pursue his already well-established administrative career, now in this new seat of government.  The royal connection lay in his hereditary office as one of the two royal 'chamberlains', a position (*regis camerarius*) which the family had obtained late in the eleventh century and continued to perform until 1263.[105]  Again like Richard fitz Nigel, the heads of the family had already become reliable and shrewd civil servants of the crown, and for their services were rewarded with beneficial marriages and estates.[106]

But Henry II's financial requirements were changing and were being serviced by two separate offices. The hereditary chamberlains remained responsible for major revenues receivable at the exchequer under its meticulous procedures, but the king's more immediate executive needs for money were being met by his own household 'chamber', to which special revenues were being assigned.

The 'chamber' was staffed by the king's own confidential officers and advisers, his *familiares*.  Some of these were also known as 'chamberlains', and their function was to receive moneys assigned to their office and to make these available to meet costs incurred by the king's day to day decisions and his other administrative requirements.  Since the king was frequently itinerant, this 'chamber' had to be able to move around with him.  So while one financial office was to act in Westminster under the Mauduits (and their fellow chamberlains, the fitz Gerolds) in their roles in the court of the exchequer, members of the staff of the other, the more personal financial office, accompanied the king wherever he moved, and became also known as officers of 'the royal wardrobe'.

When King Henry moved his centre of government from Winchester to Westminster, William (I) the current head of the main branch of the Mauduit family also began the process of transferring his own work-base from Winchester.[107]  He bought a house and land in the Longditch area of Westminster, together with some arable and meadow land in the region behind the house on the edge of what is now St. James's Park, so laying the foundation for the larger estate in the Longditch and Tothill area which his son Robert was able to build up, at and after the turn of the century.[108]

While using his base at Westminster, William as one of the king's chamberlains had

---

103  Brooke and Keir, *London*, p. 272.  But to be fair, he had been a good benefactor of the abbey in his lifetime, see p. 156 below.

104  See further Mason, 'The Mauduits and their Chamberlainship' *BIHR* 49 (1976) pp. 8-9, and Mason (ed), *Beauchamp Cartulary*; Rosser, *Med. Westminster* pp. 28-31.

105  To make matters more complicated, the family acquired a second chamberlainship as well; but it does not seem to have played a significant role.  See also pp. 271, n.21 for the elevation of the family to an earldom in 1263.

106   eg., their power-base nearest to Westminster was their estate at Hanslope in Buckinghamshire, with lands in Rutland and Northamptonshire, most of which they had received through a profitable marriage with the family of one of Henry I's 'new men'. Other, but less profitable, marriages to baronial daughters followed.  But the family did not become seriously baronial until eventually in 1263, by such a marriage tie, they achieved the earldom of Warwick; but for lack of an heir their name in the earldom was then superseded by *'Beauchamp'*.

107  He is called 'William (III)' by Dr. Mason, since the name had often been used as a family name; just as 'Robert' was.  But I will use 'William (I)' for him, as he was the first Mauduit in Westminster.

108   Mason, *Beauchamp Cartulary*, Nos. 183, 187 & 189.  The vendors of some land in Longditch bought for 40s. by William Mauduit (No. 189) were Alexander the son of William the priest of St Martin's Church

the status of a 'baron of the exchequer', becoming also known under the title 'chamberlain of the exchequer'. He was present at the exchequer sessions, seated below the table when the audits of the sheriffs' accounts were being carried out by Richard fitz Nigel, the treasurer. But the chamberlain's function in the pure formalities of the sessions was limited, compared with that of the treasurer. His main duties were financial ones, dealing for example with the collection and distribution of the resulting revenue, including the provision of moneys which the 'king's chamber' as an expanding government office had to have, and the fulfilment of all other requirements of the king.

As early as 1165, William Mauduit was also carrying out judicial duties, both in Westminster in the 'king's court' and elsewhere as one of the itinerant judges, in eg. Northampton and York. His record of judicial duties ranges from that date until 1193, shortly before his death. But another special task which regularly fell to him during Henry II's reign as one of the royal chamberlains was the transport of treasure or bullion for royal purposes. This often took him and his fellow chamberlain far afield from Westminster, not only to different and distant parts of England but also by boat, with powerful contingents of armed guards, to the continent where the king was frequently engaged in war, with his soldiers waiting (often in vain) to be paid.[109] In a world where all debt payments had to be made in coin, the transport of money was laboursome and had to be rigorously supervised and carried out, and it therefore fell to senior officers close to the king to be personally responsible, aided later by serjeants or clerks from their own offices or from the treasury, for this important task.

In addition to other offices (such as that of sheriff, which he held in Rutland where some of his estates lay) William Mauduit had one distant post which had an indirect effect on Westminster. He had inherited from his father the position of castellan of the castle of Rockingham, a royal hunting lodge in the king's forest of Rockingham in North-amptonshire, a post which after his death in 1194 passed to his son Robert. As a consequence of the influence in Rockingham which this post gave both him and his son, the names of several other important residents in the town who held the locative name 'of Rockingham' and were closely connected not only with the Mauduits and their royal duties in Westminster but also with the court of the exchequer.[110]

Another place with which William was closely connected was Hanslope in Buckinghamshire, the centre of his small baronry there which his father had acquired by marriage. As a result of this link, a number of people bearing the locative name 'of Hanslope' are also to be found among the residents of Westminster.[111]

When William Mauduit died in 1194, his son Robert inherited his office and lands, and under him the Mauduit estate in the Longditch / Tothill area continued its growth.[112]

---

(which stood near the crossroads at Charing, as the modern church 'in the Fields' does) and Alexander's wife, Alice. Alice, it seems, had inherited the land from her father 'Thedric of Eye', apparently an Englishman and an early resident in the nearby rural village of Eye, the manor adjoining Westminster. For later Mauduit acquisitions, see pp. 159-164 below.

109  Mason, 'The Mauduits & their Chamberlainship', p. 4; Richardson, 'Wm. de Ely', p. 73ff. After about 1182, the treasurer's clerk assisted in the carriage of the treasure, and the chamberlains' clerks some-times also acted on behalf of their principals. Royal treasure, when not being used, was now kept mainly at Westminster, the New Temple or the Tower of London. Such escorts ranged from 10 to 100 armed guards, Richardson, *ibid.*, p. 77.

110  See pp. 174-5 below. But the castellanship of Rockingham was taken from Robert in 1205 by King John.

111  eg. William of Hanslope (otherwise William of the Temple), see pp. 176-8 below.

112  For the continuation of the Mauduits' story in Westminster, see pp. 159-164, 269-71 below.

## (13) Alexander of Barentin – the king's butler

Henry II's butler (*pincerna*), Alexander de Barentin, was another royal officer at work in Westminster from at least 1173, even if he did not (so far as we know) occupy a house in the town.[113] However, he spans both town and country in this book, because he was also the holder of the manor of Hampstead until the time of his death in about 1191-2.[114] It may be that he used either that nearby estate or one of his London properties, instead of a house in Westminster, as his place of residence whenever his personal duties towards the king required his presence in Westminster.[115]

He was a kinsman, perhaps even a brother or brother-in-law, of the powerful Richard of Ilchester, one of the king's chief personal advisers.[116] Richard of Ilchester was the baron of the exchequer who had been specially appointed to that office by the king to perform a supervisory role, and occupied a special position at the previously checkered table, sitting between the treasurer and the justiciar.[117]

Alexander, like other royal servants, held the office of the king's butler as a serjeanty.[118] He ran a large administration, ordering wine and ferrying it from those ports where it arrived in England from the continent to the king and his itinerating court, or to the garrisons of royal castles and even to the army.[119] His duties also included the escorting of the closely-guarded consignments of money and other treasure around the country and even to the continent when needed.[120] Apart from his butlering duties, as early as the 1170s he had also performed other roles such as holding courts as a justice on circuit.

Other properties besides Hampstead came to him through his kinsman Richard of Ilchester, or in right of his own wife, Margaret.[121] But one separate property

113 Barentin was a town and area on the Seine in Normandy, 15 kilometres below Rouen.
114 VCH, *Mdx* 9/92, and see pp. 368 ff. below. Hampstead included an area called Chalcots, but by 1204 Barentin had given Chalcots to the leper hospital of St. James in Westminster, VCH, *ibid.*, p. 99. For Chalcots, see also p. 369 below, and *The Westminster Corridor*, p. 127. The other Hampstead lands passed to Barentin's heir, and soon went to descendants, but the abbey recovered them in mid-C13; see pp. 216 and 369 ff.
115 WAMs 659 (WAC 144); 660 (WAC 135), and 662 (WAC 139).
116 Alexander's sons, Richard and Thomas, were often described as 'nephews of the bishop', ie. of Richard of Ilchester, after he had been given the bishopric of Winchester, see next note and WACs 144 (1189) and 139 (1181 x 87). Moreover the bishop was clearly generous towards the Barentin family. The bishop's background is shadowy, save that he was also a kinsman of Gilbert Foliot, the bishop of London; see Duggan, 'Richard. of Ilchester' TRHS (5th) vol 16 (1965) at p. 3. Since Richard of Ilchester was related to both Alexander of Barentin and Gilbert Foliot, it follows that the latter two must also have had some family connection, if not a blood one.
117 Johnson *Dialogus* pp. 17 and 26-7. The treasurer in his *Dialogus* does not accept that Richard of Ilchester was there to supervise him. But the effectiveness of the exchequer was due in great part to its system of checks and counterchecks, whereby those who were present saw and heard everything and, being on the spot, could ensure that the rolls accurately recorded what had happened. Once finalised, the rolls were inviolate, and could not be altered save by or at the instance of the king himself. For Richard of Ilchester, who became the bishop of Winchester, see *DNB*, and Duggan 'Richard of Ilchester', *ibid.*, and see also App. A, at p. 392. Richard had been at bitter odds with Becket the Archbishop, but after Becket's murder Henry II was able to nominate Richard for the Winchester bishopric with a notorious writ, *'I order you to hold a free election, but forbid you to elect anyone but Richard my clerk'*, Warren, *Henry II*, pp. 311-312..
118 See WAM 661 (WAC 134, 1175). All the royal charters still held at WA in favour of Alexander of Barentin. are originals, sealed with the Great Seal.
119 Mortimer, *Angevin England*, p. 64. In this role, Alexander appeared frequently in the Pipe Rolls of the exchequer in H. II's reign, when accounting for sums received and when being paid his own expenses and fees.
120 Richardson, 'Wm. of Ely', TRHS (4th) 15 (1932) pp. 72n and 74-5.
121 See also WAM 660 (WAC 135, 1175 x 1177); WAM 661 (WAC 134, 1175); WAM 662 (WAC 139, 1187).

apparently held by him has an indirect but close connection with the royal palace at Westminster. This was a garden near the river Fleet on the edge of the city of London, adjoining the 'gaol of London' (later the Fleet Gaol) and almost certainly belonging to it, together with certain houses which also went with it. All of these had been held earlier by an uncle of his, Henry Arborarius and another relative, ' Ralph Arbor' , earlier wardens of that gaol.[122] Its significance for Westminster history was that the office of the custody of the Fleet prison was recorded as being conjoined (surprisingly) with the keepership of the king's palace in Westminster. And five or six years after Alexander's death in 1191, the two offices were held to belong to the current member of the Levelond family, the palace-keeper.[123]

Exactly how and when this conjunction of the two offices had come about is not certain.

But whenever the conjunction occurred, the two offices continued to be held together as a joint serjeanty for the time being, and in 1303, more than a hundred years later, they reappear in Westminster history, when the deputy keeper of both the palace at Westminster and the Fleet gaol was directly implicated in the famous burglary of King Edward I's treasure housed under the abbey's chapter house.[124]

Alexander held much other property in London, some due to the help of his 'brother' Richard of Ilchester. He had also become the hereditary Forester of Essex, perhaps inheriting the hereditary office through his Arborarius relatives.[125] Other lands he held in Barentin and in Sussex.[126] When he died in about 1191, leaving sons still under age, his estate was sufficiently valuable to attract bidders who were prepared to pay large sums (eg. £100) to become custodian of his heir. Not that it did his heir much good.[127]

---

122  *Coll. Top. & Gen.* vol iii, p. 285, and Clay, 'Keepership of the Palace', EHR 59 (1944) pp. 5-6.  Henry Arborarius had also witnessed a Westminster abbatial charter dated 1125: WAC 247, and Alexander of Barentin had figured as a witness to two charters with which Richard of Ilchester was involved, WACs 277-8 (1158- 83).  Alexander however is not known to have held the office of keeper or deputy keeper of the palace, so his Fleet Gaol position is mysterious. Later his granddaughter and heiress Sibilla was sued for some of her Hampstead lands by a Geoff. d'Arbrier, who was surely connected to Alexander's Arborarius relatives?; see p. 370 below.

123  This fact had been established, when in an action as to the identity of the true keeper of the palace it was held that Nathaniel de Levelond and his son Robert were entitled to the serjeanty of both offices, *'as held since the Conquest'.*  If this last clause was not just an invented or inaccurate archaism, it means that the conjoining of the two offices had already had a long history, stemming presumably from some royal grant of both together. For the palace keepership, see p. 106 ff. above.

124  See p. 318, n.31, and p. 106, n. 63 below.

125  Turner, *Men raised from the Dust*, p. 26 and 163. Another probable link is with Eustace de Barenton, a serjeant of H. I who in the 1120s became Forester of Hatfield (Essex), see *Regesta A-N*, 2/1518 and 3/39-41.

126  See VCH, *Mdx*, 9/93 and PRS, 3 & 4 R. I, p. 305.

127  PRS, *ibid.* & 6 R.I, 20, 182; Turner, *ibid.*  His son Richard died in debt, VCH *Mdx* 9/92, and p. 369 below.

# CHAPTER 7

# At the turn of two centuries: 1189-1216
# trends and further abbots

As the twelfth century turned into the thirteenth, the year 1200 can be seen as a signpost in the development of both the nation and Westminster.[1]

The decades on either side of that year were so loaded with new events and trends as to shape the direction of the next century in its administrative and social evolution. The town of Westminster and the abbey, being at the centre of the changes already made, were among the first to feel these consequences. This period of less than thirty years, after the death of Henry II in 1189 and through the short reigns of his two sons Richard I and John, was the threshold of a new order both in Westminster and in the administrative framework of the nation.

## A. Trends in Westminster

### 1. Government people proliferate

To begin with, there were the widening effects of the changes in government and the judicial system which Henry II had initiated. After these changes had been made, the new order had already begun to raise the profile of Westminster as a town, with the arrival of fresh and important blood. However this expansion which had begun in the town well before King Henry's death in 1189 was as nothing compared with the ensuing course of events. In the 1190s the size and nature of the town were already changing, and both with

its own momentum and with further initiatives by both the king and the abbey this transformation accelerated at an even greater rate during the century ahead.

One of the main features of this expansion was the growing number of royal servants and professional administrators in positions of influence at court and in government, in place of the members of old baronial families who had once been accustomed to serve the king administratively. More and more 'new men' and 'men raised from the dust' are to be seen assisting the king and his principal ministers; with many of them working and living in Westminster.[2]

There were plenty of opportunities for these incomers. Not only was the exchequer already well established in Westminster as the main financial instrument of the administration, but also the king's 'chamber', his personal finance office, had emerged as another effective, if still shadowy, office of government.[3] Both contributed to the influx of newcomers to Westminster.

Into the exchequer and the chamber, as two separate destinations, sums of revenue were being directed during Henry II's reign. Some sources of the revenue were allocated specifically to one or other destination: as one example, the profits of 'vacant abbeys' were assigned directly to the 'chamber'. That office had acquired the role of an effective 'bank' of

---

1   For the three abbots in the decades surrounding the turn of the centuries, see below at pp. 129 ff.
2   This local experience in Westminster mirrored what was happening elsewhere in the country. The royal practice, renewed by Henry II, of using 'new men' was not limited to a town such as Westminster. Like his grandfather Henry I, Henry II had also introduced it further afield, even to the point of choosing sheriffs, his own agents in the counties, from the ranks of his own 'new men', instead of from the 'old guard' : cf. Warren, *Henry II*, 291.
3   See Richardson and Sayles, *Governance of Med. Eng.*, chap 12, pp. 229 ff.   The role of the chamber as a financial office had probably begun very early in the 1110s, when Henry I had recovered the lost

funds for the king's executive use.[4] Using his personal confidants and advisers as his officers, the king was thus enabled to draw at once on all 'chamber' funds for immediate purposes of government as well as for his own domestic expenses. These were of course in addition to the greater funds which he could call for, from the more cumbersome processes of the exchequer. Such members of the king's personal staff were added to the corps of officials who were now working and living in Westminster.[5]

But a third group of other officials was also emerging in Westminster by this time. As a result of legal reforms which Henry II had first set in motion, 'the Bench' of royal justices (or 'the Common Bench', or 'the court of the Common Pleas', as it later came to be called) was sitting in Westminster separately from the court of the exchequer – even though it shared many of its personnel both with that court and with the senior itinerant justices who were being sent out into the provinces.[6] The sittings of the new Bench, as one sector of 'the king's court', were now being held more regularly in Westminster, on a rota of four terms in the legal year. This established a more static judicial presence in the town, which in effect complemented the carrying of more flexible royal justice into the provinces, a function which the mobile 'king's court', and the itinerant justices and other royal commissioners performed. The sittings of the Bench now took place more frequently in the king's great hall at the palace, and members of its staff were to be seen living as well as working in Westminster.

In turn the added legal business before the justices both in Westminster and elsewhere in the kingdom led to more work also for the office of the king's chancellor, operating from its quarters in the palace. This office was the one responsible for the writing and sealing of the writs needed by litigants for the new forms of legal action which had been created by the king's legal reforms. The resulting huge increase in the number of judicial writs meant that more chancery clerks had to be employed to write them, and so yet another group of new-comers were needed in Westminster.[7]

### 2. *Inflation strikes*

Then there were the consequences of a wave of inflation which was breaking over the country towards the end of the twelfth century. After a period of stability, economic conditions in England in the quarter century before 1200 were changing radically. Prices of the two staple foods, grain and animal-products, had recently been rising steadily, to culminate in their sharpest rise just as and after the centuries changed.[8] By then, prices had more than

---

Normandy and the English and Norman 'treasuries' were being brought into line, but it is only after 1154, when Henry II became king, that a less obscure history of the office can be traced.

4  Mortimer, *Angevin England*, p. 64. Hence an incentive to a king or his agents to delay the appointment of a new abbot. For eg. the vacancy at Westminster, between Abbots Laurence and Walter, in the years 1173-1175, see p. 89 above. For the 'chamber', see Jolliffe,"The Camera regis under H. II', *EHR* 68 (1953), pp. 1 and 337.

5  Examples of such royal confidants (the king's *familiares*) are Ralph fitz Stephen and William Turpin, see pp. 172-3 and 157-9 below; each of whom was labelled 'chamberlain of the *camera*'; to be distinguished from the two 'senior' royal chamberlains in the Mauduit and fitz Gerold families. For the Mauduits in Westminster, see pp. 113-4 above and 159-64 below.

6  Poole, *DB to Magna Carta* 411-4; cf. Turner, *Men raised from the Dust* 48-50. Within a short time Magna Carta (1215 and after) confirmed the new practice, whereby the Bench did not follow the itinerating royal court but sat at a fixed place, usually Westminster (with some sittings held at eg. Northampton or Oxford). See also Mortimer, *Angevin England*, 59-63 and 73-4.

7  See Mortimer *ibid.* pp. 64-65 and Clanchy, *Memory to Written Record,* pp. 57 ff. See p. 67 n. 20 above, for some of the new forms of legal action established by Henry II.

8  See eg. Miller and Hatcher, *Medieval England, Rural Society and Economic Change 1086-1348*, p. 64-69; Bolton *The Med. English Economy 1150-1500*, p. 72-6. Mortimer, *ibid.*, 154-6, lays more emphasis on the decade immediately following 1200. This inflation contrasts with the much more stable pattern of

doubled. It was 'the price-revolution of the middle ages', according to Lord Beveridge, and it was followed later by a period of much slower but still progressive inflation in the course of the ensuing century. The differing arguments about the reasons why this extraordinary rise had taken place at this time do not matter here; but there is no contention that it happened at a time when 'boom' was in the air, when the population and the prosperity of the kingdom were expanding, and when old towns were growing in size and new towns and markets were being created throughout the country.[9]

In Westminster similar changes were particularly marked. The quantity of transactions relating to houses and land which were taking place in the town, both when the centuries were about to change and afterwards, appear to have increased enormously. The extent of the town grew significantly; and to us the geography of both the town and its rural neighbourhood becomes more perceptible, because of the increasing flow of information in documents. At the same time the lives, the numbers and identities of the residents and their trades and other occupations become more visible.[10]

The wave of inflation had another important consequence for Westminster. The monks of the abbey found – as almost every other landlord throughout the country did –

that in all those cases where (within the hundred and more years since the Norman invasion) an estate of theirs had been 'leased' by their abbey to a tenant 'and his heirs' at a fixed money-rent and was still retained by that tenant or his heirs or other successors, the new price-rises for farm produce meant that the additional profits arising from the inflation were now being enjoyed solely by the tenant and his successors and not by the abbey.[11] For their part the monks, like other estate-owners, were saddled with a low rent fixed in some cases as much as a century before, while the tenant had the benefit of all the higher prices for his produce. Moreover this was a period when for other reasons the resources of the abbey were already beginning to be strained to the limit.[12]

So the monks of Westminster soon after 1200 followed the example of other landlords and started a serious policy of recovering, where they could, possession of those estates which were in the hands of such tenants, with the intention that their abbey would then be able to farm the land for itself and thus benefit from the now inflated prices for its produce, or at least to relet some or all of the land at current rates.[13] Their main difficulties were the forms of the leases originally granted and the uncertain or ambiguous state of the law as regards the recovery of land.

---

prices in the preceding two or more centuries; and it has been suggested that part of the price increases around 1200 were perhaps the result of economic forces which had been 'dammed up' in those much earlier years.

9  Miller and Hatcher, *ibid.* p. 70-83; Rosser, *Westminster*, p. 18, text and notes. Other causes assigned for the inflation have been the growth in the market economy, the rapid circulation of money, population outstripping the means of subsistence, pressure on land, large inflows of bullion into England due to increasing demand for our wool exports, bad weather, poor harvests, etc.

10  Although this is the clear impression which one gets from the scale of the existing evidence, one also has to remember, in making comparisons between different periods, that the extant charters at WA, and other dealings revealed in WAD, are an accidental factor; other charters made in earlier times which have not survived might make a difference. Equally the charters which the abbey still possesses, or once possessed, may have been only a proportion of the transactions which were taking place within the town.

11  Miller and Hatcher, *Medieval England*, pp. 213 ff.; Bolton, *Medieval English Economy*, pp. 87 ff.; Postan, *Medieval Economy and Society*, pp. 111 ff.; Harding, *England in the 13C.*, pp. 68-9.

12  Harvey *WA Estates*, p. 64.

13  Harvey, *ibid*, pp. 65 and 131. The radical change whereby estate owners (such as the abbey) now set about (a) recovering or trying to recover lands which had been let to other 'farmers', and then (b)

In one local case, in Paddington, they had already managed to anticipate their later policy by recovering as early as 1185 an estate in that manor, which at some earlier unknown time had been let to two brothers, 'Richard and William of Padington', or to their family predecessors.[14] But as regards the other areas of land in their nearby 'Corridor' estates which were still held by such tenants, the monks' success was limited. It was not until much later in the next century that, in spite of strenuous efforts, they were able to recover some of their lands in Hampstead and in Hendon.[15] The manor of Chelsea was an even harder nut to crack, and although the monks continued to receive rent for it until the sixteenth century (still at the rate of £4 p.a., set in the twelfth century), they never managed to recover full possession of the manor – all this in spite of the great and continuing inflation.[16]

### 3. The recovery of Westminster properties by the abbey

Another series of events which had remarkable results in the town during the next century had been set in motion before 1200. The abbey had embarked upon a policy of recovering possession of its own former lands within Westminster itself. The principal motive for this was of course the economic one, that is, the same motive as that noted above, which led to the monks' decision to seek to recover the abbey's lands in other manors. But one can also infer that so far as Westminster was concerned, the motive had

overtones of an 'imperial' kind as well, even if such a motive might not have been admitted by those who held it. The abbey had long ago left behind its simple founding theme, of a house of humble monks in a purely rural setting. Its now established prestige may have required that its local empire should again include important holdings in Westminster which had been granted away in the period since the Norman Conquest, and so embrace more closely the people who lived on its doorstep and were subject to its formal jurisdiction and courts.[17]

Of this policy, two separate results appear. With their eye on the benefits arising from such an inflation, the monks became 'leading participants in a boom of investment in local property' in Westminster, re-purchasing houses, empty plots and rents where they could.[18] Even rural land fell within their sights. But secondly and more importantly for them in both materialistic and religious terms, they were able, by the end of the twelfth century, to take advantage of, and themselves to fuel, a growing blaze of popular and charitable devotion and donation to the cult of the Virgin Mary, which was being shown both nationally and locally among the residents of Westminster and other benefactors of the abbey.[19]

Within the abbey at this time St. Mary had her own altar. It was this altar which became the object of a remarkable flood of devotional property-giving to the abbey, principally by those who felt the need to ease the passage of their own souls (with or without the souls of others dear to them) towards heaven.

---

themselves farming them led to the period known as the 'high farming era'. This lasted for 150 years or more, until the time of the Black Death in 1349, Miller & Hatcher, *ibid*. For Hampstead, the recovery was protracted until 1258, p. 370, below.

14 WAM 16194 (WAC 296). For the recovery of Paddington, see further pp. 92-4 above.

15 For the final recovery of lands in Hampstead, see pp. 217 and 370-4 below; in Hendon, p. 305 & n. 58. below.

16 WAM 4799, *Cal.Cl.R.* 1364-8 pp. 385-6. For one brief period in 1367 the tenant let it back to the abbey for his lifetime. Chelsea had been granted by Abbot Gervase, King Stephen's natural son, to his mother Dameta during or after the civil war, to the scandal of the monks: see pp. 78 above, WAC 262, and Harvey, 'Fee Farms of WA', BIHR 40 (1967) 131.

17 For 'fees' in Westminster granted away, see pp. 21-3 above; for a list, see App A, at pp. 391 ff below.

18 Rosser, *Medieval Westminster*, p. 6.

19 Rosser, *ibid*., p. 47.

Generous, or well-aimed, donations of town property, land and rents flowed to the 'support of the Lady Altar' (as the donors' charters put it); and if the sellers of other properties felt no such charitable urge, the abbey would often buy them, sometimes at full price and sometimes at more. Starting mainly within the ten years of Richard I's reign, the cult then flourished during the troubled years of his brother John's reign (1199-1216).

But as in so many other aspects, this short but pivotal period at the turn of the centuries was merely the threshold of much more to come. By 1220, as we shall see, an *altar* alone was regarded as not adequate as the object of such fervour. So a project for the building of a new *chapel* to St. Mary at the existing east end of the abbey was started by the monks in that year.[20] However although the floodgates of donation of property or rents for the proposed 'Lady Chapel' thereafter failed to open as wide as the monks may have hoped, a more generous and illustrious benefactor of the abbey had already appeared, in the shape of the young King Henry.

### 4.  An upsurge in record-keeping and literacy

Yet another factor converted the decades on either side of 1200 into a turning point in the recorded history of England, which had consequences also for the local history and development of Westminster.

This was the example and standards set by one man, Hubert Walter, the Archbishop of Canterbury, who also became successively the justiciar and then the chancellor of the kingdom. When Henry II died in 1189, he had been succeeded by his son Richard I (Coeur de Lion), but Richard spent only six months of his reign of nearly ten years in England. The rest of his life was spent almost in continuous fighting both on the continent of Europe, defending the lands (in modern-day France) which he had inherited from his father, and on crusade to the Holy Land. But his long absences from this kingdom meant that England, in some respects fortunately, had to be administered by others. For five years, from 1193 to 1198, Archbishop Hubert Walter became Richard's justiciar, adding a principal secular role to his ecclesiastical one, and administered the kingdom with considerable diplomacy on the absent king's behalf. And for another six years, between 1199 and 1205, he served as chancellor under King John who had succeeded his brother in the former year.[21]

The significance of this background is that Hubert Walter was a remarkable administrator, whose two periods of secular office were responsible for many administrative improvements, including the start of regular record-keeping in most branches of government.[22] He himself had had some early training in the exchequer, with its tradition of preserving necessary information in written form on 'the great roll' (the Pipe Roll made at sittings of the court). As to the law, he had gained acquaintance with legal procedures when serving in the household of his uncle the great justice, Ranulf Glanvill. It was under Hubert's influence that general record-keeping in government now began. The charters made by the kings; other royal decisions pronounced in the kings' 'close' (closed) letters and 'patent' (open) letters; records of legal court arguments and settlements of court actions; records of the hearings and decisions made by the newly appointed coroners; records of all loans made by the Jews (data preserved for administrative purposes) – all these and others were now to be made and kept in official repositories.

One of the important practical effects of this new record-keeping, which still plays its part in helping to establish the history of

20  See pp. 129, 249 and 261 below.
21  Cheney, *Hubert Walter,* passim.
22  Clanchy *Memory to Written Record,* p. 48-53; Poole *DB to Magna Carta,* p. 442-3. It is known that some record-keeping (in addition to the pipe-rolls kept by the exchequer) may have begun in the years before Henry II died, but it was at best spasmodic and ad hoc. In spite of his achievements Hubert Walter, like many in his time, was a greedy and at times unscrupulous man.

Westminster, was a development of the 'fine' system adopted by the royal court in recording compromises reached in legal disputes about the ownership of land. In a new community like Westminster, where valuable land was involved, such disputes arose more regularly than in outlying parts of the country. Henry II had made it possible for people involved in disputes about land-ownership to have the issues tried by a jury in the royal court, instead of by 'trial by battle' – the antique feudal method of trial on such issues, by a duel between the parties either in person or by their paid 'champion'.[23] However so great were the complications and delays of proprietary actions in court that often the parties would reach a compromise before the ultimate trial, and then wished to ensure that the effect of their compromise was securely recorded. Since about 1170 the court had (for a price, of course) been prepared to make a court order called the 'final concord' or 'fine', recording the compromise in duplicate on the same sheet of parchment, which was then cut into two and a copy given to each of the parties.[24]

But in 1195 a further refinement of this process was developed by Hubert Walter, whereby the compromise was recorded now in *triplicate*.[25] While the first two copies were still given to the parties as evidence of their settlement of the dispute, the third copy at the foot of the parchment was retained and preserved in the treasury at Westminster as the court's own record of the order made; and it could thereafter be consulted if any subsequent issue arose as to what had been agreed. The third copies kept by the court of such compromises came to be called the 'Feet of Fines', because of their position at the 'foot' of the record. This meant that early records made by the judges in Westminster of transactions relating to property, including of course many houses and land in Westminster itself, begin to figure prominently.

Those who knew their way through the new and growing legal process (much of which was taking place in the town) were able to use similar methods to ensure that their transactions were permanently recorded and therefore could not be frustrated subsequently by lack of proof. Thus in 1214, when Peter fitz Herbert, a prominent member of King John's court, had made a settlement with the abbot of Westminster, resolving a long-standing dispute over the manor of Parham (Sussex), he wrote a letter to 'the barons of the Exchequer and the royal justices of the Bench', requesting them to make a special 'cirograph in the king's court' recording the settlement.[26] Even twenty five years earlier, in 1189, the abbey prior had shown that he was aware of the advantages of getting a permanent court record made to enshrine such a settlement. Following the resolution of a dispute between a lay tenant and the prior and convent about rights over the vill of Benfleet in Essex, the prior made a payment of one mark to the exchequer to get a record of the compromise enrolled on its Pipe Roll.[27] There it would be safe, and no one could later gainsay it.

---

23  For 'Brungar the champion', a professional fighter, who lived in Westminster in the second half of the twelfth century, leaving a daughter, Beatrix, see WAC 406 and WAMs 17109-10, and p. 49 above.

24  The Latin name *finis* may have meant the *finis duelli*, ie. the avoidance of the bloodshed which the old feudal remedy of a duel could result in, according to 'CJ', *EHR*, 58 (1943) 496. For the date 1170, see Brand, *The making of the Common Law,* p. 87; cf. Round, *EHR* 12 (1897) pp. 300-1 and Maitland, *Select Pleas of the Crown,* p. xxvii. Of course the recording of such compromises was to be only a small part of the work of the royal court, which had to deal with all disputed cases.

25  This was an anglo-saxon practice (in different format), revived by HW; Clanchy, *From Memory to Writing,* 88.

26  WAC 487. It is not clear why the simpler Feet of Fines procedure had not been followed. Notice the way in which the exchequer barons and the judges of the bench were still coupled together as members of the 'king's court', although the two tribunals were by now sitting separately and had their own jurisdictions and procedures.

27  WAC 344 (1189). The prior was William Postard who was to be the next abbot (see pp. 129 ff. below)

Another motive in making use of this legal process was that, in an age in which the survival of private documents was uncertain and in which the opportunities for later forgeries were substantial, people who made some uncontentious but important agreement, such as a normal sale of land, could if they wished ensure that a permanent *public* record of their transaction was made. A 'friendly' action about the land could be started by one of them against the other, as though they were in genuine dispute about it, and an official court record of their agreed 'compromise' could thus be obtained – at the price, of course, of the legal costs.

The 'ineffaceable mark' which Hubert Walter left behind him has led not only to the centuries-long survival of knowledge, but also to less visible but more far-reaching consequences: namely, the wider proliferation of literacy, the further spread of the practice of making documents in matters where oral testimony would once have been regarded as essential and sufficient, and the better retention not only of official documents but also of more personal records and accounts.[28] In all these respects it left imprints on Westminster.

The large increase in the number of personal charters executed in Westminster in and after the 1190s and lodged by donors at the abbey, for retention as 'title deeds', shows the importance which had already been attached to this form of record-making and

record-keeping. We have already noted how in about the middle of the next century (c. 1250) the monks of the abbey also began (a little belatedly compared with some religious bodies) to make and keep written records of the annual accounts of their own demesne farming in the abbey's manors.[29]

## 5. *The 'division of goods' between the abbot and his monks*

With the surge of emphasis, during this period and the rest of the thirteenth century, on material possessions such as land, houses and rents in Westminster and on an enlarging economy in the town, a parallel movement was taking place within the abbey cloister as well. While this was a purely internal development within the abbey which had little influence on the town, it had been an escalating movement among the monks which had had its roots in the distant past. The movement was far from unique to the abbey at Westminster, and indeed had begun at other monasteries before it can be traced at Westminster.

Under the old Benedictine regime, an abbot had been intended to be the 'father of all', holding the property of the abbey in his own hands and, in a paternalistic way, using it as he saw fit in the interests of his monks.[30] But it did not follow that his flock would necessarily agree with what he saw fit to do for them on his own initiative. Still less if he did nothing. But since its early days the abbey

after Walter of Winchester (pp. 89-94 above), and he made this charter in conjunction with his convent of monks. In Walter's abbacy the whole manor and church of Benfleet had been confirmed to the convent by the abbot, but after about 1200 a new abbot, Ralph of Arundel (see pp. 131 ff. below) had apparently taken possession of the manor from the monks and was farming it himself. But they clearly wanted to recover possession of it (probably because of its inflated value), and after some bargaining got his agreement and a charter from him; see WACs 299, 345 and 332.

28 Michael Clanchy, in his great study *From Memory to Written Record*, (1993), chapters 2 and 3, has illuminated subjects such as 'The proliferation of documents' and the differing 'Types of record'. I would only question, with due diffidence, on the evidence of the private charters held at WA, whether he has emphasised sufficiently the burst of *private* documents relating to transfers of urban land in and after the last years of the C12.

29 See p. 105 above. The earliest extant ecclesiastical manorial accounts were those kept for the bishops of Winchester from 1208, Clanchy, *ibid.*, p. 92. The abbey's surviving records of accounts, relating to the farming business of each manor, which were made and kept by Westminster Abbey from mid-C12, will feature in relation to two of the 'Corridor' estates, Eye and Hampstead, discussed later in this book in chapters 19, 20 and 22, at pp. 339 ff. and 357 ff. (for Eye); and pp. 378 ff. (for Hampstead).

30 *The Westminster Corridor*, pp. 56 and 157.

at Westminster had become much more sophisticated and wealthy, with more property and income to its name. Even by the time of the Domesday Survey, the abbey had an annual income of £515, a figure which entitled it to a position in 'the top flight of monastic wealth' at that time.[31]

Within thirty years after the Domesday Survey it had become necessary for Abbot Crispin to assign certain fixed funds out of this income for the benefit of his convent. He had had to allocate a secured amount of £70 annually towards the monks' 'chamber' (principally towards their clothing); and this must clearly have been done after negotiation and agreement between the abbot and the convent, and in particular with the abbey chamberlain.[32]

Similarly, other sharing arrangements to benefit the monks had been made for the other two main requisites of life, namely food and fuel, and for other additional needs as well. From that time it is clear that the whole question of the abbot being obliged to make an 'agreed provision' for the necessities and indeed (by this time) the comforts of the monks was a running issue between the abbot and the convent. With the recognition, as we have seen, of the almonry, the kitchen, the chamber and other services as distinct units within the abbey, the 'obedientary system' of separate departments within the abbey, each managed by one of the monks with his own accounting duties, was already well in place.

It had always been important to ensure that charitable gifts made to the abbey were actually used for any specific purposes named by donors, and were not swallowed up in the general funds of the abbey. This gave the donors some security as regards their own wishes, which are also well illustrated by the large number of charters made during the twelfth and thirteenth centuries, granting properties, rents and other assets specifically for the personal needs of 'the monks', or for one or more of the named 'offices' which managed the abbey's different roles and duties. Kings, popes, bishops, abbots and private individuals vied in making donations to 'the convent' itself, or to 'the monks' clothing', their 'diet', 'the monks in refectory' or their 'pittances', or to one or more of the departmental officers – to the sacrist, the infirmarer, the chamberlain, the kitchener, the almoner, or the precentor.[33]   But this generosity was unpredictable and spasmodic, and clearly the convent yearned for regularity and security and for an even greater sphere of fixed support from some of the abbey's growing assets.

Meanwhile one of the factors which continually aggravated the situation during the twelfth century was that, according to the convent's perception, some of the abbots were acting high-handedly from time to time in disposing of property which belonged to the whole abbey, without obtaining the convent's consent and/or without procuring satisfactory value. Such actions, in the monks' eyes, were contrary to the strict requirements of canon law, and even to less-severe injunctions pronounced against the practice by the popes from time to time. They also served to reduce the monastery's assets in which the convent was seeking the formal allocation of a regular and proper share.[34]

Since daily food is the basic human need, the monks' concerns had centred naturally on the question as to how their food was to be paid for and provided. The funding of its

31  Harvey, *WA Estates*, pp. 28 and 55-6.

32  Harvey, *ibid*. pp. 85-91, where details of the allocation of funds are discussed. Indications of earlier sharings of assets at Westminster and other monasteries during the Anglo-Saxon period before the Conquest are dealt with in *The Westminster Corridor*, pp. 159-60. See also Harvey, *Obedientaries of WA*, Introd. pp xix ff.

33  Mason, *WA Charters* and *WA People*, passim.

34  See eg. pp. 77 ff. (Gervase); and 129 ff. (William Postard).

provision had passed through various stages. Initially an ancient custom (starting from an unknown period, no later than the mid-twelfth century) had grown up, whereby the convent's kitchener had received a food fund made up of an allowance of 8s. per day (£146 per year) from the abbot's general funds for the abbey.[35] But in the monks' eyes, they had no security about this. They had no control at that stage over the abbey's general funds, and would be at risk if any shortfall in them should occur.

In the last decade of the twelfth century, Abbot William Postard gave them in effect a small degree of security. He gave them a valuable asset by assigning to them the whole 'vill of Parham' (Sussex) with all its lands, but only on condition that the monks should themselves pay £8 to their own kitchener for their food (incidentally so relieving the abbot to that extent).[36] As a security for their food, this was minimal; but the convent were duly grateful for the abbot's gesture and for the additional valuable asset which at least they now had, even if some of the income from it had to be spent on their own food. When the next abbot, Ralph of Arundel, tried to claim Parham back from them, they fought back and appear to have compelled him not only to confirm their entitlement to it but for good measure to include with it the abbey's advowson, the abbey's valuable right to select and put forward incumbents for the church at Parham.[37]

But the significance attached to the convent's food in the early thirteenth century is reflected in the more effective arrangements which had to be made by the next Abbot William Humez in 1214-15 (specifically *'at the instance and petition of the convent'*) to endow the convent kitchen with an increased amount of £150. 10s. 9d. annually, and to secure this amount by defining the actual contributions which would be charged on nine named manors of the abbey.[38] And shortly afterwards the same abbot (with, of course, 'the convent's consent') increased the kitchen fund by a further £2 annually from the income receivable by him from the manor of Hampstead.[39]

These rather sporadic arrangements made for the monks' maintenance and to meet their wishes to participate more directly in the abbey's empire were to lead ten years later to a complete change in relations between the abbot and the convent. As we will see, in 1225, under a new and confident abbot, an extensive compromise was reached, with a division of abbey properties between them and a new definition of their respective roles. The convent were to be master of their own part of the house.

But even then that was not the end of their arguments. Indeed it can be seen as the beginning of much more serious contentions between them and each of their abbots during the thirteenth century, which by the end of that century were to sour relations between the

35 This custom was described as the 'ancient levy', alluded to in the middle of a later charter of Abbot William Humez (1214-1222), printed in Harvey, *Walter de Wenlok*, p. 216. For Abbot Humez, see pp. 134 ff. below.

36 WAM 4064 (WAC 326, 1191 x 1200). The grant was elaborately-phrased, to reflect the scene: *'with the whole chapter of Westminster standing by and endorsing the decision made and rendering all manner of thanks to me [the abbot] for this benefit'.* For Abbot Postard, see pp. 129 ff. below.

37 WAC 335, and see Mason, *WA People*, p. 74. It was valuable because incumbents would have to pay for holding the post. I have not found the evidence for the dispute on which Dr Mason relied. An obscure part of the charter suggests that the abbot was still having to account for the whole of the original £146 per year, (without the convent accounting for anything). For Abbot Ralph, see pp. 131 ff. below.

38 WAD 629a-b, printed in Harvey, *Walter de Wenlok*, 215. The charter made the total £150. 11s. 9d. The named manors included Hendon (with its northern territory, Brent), which was to contribute 'its whole farm in wheat, grout and malt'; and Chelsea, to contribute £4, the full amount of the unaltered rent which it contributed to the abbey for over 400 years, see pp. 71 and 78 above.

39 WAM 32354, see also p. 135 below. £2 was the whole rent for Hampstead since c. 1121, see p. 365.

abbot at that time, Walter of Wenlock, and some of his monks and to lead to dramatic confrontations betweeen them, to accusations of arrogance, deception and fraud, to appeals to the Pope in Rome and finally to the excommunication of the Westminster prior by his own abbot.[40]

So it is that the explosive thirteenth century came to be reflected even within the cloister. While land and houses were changing hands in the town, and wealth and power were increasingly the standards by which lay men were learning to live, even monks had learnt to look beyond their devotions. An added share in material prosperity, and the increasing power which abbey offices and the administration of their widening territories provided, were now to be added to the religious benefits of a monastic life.

### 6. *The Virgin Mary: the 'cultivation' and administration of a cult*

Since the time of the Norman Conquest the altar of the Virgin Mary had stood towards the east end of Edward the Confessor's rebuilt abbey. It could not of course stand in the central apse, which was occupied by the High Altar, the altar of St. Peter to whom the abbey was dedicated. 'The Lady Altar', as it came to be known, had no chapel of its own at that time: and indeed the abbey may have had no ambulatory at its east end, off which a chapel could stand.[41] But towards the end of the twelfth century the Lady Altar by itself had become an object of increasing devotion in Westminster, as it did elsewhere. The cult had been spreading from the continent, inspired mainly by the teachings earlier in the same century of St. Bernard at Clairvaux in France.

Cults attracted donations, and the abbey was quick to recognise both the religious and the secular advantages of a promotion of this new cult.[42] It was probably part effect and part cause of the growth of devotion to St. Mary that the monks created a separate department to administer the donated properties and moneys which the Virgin's altar was beginning to draw to the abbey. From about 1189 a succession of new 'wardens of the Lady Altar' were appointed to oversee this task, and their efforts redoubled the flood of both charitable giving and self-interested selling to St. Mary and her altar.

The precentor of the abbey, Brother Robert of Moulsham (a Westminster estate in Essex), became the first master-mind behind the campaign to win back Westminster property to promote the Virgin's cult. He became the first and the most successful of the 'wardens', holding that office together with his precentorship for about ten years, and when at the turn of the century he became the prior of the abbey, he remained in charge of the Lady Altar as well.[43]

During his period in charge of the Lady Altar, the altar received at least nine grants of property in which Robert was actually named in the charters as the warden: and in most of them he acted as a buyer, not just a receiver of gifts. Of his nine acquisitions, four were

---

40  See chapter 12 (Abbot Richard of Berking) at p. 195 ff; chapter 13 (Abbot Richard of Crokesley) at pp. 212-3; chapter 14 (Abbot Richard of Ware) at p. 226; and chapters 17 and 18 below on Abbot Walter of Wenlock, at pp. 292-5 and 319-26.

41  Rebuilding of WA', *A-N.S.*, 3 (1981) 35, 40 and 205. There is a wealth of erudite literature about the east end of the old church, mostly in the Archaeologia journals.

42  However the cult of St. (King) Edward the Confessor, while an important one for the abbey, had not been hugely popular, see Rosser *Westminster*, p. 35.

43  In eg. WAC 411 (1197 x 1200), Robert as 'precentor of the church, and procurator of the altar' effected a purchase of 'all the land' in Westminster of Simon of the gaol, for a price of five marks (£3. 6. 8). When he purchased 'all the land' of Peter Fauset for 7s. 2d. in about 1200, he was still precentor, but by the time that he came to let the same land out to Adam, one of the abbey serjeants, he had become the prior: see WACs 430 (c. 1200) and 348 (temp. John). Pearce, *Monks*, p. 46, and Rosser *Westminster*, p. 48 attribute his priorship to the earlier period of 1189-1197, but this does not seem to be borne out by the contemporary charters, which indicate progressive promotion, probably as a result of his success as warden of the altar.

purchases of rents in Westminster, and one seems to have been a gift of rent, amounting in all to an annual income of 23s. 10d. for the altar. Of the other four, one was apparently a gift of a house (a messuage) and three were purchases of 'land' (in one case, including a 'tenement' as well). By subsequent dealings with three of the latter acquisitions, Robert was able to raise a further increment of annual rents, amounting to an additional 7s. 2d. for the Lady Altar and 3s. 4d. for the abbey as the 'chief lord'.[44]

All this was extremely good business for the abbey. Already substantial 'lost' assets in Westminster had been re-acquired by the abbey, and the Lady Altar was now to receive annual rents amounting in all to 31s, for a combined purchase price of £15. 7s. This represents a 'purchase' figure of about ten, which was no more than a normal commercial rate at the time. Moreover (quite apart from the ever-increasing value of *gifted* assets in a spectacularly inflationary age) the renewed participation of the abbey as recipient of the *purchased* rents of Westminster properties raised the expectation that the abbey might be able in the future to enjoy the increasing *values* of those properties as well. There was plenty of jam, or at the least, 'jam tomorrow', on an already well-buttered slice of bread.

So, even on the surviving documents in which Robert of Moulsham was actually named, the campaign on behalf of the Lady Altar had got off to a flying start. It is small wonder that after his death Robert the prior was 'granted an anniversary' (an annual celebration of his memory, in his case on the 8/9th December each year, for which 100s. was assigned) at the expense of the altar which he had so fostered.[45]

But this was far from all. The nine cases in which Robert's name actually appears in the legal charters were only a small proportion of the total of 35 grants of property which the

Lady Altar received during this period when he was the warden, in the decades on either side of 1200. So there were another 26 grants in which the warden is not mentioned at all by name. It is very noticeable that there was a wide difference in character between the original group of nine and these other 26 cases. Of the original nine, seven were purchases and only two appear to have been gifts. But of the other 26, twenty were expressly charitable gifts (granted to the abbey 'in soul alms'); and of the remaining six cases, four were also clear gifts (although not expressed in such charitable terms), and only two could even be argued to have involved some element of give-and-take (ie. they were perhaps purchases). So all or virtually all of the second group of 26 were gifts, rather than purchases. By them the Lady Altar and the abbey itself benefitted spectacularly, both in financial terms and in the monks' policy of recovering their 'lost' properties.

So the contrast between these two groups of acquisitions by the Lady Altar suggests that, as a matter of practice, the involvement of the warden and his name were usually only recorded in the legal documents when purchases were being made, no doubt because greater responsibility had to be shouldered for the necessary expenditure. Moreover, so far as the dates of all the transactions can be estimated, most of the purchases (among the group of nine) seem to have taken place in the 1190s, and almost all of the gifts in the 1200s. So after a kick-start from the early purchases, the charity machine was already running smoothly. Robert of Moulsham was obviously well equipped to promote the monks' cultivation of the public's new-found devotion to the Virgin Mary, and it is not surprising that with such organising ability he had been promoted to the office of prior.

When Robert died, he was succeeded by two joint wardens, Brothers Stephen of

---

44 The above summary is based on WACs 346, 347, 348, 408, 411, 425, 429, 430, 433, 441 and 442.
45 WA Customary, (ed. Maunde Thompson), ii. 92. This was a rare honour for a prior at this time. Robert, as the prior, had also earned the monks' gratitude by securing the restoration to them by the abbot, Ralph of Arundel, of the manor of Benfleet in Essex, see WACs 345 and 332, and p. 132 below.

London and Walter of Hurley, and this doubling of staff may be some measure of the size of the task by this time. The gifts of property to the Lady Altar had been flowing fast during the first period after 1200, and only the acquisitive John, son of Edward the reeve, who rarely gave anything away free, was costing the altar any appreciable amount during this period, with his two sales of rents to Robert of Moulsham for a total price of £7. 13s. 4d.[46] The flow of gifts from others is the best evidence of the lay support for the altar.

But even if charity carried its own reward in heaven, there was another benefit which donors could now expect. Robert Mauduit, the royal chamberlain who kept the large Mauduit establishment in Longditch/Tothill, and his wife Isabel Basset (who made two generous gifts of houses and rents of 7s. 8d. to the Lady Altar) had successfully petitioned that the names of all donors should be inscribed in the abbey's 'book of martyrology', and should share in the 'spiritual benefits' which the abbey could provide in the shape of remembrances in all 'prayers, fasts, vigils, masses, disciplines and all other alms': perhaps a more comfortable reward than for other forms of martyrdom.[47]

The general motives of most of those who donated property are clear enough. Their charitable gifts were either made 'in soul alms', or (with or without that ultimate seal of full charitable intent) were usually expressed piously to be 'for the good of the donor's soul', and/or 'the souls of his or her spouse, parents, heirs, predecessors or successors' or any combination of such beneficiaries.

But occasionally special considerations arose. When Adam of Westminster (an officer at the exchequer) granted a 1s. rent 'in soul alms' to the Lady Altar, he did so evidently at the wish of his wife, Matilda; and the soul and the name of his wife's mother, Scolastica, were specifically included in his charter for recognition.[48] And when Rose the seamstress and Ralph Mauduit (two unmarrieds, it seems) gave a house to the Lady Altar, they asked for the soul of King Henry II to benefit, along with their own: apparently because Ralph had been in royal service before King Henry had died.[49]

Similar motives inspired some of those who gave property to the abbey itself, rather than explicitly to the Lady Altar. For example when the king's former treasurer, William of Ely, towards the end of his life restored all his houses in Westminster to the abbey, he thought fit to bracket the souls of all the three kings under whom he had served – Henry II, Richard and John – with the soul also of his predecessor and kinsman, Richard fitz Nigel, the former royal treasurer, from whom he had obtained his Westminster houses.[50]

This wave of charity towards the Lady Altar probably continued for about twenty years after

46  See WACs 408 and 441; and for John, son of Edward, see further pp. 143-5 below. For his sales, John collected sums of five marks and six and a half marks from the warden of the altar. Other purchases by the later wardens did not entirely dry up, since Stephen and Walter paid 7s., a cheap price, for a 12d. rent in Westminster in the early part of the C13, see WAM 17442. Another later warden was Bro. Henry of Colchester, see WAM 16218 and WAD 509, probably just before the proposed chapel replaced the altar as the object of the promoted cult.

47  For the grant of this reward, see WAC 329 (1200 x 1214). The book contained a calendar of martyrs, saints and benefactors of the abbey. For Isabel's gifts, see pp. 144-5 below and WAM 17327 (WAC 422, temp. John) and WAC 450 (temp John). Robert had also made donations to St Mary's Altar and Chapel, WAC 329 and WAD 507b. For the Mauduits in Westminster, see pp. 113-4 above, and pp. 159-64 below.

48  See WAM 17437 (WAC 412, temp John). For Adam of Westminster, see p. 180-1 below.

49  See WAM 17438 (WAC 435, temp John); Mason, WA People, p. 173. Rose's first husband, William Turpin, had also been a significant figure in Henry II's service, see pp. 157-9 below. Ralph was probably a nephew of Robert Mauduit, the king's chamberlain, see pp. 159-64 below.

50  See WACs 439 (1218 x 21) and 219 (1196). One of the more poignant motives, in a very different context, for generosity shown at about this time by a son, in expressly giving up his hereditary rights, when his widowed mother sold her house (to another lay person, not to the Lady Altar) was that he himself, the heir, had 'neither any children by his wife, nor any hope of having any', WAC 438 (1196 x 1212).

1200, by the end of which the monks were entertaining even greater ideas. In other large monasteries (such as Glastonbury), the now thriving cult of the Virgin had already given rise to the building of ornate 'Lady Chapels', to celebrate the mother of Christ and to contain her altar. Meanwhile in 1216 the young King Henry III, aged only nine, had succeeded his father King John and within a few years was already showing a precocious interest in the cult of St. Edward (King Edward the Confessor) and in the abbey at Westminster. It was in this context that under Abbot William de Humez the monks at Westminster adopted a plan to follow the example of their colleagues elsewhere, by building a Lady Chapel to the east of the eastern end of the abbey. This new plan and the young king's enthusiasm came together on May 16th 1220 when, still a minor of 12 years old, he laid the foundation stone of the projected new chapel and was himself crowned, for a second time, in the abbey on the following day.[51]

The campaign for the Lady Altar by itself was over. It was now to become a campaign for a Lady Chapel. Both the project of a new chapel and the active participation of the king in 1220 were small omens of the changes and the much greater building programmes which were to transform Westminster over the next fifty years.[52]

## B. Three more abbots of Westminster – as the centuries turned

During this crucial period, before and after the pivotal year 1200, there were three abbots who successively held the reins at the abbey.

## Abbot William Postard (1191–1200)
### The cost of a new abbot

After the death of Abbot Walter of Winchester in 1190, the monks of Westminster had been able to achieve their constant aim to have an abbot of their own choice, rather than one imposed on them by the king or his agents; but this had only been achieved at a great cost.[53] The new abbacy of William Postard therefore began with a heavy 'fine' of 1500 marks (£1000) to the Crown, probably exacted for the monks' right to hold a free election of their abbot. This placed a sudden burden on the monks and particularly on the new abbot to raise sufficient moneys to discharge the debt to the Crown.

The new abbacy also began, as earlier abbacies had done, with expensive embassies to the pope in Rome. However these secured for the abbey, (a) a renewed confirmation of the abbey's now time-honoured exemption from any ecclesiastical control save the pope's and (b) the right for the abbot to wear the mitre and other special vestments.[54] More significantly the pope's 'bulls' made it clear that the abbey had obviously been suffering from violent intrusions and depredations during the recent vacancies, against which the pope could give at least a verbal protection for the future, but no redress for the past.[55]

### Sources and destinations of income

These expenses and the large fine increased the financial difficulties under which the abbey was labouring towards the end of the century.[56] But the abbot was

---

51 Henry had hurriedly been crowned for a first time in 1216 at Gloucester when his father had unexpectedly died, at a time of continuing disputes with the barons. London, Westminster and the abbey were unsafe, because of fighting and military presences, see pp. 131-2 and 137 below. Henry also donated his gold spurs to the chapel.

52 For the building of the new Lady Chapel, see pp. 245 ff. below. For the building development by the monks in Tothill Street, designed to help pay for the chapel, see pp. 47 and 271. For the rebuilding of the abbey itself, see pp. 247 ff.

53 For the vacancy of one year after Abbot Walter's abbacy and before William's election, see p. 94 above; and for the previous vacancy before Abbot Walter was appointed, see p. 89.

54 WACs 181 (exemption), and 180 (vestments), both made on the 13th January, 1192.

55 WACs 181 and 182. (also 13th January,1192). The word 'bull' stems from the latin *bulla*, meaing the leaden seal attached to the pope's edicts.

56 Harvey, *WA Estates*, 64.

apparently able to discharge the whole amount of the fine in seven years from his election, according to the fifteenth century historian of the abbey, John Flete. It is not at all clear how he did this. He did make some small-scale land transactions in London and Westminster, and others in more distant estates, but it is difficult to believe that these were sufficiently fruitful to make any great impact on the discharge of the spectacular debt with which he was faced.[57] Like his predecessors he also made it his task to protect and increase the revenue which could flow from the abbey's rights to present priests to livings in parishes and its ability to require annual 'pensions' from the incumbents in its churches, but again the figures involved hardly account for his apparent success in restoring the abbey's balance with the Crown.[58]

One other potential source of new revenue for the hard-pressed abbot was one which arose directly from the abbey's estate in Westminster itself. Two major grants ('confirmations') of lands in Endiff and Longditch were made by the abbot to the two major royal officers who replaced their predecessors during William's abbacy; namely the king's new treasurer, William of Ely, and the new royal chamberlain, Robert Mauduit.[59] In addition two important licences were granted by the abbot, to Robert Mauduit and to Henry Marshall, the bishop of Exeter, for each of them to have his own private chapel on his Westminster property, which he could attend more conveniently than having to attend the parish church of St. Margaret.[60]

Unfortunately none of the records of these four transactions reveal how much the recipients had to pay by way of premiums for these benefits; and only a comparatively small sum of yearly rents is known. We could guess that some appreciable premiums were paid: but of course the abbot and convent may have preferred to be generous and undemanding towards such powerful persons, on the grounds that they were able and might be willing to benefit the abbey in other ways. So this otherwise good source of additional revenue must remain merely a potential one, so far as we can tell.

Another main feature of William's abbacy suggests that, so far from accumulating and diverting revenue in order to pay off the debts incurred by the abbey in his early years, he was unusually generous in assigning income and sources of income to other recipients, such as the whole convent of monks or one or other of the monastic departments within the abbey which served the abbey's daily needs. The convent, the infirmarer, the kitchener, the chamberlain and the sacrist were successive

---

57  WACs 307, 309, 314, 316, 319, 322, 324, 395. These are all listed in Mason, *WA People*, p. 71, but it does not appear to me that overall they were significantly profitable, unless of course the now-unquantifiable effects of progressive inflation soon converted these dealings into appreciable profit. By one largish grant, of a Lincolnshire manor (WAC 322), the abbot managed to secure a good income of £12 for the monks' 'chamber', but this was already-hypothecated income and gave the abbot little room for repayments of the major debt. In any case how does a figure such as £12, even annually, weigh against a debt of £1000, let alone other expenses which had also been incurred under the new Abbot William?

58  The abbot and the convent had been receiving support from Richard fitz Nigel, the king's treasurer who was now the bishop of London as well, see WACs 212 - 218, without any apparent signs of the friction which the abbey's relationship with the bishop of London sometimes created.

59  WACs 313 (1196) and 311 (1194 x 1200). For William of Ely, see pp. 156-7 and 159 below, and for Robert Mauduit, see pp. 159-64 below.

60  WACs 312 (1195 x 1200) and 230 (1194 x 1198). For these two other chapels, see p. 161-2 below.

61  The convent, for the pittancer : WAC 317. The infirmarer : WAC 321. The convent, for the kitchener : WAC 326. The chamberlain : WACs 315 and 322. The sacrist : WACs 225, 323, and 481. But the assignment (of as much as £14 pa., by WAC 321) to the infirmarer had a dual function, both to pay for the needs of the sick monks in the infirmary and to pay for the celebration of an 'anniversary' for the abbot, for which the infirmarer was made responsible.

beneficiaries of this policy.[61] This is hardly the picture of an abbot with a strict programme for building up assets in order to pay off the abbey's debts. And yet according to the only authority we have, he did succeed in his aim to pay off the huge debt to the Crown, but without there being substantive evidence as to how he managed to do so, and in the face of evidence that he was not sacrificing the interests of the convent in order to achieve this discharge.

### Complaints from the monks

It may therefore be ironic that shortly before William Postard's abbacy ended, he appears to have been the subject of complaints addressed to the pope by disgruntled monks, including certainly the sacrist and maybe other departmental heads. A delegation from the abbey had reached the pope in the spring of 1199, a year before the abbot's death. The papal bulls which resulted included some favourable ones which confirmed the privileges and immunities of the abbey and ordered that everyone was to comply with them. But others were condemnatory. In particular the abbot was ordered not to alienate churches and other possessions which belonged to the whole community of monks, without the consent of the convent *or the greater or wiser part of it*.[62] But these surviving records of the abbacy show that Abbot William regularly obtained the convent's consent to his actions, except in a few instances when he was assigning income or assets *within the abbey, ie. to the convent itself or to one of the monastic offices.[63]

So in May 1200 he may have died a disappointed man, 'seemingly under a cloud', as Dr. Mason has suggested. However one has to remember that more records of that period may be missing than one would normally expect; the missing ones might have painted a rather different picture, and it is

clear that the historian John Flete, writing more than five centuries ago when surviving documents may have been more numerous than now, regarded Abbot William as *'having conferred many benefits on the abbey'*, in addition to clearing the huge debt off the abbey's slate.[64]

## Abbot Ralph of Arundel (1200 –1214)
### Another deposition

Like his earlier predecessor Gervase, Abbot Ralph occupies a distinctive place as another abbot of Westminster who after about thirteen years in office was deposed; this time by order of the pope's legate Nicholas de Romanis, Bishop of Tusculum. Ralph's abbacy seems to have been undermined by dissensions with his monks, and there can be little doubt that this was part of the background to his eventual deposition. A good deal of the responsibility for this situation lay with him, but one can also see that the general body of monks were too ready to find fault initially with their abbot.

It should also be said in Abbot Ralph's favour that the times were out of joint for him. His abbacy coincided substantially with the very troubled years of King John's reign, when strong ecclesiastical and secular conflicts raged – between the king and the Pope Innocent III (leading to England being placed under a papal 'Interdict' for a period of five years), and between the king and his barons (leading eventually to civil war and the making of Magna Carta after the abbot's deposition). Such international and national antagonisms, affecting all churches in the kingdom and the atmosphere and functioning of all surrounding civil institutions, were hardly conducive to happy relations within the abbey. Indeed during the civil war the town of Westminster was the scene of military confrontations, and the king had even had to give orders forbidding the soldiery in his own garrison at Westminster

62 WAC 186 (30th April 1199). Strictly speaking, canon law prohibited any alienation, with or without the consent of the whole body of monks, but neither the papacy nor the body of monks insisted on this degree of strictness, provided that the consent was obtained; see Harvey *WA's Estates*, pp. 83-5.
63 See Mason, *WA People*, p. 72.
64 Flete, *History of WA*, ed. Robinson, p. 98.

from entering the abbey itself or its cemetery and from injuring any of the monks or other residents.[65]

### Conflicts between the abbot and his monks

However disputes about the alienation of abbey property by the abbot did lie behind much of the 'controversy and contention' between Ralph and his monks.[66] For many years this had now been a familiar theme in the wrangle between the abbots and their monks, and it was one of the factors which led to an eventual large-scale 'division of goods' between them in 1225, for which the monks had been arguing. But disposals to other people of properties belonging to the abbey were not the only subject about which Abbot Ralph and the convent disputed. For his part the abbot also acted high-handedly in his attitude towards certain assets which on any view now belonged to his monks in their own right.

For example his predecessor, William Postard, had confirmed to the convent their ancient claim to hold the manor of Benfleet, but it seems that Abbot Ralph had again received possession of it and retained it himself for several years, with a consent from the monks which was given only reluctantly and presumably under some form of duress. Led by Robert of Moulsham, the first leader of the campaign on behalf of the Lady Altar and now their prior, the monks continued to be unhappy

with this. In due course they managed to obtain the abbot's concession to restore the manor to them, but only at the price of their agreeing, at his 'request and wish', to pay for the celebration each year of four additional feasts with 'copes and processions', and with suitable drink and food afterwards; all to be provided at their expense by their obedientary, the pittancer, to whom the manor had been assigned.[67] So all was resolved apparently amicably in smooth Latin, but it must have been a bitter negotiation: the convent were being forced for a second time to accede to the wishes of the abbot, in order to get their manor back.

Analogous pressures were brought to bear upon the convent by the abbot in relation to rights held by the convent in two other manors.[68] But in each case the convent came back fighting, and the abbot had to be content with a dignified withdrawal, dressed up in some more smooth and obscure Latin. However it cannot have made relations between them any happier.

As regards the main theme of contention, namely the alienations of abbey property by the abbot, there is no doubt that he was guilty in several instances of doing this without obtaining the concurrence of the convent. Indeed his successor Abbot William de Humez had subsequently to indulge in litigation in order to recover three large areas of land, in Wheathampstead (Herts), Feering (Essex) and in Pershore (Worcs), which Ralph had transferred away from the abbey without the

---

65  WAC 151. This was in October 1215 while King John was besieging Rochester Castle which the rebels had occupied. In 1216 a rebel group in Westminster was denied entry to the abbey and in revenge seized the royal regalia.

66  Flete, *ibid.*, p. 100. See also Harvey, *WA Estates*, 83-4.

67  WACs 345 and 332 (1200 x 1214). Dr. Mason, *WA People*, at p. 74, reads the charter as indicating that the proposal to have the four extra feasts was that of the prior and convent alone, but I would think that both parties were happy to have the additional ceremonies; while it was the abbot who was demanding *payment* for these as the price of his restoration of the manor. Naturally it was the convent who requested restoration of 'our manor', but the falling of the expense on the convent was at his request, as the Latin indicates. The celebrations would of course add to the ceremonial dignity of the abbey; and provided that the cost did not fall on him, the abbot was happy to have the opportunity to preside on such occasions.

68  WACs 335 (the convent's manor of Parham, Sussex); and 336 (the convent's 'pension' of £14 from the churches of Oakham and Hambleton in Rutland), Mason, *WA People*, pp. 74-5. For Parham, see also p. 122 above.

69  *CRR*, vol. VIII, pp. 212 and 265; vol. X, p. 187.

monks' consent.[69]  We have few coherent abbey records about such disposals by abbots,[70] but the legal actions instituted by his successor indicate that some at any rate of the monks' complaints were justified.

### The pope's Interdict, and the deposition of Abbot Ralph

But in any case between 1208 and 1213/14 there had been no one to whom the monks could appeal about the abbot's actions, because of the great gulf which had separated England and the Roman church.  During this period King John and Pope Innocent III were at complete loggerheads, over the existence of any right on the king's part to choose, or at least to share in the choice of, a new archbishop for the see of Canterbury, which had become vacant.  As a result of the king's indignant refusal to accept the pope's choice of Stephen Langton as archbishop, England had been placed under the pope's 'interdict', debarring it from the exercise of any ecclesiastical functions by the clergy,[71] and in 1209 the king who had defiantly seized ecclesiastical property was himself excommunicated by the pope.  It was not until 1213 that the king surrendered, accepted Langton and agreed to be the pope's vassal.  So peace was restored and the interdict was lifted.

At the king's invitation, the pope then sent Nicholas the Bishop of Tusculum to England as his papal legate, who (among his other functions) visited and stayed at Westminster Abbey for eighteen days in the autumn of 1213, having long discussions with the convent about their grievances against Abbot Ralph and the reform of the administration.  The sequel was that soon after Christmas in 1213 Abbot Ralph was sentenced by the legate to be deposed.  On the 23rd January 1214 the sentence of deposition was carried out by an external abbot, Nicholas of Waltham Abbey, and Ralph's seal was symbolically broken before the whole chapter of the Westminster monks.[72]  But, although Ralph had been deposed, he lived for another nine years at the abbey and was treated better than Abbot Gervase had been, since the manors of Sunbury and Teddington (Middlesex) were provided for his separate maintenance.  And when he died, his body was even allowed to be buried in the nave of the abbey.

### Protecting abbey interests

In spite of the disgrace which finally overtook him, Ralph had in other respects sought to promote and protect the interests of the abbey during the difficult years of John's reign.  Recognising the advantages which the abbey could gain from the support of powerful figures, he had cultivated them with appropriate grants (all made with full assent and participation by the convent).  Such figures included **Geoffrey fitz Peter**, the justiciar and Earl of Essex, to whom the abbot and his monks granted for his lifetime the vill of Claygate in Surrey (a vill which had been assigned to the almonry, and so the justiciar's rent of £3 was now to be paid to the almoner); **Ralph fitz Stephen**, the king's close confidant and personal chamberlain, who received a grant of 'all the land' in Longditch which a serjeant of the abbey's sacristy had restored to the abbey, with a full record of the grant inscribed in the abbey's great book, the *martyrology* (because no doubt Ralph fitz Stephen had been a great benefactor to the abbey); and **Alexander of Swerford**, the learned officer of the exchequer and a canon of St. Paul's church, who received from the

---

70  cf. eg. WAD 129, a ragged note about disposals by some abbots.  It is probable that the 40 acres in Feering for which the next abbot had to go to law was the 'land' called Little Coggeshall which Ralph had let to Aubrey de Vere, in exchange for Aubrey surrendering a claim to the manor of Feering: WAC 331 (a final concord in 1201, in a legal action between the abbot and Aubrey).  Little Coggeshall had been part of Feering, as the concord states.

71  See also p. 166 below for the effect of the interdict. For Matthew Paris's 'silent' bell, see Plate 8, at p. 167.

72  See Mason, *WA People*, pp. 77-8.

abbey the stone houses and lands at Ludgate which had once belonged to one of Henry II's closest confidants, **William Turpin**.[73]

It is noticeable how both Abbot Ralph and his predecessor, Abbot William, were involved in more court actions ending in final concords ('fines'), all duly recorded before the justices of the Westminster Bench, than any abbots before them had been. This probably reflects the easier availability, since Henry II's reign, of royal justice before the Bench when it sat regularly in Westminster during the decades on either side of 1200, rather than any greater personal sense of litigiousness (or compromise) on the part of the later abbots. Abbot William Postard had been involved in six, and Abbot Ralph in four, of the surviving final concords before the Bench in Westminster, whereas Abbot Walter (1175 - 1190) had taken part in only two.[74]

## Abbot William of Humez (1214–1222)

### Early problems

The deposition of Abbot Ralph, which must have been as humiliating to the abbey as it was to him, was quickly followed by the appointment of another outsider. A Norman, William of Humez, who came from Le Hommet in Manche and had recently been serving as the prior of Frampton Priory in Dorset, was chosen and put in post at Westminster, within scarcely more than three months from the deposition.[75] Although he was known to have diplomatic

skills, the new abbot quickly found himself facing two quite different but linked problems.

Both these problems stemmed from the same root, namely the controversy which, as we have seen, had been progressively growing between the abbots and the convent of other monks, about a beneficial distribution of the abbey's assets between the abbot and his monks, and the issue of an abbot's power to dispose of these if he did not have the consent of the convent.

The 'losses' of property which the abbey had sustained during Abbot Ralph's time, without the convent's consent, had led to his deposition. Such losses were wrongful, but the convent could not challenge the new holder until after that abbot's death, and then only by action in the courts.[76] We do not know how many properties Abbot Ralph had alienated, but as already described, his successor soon started at least three legal actions to recover rural properties wrongly disposed of by Ralph – one of them to Robert Vere, the earl of Oxford.[77]

None of these three lost areas was an inroad on the estate of Westminster itself. But it seems that there was at least one other area, a nearby fourth one, which Abbot Ralph had let to the same earl without the convent's consent. This area included a wood called Eastgrove (*Estgrove*), formerly part of the Knightsbridge estate of the abbey, which

---

73  WACs 484, 476 and 477 (Geoffrey fitz Peter); 328 and 306 (Ralph fitz Stephen); 327 (Alexander) and 386 (Turpin). See also below at pp. 166-9 (Geoffrey fitz Peter); pp. 172-3 (Ralph fitz Stephen); pp. 170-72 (Alexander of Swerford); pp. 157-9 (William Turpin) for each of them respectively. There may well have been an earlier contact between the justiciar and Abbot Ralph, because the justiciar (through his wife who had been the heiress of the Mandeville family, old-time benefactors of the abbey of Westminster) had a patronal interest in Hurley Priory (which Geoffrey of Mandeville I had given to WA), and the abbot had been the prior of Hurley before becoming abbot at Westminster, see Mason, WA *People*, pp. 72-3 and 75. For the connections between Geoffrey fitz Peter and the abbey, see also Turner, *Men raised from the Dust*, pp. 61-2, 63 and 64. Geoffrey fitz Peter was the epitome of all 'new men', whom the Angevins, and Henry I before them, had made their officers, advisers and 'familiars', see the extensive biography of him in Turner, *ibid*, p. 35 ff.

74  Abbot William: WACs 310, 314, 316, 320, and 325. WAC 324 also involved Abbot William, but the court had sat at Northampton. Abbot Ralph: WACs 330, 331, 334, 338. Abbot Walter: WACs 287 and 296.

75  Although he was said to have been 'elected' (*Flete*, 101), in the context this probably means that he was first nominated, presumably by the king, and then elected by the monks. Cf. Mason, *WA People*, 86.

76  Sutherland, *Assize of Novel Disseisin*, p. 212.

77  CRR. vol. VIII/212, 265, 288, 304, and vol. X/187. See p. 132 above for the three main areas reclaimed by Abbot William of Humez in the king's court.

Abbot William was now able to recover from the earl in another compromise of a legal action.[78]

### The abbot's appeasement of the convent

More significant in the long run was the wider problem of the distribution of abbey property between the abbot (St. Benedict's supreme manager for a whole abbey) and the rest of the monks. This issue has been put into its historical context above.[79] There seems no doubt that now in the thirteenth century the problem was coming to a head, with the convent becoming more restive and applying more pressure on the abbot. It is not surprising therefore to find that William Humez had to tackle some of the convent's concerns, but even at this late stage the treatment of the problem was still piecemeal, rather than a comprehensive attempt to still the convent's complaints. The first comprehensive attempt had to wait until 1225, three years after this abbot's death.

The first step taken by William Humez was to allocate in 1214-5 the sum of just over £150 pa. to the convent's kitchener, contributed in specified sums from named manors.[80] This was in place of, and an increase on, the daily sum of 8s. which by custom had been the income within which the kitchener had previously had to work. It may be that this new yearly income enabled, or was thought to enable, the kitchener to plan further ahead and with more assurance, and that the named sources of his income and the amounts of the named manors' contributions towards it gave him a degree of security over it. But in view of the fact that we know of no document formally recording a *grant* of the earlier allowance of 8s. per day (called 'the ancient levy'), it may be that it was William Humez's action in actually recording the new income *in writing* which conveyed a sense of the security which the kitchener or the whole convent really sought.[81]

But the abbot later had to add two other grants to increase the convent's assets. First the annual income of the monks' kitchener was further supplemented by an assignment of 40s. from the profits receivable from the manor of Hampstead, and the infirmarer was granted in about 1215 *both* a similar annual sum of 40s. (the recovery of which the abbot had, in effect, just won in a legal action in the king's court against Ivo of Deene, referred to below), *plus* certain tithes (which the abbot had won in a compromise reached in another dispute).[82] So the abbot was using the success which he had had in resolving disputes with two tenants of abbey lands, to increase the income which two of the monks' officers in charge of abbey departments could draw on.

We do not know for certain what need had given rise to the additional grant of 40s. pa. to the convent's kitchener, but presumably even with the substantial annual sum of c. £150 which the abbot had already provided, the kitchener had found himself short of sufficient income to provide properly for the monks'

---

78 CP 25(1) 146/6/34. Westlake, *Westminster Abbey*, vol 1/59. The reasons for my thinking that this small but more local recovery was on a par with Abbot William's three other claims in more remote parts are that both the earl and a member of his family (Aubrey de Vere) were implicated in one of those three other actions *and* in the Estgrove action, *and* that an area in Feering was also a subject of claim in both actions. So these three elements were common to each. In effect Eastgrove had been taken from Knightsbridge and let to the earl, who held the adjoining manor of Kensington and seems to have wanted and had obtained the valuable wood.

79 See pp. 125-7 above.

80 WAD 629a-b; printed in Harvey, *Walter de Wenlock*, pp. 215-6. See pp. 124-5 above.

81 The only references to the former daily allowance of 8s. are *indirect* ones, (a) in WAC 335, relating to Parham, during Abbot Ralph Arundel's time, and (b) in Abbot William Humez's allocation of the yearly income of c. £150, WAD 629. Even after the latter, the 'ancient levy' of 8s. daily was still to be the basis for the kitchener's income, if any of the named manors failed to produce their contributions, see Harvey, *ibid.*, p. 216.

82 WAM 32354; and Stenton, *English Feudalism 1066-1166*, p. 267. See also p. 125 above.

table. But the abbot's more immediate motives for his other grant to the infirmarer, were that the abbot wished to provide for an 'honourable' anniversary for himself (which the infirmarer was to administer) and, as part of the celebration each year of that anniversary, to furnish alms for 100 poor persons and some 'relief' as well for the convent itself.

The abbot's successful legal action in the king's court which provided part of his above donation of 40s. to the infirmarer's funds is illuminating about the obligation of hospitality which certain tenants owed towards the abbot and his retinue when he visited them in the course of his periodical circuit of his manors.

### The scale of 'hospitality' for the abbot

Ivo, the tenant of the manor of Deene in Northamptonshire, had refused to provide the annual hospitality which (in addition to rent) the terms of his tenancy had in fact laid on him, and as a result the abbot had suffered damage in having to pay all the costs of a visit which he had made to that part of Northamptonshire on his circuit of visits to outlying manors. Ivo's attitude had been an outright refusal in principle to provide any hospitality, but in taking so extreme a position he may have been trying his luck in the face of, perhaps, demands for additional rent on a renewal of the tenancy, or (in his eyes) excessive demands as regards the scale of the hospitality owed. However he agreed in due course that he did owe an annual hospitality, and in view of the costs he had caused the abbot, he agreed to pay a new annual rent of £18, increased from the £16 which he had paid hitherto; but in return he succeeded in securing a perpetual tenancy for himself *and his heirs*. As a result, the abbey never recovered possession of the manor over the following centuries.

The details of the free hospitality which Ivo owed to the abbot are spelt out in a detailed list in the 'final concord' which was reached and registered before the court at Westminster in February 1215.[83] They show that the abbot had seven principal officers, who would look after the different departments of his household: his steward, chamberlain, pantler (ie. the provisioner), butler, usher, cook and marshal. The abbot had to give two weeks' notice of his intended visit, and his seven officers would then precede his eventual arrival, each to be allowed to take charge of his own scene of action in Ivo's establishment. After an honourable reception of the abbot, food and drink were to be supplied on the day of arrival, and a midday meal on the following day; but Ivo had also to make additional payments of money, because he was expected to hand over twelve pence to each of the abbot's seven officers: no doubt this was because, as the host, he would otherwise have had to provide staff to do the work which the abbot's servants were to do. After the meal on the second day, if the abbot wished to stay longer, including another night, he would have to pay a reasonable price for everything needed by himself and his retinue.

So one gets a fairly clear picture of the style in which an abbot of Westminster expected to be accomodated, and this no doubt reflected the scale and manner in which his own household needs were provided for at the abbey and at his country house at La Neyte. It seems that William Humez had set himself to sort out his entitlements to distant hospitality, because he also made a similar agreement with Robert Foliot, the tenant of the abbey's manor of Longdon in Worcestershire, who was under the same obligation.

In that case the abbot did not have to resort to legal proceedings, but there were clearly arguments with the tenant who had lost, or perhaps pretended to have lost, his original charter (which may have contained inconvenient material). However the abbot not only secured the same terms for the

---

83 Stenton, *ibid*. pp. 70-2, and 267-8; see also Mason, *People*, pp. 84-5.

hospitality which he could expect in the 'western parts' of the country, but he was also able to increase the rent for the manor from £24 to £28.[84] This increase of more than 16% was probably the best the abbot could obtain to reflect the results of inflation which had been raging, rather than extra costs caused by any outright refusal to provide hospitality, as had happened on the abbot's visit to Ivo at Deene.

### The aftermath of civil war, and the Dauphin

Another pressing problem which arose in Westminster itself and had had to be faced by the abbot early in his abbacy was the result of the disputes and civil war between the barons and King John which marked the last years of his reign. These events had brought the baronial rebels to London, which they crucially occupied in and after May 1215. So the abbey and the palace were now only a mile away from a rebel stronghold. The king at first decided to come to terms with the barons, and there was a brief interlude while Magna Carta was negotiated and signed in June 1215.

But by August the great Charter had been annulled by the pope, whose vassal King John now was, and it became a dead letter. London was still occcupied by the rebels (as the Charter itself had allowed), and fighting began again. Almost certainly the precinct of the abbey at Westminster was invaded by soldiery from the king's forces, or at least was under severe threat of violence from either side. The abbot and monks had to petition the king for protection, and by the end of October 1215 John, in the course of his siege of Rochester, had issued an order forbidding his knights, sergeants and other soldiers from entering the abbey precinct

or the church itself or its cemetery, and ordering them not to cause injury to the monks or allow others to do so.[85] It seems that with London acting as the rebels' stronghold, Westminster had been made into a royal base with a garrison and that the king's soldiers, meant to be guarding the palace, the abbey and the town, were misbehaving, as soldiers do.

But in 1216, the following year, England was invaded by Louis the Dauphin of France, who had been invited over the Channel by the rebellious barons, and he now joined them in London, a mile away from Westminster. Both the treasurer, William of Ely, and the royal chamberlain, Robert Mauduit made the grave mistake of joining the rebels, and were each rewarded by King John with the loss of their posts and forfeiture of their lands, both in Westminster and everywhere else.[86] But the abbot, having little choice, made no such mistake. Louis, for his part, ended up in unusual possession of many of the (comparatively recent) English exchequer and chancery records, which were either seized by him from Westminster or the Tower of London, or delivered to him by the absconding treasurer, William of Ely. When, after King John's death, Louis eventually was handsomely paid to leave the country in 1217, he had to agree in the treaty of peace to hand all the records back.[87]

### The Virgin Mary – her altar and chapel

The cult of the Virgin Mary and her 'Lady Altar' within the abbey was still being promoted while Abbot William Humez was in post, but it may be that the original campaign which Robert of Moulsham, the earlier precentor and prior, had initiated before 1190 was beginning to flag towards the end of the

---

84  WAD 304.
85  WAC 151 (24th October 1215). According to the charter, there were even 'king's men dwelling' in the precinct. Had they previously been licensed by an abbot to be there? By Ralph, or by William?
86  See p. 159 (the treasurer) and p. 164 below (the chamberlain). Fortunately for both of them John died in the same year, and they each did penance to the regency council (for young Henry III) and recovered their lands. For the Dauphin's invasion, with mercenaries, see Plate 8 on p. 167.
87  Richardson, 'William of Ely', *TRHS* 15 (1932) p. 58 and Smith, 'Treaty of Lambeth', EHR 94 (1979) at 577. Louis was paid 10,000 marks (nearly £6667) to go.

second decade of the next century. It must have been with the abbot's blessing that, to give the campaign new life, the grander concept of a new chapel for St. Mary, to be built at the eastern end of the abbey with the Lady Altar in it, was developed before 1220. And it must have been William Humez who was present to represent the abbey both on the 16th May 1220 when the twelve-year old king, Henry III, laid the foundation stone of the new chapel, and on the following day when in a great ceremony before the abbey's High Altar the young king was crowned for a second time, on this occasion by the once-disputed archbishop of Canterbury, Stephen Langton.

### The great arbitration

The final significant act of William Humez's abbacy was the abbey's participation in the great arbitration about (once again) the abbey's claim to 'exemption' from the powers of the bishop of London, and about the geographical extent of the parish of St. Margaret's of Westminster (which was accepted to be co-extensive with the abbot's ecclesiastical jurisdiction in Westminster). This arbitration has been dealt with in Chapter 2 and Appendix B, so far as the second of these issues is concerned.[88] But the primary reason for the setting up of the arbitration was the familiar dispute as to the 'exemption' of the abbey. The bishop, Eustace of Fauconberg, a king's clerk and financial agent, who had already succeeded William of Ely as the king's treasurer in 1217, had then in 1221 been created bishop of London as well. Copying some of his predecessors and egged on by the canons of St. Paul's, Bishop Eustace returned to the well-ventilated issue whether the abbey was independent of the bishop and answerable only to the pope.[89] Challenged on this yet again, the abbey restated its now familiar assertion of its independence from the bishop of London, and on an appeal by the abbey to Rome, the pope referred the issue to three judges-delegate, led by the archbishop of Canterbury. Shortly before Abbot William Humez's death in 1222, the abbey was once again – and finally – vindicated by the decision of the arbitrators, in its claim to be exempt from the bishop's supervision. But the other issues relating to the boundaries of the parish of St. Margaret's church, which had also been referred to the same papal arbitrators and were decided by them were more complicated.[90]

88  See pp. 36 and App. B at pp. 396-9.
89  For previous occasions when the same issue was raised and decided, see pp. 75, 87, 90, and 129 above
90  WAM 12753; Major, ed., *Acta S. Langton,* pp. 69-73; *Flete,* pp. 61-3.  Again see note 88 above.

# CHAPTER 8

# Abbey servants as residents in the town
# 1189-1216

Before 1190, the first wave of government men had been flocking into the town. But the abbey's 'serjeants' and other senior servants had already been present for a century and more, and they too were now flourishing in the decades on either side of 1200 – or perhaps they have become far more visible to us, because of the proliferation and survival of records. In favour of some of these senior servants, a number of estates in the Longditch and Tothill districts had already been created by the abbey; and in turn lesser members of its lay personnel had received smaller properties.[1]

So as the turn of the centuries approach, we can see the convergence of three factors : -

(a) the growing detail of the abbey's organisation;

(b) the extent to which the monks had made houses and land in Westminster available to their servants; and

(c) the means by which the monks were achieving their aim of recovering, or were being helped to recover, some of their 'lost' lands within the manor.

Let us look at some of these members of abbey staff, as residents in Westminster near the year 1200, whose lives and activities illustrate some aspects of this convergence.

**Master Geoffrey Picot,** was the first of the seneschals (stewards) of Abbot William Postard, whose abbacy began in 1190. He may have been appointed by Postard as soon as the latter became abbot, or have already been in the steward's post under the previous Abbot Walter. Geoffrey was probably already living nearby before he became steward, but certainly the Westminster property held by him in the early 1190s stood in Longditch Street near the abbey. In about the middle of that decade, perhaps when he retired or lost his post, he sold his interest in his land there to Henry Marshal, the bishop of Exeter, who bought it on behalf of the see of Exeter. The bishop was the brother of another famous house-owner in Westminster, the great William Marshal, who served each of the first four Angevin kings in turn and held property at the Charing cross-roads.[2] The bishop was subsequently able to build a private chapel at this property, with the abbey's permission, to go with the house which served as a base for the bishop and his successors in Westminster.[3]

This property provides a good illustration of the way in which different interests derived from land could continue to survive after physical possession of the land itself changed hands, and how the people involved then dealt with such interests. Geoffrey had himself been a hereditary tenant of this land from another 'landlord', who stood between Geoffrey and the abbey. For his tenancy Geoffrey owed an annual rent of 4d. to this landlord. Even after he had sold his own interest to the bishop and given him possession of the land, he continued to owe this rent to his own landlord. But shortly afterwards this landlord made a charitable donation, 'in soul alms', of

---

1   See pp. 20-1 above.
2   See p. 29 above. The bishop had owed his ecclesiastical promotions entirely to the influence which his brother the marshal had at court, Crouch, *Wm. Marshal,* p. 143.
3   WAM 17312 (WAC 230; 1194 x 1198] and Mason, *WA People*, pp. 71-2. Cf. also the Mauduit chapel, and the conditions imposed by the abbey, see p. 161 below.

Geoffrey's annual rent of 4d. to the Lady Altar, so giving the warden of the Altar the right to receive the annual 4d. from Geoffrey.[4]

Geoffrey's stewardship can have lasted no more than about five years after Postard became abbot, because by at least the autumn of 1195 he had retired or been replaced by a new steward called **Theobald**.[5] This was probably the occasion for Geoffrey giving up his Longditch property to the bishop.

But like many other Westminster people (such as Theobald, his successor, who came from Feering, an estate of the abbey in Essex), Geoffrey also had had roots in places outside Westminster. Aldenham in Hertfordshire (another manor belonging to the abbey, but one giving rise at this time to bouts of friction with the neighbouring abbey of St Alban's) was apparently his home town. There he already owned a number of 'houses', before receiving in the 1190s another two virgates (about 80 acres) of newly assarted land also in Aldenham from the abbey at Westminster. As an Aldenham property-holder, he was also useful as a suitable witness when an Aldenham messuage and land changed hands between other lay people in Westminster.[6] Geoffrey's large interests in Aldenham are comparable with the interests which Hugh of Colham, his predecessor as steward nearly 100 years before, had possessed in Cowley on the western boundary of Middlesex.[7]

Later, probably in about 1210, the abbey let to Geoffrey the house standing nearest to the abbey itself *within the precinct,* which Gilbert of Claygate, a serjeant in the almonry, had restored to the abbey before he joined the Third Crusade and left for the east in about 1189.[7] Since the grant to Geoffrey was made by the warden of the Lady Altar rather than by the abbot, it may be that even though the grant was made ostensibly on commercial terms, it was made as a favour, and that Geoffrey had himself made some previous donation to the Altar, for which the warden's grant was a form of acknowledgment. On the other hand it required at least one further significant annual rent: while the rent payable to the Lady Altar was 8d pa., that due to the 'chief lord', ie. the abbey itself, was 3s. 4d. This latter figure was one of the larger 'ground rents', probably because it was a special house in a special position close to the abbey. So Geoffrey was having to pay well for it, and this may indicate the depth of his pocket.

Geoffrey also held several other properties within Westminster. For example, he established (by a compromise) a right to an acre of meadow in the area of Longditch, probably near his own house, against the

---

4   WAC 445 (1194 x 1198). This shows how in the then condition of the law Geoffrey's liability to pay rent survived his disposal of the land. Geoffrey in his turn would probably have required a rent from the bishop, but we do not know how much that rent was. Because of the inflationary trends at this time and his own practical experience as an abbey steward, we can be sure that he had required at least no less rent from the bishop than the 4d which he himself still had to pay (now to the Lady Altar). So in effect the abbey now held both the 'reversion' to Geoffrey's landlord's interest (plus any rent payable to it by that landlord), and under the name of the Lady Altar, the 4d. rent due from Geoffrey – who in turn would receive whatever rent was due from the bishop, the tenant in possession. This result is made clear by the terms of WAC 445.

5    Mason *WA People*, p. 177; Maitland (ed), *Three Rolls of the King's Court* PRS XIV (1891) p. 127. It was shortly after this, in 1198, that a claim was made by a later relative of the first known steward, Hugh of Colham, that the post was a hereditary one, which he was entitled to hold: and the abbey had to buy his claim out, see p. 98, n. 21 above and WAC 310. Little is known about Theobald, and it is not known where he lived in Westminster, although there can be little doubt that he was already, or became, a resident. As steward he played his part as a fairly regular witness to charters (fifteen in all), and acted as proctor for the abbot in legal proceedings in the king's court.

6   WAC 319 (1191 x 1200); WAM 4461 and 4460 (WAC 466 and 467, 1200 x 1214). The Aldenham virgate was apparently about 40 acres, rather larger than usual: Harvey, *WA Estates*, p. 205.

7   See p. 98 above.

8   WAC 347. For Gilbert of Claygate, see pp. 101, 181-2.

engineer Roger Enganet in legal proceedings in October 1197 in the king's court in Westminster.[9] By another compromise in 1199 he also secured rights in four other houses in the town in other legal proceedings.[10]

The Picots were clearly a long-established Westminster family, but still held considerable interests in Aldenham. They were also favoured servants or associates of the abbey, with various members appearing frequently to witness charters in the abbey courts. A William Picot is also described as one of the abbey knights ('our knight') in the 1190s, when receiving a grant of a manor in Lincolnshire from the abbey, and he may have been a nephew or other kinsman of Geoffrey.[11]

**Richard of Dol**, the successor to the elusive **Theobald** (the intervening steward), was steward under the next abbot, Ralph of Arundel (1200-1214). His locative name, derived from Dol in Brittany, was one of many similar foreign names which may reflect the growing cosmopolitan character of Westminster, due in part to international trading at early fairs in the town.[12] Richard's official designation alternated between 'seneschal of the abbot' and 'seneschal of Westminster', so underlining again the personal lordship of the abbot over the whole of the abbey's 'liberty' of Westminster. During the whole of Ralph Arundel's abbacy, Richard

of Dol was playing a vigorous role, close to the abbot. His appearances as a witness to extant charters which were being executed or registered in the abbot's courts were frequent and number at least 34, and he was usually named in the charters as the first or principal witness and sometimes identified specifically as the seneschal.[13]

One property in Westminster which we know was held by Richard is recorded as 'land' which, we can deduce, lay probably on the east side of 'King Street'. Although no house on that 'land' is mentioned, it is highly likely in view of the 3s. rent which the property could command that there was one already standing on the land, and that this had been the residence in Westminster which Richard of Dol himself used. It had a frontage to the street of 22 feet, and its length was nearly 109 feet. Almost certainly it had been granted to him by the sacrist of the abbey, and probably a rent of 2s. was payable to the sacrist.[14] When Richard decided or had to move from it, he let it in the decade after 1200 at a rent of 3s. to Ralph son of Richard Testard, the reeve of Westminster at about that time.[15] Contemporaneously Richard of Dol made a charitable donation 'in soul alms' to the abbey (to provide lights for the high altar of St. Peter, which the sacrist administered) of 2s. per year, out of the 3s. rent which Ralph had now to pay to him.

9   CP 25(1) 146/1/11, and see Clay, 'Keepership of the Palace, 59 *EHR*, p. 7. The claim, made in new *mort d'ancestor* proceedings, suggests that there may have been some family relationship between Geoffrey Picot and Roger Enganet and, through the latter, with Ailnoth the engineer, Roger's father, whose widow Matilda was involved in the case. For Ailnoth, Enganet, and Matilda, see pp. 107-9 above.
10  CP 25(1) 146/2/3.
11  WACs 304, 322. The William Picot who was called the 'nephew' of Geoffrey (in WAC 304) may have been the son of the abbey knight William, rather than the knight himself. Geoffrey's son Richard also appears in that charter. Other members of the family in Westminster included 'Picot', the much earlier member of Abbot Crispin's household in about 1116, see p. 95 above; the Paul Picot who witnessed an important grant of the manor of Hendon, in WAC 245 (1121 x 1134); the Walter Picot who joined with Geoffrey Picot in witnessing the grant of a Lincolnshire manor to the knight William Picot in the 1190s (WAC 322), so making three Picots in one document; and Thomas Picot, who also owned property in Aldenham and was probably a later descendant of Geoffrey, see WAMs 4483 & 4485, and cf. Harvey *WA Estates*, pp. 115-6.
12  Rosser, *Med. Westminster*, pp. 97 and 191. For Henry III's later grant in 1245 to the abbey of a right to hold two fairs in Westminster, see p. 204 below.
13  Richard of Dol was named as a reeve of Westminster by Dr Rosser, *ibid.* pp 30 and 328, but I doubt this. Mason, *Beau. Cart.*, No. 191 which is cited does not support it. See also Mason, *WA People*, 353.
14  See WAD 357 (WAC 420) and WAM 17597.
15  WAM 17316 (WAC 419).

This house in 'King Street' is of particular interest, because it was one of the few houses, or plots of land, whose history can be traced over a long period of the thirteenth century, so that one can follow the trail of all its holders from probably before 1200, before it ultimately came back to the abbey in the second half of the century by way of charitable gift. So after a long sequence of years the abbey, at last in renewed possession of the house, was again in a position to relet it at a current rent, instead of the original rent fixed up to 70 years before. But as its history would take us into more distant parts of the century, after 1216, its detail is dealt with in a later chapter.[16]

At a later date, in 1225, someone also called Richard of Dol and identified as the steward of Westminster as well held a customary tenancy in an area of Battersea and Wandsworth, across the Thames, which was known as 'Bruges'. This may have been a son of the steward, rather than the old steward himself, since the latter must have been in office at least at the beginning of the century.[17]

**Edward the reeve**, who served as the reeve of Westminster for the period from at least some date in the 1180s until the mid-1190s, held probably the largest estate occupied by any abbey servant. It lay principally in the Tothill area, but he also probably held lands in three other areas further afield in Westminster. We cannot be certain whether the whole estate had been originally granted to him or to some earlier ancestor of his in the abbey's service; or which properties, if any, may have been subsequently purchased by himself, or indeed by his son John. But his own personal identification with Westminster and the abbey as a long-serving reeve became strong enough to secure for him the name 'Edward of Westminster'.

His Tothill estate lay on the north frontage of Tothill Street itself and in the area behind that frontage, in the sector bounded on the east by Longditch. The well known Mauduit family (both William Mauduit 1 and his son Robert, in turn) had been busy in buying up lands from various holders in those areas, after they had come to Westminster in the course of Henry II's removal of government offices to the town; and there is little doubt that much of the land so bought by them had previously been part of Edward's estate.[18]

Apparently a few houses already existed or were now in course of construction on the north side of Tothill Street. Edward himself sold half a house on the street to a Mauduit clerk, William of Hanslope (otherwise, 'William of the Temple'); and another house next door to Adam of Sunbury, the abbot's chamberlain, both at the nearer end of the street.[19] But further along the 'street' it is clear that there was still at least one arable field (or fields) actually bordering the 'great highway of Tothill'.[20] So the 'street' was far from built

---

16  See pp. 276-78 below.

17  WAM 5705* (dated 1225). The name Bruges was perhaps a corruption of *brycg*, OE, a bridge on the river Wandle, or even *bryggia* (old Norse), a quay on the Wandle or the Thames; cf. Gelling, *Place Names in the Landscape*, pp. 64-6. As regards the identity of this later Richard of Dol, cf. Mason, *WA People*, p. 250n. (the son?); Harvey, *Walter de Wenlock,* p. 217 and note, Rosser, *Medieval Westminster*, p. 330.

18  For the Mauduits, see pp, 113 ff. and 159 ff. See the charters Nos 183-200 printed in Mason, B*eauchamp Cart.*, pp. 107-117 for a long list of vendors to the Mauduits. Of these, charters Nos. 194-6 name Edward as an original source of two holdings of land, for each of which a large rent of 7s. was payable; and there may have been others which did not disclose *earlier* sources such as Edward's estate.

19  See WACs 446 and 409, and pp. 176-7 and 148 below. The half-house had already had an earlier tenant called 'Geoffrey the priest of Tothill', so it was not brand new. Another nearby tenant was Ulviva the laundress. and a next-door neighbour of the laundress was Master Arnulf Postard (the brother of Abbot Wm. Postard) and subsequently Robert of Croxley (who later became reeve of Westminster in about 1225), see WAC 441, CP 25(1) /146/5/22 and Rosser, Med. Westminster, p. 328.

20  Rosser, *Med. Westminster*, p. 30; Mason, *Beau. Cart.*, Nos. 197 and 198; and WAC 446. The arable field, of three acres in extent, had stretched from a 'meadow', belonging to the leper hospital of St. James, as far as the Tothill highway; so perhaps the arable field was a narrow close stretching across the modern St. James's Park.

up yet, and bigger 'commercial' developments of it remained to be carried out twenty or thirty years after 1200.[21]

The three other locations of properties in Westminster which were probably part of Edward's estate (and subsequently of his son, John) were in the area round the leper Hospital of St. James, the district of Aldwych, and the fields near the other leper Hospital of St. Giles, near Holborn. These are discussed below in relation to his son, John who is recorded as dealing with them.

It is not certain where Edward himself lived with his wife Cecily. It may have been at a house on Tothill Street or in the Tothill area where his main 'fee' lay.[22] Or another possibility for a residence of his was the large house which he finally let 'in perpetual inheritance' to Ralph Clerk and his heirs, at a satisfactory rent of 3s. 4d., probably in his last year or years as reeve.[23] Since this large house had once belonged to Brungar the champion, who had connections with the Spitalstrete area (between Charing crossroads and the leper Hospital of St. James), Edward may have retreated from the increasingly busy area at Tothill to that other, probably quieter, neighbourhood.[24] His tenure of the post of reeve ended in or before 1197, when he described himself in a charter as 'former reeve'.[25] He had two sons, Alan and John, of

whom Alan was probably the elder but seems to have disappeared; it was John who finally inherited his father's large estate.

A year or two before 1200, some of Edward's assets were set aside by him for a special purpose. He 'founded an anniversary' for himself, by donating rents to the value of £1. 10s. to the abbey, to pay for the provision of an annual celebration in his own memory each year, by processions, prayers and alms-giving.[26] While successive abbots and priors of Westminster had already been arranging such anniversaries for themselves or their relatives during the past century and before, this form of commemoration at the abbey in honour of an abbey servant, even if he was important both in his post and as a local landholder, was unusual.[27]

**John, son of Edward the reeve** came into his own when his father died in or shortly after 1197. Like his father, he too came to be known as John 'of Westminster', but he is curiously elusive in his position in Westminster society. We know of no employment of him either by the abbey or by the king, and he poses the question, Did he obtain the title 'of Westminster' simply by virtue of his large estate and the sales of properties which he made to the abbey?[28]

The main properties which he inherited

21 See pp. 270-1 below.
22 Such as his messuage next door to his own tenant, Master Wm. of Hanslope, the Mauduit clerk, see WAC 409.
23 WAC 406 (late C12, before 1197). This charter refers almost uniquely to the fact that an original occupational description, Ralph 'the clerk', had already by that time merged into a proper cognomen, 'Clerk', like a modern 'surname' - *non officio ita vocatus, sed cognomine*. This had happened often elsewhere, but not so explicitly.
24 For Brungar, see pp. 16 and 49 above.
25 WAC 446.
26 WAD 552; and see WAM 17323 (WAC 411, 1197 x 1200).
27 See Harvey, *WA Estates* 387ff and 373. Celebrations of 'anniversaries' for royal benefactors were also arranged by the abbey, see *ibid*. Edward was the first *abbey servant* for whom an anniversary is recorded; and the only earlier *lay people* possessing that honour were two members of the powerful Haverhill family of London, which had made large charitable donations to the abbey and had received rights of confraternity and burial in the abbey itself for their generosity; WACs 355 and 388, and see Harvey, *ibid*.
28 For his title, 'of Westminster', see CP 25(1) 146/5/22, where his widow Avicia called him by it. It may be that John only inherited it by virtue of the high-standing which his father the reeve had had. For John, see also CP(1)25 146/1/10, 146/2/5 and 146/2/25, re. 3 messuages, 1 curtilage and 6 acres in Westminster.

from his father were naturally in the Tothill area, but he also received or acquired lands in the neighbourhood of the leper Hospital of St James (including some land which actually lay within that hospital's churchyard), and further agricultural land in the Field of Westminster near Aldwych, and also in the Field of the other leper Hospital, St. Giles.[29]

John appears to have pursued a policy of splitting up the estate and selling off a considerable part of it. Many of his properties or the rents derived from them ended up back in the hands of the monks, no doubt to their great satisfaction. But there is not much evidence of pious generosity towards the abbey on John's part in reaching this result.

Most of his grants were sales at commercial prices; eg. a bundle of Westminster rents worth 8s. pa., sold to the prior for £3. 6s. 8d; and a sale of other rents worth 7s. 8d. to the Lady Altar for £4. 6s. 8d.[30] A sale of yet another group of rents also worth 7s. 8d. was made by him to Isabel Mauduit, wife of Robert Mauduit the king's chamberlain, for the price of £4. But when he sold these rents to Isabel, John knew that she wanted them specifically to donate them, as she quickly did, as free charitable gifts to the Lady Altar at the abbey.[31] So John collected his material reward, and Isabel perhaps collected her, no doubt greater, spiritual one.

When John did make a charitable gift to the Lady Altar, labelled 'in soul alms', of other land (probably near the leper Hospital of St.

James) worth 3s. 4d., it turned out to be not entirely charitable, because John required the payment to him of an annual rent of 2d. p.a. for his 'gift'.[32] Even when he granted a rent of 4s. pa. (for other Tothill land) to the Lady Altar 'for the souls of his parents and ancestors', it was because his mother Cecily had asked him to do so. Moreover the warden of the Altar had to pay a rent of 6d. back to John himself, so the gift was worth only 3s. 6d., not 4s. pa.[33]

In all, John received the large total of £12. 5s. 4d., plus two annual rents of 6d. and 2d., for his recorded disposals of some of the properties which he had inherited or had himself acquired (and these included one or two other grants to lay purchasers). For its part the abbey received land and rents, together worth 24s. p.a., from John himself (paying him £7. 13s. 4d., plus the two annual rents of 6d. and 2d., for the privilege).[34] And it also received free the further 7s. 8d. worth of John's former rents from the more generous Isabel Mauduit.

So we can see some hard business being done by Edward's son at various times during the sixteen years of King John's reign, amounting to the dispersal of a substantial part of one of the largest of the estates assembled by a principal servant (or his forebears). And, for a price, the monks were able to recover, via the market and Isabel's well-aimed generosity, considerable property

---

29 WAD 520-1 (WAC 441, temp. John); WAD 557b (WAC 408, temp. John). It is also worth noting that he appears to have entered into legal transactions with both the two abbey 'gardeners' mentioned below in the text at pp. 149-51 below.

30 WAD 557b (WAC 408, temp. John); WAD 520b-1 (WAC 441, temp. John). The purchase rates for these were, respectively, a little below and a little above the commercial average of ten.

31 WAC 449 & 450 (both temp. John). John son of Edward had agreed that Isabel might dispose of the rents as she wished, 'even to a religious house', so he contemplated such a gift; see p. 163 below. The purchase rate in this case was about the average, ten. Her gift to the abbey probably was connected with her husband's and her petition for donors' names to be entered in the abbey's 'book of martyrology', WAC 329 see p. 163 below. If so, there was a religious quid-pro-quo for Isabel's gift, which was also generous in secular terms.

32 WAD 557 (WAC 407, temp. John). The demand of even a small rent in return offended against the status of the label 'in soul alms', a label which should have represented a gift of 'pure' charity.

33 WAM 17393 (WAC 451, temp. John).

34 Disregarding the rents of 8d. pa. which John would receive, this gives a purchase figure of over 6 (quite generous to the abbey), but if one includes the 8d. rents, the figure is less generous. John got a fair commercial return.

in a fee which it had earlier 'lost'.

In addition to the Tothill properties whose rents John sold in these ways, his sales also revealed that he had held other properties elsewhere. These included: -

(a) one and a half acres of land which were actually enclosed in the churchyard of the church of the leper hospital of St. James;

(b) another meadow near the hospital;

(c) a messuage and land, near the hospital, which had been let to Ralph Clerk by Edward;

(d) seven and a half acres (probably arable, or land already used as market-gardens) in the 'Fields' near the Aldwych area, meaning probably the Field of Westminster and the Field of St. Giles.[35]

Even after all his sales of assets, there were still plenty of interests retained in his estate, when he died by October 1218. His wife Avicia, who survived him, was able to claim her dower-interest of one third in at least twelve different properties.[36]

**Roger Enganet** the engineer, who worked in Westminster for both king and abbey, spanned several of the decades on either side of 1200. But to avoid breaking up his career too much, his story has been completed in the previous section of this book.[37]

**Richard Testard and Henry Sumer** were members of two families which already were, or were becoming, prominent in Westminster; and unusually the pair of them became *joint* reeves of the manor in about 1198, probably following next after Roger Enganet. There are some reasons to think that Richard Testard and Roger Enganet, and possibly even Henry Sumer, were related to one another by family connections; and this might explain the joint appointment, particularly since there is a possibility that they may have been standing in for Roger Enganet and so relieving him of his position as reeve when his duties for king and abbey conflicted with one another.[38]

Before **Richard Testard**, there had been at least three earlier generations of his family living in both Westminster and the adjoining manor of Eye. And there were at least another two further generations to come after him. Of the latter we have already met Ralph Testard, Richard Testard's son, who bought from Richard of Dol (and eventually sold to Robert Vannator, 'the winnower') an important house in 'King Street'.[39]

In 1135 the first known ancestor of the Testards, Thovy or Tovius, had apparently held as many as three houses in Westminster; and in Eye, a whole hide (c. 120 acres, probably most of the cultivated land there).[40] By the end

---

35 WACs 441, 407 and 408. Such Tothill rents as John sold or gave included those named in WACs 449 (four rents sold to Isabel); 441 (one sold to the Lady Altar); 407 (a rent of 1s., Fot's, 'charitably' given to the Lady Altar).

36 See CP 25(1) 146/5/ 2, 3 and 22. 'Another' lady called Avicia, 'Avicia of Longditch', lived at the same time as John son of Edward (and earlier) and was herself the holder of a fee in Tothill, see WACs 446-8 and App. A at p. 393 below. The temptation to equate these two Avicias is strong, but it is difficult to reconcile that with WAC 447 which suggests that they were two contemporaries, but gives no clue about any connection.

37 See pp. 108-109 above, relating to the period when Roger Enganet had begun work, before 1189.

38 This inference is based on the following facts: the rare name of the original known ancestor of the Testards, called Thovy or Tovius; the witness Tovius Ganet in the early charters WACs 242 and 340 (and see also p. 96 n. 5), which may be a corruption of Tovius Enganet; the use of the name Ganet for Roger Enganet (WAC 291, and cf. 288); the later legal action relating to family land between Ralph Testard and Walter le Brun, who was the heir of Roger Enganet, see Rosser *Med. Westminster* 330(4); CRR Vol. XIV, p. 339, No. 1584; and the unusual joint reeveship itself of Richard Testard and Henry Sumer, see WACs 437 and 438. For Roger's conflicting duties, see p. 109 above.

39 For Dol's sale to Ralph, see also p. 141 above. For Ralph's sale to Robert Vannator, see p. 277 below.

40 *CRR*. vol. xiv, p. 339, No. 1584 (a legal action brought in 1231 by Ralph, Richard Testard's son, which gives a good pedigree of the Testard family). In that action Ralph claimed the three houses in Westminster and the hide in Eye from Roger Enganet's heir, Walter le Brun, but failed to recover anything,

of the century when Richard Testard became a joint reeve with Henry Sumer, there was still considerable other property in the Testard family. We know that Richard certainly made four gifts of rents of Westminster properties to the Lady Altar (three of them expressed to be charitable 'in soul alms'), amounting in total to 6s. 2d per year; and also that he held three acres of land in the fields between Tothill Street and the leper Hospital of St. James, before letting them to Robert Mauduit, the royal chamberlain and his heirs.[41] Richard's mother, during her widowhood, had sold one acre in the meadow of Lousmede (west of the 'King Street' properties) to Robert Mauduit, and Richard gave up any claim he might have had, as his father's heir, to this land by in effect confirming his mother's sale.[42]

Because of the absence of records it is not clear where Richard and his family actually lived in Westminster, but in view of his standing it was probably in the 'King Street' area or a similar high-class position.

His brother **John Testard**, who was also a prominent resident and property holder, gave an indication of the standing of the family, when he let to Isabel, Robert Mauduit's wife, two messuages which stood in 'King Street' on the 'fee' of the Bishop of Salisbury, and released to the Lady Altar an annual rent of 2d. which the warden of the Altar owed him for other land on the same bishop's estate.[43] The grant which he made to Isabel Mauduit seems to have run in

parallel with the similar grant (of rents) which John, son of Edward, made to Isabel at about the same time, and both sets of property, the two 'King Street' houses and the rents, were clearly being acquired by Isabel to enable her to pass them on, as charitable gifts, to the Lady Altar – as she did.[44]

For his part, **Henry Sumer**, the other joint reeve in c. 1198, had already established himself earlier in the previous decades as a favoured serjeant of the abbey, and he was regular in his attendances at the abbey courts to witness charters executed there. Initially he appears to have been granted property outside Westminster by the abbey. In about the 1180s Abbot Walter of Winchester let a mill in Wandsworth (an abbey manor, joined with Battersea) and 30 acres of land in Sutton to 'Henry [Sumer], our serjeant'. The mill, which the abbey had been able to recover from a previous tenant was probably a fulling mill: more than thirty years before, the then abbot, Gervase, already held a mill or mills on the river Wandle and obtained extra land in Wandsworth on the side of a mill in order to assist the siting of mills on the river: and the mill now held by Henry Sumer was probably one of those abbey mills.[45]

Although he was clearly employed by the abbey, Henry's base from that time, if not before, appeared to be in Wandsworth; and when a 'Custumal' was later drawn up by the abbey in 1225, the free land identified by it in

---

as a result of a legal technicality which Ralph had to concede. Whether he returned to repeat his claim on the merits is not clear, but at *CRR* vol. xv/410 and 1854, and vol. xvi/820 it is recorded that a duel (ie. a trial by 'battle') had previously been fought between the parties, Ralph Testard and Walter le Brun, in or before 1232 or 1233, but that the abbot had not yet made any 'record in his court' about it. So that it appeared to be of no effect. Cf. the other legal 'battle' in Westminster, referred to on p. 34 and 49 above.

41  WAM 17330, 17433, 17435, 17318 (WAC 423, 424, 426, 427, each temp. John). For the rent in WAC 423, see also WAC 412. For the three acres, see Mason *Beau. Cart.* No. 198 (1200 x 1214).

42  Mason, *ibid.*, Nos 199 and 200 (temp. John).

43  WAM 17328 (WAC 421, temp. John) and 17430 (temp. John)

44  WAM 17328 (WAC 421) and 17327 (WAC 422, by 1214). Again John Testard gave Isabel the right to give the properties to a religious house, as John son of Edward had. Such a grant would be a permanent one.

45  Grant to Henry: WAC 297 (1175 x 1190). Siting of mills: WAD 370 (WAC 268, 1138 x 1157). The resisting tenant still retained a patch of ground 44 yards by 22 yards, which was important for the mill (on the millpond bank), and it was left to Henry to recover it if he could – but if he did, he would have to pay a higher rent!

Wandsworth as the 'Sumer land' almost certainly represented some of Henry's holdings there.[46]

However his precise role as a serjeant within the abbey is not identified, and equally, unlike the Testard ancestors, the names of his Sumer forebears are unknown. Later Henry certainly also held lands both 'within the vill of Westminster' (which probably means in this context on or near the west side of 'King Street'), and in the meadow behind, Lousmede (which is actually named), lying among the fields round the Hospital of St James in the present-day St. James's Park.[47]

There was also other land which Henry held much further afield, namely a virgate of land in the vill of Deene (Northants) which he had been granted by the lord of the manor there, Simon of Deene and his son, Ivo. Henry now gave this land to the abbey for the Lady Altar, as a charitable gift 'in soul alms'.[48] The land still carried a rent of one pound of pepper owed to Simon and Ivo, and the monks agreed to discharge Henry of the need to pay this, by paying it themselves. This did not offend against the principle of making a charitable gift 'in soul alms', because the existing rent to an intermediate landlord was simply a limitation of the gifted land itself, not something imposed by the donor, like a rent in his own favour.

The Sumer family did not end with Henry, but continued at least into the later part of the thirteenth century, with descendants called Ralph, Richard and John.[49]

It is not known how long the unusual joint reeveship of Henry and Richard lasted. But there is evidence that Odo the goldsmith became reeve during the first decade of the new century, so it seems likely that the joint appointment did not continue for long.

**William of Hurley** was the usher (and at another time, the butler) of Abbot Walter of Winchester (1175-1190), an important abbey servant whom we have already met briefly.[50] With his wife Pavia, William had held a good fee of lands and meadows in Longditch, which had either been granted by the abbey to him or to a forebear, or come to him in right of his wife whose family may have had abbey connections. Some or all of these Longditch lands, with houses on them, were now received back by the abbey, by way of a gift from William before he died.[51]

But after his death other parts of his estate passed into different hands, when his widow Pavia (with her son's agreement) sold them

---

46 'The Sumer land': B.L. Add. Ch. 8139, WAM 9287, Harvey *WA. Estates* p. 115-6. This 'custumal' (the first surviving one at WA, see pp. 199-200 below) was a collection of established 'customs' or usages and other data relating to various manors held by the abbey, based on surveys and showing in effect the identities of tenants, their status and the customary terms on which land was held by tenants in such manors. The manors in question were those 'assigned to the convent', ie. to be held for the benefit of the general body of monks and no longer administered by the abbot, on the occasion when the abbot and the convent agreed (in 1225) to make a general division of the abbey estates between them in agreed portions: see pp. 195 ff.

47 WAM 17143A (1230s). Harvey, *ibid*, 116 and Rosser, *ibid.*, 330 say 'at Charing', but I distinguish the St. James's area from Charing. By mid-C13 John Somer (*sic*) of Eye faced claims about lands near the Hospital, CP25(1)/147/20/400; and for this John Sumer (*sic*), see also WAMs 4828, 17343 and 17152.

48 WAC 480 (temp. John). The manor of Deene was one of the manors, like Hendon, which were held subject to an obligation on the part of its lord to provide hospitality to the abbot when he visited, see pp. 136 above and 301-4 below, and Mason, WA Peop*le*, pp. 84-5.

49 See Harvey, *WA Estates*, p. 116, and note 47 above.

50 See also p. 96 above.

51 WAM 17614 (WAC 311 (1194 x 1200). William of Hurley must also have let other land to William Little ('William Parvus') of Eye, because when he witnessed a charter made by William Little, he is called 'my lord' by Little, WAC 413. William Little may have had his home in Eye, over the boundary from Westminster, but he also owned a messuage in Westminster, probably in 'King Street' (according to the details of the house), which he sold to Alexander, 'clerk of the exchequer' and his partner Edith, see WACs 413 & 414; & pp. 171 and 330-1 below.

after 1200, not to the abbey, but to Robert Mauduit who was amassing his own estate in the Longditch area.[52] These latter properties did not return to the abbey's control until nearly another 150 years had passed, when the former Mauduit lands in Westminster were re-sold to the abbey in 1344 by Thomas, Earl of Warwick (a title which one of his Mauduit predecessors had attained in 1263, through a maternal line).[53]

**Adam of Sunbury** was the chamberlain of Abbot William Postard (1191-1200). When we encounter him, he was a firm resident in Westminster, though still with connections with his home town Sunbury (Middlesex). He was living in a 'half-house', in effect a large divided property in Tothill Street, which he had first bought at an annual rent of 4s. 2d., from Edward the reeve, the main estate-holder in the Tothill-Longditch area. Adam's immediate neighbour in the other half of the house, which had its own 'curtilage', was William of Hanslope (also 'of the Temple'), the personal clerk to Robert Mauduit the king's chamberlain. So appropriately the split-house already reflected the town's mixed interests of both the abbey and national officialdom. Equally appropriately, in the house on the further side of William of Hanslope, it was the commercial interests of the town which were represented by Ulviva *lotrix* (the laundress); while in the house on the other side of Adam, William *palmarius* (the pilgrim) was perhaps an independent resident who was now returned from religious travelling to other places.[54]

Subsequently when Edward the reeve died near the end of the century and John his son had inherited the estate, Adam had then to renew his holding, by in effect 'buying' it again, (with John 'confirming' it to him, for the price of 10s), bearing still its substantial rent of 4s. 2d p.a.[55] In effect one land-rich abbey servant had enabled another to live near his duties, and the former's son was prepared to continue the accomodation, with of course a new (though reduced) price-tag attached.

After Adam's death his widow Juliana continued to live in the same property, and its value, namely the rent of 4s. 2d. p.a., which she was at first liable to pay to John son of Edward the reeve, found its way in due course to the abbey coffers, when John included the 4s. 2d. rent in the bundle of rents which he assigned (for a price, of course) to Isabel Basset, the wife of Robert Mauduit the royal chamberlain – for her to donate them in charity to the Lady Altar.[56]

## Two more serjeants, and two gardeners

**Walkelin** was a serjeant of the abbey almonry at about the turn of the centuries, and was probably a successor in that position to Gilbert of Claygate, after Gilbert had abandoned his serjeanty and other benefits in order to join the Third Crusade.[57] Like other abbey servants, Walkelin too held land in Longditch; this land may have been annexed

---

52 Mason *Beau. Cart.* No 191-3. When she sold two messuages and a meadow in Longditch to Robert Mauduit, Pavia had needed a dowry for her daughter and provided her with the 10 marks paid.

53 WAM 17635-7 (in 1344). See also p. 271 below.

54 WACs 409, 446, 447, 448 and 449.

55 WAC 409, and see also WACs 446-450. We do not know the financial premium on which the original letting to Adam had been 'bought' from Edward, but when Adam's neighbour William of Hanslope died, William's son charged six marks (£4) to Lucy of Berking who became the new tenant from him, plus rent of 1 lb. of cumin pa., WAC 447 (temp. John). And John son of Edward, 'as if chief lord', was to get 2s. pa., WAC 448 (plus 2s. 6d. pa. for the other half, WAC 447). For Lucy, see p.177 below.

56 See text, under 'John son of Edward', on pp. 143-5 above.

57 For Gilbert, see pp. 100 and 181-2. For Walkelin, see WAC 328, 417-9, 444 (all in the period 1200 to 1216) and pp. 100-1; and for an earlier Walkelin (perhaps a relative) in Abbot Gervase's time, see also p. 100 above. A later reference to a Walkelin makes him one of the tenants of free land in Wandsworth in 1225 (see Harvey, WA Es*tates,* 116), and this could just be the serjeant again or suggest a further family relationship, in view of the unusual name. For none of these Walkelins is any other name given.

to his serjeanty and his holding there was clearly described as a 'fee' (probably a sub-fee).

His 'landlord' (Nicholas son of Geoffrey son of Fredesent) donated his own interest in the whole estate 'in soul alms' to the Lady Altar in the first decade of the new century, together with the annual rent of one shilling which Walkelin was due to pay.[58]

**Thomas,** a serjeant of the sacristy and described as 'brother of Pancras' was another holder of land near Walkelin's property in Longditch. But unlike Walkelin, Thomas had donated his land there to the abbey's high Altar of St Peter at some date before the turn of the centuries, and St. Peter's altar was one of the special responsibilities of the sacrist whom Thomas served.[59] It is likely that Thomas's 'land' had been more extensive than Walkelin's, since Abbot Ralph of Arundel (who happens to refer in a later charter to Thomas's earlier donation of his property to the abbey) describes it as 'the whole of our land', which suggests something more than one piece of property. Moreover Thomas's holding lay apparently between two separate 'fees' – those of Walkelin and Stephen of Berking, which were themselves probably more extensive than one plot of land.[60]

These two serjeants are merely examples of the many lay serjeants and other servants who can be identified as holding lands fairly close to the abbey where they worked. In the decades when the two centuries were merging, such lay employees were regularly present in the abbots' courts when charters were being executed, and appear to have been 'drafted in' to act as named witnesses to them. So much so, that various groups of serjeants, containing members named as Geoffrey, Adam, Ralph, John, William and Alan (without further identification other than their group-description, *servientes ecclesiae*), appear often in a bunch at the end of the witness list in many charters executed at this period.[61]

**Eadric of the garden** was a senior servant of the abbey, holding a post of authority, almost certainly at the 'great garden' (in the present area of Covent Garden), north of Charing Street. His task, with his assistants, was to care for the fruit trees and vegetables, to foster the annual crops, and to gather and deliver them to the abbey, for consumption there or even for sale. This was well before the period when a formal obedientary office of monk 'gardener' was created at the abbey – shortly after 1227.[62] It is clear from a later charter in the thirteenth century that by then an official obedientary monk-warden at the abbey was now called 'the gardener of Westminster', and it may be that Eadric, as a lay man, had held an earlier position of a similar but less formal kind.[63]

Eadric certainly lived 'above the shop', with a house in Charing Street itself, between the street and 'the garden of the abbot', and it was in that area that he held what was called a 'fee' (*foedum Edricis gardinarii*) in one

---

58  WACs 328 (1200x 1203) and 444 (temp. John). For Geoffrey and Nicholas, see p. 100 n. 30.

59  WAC 328 (1200x 1203). Since this reference to the brothers Thomas and Pancras is in an elaborate charter executed by Abbot Ralph before all the monks present and expressly consenting in the chapter house, it is likely that Pancras was well known to all present and was yet another serjeant or other servant of the abbey.

60  For Stephen of Berking, see pp. 178 below.

61  eg. WACs 360, 387, 407 and 443. Other identified serjeants or servants were 'William of the infirmary', 'Nicholas of the cellar', 'Gervase of the kitchen' or 'Ralph of the brewery'. See also Mason, *WA People*, pp. 253-4.

62  Rosser, *Med. Westminster*, p. 136. For the Convent Garden, see pp. 33 above and 199 below.

63  WAM 17419 (1240s) by which, on a gift of a house to the Lady Altar, a rent of 2s. was to be paid to 'the gardener of Westminster', now a monk who could collect rents and be accountable for them. This was after the 'great garden' in Charing had been assigned to the convent by Abbot Berking, see p. 199..

charter.[64] He also had connections with families in Charing Street and Aldwych, and appears as a witness to other charters relating to Aldwych and the 'fields' round the leper Hospital of St Giles.[65]

However there is no doubt that he held other property as well, both in King Street and in Tothill Street, which he held from John, son of Edward the reeve, and probably had been granted by John or his father.[66]

Save that he was recorded as the holder of a fee or fees, Eadric may even have been one of those rare recorded creatures in Westminster, an individual still owing some obligation or obligations of physical labour in person, since in another transaction he is bracketed (as a joint-holder of land) with an authentically 'servile' man who could be assigned by one 'lord' to another, and who still owed work-services arising from his holding of at least one parcel of land, by name William son of Herbert. The 'ownership' of this villein, William, and his tenement of one acre of land (perhaps with a cottage), had been held by Hugh *de fonte*, a resident in the Charing area towards the end of the twelfth century, and was donated by him to his daughter, Margaret, together with another acre of land. But Margaret and her husband Simon then donated to the Lady Altar a 2s. annual rent due to them from "William son of Herbert and Eadric of the garden" for the land in question. So there was some curious connection between William, still a serf, and Eadric who nevertheless held a responsible position at the abbey and was a substantial landholder.[67]

Although married, Eadric later died 'without *lawful* heirs' and left all his lands 'to the Virgin Mary', ie. to the office and fund which supported St. Mary's altar and later her new chapel.[68]

**William of the garden** was apparently a younger colleague of Edric. He certainly held at least two acres of land in the area of Aldwych or the fields near the leper Hospital of St Giles, which he had rented from John son of Edward.[69] As in the case of Eadric, his association with the Aldwych area seems to suggest that his duties too lay with the 'great garden'. On the other hand he also held additional land, probably on the west of 'King Street', backing on to the 'smaller garden of the abbot' which apparently lay towards the present St James's Park.[70] As a gardener himself, and with the good example next door of the abbot's 'smaller garden', William may have been able to use this further land of his as a private orchard and 'smallholding'.

The Westminster gardeners, whether employed by the abbey or by the king for his palace garden, appear to have been a close-knit group, perhaps living near one another and/or standing together in their dealings. For example, later in the century we find the son of Thomas *de gardino* taking a tenancy of a 'curtilage', with Robert *de gardino* and Roger *de gardino* (son of William *de gardino*, who was probably our William) acting as witnesses to the same charter.[71] Certainly, as is shown elsewhere, Westminster was full of gardens which must have provided much work for those who tended them, particularly in the Covent Garden area.[72]

---

64  See WAM 17453, and cf. WAM 17449. Before the great garden was assigned to the convent in or after 1227, its name had been 'the garden of the abbot', see p. 33 above.

65  See eg. WAC 408 (temp John), WAM 17453 and p. 35 above.

66  WAM 17449; WAD 520 (WAC 449 & 450, temp. John); in the first of which his tenancy (for 1s. 6d. rent) is also called a 'fee', as is the holding of 'William the waller' (also 1s. 6d. rent). The latter two were 'sub-fees'.

67  WAM 17320 (WAC 416, late 12C), and WAMs 17432 (WAC 417), and 17413.

68  WAD 515. For the altar and new chapel for the Virgin, see pp. 129 and 137-8 above.

69  WAD 557b (WAC 408, temp. John).

70  WAM 17370 (? 1220 x 30). Perhaps he was the gardener at the abbot's 'smaller garden', for which see p. 199.

71  WAM 17434 (? 1240 x 50); and cf. 17431 (Tockesgardin, Richard Tocke, William de gardino, and his son Roger de gardino) and 17368 (? 1240 x 50s). For Tockesgardin & Richard and William Tockes or Toke, see pp. 33-4 above

**Odo the goldsmith** was one of the most interesting and important personalities on the Westminster scene at this time. His family and background are unknown, and in spite of all the public notice which he received he remains something of a mystery, in these respects and in other silent corners of his life. He seems to have been curiously detached as an individual, but in two apparently separated periods of his life he straddled the two worlds of initially the abbey and thereafter the king's service.

On the one hand he seems to have held no official domestic post at the abbey, but as an independent and self-sufficient resident he grew into a close relationship with the monks during the first half of his life. He became, in this phase, the abbey's reeve probably just after 1200 and acted in this capacity for a number of years, just as Edward the reeve had done during the 1190s.[73]

But his involvement with abbey business went well beyond his position as reeve. He acted on no less than 56 known occasions as a senior witness to extant charters in the abbey courts (probably more than any other witness), and in many of these transactions he was also accorded his title 'of Westminster'.[74] On at least one occasion in 1210 he appeared as proctor for Abbot Ralph (1200-16) in the king's court, in reaching a settlement in the abbot's dispute with Simon of Deene (Northants), over the right to present a

priest to the church at Uppingham (Rutland).[75]

So close was Odo's association with the abbey that he had been granted considerable properties, both on an important site in the Thamesbank area, north of the palace and 'near the sluice', and also in Longditch. In the former he lived in style in a 'capital *curia*' or complex of buildings. Later he obtained a special privilege there, in being allowed to have his own chapel built within this complex of buildings near the palace.[76] In fact, when he was not far from death in 1241, about thirty years or more after he had obtained these properties near the palace, he referred to 'the grace and generosity of his beloved lords, the abbot and convent' which had been shown to him in their grant of the special additional permission for a free chantry in his private chapel. But the abbot was not prepared to let the property with its chapel fall into 'foreign' hands, and so Odo had had to promise that if his estate should at any time be sold or given away by him or his natural heirs, the abbey's grant to him should be null and void.[77]

At least six other properties are known to have been held by Odo in Westminster: (a) a house in 'King Street' next door to the property which had been been sold by Richard of Dol, the abbot's steward, to Ralph Testard;[78] (b) another house also probably on 'King Street',

---

72  For other gardens as well in Westminster, see pp. 33-5.

73  Odo's period of office as reeve has been dated rather later, but I am sure it started near the beginning of the century and must have lasted for several years. There are about twelve charters witnessed by him *as prepositus* (reeve), which are thought to have been made in the first sixteen years of the C13, some 'early' in that period.

74  WAC passim. Odo's only rival as a constant court-witness was Stephen of Berking, a clerk who was probably the brother of Abbot Richard of Berking and appeared at least fifty and more times as a witness, see p. 178.

75  See WAM 20616 (WAC 338, dated 1210), and CP25 (1) 192/2/21 for the settlement of the dispute. It was one of the occasions when the king's court sat at Northampton, away from Westminster. As the price for Simon giving up his claim to the advowson, Abbot Ralph 'received Simon and his heirs into the spiritual benefits and prayers of the abbey'. Cf. the other trouble at Deene, over hospitality, with Simon's son, see pp. 136-7 above, and Stenton, *English Feudalism*, pp. 70 and 267.

76  WAM 17454. He granted the abbey a rent of 4s., payable to the sacrist and charged on his own 'capital messuage', in return for his receiving the offerings and oblations from his chapel. Cf. the chapel grants to Robert Mauduit, and to the Bishop of Exeter, see pp. 161-2 below.

77  WAM 17333 (18th. Oct., 1241).

78  WAM 17597 and 17316 (WAC 419). See also p. 141 above. Odo's house next door was mentioned in charter 17597.

which he held 'in fee' from William of Leigh for a rent of 2s.;[79] (c) a third property standing immediately to the west of the gate leading into the abbey cemetery, which was held by Odo later in the 1220s from John (the) skinner at a rent of 5d;[80] (d) two properties in Longditch;[81] (e) a house in Charing Street.[82]

But in spite of his close association with the abbey and his acknowledgment of generosity on the part of the abbot and convent towards him, I have not found any records of any purely charitable donations by Odo to the abbey. Even when he gave a rent of 4s. to the sacrist of the abbey, he did not do so 'in soul alms' but openly pointed out that he was doing so *'in return for for the offerings and oblations'* granted to him from his free chantry in the licensed private chapel which he had been permitted to keep in his *curia*.[83] One gets the impression from a number of factors like this that usually, with Odo, 'business was business'.

Nor can it be said that Odo was generous with his sales to the abbey. One of his houses fronted onto 'King Street', next door to the house of Andrew, clerk of the Exchequer, and shortly before 1200 he sold a rent of 20d. pa. from this house to the Lady Altar for the price of £2. This was a heavy price for Robert of Moulsham, the warden of the Altar, to pay for this rent, at a high purchase rate of 24. Shortly afterwards Odo made another similar sale to the Lady Altar of rents amounting to 3s. 6d. from two Longditch properties, at the same price of £2; but even this gives a purchase rate of 11.4, still rather above the average commercial rate of about ten.[84]

However it is also noticeable that when he was making grants of property by way of sale to the abbey, he did not dress them up or use pious invocations of succour for his own soul or for the souls of his family, as others so often did even when making commercial deals with the abbey. One gets the impression that he disdained such gestures, or that his religious beliefs were private to himself.

On the other hand he was very careful in his charters to provide against predictable and practical eventualities which might affect the abbey as recipients of his sales. When selling the rent of 3s. 6d. from his Longditch properties (which included a house) to the warden of the Lady Altar, he agreed that if the house should be destroyed *'by fire or other misfortune'*, he and his heirs would nevertheless account for this sum from their other properties. He also declared that he had instructed his tenants in Longditch to pay their rents direct to the warden of the Altar, if he himself should be absent or gone to distant parts when his own assigned rent to the abbey became due from him - *'lest I or my heirs could be unjustly slandered about the payment of the said rent'*. He further gave express permission to the warden that if there was any failure to pay the rent, the warden could distrain against not only the Longditch properties (this was the normal right of distraint ), but also against any other properties which he (Odo) held in Westminster.[85]

79 WAM 17435 (WAC 426). The rent of 2s. had apparently been assigned to Richard Testard who now gave this rent to St. Mary's Altar.

80 WAM 17374. John (the) skinner too gave this rent, and another 2d. rent, to St. Mary's Altar 'in soul alms'.

81 WAM 17452 (WAC 442). See further text below. One was let to the king's chamberlain, Ralph fitz Stephen, and the other was let to Thomas son of Pavia, the widow of William of Hurley.

82 WAD 349. Odo's niece donated this house to the abbey after his death.

83 WAM 17454.

84 The first sale : WAM 17452 (or 17414, a copy) (WAC 425, late C12); Robert was named, in the charter, in his role of *precentor* rather than as the warden, or as prior, as he later became, see pp. 126-7 above. The second sale : WAC 442 (c.1200). For purchase rates, see also pp. 144, nn. above.

85 WAC 442 (c. 1200).

These were unusually careful (and objective) provisions at so early a period. A similarly careful provision had been written into his even earlier charter of sale to the abbey of the 20d. rent from one of his 'King Street' houses.[86] In giving the standard 'warranty' for the grant of the rent (a form of legal underwriting, which entailed his support of the abbey in any court action in which the abbey's new title to the rent might be later challenged by anyone), he provided that if he or his heirs could not comply with the warranty, he and they would provide *a reasonable substitute, up to the value of the said rent*. Discerning and dispassionate provisions like these at this early date must have reflected a methodical and usually even-handed nature in the man. It is hardly surprising that such professional attitudes and skills were later secured for employment in the king's service.

But there are several unusual features to Odo. His parentage is a mystery, although we know that he had a sister called Margery, whose daughter was called Joan. Unlike his contemporaries, he avoided public protestation in his charters about religious feeling or the catholic church, but he nevertheless sought and obtained the right to have a private chapel of his own. Although he knew that the abbey had been generous towards him, he showed a remarkable lack of financial generosity in return, at a time when many were falling over themselves to subscribe to the monks' campaigns. He was hard-headed in most things and materially successful in business transactions, but clear-headed, objective and fair, without selfish sentiment.

As regards the employment of Odo's other personal skills as a professional goldsmith, whether on behalf of the abbey or any other

principal during this period of his life, we know nothing.

## A change of life and career for Odo

But shortly after King John had died in 1216 and his young son, aged only nine, had been crowned Henry III, Odo's life appears to have changed dramatically, when he received a royal post as the keeper of the 'king's works' in Westminster. The civil war (between King John and the barons) was now over, and more peaceful needs had to be met. No doubt, Odo and his administrative skills had come to the notice, some time before, of Henry III the new king or, more likely, of his regency advisers. From this time on, for another twenty years until 1239, Odo's priority was to do the king's business, principally in connection with the maintenance and improvement of the palace buildings in Westminster.[87] But in this period he became more and more involved with the king himself and his demands, as the young monarch threw off the shackles of his minority and began to contemplate grand ideas for the rebuilding of the abbey itself.

But the inheritance which Odo passed on went much deeper than that. His real contribution to history was the training of his son Edward at his side in Westminster, not only to take his place as a skilled administrator but also to act as the king's personal agent and cultivated adviser in his project for the rebuilding and refurnishing the abbey. This was to dominate the physical life of Westminster from 1245 until 1269, and beyond.

But all this will take us well beyond the period here in question, which ended with the death of King John, and so the progress of Odo's second career must wait until we embark on the history of the great rebuilding of the abbey at Westminster.[88]

---

86  WAC 425 (late C12).
87  Kent Lancaster, ' H III's Artisans, Suppliers and Clerks', *Jo. of Warburg and Courtauld Insts.* xxxv (1972) 81 ff.  So thick are Odo's appearances in the 45 years between about 1197 and his death in about 1242 that the question must arise whether in reality there could have been two successive Odos, one in the 'abbey period' and one in the 'king's period', but there is much evidence against this.  Later in the C13, however, there *was* a second 'Odo the goldsmith', namely his grandson, the son of Edward.
88  For the other half of Odo's life, and for his son and successor, Edward, see Chapter 15, at pp. 242 ff. below.

# CHAPTER 9

# The gathering of the king's senior ministers

## The evidence of numbers

The second half of the twelfth century had seen the first swallows of the migration of government officials arriving in Westminster. The pace of the immigration had then grown gradually until the last decade of the century, when it became an invasion. The newcomers, both senior and junior officers, needed houses or at least land on which to build, and their needs were evidenced by the number of legal transactions which they had to make in order to acquire places to live. And while they were congregating in the town, a flourishing market of land-transfers between other residents was also developing, so that the pace of dealing was increasing.

The collection of surviving original charters still held at Westminster Abbey is a remarkable, if biased, record of this invasion. Even if one makes allowances for all the historical factors which may have influenced the total numbers of charters retained at the abbey at different periods of time, this collection by itself indicates the increasing rate at which the market was operating towards the final years of the twelfth century and the initial years of the next.

Let us take the 29 years *before* the death of Henry II, from 1160 until 1189, and compare them with the succeeding period of 27 years *after* Henry's death, from 1190 until the death of King John in 1216. In doing this we cannot achieve strict accuracy for a number of reasons, such as the problems about the precise dating of most of the charters; so we have to look for trends rather than exact details. Making fair allowances, we can say that in the earlier period there are only about five extant charters involving properties in the Westminster area, while in the later, and slightly shorter, period there were sixty or more, a significant contrast.

There are of course several reasons why we should expect the number of surviving records from the second period to exceed the number from the first period. We know that a number of charters, particularly in the first period, are now missing, whether through accident or deliberate action; or even perhaps because some early deals were not recorded in writing.[1] And we also know that the years of the second period were marked by the changes made by Hubert Walter in the formal making and the preservation of many kinds of records, which began first with official documents but created also a similar trend in the field of private land transactions.[2]

But even if we make considerable allowances to reflect such factors, the contrast between the figures of five and sixty is so striking that it at least points a finger towards a conclusion that the market itself, and not just the recording process, was growing dramatically at the turn of the two centuries.

But to test the matter, we have to look elsewhere – to pursue further the occupations and histories of some of the people who within these years now lived and worked in Westminster.

---

1  For missing charters, see, for example, most of the 'fees' discussed above on pp. 21-23, and listed in Appendix A at pp. 391-5.
2  For Hubert Walter's 'ineffaceable mark' on the making and keeping of English records, see above, pp. 121-23.

The most senior group of new administrators who are known to have been resident about now and active in Westminster consisted of two of the king's treasurers, three of his chamberlains and two of his justiciars – with some of the people associated with them and their households. These are the subject of this chapter. A second group is made up of other important but less exalted officials, who were protégés or staff of the senior ministers and who circled round them, like planets round their suns. These appear in the next chapter.

## The senior ministers

### A. *The royal treasurer – with members of his household*

In 1190 **Richard fitz Nigel**, the king's treasurer and administrator of the revived court of the Exchequer, was still the holder of his large establishment which lay north of Endiff lane in Westminster.[3] He had also been made the bishop of London in 1189 by the new king, Richard, and therefore had a second centre of administration, at St. Paul's, his ecclesiastical seat. Like a stone falling into water, he had also made local ripples in his own two pools.

Two of those ripples were his personal chamberlains (probably holding office in succession). One of them, William Creeton, held a 'messuage' of his own in the main street of Westminster, 'King Street', not far from his master's establishment. There he could be close to his master and able to carry out his duties in Westminster more easily. This house was probably the large and identifiable one which stood 'opposite the end of Endiff lane', with a well-recorded history which can be traced for about sixty years from the late twelfth century, until it was bought back by the abbey in the second half of the thirteenth

century.[4]

The other known chamberlain of the treasurer, probably William Creeton's successor, was called Walter, who with his wife Mary also owned at least one plot of 'land' in Westminster, probably containing their house. This 'land' cannot now be identified, but it still had a role to play, before it was donated later as a charitable gift to the Lady Altar at the abbey.

In addition to his two personal chamberlains, the treasurer also had two personal bakers of his own; and we can see that there was a subtle crossing of paths between these two different groups of the treasurer's servants. One of the bakers was called Arnulf, who with his wife Emma took the step of purchasing the property of Walter the chamberlain and his wife Mary. Then Arnulf died, and received the unusual honour, for a layman, of being given burial inside the abbey, near the Lady Altar itself. This must suggest that he had had other property of considerable value, which as a benefactor he had already bestowed upon the Altar. At all events the Lady Altar also received from his widow Emma a further charitable gift of the property which Arnulf had purchased from Walter, their employer's chamberlain.[5]

The other baker was Reginald, who with his wife, also called Emma, held 'lands' outside the limits of Westminster near the river Fleet, the original boundary of the City of London.[6] Some of these lands lay 'outside Ludgate', and others within the parish of Ludgate, together with other 'land' in Fleet Street (*Flietestrate*); none of them far from St. Paul's church, the hub of the diocese of London where the treasurer (now also the bishop of London) had to be, when performing his episcopal duties. There were 'buildings' on that part of their land which

---

3   For this first treasurer's arrival in the reign of Henry II, and the revival of the Exchequer, see pp. 110-13 above.

4   WAM 17443 (WAC 434), 17317, 17373, 17379. For a fuller history of this house, see pp. 275-76 below.

5   WAM 17428 (WAD 547, 1210 x 1220?). The charter itself records Arnulf's burial near the altar.

6   The original anglo-saxon boundary between Westminster and London was later held in 1222 to have been reduced, away from the Fleet, see p. 36 above, and Appendix B, at pp. 396 ff. below.

lay 'outside Ludgate', and these buildings (perhaps where Reginald and Emma lived?) lay between *'the gate of London which is called Ludgate'* and the Fleet Bridge.[7] It is not recorded whether any of the other nearby lands held by Reginald and Emma had houses on them, but very possibly there was at least another one on their 'land' in Fleetstreet, which was partly built up.[8]

So one can now see the treasurer esconced in his large Westminster complex in Endiff and, in alternate use, his quarters at St. Paul's, looked after by his successive chamberlains (with at least one of them living nearby in a large house in 'King Street', Westminster) and fed by his personal bakers, one of whom had been buying property from one of the chamberlains, and the other a wealthy landowner near St Paul's. It would only need a fertile imagination to see Reginald as perhaps having married Arnulf's widow and so keeping the bakery business going with new capital and energy.

In his new added role as the bishop of London, the treasurer was able in the 1190s to be generous with his patronage towards the abbey which lay on his doorstep. By various gifts made during his lifetime and derived from churches within his diocese he was able to assist financially those departments in the abbey which appeared to be in need of support: first, the sacristy (responsible for the fabric of the church, its lighting and interior, and facilities for the services conducted in the church); second, the chamber (responsible for the clothing, bedding, the dormitory and laundering for the monks): and thirdly the pittancer's office (responsible for special foods and other allowances for the monks).[9]

## B. *The new treasurer – William of Ely*

But by 1197 the old treasurer had retired, and his semi-official residence off Endiff lane had been passed by way of gift to his successor, **William of Ely,** a canon of St Paul's.[10] By the transfer of the treasurership, the office had once again been kept in the family, for William of Ely was Richard's 'kinsman'. Now the Exchequer, the court of national finance, was to spend its next twenty years in the hands of the third generation of the same family; in all, a period of a hundred years or more of family control. The abbot of Westminster, as chief lord of the treasurer's land, formally confirmed the gift by Richard fitz Nigel to his kinsman, and also was careful to put on record that William of Ely was his 'very dear and special friend'.[11]

Although the complex of houses which William of Ely had received from his kinsman was already extensive, he was apparently not content with them alone. In the following years he purchased at least two further Westminster houses, one of them (which stood actually within his own complex of buildings) from Roger Enganet, the former reeve and 'engineer' employed by both the abbot and the king.[12] The other house also stood nearby in Endiff, but William of Ely was unable to get immediate vacant possession of it and had to allow the two married occupants (the vendor's son and daughter in law, William and Alice) to remain there; but in return he clearly insisted that it was accepted and recorded in front of the whole 'halimote' (the formal court of Westminster) that the male occupant had no legal rights in the house, that he and his wife had 'no children nor any hope of any', and that the wife confirmed that she had no claim in dower on the house.[13] The treasurer,

---

7 The gate itself stood halfway up the hill, towards St. Paul's; Honeybourne, 'The Fleet', *LTR*, xix (1947) p. 15.
8 WAM 13846 (WAC 390); WAM 13847 (WAC 392); WAD 475 (WAC 391).
9 WAM 16738 (WAC 216, 1192 x 1196); WAD 504b (WAC 217, 1196); & WAD 617b (WAC 214, 1190 x 1192).
10 WAD 341b; printed in full by Richardson, 'Wm of Ely', *TRHS* (4th) 15 (1932), p. 79; calendared in WAC 219.
11 WAM 17313 (WAC 313); also printed Richardson, *ibid*. p. 80-1.
12 Rosser, *Med. Westminster*, p. 20. For Enganet, see pp. 108-109 above.
13 See the detailed terms of WACs 437 and 438 (1196 x 1212); and Rosser, *ibid*. The halimote was a 'moot',

it seems, was resolute in his determination that he was not going to be defeated by later claims which, in the uncertain state of the law and legal practice, might thereafter be raised; and he achieved that aim. These further purchases meant that when William of Ely the treasurer eventually restored all his property to the abbey, it had grown even more and was large and grand enough to attract the attention of Hubert of Burgh the justiciar, an even more powerful tenant to come.[14]

Meanwhile William Creeton, the former treasurer's old chamberlain had also sold his Westminster house in 'King Street', opposite Endiff lane. A few years later the holder of that house was 'Peter of Ely'. Hailing from Ely, Peter was no doubt another relation or a follower of the new treasurer, and he himself certainly held the post of a treasury serjeant at the exchequer. He was important enough to procure both the treasurer himself and Master Jocelin Marshal, the deputy marshal of the exchequer to act as the primary witnesses to the charter by which he (Peter) acquired the property.[15] It seems that one of Peter's principal tasks as a reliable exchequer serjeant over a period of more than the next 16 years (indeed throughout King John's reign) was to accompany and guard consignments of money which were being transported from the treasury across the country or to places abroad.[16]

For his part Reginald, one of the former treasurer's private bakers, also followed suit in disposing of his lands. His master, Richard fitz Nigel, had died in 1198, shortly after retirement, and Reginald and his wife Emma decided to surrender some at least of their assets, as alms, to the abbey. To pay for 'lights' (candles, or lamps) on the Lady Altar they first assigned a rent of 6s. from one of their lands which they had let in Ludgate; and then later they donated their interests in the Fleet Street property and also their land and buildings 'ouside' Ludgate to the abbey, also probably for the Lady Altar itself.[17] It is noteworthy that the fairly new leper Hospital of St. James, standing in the central fields of Westminster on the site of the present St James's Palace, was Reginald and Emma's immediate 'landlord' for their Fleet Street property; and that the hospital was also the holder of other adjoining land within the parishes of Ludgate and St. Andrew of Holborn, quite separate from the rural land which it held round its own site in Westminster. The tenure of its 'land' along Fleet Street was expressly described as a 'fee' by the Master of the hospital.[18]

### C. *William Turpin, the chamberlain of the king's 'chamber'*

Moreover other Westminster officials had also arrived to work in Westminster, but to live just outside it in the area between the gate of Ludgate and the Fleet Bridge. It was there in the Ludgate Hill area that another Westminster official, William Turpin (who in the reign of Henry II was a *familiaris* of the king and an officer of his 'chamber', his private finance office) had had the distinction of holding 'houses made of stone', together with other land. In about 1177, long before his death, he had transferred these Ludgate stone houses and his other lands to his wife Rose (known as 'the seamstress' or 'cushionmaker'), and after his death in or before 1194, Rose gave all

---

a meeting of all the tenants, held in the lords 'hall'. It could take place in the large refectory of the abbey or, as suggested by Rosser, *ibid.*, 231, in the open, in the abbey churchyard.

14 For William of Ely's restoration of his houses to WA, see WAC 439 (1218 x 1222). For Hubert of Burgh, the justiciar during the early part of Henry III's reign, see pp. 186 ff. below.

15 WAM 17443 (WAC 434, temp. John). For Master Jocelin, see pp. 178-9 below.

16 *Liberate and Close Rolls*, passim. The king's chamberlains of the exchequer also carried special overall responsibilities for this task of transporting treasure, see Richardson, 'William of Ely', *TRHS* 15 (1932), p. 74.

17 WAM 13846 (WAC 390); and see also WAM 13847 (WAC 392); WAD 475 (WAC 391)

18 WAMs 13847. For the leper hospital, see App. A at p. 392 below. For St. Andrew's, Holborn, see p. 44 above.

of the properties to the abbey, to pay for lights on the Lady Altar. She made it a charitable 'soul-alms' gift, although subject of course to the rendering by the warden of the Lady Altar of intervening 'services' (ie. payment of rents, totalling 7s. 6d.) due to superior landlords of the properties.[19]

Turpin had been a man of great importance in the king's confidential office. He had had the comparatively new post of 'chamberlain of the king's chamber', and was known well after his death as 'William Turpin of King Henry's chamber' (although he had continued in the same position into the reign of Henry's son Richard I as well).[20] He combined the main functions of receiving revenue into the royal 'chamber', and of the provisioning and conduct of the royal household. However his work was not limited to supervisory tasks, but included carrying out in person jobs such as conducting the transport of the king's harness by ship across the Channel to France.

When Turpin had made his properties over to his wife Rose during Henry II's reign, he had even had the royal seneschals of both Normandy and Anjou as witnesses to his charter, together with the king's own household steward, a baron of the exchequer, and other important persons not connected with Westminster. This shows that this charter was made when King Henry and William Turpin were across the Channel in France, and it is an interesting commentary on royal government of the time that a purely personal and domestic matter of this kind relating to some private property back in England, near the original Westminster/London boundary, could come up for formal execution in the king's household at a time when, having won a great war a few years earlier, Henry was again busy in France negotiating a non-aggression pact with Louis, the French king.[21]

As a side-light on some other domestic or personal issues of the time, there are questions still to be answered about William Turpin. He had earlier owed his interest in the Ludgate stone houses and their annexed lands to a couple called Osmund the carter (*Osmund caretarius*) and his wife Ermengard, who from being notable landholders in this area had apparently made Turpin 'their heir in the court of King Henry' (ie. after proceedings in the *curia regis*) and had handed over to him 'the charters and all the muniments' relating to the land and houses. Was there a family relationship between him and Osmund and Ermengard; or a friendly connection, unrelated to family. Or had he been given a pledge (in exchange for a loan, ie. a 'mortgage') on their property, and had he foreclosed or made a deal with them?

When Turpin transferred the stone houses and land over to Rose in about 1177, his charter records his agreement with her that she could bestow them on any church she wished, for the good of their joint souls 'and of the soul of King Henry' (the latter because of Turpin's service with the king). Was this transfer made because Rose herself had had a family interest in the houses and land, which had become William's only through her as his wife, and which he was now restoring, for her ultimate disposal? If so, was Rose the daughter of Osmund and Ermengard? Or was William simply making an endowment for her, long before his death? Rose did not grant the properties away during Turpin's lifetime, but waited until much later, after he had died. So it had probably not been a transfer on the point of death.

---

19  WAMs 13844 & 13845 (WACs 386 & 387). Such stone houses almost always received special mention when they appeared in charters, eg. Roger Enganet's house, WAM 17438 (WAC 435), see p. 109. They were of course more common in or around London, see eg. WACs 370, 386, 387, etc. In her charter of gift to the abbey, Turpin's widow, Rose, called her dead husband 'my lord'. Rose had a later liaison, apparently unmarried but living with Ralph Mauduit, a royal officer, WAC 435, Mason, W*A People*, 172-3, and p. 128 above.

20  WAC 390 (WAM 13846, temp John), and Jolliffe, 'The Camera Regis under Henry II', *EHR* 68 (1953) 340-1.

21  Warren *Henry II*, pp. 143-7. For the 'chamber' as the king's new financial office, which was more accessible for the king than the exchequer, see also pp. 117-8 above, and 172-3 below.

Eventually after recovering these Ludgate properties from Rose, the monks proceeded during John's reign to let some or all of them out again at a current 8s. annual rent to Alexander of Swerford, a well-known exchequer officer who also served as an abbey clerk.[22]

### D. *William of Ely – the treasurer continues*

For his part, **William of Ely** continued as the treasurer until about 1217. His span of office had included the whole of King John's reign, and came to an end during the civil war between the king and the barons. Unlike his predecessor he sat rarely as a judge in the king's 'chief court', so one has to picture him spending most of his time in Westminster on the growing exchequer work, during which he made significant improvements in its procedures, or at St. Paul's where he had duties as a canon.

However for a limited time during the years 1215 and 1216 even the exchequer business was interrupted as a result of the disputes and final break between King John and the barons. It was a time of tumult, leading up to and following the signing of Magna Carta, with Louis the Dauphin of France invading England in May 1216 at the rebel barons' request, winning over a large part of the country and himself joining forces with the rebels who held the city of London, only a mile from Westminster. Louis even ended up in possession of the records of the exchequer and some judicial and chancery documents,[23] which (according to one source) he had ransacked from the treasury at Westminster.

The treasurer himself had been unwise enough to join the rebels and may even have been responsible for the loss of the above official records. So with the ultimate defeat of the rebels after King John's death in 1216, the treasurer inevitably lost his post and his lands. In due course, after becoming reconciled to the new regency (set up to govern on behalf of the young Henry III, aged only nine), William of Ely was allowed to keep his property in Westminster, although he was no longer the treasurer. He ended his Westminster official connection when, named now as 'the former treasurer', he surrendered possession of his whole establishment in Westminster (including a *curia* and a stable) to the abbey, although apparently he retained a form of contingent licence to remain in residence himself, at an additional rent of 'one pound of free incense' pa.[24]

### E. *The king's hereditary chamberlain, of the exchequer – Robert Mauduit*

After establishing a home in Westminster, William Mauduit (I), chamberlain to Henry II and Richard I, had died in 1194.[25] Robert his eldest son succeeded to the family's ancient hereditary post as one of the two royal chamberlains to the king (still Richard I), and also inherited the family estates, including the houses and lands which his father had purchased in the Longditch-Tothill area of Westminster. Robert himself remained chamberlain to three kings, Richard, John and Henry III, dying in 1222. For a hundred years now the Mauduit family had been close to the king and active with him on his business, but it is clear that as the two senior chamberlains became more and more involved with the developing exchequer, their personal association with the king became less close.[26]

---

22  WAC 327. For Alexander of Swerford, see pp. 170-2 below.
23  Richardson, 'William of Ely', TRHS 15 (1932), p. 58.
24  WAD 342b (WAC 439); also printed by Richardson *ibid*. p. 89. William's previous rent to the abbey had been a candle of two lbs. in weight, p.a., WAC 219. The surrender included a prayer for the souls of the three kings, Henry II, Richard and John. William of Ely died in 1222, after a retirement spent in his religious duties and the farming of manors which belonged to St Paul's church. He left a son and a daughter. Of these, Ralph his son still owned property in Westminster, as we shall see (p. 187); and to his daughter, Agnes of Ely, William had given a stone house, apparently in London; Richardson *ibid*. p. 60.
25  For William Mauduit's arrival in Westminster, see pp. 113 ff. above.
26  Henry II had preferred his own circle of confidants and advisers whom he himself could appoint within his own household, and his sons Richard and John followed suit. This has the result that

So the Mauduits now had an altered but still very powerful sphere of influence, and were sometimes more appropriately referred to as 'chamberlains of the exchequer'. But their main family estates elsewhere were still comparatively small, and they lacked baronial authority. Therefore their Westminster connection close to the seat of power was important to them, and Robert (who noticeably liked to emphasise his royal association) set out to improve the Westminster estate still further.

His major purchase was an acquisition from the abbey of a group of houses with other land and rents, which had been restored to the abbey not many years before by one of the abbot's *familia*, William of Hurley, the abbot's usher.[27] These houses stood in the district of Longditch, and were added to the messuage which Robert's father had acquired there. Together with that earlier Longditch house and other new purchases by Robert, they began to form a courtyard of buildings (his *curia*), with a mansion house for the chamberlain himself, and other lands which over time were to extend further westwards for a considerable distance, with a large garden at the further end. Although the complex of buildings may have already extended southwards to Tothill street, its main access was clearly from Longditch; but there is no doubt that some of the other acquisitions made by Robert enlarged his estate up to part of the expanding street of Tothill itself.

But not all of the properties which he acquired were buildings. For example, as a result of two purchases he ended up with an area of six acres of 'land', probably arable, which extended from the very frontage of Tothill street itself northwards into the site of

the present St James's Park, as far as a meadow there which belonged to the leper Hospital of St James.[28] This rural holding bordered in part on a lane *'which ran from Tothill to the Hospital of St James'*. A trace of this lane may still just be visible. It may have run along the road and passageway at the western end of the present Queen Anne's Gate, through the surviving narrow gate into what is now a new roadway and park (Birdcage Walk, and St. James's Park) but was then a series of fields leading (across the rural fields which now form the present park) to the Hospital.[29] While there certainly was some marshland in those fields, the water in that area was never recorded as being as great as the present man-made lake in the Park itself.

In addition to the future rents which Robert Mauduit was to pay in future for all the properties bought by him (amounting to 25s. 1d. each year), the total of the premiums or prices ('gersums') which he had to pay in making the purchases exceeded £26, a considerable sum.[30] There was little meanness in his estate-building.

The huge garden in the Mauduit estate, later extending from Longditch as far westwards as (probably) Rosamunds, became a notable feature of the neighbourhood, and was known by the name 'Mauduitsgarden'.[31] It must have contained a large orchard. It still retained the same name when over a century later in 1344 it was sold back (with another croft, called unsurprisingly 'Mauduitscroft', and with other Mauduit land) to the abbey by Thomas Beauchamp, the Earl of Warwick (a title which the head of the former Mauduit family had acquired in 1263, only to be replaced shortly afterwards by the Beauchamp

---

(confusingly) we find another line of 'chamberlains' (such as William Turpin 'of the chamber', p. 157) being created, who managed the finances of the royal household and its growing administrative role, with income fed to it from parts of the revenue.

27   WAM 17614 (WAC 311 and BC 190). For William of Hurley, the usher/butler of Abbot Walter in the 1180s, and his wife Pavia, see pp. 96 and 147-8 above.

28   Mason, *Beau. Cart.*, Nos. 197 and 198.

29   See p. 51-2 above.

30   Mason, *ibid.*, Nos 184-186, 188, 190-200.

31   One early charter, *ibid.*, No. 199 (1195 x 1215), already refers to 'the garden' of Robert Mauduit, and Nos. 194 and 196 to his 'messuage' or 'house'.

family and name).[32]    In due course the old garden, and no doubt other ex-Mauduit land, amounting in all to about 80 acres, became the site of the great house which in Tudor times became known as Pety Caleys (Little Calais), so giving rise to the new name 'Petty France' for the road which runs towards that site from Tothill.[33]

So, measured against the comparatively small size of this central part of Westminster, the Mauduit property grew to be a substantial block of territory. With their large landowning in the neighbourhood and the influence which they derived from their royal connections, the family must have enjoyed a powerful standing in the local community.  One of the major factors contributing to the Mauduits' prestige in their capacity as residents was the private chapel which they were granted permission by the abbey to have within their *curia*, the family complex of houses.[34]  This form of permission was a special favour because, without more, it could derogate from the authority and the financial rights of the nearby parish church of St Margaret alongside the abbey, which normally stood to enjoy dues for all personal religious services such as marriages, christenings and funerals.

Therefore when the permission for the chapel was given, it was made subject to strict conditions that it was not to infringe the parish church's rights; that marriages and the churching of women parishioners should be held at the church and proper dues paid there; that even if members of the household became seriously ill, all confessions and the giving of unction and communion should be undertaken from St. Margaret's, and the fees paid to that church; and that when the Mauduits were away, their caretaker (and by implication his family) should attend the church and pay their dues, rather than make use of the chapel.[35]

The standing of Westminster is reflected in the private chapels which were permitted in the town.  Two other analogous permissions for chapels in Westminster were given.  One was to the bishop of Exeter, in a property not far distant from the Mauduit complex of buildings.  Bishop Henry Marshal, the brother of William Marshal who held property in Charing, had also bought land in Longditch Street (from Geoffrey Picot, the abbot's steward)[36], and in the mid-1190s with the monks' permission the bishop had built himself a chapel there for the use of his see of Exeter and his successors.  If an actual charter was made by the abbot in order to grant that permission, it has not survived; but the bishop for his part recorded, in a charter of his own, the building of his chapel with the consent of the abbot and convent, and acknowledged that

---

32  WAM 17635-7.  For other Westminster gardens, see pp. 33-4. above.

33  Rosser, *Med.Westm.* p. 30n., and p. 24 above.  See also the high-flown legal description of Pety Caleys with its 'buildings, barns, stables, dovecots, orchards, gardens, ponds, fishpools, waters....' in Henry VIII's Private Act. 23 Hy. VIII, c.33, conveniently printed in *Survey of London*, vol. XIV, App. A., p. 257ff. As late as 1755, the Westminster map of St Margaret's Parish still showed a great house not far from Rosamunds, which should be the mansion called Pety Caleys. The *Survey of London*, vol. X, p. 8 appears to position the mansion further to the east ('the *south-east* angle of the park').

34  WAD 352a-b (WAC 312, 1195 x 1200).  The grant of a chapel was made, it seems, 'at the petition and request of the king's barons', with many important witnesses.  So was it designed also to help the barons who sat in the exchequer?  Or had Robert Mauduit simply asked his fellow barons to back his own request to the abbey?  He had to pay a 'pension' of 4s. p.a. to the abbey for the chapel.  And this was not the only chapel which Robert Mauduit got permission to build; in addition to this Westminster one, he had bought another *curia* at Mitcham in Surrey, one of his estates, and obtained permission for another chapel there, Mason, *Beau. Cart.*, Nos. 204 & 205.  Establishing religious buildings ran in the family.  His grandfather had earlier established a parish church in Hanslope, the centre of his small barony in Bucks.

35   Mason, 'Mauduits and Chamberlainship' p. 8 and App. V suggests that the Mauduits' Westm. establishment was used only infrequently, but I wonder.  WAC 312 (her App. V) does not seem to support so strong an inference.

36  For Henry Marshal, see under Picot, pp. 139 above.  For Wm Marshal, see pp. 29 above, and 178-9 below.

it was not to prejudice the rights of either the parish church or the abbey itself.[37] In the eyes of the monks this may have been an adequate (and cheaper) substitute for a charter of their own, even if it did not set out carefully the specific conditions which had qualified the permission given to Robert Mauduit.

Another permission for a private chapel granted by the monks was in favour of Odo the Goldsmith – a layman but the holder of important offices both with the abbey and later with the king, and a Westminster resident in a large establishment north of the palace.[38]

Two other, though rather different, 'private' chapels which were being used independently of the parish church of St. Margaret at this time were the chapels, St. John's and St. Stephen's, within the king's palace. The former had been in place before the end of Henry II's reign, and the latter during King John's reign.[39]

After Robert Mauduit had succeeded his father in 1194, a significant change took place in the character and standing of those who surrounded the Mauduit family. This can be seen by reference to those who were present as witnesses to the charters made by the family. When William Mauduit had come originally to Westminster and started to buy property, there were no, or very few, recognisable officials from the exchequer or other administrative office among those witnesses to his charters.[40] Most of the witnesses at that time were from the abbey, including the abbot himself in one case.

But ten or twenty years later, in the early thirteenth century, when Robert Mauduit was buying property in Westminster, the witnesses present at his charter-making ceremonies were predominantly officials who now worked at the exchequer or held other administrative posts in Westminster. Moreover these were usually men who were already living in Westminster, and in many cases we know the places and even the houses where they lived.[41] Probably this change was the effect of one or both of two factors: the number of officials now living in Westminster had increased greatly within these few years, and the status and circle of the Mauduits had grown even more, sufficiently to warrant a greater and more official recognition of their presence and growing influence.

Robert Mauduit married Isabel Basset, the eldest of six heiresses from a family clan which was wide-spread and rather grander than Robert's.[42] She brought him more lands in the home counties, adding to his wealth and prominence. Both she and her husband could afford to be generous, and two examples of their charity in Westminster towards the abbey are recorded. For the sum of £1. 13s. 4d. Isabel purchased two large houses on the west side of 'King Street', standing next door to Peter of Ely's house 'opposite Endiff lane', with an express right on her part to dispose of them as she wished, *even to a religious house*.[43] She then made a charitable gift 'in soul alms' of the two houses (with a sitting tenant in one of them) to the Lady Altar of the abbey, to purchase 'lights' for the Altar.[44]

---

37  WAM 17312 (WAC 230, in 1198). This was not the only property in Westminster already held by bishops or other high ecclesiastics at such early dates, see eg. the bishops of Salisbury, pp. 43 and 392; and Abbot Samson of St. Edmund's Abbey, see p. 182 below.
38  For Odo, see pp. 151-3 above and 242-5 below.
39  Colvin, *King's Works*, vol. 1, p. 493.
40  Mason *Beau. Cart.*, Nos. 183, 187 &189.  Richardson '*William of Ely*' TRHS (4th) 15 (1932) at 63.
41  See *passim* this and next chapters.
42  The ramifying Basset family (a name meaning in Norman French, 'of low stature', hence Basset hounds) produced more royal officials than probably any other family; Reedy *Basset Charters*.
43  WAM 17328 (WAC 421).  Her purchase was from John Testard, of the important Testard family, and brother of Richard Testard who as another reeve of Westminster was or had been a servant of the abbey, see pp. 145-6. The reason for her disposal-right to a religious house was that such a house was an undying body, and therefore a grant to such a body meant that the grant was a permanent one, with little hope of recovery: to be avoided normally, in the then state of the law, by *other* lords. But for the abbey in this context, it meant restoration.
44  WAM 17327 (WAC 422).

Her other gift took the same pattern, of purchasing property and then giving it to the Lady Altar; but this time it related to the western end of Westminster. For £4 she purchased, not houses, but rents owed by tenants of properties on Tothill Street. Her purchase was from John the son of Edward the former reeve of Westminster, and the rents which she bought from him amounted to 7s. 8d pa.[45] Edward had been the servant of the abbey, both as the manor reeve and no doubt in other capacities when he was not acting as reeve, and he (or a forebear) had become an extensive property-holder in the Tothill area. Some of his large land interests on the north frontage of and behind Tothill Street had already been absorbed into the Mauduit complex,[46] and others were now bought from his son John. It was another classic case of abbey servants giving way to new government officials in Westminster; with the new increased rents of the properties then finding their way (back, in a sense) to the abbey, thanks to the new fashion of devotional generosity.

These charters also confirm that many of the tenants on or behind Tothill Street were other servants of the abbey (or the family of such servants), viz.:

- *William the waller* (employed to build or repair the Thames walls, a major task);
- *Eadric of the garden* (employed on probably the 'great garden', the Convent Garden, north of Charing Street);
- *Juliana*, widow of Adam of Sunbury (Postard's chamberlain, and holder of an expensive property, paying 4s. 2d. p.a.);
- *Gervase of the kitchen*, one of the known

departmental serjeants in the abbey; and
- *Martin Smud*. The resident Smuds were also probably connected with the abbey.[47]

So not only had the large fee bordering on part of Tothill Street been granted in some earlier period by the abbey to one of its major servants (Edward the reeve), but he in turn had then sub-let individual properties north of the street to several other abbey servants as well.

These dealings had all been in the name of Isabel, Robert Mauduit's wife, but Robert made other donations to both St. Mary's Altar and later the Chapel project. It was both of them who, expressly on behalf of all donors, petitioned the abbot that those who made gifts 'for lights on the Lady Altar' should have their names inscribed in the abbey's book of 'martyrology' and should share in all 'spiritual benefits' afforded by the abbey.[48] These benefits included having their names remembered in all prayers, readings and teachings. The abbot, Ralph of Arundel, granted their request, and henceforward these advantages were an added inducement for the faithful to donate land, houses or rents to the altar. However, in spite of the appeal of a spiritual quid-pro-quo for a donor who favoured the Lady Altar, there were still those who preferred to make their donations to other parts of the abbey, such as the sacristy (or the high altar itself), the almonry or the precentorship.

For all their local grandeur in Westminster, the Mauduits were but the tip of an iceberg. Below that tip the town was becoming thick with the officers of the exchequer, royal servants and Robert's own protégés and officials. To these we will turn in the next chapter.[49]

---

45  Her purchase from John son of Edward: WAD 520a-b (WAC 449). Her transfer to the Lady Altar: WAD 520b, (WAC 450). For both Edward and John his son, see pp. 142-5 above.

46  Mason, *Beau. Cart.* No 194, 195 & 196.

47  For the 'walls' to keep the Thames out, see *The Westminster Corridor*, p. 59; and pp. 201, 298, 362 below. For Eadric, see pp. 149-50 above. For Adam of Sunbury and Juliana, see p. 148. For Gervase of the kitchen, see p. 149 n. above. Martin Smud and his son Osbert witnessed WAM 17406 in the 1220s, but Osbert was killed in Westminster in 1236, in circumstances which gave rise to an inquest, *Cal. Cl. R.*, 1234-37, 256.

48  WAM LIII (WAC 329, 1200 x 1214). The book contained a calendar of saints and benefactors of the abbey. It was the benefactors who sought this credit; the saints did not, and presumably did not need it.

49  For the Mauduit officials, see chapter 10, pp. 173-5 and 176-8 below. The rest in chapter 10 are royal or exchequer officials.

But meanwhile – on the national scene – when the long-smouldering friction between King John and the barons flared into renewed civil war in late 1215 and 1216, Robert Mauduit was still active as a royal chamberlain. Until that time he had avoided becoming implicated in the violent politics of the day; but his son William (like the king's treasurer, William of Ely)[50] now joined the rebel barons and the foreign invader Louis the Dauphin of France, and the Mauduit lands in the Midlands were under threat from the king's forces. So Robert followed his son into revolt. In the ensuing fighting both father and son were captured, and at the outset all their lands, including their Westminster establishment, had at once been confiscated.[51] But King John died in October 1216, and the Mauduits (again, like the treasurer) were able to recover their Westminster property, by changing sides and becoming reconciled to the regency council appointed on behalf of the new boy king, Henry III, to whom they now swore their homage.

### F. The two Justiciars – Hubert Walter, and Geoffrey fitz Peter

Like the above two officers of the royal executive, each of them at work and at home in Westminster, there were two notable justiciars during this period, whose presence in Westminster was dictated more by their work there than by any proven residence in the town. These were Hubert Walter and Geoffrey fitz Peter.

**(i) Hubert Walter** has already appeared in this story, as the main architect of the new systematic practices of making and keeping records of some of the royal, judicial and other

official decisions.[52] He carried out these reforms principally in his successive capacities: under Richard I, as chief justiciar (presiding over the exchequer, and acting in effect as regent of the kingdom in the king's long absences) between 1193 and 1198, and then as chancellor between 1200 and 1205 under King John. For good measure he had also been made archbishop of Canterbury shortly before becoming justiciar, and later in 1195 Pope Innocent III appointed him as his legate in England. So the authority of Hubert's reforms was supreme in both the secular and the ecclesiastical fields.

Since Westminster, as the main centre of government, was now the place where many of the administrative and judicial decisions were made, the result was that the town became the seat where many of the new records were actually made and where many of the total number of records made were thereafter stored. Others were kept at the New Temple and the Tower of London.

But in his judicial role Hubert also played a personal part in Westminster in relation to both the abbey and the town. At first, as one of the justices under Henry II and later as justiciar under Richard I, he was sitting on the 'Bench', the regular Westminster sector of the *curia regis*, and some of the cases which he dealt with related directly to the abbey. In 1185, before he acquired his later fistful of higher offices, he had been a member of the bench of justices who were due to hear the legal action, already described, between Abbot Walter and the Paddington brothers, Richard and William, about the brothers' estate in Paddington which they held from the abbey. The justices would indeed have heard the full action, if it had not finally been compromised

---

50  See p. 159 above.
51  'Confiscation', a simple word, must have been a dramatic and, for some, a frightening event.  One has to envisage the orders being given at the highest level; writs sent by horse to all the sheriffs involved; mounted serjeants with soldiery being sent at once to impose control on all buildings and lands, and if need be, to break into them; officers being appointed to administer them on behalf of the king; tenants being ordered to hold 'from the king' and to pay rents to his officer; local 'lords' and their agents, such as reeves, being informed of the change in possession; etc.
52  For the increase in the keeping of records, see pp. 121-3 above.

and the terms recorded before them.[53] Even before Hubert had become still more distinguished, the calibre of the justices on that occasion was such that it may have reflected the influence which the abbey could exert in securing the attention of important judges.[54]

Later, when Hubert Walter had become archbishop, justiciar and papal legate, he was again in the 1190s to be found involved, in a judicial capacity, in other disputes in which the abbey was a party to legal proceedings, though in each case (where records survive) the action was once again compromised at a Westminster hearing between the abbey and its opponents. By that time Hubert was the presiding judge on the bench, sitting under the title of 'archbishop', not simply as a justice.[55]

The employment of such ecclesiastical titles by a judge in a formal court of law only serves to emphasise the versatile abilities which the holders of multiple medieval offices were able to exercise. More significantly they were *able to do so*, largely because of the near-monopoly of literacy which clerics held and the tolerance by medieval society towards the conflicts of interest to which such protean appearances in formal roles could give rise. But even Hubert had to resign his justiciarship in 1198, when complaints were made to the pope that he was so involved with affairs of state that he could not pay due attention to his religious obligations.[56]

As justiciar he was succeeded by his friend and colleague, Geoffrey fitz Peter, but Hubert himself continued as archbishop, and in 1200 the new king John, on acceding to the throne, made him his chancellor as well. Almost at once Hubert both repeated the lesson of his earlier reforms of legal and royal practice, by instituting the making and keeping of written records of chancery writs and charters, and also published for the benefit of future petitioners and respondents in chancery a schedule of all the fees chargeable for documents issued under the Great Seal on the chancellor's authority.

On one occasion, as archbishop, he attended personally at a meeting of the full chapter of the abbey to act as a witness to a charter which was executed by a member of his own *familia*. James le Salvage, a clerk, was the maker of the charter in question, and at that time he was in the service of the archbishop. As the archbishop's clerk, and probably at the archbishop's request to the abbey, he had been granted by the abbey the benefices of the two churches of Oakham and Hambleton (in Rutland), at what were *increased* annual dues to the abbey of thirty marks (£20) and twenty marks (£13 6s. 8d) respectively. These were high figures, and he had therefore been required by the shrewd monks to make personal promises before their full chapter ('*in pleno capitulo*') to pay these sums, and also to record his promises in formal documents executed before the chapter of the monks.[57]

To the charter relating to Oakham the archbishop gave his formal attestation, but not to the other one. The reason for this distinction was that James le Salvage had also been required by the monks to give, as it were, security for the payment of the thirty marks (from Oakham), by promising also, as a fail-safe measure, to pay that sum out of the profits from two other churches which he happened to hold in Kent, if he were refused papal or episcopal permission to pay the increased sum

---

53  See WAC 296, and pp. 92-4 above for the context of the Paddington action, the details of the compromise and the calibre of the justices on the Bench.

54  cf. Harvey, *Living and Dying*, pp. 196-7 and 204.

55  See WACs 316 (16th November, 1197) and 310 (27th August 1198). In any event, by the time of the latter charter (a 'fine' in a legal case which involved the issue whether the stewardship of the abbey was hereditary or not, see p. 98 n. 21, above), Hubert had already resigned his office as justiciar and was named (only!) as 'archbishop'. Much earlier in 1187 Hubert had been a papal judge-delegate, sitting in a case involving canon law in St. Katherine's Chapel in the abbey itself, Cheney, *Hubert Walter*, p. 26. See coloured Plate 4.

56  Poole, *Domesday Book to Magna Carta*, pp. 222-3.

57  See WACs 482 and 483 (probably before 1197).

of thirty marks from Oakham church. Having been 'invited' and having agreed to witness the charter, the archbishop could no doubt be relied on to lend his heavy weight to the seeking of the necessary permissions, as (one can be sure) the even shrewder monks had carefully in mind.[58]

On one other occasion the archbishop played an important role in procuring a compromise of a dispute between the abbey and the nunnery of Godstow in Oxfordshire. This dispute related to the church of Bloxham, also in Oxfordshire, which until about 1176 had been an asset of the abbey.[59] The king, Henry II, had then high-handedly intervened over the head of the abbey, by granting the advowson of the church to the nuns of Godstow, because his mistress Rosamund Clifford had been re-admitted to the nunnery and was buried there when she died.[60] The abbey disputed this transfer and claimed the church back from the nuns. The dispute, being an ecclesiastical one, was referred by the pope to three papal judge-delegates and awaited decision by them.

It was at this point that, clearly with the assent of the abbey and the nunnery, Hubert Walter acted as a mediator between them; not in person himself but acting through an agent in whose decision he would have participated. The compromise reached was that the nuns should keep the church (with suitable face-saving expressions by the abbey of 'pity for the nuns' poverty'), but pay an annual 'pension' of five marks (£3. 6s. 8d) to the abbey sacrist.[61]

When Hubert died in 1205, his death led to the angry conflict between King John and Pope Innocent III about the the king's right to choose or influence the choice of a new archbishop and his fierce objection to the election and the consecration of Stephen Langton, the pope's nominee for the archbishopric, who had been elected by the monks of Canterbury.[62]

In the course of the furious stand-off between king and pope, the 'interdict' was pronounced by the pope against England in March 1208 and lasted for more than five years. In theory this meant that all religious rites in England were suspended, and that therefore, as in the rest of the country, all inhabitants of Westminster should officially have ceased to enjoy valid sacraments and the other services normally performed by the clergy.

But apparently all baptisms were still permitted, and in some but not all places, rites for the dying and dead were still carried out. Practices varied from place to place. One general exception, made a year later, benefitted the monks at Westminster and elsewhere, but not the lay people of the town, when the pope permitted all conventual churches to celebrate mass once a week behind closed doors. In the abbey records there is a noticeable secrecy about what really went on in Westminster, and one has to suspect that many compromises took place. Still objecting, John was excommunicated and in revenge carried out greater confiscations and threats against church properties and personnel. These grew progressively; and many bishops fled the country. But finally under threats of deposition and foreign attack, John made an old-style 'feudal' submission of himself and his kingdom to the pope, and accepted Langton as archbishop.[63]

(ii) Meanwhile, back in 1198 **Geoffrey fitz Peter** had taken Hubert Walter's place as justiciar, when Hubert bowed to pressure and

---

58  WAC 226 (1197 x 1198) may be a record enshrining the episcopal permission.
59  Abbot Laurence had once granted this church to Master Ralph of Beaumont, a doctor in Westminster whom Henry II and the abbot shared, but the doctor had then died crossing the Channel in 1170; see pp. 85 and 103 above.
60  For Rosamund Clifford, and the sub-manor of Rosamund in Westminster, see pp. 50-1 and 285-7.
61  WAC 225 (14 June 1197).
62  See Turner, *King John*, pp. 155 ff. See also p. 133 for the period of the Interdict.
63  See Poole, *DB to Magna Carta*, pp. 445-9 and 456-8, Cheney, 'King. John and Interdict' BJRL 31/295 and 'King. John's reaction' TRHS (4th) 31/129; Mortimer, *Ang. England*, pp. 121-2. 'Tribute' was paid to the pope for 130 years. For the unused bell-rope, see Plate 8 on the next page.

*(a)*

*(b)*

*(c)*

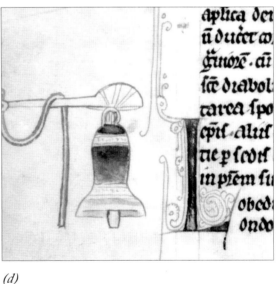

*(d)*

**Plate 8. Drawings, originally in colour, made by the monk-historian Matthew Paris, of events which affected Westminster:**
  (a) the Hospital of St. Giles, the first leper hospital outside London, founded by Queen Matilda in about 1115, see p. 35 and Map A, Plates 2-3;
  (b) the first two Knights Templar, in about 1118; at that time they were so poor that they had to share one horse. But the Templars' fortunes later became very different, see pp. 176-7, 42-3;
  (c) Prince Louis, the Dauphin of France, invading England with mercenaries in 1216, to support King John's rebellious barons, see pp. 137, 186 n.3;
  (d) the silent church bells in England between 1208 and 1213, as a result of the pope's Interdict, see pp. 133, 166.

resigned the post. Like Hubert, his rise to fame had begun in the service of both Henry II and Richard I, but unlike Hubert he was not a cleric. As a member of an obscure knightly family, he had absorbed his learning and administrative skills in the practical classroom of the king's court. He became in fact an early member of the class of 'lettered knights', those who appear to have had no formal education but achieved full literacy. His career was a straightforward one, mainly in the judicial field and leading to the justiciarship in which he spent fifteen years. His great ability had been recognised by his friend and colleague Hubert Walter with whom he served for many years, before eventually succeeding him in the top post.

Two factors brought him close to the town of Westminster and the abbey. Although he had no doubt worked at the palace when his earlier duties in the royal service required his presence there, it was his ten-year rise in the judicial sphere, from 1188 until he became justiciar, which first brought him regularly to Westminster. There he attended sessions on the Bench, combining this with work as an itinerant justice with the other sector of the *curia regis* which followed the king on his journeyings, and acting also as an independent justice on circuit both in the counties and (since he had been made Chief Forester earlier in 1184) in connection with the royal forests. Later, when he had become justiciar, he had to concern himself with the general business of the exchequer and its bi-annual sessions.

The other factor which created a link between Geoffrey and the abbey was his marriage to Beatrice de Say, a great heiress who (among other inheritances) had a claim on the huge estates of the Mandeville family, the holders of the earldom of Essex.[64] When the current earl died in 1189, Geoffrey pursued this claim in right of his wife and eventually succeeded in winning it, so becoming the new earl and one of the largest and richest landholders in the country.

The Mandeville family had been patrons of the abbey ever since the eleventh century. The first Geoffrey de Mandeville, who was one of the Conqueror's Norman barons in 1066, had subsequently endowed the abbey with his 'little manor' of Eye, adjoining Westminster to the west, and also with the church and vill of Hurley in Berkshire.[65] Later members of the family, who had since become Earls of Essex, had also made donations of both rents and lands to the abbey.[66] So the connection which Geoffrey fitz Peter had acquired with this patronal family may well have raised the hopes of the monks that the powerful and very wealthy Geoffrey, who himself was often to be seen on business in Westminster and had eventually, if belatedly, been created Earl of Essex, would follow the example of the Mandevilles and prove a generous donor to their abbey.

Such hopes, if they were entertained, appear to have been dashed: there is no evidence that he bestowed any of his enormous wealth or land on the abbey, although he was generous towards some other ecclesiastical bodies.[67] On the contrary, it was the abbey which had to make positive moves in their relationship, to try to procure the favour of the great man.

Thus in the early 1200s, almost certainly at Geoffrey's request, Abbot Ralph Arundel leased the vill of Claygate (Surrey) to the justiciar for

---

64  For these early Mandevilles, see Hollister, 'The Misfortunes of the Mandevilles', *History*, 58 (1973) 18-28.

65  See p. 19 above, and WACs 436 and 462.

66  eg. WAC 350 (a grant by Earl Geoffrey de Mandeville, II, c. 1141, of £1 worth of lands in London 'for the use of the monks in refectory', to fund an anniversary for his mother; WAC 470 (a grant by Earl William de Mandeville, II, 1166 x 1189, of the very valuable church of Sawbridgeworth, which the Mandevilles had earlier held, lost and recovered; see Hollister, *ibid*, 19-21 and 27).

67  See Turner, *Men raised from the Dust*, pp. 63-7. Turner attributes the gift to WA of £1 worth of land in London (WAC 350, see note 66 above) to Geoffrey fitz Peter, but this was the gift of Geoffrey de Mandeville II, at an earlier date.

his lifetime at a favourable rent of £3 pa. And again at the express request of Geoffrey, Abbot Ralph also made another grant, at an annual rent of £1. 10s., of certain tithes to the nuns of Shouldham Priory in Norfolk which the justiciar had previously founded and endowed. This Gilbertine 'mixed' Priory, of both nuns and monks, was the only religious house which Geoffrey himself founded and was clearly close to his own heart, since both his first wife's body and eventually his own were laid to rest there. It would have been difficult for the abbot to resist such requests from the justiciar, but it was all to no or little avail, and we know of no demonstrable benefits for the abbey.[68]

In his professional role as justiciar, Geoffrey was present on the Bench in Westminster between the years 1198 and 1204 in at least five legal cases in which the abbey was one of the litigants, and on one other similar but earlier case he had been sitting as a justice in the *curia regis* sitting in Northampton in 1192.[69] But as happened so often in the abbey's disputes, each one of the six was compromised by agreement between the parties. In the last three of the cases, Geoffrey was sitting as the presiding judge on the bench, and several of the justices sitting with him were men who had links with him and owed much to him. In all these cases in which the abbey was a party there is no indication that Geoffrey in fact played any part

in influencing the results reached by compromise, but that would not exclude the possibility that in advance of the compromises the abbot had hoped that Geoffrey and his colleagues would prove favourable to the abbey if the cases had had to be fully heard.[70]

The justiciar's authority among those with whom he sat, both on the bench and later in the exchequer, was so great that, if on some case he was not himself present in the court, the other justices or barons of the exchequer would often not reach a decision until he too had been consulted and had given his opinion to them. His learning was such that he too was once nominated as a candidate for the personal authorship of the legal treatise known as *Glanvill*, but on grounds of dating this is no longer tenable.[71]

Like his predecessor he was exacting and sometimes unscrupulous in pursuing King John's interests in the exchequer and also in the raising of moneys for him. There is no doubt that he also lined his own pocket in the process. But before the time of his death in 1213, he had lost the confidence of the suspicious king (whom he had served so well), and this may partly account for the significant fact that the regular Bench sittings in Westminster were closed by the king between 1209 and 1214, and cases were referred instead to be heard in the *curia regis* before the king himself, wherever he might be.[72]

---

68  For Claygate, see WAC 484 (a record of an interesting and succinct life-lease, under which any claims by heirs were expressly prohibited, and the justiciar envisaged, or even undertook to carry out, the stocking of the land and the making of improvements by himself, which were to enure to the abbey, and also undertook to prevent waste). Abbot Ralph is said to have the convent with him, as sellers. For Shouldham Priory, see WACs 476 and 477; Turner, *Men raised from the Dust,* 64; Mason, *WA People,* 75, 247.

69  WACs 324 (1192, in Northampton). WACs 310 and 314 (1198), 325 (1199), 331 (1201) and 330 (1204), each in Westminster, during his justiciarship.

70  Cf. Mason, *WA People,* 171, where Dr. Mason speaks of the apparently smooth relationship between the abbey and the judiciary in this period, and the abbey's hope or expectation of favour.

71  The lawbook named *Glanvill* was written shortly before the death of Henry II, probably under the auspices of Ranulf Glanvill, the chief justiciar from about 1180, see p. 93 above. Its authorship has been questioned, see Turner, 'Who was the Author of Glanvill?', *Law & HR,* viii (1990), pp. 97 ff., and Clanchy, *Memory to Written Record,* p. 73.

72  See WAC 338 (1210, heard in Northampton). As early as 1208 and in the absence of the justiciar, the king had also heard, in Westminster, another case to which the abbey was a party, see WAC 334 (1208).

# CHAPTER 10

# The town invaded by lesser officials

Having observed some of the major stars in the firmament at Westminster, we can turn our gaze on some of their planetary colleagues, who were also arriving to work and live in the town. These too were powerful men, even if less exalted than their seniors. Their number, so far as we know them, amounts to over thirty, but there were probably many others who are unknown.

The town was now beginning to hum, not only with the volume of government work being conducted there, but also with the working-out of the relationships which a developing community with common interests enjoys. Although this chapter is aimed at the secular residents of the town who made up this community, one has to remember as well the pervasive presence of the abbot and his monks – with the abbot as the watchful and powerful 'lord of the liberty of Westminster', and the body of monks as an acquisitive market force at this time, seeking to reap the benefits of the current and future inflation, by regaining possession of lands and houses lost in an earlier age.

Most conspicuous among the working officials who were resident in Westminster were those who were employed at the Exchequer; and in particular the clerks in that office. These were influential people, with a wide range of tasks which extended from duties as deputies of the 'barons', to the writing of the 'great roll' and its copies during the sittings of the court, and to the performance of other numerate and practical duties which the national audits by the court entailed. Indeed one of the main impressions which one gets from these public servants is their versatility in lending their skills to a variety of differing roles which they were expected to perform.

But other significant figures also chose to live near their place of work in Westminster. Principal among these were members of the king's own circle of advisers and the officers of his household. Even those who had residences in Westminster were not necessarily present there for much of their time: some had to follow the king on his journeyings, and others had to ride off, with servants to escort them, in whatever direction they were sent on tasks dictated by the king or his senior officers. Even more than those who were employed in different capacities at the exchequer, these royal *familiares* demonstrated a dexterous ability to adapt to any task given to them. But it is also certain that many of them, like their seniors the Mauduits, deliberately maintained houses in Westminster which would be available to them whenever they returned.

The following are a selection of some of these 'new men' of Westminster during this period while the centuries turn, with such details of their lives, homes, work and families as emerge.

**Alexander of Swerford** became a prominent officer of the exchequer, having previously started as a clerk employed by the abbey during the late 1190s. Indeed while still working for the abbey, he had then begun working for the exchequer at about the turn of the century, and during King John's reign acquired from Abbot Ralph of Arundel certain houses just beyond the river Fleet.[1] These were the stone houses on Ludgate Hill which

---

1   WAD 561 (WAC 327: 1206 x 1214) and see Mason, *WA People*. pp. 109 & 172; Richardson, 'Wm. of Ely' *TRHS* (4th) 15 (1932), pp. 48, 54, 59 and 65. The new rent for the houses was an 'inflated' one, 8s., as one can see from the previous rents of 1s. 6d., 4s. and 2s.

William Turpin, of the king's chamber, had once held, and which his widow Rose had donated to the Lady Altar at the abbey after his death.[2] Since Swerford also became a canon of St. Paul's, it is likely that his acquisition of a residence, with other investment properties on Ludgate Hill, was convenient for his duties at the cathedral.

So the grant to him by Abbot Ralph (for which even the king's treasurer acted as a witness) looks like a retaining fee from the abbey, to keep his good will and readiness to serve the abbey, at a time when he was becoming laden with other duties both in the exchequer and at St. Paul's.[3] At that stage Alexander was still described as 'our clerk' in the abbey's charter, and in that same capacity he was also a witness at the making of many of the other charters executed or recorded in the abbey's courts.

But Ludgate may not have been the only place of residence which Alexander of Swerford had obtained in or near Westminster. Unfortunately for us the name Alexander happened to be a common one in Westminster at this time, and we cannot always be certain which was which. There was one called 'Alexander of Spitalstrete'; and yet 'another' clerk of the exchequer called Alexander (who in fact may well have been Swerford, although without his usual locative designation) was already living in a *'capital messuage'* in or near 'King Street', and held another house nearby as well. At about the same time as Swerford was acquiring his Ludgate complex of houses, this 'other' Alexander donated to the Lady Altar at the abbey the second of his 'King

Street' properties (while retaining the *'capital messuage'* there);[4] and these two transactions may have been related – suggesting that it may have been Swerford who was divesting himself of one property in central Westminster (though retaining his main residence there), while obtaining the other large complex in Ludgate.

Whether or not these two Alexanders were the same person, the domestic situation of the 'King Street' Alexander is interesting. He apparently lived with a lady named Edith, daughter of Geoffrey of the Bar, by whom he had sons, although apparently he was not married to her. This was revealed without apparent inhibition, and presumably as a well-known fact, in another formal deed (one made before the whole court of the *'halimote (hall-moot) of Westminster'*). For Alexander and Edith had bought, for themselves 'and their heirs', a plot of land from William Little (*Parvus*), the Westminster resident who came from Eye: and in the charter recording the sale William Little had expressly permitted Alexander and Edith to designate whichever of their sons they chose to be their heir, for the purpose of the inheritance of the plot of land being sold.[5] Nor does their unmarried state appear to have met with any scruple on the part of the monks against receiving the messuage in 'King Street' from persons living in an unhallowed relationship.[6]

For his part the authentic Alexander of Swerford, who hailed from the west country and became the archdeacon of Salop (Shropshire), had evidently both started his career, and to some extent continued, as an

2 See pp. 157-9, above.

3 Mason, *WA People*, p. 172.

4 WAM 17416 (WAC 414: 1200 x 1210); and see also WAM 17321 (WAC 413: 1200 x 1210), which shows that this 'other' Alexander obtained another plot of land, probably in the present St. James's Park area, granted to him by William Parvus (for whom see p. 22 n. 38, and App. A at p. 393).

5 See WAC 413 (above) and cf. WAC 414. Because their sons would have been illegitimate, none of them could become an heir in law, but the *appointment* of an heir or heirs would preclude later dispute about the inheritance of the plot. Sometimes the reason for reticence about an unmarried state was that the man involved was an ambitious clerk hoping for ecclesiastical benefits (as Alexander probably was), who preferred not to parade his domestic situation, see Mason, *WA People*, p. 172. Cf. Ralph Mauduit and Rose, the widow of William Turpin, apparently cohabitees, WAC 435, see p. 158 n.19 above, and Mason, *WA People*, pp. 172-3.

6 Of course this assumes that the 'two' Alexanders *were* the same person.

abbey man. But he also acquired immense experience and acknowledged eminence in exchequer business as the clerk of the treasurer, William of Ely, and he later became the compiler of the famous 'Red Book of the Exchequer'. He was subsequently said by his friend Matthew Paris to have had an outstanding knowledge of exchequer sources and practices, and personally to have been *'a handsome, agreeable, and well-informed man, who left no one like him in England':* perhaps a model obituary.[7]

The Red Book was a great collection (now running to three modern volumes) of treatises on exchequer procedures and details of the king's household practices, of lists of knights' fees and scutages, and other detailed records.[8] This task of compilation had started from the day when the treasurer had first instructed Alexander to start digesting the massive details of knights' 'fees' which had been supplied to Henry II in 1166, when the king had wished to update that information for the benefit of the exchequer and had ordered all the king's tenants-in-chief to supply the necessary details of their dependent military men and their lands.[9]

Later Alexander also became a favoured royal clerk, and under Henry III was often at court where he performed many duties for his master, being rewarded in return with much land and remuneration. Throughout he maintained his position in the exchequer, and in 1234 he was himself made a baron of the exchequer, with a large annual pension of 40 marks (£26. 13s. 4d.).[10]  However by now Alexander had also become a canon and the treasurer of St. Paul's, and his connection with the cathedral was closer than his old link with the abbey at Westminster. So when he died in 1246, he was fittingly buried at St. Paul's.

**Ralph fitz Stephen,** by way of contrast, was a 'king's chamber' man, not an exchequer expert. Starting under Henry II, he was one of the king's *familiares,* the royal group of confidants, a member of the royal household and finance office, who established a base for himself in Westminster at this time. But like Alexander of Swerford, he also was well-known already to the abbey. During Henry II's reign he had received a grant of a piece of land in Gloucestershire from Abbot Walter of Winchester, to enable him to strengthen his own existing mill-pond there;[11] and later on, shortly after the turn of the century, he was granted further land (with probably a house on it, to judge from its 7s. rent) by Abbot Ralph of Arundel (1200 - 1214), this time in Longditch Street in Westminster.[12] The charter by which he received this second grant makes it clear that by then he was regarded as a great benefactor of the abbey, because the grant which was made in the abbey itself before the whole chapter, was ceremoniously written into the abbey's 'martyrology', the book in which benefactors and saints were recorded 'so that it may come to the notice of posterity', and the deed of grant to Ralph was deposited in the abbey treasury.

7   *Chron. Maj.* iv, RS. pp. 587-88. With Alexander's help, Matthew Paris had been able to consult some of the records kept at the exchequer,

8   See Powicke, *Thirteenth Century*, p. 65, and *Henry III and Lord Edward*, i, pp. 90-91.

9   For eg. the list of those who held knights-fees from the abbey in 1266 see Red Book of Exch., vol. 1, pp. 188-189. Most of these were in Worcs and Glos, but nearer home there was one in Bucks, one in Surrey, one in Essex, and one in Middlesex. Every one of these had received his fee from the time of Henry I; *'and none since.'*

10  Harding, *England in C13*, p. 276; Powicke, *ibid*, p. 94. Alexander was appointed with two others as 'professional' barons, instead of the usual magnates; and becoming chief baron, he introduced reforms.

11  WAD 324 (WAC 306: 1175 x 1190). In return Ralph promised to grind the abbot's corn for him, when and while the abbot visited the manor in question.

12  WAD 355a-b (WAC 328: 1200 x 1203). This was land which Thomas, serjeant of the sacristy, gave to the abbey, see p. 149 above. For Abbot Ralph, see pp. 131 ff. For Ralph fitz Stephen, see also Warren, *Henry II*, p. 308. In this charter (and WAC 442) Ralph was also called by the title 'of Boulogne', and Dr. Mason points out that his first wife had been Vicomtesse of Rouen, see WAC 328, note.

In the earlier of these two abbey charters Ralph is named as 'the king's chamberlain', of the royal 'chamber', a position which was now closer to the king than the two more ancient posts of 'chamberlains' held by the Mauduits and the fitz Gerolds whose main sphere was the exchequer. Ralph fitz Stephen, as a chamberlain in the king's household, was responsible for receiving revenue into the royal chamber, as well as discharging moneys from it for the provisioning and conduct of the king's household and his executive expenses in national administration.[13]

But in addition to such tasks, any member of the king's close circle was bound, at the royal command, to perform whatever other job was required of him: Ralph was no exception to this and his duties carried him far from Westminster. He acted as a justice in eyre, as a collector of taxes and as a surveyor of the treasure of England. On other duties it had been his task to ferry money across the Channel, to take charge of baggage for a noble visitor, to act as custodian of Queen Eleanor of Aquitaine whom Henry II had imprisoned, and to supervise the building of a religious house which the king had founded. And among yet other roles he was made sheriff of Gloucestershire for a number of years, acted as an itinerant commissioner, and was appointed assessor of taxes in certain royal forests.[14]

So this was the versatile man in the king's close employ who from at least about 1203 held land and probably a house in Longditch from the abbey. But in any case he already had one other house, also in Longditch, where he held a tenancy of 'land and a messuage' from Odo the Goldsmith, for which he was paying another 2s.

pa.[15] So between his varied royal duties, he had a good base in Westminster to come back to, available to him whenever he returned from his various assignments.

**Louis of the Exchequer,** otherwise known as **Louis of Rockingham,** was a clerk who during this period became conspicuous in Westminster in several different capacities.[16] His locative name suggests that he came to Westminster through the influence of Robert Mauduit, who had inherited the post of castellan of the castle at Rockingham and retained it until 1205. Certainly Louis was very closely connected with Robert Mauduit throughout his career, being responsible for writing many of the most important charters relating to the Mauduit presence and influence in Westminster. Of the extant charters relating to the Mauduits, he wrote at least fourteen, and the clause 'Louis the clerk, who wrote this charter' becomes a familiar refrain in many of them. In his professional capacity as a scribe he also attended Robert Mauduit, when Robert went to visit his baronial centre at Hanslope (Buckinghamshire) or his other mansion at Mitcham (Surrey).

Curiously there appears to be no clear extant record as to which part of Westminster Louis resided in. But there can be no doubt that he must have had a base in Westminster, and it is likely that as a close protégé of the chamberlain, he occupied one of the various houses in Robert Mauduit's expanding complex of buildings in and west of Longditch. If this was a matter of grace and favour towards a loyal servant, it may not have merited documentary evidence of the kind we would otherwise have expected.[17]

13 cf. William Turpin, pp. 157-9 above, a seemingly more favoured member of the financial 'chamber'.
14 Warren, *Henry II*, p. 308; Jolliffe, 'The *camera regis* under Henry II', *EHR* 68 (1953) 337-8.
15 WAD 520b-521 (WAC 442, temp. John). For Odo, see pp. 151-3 and 241-3.
16 Mason *WA People*, p. 109; and *Beau. Cart.* p. xxxij. See also Lady Stenton, *Pleas before the king*, Selden Soc. vol. 83, pp. cccxviii-ix and refs given there. See n. 26 below.
17 Or it is possible that Louis of Rockingham was the Louis *'atte walle'* or *'extra muros'*, who lived in a house just outside the walls of the abbey precinct, near the great west gate and Longditch, WAMs 17362, 17550, 17553; see also pp. 273 n. 30 below, for his probable neighbours there, the Cantilupes, the royal stewards.

But Louis also served in other roles. He clearly developed another close relationship, this time with the abbey, writing or witnessing a number of charters made by Abbots William Postard and Ralph Arundel.[18] He did the same with many of the deeds whereby lay residents were giving property or rents in Westminster to the Lady Altar during this period at about the turn of the centuries.[19] So he was a visible and much-courted resident, known to and trusted by many in the town who wished to protect their heavenly future by reliable deeds of charity. Another role in which he had served the Mauduit family was in acting as an attorney in court for Robert and Isabel, his wife; and in the same capacity he also represented others.[20] As clerk of the exchequer, his main work was as a subordinate to Robert the chamberlain, perhaps acting as his deputy when the need arose, or writing his roll for him. In this role as Robert Mauduit's clerk he even can be sighted accompanying and guarding 'treasure' (usually sacks of money) on the chamberlain's behalf, when it was being transported from Westminster after its receipt before the barons of the exchequer.

**Robert of Rockingham** was another senior clerk of Robert Mauduit, the royal chamberlain. Like Louis, he too probably came to Westminster from the small town of Rockingham as a result of a connection with the Mauduits, but it is not known whether he was any relation of Louis. Although he acted as a witness to several of the Mauduit charters, he was ostensibly not the scribe for any of them. But he appears to have had a post at

the exchequer and was described as a clerk in that organisation; it is likely that as also a senior clerk of Robert Mauduit, his other public activities were in connection with the financial affairs of his principal.

However, his standing in Westminster was considerable. His position in the lists of those appearing as witnesses in the abbots' courts makes it clear that he was seen as the peer if not the superior of many of the other stalwarts of the town. And he proved acceptable to the abbot as a suitable witness for some of the abbey's more ceremonial charters, standing there amid the full convent of monks at a meeting of the chapter. On one such solemn occasion, we are told, the whole convent was present 'with candles lit'; and on another (when Ralph fitz Stephen received his land in Longditch from the abbey in the presence of the full chapter), the grant was formally recorded in the abbey's book of martyrology, 'to inform posterity'.[21]

But perhaps more significant than these as an indicator of Robert's status was his property-holding within Westminster. It is certain that before 1197 Robert had acquired land and/or houses 'behind' the church of St. Clement Danes, near the top end of Fleet Street.[22] He probably also held other property along Charing Street (the western end of our modern Strand), for it was in or near Charing Street that his son, William, also 'of Rockingham', later owned what may have been a large 'fee' of property, including at least one house, land and a garden, which had probably been inherited from Robert.[23] It is revealing that some of the charters to which

18 eg. WAM 17614 (WAC 311), WAD 352a-b (WAC 312), WAD 578 (WAC 321), WAD 572-3 (WAC 335), etc.
19 eg. WAMs 17416 (WAC 414), 17433 (WAC 424), 17435 (WAC 426), 17437 (WAC 431)
20 See CRR 4/53 (1205) for his appointment by Robert Mauduit in one case. As regards other principals, it is clear that at this time many of the exchequer officials were beginning to act regularly as attorneys for principals with whom they had previously had no other bond or connection; Richardson, *William of Ely*, pp. 66-67. At this time most of the lay men who were appointed 'attorneys' for litigants were not professional legal pleaders, but acted as, in effect, lay proxies, but usually with some practical experience of legal process and advocacy.
21 See WACs 335 (1206 x 1214) and 328 (1200 x 1203). For the book, see p. 163 above.
22 WAM 17080 (WAC 395: 1197 x 98)
23 WAMs 17152 (1230-1240s) and 17138. It seems unlikely that this fief had been created in the C13; and if so, then it may have been part of the estate inherited from Robert of Rockingham. See also WAMs 17150, 17420 and 17445 for William's other holdings: his garden lay between the churchyard of St

Robert was a witness related to premises in the area of St Clement Danes and also in the 'Soke of Mohun', the fief belonging to the Mohun family, which lay in the area between the church of St Martin's and Charing Street.[24]

So it looks certain that this Rockingham connection in Westminster lay principally in the 'ribbon development' which lay along and around the present-day Strand, of which the medieval Charing Street was part joining Fleet Street and the City of London to 'King Street' in Westminster. It can be no coincidence that Robert's wife was Hawise, daughter of Ailward Hut 'of Charing', a prominent member of the Hut family which owned property along Charing Street. As Robert's father in law, Ailward joined him in also witnessing two of the charters relating to properties in the Soke of the Mohun family in the parish of St. Martin.[25]

Robert also appears to have spent a good deal of his time on a considerable private practice as an attorney, acting even for more distant clients in disputes in the king's court and in negotiations. For example one of his regular clients was the Bishop of Durham, for whom in the years after 1200 he acted in relation to lands in Lincolnshire and to land and a church in Yorkshire.[26] He also used to be regarded as probably one of the earliest group of professional pleaders before the Bench in Westminster, the 'serjeants' (or *prolocutores*, more commonly known as *narratores*), who at that time were skilled in the rigid intricacies of oral pleading at the outset

of a legal case and could either win or lose a case on pure legal technicalities. Very few such men can be identified as falling into this group, who represented the earliest members of an incipient legal profession in the years round 1200. But the latest view is that Robert (in addition to his positions at the exchequer and in the Mauduits' household) was more probably a recognised attorney, a member of a group who in due course during the course of the thirteenth century began to form another part of an emerging profession, but not that part which the special pleaders or 'serjeants' represented.[27]

**William English** was the brother of the former treasurer, Richard fitz Nigel, and was also known both as 'William of Westminster' and 'William of the Exchequer'.[28] And since William of Ely, the new treasurer, was another kinsman of the former treasurer, William English must also have been related in some way to William of Ely. He was a clerk in the exchequer, who also practised as a writer of charters including at least one personal charter for Robert Mauduit. In addition he was a serjeant of the exchequer (unless there were two men with the same name in an exchequer post). In this latter capacity he was responsible for transporting treasure on many different occasions.[29]

As befitted someone related to each of the successive treasurers of the exchequer, William English and his wife Isabella lived in a large house which can probably be identified as standing at or near the corner of Endiff,

Martin's church and the great Convent Garden.

24 See WAMs 17141 and 17142 (WACs 398 and 399, (temp. John). And some of William's property also lay in the Soke of Mohun, see WAM 17420 and 17445.
25 See WAM 17155A (1225 AD), by which Hawise (after Robert's death) received one of the family holdings in Charing Street. For charters witnessed by Ailward, see WAMs 17141, 17142; and cf. WACs 437, 438 and 440. Ailward and his wife (also called Hawise) were landowners too in Teddington, see WAC 316.
26 Lady Stenton, *Pleas before the king*, Selden Soc. 83, pp. cccxviii - ix, and refs. there given. See n. 16, above.
27 cf. the assessment made by Brand, *The making of the Common Law*, pp. 5-14 of the earlier work by Lady Stenton and his own later researches about the components of a real legal profession which emerged during the C13, well before 1300. The serjeants at law and the attorneys of this early period were not identical with the categories of modern barristers and solicitors, although there are some features similar.
28 Richardson *Wm. of Ely TRHS* (4th) 15 (1932), pp. 47 and 87n; WAM 17326 (WAC 346, 1199 x 1207).
29 Mason *Beau. Cart.* No 204 (1206 x 1207); Richardson *ibid.* p. 87.

between 'King Street' and the Thames.[30] William had been granted this house by Geoffrey, son of Jocelin the smith at a rent of 3s., and he then obtained a fine cirograph (a formal indentured deed) from the warden of the Lady Altar, confirming Geoffrey's grant as one 'in fee and inheritance'. But, apart from an additional rent of 4s. 6d, one of the quid-pro-quos for this latter confirmation was that William and Isabella went through a formal ceremony, before *'the better and more law-worthy men of the vill'* in the whole halimote of Westminster, making St. Mary and the warden their heirs; so that the house would in due course come back into the possession of the Lady Altar. This purchase was made at the height of the campaign in favour of the Lady Altar, and Geoffrey the seller also donated the 3s. rent due from William English to the Altar. So the monks gained two substantial assets, and succeeded once again in their policy of land recovery.

In the impressive location of Endiff, William and Isabella would have been near his respective kinsmen, although not living within the complex of buildings which the treasurers had each successively acquired. William died in or after 1207.

**Master William of Hanslope,** known also as **William of the Temple**, was another clerk of Robert Mauduit, and his Westminster residence was at Tothill.

His connection with the Mauduits is demonstrated in many ways. Since Hanslope in Buckinghamshire was the 'capital' of the Mauduits' small barony in that part of the country, it is virtually certain that, like other people who came from Hanslope, he had been a protégé of the Mauduits (in his case, Robert Mauduit). He had not figured in the previous period when Robert's father, William, had started to build the Mauduit complex in Westminster. But later, after 1200 William of Hanslope becomes labelled 'William of the Temple, the clerk of Robert Mauduit of Westminster', and this connection with the Temple appears puzzling until one sees the context of that time.[31]

The answer probably lies in the developments which had arisen in one of the roles which the Knights Templars now performed. In about 1161, the English 'Province' of the Templars had moved from the site of their former base at the Old Temple in Holborn (between Chancery Lane and Staple Inn), to the New Temple on the bank of the Thames, centred on the present-day round Church at the Temple. Founded in about 1118 as a military and monastic order to assist and protect pilgrims going to the new Latin Kingdom of Jerusalem, the Templars had been allowed wide fiscal advantages because of their international functions. As a result they had already become financial agents, providing in effect banking services across Europe, such as lending money, acting as transmitters of money and bullion, and guarding deposits of money placed with them.[32]

In England the New Temple (like the Old Temple) became in effect, among its other functions, a safe-deposit for both private and public monies, a treasury where eg. moneys collected by the exchequer could be consigned for security. It even became a secure place of deposit where, for example, in 1204 King John was able to consign articles of insignia and the

---

30 WAC 17326 (WAC 346: c.1199 x 1207)), 17322 (WAC 433). The position suggested for this house can be traced through these charters and WAM 17331 (WAC 440: 1200 x 1209).

31 cf. WAC 446 (1194 x 1197) and 447 (temp. John). Wm. of Hanslope is called Robert Mauduit's 'secretary', in Rosser, *Med. Westminster*, p. 30.

32 Burman, *The Templars, Knights of God*, pp. 74ff.; Sandys, 'The financial and administrative importance of the London Temple in the thirteenth century', in *Essays presented to T. F. Tout*, (eds. Little and Powicke) 147. In France the Paris Temple became the sole royal treasury, but in England other treasuries such as that at Westminster Abbey and the Tower of London were also used. In their business as commercial agents, the Templars funded and in other ways facilitated the transport of supplies and pilgrims to the Holy Land.

crown jewels. Indeed the New Temple also acted as a financial office as well as a place of security, and when orders were made by the court of the exchequer that moneys were due from a debtor, payment was sometimes ordered to be made 'at the exchequer or at the New Temple'.

In view of Robert Mauduit's position at the exchequer, it is probable that William of Hanslope, as Robert's clerk, was used by the chamberlain as his agent for dealing with the Templars over deposits of coin and bullion collected by the exchequer and placed at the Temple. By reason of a repeated association of this kind, he may well have acquired the name, William of the Temple. Alternatively it may be that in the interests of a closer liaison he had been given some form of accomodation or membership at the Temple, or even allowed perhaps to become one of the small group of associated lay members of the order of Templars.[33]

It was under his Temple name that in the 1190s William of Hanslope was granted a '*half messuage in the street towards Tothill*', together with other land acting as its curtilage in Longditch, by the former reeve of Westminster, Edward.[34] This divided but substantial property was near the Longditch home of his principal, Robert Mauduit, and so was convenient for the business which William had with him.

The other half of the same building was held by Adam of Sunbury, Abbot Postard's chamberlain;[35] and on the other side in the next-door house a laundress named Ulviva lived and no doubt plied her trade. So in just this one pair of buildings in Tothill Street in the period after 1200 we see evidences of the king's business, the abbot's business and a private laundry business all side by side.

William of Hanslope was a family man, and he and his wife Clarice had a son, Simon. Equally his 'landlord', Edward the former reeve of Westminster, and his wife Cecily had a son, John. After 1200 we find both these sons, who had each inherited his own father's rights in the 'half messuage' in Tothill Street, selling their respective rights in the half-messuage to the same widow, Lucy the widow of Richard of Berking.[36]

So now the widow Lucy had all the present rights in the house, subject only to the abbey's right (clearly expressed in each charter) as the 'chief lord' to be provided by her and her heirs with the very limited labour of one man for mowing or reaping on one day of the year. She had had to pay a handsome price (£4) for the interest purchased from William of Hanslope's son, but only 2s. for the former reeve's reversionary interest. Clearly the former was regarded as a secure (ie. long-term) legal interest and investment, with the corresponding result that the immediate reversioner's interest was worth much less.

It may be that Edward the reeve had also come from Barking, lying east of London; and if this were the case, there was perhaps a family relationship involved in this latest transfer from his son John to 'Lucy, widow of Richard of Berking'.[37]

The legal interest which William of Hanslope had had in the Tothill house leads indirectly to an interesting inference, because this Lucy, his successor, can make a special claim to local fame. 'Another' Richard of Berking was a monk of the abbey in the early thirteenth century, and later became prior and

---

33 For various grades of membership of the order, see Lees, *Records of the Templars*, pp. lx-lxi.

34 WAC 446 (1194 x 1197). For Edward, see pp. 142-3 above.

35 See WAC 409 (1197 x 1200) for the chamberlain, and WAC 449 (temp. John) for his widow Juliana, after his death. The rent for that other half was 4s. 2d. pa., which was a high rent. For Adam, see pp. 148 and 163 above.

36 WAC 447 and 448 (each 1200 x 1216). Clarice was still alive and gave her consent to the transfer by her son Simon. John's position as now the 'lord of [Edward's] fee' was expressly recognised in Simon's charter, even though the residual rights of the abbey to have a limited amount of physical labour were unusually preserved. 'Berking' (so spelt at that time) was the vill of Barking, east of London.

37 The C13 endorsements '*Berkinges Tothull*' in WAC 447 (cf. WAC 448), and *Edward 'de Totehull' Berkynge* in WAC 446 raise this suspicion.

then the enterprising and successful abbot of Westminster from 1222 to 1246.[38] His mother is known to have been called Lucy, and it seems likely that this Lucy and her husband Richard of Berking were the mother and father of the later abbot. The timing is right, and there are other indications in this direction.[39] The Richard of Berking who had been Lucy's husband had also had connections with the abbey at the time of Abbot Walter of Winchester (1175-90) and acted as witness to at least five major charters of that abbot.[40] Then he was followed by another Barking man, Stephen of Berking (possibly another son of Richard) who became a clerk at the abbey and was not only the holder of a recorded 'fee' (again in the Longditch area), but also became one of the most constant attenders at the abbot's court at this time, as a witness to charters.[41]

So while it is not possible to eliminate a coincidence of names, it seems more likely than not that the widow Lucy, now the holder of the half-messuage on Tothill Street and land behind it in Longditch, was the mother of Richard of Berking, the future abbot, and perhaps mother of Stephen as well; and that the two brothers (if indeed they were) had each professed religious orders, one as a 'secular' clerk, and the other younger one as a monk, later to become Abbot of Westminster. If so, then since she is not referred to in her son's abbacy, she was probably dead before he was elected.

**Master Jocelin fitz Hugh**, another leading officer of the exchequer for many years on either side of 1200, was also able to combine his post there with the performance of other professional services as an attorney for private clients.

The post which he held at the exchequer was as deputy marshal of the court, although he himself was a beneficed clerk rather than a man-at-arms (as the office of marshal of the exchequer had once required). In this position he served as a clerk and deputy of the great William Marshal, the king's marshal, who as a baron of the exchequer had a formal place allotted to him at the exchequer table.[42]

But this formal role was in fact performed for the royal marshal by Master Jocelin, as his deputy, who may indeed have been the first clerk to shoulder this office in place of his principal. As a result Master Jocelin himself became more grandly known as 'Jocelin Marshal', or 'the marshal of the exchequer', or the 'king's marshal', although in reality he sat only as a deputy.[43] His duties in the court included keeping the court prison, administering oaths, passing writs of summons to the usher for delivery to the sheriffs who had to appear before the court, and keeping vouchers produced in court.[44] All such duties were performed by him in Westminster, save on those rare occasions when exceptionally the exchequer sat elsewhere.

In addition to his exchequer duties, Master Jocelin was able to conduct a flourishing private practice as an attorney in the king's court, on occasion acting for the Earl Marshal, but generally for other principals. For example he is named as acting as attorney for a noteworthy member of the king's *curiales*, Peter fitz Herbert, when Peter was unable

---

38 See chapter 12 below, pp. 194 ff.
39 For example, it may be significant that Lucy was granted the honour of an anniversary at the abbey, Pearce, *Monks*, p. 48. Such an honour for a lay woman was very unusual.
40 WACS 288, 297, 298, 303 and 306.
41 For his fee and clerkship, see p. 391, and WAC 328 (1200 x 1203) and 461 (1206 x 1213). Stephen witnessed at least 50 charters among the charters in Mason, *WACs*, and more among charters executed later than 1216. For another regular witness, the important Odo the Goldsmith, see pp. 151-3 and 242-5. Stephen's fee may have been inherited from his father, the first Richard, Lucy's husband, (who may not have been even the first holder).
42 For William Marshal, the earl of Pembroke, also known as the Earl Marshal, see p. 29 above.
43 In the charter at Mason, Beau. Cart., No. 199, Jocelin received the title 'Master Jocelin the marshal'.
44 Johnson, *Dialogus*, pp. xxxi-ii; Richardson, 'William of Ely', *ibid.*, pp. 85-6; Crouch, *William Marshal*, pp. 146, and 168.

(because he was engaged on 'the king's business') to be present himself in the final stages of an action in the king's court, in order to complete a compromise arrangement of the action, made between himself and the abbot of Westminster.[45] Jocelin also served judicially on occasion as a king's justice.[46]

One benefice which Jocelin enjoyed as a priest was the rectorship of a Westminster Abbey church in the city of London, St. Matthew's in Friday Street. But this cannot have been a sinecure: even if he sought to discharge his duty there through a vicar (as may have been necessary, in view of his other tasks), it would still have demanded some personal attention from him.[47]

His residence was apparently provided for him by his principal, William Marshal, who held a fee at Charing which contained at least one large property. This was a site running down to the Thames from the crossroads, and it held a number of houses which the marshal let to his deputy at some date before 1199. It may well be that in addition to being the marshal's deputy in the exchequer, Jocelin also acted as his personal financial officer in charge of a private 'wardrobe' or finance office for the marshal at this site.[48] In addition William Marshal himself retained a right to make use of the Charing property as a place in which he and his staff could lodge, when he was needed for attendance on the king in his palace in Westminster; so the property was large enough to house a great man and his retinue, as well as Master Jocelin and his.[49]

William Turpin, of the king's chamber, had been a friend and colleague of Master Jocelin in the government bureaucracy, and having no children of his own and perhaps being also related to Jocelin, granted some of his Warwickshire lands to him.[50]

**Andrew of the Exchequer** was an official who illustrates another quite different function at the exchequer, but as a resident lived, like his colleagues the other clerks, in the area bordering 'King Street'. He was both a serjeant and a clerk employed in the court of the exchequer, and he certainly held, but only for a period, the office of 'melter' there. He obtained this post in the first half of the 1190s when he bought from the king the wardship and thereby the rights of the heir of 'William the melter' during the heir's minority.[51] The office of melter was a serjeanty, with (unidentified) land attached; and in view of the importance of his function and the essential incorruptibility of the holder of such post, the melter had to be a servant of the king himself and not of the exchequer or any of its barons.[52]

The melter (the *fusor, funditor* or *le fundur*) was an officer of the Upper Exchequer where the accounts of the sheriffs of the counties and other accounts were presented, checked and quantified. His role was that of a metal smelter for the purpose of checking the silver content of the coins submitted to the exchequer, and for the purpose of smelting he operated a furnace.[53] Under the later 'Gresham's law',

---

45  WAC 487 (1214).

46  Richardson, *ibid.*, pp. 64 and 84-5.

47  Mason, *WA People*, p. 172. Jocelin also held a rectorship of a benefice in Glos., given him by the Marshal.

48  Crouch, *William Marshal*, p. 168. For the Charing site, see also p. 29 above.

49  Crouch, *ibid.*, p. 146. When Jocelin died, he was succeeded by Wm. Toke of Aldewych, see p. 33 above

50  Mason, 'Mauduits and their chamberlainship', *BIHR* 49 (1976) p. 9. For Turpin, see pp. 157-9 above.

51  By 'regalian right', the king was entitled to assume the rights of an heir who was under age at the time when his father died. The sale of such rights was a profitable source of income for the royal purse. In modern terms, it became an opportunity for a virtual auction, for sale to the highest or most favoured bidder. This was a similar royal right to that which enabled the king to take over for a time the assets of a monastery when the abbot died.

52  Johnson *Dialogus* p. xxviii. For the importance in Westminster of the office of melter in the C13 and its eventual surrender to the king by Odo son of Edward of Westminster in 1285, see *ibid.*, p. xxix.

53  Johnson *ibid.*, pp. 36-38. For the authorship of the *Dialogus*, see p. 111 above.

coinage deteriorates, and it did so particularly in medieval times when it was frequently abused by clipping or forgery. So it was the melter's task to smelt and to convert, into one ingot of silver, as many of the silver penny coins – *as proffered by a sheriff or other accounting officer* – as would make a 'true pound' (ie. 240 pennies of the correct silver content).

A sample of the coins so proffered was brought to the melter and his furnace, for the purpose of an 'assay' of the sheriff's actual moneys. The melting of the coins required great care on the melter's part, to avoid either over-heating or under-heating the metal. The resulting ingot was then brought back to the barons and weighed against a certified 'pound' weight, and any underweight of silver so detected had to be made up with additional coins.[54] The calculation obtained on this single sample of one pound weight was then taken as representative of the *whole* of the sheriff's proferred monies, and any necessary adjustment was made against him throughout the whole of his account with the exchequer for that year.[55]

For his labour the melter received the sum of two pence for each 'pound' assayed, and it was the relevant sheriff who had to pay this fee. In addition the melter was entitled to standing wages of 5d. per day during the sessions of the exchequer. These were the remunerations which Andrew would have received throughout the period while he remained the custodian of the under-age heir and the vicarious holder of the heir's office.[56]

It is not clear what Andrew's other functions in the exchequer had been, although his name appears in the documents almost invariably as 'Andrew *de scaccario*'. It may be that as a clerk he was employed in writing one of the rolls recording the proceedings. But confusingly there were also other officials each called Andrew, who had business in connection with the exchequer. For example another Andrew was a well-known clerk of Richard fitz Nigel, the former treasurer, who regularly rode in company escorting treasure from the exchequer when it was being transported across the country.

However apart from his exchequer duties, 'Andrew of the exchequer' also had time enough to practise as an attorney in the king's court.[57] He became prominent too as a familiar figure in the abbot's courts, as one among his fellow residents who 'made suit' there in person and acted as a witness to the making of deeds recording land transactions in the town.

It is therefore no surprise to find that he too was the owner of a house and land in the significant area between 'King Street' and the Thames, next door to the mansion house and other houses of Odo the Goldsmith, one of the leading residents of Westminster.[58] Andrew was clearly a family man since a son of his, William, also appears as a witness listed immediately after him during King John's reign and was presumably another resident, maybe to follow in his father's footsteps in the exchequer.[59]

**Adam of Westminster** was a ubiquitous figure on the Westminster scene in this period. Although he was on one occasion called 'son

---

54   In overall charge of the assay operation there was another officer, a knight called the *miles argentarius* (the 'knight silversmith'), who later became known as *le pesour*. see Thomas of Windsor, p. 184 below.

55   Presumably if the ingot weighed *more* than the certified poundweight, there should have been an adjustment in the sheriff's *favour*. But no provision is envisaged for this in the *Dialogus*: the treasurer reiterates, 'it is the king's profit that is served in all these matters', ie *not* the sheriff's, see *Dialogus*, p. 38.

56   Since Andrew's period of office was only temporary and probably performed by deputies, one finds mention of the names of at least four other melters about now, during a period of about thirty years. The names were Richard, Alexander, John and Adam. See WAC 446 (1194 x 97); Richardson, 'William of Ely', *ibid.* pp. 64 and 89 (1217 x 1221); Rosser, *Med. Westminster* p. 152 (c. 1230); WAMs 17372 and 17374.

57   Richardson, *ibid.* p. 66.

58   WAMs 17414, 17433 & 17452. For Odo, see pp. 151-3 and 242-5.

of Henry', Adam was more often known – and perhaps pompously liked to be known – as 'Adam the bishop's nephew', since he was related to the king's confidant, Richard of Ilchester, the bishop of Winchester, who had been appointed to the exchequer by Henry II to watch proceedings there on the king's behalf. Throughout his life the bishop had been Henry II's candidate for many posts, but his special monitorial role in the exchequer had probably the most important influence in furthering his nephew's interests. Adam's constant reiteration of his relationship with the bishop when witnessing charters, coupled with his appearance as a witness of the royal treasurer's purchase of a further large house at Endiff, suggest that Adam too held a post in the exchequer.[60] But no detail of his role there is known.

It is however clear that Adam had been a significant resident in Westminster, and had the title 'of Westminster'. With his wife Matilda, he owned various properties in the area between Tothill Street and the leper hospital of St James (now St James's Park), some or all of which had come to him through Matilda. She was the daughter of Robert of Deerhurst, who had been a landowner in that area of Westminster. Several of the purchases of land and houses made by Robert Mauduit, and indeed by William Mauduit, his father before him, were from Adam and Matilda.[61] And by 1207 Adam was sometimes using another name, 'Adam of Deerhurst', acknowledging his father in law as the original

source of at least one house sold by Adam and Matilda to Robert Mauduit.[62]

**Geoffrey and Robert of Claygate** were two brothers who served as lay serjeants of the treasury, escorting treasure on its way to the armies or a place of security, but they also found time to appear frequently in the abbot's courts as witnesses, often in tandem.[63] A third brother, Richard, also similarly appeared as a witness in a few instances, but it is not clear whether he too was employed at the exchequer. In spite of the constant references in the charters to Geoffrey and Robert as witnesses, they seem not to have indulged (so far as I can see) in land transactions in Westminster. There is no clear evidence about the place or places in Westminster where they may have lived, but a clue emerges from the history of another Claygate man, Gilbert of Claygate. Claygate was an old estate which the abbey had held before the Conquest but had lost in the C12.[64]

It is possible, even probable, that the three brothers were the sons of Gilbert, who during Henry II's reign had re-granted his estate in Claygate (Surrey) to the abbey, in return for very substantial benefits. In this transaction, as a recompense for the donation of his Claygate lands, Gilbert had received a perpetual serjeanty at the almonry, together with two houses standing within the abbey precinct (described as *the nearest to the abbey*) and two corrodies.[65] This was generous treatment for Gilbert and his wife Alice, and it may have reflected a protracted yearning on the part of

59 WAD 567b-568 (WAC 480)
60 WAC 437 (1196 x 1212); cf. Richardson 'William of Ely', *ibid.*, p. 86. Rosser, *Med. Westminster*, p. 30 has also deemed Adam to be an exchequer officer. For other 'nephews' of the bishop, who were presumably related therefore to Adam as well, see the sons of Alexander of Barentin, the king's butler, at p. 116 above. For Richard of Ilchester, see also pp. 43, 87, 111 n. 97, and 392.
61 Mason, *Beau. Cart.* Nos 183, 184, 185, 186. See also Richardson, *ibid.* pp. 63 and 86. For Robert Mauduit's purchases, see pp. 159 ff. above.
62 Mason, *Beau. Cart.* No 184.
63 Richardson 'William of Ely' p. 88n.; *Rot. Litt. Claus.* I. 74; *Rot. Norm.* p. 24; for appearances as witnesses, see eg. WAM 17445; *Beau. Cart.* No 185, 186; WACs 395, 403, 414 and 416-8; but there are at least another twelve charters to which one or other of them, or both, appeared.
64 Harvey, *WA Estates*, p. 358.
65 WAD 465b; Harvey *Living and Dying*, p. 240; Mason *WA People*, pp. 254, 219, and see also WAC 485. For a 'corrody', see p. 99 n.27 above. One of the two corrodies which Gilbert received was the customary one which went with the office of serjeant of the almonry. See p. 168 above, for the reletting of Claygate.

the monks to recover his Claygate land from him, at whatever price was required.

Thereafter Gilbert and Alice probably lived in one of the two houses within the precinct and close to the abbey, but later in about 1188 Gilbert decided to join the Third Crusade which was mustering at that time. However before he *'took the road for Jerusalem'*, he donated the house in which they lived back to the abbey; but to protect his wife Alice he postponed the gift by providing that it was not to take effect until after she had died.[66] We have no evidence that he returned from that crusade. Later, in King John's reign, another probable member of the same family, Agnes of Claygate (the widow of one of the brothers ?) was living next door, in the second of the houses.[67]

So it may be that one of the two houses within the precinct had been a family home where the Claygate brothers had lived with their father and mother, and that later the second house had become the home of one of the brothers and his wife Agnes (who had then survived him).

**William 'de Castello'** and **Laurence 'de Castello'** (sometimes 'Castellis'), were contemporary clerks of the exchequer in the years after 1200, and were each resident in different houses in the 'King Street' area. It is not clear where the 'castle' or 'castles' were from which their locative name came; it was unlikely to have been the Tower of London, which was usually known by the name 'Turris', eg. Robert de Turri, a familiar figure in Westminster later in the thirteenth century.

William obtained his 'land with a building

on it' in Westminster from Abbot Samson of the great abbey of St Edmund in Suffolk. These 'King Street' premises were clearly large, being later described as a *curia*, a courtyard or close of buildings. Up to the time of the transfer, the abbot of that abbey had held the house as an 'inn' to stay at, when he came from the country to meet the king at Westminster. In now granting the property to William de Castello, the abbot reserved to himself and his successors the substantial right to stable fifteen horses there, whenever he or they should come to court in person. Even with this limitation on William's rights as the new occupier, the rents were high, 11s. per year, payable to Wimund the baker, his next door neighbour (from whom the abbot of St. Edmund's abbey had held the property), with another 2s. 4d. payable to the archdeacon of London, Walter of London.[68]

The number of exchequer officials who were already living in or near 'King Street' in Westminster is highlighted by the fact that William's house was probably only two doors away from one of the houses which his colleague, Alexander clerk of the exchequer, held and ultimately donated to the Lady Altar at the abbey. Moreover William's house was also in the same close neighbourhood as the property of Laurence de Castello.[69]

William's position in the exchequer is unknown, though as a clerk he may have been responsible for writing one of the rolls. But as late as 1227 he was apparently acting as the personal clerk of the treasurer in paying out moneys at the exchequer *'towards the work of Dover Castle'*.[70] He had also been an assiduous attender and witness in the abbot's court; and,

---

66  WAM 23638e, (WAC 347, temp. John).   Cf. Andrew Bucherel of London, a pilgrim to Jerusalem, WAC 353.

67  *ibid.*   Agnes's house was next door to one granted by the warden of the Lady Altar to Master Geoffrey Picot, the former steward of the abbey, see *ibid.*, and p. 139 above.

68  WAM 17315 (1206 x 1211), 17372 (1230s ?).   Wimund was the abbey baker, a prominent resident in 'King Street' and a frequent witness of charters.   He may well have held a 'fee', but is not named as a holder of one.

69  For Alexander, see p. 171 above. The close proximity of his and William's houses can be deduced by comparing the details of WAM 17315, 17372 and 17416 (temp. John). For the closeness of Laurence de Castello's house, see text below.

70  Colvin, *Building A/cs of H III*, p. 65. It is suggested there that William was probably an 'under-treasurer of the exchequer' at that time.

like many of his brethren, had a private profession as well, practising as an attorney before the king's justices. So he had not only still been living when King John died in 1216, but he also survived for more than another ten years under King Henry III. Many years later after his death, his house, described then as 'a messuage and curtilage' was bought by the pious King Henry and donated in 1253, in soul alms, to the abbey in aid of the precentor's office.[71]

For his part, **Laurence de Castello** (otherwise known as 'Laurence of the Exchequer') also held 'land', which in this context meant a house with land, on the same side of 'King Street' and in the same area as the houses of William de Castello and Alexander the clerk, his colleagues at the exchequer.[72] Laurence was witnessing deeds in the abbey court in the decade before 1200, and was also active in the period after the turn of the century. He apparently had another property in Endiff Lane, but his main house in 'King Street' was two doors away from a house of Odo the Goldsmith, a pivotal house of that important resident.[73]

Laurence's house was passed on to his son, who was also named Laurence and may at first have followed his father into the exchequer, but in due course became more closely connected with the personal service of King Henry III. In the 1230s he was again coupled with Odo the goldsmith (in the second phase of the latter's professional life, now in the service of the king), as joint keepers of the works needed on 'the king's houses in Westminster', responsible for their maintenance and repair.[74] In that role

Laurence II appears to have had a warm personal relationship with the king (as Odo had), because we find the king ordering his Constable of Windsor to supply each of his two 'keepers' with three good tree-trunks, *'for their hearths'*.[75]

**Executive officers of the Exchequer.** Four other officials, named below, who played executive roles in the procedures of the exchequer illustrate for us some of the practical tasks which had to be performed when the court was in session. Their tasks started initially in the Lower Exchequer or 'Receipt', the chamber where the heavy sacks or cases of silver penny coins, which had been collected by the sheriff of each county from the payments of taxes and other due sums, were initially handed in. But because many coins were subject to forgery or illegal clipping, they had first to be subjected to a process of lengthy counting and examination, with the taking of a first sample of the coins and the re-packaging of the rest of them – all this conducted in the Lower chamber.

Then the scene passed to the hall of the Upper Exchequer, where the barons of the court and their clerks sat around the exchequer table. There they witnessed the weighing of the sample coins, and when the weighing and the assay of their silver content and the consequent adjustment of the sample were completed, the treasurer and other barons proceeded to determine the true state of account between the sheriff and the exchequer, taking into account the value of the tendered coins as shown by the assay. As they went, they resolved any questions of legal right which arose.[76]

---

71 WAM 17357 and *Cal. Ch. R.* 1226-57, p. 422. See also WAM 17359 for the extinction of the dower rights of a subsequent owner's widow in this house. Before he died, William had also bought a convenient right of way for his house, from another neighbour, in perhaps the 1230s, see WAM 17372.

72 WAM 17367 (1240-60). It is also noticeable that 'Laurence *clericus*', as a neighbour, was a witness to WAM 17372, one of the charters which helps to identify the area where William's house was.

73 WAM 17367 (1240-60); and cf. WAM 17353.

74 *Cal. Cl. R,* 1231-34, p. 90; Cal. Lib. R, 1226-40, p. 248; WAM 17384 (1240-50s).

75 *Cal. Cl. R.* 1234-37, p. 133. For Laurence I and II, see further pp. 242, 269 below.

76 The shortened descriptions given here are all extracted from the discursive *Dialogus* written by the Treasurer, Richard fitz Nigel in the 1170s, see p. 111 above. Details of the process and roles described changed later.

(1) **Albinus the clerk** was one of the four 'tellers' (*computatores*) in the Lower chamber. Theirs was one of the first jobs: to count the massive quantities of coins (all silver pennies; there were no other coins in use), which the sheriff or other accounting officer had amassed and had now tendered to the exchequer. The pennies were counted in batches of 100 shillings-worth (1200 pennies per batch), which were packed into large leather cases (forels), each case containing 100 'pounds-worth' (24,000 pennies). But one 'small' sample of forty four shillings-worth (528 pennies in all) had been taken and placed in a separate purse, for transmission to the Upper chamber. Meanwhile wooden tallies of receipt were cut and given to the sheriff for his deliveries.

(2) **Thomas of Windsor** was the 'weigher' (*le pesour*), or the 'knight silversmith', as he was known earlier. His duties followed after the tellers' task was completed: he had to bring the sample coins in their purse to the Upper chamber, to empty them onto the exchequer table in front of the barons or their representatives, and to mix them all up. On his weighing balance, he then found how many of the 528 mixed coins were equivalent to a certified 'pound' weight (worth 240 'true' pennies with the right silver content), and if the number was more than 240, that number of the sheriff's tendered pennies then became an adjusted sample chosen for assay.

So the weigher then had to take this adjusted sample of 240 *or more* pennies to the 'melter's' workshop, for the smelting of the coins by the melter in his furnace and the making of an ingot of their silver content.[77]

The weigher then brought the ingot back to the barons and in their presence weighed it against the certified pound weight, and if there was any underweight of silver, it had to be made up by adding further coins to the balance from the original sample purse of 528

pennies. The adjusted number of coins (ie. 240 *plus*, to a pound) was then taken as the measure for calculating the value of the whole of the sheriff's proffered load of coins.

Thomas of Windsor had been preceded in his post by Gervase of Windsor who was probably his father.

(3) **John of Wyke** was both a lay serjeant of the exchequer in the 1190s, who became one of the two ushers of the Upper chamber. As a lay serjeant, he was employed in the usual role of the exchequer serjeants – as a responsible person in charge of armed men accompanying moneys or other treasure, when it was transported about the country or abroad. But as an usher, his main duties were to admit only the right people into the chamber, and to produce articles needed in any of the exchequer proceedings, such as the large leather cases in which the majority of the coins were packed after being counted, and the wood for the wooden tallies which were cut and used as receipts for the moneys received.

John also 'kept the door' of the 'privy chamber', which was provided for the barons so that they could withdraw for their private deliberations; and he was responsible for ensuring that no one other than the barons themselves or persons summoned by them could enter that room. It was also his task (a) to make all necessary arrangements about the furniture in the hall where the barons of the Upper Exchequer sat, and (b) to deliver *'in person or by a trusted messenger throughout England'* all summonses issued by the barons after each session of the court and addressed to every person required to appear at the next session.

(4) **John of Stortford** was a clerk and notary known as the Treasurer's Scribe, who was responsible to the treasurer himself for writing the great Roll, the official record of the court proceedings in each year. The Roll was called the 'authoritative Pipe Roll', whose

---

77 For one of the melters, and the method of assay, see Andrew of the Exchequer, at pp. 179-80 above. If the proffered sample had *too much* silver content on the assay, the sheriff apparently received no credit for this, because it was *'only the king's profit'* which was to be considered.

wording was sacrosanct after it was completed, save that the king alone ('who can do no wrong') could make a retrospective alteration.

It was the treasurer himself who dictated the wording of the record to his scribe, and the other scribes making copies (for their own masters among the other barons) had to take care to follow the precise wording of the official record *so that no iota is missing*. The record had to be written on sheepskin, on skins joined end to end in long lengths called 'pipes', which were sewn together at the head and then rolled up. No erasure was permitted in the writing, but any clerical error had to be corrected at once, by drawing a fine line underneath the error and writing the correct version immediately afterwards.

# CHAPTER 11

# The boy-king and the justiciar
## 1216-1232

While Westminster was still filling up with its new bureaucrats, a different chapter in its story began. With the rebel barons and Prince Louis, the Dauphin of France, still holding London and Westminster after King John's death in 1216, the young Henry, John's son, could not be crowned in the abbey at Westminster, but was 'made king' in the west of the country by loyal magnates in a hurried ceremony in Gloucester Abbey.[1] But the accession of the boy king, aged only nine, meant an initial period of instability and changing influences.

One of the major influences during the next sixteen years was Hubert of Burgh, whom King John had made his justiciar and the constable of the crucial castle of Dover in 1215 in the course of his struggles with the barons. Like the venerable William 'the marshal', now over 70, who reluctantly agreed to act as the 'Regent' of England during Henry's minority, Hubert also remained in political favour on the accession of the young king in 1216.[2] In the course of the next three years, while the marshal survived as the regent of England, Hubert was to play at first a vital military role as the custodian of Dover Castle, in both the defeat of Prince Louis and the rebels and then in Louis's withdrawal from England under treaty; and thereafter, an important role as justiciar in legal and administrative matters in Westminster itself, during the short period while he was still overshadowed by the authority of the old regent.[3]

But Hubert's main significance in this story is that after the regency had finally ended with the great marshal's death in 1219, Hubert was to act as the main administrator of the nation, closest to the young king, and the head of judicial process in Westminster for most of the king's minority, and beyond. He also became the prime resident, if often absent, of the town itself – after the king.

In the meantime, however, while William the marshal was still alive and remained in the office of regent, the lapsed legal administration was restored. The regular sittings of the 'Bench' of justices in Westminster, which had been suspended by King John in 1209, were revived in accordance with the requirement, which had now been made by clause 17 of Magna Carta, that the hearing of 'common pleas' (civil lay actions) should take place *in some fixed place*.[4] So pleas

---

1  For the rebel barons and the Dauphin's arrival, see p. 137.
2  For William the marshal, see pp. 29 and 178-9. Like other men greater than the great, he was usually known under that common name, but he had been raised to the peerage in 1199 as the Earl of Pembroke by King John. By his example he had made his 'commoner's' name the more illustrious of the two. Both William and Hubert, and others, had been and remained loyal 'king's men'; but the rebels had been and still were many. The boy-king even called the marshal, 'the ruler of us and our kingdom' (EHD 3/338).
3  Hubert had held the pivotal Dover Castle against all Louis's and the rebels' attacks, and had then defeated the French fleet in a naval battle off Sandwich in the Strait of Dover. These royalist successes and a victorious battle at Lincoln meant the end for Louis in England, who in 1217 departed with a treaty and 10,000 marks in his pocket.
4  Although the original Great Charter of 1215 had been annulled by the pope, revised versions were issued after John's death, in 1216, 1217 and 1225, with some provisions added and some omitted.

before the Bench began again in the great and little Halls within the palace complex in 1218, with the marshal at first presiding and Hubert present on some occasions. Salaries for the justices were instituted, to reduce temptation from bribes, a further spur to their becoming a progressively more professional body.

Sittings of the exchequer which had also lapsed were again reinstated in 1217 (though without the presence of Hubert, for the time being); and the judicial circuits of the general eyre throughout the country were also restored in 1218, with the country parcelled out among eight organised groups of justices.[5]

However it was after 1219 that Hubert's star really began to shine. In April that year William the marshal, an old man now very close to his death, resigned his office as regent. From the manoevrings which followed his resignation, there emerged a triumvirate of power in England. It was Hubert, as justiciar and now the controller of the king's seal, who was soon to secure the premier position in this triumvirate, and finally to become the sole survivor of the three regents.[6] Over the next four years one of his two colleagues had withdrawn, and the other had been forced, from their positions in the triumvirate. For the next eight years Hubert remained as the foremost liberator of the crown's castles and other royal properties which had been seized by rebelling barons during the civil war, and thereafter he remained the defender of the young king's position, acting in effect as his first minister and champion.[7]

By 1222 Hubert had already been carrying the main burden of day-to-day government, making hundreds of administrative orders with the royal seal entrusted to him, and at the same time directing in Westminster the sittings of the exchequer and maintaining control of the Bench of justices. His duties also meant that he regularly was making journeys to other parts of the country to carry out administrative acts or to visit his own growing estates. It was clearly time for him to acquire a permanent home in Westminster where his power lay.

## The justiciar's establishment in Westminster

It was in that same year, 1222 or shortly afterwards, that Hubert bought one of the largest residences in Westminster itself, not far distant from the palace, the real seat of power where his presence was regularly needed both for the judicial sittings of the bench and financial sittings of the exchequer, and for consultations with the young King Henry. He paid to the abbey the massive price of 140 marks (£93. 6s. 8d.) for the large complex of houses on the bank of the Thames north of the palace, which the royal treasurers, Richard fitz Nigel and William of Ely, had earlier held.[8] He even went further and acquired other adjoining houses and a 'grange' from Ralph, the younger son of the old treasurer William of Ely, and yet other nearby properties as well.[9] Both from there and from Westminster Hall he was able to carry out his loyal policies both as

---

5   Carpenter, *Minority of H. III*, 64-6, 96-100.
6   The other two members of the triumvirate were the pope's legate, Pandulf (now present in England, which had become a papal fief after King John's submission to the pope), and Peter des Roches, the autocratic bishop of Winchester, previously a minister to both Kings Richard and John. The legate resigned in 1221, and the bishop in effect was forced from power in 1223/4 after an explosive meeting between him and Hubert and their respective supporters, held at the New Temple in Fleet Street. The purge of the bishop left the arena free for Hubert, at least for the next eight years – but the bishop still lurked and finally had a temporary revenge, as we shall see.
7   For all his loyalty to the king, Hubert was greedy for power and great possessions, like others in this period. But these others, barons and military men who had snatched royal castles and estates during the civil war, were the cause of self-serving struggles in the next four years: see Stacey, *Policy, Politics & Finance*, pp. 11-18.
8   WAD 347, Rosser, *Med. Westm.*, p. 21; for the treasurers, see pp. 110-13, 155-6, 159.
9   For Ralph's sale to Hubert, see Richardson, 'William of Ely', *ibid.*, p. 90; and for at least two other properties, see Rosser, *ibid*, p. 21.

justiciar and as the most powerful counsellor of the young king during the years from about 1224 until 1232.

There can be little doubt that Hubert had previously eyed this property in Westminster, as one suitable for himself, ever since he had made one of his rare appearances as a witness to a recent private Westminster charter, by which the previous tenant William of Ely, the former king's treasurer, had restored the same property to the abbey.[10]

As his predecessors had done, Hubert himself continued to add yet further properties to his Westminster establishment and so helped to contribute to its description, *a noble palace'*, which the monk-historian Matthew Paris later gave to it.[11] We know that apart from an unknown number of 'houses' in this complex, there was also a courtyard or close, round which presumably the houses stood, a garden, a grange or barn, and an adjoining stable.[12] Here from time to time he no doubt brought his third wife, Margaret the sister of Alexander, the king of Scotland, whom he had recently married in 1221: a marriage with royalty – resented by older barons – which now related him distantly to the young English king and cemented the social and political position of the ambitious and covetous Hubert, whose father had been only a Norfolk knight.

## The London – Westminster riots of 1222

In July 1222 there occurred an episode in Westminster and London which reveals the real flavour of the unsettled and violent times which the civil war and the invasion by Prince Louis six years before had left behind. This interlude also demonstrates the equally violent ruthlessness which Hubert could show in countering such violence and the seditious unrest which he believed it exposed.[13]

On the 25th July of that year, a wrestling match near the Tower of London between teams from London and from the 'suburbs' (meaning Westminster) had been won by the Londoners. The bitter rivalry between the teams was such that the steward of Richard of Berking, the very recently elected abbot of Westminster, quickly made a plot to reap revenge.[14] The steward announced another match, to take place six days later, on the 1st August, this time in Westminster, with an invitation to all to come and take part. The place for this was in or near the nearer part of the Tothill Fields, *'where champions fight'*, the site where judicial combats took place.[15]

The wrestlers and citizens of London came in crowds to this new match, but during the combats many Westminster supporters,

---

10  WAC 439 (1218 x 1221), Richardson, *ibid.*, pp. 89-90. Hubert was not alone as a leading witness to this charter, since the pope's legate, Pandulf, the senior member of the triumvirate, and Eustace of Fauconberg, the new royal treasurer and future bishop of London, made a trio with him. William (a rebel in the civil war) had lost the property, by confiscation, see p. 159; it was after his later recovery of it, that he restored it to the abbey.

11  Paris, *Chron. Maj.* iv, 243-4. Hubert and Matthew Paris later met and talked, and in a number of places the historian appears to have used information fed to him by the justiciar, and probably also visited his grand residence in Westminster. But see Carpenter, *Reign of H. III*, p. 137 ff, for questions about Paris's reliability.

12  For the various parts of the whole property, see WAM 17376, in which the garden and stable adjoin a messuage which is being conveyed by that charter; and WAD 342b. for the houses, the courtyard and stable; and Rosser, *Med. Westminster*, p. 21.

13  The episode is described in greater detail in Norgate, *The Minority of Henry III*, pp. 184-6 and Ellis, *Hubert de Burgh*, pp. 69-73; Carpenter, *The Minority of Henry III*, pp. 290-1. The main chronicle sources are Matthew Paris, Roger of Wendover and the Dunstable and Waverley Annalists.

14  For the new abbot, Richard of Berking, see next chapter, at pp. 194 ff. He had certainly been elected before the 7th July (only 18 days before the match), but the pope had doubts about the election, Pearce, *Monks*, p. 48.

15  See p. 49 above. For Matthew Paris's drawing of a wrestling bout, see Plate 9 on p. 191.

whom the abbot's steward had secretly armed, fell upon the unarmed Londoners when the signal was given, and beat and wounded many of them. The Londoners fled back to the city, where uproar soon ensued. The common bell of London was rung; a mass-meeting of the citizens resolved on summary action. The *'prudent and peaceloving'* mayor, Serlo, advised that no more than compensation should be sought from the abbot, but the citizens were reported to have rejected him and to have chosen a new mayor and war leader. After an inflammatory speech from a former sheriff of London (now an alderman) called Constantine fitz Alulf, they marched out in armed bands, with the intention of razing all the houses of the abbot in Westminster and the house of the steward to the ground.

A riot in Westminster followed. Fortunately the mobs were dissuaded by some 'wise man' from attacking the abbey itself, but they tore down the steward's house and looted his goods. It was a scene of tumult, and the inciter Constantine was reported to have shouted out during it the old French battle-cry of the civil war, *'Mountjoy ! Mountjoy ! May God and our lord Louis help us'*, and two others took up the cry. And so, in Hubert de Burgh's view when he heard of it, a riot had become a seditious rising.

Hubert at that time was at Gloucester, but on receiving the news, he set out for the capital. Meanwhile the abbot of Westminster had already arrived in the city of London with a troop of mounted servants including some men-at-arms, to report the matter and complain to a friend of the king who was there. But round the house where they met,

the citizens gathered 'like bees' and seized twenty of the abbot's horses, beat up his servants, maltreated the men-at-arms and aimed to capture the abbot himself. Slipping out of the backdoor, the abbot was able to escape to the Thames; there he left in a boat under a hail of stones from the thwarted citizens, but came home safely to Westminster.

The pendulum then swung abruptly the other way, with the arrival of Hubert on the 13th August. He had come to teach the citizens a lesson, with the help of the military commander, Falkes de Bréauté, and contingents of his soldiers.[16] Hubert summoned the citizens and demanded to know who was responsible for the outrage. Constantine stood forward and boasted of his actions, whereupon he and two others were arrested by Hubert and delivered to Falkes and his soldiers. The next day they were all taken secretly to Tyburn and hung, in spite of Constantine's last-minute offer of 15,000 marks for his life. Some other citizens were arrested for seditious behaviour, and had their hands or feet cut off. Many others fled in fear, never to return. The mayor and aldermen were deposed, sixty hostages were taken, and a great collective fine was imposed on the city.

But the spirit of Magna Carta was now abroad. So however much the temper of the time, and of earlier times, may have tolerated such savage punishments, the verdict of a London chronicler was an indirect complaint: *'Constantine fitz Alulf was hanged, and without judgement'.*[17]

But we do not hear what happened to the abbot's steward, who had started it all.

16  For Falkes, see p. 192, n. 24, below.
17  *Liber de Antiquis Legibus*, (Stapleton, ed.) Cam. Soc. vol 34, p. 5. Constantine was a wealthy man with considerable land, some of it in Middlesex, but he had holdings also in London, Essex and Herts, all of which were confiscated, but later restored in 1225 to his son Hamo, see *Rot. Litt. Claus.* (Hardy ed.) ii, p. 39 (a); but in Jan. 1247, they were given by Henry III to the House of (Jewish) Converts, *C. Cl. R* 1242-47, p. 496. For the House of Converts established by Henry, see p. 284 below. Constantine had also held land in Hampstead, see VCH *Mdx* 9/92 and p. 369, n. 41 below.

## The boy king grows up

While Hubert had been making his way to the ultimate power which a lay man could achieve, the young king had of course been growing up. Some of his first official appearances, after his coronation at Gloucester in 1216, were at 'great councils' held in 1217 and 1218 in the Great Hall at Westminster. These were meetings of the lay and ecclesiastical magnates who had been summoned to express their counsel and consent, or dissent, for the regent's proposals. At the first of these, many of those who had rebelled against Henry's father were summoned to Westminster to swear fealty and homage to the boy-king and to lay claim to recover their confiscated lands; and in 1218 the king's increasing age and acknowledged maturity of character was recognised by a decision in the great council to make a formal but restricted grant to him of a seal of his own, on which he was depicted as already a grown man, in full armour on horseback.[18]

By 1220 it was time for the king's authority to be asserted, because his boyhood and the problems which it caused for those who meanwhile had to administer his kingdom had become a focus for derision and subversion in some quarters. So a splendid second coronation was planned for him, this time to take place at its proper site, in Westminster Abbey, at the hands of Stephen Langton, the once-disputed Archbishop of Canterbury. On the 17th May 1220 the ceremony was carried out, and a monastic chronicler who probably saw the event wrote, *'a greater celebration has not been seen in our days'*.[19] So Henry, a zealous enthusiast for ceremonial and religion in later life, had already had two coronations before even

reaching the age of thirteen. Even though the second coronation was initiated by his ministers, there can be no doubt that the king was already delighted to cooperate and play his ceremonial part to the full.

But his formal bond with the abbey, which was to dominate much of his life, had already been forged on the day before this second coronation. On the 16th May he had performed his act of devotion at the abbey, in laying the foundation stone of the projected new Lady Chapel at the east end of the abbey (as it was then), and so associating himself with the ambitions of the monks both to enhance the abbey and to recast their cult of the Virgin Mary which they had been promoting for the last thirty years.[20] Perhaps as a pledge of his enduring zeal for the abbey which he was later to consummate by rebuilding it, he donated to the fund for the new chapel the golden spurs which he wore on that occasion. Although this first royal act was directed to the honour of the Virgin, the king's own special devotion was to be reserved (maybe it already was) for St. Edward the Confessor, the first builder of the abbey in stone, whom the young king was later to emulate.

The next stage in the emergence of the king from the chrysalis of his youth was reached three years later in 1223 when, as a result of directions given by the pope, Henry received a greater control over his own seal and hence the power to give at least some orders of his own, without the overriding influences of others. This decision was a momentous one, made in Westminster by Hubert and the Archbishop of Canterbury, who had intervened to keep the peace in a violent dispute which had arisen between the

---

18  Both William of Ely (p. 156, 159 above) and Robert Mauduit and his son William (p. 164 above), as rebels, had to sue for restitution of their lands. The advent and ensuing use of the king's seal did not mean that the king was yet to play any full role in government. For the present the seal remained in the control of the regent and his associates.

19  Carpenter, *Minority of H. III*, p. 188; *Ann. Mon.* iii. 57. For a drawing of the crowning, see Plate 9 on p. 191.

20  See pp. 126-9 and 137-8 above.

(a)

(b)

(c)

(d)

**Plate 9. Further drawings by Matthew Paris:**
(a) the second crowning of King Henry III in 1220, by Archbishop Stephen Langton in Westminster Abbey, see p. 190;
(b) a single bout of the wrestling match between Westminster and London in 1222, which ended in riots and executions, see pp. 188-9;
(c) a legatine council (one of several), in which the legate sent by the pope delivers his instructions to the assembled clergy, see p. 82 n.57 and cf. p. 234;
(d) Henry III and Queen Eleanor coming back from France, 1243. Typically, Henry appeared in no way perturbed by the failure of his campaign in Poitou from which he was returning with his Queen, see p. 206 and n.61.

justiciar and other magnates, including Peter des Roches, the Bishop of Winchester.[21]

From December 1223 therefore Henry could now give and seal orders on his own, with the formal limitation that he still could not make permanent disposals of royal property until he came of age. In practice of course the justiciar or other advisers were usually consulted, or had themselves initiated the king's action. From this time forward, royal orders and decrees, as registered in the official rolls, were now made with the king's presence recorded as the sole formal witness: ie. 'teste rege', and no longer eg. 'teste Huberto', 'teste H.' or 'teste judicario'.[22] Often however the justiciar or one or more of the bishops was recorded as being in attendance as well, though without them being made formal witnesses.[23] But on some occasions the young king even acted alone, with no minister even mentioned.

The central importance which Westminster had already assumed, even in the continuing peripatetic form of medieval government, is demonstrated if one follows the geographical route which from the age of seventeen the king was now taking around the kingdom. Thus in the first six months of 1224, about 95 of the king's 'letters', giving royal orders and decrees, were sealed and witnessed by him in Westminster, while the remaining 60 were shared between such places as St. Albans, Marlborough, Bristol, Reading, Waltham, Ditton, Ham, the New Temple, Winton, Wallingford, Southampton, Northampton and London, where the king stayed briefly on his itineraries.[24]

Equally the 'great councils' of prelates and magnates, the precursors of more modern 'parliaments', which were summoned at intervals throughout the king's minority reveal that Westminster featured as the location for such assemblies more often than any other.[25] There in Westminster, not only were these early assemblies held in such palace quarters as the great or the little Hall, but also in different settings within the abbey, such as the refectory, or the infirmary chapel of St. Katherine, or later in the new chapter house.

So the prominence of Westminster in the government process was now entrenched, and in his own Westminster establishment Hubert had continued to survive as the tenant of the abbey, performing his national role in each of its different stations. But in 1227, more than a year before he had reached the age of 21, the king had taken to himself full regal powers to issue royal charters under seal and so pre-empted his own calendar majority. From then on Henry proved himself to be his own master in some things, with powerful and increasingly mercurial ambitions of his own.

## Hubert's fall

Although before 1232 the justiciar had already begun to lose some of the king's confidence, his fall from power, when it came

---

21 As a result, the bishop - the other remaining member of the triumvirate, see p. 187 n. 6 above was soon ousted, only to return like a vengeful demon in 1232, with Hubert's consequent fall from power, see below.

22 Carpenter, *Minority of H.III.*, 301-321. See also the rolls cited in the text.

23 A document witnessed by the king needed no other witness, although in practice it sometimes did have another person or persons present who were listed as a witness.

24 *Cal. P. R.* 1216-1225, passim ; *Rot. Lit. Claus.*, (Hardy, ed.) (1833), pp. 581 ff. From late June 1224, a huge number of royal letters were written from Bedford, but there was a single reason for this – from June to August Bedford Castle was being beseiged by the king. The fall of the castle 'concluded the triumph of central government' and spelt the end of the career of the castle's holder, Falkes de Bréauté, the mercenary captain who had begun by working for King John and had ruthlessly won power and castles for himself in the troubled times of the baronial rebellion and after; see Carpenter, *Minority of H. III*, 333-4 and 369-70. For Falkes, see also p. 189 above.

25 See eg. those councils or 'parliaments' discussed in Carpenter, *Reign of Henry III*, pp. 385 ff. and those listed in Powicke, *H. III and the Lord Edward*, p. 805. The word 'parliament' was about to become fairly

in that year, was sudden and unexpected. His former colleague Peter des Roches, the Bishop of Winchester, the very man whom he had himself 'purged' in 1223-4, had won back the king's favour, and for the next two years after 1232 Hubert was in the wilderness.[26] He lost his office, and his lands were confiscated, including his whole Westminster establishment. At times his very life hung in the balance. He had made many enemies who were now glad to harry him. There ensued an extraordinary story of drama, flights to sanctuary, violations of sanctuary, imprisonment, escape, outlawry.[27]

But, foreshadowing Henry's future swings of temperament, the royal weathercock swung round again. By the 3rd June 1234 the king had 'remitted his anger' towards Hubert, and gave orders to the Sheriff of Middlesex that some of Hubert's lands, including his 'houses in Westminster', and his personal charters were to be restored to him.[28]

But the great office of justiciar was now allowed to lapse and was not revived until the 1250s, long after Hubert's death. Even then the office was to be only a pale shadow of the central role which Hubert had personally played from his Westminster base during most of the king's minority. The brief age of an all-powerful lay individual was over. Westminster and its abbey, as the home-town now of government and the cherished objective of an impatient king's devotion, had new horizons to reach.

By 1241, before he died, Hubert redeemed an earlier but unfulfilled vow to take the cross and go on crusade to the Holy Land, in granting his whole Westminster property to trustees, for them to sell 'as God and prudence advised them' – which they did by selling it to Walter de Gray, the archbisop of York, for £266 13s. 4d., an enormous sum expressed to be for the 'support of the Holy Land'. In 1245 the property was given by the archbishop to his successors in the See, and for the next three centuries it remained as 'York Place', the residence in the London area of the archbishops of York, including Cardinal Archbishop Wolsey, until Henry VIII acquired it after Wolsey's fall.[29]

common, but not as a precise term of art. It became used for any important assembly, any occasion for 'talking', as its derivation suggested, see Powicke, *ibid.*, 338-41 and Carpenter, *ibid.*, p. 382. For the later development of 'parliament', see pp. 220-3.

26  For the purge of the bishop in 1223-4, see p. 187, n. 6, above.
27  Carpenter, *Reign of H. III*, pp. 45-60.
28  *Cal. Cl. R.*, 1231-34, p. 443 ff.; *Cal. P. R.*, 1232-47, pp. 48, 73, 81 and 100.
29  For Hubert's confirmation of the sale and the archbishop's gift, see *Archbishop Gray's Register*, ed. Raine, Surtees Society, lvi,  pp. 199-200.

# CHAPTER 12

# The three abbots 'Richard' – Richard of Berking
## 1222-1246

## Background

The rise, and later fall, of Hubert de Burgh, as Westminster's foremost resident and the kingdom's most powerful administrator had mostly coincided with the boyhood years of King Henry III. During the same period the religious half of the town, the abbey and its people, also entered upon a new phase. Most of its earlier abbots had already, as we have seen, enjoyed harmonious relations with previous kings, but in 1222 there began a sequence of three abbots who went further still. In addition to their religious role, the three of them also held, for most of the thirteenth century, powerful lay positions in the royal administration of the country.[1]

Of course any abbot of a church which was linked, as the abbey of Westminster was, to the apparatus of kingship – such as royal coronations, the adjoining palace and the structures of national administration – would necessarily be prominent. But up to this time none of the earlier abbots of Westminster had played a personal role of significance in the field of secular government. This was now to change for most of the remaining century. Beginning in 1222 the next three abbots were to forge powerful links between the world of the church and the royal and administrative worlds in Westminster, links strengthened further by the extravagant favouritism which Henry III showed towards the abbey of Westminster.

By coincidence the duration of these three abbacies overlapped substantially with the reign of that long-lived king. Unusually Henry III was king for a remarkable period of 56 years (1216-72), and the three abbots together coincided with 50 of those 56 years. Each of the abbots, and the abbey over which he presided, owed much to royal influence; and their combined periods of dependence on the king's favour contrast with the subsequent period, when Henry's son, Edward I (1272-1307), was to show less personal interest in the abbey and, after his first eleven years, in the usefulness to him of an abbot of Westminster.

Moreover, within the abbey itself, these three abbots, with the cooperation of their monks, entered upon domestic policies of greater sophistication and efficiency than had been seen before. This phase led to changes which included the following: – (1) the first comprehensive steps within the abbey to try to resolve the old conflicts between the abbots and their monks about the sharing between them of the benefits of the abbey's considerable assets; (2) an attempt to make a systematic appraisal of at least some of the abbey's land holdings and other resources; and (3) the start, at or before the middle of the thirteenth century, of methodical practices for the recording and auditing of annual accounts in each of their estates throughout the counties. None of these changes proved to be a resounding success at once, but at least they all pointed in the right direction.

But, to the confusion of record-makers and historians, each of the three abbots had

---

1   After the death of the second of these three abbots, the existing prior (Brother Philip of Lewisham) was elected abbot by the convent, but he died within three months and before he had received papal confirmation of his election. So technically he was not yet abbot, and in any case he did not survive long enough to make any mark.

the same first name. Richard of Berking (1222-1246), Richard of Crokesley (1246-1258) and Richard of Ware (1258-1283) followed one another in succession. Many records during this whole period, particularly the charters of private residents who bought and sold land in Westminster, were still undated, and so when one of the abbots happened to be mentioned in such records without his locative name (eg. simply as 'Richard, abbot of Westminster'), it is often difficult to be sure which one of the three is referred to.

Fortunately, the practice in Westminster of dating even private documents exactly did begin to grow further towards the end of the century. It became common in the 1280-90s and almost universal by the early 1300s.[2] So doubts like those which arise about identifications in some of the 'Abbot Richard' charters during the thirteenth century could not arise in relation to documents dated from about 1300 onwards.

## The new abbot and his compromises with his monks

Richard of Berking who became abbot of Westminster on the death of William of Humez in April 1222 was one of the few abbots, before the fifteenth century, who had held the office of prior before reaching the abbacy. So unlike his predecessor, he was not imposed on the abbey as an 'outsider'. Being already known and acceptable to the monks over whom he

had presided, he was quickly elected as abbot by them, certainly before the 7th July of that year, so avoiding any long 'vacancy'.[3] His native ability and competence was soon demonstrated both within the abbey itself, in which he took firm action to try to restore amity with the monks and to rebuild the abbey's financial position, and in various national administrative roles in which he served King Henry III.

No doubt it was his earlier experience as prior in charge of the convent of monks which had taught him that, as now the abbot, he had rapidly to find a solution for the ancient dispute between previous abbots and the rest of their monks, as to the correct balance in the sharing of the benefits and liabilities of the abbey's substantial assets. This problem had rumbled on for over a century, and only piecemeal attempts had been made to solve it.[4] But within three years of his election the new abbot had already succeeded, it seemed, in this objective.

He had been able to negotiate the terms of a lengthy compromise with his band of monks, and to bring it to a formal execution in November 1225.[5] It is clear from the wording used in that agreement that each side thought that this would be a satisfactory conclusion of the matter. The monks' appreciation of their abbot for achieving, as they thought, a permanent outcome with them was shown by their expressing in the

---

2   eg. WAMs 16754 (1282), 17467 (1285), 17468 (1286); 4874 (1291), 17475 (1293), 17478 (1294) etc; 17487 (1301), & passim thereafter. Rare earlier datings were given in grants or other records made *by* important people, eg. **by the king**: invariably dated, (eg. WAMs 17356 and 17357, both 1253); **by the abbot**: not always dated even by the 1260s (eg. in WAM 17337), but almost invariably dated thereafter; **by Odo the goldsmith** (see pp. 151 ff. above): a rare early date in 1241 (a special promise to the abbot, in WAM 17333). But other private grants, even to the abbot or other monk officers were usually not dated (eg. WAMs 17339-54), until the 1260s. Then in 1261, 1262 and 1270 (WAMs 17358, 17359, and 17361) private grants to the abbey were being dated; but even **Henry of Almain's** grant of his house Almaine to WA in or before 1269 was undated, see p. 273.
3   Richard may have also had grounds for acceptance by his fellow monks, if his mother Lucy and his father were known Westminster people who lived or had lived in Tothill Street, see pp. 177-8 above.
4   For the earlier history of this dispute, see pp. 123-6 and 135-6 above. Richard, in his earlier role as prior (when William of Humez was in his last years as abbot), had probably played a role *on the other side* in the arguments. He had now to see it from the abbot's point of view, but no doubt with greater sympathy for the monks' case.
5   WAM 5705*: printed (in Latin) in Harvey, *Walter de Wenlok*, pp. 217-22) and WAD 629b-631. The monks even sought and obtained a confirmation of the agreement from Pope Gregory IX in Rome.

document *'their thanks and gratitude, from one and all, to Abbot Richard as to a father and pastor'.*[6] But in fact the end of wrangling was still well out of range, and the same degree of heartfelt amity between such parties was not to be demonstrated again during the rest of the century, or beyond.

So some residual but lesser disputes between the Westminster abbots and their respective convents of monks were to continue after 1225, reaching progressive heights of greater bitterness during the rest of the century and beyond. The two main causes of this renewed wrangling were later objections made by the monks to some terms of the Berking compromise, and other complaints by them that successive abbots were not prepared to comply with their obligations under it. But none of this detracts from Richard of Berking's achievement in having at once grasped the nettle, and in successfully resolving at least many of the earlier causes of conflict by means of his first negotiated 'treaty' with the monks.[7]

### The first compromise

The principal feature of the new agreement was the abbot's full acceptance that the body of his monks should at last have their own comprehensive 'portion' or share of the abbey's assets, and that (in addition to the estates whose rents had already been assigned to the convent kitchen by Abbot William of Humez ten years before) this share should be made up mainly of

(a) six estates in the Home Counties; composed of five *'principal manors'*, Battersea and Wandsworth, in Surrey, just across the Thames; Feering in Essex; Aldenham, Stevenage and Wheathampstead, each in Hertfordshire; together with the smaller and closer estate of Knightsbridge (which included the district of Westbourne) in Middlesex; and

(b) substantial amounts of rental income from parts of other estates which had been let out, as 'fee-farms' to long-term tenants. These included amounts from the local estates of Hendon and Brent ('the whole farm, in wheat, grout and malt'), and Chelsea (£4).[8]

The abbey's estates in the Home Counties constituted the largest geographical cluster of its lands, and they were of course those nearest to the abbey itself. The next largest cluster of the abbey's estates were those in the distant 'western parts', ie. in Gloucestershire, Staffordshire and principally Worcestershire, and all of these were retained by the abbot, to become the major part of his share of the abbey's assets.

There can be little doubt that the main reason why this partition was made mainly on a geographical basis was the old Benedictine rules that no monk was to leave his precinct for any purpose without the abbot's order or consent, and that distant journeyings entailed problems about the keeping of the obligatory religious offices at set hours.[9] On the other hand, the abbot, like a lay magnate and his entourage, was free to itinerate with the officers of his household, on domestic and now also national business. However the ordinary monks remained restricted, if not scrupulously bound, by the old rules. As time went on, and as external administrative duties fell more and more on the monks who were appointed to act as obedientiaries or as bailiffs or deputy bailiffs in charge of estates, the rules against journeying away from the abbey precinct seems to have become more and more relaxed.

In addition to these six further estates and the sums of income allotted to the monks from

---

6    cf. similar thanks given to a previous abbot, William Postard, see pp. 125 n. 36, for a less exacting attempt to help the monks.

7    For these later disputes, see this and the two next chapters. It is well recognised that compromises can sometimes create more problems than those which they seek to resolve.

8    The monks of the convent liked to refer subsequently to these five as their 'principal manors'. In later years the convent's 'portion' came to consist of most of the Home Counties estates, some of them by later purchase by the convent, see Harvey, *WA Estates* pp. 65, 104-5 and 414-6. See pp. 135-6 above for Abbot Humez's grants to the convent.

9    See *The Westminster Corridor*, p. 143 and note 37; and chapters 67 and 50 of St. Benedict's Rule.

other fee-farmed lands, many other lesser assets – such as existing mills in Westminster and moneys from other sources, eg. certain named churches – were also assigned by Abbot Richard to the convent as part of their new 'portion'. But not everything was turned over to the convent: eg. the abbot in his turn was to retain all the abbey's advowsons, the existing rights which it held to present incumbents for particular churches. He was also to remain entitled to his rights to receive temporary hospitality from the tenants of certain estates in the course of his itinerations, and he retained the right to receive free milling and other treatment in the Westminster mills of his corn, grout and malt.[10]

The abbot was in effect divesting himself of immediate control of much of the abbey's 'empire', even if as abbot he still had a general oversight over the entire expenditure of the abbey.[11] Therefore a question necessarily arose as to what the effect of this divesting would be on those *obligations* which the abbot had always had under the previous regime. Would it relieve him of all of them, or would all or some of them continue to rest on his shoulders? The answer was that the principal obligations which were to remain with the abbot had also to be spelt out in the compromise document.

The abbot was to continue to be responsible to the king for all the military service due from the abbey, but in turn he would be entitled to all the services of those tenants who held their lands under obligation to provide military service for the abbey.[12] Secondly, he was also to remain liable, as

before, to 'defend' all the abbey's lands and other possessions against all civil claims, eg. by conducting and paying for all necessary legal defences and any actual litigation. Thirdly, he was to continue to be responsible for providing hospitality for the most important guests, and its cost, while the convent assumed the duty to entertain all lesser guests through a new 'obedientiary', the 'warden of hospitality'.[13] Fourthly, the provision and repair of the river-walls which were necessary to defend the abbey and its precinct against all threats from floodings of the Thames were to remain the abbot's obligation, as before, together with their cost.

The abbot's principal compromise with his monks was a remarkable agreement, when one considers the complexity of the issues which such a large division of assets and obligations gave rise to. On its face it appeared to have comprehensively picked up remaining issues, and one can well imagine the length and indeed intimacy of the talks in which the two parties must have been closetted in order to reach such apparent finality. Amongst the details, we can see that even such lesser, though important, matters as the necessary fires in the cellarer's offices were well provided for financially,[14] while the abbot was also prepared to meet his monks' demands for half the cider made from the apples and pears in the abbey's gardens in Westminster, as well as the amount of actual fruit which the convent had hitherto drawn annually from the gardens.[15] When one remembers the primacy of an abbot's original position of power, the

---

10  The abbot's main rights to receive hospitality in the Home Counties were at **Hendon** (Mdx); **Denham** (Bucks); **Ockendon** (Essex); **Islip** (Oxon). For **Deene** and **Sudborough** in Northants, Hendon and Denham, see pp. 136 above, 199 n. 22 and 202 below.

11  Harvey, *WA Estates*, 91.

12  See *The Westminster Corridor*, p. 141-2.

13  In return for the latter obligation of hospitality, the abbot endowed the convent with certain other sources of income, including a money contribution from the town of Westminster (£8) and half the hay and herbage crops from the meadows in Westminster.

14  The word 'brueria' in the translation of WAD 629b-631 (given in the WAD 'Descriptions' at the abbey) means here 'furze' or 'heath', for burning as fuel, not a 'brewery'. It is the same word in Latin. And the furze continued to be regular fuel for local cottagers on Hampstead Heath until the second half of the C19, as shown in affidavits in the Heath litigation of 1866. The word is also used to refer to the heath itself in the Survey of Hampstead in 1312.

flexibility which this abbot was prepared to show shines through the agreement.[16]

It also emerges from the document that, although this was the first time that a seemingly comprehensive 'portion' for the convent was being established, there had previously been a range of well-established 'customary' arrangements for basic accountings between previous abbots and the convent which had recognised somewhat similar entitlements on the part of the monks. These previous arrangements had probably resulted, in part, from the ad hoc smaller-scale agreements between earlier abbots and their monks, such as undertakings by those abbots to provide specified amounts to the convent's kitchener for the monk's food.[17] The importance of these earlier 'customs' was such that Richard of Berking's large-scale compromise now specifically allowed the monks to resile from its agreed terms, and to *revert to the ancient and laudable customs*, if the abbot failed to comply with some of his obligations under the compromise.[18]

### The second compromise

Although the main agreement was wide-ranging, it quickly emerged that inevitably there were other matters which still had to be sorted out between the abbot and his convent, and a second agreement had to be made, probably within a few weeks after the first. Most of the new provisions were consequential on matters already agreed, or made small but pertinent additions to the main compromise. They were apparently dealt with amicably, and the celebration of an 'anniversary' each year for the abbot after his death was also provided for. But there was no further expression of thanks to him this time.

This second agreement reveals that the abbot was already engaged at that time in two legal actions in the king's court to assert rights to abbey property – he was claiming (a) recovery of the main estate in the manor of Hendon against its sitting tenant, and (b) the advowson of the church in Sawbridgeworth (Herts) against the Bishop of London. From anticipated compromises in these two actions the abbot apparently expected to obtain certain moneys, and in this second agreement between him and his monks, these expected moneys were made the subject of new arrangements, in line with the new spirit of 'sharing' which lay behind the main agreement. Any moneys to be received from the Hendon action were to be shared between the abbot and the convent; and an expected pension of £10 pa. receivable by the abbey (apparently, in exchange for the ceding of the advowson of Sawbridgeworth church to the Bishop of London) was to fund both the celebration of the abbot's anniversary and also the provision of alms for 300 poor people on the same day.[19]

---

15   At this stage even the 'great garden' at (present-day) 'Covent Garden' was still a 'garden of the abbot', but it was soon to become the 'garden of the convent', see p. 199 below.

16   For an abbot's original primacy, which this abbot was now foregoing, see *The Westminster Corridor*, pp. 157-8.

17   See eg. pp. 123-6 and 135 above.

18   Harvey, W. de Wenlock, p. 220. The convent's entitlement to revert to *'the laudable and ancient customs'* is also repeated in the second agreement (described below) made by Berking and the monks, see WAD 631b.

19   The Hendon action was against Gilbert of Hendon, the tenant of the fee-farm there, comprising a messuage and three hides; see pp. 75-6 and 79-81 above (earlier history) and 201-2 below. The action about Sawbridgeworth church was against Eustace of Fauconberg, the bishop of London, who had claimed the advowson. However it seems that this expected funding of the abbot's anniversary did not materialise, since the ceremony had to be funded later by the rents from a new vill of Moreton-in-Marsh in Glos. which Berking built, plus an added two marks from another smaller estate in Hendon called 'Frith' (which the abbot had by then recovered), see *Flete*, p. 107. For the apparent sequel about the advowson in 1258, see Harvey, *W. de Wenlok*, p. 224 n.1 and the records there cited. The abbot had yet another legal action on foot at about this time, see n. 22 below.

Two more local assets which the convent gained from this second agreement with the abbot was an entitlement to the whole stock of pigs belonging to the abbey in Westminster, together with the right to the 'work services' which certain carters in Westminster owed to the abbey.[20] Both of these the abbot agreed to hand over to the monks, so that they would thereafter get the income-benefit of them, as part of their share of the assets.

### The third compromise

But within two years after these reasonably amicable further arrangements, the monks were back again with demands for further provision, this time specifically for the cost of their 'victuals'. The days were over when the monks of Westminster were content with the more simple diet of their forebears. They were now bluntly asserting that provision for their food was *'insufficiently made'*.

This time the abbot must have dug his toes in against further voluntary concessions, or at least found that even with goodwill he could not reach any friendly solution with the convent. The new demands had to be referred to the arbitration of three bishops in 1227. The bishops were persuaded to order some new concessions by Abbot Richard, but they only did so behind the usual smokescreen still used in some arbitrations, that this was in order *'to re-establish peace and concord, and to hush for ever all controversy'* about the monks' food. They also added strict injunctions, at the end of their award, that the convent was not to make any further demands on the abbot or his successors, having now obtained not merely a 'sufficient' but an 'advantageous' provision for their food.[21] So the over-optimistic message from the arbitrators was, No more!

The main effect of their award was that, in order to give his monks more income or produce, the abbot had to transfer two more nearby estates to them, namely Ashford and Greenford in Middlesex; plus an extra £3 pa., which he had just obtained in yet another legal action in the king's court.[22] Moreover he was also to assign to them the productive 'great garden' north of Charing Street, (which in due course became 'the Convent Garden') together with all rents which had by then been allocated to pay for the great garden and its servants. But since the abbot was to retain his other garden, known as 'the abbot's smaller garden', he was to be allowed to keep the right to use both the cider press at the 'great garden' and the services of its servants, when he wished to make cider from the apples or pears from his own 'smaller garden'.[23]

## A survey of the convent's new estates

In addition to negotiating, and in 1225 completing, the great sharing-out of the abbey's possessions, the abbot and his monks afterwards completed another practical exercise which demonstrated a more sophisticated

20  A useful illustration of the way in which the work services of those tenants still tied to the land could be transferred by the 'owners' of the right to such services. The convent of monks, alone, now became the 'owners'.

21  WAM 5683***. Since all subsequent records show that the king was violently opposed to any disputes between the abbot and his monks, it is probable that even in 1227 the wording of the award reflected royal dismay and anger at the outbreak of further confrontations between the major players in 'his' abbey.

22  (a) For the locality of these two extra estates in Mdx, see eg. coloured Plan B in *The Westminster Corridor*, after p. 96 (but Ashford should have been coloured blue there, as it was a *pre*-DB estate of the abbey). Certain woods in the two estates were to be kept by the abbot;  (b) The further legal action was against the abbey's tenant at Sudborough (Northants) who was contesting the abbot's right to receive hospitality at that manor. In the end, the tenant agreed to pay an extra £3 pa. rent, in return for the abbot's waiver of his right to hospitality on one visit: CP 25(1)172/18/124, and Harvey, W. *de Wenlok*, p. 225. So the convent gained this extra income, and the abbot lost his annual hospitality at Sudborough.

23  For the 'great garden' and 'the smaller garden', see pp. 33-4 above. For the 'smaller garden', see WAM 17370 (in about the area of the modern Horse Guards Parade?) and Appendix D, at p. 406.

approach to administration. This was the first (surviving) large-scale attempt to carry out a systematic review of abbey estates, but it related only to some of those estates which the convent had now 'acquired' from the abbot. It was intended to record the personnel in them (both the free tenants and the tied 'customary' tenants), together with their lands and rents, the work services which they owed, and the 'customs' under which each estate was ordered. However it was only an attempt, and a very patchy one. This 'Custumal', as it is called, included only eleven of the estates now held by the convent, and it also missed out quite a good deal of the relevant material, even for those eleven.[24]

One of the merits of the 'Custumal' is that it lists at least some of the 'free tenants' which the abbey now had on these convent manors.[25] But these free tenants numbered only 39, out of a total of 387 tenants, and they were spread unevenly over the total of eleven manors. Of the group of the convent's 'home' estates in the neighbourhood of the abbey, only Knightsbridge-and-Paddington (treated apparently, for this purpose, as one estate) is included among the group of eleven estates reviewed in the 'custumal'. Unfortunately no free tenants in Knightsbridge-and-Paddington are recorded, though we do know that there were free tenants present in that manor.[26]

This attempt by the monks to prepare data which would be useful in the subsequent administration of the convent's manors had been based on even earlier custumals, no longer extant. These seem to have been begun since the 1190s, when lessons were being learned from the orderly making of some national records as a regular practice.[27] By 1225 there is clear evidence, in the above documents made while Berking was abbot, that the practice of keeping and rendering written accounts and recording other data in writing was already being observed in some quarters in the abbey, however rudimentary such records may have been at that time.

For example, under the first compromise made by Richard of Berking and his monks, the convent's new *'warden of hospitality'*, the convent's officer who was to be appointed to carry out certain duties of hospitality laid on the monks, was ordered to render accounts of all his receipts and expenditure, *four* times each year. Similar accounts, to be made *twice* yearly, had been required even earlier by the abbot and convent at Westminster, relating to certain tithes of Wheathampstead church (Herts) which belonged to the abbey. Such accounting practices had been officially ordained for churches in 1222, when Stephen Langton, the Archbishop of Canterbury, at the Church Council of Oxford had prescribed a rule that accountable officers such as obedientiaries should present accounts 'four times or at least twice a year'[28]

Equally the second agreement made between Berking and his monks declared that all the live and dead stock, including ploughs, which the abbot had assigned to the monks in each of their manors, were to be 'numbered separately and plainly set down in writing', without any indication that this was an

---

24 WAM 9287. The Custumal is usually dated c. 1225, but since it includes Greenford manor as an asset of the convent, which the bishop arbitrators in 1227 had ordered to be transferred by the abbot to the convent, it should probably be dated 1227 or later.

25 See Harvey *WA Estates* p. 101 ff. for an account of the emergence of free tenants on abbey estates during the centuries after Domesday.

26 The areas of Knightsbridge and Westbourne and Paddington are treated variously at this time, sometimes as separate estates and sometimes in different combinations, as shown here. The three vills in these areas had received special mention in the great arbitration in 1222, only three years before, when they were held to be within the limits of the parish of St. Margaret's church, see App. B, at p. 399.

27 cf. Harvey, *WA Estates*, 105. For the beginnings of regular *national* record-keeping, see pp. 121 ff. above.

28 The compromise: WAD 630. Wheathampstead church: WAD 449a-b. Stephen Langton : Wilkins, *Concilia*, i, p. 590. These are drawn together in Harvey, *W. de Wenlok*, 218-9, nn.

unfamiliar practice.[29] So probably the making of written stock lists was already an existing practice in the abbey's administration of its estates, even if (to judge from similar lists occasionally to be found in the farming accounts of the abbey's manors later in the century) such lists were probably even more primitive in the 1220s than they were later towards the end of the thirteenth century.

## Abbot Berking and the improvement of the abbey's estate

Another area in which Abbot Richard was able to exhibit his practical abilities was in dealing with the financial stringency in which the abbey stood at this time.[30] The monks had very recently, in 1220, chosen to embark on the expensive project of building a new chapel to St. Mary the Virgin at their own cost, and they had done so at the very time when they were already in financial straits. Thirty years before, at the outset of Abbot William Postard's election, a huge debt of £1000 had been incurred by the abbey, and since that time other burdens had been laid on abbey funds by the loss of certain properties which had taken place under the recently deposed Abbot Ralph. On top of all, the 'great inflation' had been inflicting its damaging effects upon the abbey finances.[31]

To remedy this difficult situation, the abbot initiated a policy of increasing the abbey's landed estates and other assets, no doubt with the object of not merely increasing its immediate annual income (in rent or produce) but also, in course of time, of taking advantage of the effect of the current inflation upon both rents and produce. High on his list for acquisition were properties which had passed out of the occupation of the abbey, although lying within its own estates.[32] We have already seen that by or before 1225 he was already engaged in three legal actions – to recover the main estate in Hendon, to defend an advowson in Sawbridgeworth (Herts) against a claim by the bishop of London, and to establish his right to hospitality at the abbey's estate of Sudborough (Northants) or to exchange it for more rent.[33]

In about 1223 Abbot Berking obtained by agreement (an acquisition 'in soul alms', confirmed in subsequent legal proceedings in 1236) the repossession of the so-called 'island' ('insula', later La Neyte) within the next-door manor of Eye, west of Westminster itself.[34] The donor was a clerk, Laurence the son of 'William the small' (le petit or parvus); the former has already been mentioned above as the holder of a 'fee' in Westminster.[35] The area of the 'insula' (which included 'a close and all within the close and circuit of the island, with the mill') was described as a 'hide' in size (100 acres, or up to 120), and the existing (now reserved) rent for it was equally impressive, 100s pa., payable – not to Laurence the seller of the 'island', but to its previous owner, Willam of Hurley and his heirs.[36]

29  WAD 631b.
30  Harvey, *Estates*, 64 identifies the start of Berking's abbacy as a period of particular strigency for the abbey's finances, as a result of past liabilities or reductions of income.
31  For Postard, see pp. 129-31 above. Even his eventual discharge of the £1000 debt entailed a straitening of the financial situation. For Ralph, see pp. 131 ff. For the inflation and its effects, see pp. 118 ff.
32  On the financial side, Berking is said to have increased the abbey's annual income by about £200, through the success which he had had in acquiring new, or recovering old, properties, see Harvey, *WA Estates*, 164, and Matthew Paris's figure of £200 there cited. For the policy of re-purchase of 'lost' lands, see also pp. 120-1 above.
33  See notes 19 and 22 of this chapter, and their relevant texts, and see also in text below.
34  WAM 4772, WAD 100b, and, in 1236, CP 25(1) 146/10/144, WAD 104b. See also p. 330-1 below.
35  For William *le petit* or *parvus*, see pp. 22, n. 38; and App. A at p. 393. Shortly before 1223, a William of Hurley had sold the 'island' to William *parvus* – whose son now sold it on, to the abbot, but reserving the rent to Wm. of Hurley and his heirs. There were probably debts & mortgage between these two Williams, see WAD 100-102b.
36  This William of Hurley (and his father Arnold before him) was a 'knight', see p. 331 below. The abbey had to take over the existing rent for William of Hurley, though the grant (per WAD 100b) was 'in soul alms'; but then obtained a release of that rent, by granting land in Herts in exchange to William, WAD 102b.

At first sight, this could be seen as no more than a self-regarding acquisition of a nearby estate designed for the residence of the abbot himself and his successors, well away from the hurly-burly of abbey administration – as indeed it did become. But the large re-acquisition meant that valuable and productive meadows along the Thames, with other land and the mill, which had been in the hands of long-term tenants, once again became the abbey's property in hand, and (directly or indirectly) contributed to its finances by providing produce or other income.[37]

The abbot's legal action against Gilbert of Hendon for the manor (a messuage and three hides) did not result in recovery of the land, but by a compromise in 1225-26 resulted in a very satisfactory increase of the annual rent to the figure of £22, plus an increased farm of wheat, grout and malt. Fortunately the compromise or 'fine' also contains a record of (i) the mowing and carting services which Gilbert and his successors were to provide for the hay *in the Westminster meadows* for the abbey each year, and (ii) the rights of hospitality which were to be furnished at Hendon for the abbot and his retinue (on *'only 35 horses'*), for one night each year.[38] Gilbert's case in law must have been thought weak, to justify the advantages now gained by the abbey.

In furtherance of his policy, the abbot was also prepared in at least two cases to sacrifice rights of his own relating to hospitality, to benefit the finances of the abbey. Sudborough in Northamptonshire was one of the more distant estates on which the abbots had previously been entitled to hospitality, and as we have already seen, Abbot Berking before 1227 had agreed with the tenant of Sudborough, in a legal action between them in the king's court, to give up his right of one day's hospitality in exchange for an extra rent of £3 pa. from the tenant.[39] In a like case in 1231, the abbot also gave up his right to one day's hospitality at Denham in Buckinghamshire, in return for an agreement by Henry de Capella, the tenant, to pay a similar sum of £3 extra rent.[40]

In 1238 the abbot was also able to recover or acquire other major properties for the abbey, such as half of the manors of Longdon, with lands in Castlemorton and Chaceley, all in Worcestershire; and nearer home, the sub-manor of 'Frith' in Hendon.[41] He also built a new vill at Moreton-in-Marsh, in Gloucestershire, which brought added income.[42] In addition, different types of assets were obtained or recovered for the abbey by him: for example, by his procuring the acquisition in 1231 of the valuable church of Oakham in Lincolnshire and its dependent chapels, all at his own expense; and in addition the church of Ashwell in Hertfordshire, at the joint expense of himself and the convent.[43] John Flete, the later monk-historian of the abbey, also lists a formidable range of the abbot's additional acquisitions of smaller tracts of land, and his other actions and benefactions in favour of the abbey.[44]

---

37 cf. Harvey, *ibid*, p. 130. For some of the (printed) accounts for the abbot's La Neyte, see Harvey, *W. de Wenlok*, pp. 155 ff. For separate accounts for the manor of Eye, see chapters 19 and 20 below, at pp. 339 ff and 356 ff.

38 CP 25(1) 146/7/58. The services were:- eight men to mow for two days each year (when needed), and eight carts with two men, four oxen and two horses for each cart, to cart the convent's hay for two days each year; and provision of enough specified timbers from Hendon Wood to build a lodge to house the men who guard the Westminster meadows. For other 'foreign' mowers and carters needed in the Westminster meadows, see pp. 357 ff., and nn. For the original Hendon rent, see pp. 71-2 n. 13; altered at pp. 80-1.

39 See p. 199 and n. 22 above. The former £3 pa. became an asset of the convent, under the arbitration of 1227.

40 See *Cal. Ch. R.* (1226-1257), p. 130. The existing rent for the manor was £15 pa.

41 WAMs 32674-5, and CP 25(1) 258/5/13 (Longdon, etc, costing over £301). WAD 374b-5b (Frith).

42 *Flete*, 104 and 107, Harvey, *WA Estates*, 345.

43 Harvey, *WA Estates*, 404. The two churches were acquired by 'appropriation', which involved negotiation and the procurement of either episcopal or papal approval. In the case of Ashwell church, approval by the bishop was not given, and the abbey had to seek papal approval, see p. 209 n. 1. below.

44 *Flete*, ed. J. A. Robinson, 103-105.

But Abbot Richard himself was but a monk, with apparently few or no familial sources of serious money.[45] We may well ask, how was he in a position to make purchases 'at his own expense'? While it is not clear how many of his acquisitions were benefactions paid-for by himself on behalf of the abbey, some of these purchases undoubtedly were formidably expensive.

The purchase of half of the manor of Longdon, for example, had cost £301. 6s. 8d: an acquisition which was made at more than double the usual market rate.[46] On the one hand, it can be seen as a desirable re-purchase of an old manor which the abbey had owned from before the Conquest, only to lose it in the twelfth century when it had been let as a fee to the Foliot family and had subsequently been retained by that family.[47] But the sheer size of the cost of its re-purchase in 1238 suggests that depleted abbey funds alone could hardly have afforded such a cost, even if there was the sentimental but potent desire to recover a pre-Conquest manor. Although there is no record of any personal participation by the abbot in this purchase, it seems likely that in this transaction, as well as in the others where his generosity is safely recorded, he contributed some part of the cost. But where did any of his personal funds come from? The answer probably lies in the other half of the abbot's career.

## The abbot as treasurer of England and royal envoy

In addition to his domestic achievements as abbot, Richard of Berking learnt at the same time to play a leading role in national administration. His abilities had brought him to the notice of the king, who is said to have later 'preferred him above all the magnates of the kingdom - in all things'. Even in the days before he had become the prior at the abbey, he had been responsible and competent enough to represent the previous abbot as his advocate in a lawsuit in the king's court. Perhaps he had already been 'noticed' in such activities; at all events, when abbot, he now became the special adviser and confidant of the king, and was made 'the principal baron of the exchequer' and eventually the royal treasurer himself, 'the treasurer of England'.[48] So one can safely picture this enterprising and highly competent abbot moving calmly, but no doubt in suitable state, between his abbatial tasks at the church and the lay duties which he had to perform at the various seats of lay power within the adjoining town, whether at the king's quarters in the palace, or at the exchequer rooms or the treasurer's office.

The services which the abbot rendered to the king in these various roles were no doubt a source from which he was able to draw personal profits, and this would have enabled him to assist the abbey in his policy of extending its assets so that it could take advantage, instead of being at the mercy of the wave of inflation. But it was not merely within Westminster that such services were required of him. And equally it was not only money which the abbot was able to earn in the royal service. His position as a close adviser must have further stimulated the king's existing enthusiasms for all things religious and in particular for Edward the Confessor and his abbey at Westminster, and accordingly the abbey was to benefit in many different ways.

As illustrations of the width of his own usefulness to young King Henry, we find that on several occasions Abbot Richard was employed by the king as his own confidential

---

45 For some inferences about the abbot's family, see p. 177-8 above.
46 The realisable rent for the half manor was about £14, and a usual purchase rate was about 10 times the rent.
47 Harvey, *Estates*, 166 and 414-5. See pp. 120-1 above, as to earlier policies to recover such alienated properties.
48 *Flete*, *ibid*, 103. On a much later tombstone, Berking was called a 'prudent officer of King Henry' (III) in bad Latin, which was hardly flattering. What being 'treasurer' meant in this context is open to some doubt. Similarly Abbot Richard of Ware later became treasurer to Edward I, see p. 226 below.

negotiator, sent abroad to treat on the king's behalf in dealings with foreign powers. Thus in May 1234 he was despatched with another colleague to France to assist other royal envoys, the Bishops of Winchester and Exeter, in treating with King Louis IX of France over the extension of a truce between the two countries, which was about to expire. And again in May 1240 he was sent abroad on royal business, this time on an unspecified errand to an unidentified destination in 'parts across the sea'. He and his colleague were to carry 'the king's message' with them, receiving £10 at the king's order for certain expenses on the journey , and crossing on a ship which had to be hired for them in the port of Dover. Later in the same year, on the 5th October, the king was directing that £1000 should be paid to the abbot, for him to effect its payment over to the Prior of the Hospital of St. John of Jerusalem in France, *'for the use of the Count of La Marche'*, the king's volatile Poitevin step-father. So the abbot had become truly involved even in the tortuous complexities of the king's continental manoevrings.[49]

## The king's favours towards the abbey

As for the other benefits which the abbot's close relationship with the king, combined with Henry's existing devotion to St. Edward and the church which he had built, helped to confer on the abbey, the flow of royal benefactions ranged from acts of munificence to minor donations. The greatest gift which the king was to confer upon the monks was his grand project for building a new abbey, in place of the old one which was to be demolished; and all without expense, though with great disturbance and personal discomfort for them. Ever since the early 1220s

the young king had been bent on favouring the abbey, and after he had become his own man in about 1227, the plan for a great rebuilding must already have been maturing in his mind during the 1230s and before.[50]

After some years of gestation, that project was at last brought to a practical 'start of works' on the 6th July 1245, only sixteen months before Abbot Richard's death in November 1246. In the absence of direct evidence, one can only speculate about the degree of influence which the elderly abbot may have been able to bring to bear in person upon the king, in the slow development of the grand plan over the previous years. But it is impossible to believe that between such close confidants there was no mutual influence and indeed cooperation, directed to the same objective to urge the matter forward, even if the ever-compulsive King Henry may have needed little strenuous incitement to carry out his project. Certainly the work of making or overseeing the necessary practical arrangements arising from the forthcoming disruption in the life of the church and the convent must have fallen hard on the abbot's shoulders.

Moreover in the light of other events, it is difficult not to think that there was more than mere coincidence to the significance of that month of July 1245. For it was on the second day of that same month that the king made another grand gesture, both to benefit the abbey and to realise yet another enthusiastic vision, this time for both town and monks of Westminster. This was a royal grant to the abbot of the right to hold two annual fairs in Westminster.[51] Each fair was to last for three days, from the 5th January and the 13th October respectively: with all the benefits of enrichment for the abbey which

---

49   *Cal. Cl. R.*, 1231-34, p. 562; and *Cal. Lib. R.*, 1226-40, pp. 466, 473 and 496.

50   Curiously the evidence for the gestation of the project is slight. See pp. 241 ff below, for the rebuilding itself and its prelude.

51   *Cal. Ch. R.* 1226-57, 286. For the effect of the fairs on Westminster, see p. 212 below. In accordance with the king's custom, but reflecting his priorities, the *'Church of St. Peter, Westminster and the glorious King Edward the Confessor'* were also named as grantees in the royal charter. See also the illuminating chapter 4 in Rosser, *Westminster*, at p. 97 ff.; and pp. 308 below for some later developments as regards the Westminster fairs.

such a grant entailed.[52] So within that first week of July 1245, the monks both received the grant of these valuable fairs, and also witnessed – and no doubt themselves had already had to adapt radically to – the start of the works of gradual demolition, in accordance with the royal plan to construct a new abbey in place of the old. Following such events, the abbot may well have been able to rest content before dying in the following year, knowing that the king's enthusiasms were now under control and well set on course to enhance both the abbey and the town.

If one looks ahead, it is to be noted that three years later the abbey (no longer with the same abbot, but with his successor who was also a friend of the king) was to receive a further royal grant, for an extension of the duration of the October fair to 15 days. Added to this new display of generosity were further remarkable orders from King Henry: firstly that during the holding of this Westminster fair, all other fairs throughout the kingdom were to be suspended; and secondly (to the dismay and fury of citizens and traders in London, with whom the king was then at loggerheads) all London shops were to be closed. The intent was clearly to drive as much custom as possible, both national and local, to Westminster during its major fair.

But in addition to such spectacular benefactions, the king's bounty towards Abbot Berking and his monks ranged over other matters great and small. Construction of the new chapel for St Mary had already started in the 1220s and continued into the 1230s: and on the 24th April 1234 the king granted the abbot twenty oak trees from his forest of Tonbridge *'for his new works on the chapel of St.*

*Mary which he is carrying out in his church'*. The oaks were presumably for the roof of the chapel. Five years later the glazing of one of the chapel windows had been done, and ten years later, by January 1244, some of the remaining work on the glazing had been completed, and the king was paying the bill.[53] But progress was clearly slow.

In July of 1235 the abbot had received a royal grant of the right to receive eight deer taken from the forest of Windsor, with a further order that they were to be delivered to the abbey on the day before the 1st August (the feast of St. Peter in Chains, or Lammas day, the start of the yearly harvest), and that when they were delivered, the huntsmen carrying them were to blow two ceremonial blasts of their horns before the great altar of St. Peter in the abbey.[54] This grant of eight deer later became an annual gift to the abbot, for him during his lifetime and for his successors, with yet other gifts, sometimes larger, sometimes smaller, of deer from time to time.

One of the 'liberties' of the abbey which King Henry had in general confirmed to the abbot by charter was the financial right to receive any 'amercements' (in effect 'fines', in the modern sense, for misbehaviour or failure of duty) which any of the abbot's tenants or other 'men' anywhere were ordered to pay by any court in the kingdom. But this right was not being observed in 1236, and so the king had to spell out specific orders that all such amercements should be paid to the abbot from the exchequer or the sheriff of any county in the kingdom. This ensured that the funds of the abbey at Westminster would benefit by the amount of such fines, wherever the abbey's tenants and their faults happened to be within

52 The two dates for the start of the fairs were, fittingly, the dates of the 'deposition' (the dethronement, by death, of King Edward the Confessor in 1066; his burial following on the 6th January) and the 'translation' (the removal of his body in 1163 to a new shrine, after canonisation in 1161, see pp. 84-5 above).

53 For the twenty oaks, see *Cal. Cl. R.*, 1231-34, pp. 409 and 401. Other gifts of oak timber for building works were also being made to the abbot by the king well before his own major works in building a new abbey began in 1245. When Berking died in Nov. 1246, he was buried in the new chapel, long before the chapel and the new church were reconciled, see p. 261. For glazing work, see *Cal. Lib. R.* 1226-40, p. 442 and 1240-45, p. 212.

54 *Cal. Cl. R.*., 1234-37, p. 119 . Cf. *Cal. Lib. R.* 1226-40, p. 282 .

the kingdom. In similar fashion, the king had in 1235 conferred freedom from tolls in all markets and fairs, not only on the abbey itself but also on all its tenants. Other measures to give yet further financial assistance had been royal grants to the abbey, in various years, of rights to hold fairs or markets elsewhere outside Westminster: eg. at Staines in Middlesex, at Islip in Oxfordshire and at the abbot's newly-founded vill of Moreton-in-Marsh in Gloucestershire.[55]

Many of the years between 1235 and 1246 were filled with orders from the king for artistic objects of every kind, to beautify both the old abbey and the proposed new one, and to enhance its religious services, its ornaments and its vestments. But deeming the abbey to be *'his own'*, the king was also jealous in his protection of its rights. Since he had previously confirmed all the abbot's 'liberties' by charter, he was quick to order that no one should even enter any land belonging to the abbey without the abbot's consent; not even any of his own sheriffs nor, in one case, the abbot of Pershore, who had presumed to do so.[56] And no sheriff was even to entertain any legal claim which contravened the king's charter of liberties to the abbey.[57]

Henry's child-like delight in both giving and receiving expensive gifts to all and sundry meant that his generosity seemed to know no limits.[58] Anyone connected with the abbey was within range of it. In May 1246, nearly a year after the demolition of the old abbey had begun, the king made a large purchase of houses in 'King Street' for the heavy price of 60 marks (£40), buying up those which belonged to Thomas of Poulton, a royal serjeant who served the queen, including a large 'messuage and curtilage' which in the earlier years of the century had once belonged to William of the Castle, the exchequer clerk.[59] Henry kept the large messuage and later gave it as a charitable gift to the precentor's office at the abbey, but the other houses he donated at once to Master Henry of 'Reyns', the mason, his chosen 'architect' and manager for the building of the new abbey.[60]

In return for his generosities to the abbey, Henry required unquestioning compliance with his own demands for fitting celebrations at the church by the abbot and monks. The tone of a spoilt child can be heard in many of his orders for the abbey, whether addressed through his personal clerk of works, Edward son of Odo the goldsmith, or direct to the abbot or other officer of the abbey. When about to pay a visit to the church after his return from the continent in August 1243, the king – ever the great showman – gave orders to the abbot that *'against my arrival in Westminster let all the lights, as many as are used for the celebration of the feast of St. Edward, be burning, and let the great chandelier in the church be lit'.*[61] And in 1244 peremptory orders went out that for the feast of St. Peter in Chains (1st August), the first day of the harvest, *'as precious a chasuble as you can find in London'* be bought, to be offered up at the abbey,*'with a great mass on that day for the king'.*[62]

---

55   For amercements, see *ibid.* p. 245 (1236). For tolls, see *Cal. Ch. R.*, 1226-57, p. 208 (1235), and Rosser, pp. 104-05. For other fairs and markets, see CCR *ibid.*, pp. 67 (1228, Staines and Moreton), & 286 (1245, Islip).
56   *Cal. Cl. R.*, 1242-47, pp. 50 (1243) and 377 (1245).
57   *ibid.*, 1251-53, p. 279.
58   Henry has been aptly called 'the child king', Mortimer, *Angevin England*, p. 64. And like a child, he had almost miraculous powers of survival.
59   *Cal. Cl. R.*, 1242-47, p. 428 and 1247-51, p. 305; *Cal. Lib. R.*, 1245-51, p. 47. For William of the Castle, see pp. 182-3.
60   WAM 17357 (king's gift to the precentor, 14/3/1253), and see also 17359, for the release in favour of the abbey in 1262 by Thomas's widow of dower rights in one of the houses. For Henry the mason, see pp. 249-52 and 253-6.
61   *Cal. Cl. R.* 1242-47, p. 41. Not even the complete failure of his campaign in Poitou could dampen his enthusiasms.
62   *ibid.*, p. 209.

## Celebrations at the abbey and in the town

The abbey church was of course the scene of other celebratory rituals during Abbot Richard of Berking's administration which Henry insisted on observing whenever he was free from administrative duties, on the feasts of St. Edward (October 13th and January 5th), at Christmas and Easter and on other special feast days. For another coronation too the abbey served as the obvious and essential place. When in 1236 the king, now 29 years old, ended his search for a wife by finding the very young Eleanor of Provence, a daughter of the Count of Provence, it was of course in the abbey that the coronation of the young queen had to take place. The wedding had been celebrated by Archbishop Edmund at Canterbury, whither Henry had 'run' to meet his girl bride (puella) aged only twelve, after she had landed in England, to be married there before being brought on to Westminster by the king, to be crowned 'with unheard-of solemnity'.[63]

Seven years later in 1243 it was the turn of the king's younger brother, Richard earl of Cornwall, to marry the beautiful Sanchia of Provence, Eleanor's sister, at the abbey. The earl, now a wealthy and self-important man, was himself a resident in Westminster, having obtained a large property north of the palace from his brother ten years before. He was able to stage not only a splendid wedding service for himself in the presence of the king and queen and the sisters' mother, the countess of Provence, but also to provide an incomparable feast afterwards at his grand Westminster home.[64] This great display of worldly riches earned the equally great condemnations and perhaps some envy from Matthew Paris, the roving monk historian of St. Alban's. From his pen the fancy censures flowed: it was all *'secular pomp', 'empty glory', 'transitory luxuries', 'crowds of feasters', 'every kind of joker', a 'medley of dress', 'contemptible'.*[65]

In addition to such celebratory functions, both the abbey and the palace were also performing important political roles while Abbot Berking and his successors were alive, in providing venues where early meetings of the king's great council or early 'parliaments' could be held. Since that is a story which extends over a long period, it is deferred here until we consider the life of the next abbot, Richard of Crokesley.[66]

## Outside the precinct's walls

Since the whole town of Westminster had also entered on an era of great change during the memorable abbacy of Richard of Berking, it is worth noting briefly some of the features of that change which had been taking place before the old abbot died: –

1. The momentum of transactions relating to houses and land in the town, which had begun in the last decade of the previous century, accelerated relentlessly when the troubled years before and after the death of King John were over. King Henry's reign was to be far from trouble-free, but at least a better-ordered machinery of government was in place, centred in Westminster, and that meant more officials and administrative visitors in the town, some to become residents and to

---

63  M. Paris, *Chron. Maj*, iii, p. 336.
64  So the two royal brothers married two sisters, dd. of the Count of Provence. But as well the two sisters had two other sisters, who married the king of France, Louis IX, and Louis's brother, who was to become the king of Sicily. So the Provencals scooped the royal pool. The resulting arrival of Savoyard relations in England, and the favours shown to them, increased the dislike already felt for other 'aliens' such as King Henry's relations from Poitou and gave rise to much of the political trouble between Henry and some of his native barons in the 1250s. For the fate of Earl Richard's house, later called Almayne, see pp. 272-3 below.
65  Paris, *Chron. Maj.*, iv, 263. According to Matthew, the earl provided 3,000 dishes at the feast. If he had lived beyond 1259, Matthew might have regarded the destruction of the earl's house in Westminster, *Almayne*, in 1263 as a just desert. Later Richard and Sanchia were king and queen of Germany.
66  See pp. 220 ff. below.

work there, others just to do periodical business with the offices and courts. With them came those who aimed to provide the services which the incomers needed – the lodgings, food and drink, clothing and shoes, building and most other necessities of life. And so the wheel of property turned, and charters reflecting the rolling purchases and lettings multiplied in the abbot's court.

2. The streets of Westminster were full of new buildings, and must have been ringing also with the construction of new wholesale developments of housing. At least two, if not three, such large-scale projects can be detected during Berking's abbacy; and who knows how much else lies undetected? Tothill Street figured largely, with its two building ventures, and Aldwych benefitted with a housing enterprise undertaken by a local resident but an unusual developer, the well-known Westminster clerk Henry of Belgrave.[67] It may also be that the 'common ditch' behind the houses on the west side of 'King Street' shows that a building project had taken place there too, with the latest drainage arrangements for residents.[68]

3. The complex of houses bordering the Thames and Endiff lane which had belonged to the old treasurers, Richard fitz Nigel and William of Ely, had passed in the early years of Abbot Berking's abbacy to Hubert of Burgh, in his spectacular rise to power. His mansion there continued to grace his justiciarship until his equally sensational fall, and before the abbot's death in 1246, the whole Endiff property had become the residence used by the archbishop of York whenever he was in the neighbourhood of London.[69] Since 1188 the archbishop of Canterbury had also established his own London residence at Lambeth, and so for the rest of the medieval period the two

archbishops faced each other across the Thames; not always amicably when precedence was in issue.[70]

4. In the 1230s Abbot Berking must have watched the great stone mansion, later to be known as *Almayne*, being built by the king's brother Richard the earl of Cornwall, on a site south of Endiff lane. He must also have remembered the feasting there in 1243 after the earl's wedding. But before he died, the abbot could not have foreseen that the life of the mansion was to be brought to a violent end less than twenty years later at the hands of a London mob.[71]

5. Above all the most dramatic change which the town was to see and hear, while Abbot Berking was still alive, was the planning and start in July 1245 of the demolition of a major part of the old abbey and the rebuilding operations which King Henry had devised for his splendid new abbey.[72]

## The last days of the abbot

In spite of all the distractions which the king was having to deal with in the 1240s, he did not forget his close personal relationship with the remarkable but now ageing Abbot Berking. Three months before the abbot died, Henry was ordering *'the most precious mitre that can be found in London'* as a gift to the older man. It was to be his last gift. When the abbot died in November 1246, he was buried in a marble tomb immediately in front of the altar in the new Lady Chapel over whose construction he had presided. By that time Westminster was already resounding with the works of demolition and the early stages of the construction of the new stone abbey, which had now been in progress for more than sixteen months.

67  For projects in Tothill Street, see pp. 47 above and 270-1 below; and in Aldwych, see pp. 34 n. 36 above.
68  See pp. 53-5 above.
69  See pp. 193, and n. 29, above, and 269 below.
70  For unseemly episcopal squabbles within the abbey, and secular disputes in the king's Great Hall, see pp. 239-40 below.
71  For the violent end of Almayne, see pp. 272-3 below.
72  See chapter 15, 'The great rebuilding', at pp. 249 ff.

# CHAPTER 13

# The three abbots 'Richard' – Richard of Crokesley
## 1246-1258

So by the end of 1246 King Henry's project for the rebuilding of the abbey was well under way, and Westminster was echoing to the sound of demolition and construction. Masons, carpenters, blacksmiths, other metal workers and their dependants were about to double the transient population of the town in the next twenty-five years, before this first great stage of the rebuilding was complete. With this frenetic activity growing around them, it is hardly surprising that the monks were to find little room for the domestic peace and harmonious contemplation which their calling needed.

When his predecessor died in November of that year, Richard of Crokesley was a prime candidate for the abbacy. As a monk at the abbey, he had studied in the schools and was a 'Master', a *'vir litteratus'*, and a man *'skilled in both civil and canonical law'*. Although he had not served as the abbey prior, he had risen from the ranks of the ordinary monks, and had later been appointed the archdeacon of Westminster by the bishop of London. Apparently he had already been recognised as having diplomatic and forensic skills, and had made an early journey abroad in 1239, having been sent to Rome on a mission on behalf of the abbey.[1]

Above all, he was known to King Henry, and indeed was either his close friend already,

or in the course of time became so. In 1242 he had been selected, with another monk, by Abbot Berking to carry the abbey's relic of the Virgin's girdle, which the king had required to be brought to him and Queen Eleanor, while they were in Gascony. The reason behind this was that the queen was pregnant and the girdle, given to the abbey by St. Edward the Confessor, was thought to assist in childbirth.[2] It may be that the king's and Richard Crokesley's friendship had begun from that time, and that the king had quickly realised that Richard could be a potential member of the band of reliable and adroit men whom he could employ in enterprises involving statecraft, just as the previous abbot had been. We know that in appearance Richard looked every inch the ambassador. He was handsome and 'elegant and eloquent', and when he said mass, he was able to do so *'like a bishop in all things'*.[3]

### The abbot as royal envoy
So it is not surprising that even the very early years of Richard's abbacy saw him being sent abroad again, this time on close personal business on behalf of the king. In 1247, within eight months of his election as abbot, he was sent abroad to Germany with John Mansel, the king's closest and most trusted counsellor and clerk, to treat with the Duke of Brabant for the

1 The mission had been to secure papal confirmation for the appropriation of the church of Ashwell (Herts) by the abbey, which had been made shortly before, by permission of Pope Honorius III in 1225. But the bishop of Lincoln, Robert Grosseteste, in whose diocese the church lay, had objected, and the abbey had to seek confirmation from Honorius's successor, Pope Gregory IX, Bliss (ed); *Cal. Pap. Reg.* 1/181. For Ashwell, see p. 202.
2 Thompson (ed), *Customary of WA*, pp. 73 and xviii. The date given there was 1246, but it was 1242 when the queen was in Gascony and pregnant. In the event the queen gave birth to a daughter, Beatrice, at Bordeaux.
3 M. Paris, *Chron. Maj.*, v. 700; Flete, *History of WA*, p. 109. Appropriately one of the first gifts which the king gave him in his first year was a 'great pontifical ring', bought for £4: *Cal. Lib. R.*, 1945-1251, p. 118.

betrothal of the duke's daughter to Henry's young son, Edward, aged only eight. But *'for a reason unknown, they returned sadly with empty saddlebags'*.[4] Again in each of the two following years the abbey had to do without its abbot for some period while he was away abroad on royal business. In 1248 the payment of expenses abroad ran to more than £155, suggesting that long stays there had been required, or that certain financial 'inducements' may have had to be made by him to further the king's business.[5] But like his predecessor he continued, when at home, to receive recognition of his services, in the form of royal presents of deer from the king's forests, and in 1248 the gift of a single but special oak tree from the forest of Windsor, with which 'to make a mill'.[6]

### The casket of Christ's Blood

In 1247 there had occurred one of the grand occasions in Westminster in which King Henry revelled. The two orders of the Knights Templar and the Hospitallers, in concert with many priests in the Holy Land, had sent to England a crystal casket said to contain some of Christ's Blood.[7] Indulging his passions for religious ceremony and theatricality, the king staged a procession on St. Edward's day (13th October) in which in the company of all the priests of London, and himself wearing humble dress and walking on foot, he carried the casket held high in both his hands from St. Paul's church in London all the way to the abbey at Westminster, being met on the road by more than a hundred chanting bishops, abbots and monks. Once in central Westminster, he carried the casket round the abbey, and the palace, including his own royal

rooms there. The abbey, on which some demolition had already taken place, was packed; mass was celebrated, a suitable sermon was preached by the Bishop of Norwich, and the relic was solemnly presented to the abbot. The king changed into robes of silk cloth of gold and, sitting on a splendid throne, then performed a ceremony of conferring knighthood on one of his half-brothers and other young men.

All these details, and more, were recorded by the indefatigable Matthew Paris, who on this occasion had a compulsory reason for doing so. As a monk of St. Alban's abbey, he had been present himself at this celebration at Westminster, standing not far from the king's throne within the abbey. Being already known to the king because of the fame of his historical writings, Matthew suddenly found himself being beckoned by the king and commanded to sit down below him and to watch. He was then ordered to record the magnificent proceedings of that day – *'so that their memory cannot on any account be lost to posterity down the ages'* – a prophetic royal command. After the ceremony Matthew was invited by the king to dinner with his three monk companions, and a sumptuous meal was provided at the king's expense in the refectory of the abbey for all the monks present on that occasion.

### The abbot heads for trouble

However disputes lay ahead for the abbot – first, trouble with the citizens of London, and later, dissension with his own monks. The former trouble arose because of orders which the king made in 1248, extending the rights already given by Abbot Berking to the monks

---

4   M. Paris, *ibid.*, iv. 623-4. *Cal. Cl. R.* 1242-47, p. 533. So even the presents which they had taken had failed to persuade the Duke.

5   *Cal. Lib. R.*, 1245-51, p. 171. But in each of 1247 and 1249, his expenses were only £13. 6s. 8d.

6   *Cal. Cl. R.*, 1247-51, p. 54. The oak tree may have been for the central post of a post-(wind)mill, or for the abbey watermill on 'Millbank'. Windmills had arrived in England in the previous century, see Kealey, *Harvesting the Air*, passim. Although both Westminster and La Neyte in Eye were low-lying, the uninterrupted flow of wind along the river valley were quite sufficient to drive a windmill. For the mill in Eye and perhaps even an earlier watermill, see eg. DS, *Eye A/cs*, pp 1, 8, 14, 110, 115, 140, 228.

7   Even Matthew Paris recorded the holding of doubts expressed about the genuineness of the relic, *Maj. Chron.* vi. 638. For his careful drawing of the ceremonial walk, see Plate 10, p.211.

**Plate 10.** Matthew Paris was himself present when Henry III carried a phial alleged to hold some of Christ's Blood, all the way from St. Paul's to Westminster Abbey. All the priests of London were required to follow the king, and many bishops, abbots and priests met him in Westminster. At the abbey, the king directed Matthew to record in his history all the events of the occasion, as he then did with this careful drawing and a full description. See p. 210.

of Westminster to hold two annual fairs in the town.

The latter trouble, between the abbot and his own monks, arose because of continuing differences over a few of the terms of the great 'sharing' compromises made by Abbot Berking. Great bitterness seems to have accompanied this dissension, so much so that it caused *'disgrace and scandal to the whole order of black [ie. Benedictine] monks'*, according to Matthew Paris.[8] Worse still, from the abbot's point of view, it clearly caused petulance, if not downright anger, on the part of the king, who disliked such dissensions in 'his' abbey and seems to have regarded the abbot, rather than the convent, as being responsible for them.

The right to hold the two annual fairs in Westminster in October and January had been granted earlier by King Henry to Abbot Berking in July 1245, the same month in which work on the royal project of rebuilding the abbey had begun. The start of the demolition and building work had created a disastrous site for these autumn and winter fairs, when the time came to hold them. We know that by about the time when Abbot Crokesley was elected abbot at the very end of 1246, at least part of the abbey, at its eastern end, was already *'half demolished'*,[9] and then to make matters even worse, the rains of 1247 arrived in deluges. The fairs were already too large for the abbey churchyard, the site chosen for them. This site was reduced to mud, and in any case it held no sheltering stalls. *'Crushed, drenched and muddied, the unhappy merchants wished themselves at home by their hearths, among their families'.* [10]

This was the scene when the king, apparently not disconcerted by the chaos, managed typically to compound the whole problem, at a great ceremony at the abbey in

1248, by extending the period for the main fair in October from three days to fifteen, and even more significantly by ordering both the suspension of all other fairs in the kingdom during the October fair in Westminster, and also the closure of all shops in London during the same period. All this was designed to provide further funds in Westminster for the great rebuild of the abbey, and at the same time to penalise the citizens of London, with whom he was already on bad terms. In favour of the abbey he also planned other restrictions on the city, overruling the Londoners' furious but natural objections, and even their offers of large amounts of money failed to soften the king's determination to drive his nail home. But as a result it was the abbot who was blamed as the person thought to have brought all this about, and the king's brother, Richard Earl of Cornwall, who was well regarded as a professional arbitrator, had to be brought in, with Earl Simon de Montfort, to mediate between the abbot and the citizens of London.[11]

Meanwhile a second storm was brewing for the abbot. It is clear that by about 1250 three of the terms on which the original 'sharing' compromise had been made between Abbot Berking and his monks in 1225 were causing great dissension between the new abbot and the monks. This was the cause of the *'scandal to the whole order of black monks'* reported by Matthew Paris. The disputed terms related to: –

(a) the existence of any right on the part of the abbot officially to 'visit' (and correct any errors in) any of the estates which the convent now administered. Under Abbot Berking's agreement, the abbot had no right to 'intrude himself' into any of those estates, unless of course the convent assented;

8   M. Paris, *Chron. Maj.*, v. p. 83.
9   M. Paris's word for the physical state of the abbey is *'semirutam'* = half-broken, *ibid.* iv. 589. Even when Henry III died in 1272, his rebuilding did not extend to the western end of the nave, the rebuilding of which did not even begin until 1376 and was not completed, in different stages, until after 1500.
10   Rosser's graphic summary, *Med. Westminster*, p. 98. M. Paris, *Chron. Maj.*, v. pp. 28-9 and 333.
11   M. Paris, *ibid*, v. pp. 127-8. See also Denholm Young, *Richard of Cornwall*, p. 75. For the earlier and the later history of the fairs, see pp. 204-5 above and 212 below. In 1248 the king ordered the transfer of the fairs to Tothill, another muddy site, but this does not appear to have happened, perhaps fortunately.

(b) an obligation which Abbot Berking had undertaken, to supply meat for the tables in the monks' second dining hall called the 'misericord' during part of January each year; and

(c) the extent of the abbot's power to dismiss any monk who had been appointed as an 'obedientiary', to manage one of the convent's administrative departments. In Abbot Berking's agreement, there appeared to be conflicting rules about dismissal.[12]

On the first and third of these issues, the new abbot was clearly demanding the right to 'visit and correct', and a right to dismiss for reasonable cause. The meat issue had recently been pre-empted by a decree of Pope Gregory IX and later the Benedictine General Chapter, which had prohibited the eating of meat (even in the misericord) by any able-bodied monk, so it is hardly surprising that the abbot's obligation to provide certain meat dishes for the monks had had to be withdrawn: but, for all we know, the monks may, in exchange, have been demanding some compensatory financial adjustment.[13] However the real disputes must have been attended by considerable personal rancour; the new abbot appears to have been a more overbearing man than his predecessor, and was not content with the original agreement.[14]

At all events King Henry stepped in, because of the scandal being caused by the dissensions in 'his' abbey. By then nearly two years had elapsed. In July 1252 two mediators, the Bishop of Bath and Wells and John Mansel, the king's trusted officer and envoy, were appointed by the king, and three weeks later, with the help of their mediation, a new agreement was entered into by Abbot Crokesley and the convent on the 16th August. Apart from other lesser provisions, the three original terms were withdrawn, and the new settlement;

(a) gave a new right to the abbot, that once a year he should be entitled to 'visit', and correct abuses in, any of the convent's 'principal manors', staying there one day;[15] and

(b) defined more clearly a power for him to dismiss an obedientiary *'for reasonable cause, according to the order and rule of St. Benedict'.*[16]

This may appear to be an amicable and relaxed agreement between the abbot and the monks, but it is clear that there was much more to it than that. Not only did the king and the two mediators, impose their seals on the document, but when appointing the mediators, the king had written a letter to the abbot and convent, in which he said that it was he who *'had ordained a certain form of peace [between the two parties], which he wishes to be*

---

12 The 'misericord', which was additional to the huge refectory, must have been built before 1225 between the refectory and the kitchen. 1230 has been given (Harvey, *Living and Dying*, pp. 41-42) as the date *after* which this room was built, but the misericord is named in the 1225 compromise itself, without any mention of recent building, so it probably antedated that compromise by some years. Misericords, as additional meal rooms, were being built everywhere about this time, Knowles, *Monastic Orders in England*, p. 281.

13 Harvey, *W. de Wenlok*, p. 227. n. 3.

14 The abbot's repeated absences abroad, and his withdrawals (when in England) from the abbey to La Neyte his country house at its 'island' site in the manor of Eye may also have been causing affront to his monks.

15 One of the subsidiary terms about the abbot's visits shows that the abbot was allowed to bring 20 horses (for his retinue), and that the manor had to provide oats for that number of horses, if procurable, or if not, 3d. for each horse. Food for the humans was not provided for, but logs for burning were to be supplied.

16 WAM 5956 (WAD 632b-633b). When properly analysed, the power to dismiss an obedientiary, as given in the old agreement, had been drafted rather loosely and obscurely, and the new one was short and clear: but (disregarding lawyers' arguments) in practical terms the difference was slight. On the other hand the right of visiting the convent's manors was a new one, since the old agreement had forbidden the abbot (and, curiously, the prior as well or anyone else except appointed bailiffs) from 'intruding' into any of the convent's manors without the full convent's consent. Denholm-Young, *Richard of Cornwall*, p. 75, says that Earl Richard acted as a mediator between the abbot and convent in 1251, and that 'the abbot lost three manors' by the 1252 award; but quaere?

*inviolably kept'*, and that *'the Abbot in the King's presence has agreed to his ordinance'.*[17] Moreover the evidence of Matthew Paris indicates that the abbot was a reluctant party to the agreement and wished to appeal to Rome, so earning the king's severe displeasure and a temporary loss of his favour.[18]

The clues which suggest the apparent support of the king for the convent in their disputes with the abbot are reinforced by the fact that it was also in 1252 that the king granted a really substantial benefit to the convent, but not to the abbot. He made a charter in the convent's favour which, in effect, freed that 'portion' of the abbey's assets which the convent now enjoyed, from the old rule that when there was a vacancy in the abbacy, the king by his 'regalian right' became the temporary custodian of *all* the assets of the abbey. So now it was only the abbot's share of the assets which could be taken over by the king during the period before a new abbot was appointed.[19]

At the first opportunity for implementing this (ie., when Abbot Crokesley had died on the 17th July 1258), we find immediate instructions being given by the king on the 24th July to Adam of Aston, his newly appointed custodian of the abbey, not to take control of the convent's possessions.[20] So within one week after the abbot's death, and in the middle of his 1258 crisis with the barons, he remembered (or had been reminded of) his undertaking to the monks of the convent at Westminster.

### The abbot's continued career as a royal envoy

Yet in spite of the king's anger at the dissensions in the abbey during the early 1250s and the abbot's part in them, Abbot Crokesley was still being employed as one of the group of confidants who acted as the king's envoys to the continent. In 1251 he was sent to treat with the French king, and also to the papal court.[21] In 1252 he was again on the continent on two occasions on other business of the king.[22] And in July 1254 he was given a more far-reaching task by Pope Innocent IV, in an enterprise in which the pope and King Henry were by now jointly engaged. This project was a further crusade, for which the king had 'taken the cross' four years before in 1250. To finance the crusade, a tax on the church and clergy had been ordained, and for this purpose two bishops and Abbot Crokesley were appointed in 1254 to assess the value of all the relevant church property in the country, a massive undertaking.

In this task, all the distant western and Welsh dioceses in the country were assigned to the abbot, which can only have meant that he was absent or otherwise engaged for even longer periods from his office and duties in Westminster.[23] However by June 1256 he was again being sent off to Rome, with massive powers for him and two other envoys to obtain loans 'from merchants or others' on behalf of the flailling king who by now was extremely short of money.[24]

17 WAD 633b. My italics in the text identify clues to the background behind the agreement. Even the agreement itself speaks of it being made at the 'wish' of the king. He also 'stood over' the abbot as he executed it.

18 M. Paris, *Chron. Maj.*, pp. v. 303-5. Another issue, which cannot be resolved here, is the content and identity of another mediation award, made by four other abbots, on the same issues, as referred-to in an oath which the abbot was compelled to make four years later, in 1256, binding himself to observe the original agreement of 1252 and not to observe the abbots' award, see WAD 633b-634, and WAM 5683. There had been more ructions.

19 WAD 64, and *Cal. P. R.*, 1247-58, p. 150. Even after Abbot Berking had effected the 'sharing' arrangement in 1225, the old rule had not been changed, with the result that when that abbot died in 1246, the convent's 'portion' had passed briefly into the king's custody (and so did the abbot's); see Harvey, *WA Estates*, p. 87 and n. 3.

20 *Cal. Cl. R.*, 1256-59, p. 249.

21 *Cal. Cl. R.*, 1247-51, p. 420; M. Paris, *Chron. Maj.*, v. pp. 228 and 231.

22 *Cal. Lib. R.*, 1251-60, pp. 27 and 91.

23 Powicke, *Henry III and the Lord Edward*, i. pp. 370-1.

24 *Cal. Lib. R.*, 1251-60, p. 301; *Cal. P. R.*, 1247-58, pp. 479, 481, and M. Paris, *Chron. Maj.*, vi. 333.

With this crescendo of administrative duty to keep the abbot away from his place in the abbey, the climax came when, in his own last days, he became implicated in the last chapter of the king's tortuous career – namely, the final period of conflict with the barons, which led eventually to savage civil war in the early 1260s.[25] The abbot's involvement in this murky saga was cut short, perhaps even fortunately for him, by his own death on the 17th July 1258. More than two months before that, at a threatening meeting held in the great Hall of the palace at Westminster, the king had at last agreed, under duress, with the barons' demands that reforms of the realm and its international relations had to be carried out.[26] The reforms were to be undertaken by a council of twenty-four members, composed of twelve chosen by the king and twelve by the barons. Abbot Richard of Crokesley was one of the twelve who were then chosen by King Henry.[27] But although the abbot may have been able to take part in the initial deliberations of this council in June, his own death a few weeks later brought his role in it to an end.

## The improvement of the abbey's estate

In spite of the time which Richard of Crokesley had had to spend on royal or other public affairs, he did succeed in continuing the policy of his predecessor in adding significantly to the assets of the abbey in order to increase its income. Inflation was still in progress, so there was still every incentive to do so. His purchases included the large estate (a 'soke' in the city of London, Westminster and elsewhere in Middlesex), of the family of Mohun which was currently held by Robert of Beauchamp, a royal circuit justice, and his wife Alice.[28] For this the abbot had to pay £56. 13s. 4d., and it is possible that he may have paid this out of his own pocket, although he made no claim to have done so.

A second addition to the abbey's property, but one which may have owed more to the king's generosity than to the abbot's own efforts was a royal gift of houses lying outside the cemetery wall of the abbey precinct. These had belonged to Sir William II of Cantilupe, the king's own seneschal or steward and the head of his household. Sir William had died in February 1251, and immediately the king bought them and gave them to the abbot and the convent, for the express use of the sacrist.[29] These properties lay not far from the west gate of the abbey, and included at least one large house which Sir William had himself occupied.[30] The king was adamant that the sacrist should have the sole use of the houses, and the abbot and convent were expressly prohibited from removing them from his control. The king also granted the right to the sacrist to hold the properties freed from the power of any of his marshals to lodge or billet

25 By this time the king was bogged down in the morass of problems which he had been frenetically creating for himself – his own projected crusade (which of course never happened); a mad plan to obtain the crown of Sicily for his second son Edmund; the incurring of staggering debts to the pope, as a condition of the Sicily plan; and resulting antagonisms with his own barons, and eventual civil war in England – from which, with all the undeserved luck of the reckless, he survived defeat & imprisonment, & finally escaped alive and on the throne.

26 A group of barons and knights had arrived armed at Westminster Hall on the 30th April 1258. For further details, see p. 221 below, and Carpenter, Reign of H. III, pp. 187 ff.

27 Powicke, H. III and Ld. Edward, p. 384; cf. Cal. Pat. R., 1247-58, 637.

28 CP25(1) 147/17/318, and WAD 87a-b. This purchase was in 1252. The fee of the Mohun family in the Charing Street area of Westminster features in a number of property transactions which had occurred earlier in this century, see p. 392 below. For Robert, see Reedy, ed., Basset charters, p. 87, no. 144.

29 Cal. Ch. R., 1226-57, p. 404. His father, another William, had been a royal steward also, for King John, and had received a barony. See also pp. 273-4 below about the Cantilupes as residents in Westminster and their houses there.

30 See the evidence of the location outside the cemetery wall in WAMs 17362, 17550 and 17553. Appropriately one of the neighbours was known as Louis 'attewalle' or 'de muris.'

people in any of them, unless of course the sacrist was willing to accept such occupants.

A third acquisition of property by the abbey arose because by 1249 the king had decided to make provision for the celebration of an 'anniversary' to commemorate the memory of both himself and his queen, Eleanor of Provence. In that year the abbey was able to 'appropriate' the church (and thereby the income from it) in its own manor of Feering in Essex, as a result of a licence granted to the abbey by Pope Innocent IV, and had been supported in this action by the king. But this papal licence was expressly awarded for the purpose of paying for the celebrations required for the royal anniversary, so that although the abbey acquired a valuable new capital asset in the form of the church, the profits of the church were in effect pledged for the benefit of the king and queen's perpetual 'anniversary'.[31]

A fourth acquisition for the abbey's overall estate was the recovery by 1258, of most of the manor of Hampstead from its sitting tenants, Andrew of Grendon, a royal serjeant, and his wife Sibilla. This manor had been one of the first properties granted to the abbey shortly after its foundation in the tenth century, but lettings of parts of it had later been enforced by William the Conqueror and Henry I to military tenants. More recently the acquisitive Alexander of Barentin, King Henry II's former butler in the twelfth century, had obtained the manor, and Sibilla was his grand-daughter and (at one remove) the heiress to the estate.[32] The recovery of this anglo-saxon estate was effected through a legal action started by Abbot Crokesley against Andrew and Sibilla as early as about 1253, leading to

success by about 1257. The abbot was clearly proud of his achievement, since he recorded that it was *'by his own efforts'* that he had succeeded in obtaining this recovery – with perhaps the not-so-gentle implication that his predecessor Richard of Berking, who had merely laid a passive claim to the estate in a third-party's unsuccessful legal action to try to wrest Hampstead away from Andrew and Sibilla, had failed to seek, still less to obtain, its recovery.[33]

As a fifth acquisition, Abbot Crokesley was also responsible for the recovery, by compromise in a legal action or actions, of another estate, called West Stoke in Sussex, which like Hampstead had belonged to other holders.[34] Accordingly he felt able to assign the profits of Hampstead, West Stoke and the Mohun family fee in London and Westminster (all of them acquired by him) to pay for the celebration of an over-elaborate and too-expensive 'anniversary' of his own death, which he ordained in 1256.[35]

A sixth acquisition made by Abbot Crokesley was a substantial amount of land in Yeoveney, part of the manor of Staines in Middlesex, bought from its sitting tenant for £40.[36]

## The making of records of manorial administration

It was probably Abbot Crokesley who initiated the practice at the abbey of making and keeping written manorial accounts. The regular creation of *national* records had begun in the years on either side of 1200, promoted and guided by Hubert Walter, justiciar and then chancellor, and it is not surprising that

31   Harvey, *WA Estates*, pp. 49 and 406, and *Wenlok*, p. 229n.
32   For Hampstead's earlier history, see *The Westminster Corridor*, chapters 8 and 10; and p. 115 above and chapter 21 below, at pp. 368 ff.
33   *Cal. Cl. R.*, 1251-53, p. 442. Abbot Berking had only registered a claim against the Hampstead estate in an unsuccessful action brought by Gilbert of Hendon to 'recover' it for himself from Andrew and Sibilla in 1231-2: CP 25(1) 146/8/98. See also VCH, Mdx., 9/92-3 and 99.
34   See VCH, *Mdx.*, 9/93; VCH, *Sussex*, 4/192-3; Sussex Rec. Soc. vol. 7 § 611 and 618.
35   For the anniversary, see text below and WAM 5405, and WAD 115b; cf. Berking's lesser anniversary, WAD 376, and *Flete*, 107. Matthew Paris (*EHD* 3/125) recorded the claim that Crokesley had added 12 hides to WA's lands.
36   Harvey *WA Estates*, p. 415; WAD 140; WAM 16749 and 16750.

some other lay and ecclesiastical magnates had soon recognised the efficiency which written records could give to the administration of their own estates.[37] As early as 1208 the first surviving accounts of revenue and expenditure on the manors of the large estates of the bishop of Winchester were being made, following the lead given by the court of the exchequer.[38]

But the lesson was not learnt quickly in Westminster, probably for two reasons – the abbey's closeness to and involvement in the troubles during King John's reign, and the anxious state of the relationship between the abbots and their monks, which had come to a head in the compromised sharing of assets under Abbot Richard of Berking. Some primitive records about the manors assigned to the convent may well have preceded the making of the 'Custumal' in 1225.[39] But there had been no other attempt, so far as we know, to record in writing any accounts or other details about the state of any of the manors.

In this, the abbey at Westminster was far from unique. Elsewhere manorial accounts of any kind remained rare until the 1250s and after.[40] But in the early 1240s a significant set of *'Rules'* for estate management had been written by Bishop Robert Grosseteste of Lincoln, in order to assist his neighbour the Countess of Lincoln who had been widowed. These were strategic rules for estate-owners, not for the owners' agents – ie. their stewards, reeves or bailiffs – who were concerned more with tactical farming problems in the fields. Between about 1260 and the end of the century three other more detailed treatises about

management practices and the problems of making profits and accounting and auditing were written, together with a number of shorter tracts.[41] So the subject was by then a well-ventilated topic, and the treatises were becoming reasonably well-known among those who owned or managed estates.

But in the 1250s there was only the Grosseteste *Rules* and practical experience to go by. Among the archives of the abbey at Westminster, the first manorial accounts (limited to receipts and expenditure, with records of crops and livestock) which have survived were those for the year 1252 in the manors of Todenham (Glos) and Sutton under Brailes (Warwickshire), estates still administered by the abbot.[42] But, nearer home, the second earliest accounts to survive were those for the convent's manor of Knightsbridge, close to Westminster, relating to the period beginning on the 25th July 1257.[43]

But the third related document to survive was not an account but a 'rental' for the tenants of another 'corridor' manor, Hampstead, after Abbot Crokesley had recovered possession of it. This was a list of both customary and free tenants in that manor in the period 1258-9, with details of their quarterly rents. Hampstead was now a manor managed by the convent, not by the abbot, and its main 'issues' were assigned to the monks. So we have here two documents which were created during Abbot Crokesley's abbacy, and one which must have been made in the year 1259, following his death, probably during the vacancy.[44]

37  For Hubert Walter, see pp. 121-3 and 164-6 above.
38  Clanchy, *Memory to Written Record*, p. 92. An earlier bishop of Winchester, Richard of Ilchester (see App A, at p. 392) had had first-hand knowledge of exchequer accounting.
39  See pp. 132-3 (John's reign, abbots' and monks); 195 ff. (Berking's compromises); 199-201 (Berking, the custumal).
40  Clanchy, *Memory to Written Record*, p. 93.
41  In order of date, the three treatises were the anonymous *Seneschausie; Walter of Henley's Husbandry* (usually just called Walter of Henley); *and the* anonymous *Husbandry,* see D. Oschinsky, *Walter of Henley and other Treatises on Estate Management*.
42  The following details are based on the summary lists of accounts and court records provided at WA.
43  Knightsbridge included the district of Westbourne, lying on the west side of the river Westbourne; for which see *The Westminster Corridor*, pp. 43 and 113. Abbot Berking had assigned this manor to the convent in 1225.
44  See WAMs 25900 (Todenham); 16367 (Knightsbridge); 32360 (the Hampstead rental). Accounts for the manor of Hampstead did not start until the year 1270/71, and then the surviving a/cs are intermittent.

But the Knightsbridge account for the year 1257/58 makes it clear that it cannot have been the first such account for that manor, because it begins by referring to 'arrears' of 20s. 6d. which the reeve already owed from his 'previous account'. So the making of written accounts for this convent manor must have started in some year before July 1257. How far before, we cannot tell; but we can say with some assurance that, in relation to at least Todenham and Knightsbridge, it was Abbot Crokesley and his monks who, in joining the group of other ecclesiastical houses and lay estate-owners who had already started making and keeping written accounts for their manors, had dragged the abbey into the thirteenth century.

But it was not until the 1270s that similar accounts were made and kept for *other* manors belonging to the abbey.[45] For sixteen of the manors (including Eye and Hampstead), simple accounts of receipts and expenditure were started in the 1270s (but have survived only intermittently); and for many others a similar start may have been made in that decade but without any extant records.[46] *After* the 1270s up to the time of the Dissolution, many more but intermittent accounts for abbey manors have survived; but many more were no doubt made, though they are now lost. Unfortunately there are none extant for Westminster over the whole medieval period.

The best conclusion one can reach is that while Abbot Crokesley himself probably initiated the making and keeping, and the auditing, of manorial accounts in a few manors in the 1250s, it may have been his successor who at the beginning of the 1270s developed

the practice more extensively. But because so many documents are missing, we cannot be sure whether the practice was applied wholesale, or was introduced bit by bit and place by place over a protracted period.

In addition to the accounts, records also began to be kept at the abbey of the legal proceedings before the manorial court in each manor. But of these, only four – out of all the abbey's manors – have any surviving court records dating from the 1270s, and only six in the remaining decades of the thirteenth century. In the whole of Middlesex there are no surviving court records in the thirteenth century in any of the abbey's manors, save in Hampstead which has one record for one sitting of the manor court in the year 1295-96.

## Abbot Crokesley's anniversary

Abbot Crokesley's foundation of an anniversary for himself provides an informative picture of what could be entailed in such a celebration, and also a further powerful confirmation of the abbot's character. All the abbot's relationships reveal that he was a powerful personality, very able and imposing, but self-willed to the point of being initially prepared to oppose the even more self-willed king, on whom he so much depended. His anniversary grant is of a kind with this. While Abbot Berking had arranged a relatively simple celebration for both himself and his parents, Abbot Crokesley required ceremonies on a scale which were soon seen to be extravagant and vain. Even the charter creating it was itself a work of art, clearly designed to match the event in self-importance.

According to his instructions, each year

They are simple in form and content, limited to receipts of income and payments made (plus stock details of grain grown and grain used, and increase or decrease of livestock). But the facts giving rise to the receipts and payments, and the identifications of the people involved, as recorded in the a/cs, present a clear picture of manorial life.

45 For A/cs in Eye, see pp. 334-5, 340-1, 343-4, 350 ff., below; in Hampstead, see pp. 379-390 below.

46 A single record from Launton (Oxon) has survived from 1267. This was a manor of the abbot (then R. of Ware)

47 For these alms, £16. 13s. 4d. was correctly allocated. The rate may have been normal, see Harvey, *Living and Dying*, pp. 27-28, but the numbers of poor to be provided for were wildly excessive for such an anniversary. Abbot Berking allowed for (generous) food for only a hundred poor on just the one anniversary day.

the celebration was to start with a muffled peal of the greater bells of the abbey on the eve and the day of the anniversary, to be paid for by an allocation of 13s. 4d. Also on the day of the anniversary there was to be a massive distribution of alms to a thousand poor persons, and on each of the following six days to five hundred of the poor. The rate for the alms was to be one penny for each person each day (the rate at that time for a day's ordinary labour of a man in the fields).[47] Solemn mass, with the monks in copes, was to be said on the anniversary day, and special dishes of food and condiments were to be provided for the whole convent costing £7 each year, and the servants of the abbey were to share a distribution of 6s. 8d. Four new monks, beyond the full complement, were to be taken on, to celebrate mass every day at four different altars in the abbey, with prayers for the abbot's soul, and £20 each year was to be assigned for the maintenance of these four monks. During the celebration of the mass, four candles were to burn round the abbot's tomb in the abbey, and all day on the anniversary day itself; while in the chapel of Tothill a lamp was to burn in front of the cross, and one candle before the altar of St Mary Magdalene. All these lights were to cost £3. 13s. 4d, each year. The total cost to the abbey was to be the great sum of £48. 6s. 8d. each year. These costs were to be paid from the profits of the estates of the Mohun family & the manors of Hampstead and West Stoke.[48]

Although Abbot Crokesley no doubt sought to justify his anniversary on the grounds that it would be paid for by properties acquired by him, it is hardly surprising that later the monks did not wish to pay such excessive costs, however much the abbot may have added to the abbey's annual income.[49] At all events, within ten years after the abbot's death the new Abbot Richard of Ware and the convent appealed to Pope Clement IV against the imposition on them of such an anniversary, and received in May 1268 a 'moderation' of the annual amount which the abbey would have to pay for it.

The pope had sent instructions to the abbot of Waltham Abbey, as an independent assessor, to fix a reasonable sum *as may be just to the abbot's [Crokesley's] merits and not press too heavily on the monastery*', in place of the total cost. The annual sum was reduced by the assessor from the £48. 6s. 8d. ordained by Abbot Crokesley to a diminutive ten marks (£6. 13s. 4d.), to be provided from the manor of Hampstead.[50] This meant that any profits from the Mohun family properties and from West Stoke, and the balance, if any, from Hampstead, would now be available to meet other liabilities of the abbey. But how the reduced ten marks were to be divided between the specified items of Abbot Crokesley's over-reaching anniversary is not revealed.

## The king's feasts

One noticeable feature about the period when Crokesley was abbot is the extent to which the king appears to have increased the scale of the celebrations which it was his habit to hold in the abbey and his palace on the important religious feast days. As had been the case during Richard of Berking's abbacy, these ceremonies included not just one or more of the great seasonal feasts such as Christmas and Easter (whenever he chose to be in

---

48  Each of these lands had been recovered by the abbot's own efforts, as he claimed.

49  Crokesley's anniversary charter had received the assent of both the king and the whole convent, and was executed in chapter. Moreover later in 1256 it had even been referred by Crokesley to the pope, then Alexander IV, who had confirmed it. If Crokesley had provided the cost of the purchases or legal actions out of his own pocket, his case was that much the stronger, but even so, the abbot's 'generosity' would have principally availed his own soul, and one can see why the convent and Abbot Ware later objected to the excessive burden.

50  WAM 5400 and WAD 116b-117. On the instructions of the pope, the abbot of Waltham Abbey also had to absolve Abbot Ware and his monks from the sentence of excommunication which they incurred as a result of challenging Crokesley's charter, containing as it did the usual anathema against any challenge, WAD 118a-b.

Westminster for them), but also the special feasts for St. Edward the Confessor on October 13th and January 5th each year in the 1250s.

The scale of the secular celebrations on these occasions can be judged by the amounts of food ordered, at short notice, by an apparently frenetic king from his sheriffs and bailiffs in the Home Counties for the proposed feastings which were designed to follow the religious ceremonies. We find his orders issuing, on various occasions, for quantities such as 14 boars, 100 pigs, 25 swans, 1380 hens, 300 partridges, 500 pheasants, 36 geese, 250 rabbits, 500 white cocks, 7100 eggs, 40 ox-carcases.[51] The sheriffs and bailiffs who received such orders might be given only two or three weeks, and sometimes less, not only to gather together the demanded quantities, but also to transport and deliver them at the desired destination. The sheriffs' networks of suppliers of produce and carrying-services necessary for the rapid implementation of such orders, and/or their fear of the consequences of failure, must have been prodigious.

Since the king invited all or some of his magnates to such ceremonies, it was sometimes useful for him to combine these occasions with later administrative meetings of his common council, held after or at least in the same month as the celebrations. In the conjunction of such events, we can see a fortuitous interplay between, on the one hand, his enthusiasms for religious celebrations and secular feasts in Westminster and, on the other hand, the slow development of a wider form of parliamentary government.

## Meetings of the king's council and 'parliaments' in Westminster

The thirteenth century played a seminal role in the evolution of parliamentary government, and Westminster can claim to have been, then and more recently, the place in which most of the significant steps were taken. Both 'parliament' itself, and the 'commons' as participants in it, have been said to be 'creatures' of the century.[52] By the middle of the century, during Richard of Crokesley's abbacy, some early seed had been sown, and its germination was shortly to come. Both Westminster Hall and other meeting-places within the abbey had already acted and continued to act as the main seedbed. This part played by Westminster is reflected in the earlier history.

The baronial disputes and civil war under King John in 1213-17, and the early editions of Magna Carta, had underlined the obligation on the king to obtain the 'common consent' of (at that time) his magnates before taking certain actions. The devious but far-sighted King John had already seen in 1212 that there were other people who might be used by him, as a counter-balance in arguments with his troublesome magnates. These other people were provincial knights. In 1213 he summoned *'lawworthy and discreet knights'* (who were members of the common people, not the nobility), and even four *'discreet men'*, from each of the counties, to attend a meeting of him and his council of magnates, *'to speak with us on the affairs of the kingdom'*. These opportunistic attempts by King John to widen the debate by adding such members of the 'commons' were frustrated, but the idea pointed ahead to a revolution which was to come many years in the future.[53]

No other step was taken to implicate representatives of the people even in a limited way until 1227, when Henry III (in the first year of his self-ordained majority) ordered that four knights from each of thirty-five counties were to be elected in their county court to appear, as representatives *'on behalf of the the whole county'*, before the king in Westminster.

51  See eg. *Cal. Cl. R.*, 1253-54, pp. 105-6; 1254-56, p. 378; and the records are full of similar injunctions to the sheriffs to make preparations for the king's celebrations.
52  Carpenter, *Reign of H. III*, p. 381
53  Stubbs, *Select Charters*, p. 282 (1213). These early attempts by the wily king are generally regarded as unclear because the surrounding circumstances are not well evidenced, but the wording of the extant writ and the intention behind it seem so clear that I think they have been undervalued. It also fits so well with John's character. But see Carpenter, *ibid.*, pp. 391-2.

But the function given to them was merely to inform the king and his advisers what grievances the county had against the king's sheriffs over the implementation of any articles in Magna Carta. This was a truly limited function – to inform, not to debate, still less to decide; and in any event the king's council on that occasion was an incomplete one.[54]

So in the 1230s and 1240s decision-making still rested with the king and his council, with not even any advisory or decisive input from the commons. When for example in January 1237 the king's great council met first in the great Hall of the palace at Westminster, and then met again in the late Norman chapel of St. Katherine in the abbey, only the magnates were still participants with the king.

But one nominal but significant change had taken place by then. We know that before this time some councils of the king and his magnates had been referred to as *'parliaments'* – ie. times and places for talking, even if the talkers were restricted in number and character. In November 1236 the king himself in his own court had adjourned a legal case to the 'parliament' which was then due to be meeting in the next January. It was a new name, but for an old institution. However the name was used from then on in some official records and the chronicles, although it was still not a unique name for such royal assemblies.[55]

But again in October 1244 and February 1245 when the king's council was meeting in the great refectory of the abbey, the position was still the same. No members of the 'commons' were present as even marginal participants in the king's council, still less as representatives of the counties or other laity.

It took a national scare in 1253-54, during Crokesley's abbacy, about rumoured military threats from Spain, to bring about the summoning again of two knights from each county, chosen on behalf of all and sundry in the county, to make a renewed appearance *'before our council at Westminster'* in early May 1254. This time the reason for the calling of a parliament was the king's need to impose more taxes to meet the supposed threat, and the knights were to report *'precisely to our council what kind of aid* [quale auxilium] *they were prepared to provide for us in so great a necessity'*.[56] So the knights were at least being drawn closer to a parliamentary debate about both the principle and the size of any award of tax for the king. But they were certainly not members of the debate, still less essential members; and certainly no link between tax and representation of the commons was yet established.

In 1258, the turning point in Henry's disputes with the barons, a dramatic confrontation took place on the 30th April at the great Hall in Westminster, when a confederate party of dissatisfied barons and knights led by the Earl Marshal and Simon of Montfort, marched in armour to the palace and faced the king. This confrontation occurred towards the end of one of the most important parliaments under Henry III. *'What is this, my lords? Am I – a wretch – your captive?'*, the king asked. Even though the militant intruders had ostentatiously left their swords at the entrance of the Hall and assured the king of their loyalty, the duress imposed on the king induced him to swear to accept reforms of the realm.[57]

But in the resulting negotiation between 24 appointed 'reformers' of the kingdom, no

---

54 Carpenter, *ibid.*, p. 391.
55 Mortimer, *Angevin England*, p. 103. *CRR* xv 2047. Later the name was even used retrospectively, to refer to the old meeting at Runnymede in 1215 between King John and the barons, when Magna Carta was negotiated.
56 Stubbs, *Select Charters*, pp. 365-66; Carpenter, *ibid.*, pp. 391-2; Powicke, *The C13*, pp. 117 and 141. This 'parliament' (as it was expressly named) was summoned, in the king's absence in Gascony, by his regents, the queen and his brother, Richard the earl of Cornwall. A tax was in fact agreed, on stringent terms.
57 The Tewkesbury Annals, *Ann. Mon.* i. 163-5. Carpenter, 'What happened in 1258?' in *Reign of Henry III*, pp. 187-89.

attempt was made to include elements of the 'commons' in sittings of parliament.[58] However the provincial knights were again soon brought into the scene in another ancillary role. By that year 1258, grievances in the country about oppression by sheriffs and other royal officers were rife, and those who had suffered were invited to take their complaints to four knights chosen from each county. These knights had been ordered in August 1258 to inquire about such abuses and, more significantly, to bring the records of their hearings to Westminster at the time of the October parliament and deliver them personally to the king's council. As a result the new parliament held in the great Hall at Westminster ordered drastic measures – the appointment of new sheriffs, local men instead of king's men, with other effective steps.[59] These results served to show all parties how productive such involvement, and information, from the knights could be.

Meanwhile by this time the abbey at Westminster was rudderless. Abbot Richard of Crokesley, who had himself been due to take part on behalf of the king in the negotiation about constitutional reforms, had just died in July 1258,[60] and no replacement as abbot was confirmed until a year later. So all the most important advances in parliamentary history fell after Crokesley's abbacy. But they are included here in this chapter, in order not to break the story and to point the way ahead for the constitution of parliament.

By 1261 it seems that a subtle change had taken place in the attitudes of both the king and the magnates (who were again at loggerheads) towards other elements in the kingdom. Each of the disputing parties appear to have realised that the 'commons' were perhaps a valuable force which they should cultivate in their own interests. In September a summons went out from Simon of Montford and some of the other magnates to three knights in each county to come to consult with them at a parliament at St. Albans *'about the common affairs of the kingdom'*, the same remit as that given to magnates. In contrast the king summoned three knights in each county to come to a meeting of his royal council at Windsor, for a political but more limited purpose.[61] The sequels are not recorded. But this was the first time that any members of the commons had been called to a meeting to discuss *'affairs of the kingdom'* since the time when King John had summoned knights for that purpose in 1213.

The next step was that after the civil war had begun and the rebel barons had won the battle of Lewes in May 1264, their leader Simon of Montford issued similar invitations, by formally summoning (though still in the name of the king) a parliament in June 1264 in London; and then another, 'the famous parliament', in January 1265 at Westminster.[62] Four knights were to be chosen to represent each county and to appear at the June parliament, *'to discuss the affairs of the king and the kingdom'*. But for the second parliament, in January 1265, Simon had gone further and summoned representatives from both the counties and the boroughs: two knights from each county and also (uniquely, up to that time) two burgesses from each town, for a subject-matter which was again *'the affairs of the kingdom'*. This was a seminal summons.

---

58 Of the 'reformers', twelve were appointed by the barons, and twelve (including Abbot Crokesley) by the king, see p. 215 above. But neither king nor magnates were concerned to include the commons: each had very different objectives. The ensuing debate led to elaborate proposed reforms in the 'Provisions of Oxford', and the 'Provisions of Westminster' (as to which, see *EHD* 3/370-376).

59 See Powicke, *H. III and Ld. Edward*, pp. 399-402, and Carpenter, *ibid*, pp. 190-197.

60 It was even rumoured that Crokesley had been poisoned by the Lusignans, the king's half-brothers who had been the focus of such antagonism from the barons in their disputes with the king.

61 The king's avowed purpose was *'so that they might see and understand that we propose to attempt nothing save what we know will conform to the honour and common utility of our kingdom'*

62 Meetings of this parliament were held (between Jan. and March) in both Westminster Hall and the abbey's Chapter House.

However the example set by Simon of Montfort was not followed at once, nor indeed did it even draw written comment from contemporaries. It may even be the case that the commons had been introduced in the parliamentary summonses only in order to publicise the 'new form of government which Simon had devised'.[63] In succeeding parliaments before 1275, there are some, but not many, instances in which representatives of the commons were summoned to parliament. But in his first parliament in 1275, the new king, Edward I, summoned both four knights and four to six burgesses from every city, borough and merchant town. The parliament, twice the size of usual assemblies, was referred to as the king's 'first general Parliament' in the preamble of the First Statute of Westminster, to which the commons were stated to have given their assent.[64] Thereafter the regularity of the commons being present in parliaments grew progressively, if slowly, until shortly after the turn of the century their entitlement to be present was, at least in theory, taken for granted.[65] In practice however it was not until after 1325 that parliaments always contained representatives from the 'commons'.[66]

Between 1258, when the programme for the 'reforms' had been agreed between King Henry and the barons, and 1335, about 123 parliaments were held, and of these the great majority took place in Westminster. And from 1336 the place for the sittings of parliament began to be Westminster invariably.[67]

---

63  Sayles, *The King's Parliament of England*, pp. 63-4.
64  For the First Statute of Westminster, see EHD 3/397-410 and p. 291 below. At this parliament the 'communities of merchants' (ie. the urban burgesses) procured the passing of a statute which granted the king a right to receive customs duties on wool and hides, so giving legal authority for this form of taxation, see Prestwich, *Edward I*, pp. 99-100.
65  Carpenter, *ibid.*, pp. 393-4; *Modus Tenendi Parliamentum*, ed. T. Hardy.
66  In focussing on the 'commons', this summary has necessarily had to omit much else which may be thought to be material. At least it makes the topic briefer than some of the weighty treatises on 'Parliament'.
67  Sayles, *ibid.*, Appendix pp. 140-141.

# CHAPTER 14

# The three abbots 'Richard" – Richard of Ware
## 1258-1283

After the death of Richard of Crokesley in July 1258, there was a brief interlude of a few months in the abbacy, while the prior of the abbey, Philip of Lewisham, was first proposed and then elected as abbot by the other monks. But in a matter of months the prior died unexpectedly, before he could be confirmed as abbot by the pope.[1] The result was that it was December 1258 before another monk at the abbey, Richard of Ware, was elected as abbot and obtained royal approval. By the 16th December he was setting out on the arduous journey across the continent to Rome to obtain the pope's approval. But once there, he was delayed, and it was not until after the mid-summer of 1259 that he returned from the continent, after having secured the pope's confirmation of his election.

But until that time, as still an 'abbot-elect', Richard of Ware had not yet become 'the abbot of Westminster', and so the vacancy in the post of abbot continued for just over a year from the time when Abbot Crokesley had died (July 1258 to August 1259). For most of this period, King Henry who was as ever short of ready money, particularly for the on-going building works at the abbey, had allowed the now leaderless convent, under a sub-prior, to keep the custody of the 'whole abbey' from August 1258, in return for a huge 'fine' of 1100 marks (£733. 6s. 8d), mostly payable by them at a weekly rate of £25 against the building works.[2] Eventually on the 17th August 1259 custody of the whole abbey was transferred to the newly confirmed Abbot Richard of Ware, who had arrived back from Rome; but the balance of the 'fine' of course remained outstanding.[3]

### The abbot as royal envoy and officer

Like Richard of Crokesley, Abbot Ware had not previously served as prior of the abbey, but it is likely that he had already come to the notice of the king before his election. As Richard of Berking had done, Richard of Ware had earlier, in 1257, acted in the legal capacity of proctor on behalf of his predecessor in an action in the king's court; and in that role his potential ability as another reliable royal agent may well have been recognised by the king. By the 1260s the king was still being

---

1   The large sum of 600 marks (£400) had been borrowed to pay for the expenses of obtaining papal confirmation for Philip, and Richard of Ware, his successor, had to assume responsibility for the debt, in addition to the even larger loan of 1000 marks (£666) needed for the expenses of his own election.

2   *Cal. P. R.* 1247-58, p. 650. *Cal. Cl. R.*, 1256-59, pp. 259, 249. In effect the king exchanged his right to administer the *abbot's* portion of assets during the 'vacancy', in return for the payment of the fine by the convent. As for the convent's portion, the monks were now entitled, in any event, to retain the custody of that, thanks to Abbot Crokesley, see p. 214 above. However during the vacancy the king deliberately kept for himself (and in fact made use of) the abbey's rights to present incumbents to various churches; and by legal action against the bishop of London before the justices at Westminster, he also recovered on behalf of the abbey a further right of presentation to one church, see *Cal. P. R.* 1259-1266, pp. 11, 30, 35, 38; and *ibid*, p. 81. *Flete*, p. 113, says that the vacancy' lasted 'two years and more', but this is wrong. At most it was 'one year or more'.

3   *Cal. P. R., ibid*, p. 39. Foster, *Patterns of Thought*, 14-18, offers a different and later sequence of events which I think is wrong, but this does not in any way detract from the substance of his review of the great Westminster pavement and its meaning.

particularly hard-pressed in his disputes, and finally the civil war, with those barons who had sided with Simon of Montford, and so was no doubt grateful to have found in this third Richard someone on whom he could again depend with assurance in the various administrative and diplomatic missions intended for him.

The confidence shown by King Henry in the new Abbot Richard was to prove no less strong than his earlier link with each of the two previous abbots of Westminster. For the first eleven years of Ware's abbacy, a major part of the great rebuilding of the abbey was still in progress, and if the king, amid all the other political and military distractions which he had at home at this time, was to keep sufficient attention focussed on the abbey, it was essential that his emissaries, such as the abbot, could be relied upon to deal with pressing issues abroad.

Certainly the new abbot began at once to act in the role of one of the king's regular envoys, for between November 1259 and 1266 he appears to have served abroad in every year, as distantly as the court of Rome on at least three of these occasions.[4] On one occasion in 1262 he even accompanied the king himself when Henry visited France, and as the abbot alone had the duty at the abbey of dealing with all litigation affecting the abbey, the king in order to protect the abbey commanded that all actions against the abbey in the king's courts should be adjourned while the abbot was serving in the king's service abroad.[5] While he was away on royal business, the abbot's other duties in Westminster of course had to languish, and we find for example in 1266 that because of the abbot's

absence in that year Sir William Bonquer, a marshal of the king's household, had to be commissioned by the king to undertake the task in Westminster of 'delivering the gaol of Westminster', ie. hearing and deciding the cases of the prisoners currently in the abbot's gaol, and so effecting the process of 'gaol delivery'.[6]

We do not know all the other *domestic* assignments (within England) which the king may also have been giving to the abbot during this period. But we do know for example that later in 1266, in one of the last stages of the civil war while some of the rebel barons and their supporters were still being besieged at Kenilworth, Abbot Ware performed some special *'service in the siege of Kenilworth Castle'* for King Henry, for which the king later acknowledged his indebtedness.[7] On another occasion, in 1269, the abbot was employed by the king to carry a personal message to other important people. Henry had summoned a parliament of his magnates and bishops to take place in Westminster, but found when the time came that he had been delayed by 'a tertian fever' (an illness which he sometimes suffered from; though on this occasion it was soon over) and despatched Abbot Ware on the 21st June with orders to warn those attending that the king would be late in arriving because of the fever, but that they were all to wait there for him.[8]

But after yet other tasks abroad, one of the very last diplomatic services abroad which the abbot performed for the old king was when the abbot was again sent with other agents to France apparently on two occasions, in August 1271 and the early months of 1272, under orders to obtain for Henry, if necessary by

---

4  *Cal. P. R.*, 1258-66, pp. 59, 117, 135, 237, 280, 418, 681.

5  *Cal. Cl. R.*, 1261-64, pp. 268-9.

6  *Cal. P. R.*, 1258-1266, p. 681. The abbot's prison was in the abbey's western gatehouse, and the serjeant janitor of the gatehouse also held the serjeanty of the prison and was responsible for keeping the prisoners securely, see p. 304, n. 52 below. Sir Wm. Bonquer was also a regular envoy, proctor and factotum of the king, and a tenant of the abbey, of land in the manor of Kelvedon in Essex, Fle*te*, pp. 115-6.

7  *Cal. P. R.*, 1266-1272, p. 338.

8  *ibid*, p. 384. Even an eminent person could be used as a royal messenger on an important occasion such as a parliament.

legal action, certain lands in the south-west of France which were due to come to him on the recent deaths of the Count of Poitiers and his wife.[9]

At last in November 1272 King Henry – the creator of the new abbey, and the demanding taskmaster of, now, three abbots of Westminster – died in his palace in the town. So ended the 56 years of the longest reign of any earlier or later English king or queen, until the reign of Queen Victoria surpassed it in the nineteenth century. It was perhaps typical of Henry's crowded and tumultuous reign that even as he lay near to death, the great Hall and the courtyards of his Westminster palace were filled day by day, for about 14 days, with two clamouring swarms of Londoners, who had flocked to Westminster to dispute about the election of a new mayor for their city. All things came to the king, even when he was dying. Only five days before his death were his ears relieved of the tinnitus of this London commotion.[10]

But for Abbot Richard of Ware the pattern of his national work changed little. King Henry's son, Edward I, was abroad on crusade when his father died, but when he returned two years later, the number of the abbot's absences from Westminster continued, and if anything may have increased. Like his predecessors, he too was now being sent abroad again on diplomatic missions – including probably at least one journey to Rome because his absence on that occasion was expected to last a year. Such journeyings included other more personal missions, such as that in February 1279, when he was the senior of two envoys sent abroad by Edward I

to treat with John, the Duke of Lorraine and Brabant, for the marriage of the king's daughter Margaret with the Duke's son.[11]

But in addition he soon found himself being drafted into very different activities, on national rather than international tasks. In 1278 he was despatched as the chief justice of the 'general eyre' ordered in that year, to carry the law into the northern counties of Cumberland, Westmoreland and Northumberland; and there may well have been other occasions when (in breach of papal prohibition) he was being employed in such legal roles.[12] The culmination of his secular career was reached in 1280 when he became the king's treasurer, an office which he held for the next three years before his sudden death in 1283.[13]

In all his dealings with the royal business of two kings, Abbot Richard of Ware appears to have been an efficient and versatile personal agent, on whom both kings in whose reigns he was also the abbot of Westminster knew that they could completely rely. But in his role as treasurer, he has been dismissed as 'not a man of any great significance'.[14] Probably he had all the necessarily unsensational talents of a competent modern-style civil servant or diplomat, and the fact that he ended up as the king's treasurer may be indicative of this.

### The abbot and his monks
There seems little doubt that Ware's other role as abbot of a great monastery must have suffered considerably as a result of these national duties. Certainly his relationship with his own monks cannot have been of the warmest, since his death when it came was recorded by one of the annalists as *'little*

---

9   *ibid.*, pp. 568, 581-2, 620, 628. The English claim to these lands (the 'Agenais', between Perigord and Quercy) had arisen under the terms of the Treaty of Paris, which in 1259 had brought a long-running state of hostilities between England and France to an end.

10  Powicke, *H. III and the Lord Edward*, pp. 588-591.

11  (To Rome) *Cal. P. R.*, 1272-81, pp. 159, 162; and cf. also *ibid.*, pp. 128 and 302-3; (to the Duke) *ibid.*, p. 302. For other visits abroad by the abbot, see *Cal. Cl. R.*, 1272-4, pp. 117 and 417.

12  *Cal. Cl. R.*, 1272-79, p. 504, and cf. 262. *Cal. P. R.*, 1272-81, p. 277.

13  But as in the case of Abbot Berking, who had become H. III's treasurer, it is difficult to reconcile the duties of the abbot of Westminster with all the duties of the old-time royal treasurer.

14  Prestwich, *Edward I*, p. 234.

*mourned, because of his severity'.*[15]  Although there is no direct evidence that there were explosive disputes between him and his monks about the sharing of the abbey's possessions or its obligations, it is highly significant that very soon after Abbot Ware's death on the 8th December 1283, the prior and the convent had already formulated, and had executed by the 2nd January 1284, a long written 'agreement' of 32 prescriptive articles, for the abbots and the convent of Westminster henceforth to observe.[16]

The barbed manner in which these rules were worded – almost every one of them directed specifically to an obligation on the part of the abbot – and the speed with which the list was produced so soon after the abbot had died, leave little doubt that they reflected dissatisfactions, which had either simmered earlier, or even flared up, between the abbot and themselves at different times. Gathered together in their new and beautiful chapter house, the monks – freed now from the constraints imposed by an austere abbot – even enacted that these added rules should be inscribed in the abbey's great book of martyrology, and once every year, on an appointed day, should be read aloud to the brotherhood assembled in chapter. And all and singular were, by a corporal oath sworn in chapter, ordered to be bound now and in the future to observe all the 'compositions' in every article, ie. the previous agreements and these new articles, made (so it was said) between 'the abbots and the convent of Westminster'.

Many, but not all, of these articles reflected obligations which could be spelt out from the earlier compositions or agreements between previous abbots and their monks. But the pattern of the articles very clearly suggests that Abbot Ware's monks wished to make a definitive catalogue of obligations for abbots in the future to comply with, so that they could point to them if the necessity arose.[17]  Virtually nothing was said about the corresponding obligations which under the earlier compositions were to fall upon members of the convent.

Moreover, in so enshrining their new articles in the great book, the monks did not openly dwell on the fact that this new ordinance of theirs had in fact been formulated unilaterally, by themselves alone, without either any assent from any abbot or approval from impartial arbitrators, as all previous 'compositions' had had.[18]  It is also noticeable that although this new document used the time-honoured description 'of good memory' when referring to Abbot Ware, there were no warm expressions of love or respect for the late abbot from his monks.  As a result of their unilateral act, a fertile crop of fraught disagreements was sown, for the next abbot and his monks to reap within the following twenty five years, and a precedent for this divisive pattern of conduct by the prior and convent was established. Indeed during yet another vacancy which followed the death of the *next* abbot as well, the then prior and convent copied and enlarged upon the precedent, by producing an even larger catalogue of the abbot's obligations, as they interpreted them.[19]

## The great Pavement

In spite of the muted and unsympathetic relationship which appears to have existed between Abbot Ware and his flock, there is no doubt that the abbot made two spectacular contributions to the fame and the life of the

15  *Annales Monastici (Dunstable)*, Luard ed. R.S. vol. iii. p. 305.
16  WAD 638-9; Harvey, *W. de Wenlok*, pp. 229 ff. For a peaceful chapter meeting, see Plate 21, after p. 288.
17  But it is not clear whether the articles were meant to comprehend actual disputes which had occurred, or merely reflected the convent's desire to have in black and white a clear list of abbatial duties.
18  For the part played in this ordinance by Brother Walter of Wenlock (who then became the next abbot after Richard of Ware), see pp. 293 and 325 below.
19  For the dramas in the years of Abbot Walter of Wenlock's abbacy (1283-1307), and afterwards, see the section *'The final explosion between the abbot and the prior'*, on pp. 319-24  below.

abbey. The first of these had its origin in his first journey to Italy in 1258 and 1259, as an abbot-elect seeking confirmation from the pope. By that time the building of the new abbey at Westminster had advanced well; and the thoughts of all those living in Westminster must have continually revolved around the great new structure which they could see rising from the ground, even amongst all the dust and din which the ubiquitous workmen were creating. Such thoughts, carried to Italy by the abbot-elect, soon found a resonance in sights which he himself undoubtedly saw while he was there.

It is likely that in the early summer months of 1259 the pope, Alexander IV, was resident, not in the Vatican, but in his native city of Agnani in the hills south of Rome. Shortly before that time, the stone floors of the cathedral of Agnani had been enriched with the finest displays of marble 'cosmati' decoration in Italy.[20] This decorative stonework was akin to mosaic, but was fashioned with cut stone pieces of varying sizes and shapes, unlike mosaic work which usually employs stone squares of the same size and shape. Any ecclesiastical visitor to the pope's court, and particularly to Agnani, would inevitably have taken the opportunity, while he was in Italy, to view these marvellous pavements, devised by specialist families of craftsmen and worked in elaborate and excitingly-coloured geometrical patterns of stones.

There is no doubt that Richard of Ware brought back to King Henry tales of such spectacles to be seen in Italy. But these were not merely prodigies of stonework, but also 'patterns of thought', reflecting the interest shown by both ancient and contemporary thinkers and artists in the cosmological implications of geometry and measurement.[21] To a king already intent on rivalling the beauties of the French king's recently-completed chapel, Sainte Chapelle, in Paris, and other features of great new churches in France, this information was like manna.[22] It now became essential for him to form plans to embellish the new abbey at Westminster with an even more intricate and meaningful pavement, with religious and philosophical symbols and enigmas built into it. The king was later to recognise expressly that for the resulting marvel he was indebted to the abbot in person.[23]

But in addition to the pavement, there was also another special project to pursue further. The king wished to add yet more richness to the splendid new shrine and chapel which were being constructed to house the body of St. Edward, the abbey's and his own patron saint. Work had begun on parts of the shrine about twenty five years before, and great sums of money, and artistic skill and effort were being expended in its creation.[24] To crown this work of art, the talents which could create a cosmati pavement worthy of the rising abbey could further enhance the base of the new shrine, to make it match even Henry's ambitious fancies for his patron saint.[25]

So by February 1260 the abbot was off again, on another journey back to Rome; and

---

20 The name 'cosmati' derives from the Cosmatus family, but there were at least four other families in Italy with members skilled in the art and craftsmenship of this form of stonework: Foster, *Patterns of Thought*, pp. 21-22.

21 Foster develops this intriguing theme in detail, see his chapters 5-8. Cf. Binski, *WA and the Plantaganets: Kingship and the Representation of Power*, pp.97-100.

22 With the permission of the French king and indeed escorted by him, Henry had himself visited Sainte Chapelle in December 1254, and also the great church at Chartres which already possessed its own similar labyrinthine pavement (though less intricate than that built later at Westminster). According to a contemporary poem, after studying the French chapel closely Henry declared that he wished he could carry it back to England *'in a cart'*.

23 *Cal. P. R.*, 1266-1272, p. 338.

24 Paris, *Chron. Maj.*, iv. 156. St. Edward's new shrine was given its own workshop and its own keeper and funds, Kent Lancaster, 'Artisans, Suppliers and Clerks', Jo. Warburg, xxxv (1922), p. 96; and pp. 247-8 below.

25 See Carpenter, 'H. III and the Cosmati Work at WA', in his book *Reign of Henry III*, at pp. 409 ff.

**Plate 11.** The intricate geometric patterning, inlaid by Italian workmen in the great Cosmati pavement at the abbey is best revealed in this print made in about 1812 and contained in R. Ackermann's *History of St Peter's Westminster.* See pp. 230-231.

in January 1261 for yet another.[26] The reason, on each visit, was business for both the king and the abbey, and it is likely that the abbot was already making early inquiries for the future hire of a skilled designer and craftsmen, and for resolving any problems for the transport of both men and materials, which would be necessary when the works on the abbey at Westminster were ready to receive the installation of the desired pavement, and for the work on St. Edward's shrine and chapel. Five years later, in November 1266, the abbot was making a third journey to Rome on 'the king's affairs', and it was probably on this visit that the enterprise was settled contractually; and afterwards the conveyance was carried out, right across the continent, of the craftsmen, their marbles and other stones and their tools.[27]

Writing in the fifteenth century, John Flete the abbey's historian records that the abbot, when returning from the very first journey which he had made to Rome to receive the pope's confirmation, had brought the craftsmen and their stones back with him on that occasion.[28] But since we now know that that return of his was in 1259, and that the cosmati work in the abbey was not begun until 1267/68, it is impossible to believe that the marble-workers had to remain idle, cooling their heels in Westminster, for eight or nine years before being able to start their work. It also seems unlikely that the abbot had been able to finance the project himself, as Flete also asserts, since the cost must have been formidable and only within the reach of one such as the king (however hard-pressed as he always was to find ready cash).

It was the skills of Peter Oderisius, a master craftsman and the most outstanding member of the Italian Oderisius family, and of his workmen, which had been sought out and hired by Abbot Ware. Most of Peter's work elsewhere, it seems, was carried out on religious screens, tomb sculptures and other church furniture, and work on these was usually finer and more complex in its design and workmanship than the work on cosmati pavements, even those at Agnani. Indeed the great pavement which Peter designed for the abbey at Westminster is the only such pavement known to have been created by him, and when contrasted with such other pavements it was unique in its complexities of design, workmanship and symbolic meanings.[29]

Twenty-five feet square, it is bedded in the sanctuary at the foot of the great altar, on the east side of the crossing of the two transepts. Beginning in 1267 or 1268, the total work both on the pavement and on the new shrine and chapel for St. Edward took about two years apparently to complete. The pavement itself was finished, it seems, by the end of 1268, and one can envisage that some of the craftsmen then returned to Italy. In turn, sufficient work on the shrine must have been completed for the grand 'translation' of St. Edward's body to its new home to take place ceremonially on the saint's own day, the 13th October 1269 and for the partially-completed abbey to be consecrated, presided over by the king. This was the day for which he had waited for at least the last twenty-five years.

The pavement's cryptic inscriptions, in brass letters set in three sections both round and inside the square centrepiece, provided a few hard facts, set among masked clues and riddling mathematics, to identify, or perhaps to disguise, the dates involved and the

---

26  *Cal. P. R.*, 1258-1266, pp. 59 and 117; and 135. It is unlikely that the abbot had stayed over from his 1260 visit into 1261. These dates are clear; but I cannot find evidence to suggest a later journey in 1267-8, as referred-to by Colvin, *King's Works*, I, p. 147 and adopted by Foster, *Patterns of Thought*, p. 18.
27  *Cal. P. R.*, 1258-1266, p. 681.
28  *Flete*, p. 113.
29  See Foster, *ibid.*, pp. 21-27 and 80-110, for all the various evidential issues which arise about identities, comparisons and dates. There are several complexities in the story, and some inconsistencies in the chronology.

predicted age of the world. At least the four 'composers' of the whole work were identified, if not too clearly, as:     (a) King Henry III; (b) the 'city' (? of Rome), denoting symbolically perhaps the source of the stones used; or even some act of generosity on the part of the pope; (c) 'Odoricus' (ie. Oderisius, the craftsman-designer); and (d) the abbot.[30] The pattern of the stonework was a spiralling and interlocking sequence of concentric roundels, enclosed within a trio of squares of ascending size (one of them set obliquely), and composed of a shimmering maze of small purple, green, red, blue and yellow-ochre lozenges, triangles, diamonds, squares, rectangles, hexagons, heptagons, stars and circles, all of varying kinds of marble, serpentine, jasper, glass and some local stones, enclosed in a matrix of Purbeck 'marble'.[31]

There can be no doubt that Abbot Ware was the main agent responsible for the importation of the craftsmen and materials required for the design and construction. But his contribution in even this aspect of the venture was barely acknowledged by the niggardly words placed later on his tomb, under the north side of the sanctuary. Translated, his epitaph runs: "Abbot Ware, who is at rest, carries here [the weight of] the stones which he carried here from Rome".[32] This miserly inscription also reflects, again, the lack of close sympathy on the part of the monks towards their abbot. But in view of the king's later acknowledgment of the debt which he owed to the abbot for the pavement,[33] without doubt it had been the abbot who (on a first visit to Rome, made for a different purpose) had first seen and understood the

creative possibilities in such a pavement for the new abbey, and had taken the idea back to the king and must have helped throughout, as abbot, in bringing it to fruition. So he was responsible for more than just the bringing of the craftsmen and their materials to England.

## The Westminster Customary

The second major contribution which Abbot Ware made to the life of the abbey was his creation of a remarkable record of the rules and practices observed in the abbey at Westminster. It is usually called his 'Customary', because it reflected all the recognised 'customs' with which the monks were expected to comply, in the regulation of their behaviour together, in accordance with the Rule of St. Benedict as interpreted by later ordinances. The customs related to all aspects of their daily life – in the dormitory and refectory, in the church, cloister and choir, in the washhouse, almonry and infirmary; and in the discharge of the many duties laid upon all those who were appointed to hold the offices within the abbey, from the abbot and prior downwards, through all the monk officeholders, the 'obedientaries' who managed the day-to-day administration.[34]

Only one part of this all-embracing work has survived, but the overwhelming detail contained in this part gives an extraordinary picture of the daily lives of the monks of the abbey in the thirteenth century. The other three parts of the work have been lost, and apparently the reason why this fourth part has been preserved is that, because its contents were regarded as *'the more secret matters of our [Benedictine] order'*, it was separated from the three other parts and kept under lock and

---

30  The riddling mathematics of the inscription do not cohere precisely, but the text above is probably the best sense to be made of it.
31  The Purbeck, being locally to hand, was used instead of Carrara white marble. All the cosmati work at Westminster, and its matrix of Purbeck, have suffered extensive damage (mostly since the eighteenth century) and have been patched up and restored from time to time. All but seven of the brass letters of the long inscriptions are lost. The pavement used to be shown publicly on three days each year, but at present it is closed for conservation works. For the geometric effect, see Plate 11 at p. 229.
32  *Flete*, p. 115.
33  *Cal. Pat. R.*, 1266-1272, p. 338.
34  Thompson, ed., *Customary of St. Augustine, Canterbury and St Peter. Westminster, vol. ii.*

key.[35] It would not be the first time that an intended secrecy has ironically led to an even wider dissemination of the information secreted. But there seems to be nothing more sinister in the secrecy intended by the monks than an understandable respect for their own privacy about some quite intimate details of their lives, and a wish on the part of the order not to reveal to the world how their administration worked, or perhaps sometimes did not work.

A similar Customary for the monks of St. Augustine's Priory at Canterbury has also survived, but this seems to have been modelled later in the fourteenth century, either on Abbot Ware's Westminster one or some earlier one at Canterbury.[36]

It is clear that the Westminster Customary is not an entirely original work – in the sense that this could not have been the very first attempt to describe the daily practices of the monks. To be able, unassisted, to conjure up a first description of such exacting details of the course of abbey life would have been extraordinary. We have to postulate that there were earlier sources. It is much more likely that earlier, but no doubt rougher and disconnected, notes or summaries of the 'customs' existed in the abbey, which the scribe compiling the Customary was able to use. Moreover it seems that much of the Westminster Customary and the similar (though not identical) one for St. Augustine's, Canterbury must have been drawn from some independent common source.[37] Quite apart from the virtual impossibility of writing a coherent description of the customs without such outside assistance, the earlier observance by the monks of the detailed customs themselves would have proved very difficult,

if not impossible, without earlier records to rely on, however scrappy they may have been. However the book is certainly written with specific relevance to Westminster customs, as the many references in it to specific facts peculiar to the abbey at Westminster demonstrate.

In its detailed extent and coherence, this new Customary was certainly original. It has every appearance of having had a methodical and exhaustive mind behind it. The abbot himself was not the scribe who put it all together on parchment. That scribe was the sub-prior of the abbey, William of Haseley (Oxon), who was also the master in charge of the novices at the abbey. William of Haseley was engaged on the job from the very start and carried it through to the end,[38] but although he probably contributed substantially to the compilation and selection of both subject matter and detail and was obviously a methodical scribe, the painstaking and comprehensive nature of the Customary has all the hallmark of a business-like overseer such as Abbot Ware clearly was.

Even by itself this single, but massive, part of the Customary clearly must have taken a long time both to compile and to write out. This started in 1266. Although there is unreliable evidence to the effect that the whole work was completed in the course of that one year, it is clear that the final completion could not have been achieved until after Henry III had died in 1272.[39] But coincidentally most of the writing of the Customary was going on during the very years when the cosmati work on the pavement and the new shrine for St. Edward were being installed in the new abbey.

The surviving copies of the Customary are themselves not complete,[40] but even so its

---

35  Thompson, *ibid.*, ii., pp. vi-vii.

36  *ibid.*, vol. ii., pp. vi-vii.

37  *ibid.*, p. viii.

38  See the colophon on the extant (though damaged) copy of the original MS, as recorded at *ibid.*, p. vi.

39  See Harvey, *Walter de Wenlok*, p. 9, n. 6. This is because H. III is referred-to in the Customary in such terms as a dead person would have been. There is also the length of the work to be taken into acount. Flete, *History of WA*, p. 114, reports that the work was completed by Wm. of Haseley in 1266.

40  Apart from the missing three parts, even this surviving part contains illegible passsages, and does not deal with some topics. However it is still a remarkable document.

contents are too comprehensive to permit any attempt at a long description here. But its subject matters can be summarised. The book was an essentially practical account of abbey-life, which described the duties and activities of the great officers and their offices, and the rights and obligations and the behaviour and deportment of monks in all situations.

The main 'obedientaries' who controlled the departments of administration ranged from the **precentor**, who was in charge of all music and the choir, the library and all its books and the archives of the abbey, and (with two others) the seal of the convent and the sealing of all abbey documents; the **sacrist**, in charge of the fabric and cleanliness of the church, the ornaments, the services, the lighting of the church, the cloister and the administrative offices, the ringing of the bells, and the care of the cemetery; the **cellarer**, in charge of catering and all stores, of the servants, the transport of food and drink, of general repairs and the provision of fuel; the **kitchener**, in charge of the cooking and the whole kitchen department, including all its utensils; the **refectorer**, in charge of the refectory (or *frater*), the huge room where meals were mainly eaten, and of the other room used for the same purpose, the *misericord* which had more recently been built; the **chamberlain**, in charge of the provision of all clothing, shoes, bedding, the washing and repairing of clothes, the provision of hot water for the (very rare) baths and shaving; the **almoner**, in charge of the almonry itself (which lay outside the west gate of the abbey in Tothill Street) and the very extensive distributions of alms in the form of money, food or clothes to the poor; the **infirmarer**, in charge of the infirmary where the seriously sick monks were tended, and of others less sick who needed treatment without being hospitalised.[41]

The detail of the requirements at that time for the ordinary daily behaviour of the monks is in general precise, but there are clearly some gaps and deviations in attitudes, if one applies some modern comparisons. As was usual in Benedictine houses, monks slept in their daytime underclothes, to avoid public undressing. When these underclothes were changed, a special wash for the hands was necessary afterwards. Legs were not to be shown, when taking off shoes and stockings. Canvas mattresses contained straw, and rested on straw. It was decreed that the straw should be changed at least once a year, and the dormitory cleaned on that occasion. When getting up, one should leave the bed well covered, resulting in little airing. Washing of the feet was only a weekly requirement. Baths were mainly for the sick and were not to be taken regularly: even the old custom, a generous four baths a year, had been withdrawn by the time of Ware's Customary. Shaving was to be done in pairs once a fortnight, with one shaving the other, in a cloister open to the elements. The senior monks were to be shaved first, so that they had the benefit of the sharp razors and the dry cloths. Gloves should be just mittens: gloved fingers were a luxury. And so on.

In contrast there was considerable delicacy in some matters, where modern conduct might compare badly. Behaviour at table was carefully circumscribed. Unseemliness or impoliteness was rewarded with the need to prostrate oneself, until permission to resume one's seat might be given. Arms and elbows were to be kept off the table. Chattering and lounging were against custom. A nut had to be cracked silently with a knife: unless everyone had nuts, and then it was the meal-time 'reader' who had to suffer, in trying to make himself heard above the racket.

Above all, the moderation of the whole Customary shines through it. Severity and rigidness is to be tempered by pragmatic leniency, according to the circumstances of time and place. Although speech, when allowed, should always be low, the sacrist in speaking to royalty or a magnate can speak in a normal voice. The feelings of any one who

41 A lesser officer mentioned in the Customary was the monk-gardener (see p. 149 above, and Mclean *Med. Eng. Gardens* pp. 40-41). He had to take off his cape and boots before coming to church.

offends against a rule are to be respected, in the first place, by gentle admonition, so that he is not humiliated. Forgiveness is to be extended to the penitent. Some of the humanity demonstrated in the Customary might be a good prescription for modern manners.

## Cardinal Ottobuono and the abbey

This same period, when the Westminster pavement was being installed and Abbot Ware's Customary was in course of being written, saw a third event which also had consequences for the abbey. This was the three-year stay in England of Cardinal Ottobuono Fieschi, the pope's legate, newly appointed because of the effects of the civil war.

The mid-1260s had been dramatic in England. The decade had seen the culmination in 1264 and 1265 of the struggle between King Henry and the dissident barons under Simon of Montfort. That struggle came to a head in the two battles of Lewes and Evesham, leaving Henry defeated in the first, but victorious in the second. But the king's initial defeat and capture in 1264 had already prompted Pope Clement IV (to whom Montfort was a *'pestilent man'*) to appoint and despatch a cardinal as the new papal legate to England, where he arrived in October 1265, with threefold instructions. He was to procure the restoration of both the king (already accomplished at the battle of Evesham, shortly before his arrival) and of peace, which was still far from won; to reform ecclesiastical affairs; and to preach a crusade. The least graphic of these, the reform of ecclesiastical matters, affected various places in the kingdom including the abbey at Westminster, which still suffered from some internal problems.

Cardinal Ottobuono effected two sets of changes at Westminster. Initially he had been far too taken up with his other much more important tasks in England, but during his legation he sent two deputies to the abbey at Westminster, to investigate its internal issues. After receiving their 'very favourable report' he endorsed their decisions, which in effect applied a brake to some of the prior's and the convent's activities. The convent's officers were not to conduct or make any transactions with other parties without obtaining the abbot's consent. The prior was to relieve the abbot from duties in the church and in the monks' dormitory, the cloister and their 'other haunts', and for this purpose he was to move his chamber nearer to the cloister, by the door to the infirmary. The monks were not to make visits to the convent's manors except on infrequent occasions. All the monks were to use the same kind of cup, whether of silver or wood. Rules were laid down for the management of the infirmary and its inmates.[42] From these ordinances one can detect the kind of problems which had been arising, and it seems clear that the legate accepted Abbot Ware's point of view about issues at the abbey, rather than the monks'.

Another area in Westminster in which the cardinal legate appears to have imposed a correcting hand was in relation to the leper Hospital of St James, which was under the supervisory control of the abbey. Since its foundation during Henry II's reign, predictable troubles had arisen over the management of the hospital, where both 'brothers and sisters' were present. The legate and the abbot collaborated in laying down a number of firm but unspecified ordinances about the conduct and management of the hospital, backed by threats of exclusion from the church and the removal of the inmates' food allowances, if the rules were broken.[43]

---

42 WAD 28. The usual internationalism of the 'European' ecclesiastical scene is illustrated by the fact that the legate's deputies for this purpose were an Italian archbishop and a dean of Bayeux. So far as I know, nothing was ordained by Ottobuono about the abbey's privileges lost to London, during the civil war, see p. 238.

43 *Flete*, p. 115. For a legatine council, as Matthew Paris saw it, see Plate 9 at p. 191.

## The deteriorating finances of the king

Another role which the legate Ottobuono played during his three-year stay in England reflected the increasing involvement of the abbey in the worsening financial position of the king. Way back in 1245, when the king had started the construction works for his new abbey in Westminster, he had begun a process which meant that by the end of the 1250s his finances were in dire straits. But the construction works, costly as they were, were responsible for only part of this predicament. In other quarters also he was incurring huge debts, and by 1257 was having to borrow money in large amounts in order to meet earlier debts.[44]

By the time that Abbot Crokesley had died in 1258 and the subsequent 'vacancy' in the abbacy of more than a year had begun, Henry was desperately short of ready money and was prepared to pledge anything precious in order to obtain it. In even earlier years, he had had to sell or pawn some of his own jewels and plate in order to raise money.[45] But now in late 1258 the king persuaded (or perhaps forced?) the prior and convent of Westminster, in the absence of any abbot during the vacancy, to act as sureties for another loan which he was incurring in order to pay off part of an even earlier vast debt of £90,000, and in return he pledged some of his jewels to the prior and convent.[46]

But the position then became even worse. Henry was pawning more jewels in France in 1260-1 in order to raise money.[47] Later, after the papal legate Ottobuono had arrived in England, the king gave powers in 1267 to the legate to raise money 'for the most urgent business of the king' and to pledge not just some of the crown jewels, but even 'the Westminster jewels' – which already were deposited at the abbey for the purpose of being set in the golden decoration of the new shrine which was in course of completion at the abbey for St. Edward.[48] In this way the abbey was becoming sucked even further into King Henry's financial problems, at precisely the time when the construction of the new church was being brought to that state of (partial) completion which was shortly to be celebrated in the abbey's consecration and the translation of St. Edward's remains to its new shrine in October 1269.

After Henry's eventual death in 1272, the relationship between the abbey and the new King Edward I appears to have lost the close and indeed passionate character which King Henry had nurtured for the whole of his reign. However the abbot personally continued to play his more dispassionate administrative roles as royal envoy and legal justice, and finally became the royal treasurer to King Edward.[49]

---

44  For the circumstances, see p. 215 n. 25. Eg. in June 1256, even Abbot Crokesley was being sent off to Rome again, with two other envoys, empowered to obtain large loans 'in the king's name, from merchants and others', *Cal. P. R.*, 1247-58, pp. 479, 481.

45  This practice had began back in the 1240s, eg. when he borrowed money in 1245 from his own brother, Richard of Cornwall, secured on a pledge of gold objects of treasure lodged at the New Temple; or sold some plate and jewels to the citizens of London in 1248: *Cal. Pat. R.*, 1232-47, p. 456-7, and Paris, *Chron. Maj.*, v. 21-2.

46  *Cal. Lib. R.*, 1251-60, p. 459  Henry's huge debt was owed to the pope, as part of the price which he had to pay for his mad scheme to obtain (through the pope) the crown of Sicily for his son Edmund; cf. p. 253, n. 65.

47  See Harding, *England in the C13*, p. 297. For this, Henry even had to get the help of his own sister in law, the queen of France.

48  *Cal. Pat. R.*, 1266-72, pp. 50, 133 and 135-40; and Harding, *ibid*.  The Westminster jewels were to be transferred to the legate, who was to keep them as a pledge at the Tower of London; they are listed in full, upon six pages in the above Pat. Rolls, at pp. 135-40. The jewels were worth over £25000, Colvin, *King's Works*, I/148. WAM 9464 (referring to the 'gold, precious stones and jewels of the shrine') provides evidence that some of the jewels had already been sold by the king, and some pledged, before the rest were handed to the legate.

49  See pp. 226, and cf. 203 above.

## The acquisition and management of properties for the abbey

Like his two predecessors, Abbot Ware also continued to follow the abbey's policy of purchasing properties where these became available, in view of the rising prices during the continuing inflation. A major acquisition which he made in 1270 was the manor of Great Amwell, situated on the river Lea in Hertfordshire. The abbot must himself have known this manor and the holders of it, since it lay only a few miles south of his home town of Ware. Lying on this important river, the manor had a valuable watermill and at least two vills in it, in adjoining Stanstead and Great Amwell itself.[50] The Limesey family which had owned the manor since at least the time of Domesday had always held it directly from the king, and indeed its purchase now by the abbey from Sir Ralph of Limesey proved to be the only acquisition by the monks of a major property on the Crown's estate during the whole of the thirteenth and fourteenth centuries.[51]

Sir Ralph apparently had no direct heir, and having previously had to borrow money from Abbot Ware and having leased the manor to him during the abbot's lifetime, he decided to sell his interest in this major property to the abbey, probably because of his own poverty. At all events in 1270 the abbey acquired his interest, for a price which must have seemed formidable, 850 marks (£566. 13s. 4d.),

fortunately payable in instalments.[52] But even this was not the end of the price which had to be paid for the manor, because more than forty years later the monks found that they had to pay another 200 marks, to buy off a legal claim made by a member of the same family that he had rights in parts of the manor which had not been cleared in the original purchase.[53]

But where could such large sums have come from? No doubt the abbot himself had been making money through his administrative activities on behalf of the king, and one would have expected that he was making at least a considerable contribution towards the original purchase of Great Amwell. But if he did, there seems to be no record of it, and we find that in 1288, five years after Abbot Ware's death, the next abbot assigned the whole manor of Great Amwell to his convent of monks, on a claim made by them that Abbot Ware *'had bought the manor with the assets of the convent, and had promised to assign it to them'*.[54] If this claim were true, the price had come entirely from the convent's portion; but it is difficult to believe that the convent could produce so much ready money for one transaction, even in instalments.[55]

Meanwhile however the perils of any property situated on a river were illustrated at Great Amwell itself. One day in mid-summer 1279 the abbey's watermill and its surrounding 'tenements' in both Amwell and Stanstead were suddenly flooded by a great head of water coming down the river from its

---

50 The river Lea had been the boundary of Middlesex since later Anglo-Saxon times, see *The Westminster Corridor*, p. 22, cf. p. 16 (at an even earlier time).

51 Harvey, *WA Estates*, pp. 168 and 188.

52 Sir Ralph's poverty was probably due to the fact that he had fought on the barons' side against King Henry in the 1260s, and had had to redeem his confiscated lands after 1266. For the abbey's purchase, see WAMs 4256, 4259, 4246 and Harvey, *ibid.*, p. 191.

53 Harvey, *ibid.*, pp. 175-6, and WAM 4250.

54 WAM 4241; *Cal. P. R.*, 1281- 92, p. 416. It is hard to say whether the purchase of Great Amwell was a good investment. Its value in 1270 appears to have been £40 pa., which suggests that even the original price, at 14.5 years purchase, was excessive, If however it *later* proved to have been a fortunate purchase, the purchase was also opportune in the sense that it took place before 1279, when the Statute of Mortmain was enacted, forbidding sales of property to perpetual bodies such as the abbey, without a special licence which had to be obtained, for a further price, from the king.

55 Barbara Harvey (*ibid.*, pp. 59-60 and 63) estimated that by about this time the whole annual income of the convent was about £1100, (nearly twice that of the abbot's income from abbey assets). The £1100 had to suffice for all the convent's activities, including those of all the obedientiaries which, in effect, included the provision of all the necessities of life for the monks, as well as other obligations.

higher reaches. It turned out that another riparian owner up-river, the abbot of Waltham Holy Cross (Waltham Abbey) had begun building a lock on the river and, in so doing, had caused or allowed certain sluices to be opened without warning, and the head of water had swept down on Great Amwell, causing the flood.[56] Apparently an action was started by Abbot Ware against his brother abbot, and the latter was ordered to repair the mill, with its millpond and dam, to the same condition that they were in before the flood. Later another dispute arose whether he had in fact repaired them, and in November 1283, about five weeks before Abbot Ware died, a commission had to be appointed by the king to investigate whether the proper repairs had been carried out.[57]

Great Amwell had been the greatest acquisition of valuable property made by Abbot Ware, but we can also see that he was able to recover other smaller areas of land for the abbey. One potentially very valuable area, much nearer home, on which the abbot also concentrated was the district west of the road 'Aldewich' in Westminster itself. This was the main garden district of the town, where the abbot's 'great garden' (by that time called the 'Convent Garden') and 'Tockesgardin' (the original large garden of the Tocke family) lay.[58] Over the course of time Tockesgardin, like other existing gardens, appears to have been divided up into two or three separate areas held by different people, with the name

Tockesgardin retained for the whole area of the original family holding. But the major part of Tockesgardin had eventually been donated back to the abbey, from whom it must have originally sprung.[59]

It appears that Abbot Ware set about improving the abbey's interests in this Aldewich district, no doubt because of the value of the land there for market gardening, with such ready markets nearby in the city of London. He succeeded in acquiring, from one holder, more 'land in Tockesgardyn' which lay north of the Convent Garden and stretched from Aldewich to St. Martin's lane; and, from another holder, a house lying between the late Walter the gardener's house and the Convent Garden. He also managed to obtain remission of an annual rent of two and a half marks which the abbey had had to pay to the Bucuinte family for the major part of the old Tockesgardin since recovering the immediate interest in it. And from current members of the Tocke family, he took a lease of certain other areas of land near another house on the east side of the Convent Garden, with an additional covenant that the lessors' gardener should repair the Convent Garden's earth walls and keep them repaired as hitherto.[60] In this way the abbot was not only rebuilding the abbey's estate in the area, but doing so with a view to taking advantage of the continuing rise in prices, particularly of market-gardening produce.

The abbot also made other acquisitions of

56 *Cal. P. R.*, 1272-81, p. 346.

57 *Cal. P. R.*, 1281-92, p. 103. I do not know what the final outcome of that inquiry was.

58 For this district, see also pp. 33-35 above. For the assignment of the abbey garden to the convent by Abbot Berking, see p. 199 above.

59 The clerk, Henry of Belgrave, donated it to the abbey, in probably the 1240s, see WAM 17351. Henry, an extensive land holder east and west of the Charing crossroads, became known later as Sir Henry, WAM 17371: see also pp. 33-34.

60 WAD 622b, 621b, 623b-4. The remission of the Bucuinte rent was obtained from Adam of Stratton (see pp. 265-6 below), who must have acquired the main Bucuintes' interest in the old Tockesgardin (see p. 33 above) and then released the abbey from the rent. Knowing Adam, one can be sure that there was something to be gained by him from such generosity. For the descent of other Bucuinte interests in that garden, see WAMs 17431 and 17481. One can also see that other Londoners were by now landholders here, no doubt to profit from this valuable market garden area, eg. 'John, son of Peter, citizen of London', see WAD 622b. The Convent Garden is described as 'abutting on the Kingsway at Aldewiche' WAD 621b, names now restored within the area. For such gardens in London suburbs and elsewhere, see Dyer, *Everyday Life in Med. England*, 121-22.

lands for the abbey, but these were further afield, in Kelvedon, Essex and in Gloucestershire and Worcestershire.[61]

In managing his estates, both those which he inherited and those which he himself recovered or acquired, Abbot Ware undoubtedly employed the practice which his successor Abbot Wenlock retained and developed more fully, of using 'writs' containing written instructions addressed to his own reeves and other officers in the estates.[62] It is also difficult to believe that even earlier in this more sophisticated century other abbots had not used the same practice.

## Benefits from the king

As had happened with his predecessors, Abbot Ware's own relationship with Henry III and even with his son Edward I enabled the abbot to obtain advantages which greatly assisted the abbey's financial opportunities. For example, on the 16th September 1263, as a further step towards promoting the forthcoming fair of St. Edward (due to take place a month later, on the 13th October) King Henry repeated a previous grant that all merchants coming to this fair were to be free from 'royal prises', the king's right to take articles or produce from merchants or landholders, without paying for them then and there.[63] As the beneficiary of the fair, the abbey profitted accordingly.

This royal regrant was made in the middle of the difficult period between 1258 and 1268 when baronial disputes, eventual civil war and defeat unsettled and nearly unseated King Henry. But during the same period the abbey suffered serious losses of virtually all its special rights and privileges with which it had been endowed by successive kings, particularly Henry III. While the abbey had

been the loser, the major winners had been the citizens of London. Siding with the rebel barons, the citizens had reaped the benefit when the abbey was compelled to renounce old rights in favour of London during the barons' belligerence in 1263-64. Examples of the lost rights were express renunciations, extracted from the abbey, of (a) its long-standing entitlement to receive all 'fines' and 'amercements' payable by persons who were tenants of the abbey, wherever and by whatever court such penalties were imposed, and (b) all its 'liberties' and rights in the county of Middlesex.

Even though the king ultimately triumphed against the barons in and after 1265, this still left the abbey faced with its own charters of renunciation in favour of the citizens of London. But in November 1265-66, within a few months after his victory at the battle of Evesham, the king began restoring at least some of the abbey's lost rights by charters which were apparently made but not recorded in the usual roll of royal charters.[64] And later in 1280, eight years after Edward I had succeeded his father, a more systematic re-confirmation of the abbey's old rights was carried out. This took the form of various charters made by Edward in November 1280, reconfirming at least eleven earlier entitlements which King Henry had bestowed upon the abbey during the course of his reign, including his long and comprehensive grant of rights and privileges to the abbey whch he had made in 1235.[65] Although Edward did not share his father's extravagant devotion to the abbey, he did much else to support it in ways like this. But his help was cooler and less partial.

This was a period in which the king was concentrating his efforts on providing powerful backing for the abbey. In December,

61 In Kelvedon, a pre-Conquest estate of WA, a leased part of the estate was recovered, while in Glos. and Worcs. lands were acquired from the mortgaged estate of one of WA's corrodians, Laurence of Wandsworth; see *Flete*, pp. 115-6 and Harvey, *WA Estates*, p. 170 and *Living and Dying*, p. 241.

62 See p. 295-8 below and the facts in notes 17 and 18 there.

63 *Cal. P. R.*, 1258-66, p. 278. See a previous order in 1248, at *Cal Ch. R.*, 1226-57, p. 334.

64 These charters, made in 1265-66, were referred to later in Edward I'st charters in November 1280, see next note. The usual roll for 1265-66 is clearly incomplete, presumably because of disarray caused by the recent civil war.

65 *Cal. Ch. R.*, 1257-1300, pp. 238-9 and 241.

the following month, he made another charter granting freedom from the powers of his stewards and marshals to commandeer or to billet lodgers in the 'long house' in the abbey churchyard which Abbot Ware had just rebuilt, extending from the northern gate of the churchyard to the new belfry. This valuable building had been designed for letting to merchants at the Westminster fairs, with its profits devoted towards *'the support of the lamp of the high altar and St Edward's shrine'*.[66]

## Celebrations in Westminster

During Abbot Ware's period of office, Henry III's seasonal celebrations in Westminster at Christmas, Easter and the feasts of St. Edward continued whenever possible, but on a lesser scale than those which he had promoted during the 1240s and 1250s – and with interruptions. The king's recurring shortages of money reduced even his expensive sense of ceremony, and when war broke out sharply in 1264 at the culmination of his disputes with barons, the grand ceremonies had to be completely suspended. But after the successful conclusion of his struggles with the barons, and with twenty two years of construction works on the new abbey completed, the scene changed. Although the new abbey was not entirely complete, since the building extended only as far westwards as the fourth bay of the nave, most of it was ready. The choir itself, the sanctuary, the great pavement, the transepts, the high altar, St. Edward's chapel with his new shrine, the Lady Chapel and the chapter house were substantially finished, and the king who was nearly 62 years old had recognised his own mortality and the need to ensure that the celebration of their completion was carried out in his own lifetime.

Just as the king had marked the early years of his rebuilding of the abbey by his dramatic dedication in 1247 of a precious relic of Christ's blood, so now towards the end of the 1260s he devised a comparable drama to mark its near-completion.[67] He appointed another great celebration at the abbey for St. Edward's day, the 13th October, 1269, when the consecration of the new building and the translation of St. Edward's body to its new shrine immediately behind the great altar were to be carried out.

But predictably not everything went smoothly. At first the intention was that the king and queen should wear their coronation crowns in great splendour at the ceremony, but on its very eve this plan was abandoned peremptorily by a sudden proclamation made in Westminster Hall. On the following day the ceremonial in the abbey remained impressive, but was marred by a ludicrous ecclesiastical dispute between the bishops, which ended in some scuffling by attendants before the high altar.[68] But the relics of the saint were reverently carried in procession from its old shrine, on the shoulders of King Henry, his brother Earl Richard of Cornwall (who by now had also become a king: 'of the Germans') and their respective sons, and in the splendid new shrine the relics were restored to their interrupted rest for the last time (so far). Mass was celebrated for the first time in the new church.

At the great feast held afterwards in the great Hall, the scene was marred only by

---

66  *Cal. P. R.*, 1272-81, p. 418 and WAM 17458. The commandeering or billetting of the house would have caused loss of valuable lettings at the times of the fairs, and also when parliaments and the legal terms brought an influx of visitors to the town. For the new belfry, see pp. 248-9 and 254 below. King Henry had also given a similar freedom to houses which he had bestowed on the sacristy at the abbey in 1252, see p. 215 above.

67  For the dedication of the relic in 1247, see p. 210 above, and Plate 10, p. 211, by Matthew Paris.

68  Boniface, the archbishop of Canterbury, could not be present owing to his age, but Walter Giffard, the archbishop of York who therefore presided insisted on a right to have his cross carried in front of him, contrary to claims that he was not entitled to this within the province of Canterbury. Scuffles by attendants ensued, and the other bishops refused to follow the archbishop of York in procession round the church, but sat resentfully in their stalls; Powicke, *H. III & Ld. Edw.*, pp. 576-7. In retaliation Boniface then placed an interdict on London.

further disputes, of a secular kind this time, between the citizens of London and Winchester.[69] This mix of sanctity, triumph and occasional farce was symbolic of Henry's struggles to create his new abbey, and perhaps of his whole reign.

Another memorable day of celebration for the abbey, this time for a new king, was the 19th August 1274, when Edward I, who had been abroad on crusade ever since his accession in 1272, now returned and was finally crowned in the abbey with his queen, Eleanor of Castile, by the Archhbishop of Canterbury. This ceremony too was followed by another great feast in Westminster Hall, now newly decorated by Stephen, the king's painter. The king of Scotland attended, and 500 horses were set free by their knightly owners, for anyone to catch and keep.

In contrast to Henry III's last great occasion in the abbey and the royal hall, it was perhaps symbolic of this new reign that everything went according to plan. Enormous preparations had been carried out to clean the city of London, and instead of water, the Cheapside conduit *'poured forth white wine and red like rainwater'*. The palace of Westminster and the great Hall had been newly repaired, at great expense. Food and drink in huge quantities for the feasting were collected from all quarters.[70] Walter Giffard, the recalcitrant archbishop of York, whose own London residence York Place lay just north of the king's palace of Westminster, was excluded from taking part in the ceremonies. All other comers, rich and poor, were made welcome.

## The impact of the parliaments

The increased holding of many parliaments at Westminster, with the resulting arrivals and departures of great and small participants and

of many of the service-providers who fed upon their needs, continued to act like the tide – with the flotsam flooding into the town and flowing out again. Although some other cities and smaller places throughout the country were also the scenes for such gatherings, Westminster was already the prime site for them. During the abbacy of Richard of Ware, this tide of parliament flowed into Westminster at least twenty-three times, and ebbed out again. By itself, Westminster accounted for nearly half of the whole number of parliaments held, with London accounting for thirteen and other places less.[71]

The period when Richard of Ware happened to be abbot of Westminster saw some of the early steps which were leading to the evolution of 'parliaments' which had some representatives of the 'commons' of England.[72] But it was in the commoners' role as 'make-weights' against the magnates that both King Henry, and particularly Edward I after him, tended to view representatives of the commons in parliaments, as useful for their own royal purposes.

This gradual change in the composition of future parliaments meant in turn that the visitors who invaded Westminster periodically to take part in such parliaments, or to accompany and support the participants, were of a wider class and range of people. By 1275 during Abbot Ware's abbacy, knights from the shires and burgesses from the cities and boroughs, with their families and servants, were now beginning to appear from time to time in numbers in Westminster – to seek lodgings, food and other services in the town, so stimulating further the trade in services which was already, and was to remain, the hallmark of the town.

69 The disputes between the citizens of London and Winchester related to the right to perform the service of butlery at the feast. See Powicke, *ibid*, p. 576.

70 eg. *Cal. P. R.* 1272-79, pp. 70, 71; Prestwich *Edward I*, p. 89. For a king crowned, see Plate 16, at p. 262.

71 See Sayles, *The King's Parliament*, Appendix at p. 137 ff. Cf. shorter lists (not all agreeing) of parliaments appearing in Carpenter, *Reign of Henry III*, p. 475; Powicke, *H. III and the lord Edward,* ii. p. 840; Prestwich, *Edward I*, p. 612, and Harding, *England in the C13*, p. 345.

72 For the emergence of some of the earlier 'parliaments' which included or at least listened to 'commoners', see the previous chapter dealing with Abbot Crokesley, at pp. 220 ff. above.

# CHAPTER 15

# The great rebuilding of the abbey
## 1245-1272

During the middle of the thirteenth century, the abbey at Westminster was doubly rejuvenated. Not only was the greater part of it rebuilt – its first rebuilding in 200 years – but it also became re-endowed with the status of a royal mausoleum, which its first rebuilder, the king and saint Edward the Confessor, had originally given to it. These two supplements – to its dominant physical presence as it now towered over the town of Westminster, and to the mantle of its own national reputation – owed everything to the personality of one man, King Henry III, and in particular to his own self-identification with his saintly predecessor.

But Henry was never single-minded. Even while his ambitions fastened upon the abbey's rebuilding, one of his other fancies was a more secular one: the constant improvement of – and general tinkering with – his own residences, in particular his palace at Westminster. These two obsessions seem to have filled much of his waking thoughts, whatever other demands – about military and diplomatic necessities on the continent, or empty treasuries and recalcitrant barons at home – were made on him.

## A royal mausoleum

In the past, the abbey of Westminster had appeared to have been slighted, in one respect, by the Norman and Angevin kings. Not one of them, since the Norman Conquest, had chosen Westminster as his burial place – even if many coronations had taken place there.[1] Most of the Norman kings had preferred that their bodies should be buried at other churches, notably churches which they had themselves founded or promoted. But the two first Angevin kings (Henry II and Richard I), with their much wider continental territories within the area of modern France, had chosen the abbey of Fontevrault in Anjou as their final resting place. And King John, who in any case had lost much land on the continent, reverted to making England his choice, but favoured Worcester Cathedral for his tomb.[2]

So the early example set by Edward the Confessor, the last king of the Anglo-Saxon era, had been side-stepped by all the intervening monarchs since the Conquest. But with Henry III, everything now changed.

Before the age of thirteen, the young king had already demonstrated both his interest in a rebuilding of part of the abbey buildings, and also a personal and prophetic bond with the abbey itself. On two consecutive days, the 16th and 17th May 1220, he had first laid the foundation-stone in the monks' new project of building a chapel for the Virgin Mary ('the Lady Chapel'), and had then taken part in his second coronation ceremony, this time in the abbey at Westminster. His subsequent donation of his gold coronation spurs to the fund for the construction of the new chapel foreshadowed his later large-scale rebuilding of the abbey itself and his future liberality with his own, and other people's, money towards that grander objective.[3]

---

1   cf. Mason, *People of WA*, pp. 285-7: - 'they appear almost to have had a grudge against the abbey'.
2   *William I* was buried at St. Etienne, Caen. *Wm. Rufus* had chosen St. Peter's Abbey, Gloucester; but ended up (involuntarily, thanks perhaps to Walter Tirel) at Winchester. *Henry I*, at Reading Abbey, Berks. *Stephen*, at Faversham Abbey, Kent. *Henry II* and *Richard I*, at Fontevrault, in Anjou. *John*, at Worcester, close to his patron, St. Wulfstan.
3   See also pp. 137 ff. and 190.

Moreover two months after his coronation at Westminster, he went to Canterbury cathedral in July 1220 to witness the 'translation' (the ceremonial removal) of the remains of St. Thomas Becket from the crypt to a new shrine in the Trinity chapel. That experience almost certainly set him upon the path which led him to the culminating event of his rebuilding of the abbey in Westminster, when nearly fifty years later on the 13th October 1269 the body of St. Edward the Confessor was also removed to a splendid new shrine which Henry had had substantially completed and placed within the rebuilt abbey.[4]

Much earlier, in October 1246, in the first stages of the rebuilding, Henry had decided that he too wished to be buried in the new abbey, and in due course his wish was fulfilled when he died in 1272.[5] So both the bond of royal burial in the abbey was eventually re-established, and a renewed honour had meanwhile been paid to the memory of Edward the Confessor, the king and saint who had been the original author of such a bond.

## The king's agents for his Westminster projects

### The re-emergence of Odo the Goldsmith, 1218-39

But long before this formal bond of royal burial was re-forged, young King Henry in his early days had already begun, since about 1218, to benefit from the services of a man who was destined to figure throughout the king's renovating and rebuilding programmes in Westminster during the next fifty years. This was Odo the Goldsmith, the well-known and influential resident of Westminster, who for many years had lived as a tenant of the abbey in a large establishment in the Thamesbank area near the palace precinct, and had already served the abbey in the office of reeve of Westminster.[6] But his new role, now in the king's service, was both a direct and an indirect one. It was direct, in that he himself became the main 'keeper of the works of the king's houses in Westminster' and remained in that post for twenty one years.[7]

But Odo's role became indirect as well, because his son Edward whom he introduced to royal service in 1238 and trained to follow in his footsteps, became an even more trusted and competent royal servant, and the king's main agent in all things administrative and personal during the subsequent rebuilding of the abbey. For nearly twenty-five years after 1239 Edward, known usually as 'Edward son of Odo', followed in his father's footsteps and was at the hub of every undertaking initiated by the king, complying with all his wishes and whims.

But before his son Edward had taken over the reins, Odo's own service as a royal agent had lasted from 1218 until 1239.[8] During this period, work on the monks' project of building a Lady Chapel at the abbey had started after 1220, and the chapel, situated at the east end

---

4    For the shrine, see Carpenter *The reign of H. III*, pp. 407 ff; Foster, *Patterns of Thought*, pp. 8-9; and pp. 228 and 247-8. Foster says that before the king's promotion of him, St. Edward had been 'a minor Anglo-Saxon saint'. The new shrine was built just beyond the high altar. Binski, 'The Cosmati at Westminster', *Art Bulletin*, 1, pp. 6-34 argues that the Cosmati base of the shrine was not completed until 1279.

5    *Cal. Ch. R.*, 1226-57, p. 306. The king re-affirmed his wish in a will, made in 1253. Although he was buried by the high altar in 1272, he was 'translated' in 1290 to a Cosmati tomb, with effigy, near St Edward's shrine.

6    For Odo's extensive background, see pp.151-3 above.

7    Other officials also became 'keepers' in Westminster jointly with Odo at various times, eg. the royal clerk Robert Passelawe (see *C. Lib. R.* 1226-40, pp. 199 and 235); and Laurence II de Castello, for whom see *Cal. Cl. R.* 1231-34, p. 90 et al., and also pp. 182-3 above and p. 269 below. For the hereditary office of 'keeper of the king's houses' themselves (as distinct from the keeper of *new works* on them), see p. 106 ff above.

8    Kent Lancaster, 'Artists, Suppliers and Clerks', *Jo. Warb. & Court. Inst.*, xxxv (1972) pp. 96-8 has much of interest about Odo, but erred in saying that Odo's 'antecedents are completely unknown'. Some are unknown, but much of his long history before the king employed him is known, see note 6 above.

of the existing church, was beginning to rise very slowly during these years.[9] The slowness was probably due to lack of funds, but records of the progress of the construction are scarce, and we know only scattered details.[10] By April 1234 the king was donating twenty oak trees from his forest of Tonbridge (Kent) to the abbot Richard of Berking for 'his new works of the chapel of St. Mary'.[11] By 1239, when Odo was close to handing over his office entirely to his son Edward, it is clear that the construction of some of the windows of the chapel was completed and that the glass in them was being, or had been, installed.[12]

However there was still more to be done on the building of the chapel, and it was not until at least 1245 that the chapel, in its first version, was nearing completion. By then the work had been extended by the king's special orders to include the building of two other altars, to St. Adrian and St. Michael, on the vaulted floor of the chapel's vestibule; the king was taking over control of the project, and the problem of marrying-up the new chapel with the plans for the rebuilding of the main church had still to be faced.[13] At least by 1246 the chapel, in its first form, was sufficiently complete for Abbot Berking to be buried in it when he died in November of that year.[14]

Meanwhile however, before his formal retirement in 1239, Odo's work as keeper lay mainly with the maintenance and improvement of the king's 'houses in Westminster', since in the 1220s and 1230s the king was concerned more with his own secular buildings and had not begun to concentrate his plans on the abbey. For the time being, therefore, Odo's role related principally to the palace buildings, including the administrative buildings within its precinct, such as the king's great and little halls and the exchequer buildings. As a rich man himself, Odo was often expected to advance his own moneys (sums such as £201 or £133) for such works, including the payment of workmen's wages, and to rely on subsequent reimbursement in due course by the king. When this happened, repayment by the king was often delayed, and meanwhile the keeper remained the king's creditor. But when it was the unfortunate workmen or suppliers who sometimes remained unpaid, then it was they who had to suffer from the system.

So Odo and his fellow-keepers were in irregular receipt of large sums, to repay them for improvements or repairs which generally had been carried out already in accordance with the king's orders. Some examples of the widely-varied tasks required of him were: – the repair of the king's riverside quay, within the palace site, after it had been damaged by flooding of the Thames; the construction of a new 'private chamber' in the palace, for the king; the erasure of an existing mural of animals and birds in the king's main chamber, by a covering of green paint which, King Henry ordered, was 'to look like like a curtain';

---

9   For the context of this project, see p. 128-9 above.

10  The 'architects' or designers of such stone buildings were invariably masons. Westlake, *WA*, vol 1, chap. 4, p 59 and J. Harvey, *Masons of WA*, p. 83 suggest that that the chapel's designer may have been the prominent mason, Master Ralph of Dartford, who held a property in Tothill Street from the abbey. There are some indications that the new chapel was intended (either when it was started, or at some later date) as a first stage in the rebuilding of the abbey, Colvin, *King's Works*, I. p. 132.

11  *Cal. Cl. R.* 1231-4, pp. 401 and 409.   Since this was perhaps fourteen years after the official start of the works, the oaks were probably for the roof of the chapel.

12  *Cal. Lib. R.*, 1226-40, p. 442.   Odo's son had paid for the glass and installation, and in Jan. 1240 was being repaid five and a half marks.   Four years later, other glazing had been carried out in the chapel (*Cal. Lib. R.*, 1240-45, p. 212); but after another twelve years, in 1256 the chapel was having to be seriously remodelled to adapt it to the rebuilt east end of the new abbey, see Colvin, *King's Works*, vol. 1, p. 144, and p. 261 below.

13  *Cal. Lib. R.*, 1240-45, p. 212, and *Cal. Cl. R.*, 1242-47, p. 208.   See Colvin, *ibid.*, p. 131 n. 7 for this suggested site for the two altars.   For the king's taking of control, see Carpenter, *The House of Kings*, p. 24.

14  For the abbot's death, see p. 208 above.

the provision of moneys by Odo to Master William, the plumber and conduit-builder *'who is to bring water by conduit to our palace-court at Westminster'*; the plastering and repair of the passageway between the royal chamber and the exchequer office of Receipt; and the erection of the king's gibbet.[15]

Such orders were usually delivered by royal 'closed' letters, which were then enrolled on the 'Close Rolls' which were now in regular use as official records. But sometimes the king had himself given an advance order by word of mouth to Odo himself or even to a craftsman involved, and however given, such orders had to be complied with rigorously.

Although Odo's earlier duties had exclusively been to do with the palace buildings, during the later years of his service there were also several tasks which the king required him to carry out for the benefit of the abbey as well; and at the same time there were indications of a more personal relationship between the king and his faithful servant.

For example, after King Henry in 1236 had married his queen, Eleanor of Provence, Odo received orders from him to 'make a figure of the queen' and to place it on the existing shrine of St. Edward the Confessor in the abbey.[16] Being a goldsmith, Odo was capable of fashioning such a figure himself, but it is not certain whether he was being required to use his own professional skills for this purpose or was merely required to see that the figure was made. On another occasion in the same year he was instructed by King Henry to obtain and present two pieces of richly embroidered 'stuff' (material worked with gold thread) at the shrine of St. Edward, on behalf of the king and queen.[17] In the previous year, 1235, the king had shown a personal concern for his 'keepers' by giving instructions to his Constable of Windsor to supply to both Odo and Laurence II de Castello, his fellow keeper of works at that time, *'three good tree trunks'* each – *'for their hearths'*.[18]

### The partnership of father and son

During his last two years in the king's service, Odo took his son Edward into partnership with himself, probably at the king's express wish, and the king's orders were then sometimes addressed to the two of them together, both for works on the palace buildings and for royal works and offerings at the abbey. At the same time both of them were officially made joint 'keepers of the king's cellar', and one or other of them then dealt with inward deliveries of the king's wines received from the continent, and with outward despatches of royal presents of wine to favoured subjects.[19]

From small changes in the relationships, one may see the gradual emergence of the personal role which became both more comprehensive but also more intimate between Edward and the king. While Odo's duties for most of his service had principally revolved round his official post as the main keeper of works on 'the king's houses' in Westminster, in the later stages of his service, particularly when Edward was acting with him, his role appears to have been regarded as including a closer relationship with the king.

Although Edward had already begun to act in his own right during the course of 1239, the start of the next year marked more

---

15   *Cal. Cl. R.*, 1234-37, pp. 245 (quay), 81 (private chamber), 484 (repainting), 69 (passageway); *ibid.*, 1231-34, pp. 530 (conduit); *Cal. Lib. R.*, 1226-40, p. 243 (gibbet). The king's demands for various decorations in green paint, 'like a curtain', extended to at least three of the palace rooms. The palace quay often had to be repaired, indicating heavy use of it.

16   *Cal. Lib. R.* 1226-40, p. 243. See also *Cal. Cl. R.*, 1234-37, p. 278, a slightly earlier but related order, directed to the king's treasurer, for 'a good likeness of the queen'. Such demands from the king fore-shadowed many similar ones directed later to Edward. Eleanor and her three sisters, daughters of the Count of Provence, each married royalty, viz. the kings of France and England, and their respective brothers

17   *Cal. Cl. R.*, 1234-37, p. 41. The medieval word for pieces of this valuable 'stuff' was 'baudekins'.

18   *ibid.*, p. 133. For Laurence II de Castello, see note 7 above.

19   *Cal. Lib. R.*, 1226-40, p. 313, cf. 363 and 393, and eg. *Cal. Cl. R.*, 1234-37, p. 440.

conspicuously the complete change in his status. During the third week of the new year, Edward purchased an official hereditary post at the exchequer, with the king's knowledge and full approval. The previous holder of the office of *fusor*, the melter, at the exchequer had apparently decided to go on pilgrimage to the Holy Land, and Edward took the opportunity to acquire the post from him for the sum of twelve marks (£8). The king marked the occasion by making a special royal charter confirming the transfer of the office; he also formally notified the Barons of the Exchequer of it, and took Edward's oath of allegiance, his 'homage', in his new position at the exchequer.[20]

This step seems to have signalled the transition from father to son in the royal service, but Odo still had at least one swan-song to come. Even as late as April 1242, the new chapel for St. Mary at the abbey must still have been well behind schedule, because in that month the king made financial provision designed to effect its completion. Out of substantial moneys which he lent to the abbot and convent, he arranged for a yearly sum of £40 to be paid to Odo *le Orfevre* who was instructed to '*make* the [chapel]' of St. Mary, until the moneys were exhausted.[21] But as Edward's father is thought to have died in about the same time, 1242, the plan (so far as it involved Odo) may have been frustrated. However, as indicated above, it is clear that much work on the chapel still remained to be done, including significant additions to its initial design which were not completed until about 1246.

Throughout the years while he was acting as the king's agent for works in Westminster, Odo had remained as a resident in his complex of houses off 'King Street', north of the palace and near the sluice on the Clowson stream. After his retirement in 1239 he continued there, and it was in October 1241 during this short period before his death that he received 'by the grace and generosity of the abbot and convent' their grant of a free chantry in the private chapel which they had allowed him to build there.[22]

### The king's new agent, Edward son of Odo: his early years, 1240-45

For his part, Edward was already deeply embroiled in all aspects of the king's plans for Westminster. Some of these had involved gifts or offerings designed to enrich the abbey, such as the purchase of 'a crystal vessel to be offered to St Edward'; or the making of a 'wooden shrine for the use of St. Edward'; or the purchase of 32 pieces of gold, most of which were expressly designated as offerings for the king to donate to the abbey at the celebrations of various feast-days.[23] Other duties laid on Edward by the king were the building works on some parts of the existing abbey itself: these included the new chapel of St. Mary, to which the king in 1245 made a personal but hardly princely gift of £10. Even before 1245 something like £200 had been spent on these abbey works.[24]

But like his father, Edward was also the king's keeper of works at the palace, and other plans made by the king involved more familiar tasks required of Edward for the improvement

---

20 *Cal. Ch. R.*, 1226-1257, pp. 249-50, and *Cal. Cl. R.*, 1237-42, p. 169. The previous holder was another 'Odo': he was Odo, son of John, and the coincidence of 'Odo, son of John' selling the office to 'Edward, son of Odo' has made for disagreement among historians; see Kent Lancaster, *ibid*. pp. 97-98. For the office of *fusor* at the exchequer, see p. 179-80 above.

21 *Cal. P. R.*, 1232-47, p. 280-1. *Le Orfevre* was French for 'the goldsmith', and it is difficult to resist the conclusion that this Odo was Edward's father, who was now free of his duties as 'keeper of (palace) works' and therefore could be expected to be able to apply himself, unimpeded, to dealing with the chapel.

22 WAMs 17333 (dated 18th Oct. 1241), and 17454. In return Odo promised that the grant would cease to have effect if his estate should become alienated to anyone other than his natural heirs.

23 *Cal. Lib. R.*, 1226-40, p. 489; *ibid.*, 1240-45, p. 83; *ibid.*, p. 120-1.

24 Colvin,, *King's Works*, I, p. 131. For the king's gift of £10, see *Cal. Cl. R.*, 1242-47, 323.

or repair of the palace buildings or the royal facilities within them: such as the raising of the chimney-piece of the queen's chamber, and the repainting of it with *'a figure .... which by its sad look and other miserable portrayals of the body may be justly likened to Winter'* (a curious subject for the queen's bed-chamber); the covering of the louvre above the king's lesser hall with lead; the purchase and installation of a marble altar in the queen's chapel, and later the 'thorough' painting of that chapel; and a further repair of the king's quay at the palace.[25] In addition to these (and many more) individual assignments, all the more continuous and ordinary repair work on the palace 'houses' also fell to Edward to carry out, and like his father before him, he usually did this at his own cost or liability initially, but with periodical repayment by the king of the large sums involved.[26]

The various pressures inflicted on Edward by his importunate master can be measured by the manner in which some instructions were given to him in 1244, for the completion of a new chamber for the king's knights within the palace, which was to be ready in six weeks *'even if a thousand workmen are needed every day'*. The king's new privy chamber in the palace had to be finished and ready in time, *'even if it costs £100'*.[27] In other cases, the usual veiled threats of the consequences of failure were used, such as *'if you value our love and favour, you will ...'*. All such demands were being dictated even before the more exacting task of the rebuilding of the abbey itself got under way.

The third category of task which King Henry was already instructing Edward to carry out was the king's more personal requirements of him. When the king felt inclined, as he frequently did, to give further presents to his queen, Edward became the regular channel for their creation or acquisition. Thus one bare week before Christmas day, 1240, Edward was given a frantic order from the king for the urgent making of a present for her, a gold bowl on a stand with an enamelled interior, *'so that she may drink from it at Christmas'*; and on a later occasion *'a girdle of gold'* was to be made by Edward, for the king to give to her.[28] Or if delivery of a consignment of herrings, which the king had purchased in Yarmouth, was to be made in Westminster, Edward was made his agent to receive them from the sheriff of Norfolk; on another occasion, there were no less than 40 'lasts' (nearly 500 barrels) of herrings to be consigned to Edward, again from the same source.[29] Then the king needed a special 'gospel-book' for use in his own chapel in the palace at Westminster, and Edward was to buy it and place it ready for him there.[30]

One special task for Edward, which was also to recur over the years, was the distribution of alms to the poor of Westminster, on the king's behalf. From about 1240 Edward began to carry out this duty, sometimes jointly with the king's treasurer: the distribution was usually performed in one or both of the great or lesser halls in the palace,

---

25 *Cal. Lib. R.*, 1226-40, p. 444 and p. 478; *ibid.*, 1240-45, p.134; *ibid.*, p. 29. The louvre was a domed structure on the roof of the hall, with side slats to provide fresh ventilation by the escape of stale air and smoke. All these works, and others similar, were to be carried out in the years 1240-45.

26 Typical amounts so paid (rounded off) were £58, £79, and £42, but they sometimes rose to figures like £147 or £430. One of the highest 'debts' incurred in this way by the king, and later paid, was £1949, after the king's 'new chamber' in the palace was completed and his new conduit installed, see *Cal. Lib. R.*, 1240-5, p. 239.

27 *Cal. Cl. R.*, 1242-47, pp. 160 and 435.

28 *Cal. Cl. R.*, 1237-42, p. 258; *Cal. Lib. R.*, 1240-45., p. 121. The work on the gold bowl was to be pushed forward 'day and night', since there was only the one week to go.

29 *ibid.*, 1240-45, pp. 12 and 91. A 'last' of herrings was twelve barrels, so the full consignment was 480 barrels, a massive load to deal with. They were sometimes used as alms, as well as for court consumption.

30 *ibid.*, p. 29. About a year later, Edward was similarly instructed to obtain a missal and a book of antiphons (choral responses), bound in one volume, *ibid.*, p. 121.

and often the total number of those who received the alms was in the high thousands. For example in December 1243, Edward received over £16 for alms for 4000 of the poor; and in the next month, over £41 for another 20,000.[31]

Like other royal clerks, Edward received many gifts and benefits for himself from, or through the influence of, the king. As a married man with children, he was ineligible for a bishopric, and besides he was far too valuable to the king where he was, in the centre of the king's expanding plans for Westminster. But he received at least two valuable church livings, the profits of a die at the Canterbury mint, his robes of office, and allowances from office at the exchequer, of which he was named a 'baron'. He had of course inherited his father's palatial 'court' of houses in the area between 'King Street' and the Thames north of the palace, with the special right from the abbey to enjoy the private chapel there, and in 1244 he was granted another special right by the king to draw water for his house complex from the palace conduit which fed the great hall, via his own small pipe 'the size of a goose quill'.[32]

### First steps towards a new shrine for St Edward

One of the first stages on which King Henry concentrated, as a preliminary to his larger rebuilding plans for the abbey, was the construction of a new shrine for the body of his patron saint, Edward the Confessor. As the first rebuilder of the abbey in stone, King Edward had originally been buried in an underground tomb in front of the high altar, but in 1163 after his canonisation his body had been 'translated' to an above-ground shrine on the site of the original tomb, again directly in front of the high altar.[33] But at least by 1241 King Henry had already set work in motion on a casket (of 'purest gold', over a wooden frame) for the saint, which was eventually to be positioned on a new base for a shrine *behind* the altar, and the work was to be carried out by goldsmiths selected in London. In that year, in addition to his general office of *'keeper of the works of the church of Westminster'* Edward son of Odo was made the king's *'keeper of the works of the shrine'*, a position he retained until his retirement in 1263.[34] A workshop for the shrine work was set up, and the work had its own funds.[35]

The shrine, which was not substantially completed until at least 1269 (and perhaps beyond), had always been designed to be a sumptuous structure. And in no way was its new position *behind* the altar intended to be a demotion. At that time no screen existed behind the high altar, so that the view, seen from the sanctuary and the choir, of the elevated shrine rising majestically *above* the intervening altar would be uninterrupted.[36]

However we do not know all the stages by which the plans for a new shrine were finalised or later altered over the years between 1242 and the shrine's completion in 1269. But we do know that by May 1242 marble work was already proceeding on it, with the goldsmiths being paid for their professional work on, presumably, gold images or other similar decorative features, because Edward son of Odo, the appointed keeper, was being provided with royal money expressly to pay for the continuance of that work.[37] At that early stage, or perhaps even earlier, it is not impossible that work was being carried out on the *existing* shrine (the one in *front* of the altar,

31  *Cal. Lib. R.*, 1240-45, pp. 204 and 210.
32  See generally Colvin, *King's Works*, p. 103. For his father's houses and private chapel, see p. 151 above. For his right to draw water from the palace conduit, see *Cal. P. R.*, 1232-47, p. 430.
33  For the history of the canonisation, see pp. 84-5 above.
34  M. Paris, *Maj. Chron.*, pp. 156-7; Kent Lancaster, *ibid.*, p. 101.
35  Kent Lancaster, *ibid.*, p. 96. According to Colvin, *King's Works*, I, p. 148, the workshop was probably built in the palace grounds.
36  See Foster, *Patterns of Thought.*, p. 35.
37  *Cal. P. R.*, 1232-47, p. 285, and *Cal. Lib. R.*, 1240-45, p. 134.

dating from 1163), which at that time was perhaps being improved rather than being scheduled for complete replacement.[38] At all events it is clear that special work by the chosen goldsmiths in relation to St. Edward's shrine was already in progress, and more importantly, that it was the king who had originally instituted the project and was paying for it.

Moreover the work on the shrine appears to have continued on the same basis until 1245-6, when it was overtaken by the greater rebuilding scheme for the whole abbey, which by then had already started.[39] In June 1246 Edward son of Odo was receiving 60 marks (£40) 'for works on the shrine of St. Edward', and while other works on a much larger scale began on the general rebuilding of the abbey, special payments on behalf of the shrine continued to be made to Edward throughout the succeeding twenty years, for the purchase of cameos, precious stones, gold and marble destined for the ever-greater adornment of the shrine and for the payment of the long-serving goldsmiths' wages.[40] But, as we shall see, the new shrine figured again in King Henry's special plans twenty years later, when the hectic rebuilding of the church was approaching its contemplated end, and (after Edward of Westminster's retirement and death in the 1260s) the remaining work on the ornate but still-unfinished shrine was put into the special charge of the king's 'royal goldsmith', Master William of Gloucester, for him to complete, together with 'cosmati-style' patterned stonework added by Italian craftsmen to the base of the new shrine.[41]

### The start of work on the belfry

Another prelude to the ultimate rebuilding of the abbey itself was a plan to build a new belfry for the church. This was to be a detached structure, rectangular in shape, on about the site of the present Middlesex Guildhall, a site which then lay within the precinct of the abbey.[42] It may well have been a plan formulated in the first instance by the abbot and the monks, rather than by the king, but the king certainly embraced it. In 1244 he had instructed Edward son of Odo and his associate keepers of works to let the abbot, Richard of Berking, have *a good strong beam, to support the bells of Westminster'*, with delivery to be made to the abbey sacrist.[43] In the previous year he had made a gift to the abbot of ten oak trees, and it may be that they too were materials being collected for the future construction of the belfry.[44]

After the start of the work of rebuilding the abbey itself in 1246, the belfry was a feature which was probably delayed by other more urgent requirements of the greater scheme, since the actual construction of the detached

---

38 Even as early as August 1239 Edward son of Odo had been instructed to 'make' two images out of pure gold *'for St. Edward's shrine'*, and it looks as if this may have been work on or for the old shrine: *Cal. Lib. R.*, 1226-40, p. 404, unless the shrine was already destined for replacement even by that date.

39 In July 1244 Edward son of Odo had been paid £100 for the wages of the goldsmiths working on the shrine for St. Edward, and for the gold which he had had to buy for them to work with, *Cal. Lib. R.*, 1240-45, p. 248.

40 Colvin, *ibid.*, p. 147; and in the 'Accounts of the works of the church of Westminster' for 1266-67, we can see £614 being paid for 'the services of masons, paviors ... carpenters, painters, plumbers, glaziers, labourers, and in works put out at task to masons, carpenters and painters .. etc.' for the shrine, Colvin, *Bldg. A/cs*, pp. 422-3.

41 See p. 265 below, and Kent Lancaster, *ibid.*, p. 96. Before his own death in 1269, William and a team of colleagues and Italians completed the remaining work, so that the shrine could at last receive the 'translated' remains of the saint at the old king's celebration to mark the completion of the rebuilding.

42 See Colvin, *King's Works*, i, p. 143. After the belfry, the site later became that of the 'old Middlesex Sessions house'. External belfries were also built at Chichester, Norwich and Salisbury cathedrals; and of these, that at Chichester still survives.

43 *Cal. Cl. R.*, 1242-47, p.186. The involvement of the abbot and sacrist reveals the participation which the monks too had to provide in the building operations, and not merely the 'keepers'.

44 *ibid.*, p. 132. Alternatively these trees may have been destined as further beams for the roof of the new chapel, like the twenty oaks given by the king in 1234, see p. 243 above

belfry does not appear to have got under way until 1249 when the piles for its foundations were still in course of supply.[45]   As we shall see, the casting of the bells had been started by the chief metal-craftsman Master John the Senter, and the lower structure of the belfry and all the bells were ready for their hanging in the early 1250s.[46]   The avoidance of the engineering stresses which would have been entailed by hanging the bells high within the abbey itself meant that the bells of Westminster in their detached and lower structure could be particularly large.

## The beginnings of the great rebuilding

### Arrival of Master Henry de Reyns

So the years 1220 to 1245 had seen the start of three enterprises, as fore-runners to the ensuing rebuilding of the whole abbey of Westminster – these were the new chapel of St. Mary, the elaborate shrine for St. Edward, and the free-standing belfry.  But what had been happening meanwhile about plans for the greater rebuilding ? Obviously some designing and groundwork were essential, but it is a curious thing that the evidence (even among the king's own documents) of preparations carried out before the actual start of work in 1245 is unusually sparse. It was fortunate that the king already had an existing building organisation established in Westminster for other purposes, under the control of Edward son of Odo, which could perhaps cope with some of the practical problems which such a rapid start must have entailed.

King Henry's high ambition was to use the latest developments in Gothic architecture and to rival the great churches recently begun in France, not to mention new cathedrals and abbeys already rising in England.  Bearing in mind such religious and artistic enthusiasms, one could have thought that the preparations for the new enterprise would have been spectacular and extensive.  But the king, as always, was also massively engaged during the years leading up to 1245 in other calls on his time and presence, such as continental wars and diplomacy.  Moreover medieval building practices were empirical, pragmatic and, by modern standards, unceremonious. So it was that even the man, who was to be (in modern terms) the combined architect, structural engineer and practical manager of the first stages of the works at the abbey seems to have been chosen only a month or two before the actual start in July 1245 of demolition of the eastern end of the old building.[47] This was Master Henry 'de Reyns', who had been given a robe of office (a tunic and a very necessary over-tunic) as the 'master of the king's masons' two years before, while engaged at Windsor on building operations which were (at that time) the largest in the kingdom.[48]

But in addition to the process of disengagement from his duties at Windsor, Master Henry 'de Reyns' was also sent up to York in March 1245 with his colleague the king's carpenter, to confer with other master craftsmen and advise about the fortifications of the castle there.[49]  And this was only four months before the work of demolition at the abbey of Westminster began in July.  So the master-mason was missing from Westminster for at least some part of those preparatory months, and we know nothing about the consultations between him and the king, or with Edward son of Odo, about what the king wished to see in the designs for the new abbey.

---

45   See Scott, *Gleanings*, p. 248, and Colvin, *King's Works*, p. 143, n. 3.

46   For the later completion of the belfry, see p. 254 below.

47   Colvin, *ibid.*, p. 104.  Perhaps one modern equivalent for Henry the mason's role might be that of the 'project manager' – although this would do no justice to the mason's overall *design* responsibilities.

48   J. Harvey, *E. Med. Architects*, p. 251; Colvin, *ibid.*, p. 104

49   *Cal. Cl. R.*, 1242-47, p. 293. The sheriff of York was to meet them and bring the other experts.  Master Henry's skills probably included a knowledge of French military architecture, Colvin, *ibid.*, pp. 105 and 116.

**Plate 12.** A private charter, which in most ways was typical of about a thousand such charters relating to houses and lands in Westminster. But this charter is special. It identifies King Henry III's great 'architect' of the abbey by his full name, the master mason Henry 'of Reyns', nearly ten years after his death. It was made by the mason's son Hugh, and it was specifically dated the 20th March 1261, an early date for a private charter to receive a precise dating. It recorded a charitable gift by Hugh of a rent of 5s. pa. to the abbey, for a house which had been his father's. See pp. 249, 251 and 253-6

It was only in December of that same year that Henry the mason was appointed one of the three 'keepers of the works of the church of Westminster'. The other two keepers were, of course, Edward son of Odo, and (as representative of the elderly abbot and the convent) Richard of Crokesley, a monk at the abbey, who was also the archdeacon of Westminster and about to become abbot himself within a year.[50] These three were to be in charge of a separate financial office, called the 'New Exchequer', to deal with the great enterprise. In the usual way of the world, the practical and professional man on whom the design, management and safety of the whole construction depended was listed the last of the three.

It appears that while undertaking the first stages of his new assignment, Henry 'de Reyns' may have had to find lodgings somewhere in the town of Westminster for the time being. It was not until May of the following year (1246) that the king provided a house in the town for him, by purchasing a large complex of houses in 'King Street' from Thomas of Poulton for 60 marks (£40) and giving some of the houses to his 'architect'.[51] So the king's endorsement of him was doubly assured, and the mason's post was the greatest professional accolade any man could have; in setting the general design of the new abbey he made it his own memorial.[52] However he did not survive to see it even half finished, since by 1253 he must have become ill or had died and had to be replaced by another master mason.

Henry's name 'de Reyns' has left a conundrum, on which historians take sides. The spelling 'Reyns' could apparently mean Reims in the Ile de France, or it could mean Rayne, near Braintree in Essex. The odds appear at first sight to be stacked heavily in favour of the former. The great church at Reims was already being built at this very time, having been started in 1211, 34 years before Westminster. So here was a man who could have already had personal experience in the building, and even perhaps the design, of a cathedral church with which the later design of the abbey at Westminster had architectural connections.[53] But a more local patriotism also stakes a claim to Henry. The present small village of Rayne in Essex had been the baronial seat of the estates of the great Rames family, who had come over from Normandy with the Conqueror, and the family still had large interests there and elsewhere in East Anglia.[54] Indeed King Henry was a visitor to Rayne, and had been staying there for several days in August 1238, a date when he might well have been thinking ahead to prospective building projects, such as Windsor or even Westminster. But although there is no reason why a mason should not have come from Essex (even if the county was more famous for its carpenters),[55] the balance of probability still favours the French connection with Reims as his professional background and experience, whether or not he was an Englishman.

So on the 6th July 1245, with little time for much preparatory work, demolition of most of the east end of the church and of the

---

50  *Cal. Lib. R.*, 1245-51, p.15. For the abbot, see p. 209 above.
51  *ibid*, p. 47 and *Cal. Cl. R.*, 1242-47. p. 428. See also pp. 206 above and WAMs 17357 and 17359. It is possible that one or more of these buildings had to serve as the design office for the huge project.
52  "The greatest of Henry's craftsmen, and the only one whose work is still known and admired at the present day", Colvin, *ibid.*, p.105. For a house of his in Westminster, see the charter at Plate 12.
53  Medieval masons were often known by the name of a place where they had practised, rather than their place of origin, and experienced professionals often migrated between countries. It is arguable whether WA is more 'English' than 'French', see J. Harvey, *E. Med. Archs.*, p. 252 and Colvin, *King's Works*, p. 151. In the barrier-less world of medieval Europe, Henry could have been a repatriated English mason, or an expatriate French mason. See also Binski, *WA and the Plantaganets*, pp. 15 ff. and 34-42, re. the influence of Reims on WA.
54  See DB *Essex* (Phillimore), section 39/1-12; *Suffolk*, sections 38/1-27 and 76/22; Norfolk, section 43.
55  This is one reason which Colvin, *ibid.*, p. 104, gives for not preferring Rayne to Reims.

central tower began, according to the chroniclers.[56] We know nothing about the arrangements for the sheltering and convenience of the monks who of course had continuing choral and other 'monastic office' duties, but a new and temporary choir must have been created for them, presumably in the nave, which for the time being was left intact. The only part of the nave which was rebuilt in this period was the group of four bays surrounding the choir.

No financial organisation had yet been set up, and it was only in the December of that year that the three 'keepers' of the new works were appointed. Even when that had been done, it seems that there was no fund of money for the works, because it was only in the first months of 1246 that the king made financial arrangements for the project.

### Funding of the 'New Exchequer'

A 'New Exchequer', the new accounting office for the rebuilding works, separated from the central exchequer, had been established in Westminster by December 1245. During the course of that year the king had been raising money by 'tallaging' (taxing) the helpless Jews throughout England, by demanding 60,000 marks from them, to be paid in instalments over the following seven years.[57] On the 15th February 1246 the king obtained 3000 marks (£2000) from a Jew, Moses son of Hamo, and assigned both that sum and *other money which the king will assign* to *the works of the church of Westminster*. The three financial administrators of the fund were to lay the moneys out in instalments, at the rate of £50 at Easter and Michelmas each year.[58] Two months later, the king became entitled to receive another sum of £2591 from the widow of another Jew, David

of Oxford, and that sum, and other moneys from other persons, were given by King Henry to the abbey *'for the fabric of the said church'* and ordered to be paid into the New Exchequer, of which Edward son of Odo and Abbot Richard of Crokesley had been named as 'treasurers'.[59]

Not only at the outset, but also throughout the next twenty to twenty-five years, it was the king's funds which paid for virtually the whole cost of the new abbey works. At some point in these early years the king also ordered his treasurer to begin making a regular annual payment of 3000 marks (£2000) to the keepers of the abbey works. But in the 1250s the treasuries became increasingly more hard-pressed for money, and to keep the abbey works going at all costs, the king responded by ordering those who owed substantial sums to the crown to divert them, by paying them direct to the keepers of the abbey works, instead of into the national exchequer. In spite of such measures, the shortages of money at the work-face are revealed by events such as overdue payments of wages to the workmen on site or the treasurers' inability to pay for materials.

On one occasion in February 1256, 'the masons and other workmen' who had been at work on the new abbey were actually about to leave the town of Westminster because they had not been paid and were short of money, and the king quickly had to instruct his own treasurer to *'examine the debts owing to the king'* and to obtain money *'from whatever source he thinks best ... up to £400, so that that work shall not be hindered for lack of money'*.[60] More than a year before that, the workmen had actually left Westminster (*'as the king is informed'*), and the treasurers had been ordered to find money in

---

56　M. Paris, *Maj. Chron.*, iv, p. 427; Rishanger, (Riley ed.) RS p. 429.
57　Powicke, *ibid.*, pp. 310-313.
58　*Cal. P. R.*, 1232-47, p. 474.
59　*ibid.*, p. 478. Colvin, *King's Works*, I, p. 134 and n. 2, does not appear to refer, as I understand it, to these important sums, but draws attention to a later annual payment to be made by the treasurer, which cannot be earlier than 1249. I do not understand this, as the Jewish moneys must have formed the main early funds on which the fabric treasurers could now begin to draw in the succeeding months.
60　*Cal. Cl. R.*, 1254-56, p. 274, reprinted at Colvin, *Bldg A/cs*, p. 195. Wages were often paid late, but this must have been an exceptional occasion. Official 'strikes' as such do not appear until the C14. One can see that the king's concern here was for the work, not the workmen.

order to be able to recall them.[61] And there was one later occasion when even the royal treasurer, and the chamberlains of the king's personal financial office, the chamber, had to complain to the king that they did not have *one single penny*' left with which to pay for the abbey works.[62]

So an organisation for the funding of the building works was in place throughout the quarter-century of the construction, but the funding itself tended (like most things in the mercurial king's court) to become hand-to-mouth during these years of King Henry's indigence. Yet the rebuilding works – with urgently-repeated insistence from the king, even when he was abroad or at war, or at loggerheads with his barons, or engaged on other building projects – were driven forward until the celebration of their 'substantial completion' in a great ceremony on St. Edward's day, the 13th October, 1269 at the abbey.[63] The total cost to the king of the rebuilding of the abbey over this whole period was clearly well in excess of £40,000, an enormous sum equalling most of the king's total income over two years.[64] But to put this expenditure into some perspective, one has also to compare it with the money which throughout his reign the king was spending on his castles, palaces, manor houses and other buildings which has been estimated to have

exceeded £113,000. It is hardly surprising that, with such burdens on top of other problems, his treasury was in continuous straits.[65]

## The progress of works under successive managers

### A. *Master Henry de Reyns (1245-1253) and Master Alexander the Carpenter (1234-1269)*

Although Edward son of Odo continued to be a constant force for a period of nearly twenty years on the administrative sector of the rebuilding, the personnel on the executive side of the works changed more often. The master mason, Henry de Reyns, the main designer and first 'master of the works', remained in charge for eight years; but disappeared from the records in 1253. Probably the last mention of him was on the 9th September of that year, when he received deliveries of 'coloured glass' and 'white glass', perhaps additional glass for the altered chapel of St. Mary.[66] It cannot be coincidence that on the 11th June in the same year the king had ordered that a robe be given to Master John of Gloucester as 'the king's mason of Westminster', who later took Master Henry de Reyns' place, and that his 'wage' was to be 12d a day. Since we do not know what happened to Master Henry, we can only infer that he may have been ill and died or retired through ill-health,

---

61 Patent Roll printed at Colvin, *ibid.*, pp. 194-5. On an even earlier occasion in July 1250 the royal treasurer and Edward son of Odo had been directed by the king to obtain £200 '*by loan or by any other means, as best they can*' and to pay it to the keepers of the abbey works, so that the work was not held up: *Cal. Cl. R., 1247-51*, p. 307, reprinted Colvin, *ibid.*, p. 192-3.

62 *Cal. Cl. R., 1268-72*, p. 227. For the king's 'chamber', see pp. 117-8 above.

63 For the ceremony at the abbey and feast in Westminster Hall, see pp. 239-40 above. 'Substantial completion' is the modern term for the main completion of a building contract, even when there inevitably remain some works to be done. This is not inappropriate for the medieval situation at the abbey, where there were still many works to be done after October 1269. But it would be difficult to pursue this analogy further to include *the rest of the nave*, which was not begun until over 100 years later or completed until another 150 years after that!

64 See the discussion of abbey costs in Colvin, *King's Works*, I, pp. 155-57. The secular building costs are given at *ibid.*, p. 109.

65 Another staggering liability which Henry incurred was his bizarre promise in 1256 to pay the Pope's debts, of about £90,000, when striking a deal with him so that Henry's son Edmund might become king of Sicily (which in substance he never did). Fortunately for Henry, he secured a release of the money obligation two years later.

66 Colvin, *Bldg A/cs*, p. 287. Earlier deliveries of glass were made on the 4th August, for insertion on task work. For earlier glasswork in the chapel, see p. 243 above.

and that perhaps Master John had already had a period of 'running-in' alongside Master Henry, before taking over the role in the autumn of 1253.

During Master Henry's period of office (1245-53), the demolition of the eastern end of the old church took place, with the virtual completion of the structure of the new chapter house, the first and central section of the new church and the detached belfry in the precinct.[67]

After the initial demolition works eastwards of the nave were over, construction had begun on the vault below the chapter house and then the innovative superstructure of the chapter house itself, supported only at that stage by its (still existing) one central pillar, light buttressing and some metal tie-bars. This had been followed by other structural work on the side of the cloister leading to the chapter house, and on its imposing entrance.[68]

At the same time, the church itself was also rapidly rising from the ground, and by October 1252 the five main piers of the nave nearest to the choir, which were to be surrounded by 'marble' shafts (of Purbeck marble), were already built, and Master Henry was being ordered by the impatient king to have all the 'marble' work raised during the forthcoming winter, so far as it could be done 'without danger'.[69] Towards the end of 1252, timber was being sought for the roofing of the new church and for the making of the monks' stalls in their new choir. The speed with which

all this main central structure had been built since 1246 is quite astonishing. But at this stage the problems concerning the way in which the new east end of the church would be joined to the nearly completed chapel for St. Mary had not yet been faced.[70]

Meanwhile in the abbey precinct surrounding the new building, the construction of the belfry had also been proceeding almost to the point of completion in 1253 when Master Henry's place was taken by Master John. The bells had been cast by the bell-founders in the period after February 1250. One of the bells was called *'the great bell of Westminster'*, and there were probably four others, weighty but not so large as the great one. The king gave instructions for the *'great new bell'* to be hung at the end of 1252, in time for it to be rung at the next feast of St. Edward on the 4th January 1253, even before the final completion of the belfry itself.[71] After the great bell had been hung in place, and later the other bells, the wooden roof of the belfry had to be built by the carpenters and then covered with lead by the plumbers during that year, 1253.[72]

Although Master Henry had been the principal designer and officer in charge of the whole construction, he had had a colleague who was responsible for all the carpentry, including the scaffolding needed for the rebuilding. This was Master Alexander, the king's master carpenter, a towering figure who had already been working for the king since at least 1234, both on the palace in Westminster

---

67   J. Harvey, *E. Med. Archs.*, p. 252. The site of the belfry was the site of the later 'sessions house' of Middlesex; itself rebuilt later and called the Middlesex Guildhall, which still stands on the west side of Parliament Square.

68   The chapter house was to have a splendid lectern, which was to be made by Master John of St. Omer, a Flemish carver, who was ordered to copy one at St. Albans, but to make it *'if possible, even more handsome and beautiful'*; *Cal. Cl. R.*, 1247-51, pp. 203 and 245; and Colvin, *Bldg. A/cs.*, pp. 190-1, 236 and 266. For the chapter house and some of its tiles, see Plate 13 at p. 255, and Plate 21.

69   *Cal. Cl. R.*, 1251-3, p. 174, printed at Colvin, *Bldg. A/cs.*, p. 192. This did not, at that stage, include any of the other main piers of the *nave*. Only five of these (on each side) were rebuilt by 1272; for the rest, years later, see note 63 above.

70   For the problem about joining the chapel to the east end of the new church, see p. 261 below.

71   *Cal. Cl. R.*, 1251-3, p. 280, printed at Colvin, *ibid.*, pp. 192-5. Both the shrine and the bells figured in a drawing of the church made by Matthew Paris, Lethaby, *Craftsmen*, p. 156 and Fig 40.

72   See Colvin, *King's Works*, p. 143. 26 carpenters and 9 plumbers were at work on this during 1253, and iron nails supplied by Henry of (London) Bridge were in frequent demand, Colvin, *Bldg. A/cs.*, eg. pp. 239, 270-4.

**Plate 13.** In King Henry's rebuilding of the abbey, the Chapter House was one of the first parts of the abbey to be begun and completed. With its innovative support by one central pillar and its spectacular tiled floor, it not only provided an imposing space for the monks' daily 'chapters' for prayer and administration, but also came to be used for secular purposes such as meetings of the king's council or later the house of commons. Even later, after the Dissolution, it was misused for the storage of public records. See p. 255.

and elsewhere; and he continued to do so on the abbey and the palace until shortly before his own death in about 1269. In the length of his office-holding, Alexander rivalled Edward son of Odo, the king's 'beloved clerk'.

As the chief carpenter for the works at the abbey (and also at the palace), Alexander was in charge of, and personally carried out, the purchasing of timber in specified amounts, mostly at Kingston or the king's park at Havering, from where the timber had to be carried by boat to Westminster down or up the Thames;[73] and he was of course responsible for the design of the timber works themselves. However in the records one can also see him doing quite different jobs as well, eg. 'weighing and transporting' metal, carrying charcoal for the purposes of the firing of the metal, and 'buying a whole wood', probably both for timber and firing. Alexander also became a substantial local land-owner.[74]

When Master Henry de Reyns ceased to be chief mason in 1253, Master Alexander survived him, continuing in his own role as the king's master carpenter, in collaboration with the new master mason of Westminster, John of Gloucester. In November 1256, as we shall see, both he and the chief mason reached an even more responsible position in the king's service.

### B. Master mason John of Gloucester (1253 - 1260), with Master Alexander the Carpenter

Unlike his predecessor, John of Gloucester was a more identifiable figure. He was the holder of properties in Gloucester, and had been working for the king since before 1249 when he was already 'Master John the king's

mason'. His new robe of office given to him in 1253 as 'king's mason of Westminster' and his assumption of Master Henry's role in that year were significant professional advancements for him, and he remained in charge of the abbey's new works until his death in 1260.

However Master John was not restricted to his duties in Westminster, and during the next five or six years worked as well on royal buildings at the Tower of London, Windsor, Oxford, Gloucester, Guildford and elsewhere. Clearly he had found considerable favour with the king, and it is not surprising that in November 1256 both he and Master Alexander, the king's carpenter in Westminster, were jointly appointed as keepers and inspectors of all the king's works south of the rivers Trent and Humber, because the king had become dissatisfied with the efforts of his sheriffs and other royal officers in looking after his castles, palaces and other buildings.[75] This new office meant that the two master craftsmen had to travel and inspect many distant properties, and so the extra costs which they would incur were compensated by an award of double fees.[76]

The absences from Westminster which this new joint office clearly entailed for the two master craftsmen surely means that by the middle 1250s the designs and rebuilding of the abbey had reached a stage when most of the main works were 'on track' and did not require their unremitting attention. Indeed each of these two 'chief masters' had several of his own competent and managerial colleagues working at the abbey who were themselves 'masters' of their craft. Specialist jobs for masons (like the making of the intricate stone

---

73  Carriage of timber by boat from Kingston was a constant requirement. As late as 1272, when the abbey had already been consecrated, a barge which had belonged to a felon was seized by King Henry and drafted into the task of carrying building materials to the abbey, *Cal. Cl. R.* 1268-72, pp. 459-60.

74  He ended up as the holder of one or more houses between 'King Street' and the Thames, and of lands in the Field of Westminster near the leper hospital of St Giles; in the Ossulston area of Eia; and in Knightsbridge. See WAMs 4875, 17440/17551, 17383/17468, 17544; CP25(1) 147/21/417; and J. Harvey, *E. Med. Archs.*, pp. 5-6. He also received royal gifts of other houses in Canterbury.

75  *Cal. Cl. R.*, 1256-9, p. 14, and *Cal. P. R.*, 1247-58, p. 538.

76  The king also gave Master Alexander £2 to buy a very necessary horse, *Cal. Lib. R.*, 1251-60, p. 350. In spite of his opportunities for wealth, Master John appears to have died a poor man, J. Harvey, *ibid.*, p. 120.

**Plate 14.** In several places in the new abbey, sculpted stone heads of men were used as corbels, perhaps serving as portraits for posterity of a few of the actual masons working in the construction, or of other male 'characters' known to the masons in charge; and in one case a woman's head has been used, with a cloth cap, and a cloth strap under her chin. Such a cap and strap appear in a medieval picture of a woman milking a cow, so perhaps the woman whose head appears here, was working in the fields nearby and was used as a model. Or maybe the folds of her dress around her shoulders suggest a wealthier background for her: was she Argentine, the wife of the king's master-carpenter, Alexander? Or Agnes, the wife of the master-mason, John of Gloucester? See p. 259. For some names and numbers of the workmen on the site, see pp. 259-60.

*(a)*

*(b)*

*(c)*

**Plate 15. A royal effigy, and more heads:**
   **(a)** buried at first before the high altar, Henry III's body was moved in 1290 by his son Edward I to a splendid new Cosmati tomb which Edward had had made, with a fine bronze-gilt effigy made by William Torel, the goldsmith and sculptor, see also Plate 20, after p. 288;
   **(b)** a stone head, sculpted realistically, overlooks the north transept: it is thought to be a possible likeness of Robert of Beverley, Henry's third master-mason in charge of the rebuilding from 1260 until after the king's death in 1272, see pp. 261-3;
   **(c)** a wooden painted head, fixed above the sedilia in the choir, may have been intended to be a likeness of either Abbot Ware or Abbot Wenlock, see chapters 14 or 17.

traceries of abbey windows, carved stonework on capitals in the cloister, or the elaborate arches of the entrance into the new chapter house) were already in the hands of experts like Master Aubrey, who is recorded as carrying out many such 'task works' (jobs where the whole price was agreed in advance).[77]

Equally Master Alexander the carpenter was supported in his Westminster duties mainly by another principal colleague, Master Odo the carpenter, a resident living at a house fronting 'King Street' and also owning land in the Field of Tothill. Odo the carpenter worked professionally in the abbey's rebuilding from the 1240s through to the 1260s (with perhaps a special responsibility for the wooden scaffolding), and later in the repair of the palace after a big fire in 1262.[78] Both Alexander and Odo also played additional parts in much abbey business, as witnesses in the abbot's courts, often appearing together in that capacity.[79]

Other senior and experienced craftsmen were of course also present on the building site, acting as specialists in their various fields; such as: -

Master Edward the glazier;

Master Henry of Lewes, the ubiquitous smith;

Master John 'le senter', the metal-worker and bell-founder, who made the 'great bell of Westminster', and other bells, to hang in the new detached belfry;

Master Peter of Spain, the king's favourite painter, who also painted many of the palace chambers as well as numerous parts of the abbey; supported by the Westminster monk 'Brother William the painter of Westminster', another 'beloved painter' of Henry III; [80] and

Master William of Strand, the plumber, who with his assistant Roger the plumber installed the lead roofing of the detached belfry, and doubtless was also responsible for the leadwork of the north porch which Roger fixed.[81]

It was customary for the king to make an annual gift of a robe of office to some, but not all, of his senior craftsmen at Westminster, in time for the Whitsun feast. Even Agnes and Argentine the wives of the two most senior masters of all, namely John of Gloucester the chief mason and Alexander the chief carpenter, also received annual robes, which were presumably complimentary rather than symbolic of any office.[82] For their part, these two most senior masters from about 1255 received, in addition to their fees and other allowances, two annual gifts from the king of *furred* robes *'such as the knights of the our*

---

77  Colvin, *Bldg. A/cs*, pp. 219, 251, 279, 287 and 236. Other masons working on the abbey, and also on the palace buildings, were Masters Richard of Eltham and William 'de Wauz'. At this time, task works were often used in the abbey rebuilding, and elsewhere, eg. manor a/cs, having been comparatively rare previously in England, see Colvin, *King's Works*, I, p. 107. Both task works and ordinary day works (works carried out without prior agreement of prices, but paid for at acceptable rates for the workmen, plus cost of materials) were sometimes paid for in advance, see Colvin, *Bldg A/cs*, eg. pp. 218-9.

78  WAMs 17511 and 17389; J. Harvey, *E. Med. Architects*, eg. p. 220. A group of about six to eight other less-qualified carpenters, which included another William 'de Wauz' and three local carpenters, Henry of Knightsbridge, Roger of Westminster and John of Paddington, often appears in the surviving accounts.

79  eg. WAMs 17349, 17379, and 17441.

80  Pearce, *Monks*, p. 53.

81  Colvin, *King's Works*, I, p. 141. William was probably also the plumber who had to carry out the king's orders in April 1259 to make a conduit to carry the waste water from the palace kitchens to the Thames, *'because the stench of the dirty water which is carried through our halls infects men frequenting them'*, Cal. Cl. R., 1256-9, p. 380.

82  *Cal. Cl. R.*, 1256-9, pp. 56, 159 and 218-9, printed by Colvin, *Bldg. A/cs.*, p. 194-5. There was also a woman lime-burner called Agnes of London who regularly supplied lime in large quantities for the mortar at the abbey, but there is nothing to connect her with the chief mason's wife. The other master craftsmen in Westminster favoured with robes were the masons Richard of Eltham (a Tothill Street resident, whose brother, John of Eltham, was another master mason) and William 'de Wauz'; the carpenter Odo; the glazier, Edward; the smith, Henry of Lewes.

*household receive'*, having previously had just one ordinary robe.[83]

For every one of such master craftsmen, there were of course many less skilled members of the same craft who are named in the (incomplete) records of the rebuilding, and very many more who are accounted for but not actually named. If one takes the year 1253, the only well-recorded year, one can see that during the 'high season' of nine weeks between the 23rd June and the 24th August, on average about 145 masons (the most numerous of the craftsmen, when the differing categories of their craft are added together) were working at the abbey: with no very great variation from week to week. During the *rest* of the main working period in that year (taken as, from the end of April to the 9th November, but excluding the above high season), the average number of masons on site at any one time fell to about 107, but with rather more variation from week to week.[84]

This pattern was obviously not a constant one, because the number of members of any craft who were at work on the abbey during any period depended principally on the demands of the building programme at that time, and these demands must have varied enormously. The same is also true of the number of unskilled labourers, which varied (during the whole of the main working period in 1253) between 91 and 220 – although, in their case, the three weeks in August-September of that year, when only 91 labourers were working at the abbey, no doubt reflected also the demands of the harvest, to which many labourers, and some craftsmen too, were likely to have been drafted away.

The total weekly number of all categories of workmen on the abbey site, over the same main working period in 1253, varied between 216 and 433; and again if one excludes the harvest period, the variation falls to the difference between 267 and 433. These figures are significant if one compares them with the figures of workmen on site which the impatient king demanded or expected, when he was cajoling his managers to hasten the works or to get particular tasks done. For example, two years before, in 1251, King Henry had ordered his faithful Edward son of Odo to pay the (probably overdue) wages of the workmen with moneys which the sheriff of Norfolk was sending to Westminster, adding *'taking care that 600 or 800 men are working there when the king arrives'*.[85]

There is no doubt that royal impatience ran away with the figures, when the king found that realities were not matching his expectations. There was his famous remark, already noticed, about expecting *'a thousand workmen'* to be employed *'every day'* in order to get a job done at the palace within six weeks.[86] But even allowing for his exaggerations, there can be little doubt that the limited abbey site must have resounded like a giants' foundry for most of the time. Three or four hundred workmen on and around the site each week, with all the sheds, storehouses, workplaces for cutting and carving stonework and the cutting and forging of metalwork, and perhaps even workers' 'lodges' necessary for such a colossal undertaking, would have presented an astonishing spectacle and created a deafening noise across the town.[87] And if

---

83  J. Harvey, *E. Med. Architects*, pp. 5 and 118, and Colvin, *King's Works*, I, p. 105. The fur was 'good squirrel'. When travelling, they were now to get double, meaning four robes, no doubt necessary in view of wear and tear.

84  Calculated from the useful numerical table in Colvin, *Bldg. A/cs*, p. 7. The different categories of mason were 'white cutters', 'marblers', 'layers' and 'polishers'. The weekly variation during the 'high season' was between 138 and 158 masons on site (ie. 20). The variation in the rest of the working period was between 86 and 123 (ie. 37). The specified periods exclude (roughly) the six months from early November to the end of April, when weather conditions limited the levels of *open-air* work.

85  *Cal. Cl. R.*, 1247-51, p. 423, printed at Colvin, *ibid.*, pp. 192-3.

86  *Cal. Cl. R.*, 1242-47, p. 160. See p. 246 above. For sculpted workmen's heads, see Plate 14, p. 257.

87  Rosser, *Med. Westminster*, p. 150, attributes the 'continuous din' in Westminster to the whole period from 1200 to 1540, with 'almost every working day, at least one part of the town resounding with the

433, the maximum number of workmen present in any one week during 1253, was exceeded in other years, then the effects on the town must have been even more extravagant.

In November 1254 the king who was then in Gascony had mistakenly thought that sufficient progress had been made with the works in Westminster to warrant planning for a consecration of the new church in October of the following year.[88] But although it was to be another fifteen years before such a ceremony could be held, it does seem that much of at least the structural work on the east end of the church had been carried out by the end of 1255; so much so that in 1256 the king, now back in England, faced the fact (no doubt after full advice from his chief craftsmen) that the inconsistency between the separate chapel of St Mary, which had been completed with a wooden roof, and the stone roofing of the new church had at last to be dealt with. So he gave orders for the wooden roof of the chapel to be taken down and for the walls of the chapel to be heightened, to conform with the adjacent new structure and to accomodate a stone roof.[89]

By the summer of 1259 all the structural work on the central crossing and transepts of the new abbey also appears to have been completed, because the king in June ordered that the 'old fabric as far as the vestry' be pulled down and rebuilt in conformity with the new work.[90] The 'old fabric' must be that part of the nave which was designated for

rebuilding, namely its first four bays west of the north transept, reaching beyond the length of the new choir. This was now the limit of the rebuilding plan, and the construction of this section of the nave (on both sides of the choir) now formed the remaining major objective. However it was another ten years before the church could be consecrated, and meanwhile within a short time after the start of work on the nave, Master John of Gloucester died in the summer of 1260.[91]

So a new 'master of the works' had to be chosen, and naturally this was to be another master mason, Robert of Beverley. But the great survivor, Master Alexander the Carpenter, still continued for another seven years in his two roles, as king's carpenter in Westminster (at both the abbey and palace) and keeper of works at royal properties south of the Trent.

### C. Master mason Robert of Beverley (1260 - 1272 ff.), with Master Alexander (1234 - 1267) and thereafter with Brother Ranulf of Combermere (1266-1272)

Robert of Beverley was already known for work both at the abbey, where he had worked in 1253 and 1259 (and also perhaps between those dates), and at the palace in 1259.[92] But his experience may well have extended to the building works on the new Minster at Beverley in Yorkshire, from where he probably came. Stepping into the shoes of John of Gloucester

noise of the mason's chisel, the blacksmith's anvil or the carpenter's saw.' If this is true of that whole period, the years between 1245 and 1269 must have been the high peak of the cacophony.
88  Undated Patent roll, printed at Colvin, *Bldg. A/cs*, pp. 194-5.
89  *Cal. Cl. R.*, 1252-56, p. 314, and Colvin, *King's Works*, I, p. 144. The chapel was the one begun, on its own, in or after 1220, before the rebuilding of the whole abbey, see pp. 241, 243 and 245 above. It had probably been built *beyond* the original east end of the old church. The unwanted timbers and lead from the chapel's former roof were given to St. Martin le Grand, a college of canons in London, for recycling in a new chapel.
90  *Cal. Cl. R.*, 1256-9, p. 390, printed at Colvin, *Bldg. A/cs*, pp. 196-7.
91  In spite of his high position and royal gifts which he had received, Master John died a comparatively poor man, and in debt to the king because, it seems, he was in arrears with his duties, J. Harvey, *E. Med. Archs*, p. 119. Yet he had had a house and curtilage in Westminster, and had received an estate in Oxon, houses in Oxford, Northampton and Bridport, double wages, etc; *ibid.*, p. 120.
92  (Abbey): see Colvin, *Bldg, A/cs*, pp. 230-1, and J. Harvey, *E. Med. Archs.*, p. 23. (Palace): see Colvin, *ibid.*, pp. 288-9, 292-3, 298-9, 342-3, 346-7, 350-1.

**Plate 16.** A crowned kingly figure (unusually, clean-shaven) is painted full-length at the back of the sedilia in the abbey's choir. The tallness of the figure and the probable date of the painting suggest that it was modelled on King Edward I, perhaps shortly after, and in celebration of, his coronation in 1274. For his coronation, see p. 240.

at Westminster in 1260, he became the king's new master mason and now the senior colleague of Master Alexander, the king's long-lived carpenter.

Between many other assignments elsewhere for each of them, these two now worked at the abbey for the next seven years in progressing the major works on four bays of the nave, and supervising many other residual works until Alexander retired in about 1267 and was himself replaced. After that change, Robert of Beverley was given another colleague in Alexander's place: this was Ranulf a lay-brother from the abbey of Combermere (Cheshire), who became one of the keepers of the Westminster works.

Like his predecessors, Master Robert of Beverley became a resident in Westminster, as a necessary aid to the carrying out of his new duties. In acquiring property in Westminster, he became a tenant of the abbey, and took part as a senior witness in the abbot's court, often doing so together with his older colleague Master Alexander, in at least thirteen extant charters made by other residents about properties in Westminster. He also became a corrodian of the abbey, and an owner of local land in the manor of Eye adjoining Westminster, in the field called the Northfield.[93]

There can be little doubt that, during the decade of the 1260s, progress on the abbey works was slowed up by disruptive events taking place in the kingdom until 1268: principally (a) the distractions of the king's disputes with rebellious barons, and the civil war between 1264 and 1266, and (b) the resulting and humiliating conflicts between the abbey and the citizens of London (who sided with the barons) over issues as to their respective privileges.[94]

The last years of the 1260s were the period in which both the installation of the splendid Cosmati pavement in the sanctuary of the abbey by Italian craftsmen and the further embellishment of St. Edward's shrine by the Italians and London goldsmiths were 'extra works' which had to be carried out before the new abbey could be consecrated in 1269.[95] Such specialised additions to the more ordinary building works originally envisaged may well have added to a slowing-up of operations. The retirement of the invaluable Edward son of Odo in 1263 may also have acted as a retarding factor. These were probably some of the reasons why the yearly expenditure on building operations at both the abbey and palace under Master Robert of Beverley during the 1260s appears to have fallen to about two thirds of the costs in previous years.[96]

The substantial building of the four eastern bays of the nave is thought to have followed the original design which Master Henry of Reyns had had in mind, though with slight innovations in decorative structures which were probably imaginative contributions added by Master Robert of Beverley.[97] But one noticeable addition in a continental style,

93  Harvey, *Living and Dying,* p. 241 (for his corrody); WAM 19/4828 (for his land in Eye); and J. Harvey, *E. Med. Archs.*, 23 (for other land in Pyrford). Robert did not die until 1285, and continued to work for the king at many other places as well as Westminster. He made a wax image of Henry III after his death, which later may have been a model for the brilliant figure made in 1291 by Torel for Henry's tomb at Edward I's wish. A stone head in the abbey may show Robert, see Plate 15, at p. 258.

94  For this period generally, see p. 238 above. In civil-war disputes with the city of London, the abbey had had to renounce to the city many of its genuine rights, but in 1265-6 had been able to recover some of them by charter from Henry III; and more in 1280 from Edward I, see eg. *Cal. Ch. R.*, (1257-1300) 238-9 and 241.

95  For the work on the shrine, see pp. 247-8 above. See also coloured Plate 19, after p. 288.

96  See the annual costs incurred between the beginning of 1264 and the end of 1272 (in Colvin, *Bldg. A/cs.* pp. 416-435), which Colvin, *King's Works,* I, p. 146 says reflect a fall of about one third from earlier years, from £1800 to £1163. I assess his component figures slightly differently, but they still reflect much the same fall.

97   Two of these innovations were the increased number (8) of Purbeck marble shafts attached to the new nave piers, and an extra intermediate rib in the stone vaulting, see Colvin, *King's Works*, I, p. 144.

namely carved models of armorial shields (both royal and baronial) in painted stone, 'hung' high in the aisles behind the rebuilt piers of the nave, was probably a design 'extra' demanded by the king himself, who had seen a display of shields in 1254 in a great hall in Paris, where he had been entertained by King Louis of France.[98]

There was of course a great deal of additional decorative work still to be completed in the new church, as happens towards the end of any great building project, but the records also reveal some of the more essential and solid items which still needed to be done. Even by 1264 the woodwork of the monks' stalls in the choir was still far from complete, because 'heavy timber' and other 'timber' were still having to be bought to make 'columns' for the stalls.[99] Extensive work on the glazing of the abbey windows was also still needed, because canvas was being bought to keep out the weather until the glass could be installed. Indeed an item described as 'things necessary for glass windows' appears regularly from 1264 until 1272 (ie. even after the consecration of the church in 1269); and this is the case even in very abbreviated enrolled accounts which have survived for this period.[100]

Again, the construction of the central lantern tower which was proposed to cover the crossing between the transepts had only been 'begun' within the period between September 1267 and December 1269 and, whatever state it had reached, still needed protection from the weather with 'tiles, litter, reeds and straw', which had to be bought for that express purpose during the same period. Apparently the tower was still either unfinished or in need of more weatherproofing even as late as 1274, when King Edward I's coronation took place, and it had had to be boarded up.[101] Moreover even though only scattered records for the completion of such a complex construction as the abbey have survived, it is highly likely that there was much else which needed doing both before and after the church's consecration in 1269.

### The abbey pavement and shrine again

In any event the situation had changed substantially in and after 1967, when Abbot Richard of Ware returned from his final Italian visit in this phase, having made arrangements for the conveyance to England of the team of cosmati craftsmen under Peter Oderisius, with stocks of their marbles. The resulting pavement was probably completed in 1268 or early 1269, and additional cosmati work had then to be added to the marble and stone base for the new golden shrine in the chapel of St. Edward, in time for it to be sufficiently ready for the translation of the saint's remains in October of 1269.[102]

The shrine itself had been under construction, probably intermittently, since 1241. It was a composite structure, consisting of the wooden chest which was to house the remains of the saint, covered with gold plating and fantastically ornamented with elaborate gold and silver statues and other figures, with inset jewels and enamels. The chest was built with sloping roofs, in the shape of an Ark. Below the

98   After intermittent years of hostility and even war over English claims to the lost Angevin lands of Anjou, Maine, Poitou and Normandy, the two Kings Henry and Louis (brothers in law) had met at an extended 'family party' when Henry visited Chartres and then Paris in 1254, see Powicke, *H. III and Ld. Edw.*, pp. 240-1.

99   Colvin, *Bldg, A/cs.*, pp. 418-9. Presumably the columns were the long vertical shafts between the seats.

100  *ibid.*, pp. 418-439. The extant accounts are the summarised and brief records in the exchequer Pipe Rolls.

101  *ibid.*, pp. 425-7 (for the tiles etc). Colvin. *King's Works*, p. 146 describes the tower as 'only a stump' by 1269, but cites only the record of Edward I's coronation, which just says that the tower was boarded up.

102  See Carpenter, 'H. III and the Cosmati Work', in *The reign of H. III.*, p. 409 ff. on the issue whether the shrine was actually completed at all by H. III, rather than by Edward I. See Plate 19, after p. 288.

chest was a great rectangular base of marble and stone, with inset niches in its longer sides into which a disabled pilgrim could creep to obtain closer proximity to the saintly relics in order to obtain a cure. Ultimately in the final year before the translation ceremony, it was this base which was made more splendid by the cosmati workmen, who covered its sides with their interlocking marble patterns of circular and square lozenges.

### After the retirement of Edward son of Odo

Well before the final stage of the embellishment of the shrine, Edward son of Odo had continued in post until 1263 as the 'keeper' of the works of the shrine. But after Edward's retirement in that year from all his posts in the king's service, his position in charge of the shrine was vacant until Master William of Gloucester, a skilled London goldsmith, was appointed in his place in 1266.

Master William had already been made the 'King's Goldsmith' in the early 1250s, and subsequently the keeper of the London and the Canterbury monetary exchanges. He was a working goldsmith and maker of valuable articles, and in that capacity had supplied the king, to his order, with many precious objects such as goblets, chalices, dishes and croziers.[103] In his royal goldsmith's capacity he had also designed the 'beautiful folly' ordered by the king in 1256 in the course of an official recoinage, a new penny made in gold instead of silver; but the coin had then proved too valuable for common use and was withdrawn thirteen years after its issue.[104] Master William had later fallen from royal favour during the civil war in the mid-1260s, because he had joined the baronial side, but soon afterwards he recovered the king's favour and was officially appointed 'the keeper of the works on the shrine' in 1266.

For two to three years he and five other goldsmiths were then working on the shrine, bringing it up to the state of perfection expected by the king. Many of the famous jewels and figures which adorned the shrine may well have been created or planned by him. But Master William died in early 1269, and the next few months, before the consecration of the abbey in October that year, were spent in final touches to the shrine made by another prominent London goldsmith, Richard Bonaventure who was appointed in William's place.

But Edward of Westminster (the other name by which the 'son of Odo' was known) had been the controller of the whole rebuilding project, as well as being the keeper of the more specialised works on the shrine of St. Edward. He had always been the axle on which the executive work of the professional master masons, carpenters and goldsmiths turned. So when he retired in 1263, another axle had to fashioned. This was to be Adam of Stratton, a man very different from the faithful Edward of Westminster. He was competent maybe, but ever devoted to his own interest, and one whose notorious self-seeking was revealed in full when the next king, Edward I, purged many such corruptibles in and after 1289.

Beginning as a small-time clerk from Wiltshire with considerable financial acumen, Adam of Stratton had already advanced in the 1250s to a position in the exchequer, as clerk in the office of Receipt, where he caught the eye of the king. He was made a king's clerk, and keeper of works 'in the king's court of Westminster', and in concert with Master Alexander the Carpenter was sometimes witnessing charters now held at the abbey and rendering accounts up to December 1259 for works within the palace.[105] So with the king's

103  See Kent Lancaster, *Artisans, Suppliers and Clerks*, p. 94.
104  Kent Lancaster, *ibid.*, p. 94-5. See also Denham-Young, *Richard of Cornwall*, pp. 59 ff., particularly pp, 63-4, where the gold penny is called 'a beautiful piece of folly', devised by the king when his brother, the Earl of Cornwall, the manager of the recoinage, was away. But nevertheless the earl made, one might say, 'a mint of money' out of the recoinage.
105  Colvin, *Bldg. A/cs.*, pp. 334, 336. Unfortunately these accounts are just the summarised enrolments made on the exchequer pipe rolls, and contain little detail beyond that already described. For the pipe rolls, see pp. 184-5 above.

favour he was later made successor to Edward of Westminster when Edward retired as keeper of the works of the abbey, and he continued to serve in that central post, inspecting and auditing the accounts for the works carried out in the abbey and the palace from 1264 to at least 1272.[106]

But Adam also had many other irons in the fire, becoming (through other influence) a chamberlain at the exchequer, with rich estates, and setting up as a moneylender in London, through which he made a fortune. He was a shameful operator, and while also acting as the steward of the lands of the self-styled Countess of Aumale in Wiltshire, he extorted an even greater fortune by buying up debts owed to Jews and hounding the debtors, finally meeting his end in a great purge of judicial and official corruption under Edward I in and after 1290.

As well as having the ear of the king and a role connected with both abbey and palace, Adam did not fail to indulge in property in Westminster, and probably became a resident in the town. He certainly owned a substantial reversionary interest in one of the largest houses and land in Westminster, on the bank of the Thames, stretching probably for over a hundred yards from Charing down to the river. This property had no less than five tiers of such interests, which the current holder had to satisfy by paying five rents; and of these interests, 'Sir Adam of Stratton's' was the most valuable, being worth five shillings each year.[107] So with at least one finger in the Westminster pie, Adam continued – before his final end – to serve the king in

the most powerful post in the last stages of the rebuilding project.

### The culmination, and after

So at the end of Henry III's great undertaking we come again to his ceremony on the feast of St. Edward on the 13th October 1269, when on the shoulders of the king, his brother the Earl of Cornwall (now also a king, raised to the throne of 'Germany'), the princes Edward and Edmund and two barons, the jewelled 'ark' was carried from the saint's tomb in front of the high altar to the new chapel behind the altar and placed on top of its resplendent base, so completing the golden new shrine on which the king's mind had been so set. After the ceremony of consecration of the church, a secular celebration was held in the great hall at the palace, where a sumptuous feast was served.[108]

Although St. Edward's day 1269 was a finale for the king's devotion, the work continued until his death in November 1272, to the value of about £3000. This shows that a considerable amount of building had remained to be done, and most of it was carried out at a rate which was little different from that which had been seen during the previous decade. Even so, it seems that when the king died, the fourth bay which was being rebuilt in the old nave was still incomplete, with both the clerestory and the vault above it missing, actually leaving a gap to be boarded over at roof level between the two constructions.[109]

Needless to say, King Henry in his will urged his son Edward, who at the time when

106  Colvin, *ibid.*, pp. 417-433. See also Powicke, *Thirteenth Century*, p. 364, and Harding, *England in C13*, p.153. Adam certainly had the king's personal confidence, because in his role as keeper he even received the description 'our beloved clerk', which was not accorded to all, see Colvin, *Bldg. A/cs.*, pp. 198-9.

107  WAM 17378; see further pp. 39-40 above for the parties. Even the abbot's interest was worth less than Adam's: a rent of only 3s. 6d. each year. As a witness in WAM 17360, Adam was named with the royal chancellor and treasurer.

108  Luard (ed.), *Annales Mon. (Osney)*, RS. iv. p. 226-7. For the unfitting wrangles, which marred the two celebrations, see pp. 239-40 above. When later the old king himself died, he was first buried before the high altar: later, see Plate 15, p. 258, and Plate 20, after p. 288.

109  The much later rebuilding of the nave is described by Rackham, 'Nave of Westminster', *Procs. B. Acad.*, 1909-10, pp 1 ff. See also his earlier 'Building at WA', *17 Archaeol. Jo. (2nd Ser.) No 3*. pp. 259, at 270 ff.

his father died was playing an iconic part as a leader on crusade to the Holy Land, to complete the rebuilding of the church, emphasising to him that he had been named after the saint himself. But Edward's different temperament was not in tune with the idea. He was a religious man and showed due respect, but not obsession, towards the abbey. It was not the cost of further works which deterred him. He had other things to do, and went on to spend about £80,000 on his eight Welsh castles, £20,000 on the Tower of London alone, £4,000 on the building of St. Stephens Chapel in the palace, and another £6,000 on the rest of the palace. And it did not end there.[110]

But if he failed the abbey in quantity, in quality he succeeded. In 1292 and after, he endorsed and enlarged his dead Queen Eleanor's munificent foundation in favour of the abbey, and both earlier and later he made generous contributions towards the glazing of the windows in the abbey, which were still unfinished.[111] The brilliance of this thirteenth century glass installed at the abbey shows, in a few surviving medallions, that it rivalled even some of the magnificent and contemporary glass which had been installed at about the same time, and still survives in greater amounts, at Canterbury Cathedral.[112] If one compares existing specimens from each church, one can well believe that all or some of them were made by the same expert craftsmen.[113]

So Henry's great rebuilding of the abbey dribbled to a close after his death. The rest of the old nave which still remained had to deputise for a completed new nave for 250 years, waiting for available funds for even the start of works in 1376, and thereafter for its final completion another 150 years later. The centre of the town of Westminster must have sunk into a comparative silence for over a century, after the frenetic quarter century of King Henry's obsession with his ecclesiastical construction site. This later history is a fitting comment on the dependence of the great rebuilding on the fanatical drive of Henry III.

110  Colvin, *King's Works*, I, p. 161. In addition to other religious building, Edward I in 1277 founded a huge new Cistercian monastery at Vale Royal in Cheshire (although later in 1290 he withdrew his support for it). For a painted king's figure, probably modelled on Edward I, see Plate 16, at p. 262.
111  For the Queen's foundation, see pp. 305-7 below.
112  Unfortunately in the first stages of the Civil War in the seventeenth century, most of the glass at an abandoned Westminster Abbey was removed, on an order made by the Long Parliament in 1642, and only a few small examples of the thirteenth century glass survive in the Abbey Museum. See Plate(s)
113  I have not seen this asserted or denied, and rely on my own observation.

# CHAPTER 16

# Lay people and places in the unfolding century
## 1200-1307

## Content and context

What about the later residents in Westminster who followed in the shoes of some of those previously described? This chapter aims to throw a little light on a few of those who came after; and this leads also to a wider net of new encounters, with other residents in the town who exemplify different *classes* of tenants during a century of innovation and advancement.

Inevitably, because of the unfair incidence of surviving documents, the scales are weighted heavily in favour of the so-called 'great' or the 'well-to-do', since their names were more likely to receive recognition in written records. But in the haphazard lottery of record-survival we can also catch sight of even the more humble and the unostentatious, those who appear in 'the small tapestried panels which surround the arras of greater events' - as I foretold in the Introduction to *The Westminster Corridor*.[1]

The years around 1200 had been a focal point for the initial growth of the town of Westminster.[2] The expansion already occurring in the town before that date had been largely due to the administrative and legal changes made by Henry II during the second half of the twelfth century, to the continuity of national history restored by his reign, and to a new climate of enterprise.[3]

The ensuing cross-currents during the later reign of King John (1199-1216) may have momentarily slowed down the rate of expansion in Westminster.[4] However there can be little doubt that in the years *after* John's death in 1216, the national scene and temper of the times were sufficiently favourable for a continuing upsurge in the town, apparently unchecked by such other problems and disturbances, as there were from time to time in the kingdom.[5] The reigns of the two kings, Henry III and Edward I, which saw out the rest of the thirteenth century, saw an enlargement of population to a peak by 1300 and an expanding land market in the town and its neighbourhood.

We have already met many of those who came to the town in the later twelfth century – such as the royal treasurers who from their complex of buildings on the bank of the Thames managed the workings of the restored court of the Exchequer; their subordinate

---

1   *The Westminster Corridor*, p. 12.

2   See p. 117 ff. above.

3   For the changes and reforms made by Henry II himself, see pp. 66-9 above; and these in turn had led to other organisational reforms made by Hubert Walter during Richard I's reign, see pp. 121 ff. above, and to other initiatives which followed.

4   For some of the cross-currents during John's reign, such as his conflict with the pope, the period of the 'interdict', and later his disputes and civil war with the barons, see pp. 131-2, 133 and 137 above. All this touched Westminster in other ways, but it is not certain whether it slowed expansion to any great extent.

5   Even the ten years of conspicuous disputes and eventual civil war between Henry III and some of his barons (1258-1268) appear to have had little effect on the growth of Westminster, although both the abbey and the town had separate problems with the city of London, and some houses in the town did actually suffer physical destruction during part of this period, see pp. 272-3 below.

clerks who staffed the court and staked out their own corners in 'King Street'; the ubiquitous Odo the goldsmith, property-owner on the Thamesbank and elusive individualist, who first served the abbey and then lived long enough to minister later to the king; the Mauduits, royal chamberlains and purchasers of much of the Longditch and Tothill area from the abbey servants who had been the earliest beneficiaries of the abbey's tenancies in the town.[6]

## A. Successors and heirs

The later relatives or successors of many of these original householders, and sometimes their surviving houses too, can be traced well into the ensuing centuries. For example in the early 1220s, as we have seen, the royal treasurers' complex of houses had been taken over, at considerable cost, by the justiciar Hubert de Burgh. But after Hubert's fall from grace and later reinstatement, the complex was bought by the archbishop of York, and given by him to the See of York. So, as 'York Place', it became the residence of the archbishops during the rest of the medieval period, ending with Cardinal Wolsey.[7]

On the other hand, Odo the goldsmith's property remained at first in the family. Edward, Odo's heir, who in his father's stead became the indispensable factotum of King Henry III, inherited his father's large complex, his *curia*, near the sluice on 'King Street', and lived there for the rest of his life while he faithfully carried out his royal master's demands in connection with the rebuilding of the abbey.[8] But the *curia* was split up after Edward's death, with his son,

another Odo, occupying part of it, while serving in a lesser role as a melter and remembrancer of the exchequer. Later, in keeping with its former ties as a royal administrator's base, another part of the large complex was sold by Thomas, the seond son of Edward, and became the home of Robert Burnell who served King Edward I as his powerful chancellor for eighteen years from 1274.[9] So the continuity of part of the site was preserved for almost the whole thirteenth century.

Laurence of the Castle was another who passed his house in 'King Street' down to his son, another Laurence, who entered King Henry III's service. In the 1230s-40s Laurence II figured alongside Odo the goldsmith (who was also his near-neighbour in 'King Street'), as one of the two 'keepers of the king's houses in Westminster', responsible for the maintenance of the palace buildings.[10] Later he had become known as Sir (*dominus*) Laurence son of Laurence. He was still living in his father's old house in the 1240s-50s, before apparently investing in an even grander house with grounds running right down to the river where it swung eastwards away from 'King Street'. This in turn he later sold in about the 1270s to Roger Chese of Westminster and his wife Elen.[11]

The Mauduits, the hereditary chamberlains, had first sunk from the heights to the depths, but then rose again to an even greater height. As rebels against King John, both Robert Mauduit and his son William (II) had suffered dismissal, confiscation and imprisonment.[12] But when each of them had made his peace with the

6   See pp. 110-13, 155-6, 156-7 and 159 above (the treasurers); pp. 170-2, 173-6, 178-81 and 182-5 (the lesser officials);   pp. 151-3 (Odo the goldsmith);   pp. 113-14, 159-64 (the Mauduits);   pp. 95-106 and 139 ff. (the earlier abbey servants).

7   See *Archbishop Gray's Register*, (Raine, ed.) Surtees Society, pp. 199-201; and p. 193 above.

8   See pp. 242-5 (Odo and Edward) and 245-9 (Edward alone).

9   Rosser, *Med. Westm.*, p. 27; *Cal. Cl. R.*, 1268-72, p. 566. Usually labelled 'great' (eg. by Prestwich, *Edw. I*, p. 136), Burnell was also acquisitive and unscrupulous, *ibid*. p. 110; greatness and greed often went together.

10  See WAM 17429 and *Cal. Cl. R.*, 1231-34, p. 90 et al.; and pp. 182-3 above.

11  WAM 17378. Cf. WAMs 17353 and 17367 (1244/45), and pp. 39-40 above. The length of the later property, from Charing down to the Thames, was probably over 100 yards.

12  A repeated warning: because I am limited to Westminster, my 'numbering' of the William Mauduits differs from that used by Dr. Mason.

regents while Henry III was still a boy, their office and inheritance as royal chamberlain at the exchequer and their lands including the Westminster estate were all restored to them. The scope for mercy was immense – if one paid.[13]

After Robert's death in 1222, William Mauduit (II) stepped into the family post and was active personally during the first part of Henry's reign. But later he seems to have acted largely by deputy, and even his clerks were allowed to act as his deputy on exchequer business.[14]

In 1234 William Mauduit (II) had to face a legal action by Abbot Richard of Berking before the bench of the king's justices in Westminster. The abbot's claim was that for six and a half years he had not received any rents for fourteen tenements on Tothill Street which the Mauduit family had built and sublet to various sub-tenants. The arrears of rent had now reached £6. 12s. But equally in turn William Mauduit had also not received (for some reason which we do not know, but presumably a collective dispute) any rents from his sub-tenants during the same protracted period.

A compromise was reached before the justices, by which William Mauduit and, more importantly, each of the sub-tenants, who had all been summoned as well before the Bench and were present there in the courtroom, acknowledged that the sum of the claimed arrears was correct and that the total yearly rent for all the tenements combined had been and would continue to be 21s. 10d for the future. In return, the abbot, having established to his satisfaction both the obligation as to the future rent, and also an agreed right for him to distrain directly against any of the sub-tenants, if rents were not paid in future, was prepared to accept a down-payment of £3 in full discharge of the arrears of £6. 12s.[15]

The names of all the sub-tenants are fortunately given in the court's record of the compromise, and from some of them we can deduce that the fourteen tenements were in fact a row of houses on the north side of Tothill Street, facing the abbey's almonry and the 'chapel of Tothill' (the chapel of St. Mary Magdalene). Four of the sub-tenants were Bartholomew *faber* (the smith), Germanus *brevitor* (the letter-writer), Gilbert *marescallus* (marshal – used here as a 'surname', not as an occupation), and Richard *le haut* (the tall), and it can be shown from other later charters that each of those people still held or had previously held houses in exactly that position along the first reach of Tothill Street opposite the almonry.[16] Of these four, Gilbert Marshal, a clerk, may have been the younger son (with that name) of the great William Marshal, the holder of a large property in Westminster, near the Charing crossroads.[17] And Richard 'the tall' hailed from the adjoining manor of Eye, but had held a number of these houses in

13  'In misericordia'; the legal label for the 'guilty' verdict usually had its payment tag attached.
14  It is likely that William of Rockingham, his clerk, who is identified in charters as holding a fee in Westminster (WAMs 17150, 17152), acted as his deputy; cf. Mason, 'Mauduits and their Chamberlainship', *BIHR* 49 (1976) pp. 13-15. Wm. of Rockingham was son of Robert of Rockingham, an early licensed-attorney, see p. 174-5.
15  Mason (ed), *Beau. Cart.*, ch. No. 201. The case well illustrates the wide tolerance in medieval times of non-payment of debts over protracted periods. In some cases, express arrangements were sometimes made for *direct* payment of rents by sub-tenants to a chief lord, in effect freeing the intervening tenant, not necessarily of his liability to the chief lord, but at least from the work of collecting rents and paying his rent over to his own landlord. Some of these plots had much the same sizes, in a 'collective' development, see App. D, p. 407.
16  The later relevant charters are WAMs 17406, 17408, 17409, 17394 and 17398. 17406 also shows that Richard Altus (= *le haut*) must have later lost his house for some reason (perhaps evicted for again not paying a disputed rent ?) and then recovered it in a legal action before the justices in a Middlesex eyre.
17  See Crouch, *William Marshal*, pp. 131 and 220; WAMs 17394 and 17398; and for William Marshal, see also pp. 29, 178-9, and 186-7 above.

Tothill Street, which two of his daughters and his widow later inherited and lived in.[18]

In view of the claim for arrears of rent (over a period of six and a half years) made by the abbot of Westminster, this line of houses in Tothill Street had certainly been in existence since before 1228.[19]   Moreover another large development, called 'the Virgin Mary's New Rent', of about twelve houses further along Tothill Street was built *by the abbey* in or after 1230, in order to raise funds for the building of the Virgin Mary's new chapel.  These two separate developments were probably made within a short time of one another, but in different sections on the same side of the street; the first by William Mauduit (II) in the 1220s at the eastern end of the road, and the second by the abbey in the 1230s further west along the street.[20]

William Mauduit (II) had acquired a contingent and unpromising right to the earldom of Warwick by marrying the daughter of the current earl, a lady with few expectations of inheritance at that time.  But in the course of years this had a dramatic result for his son.  When William (II) died in February 1257, his son (yet another William: no. III) inherited the right, and in 1263 the right did mature when the existing earl died.

Thereupon William (III) stepped into a different world.  He inherited the earldom, Warwick castle and great estates, which were grand enough to make the chamberlainship and the Mauduit possessions, including their Westminster properties, pale in comparison. From then on, the Mauduit establishment in Westminster could be rated comparatively insignificant by the grand earls, and the duties of a royal chamberlain, which had previously brought the chamberlain to Westminster whenever he was needed, were performed at the exchequer by a permanent paid deputy. The local importance in Westminster of this branch of the Mauduits was over, not because, as so often happened, a family had somehow sunk into obscurity, but because it had been swept into an even more imposing world – but with its own name to be submerged there shortly afterwards and lost.[21]

For the rest of the century and nearly another half-century as well, the earls continued to hold the properties in Westminster called 'Mauduitsgarden' and 'Mauduitscroft', with some nearby arable and meadow land and certain rents from five houses on Tothill Street. These included most of the remaining lands and buildings from the old holdings of the Mauduit family.[22]

---

18  Mason, *Beau. Cart*, Ch. No. 201.  For Richard the tall, see also p. 330 below.
19  While it is not certain whether these houses had been built only a short time before that date, or at a much earlier date, by 1200, I doubt the earlier date.  Dr. Mason in 'Mauduits and their Chamberlainship', *ibid.*, p. 16n., appears to regard the subletting (and perhaps the development also?) as having been made by William Mauduit II (ie. after 1222), but Dr. Rosser, in *Med. Westminster*, p. 30 attributes the building of 'a string of houses' to an earlier period, before 1200.  There is no doubt that *land* and a few houses along the roadway were the subject of transactions before 1200, but I doubt whether it can be established that a *collective* development (of at least 14 houses) took place in Tothill Street at that early time.  The firm reference to 'our houses' made by Abbot Wm. Humez (1214-1222) in WAM 17614 relates expressly to Longditch, not Tothill Street.
20  Dr Rosser attributed this later development by the abbey to c. 1230, see *ibid*. pp. 152 and 48.  For the 'New Rent' development, see pp. 47 above.
21  But five years after 1263, the Mauduits' *direct* connection with the earldom was lost when Wm. Mauduit (III) the new Earl of Warwick, died childless and was succeeded by his nephew, Wm of Beauchamp, who became the first Beauchamp earl of Warwick.
22  In 1344 the abbey repurchased the whole of these properties from Thomas the existing earl, and in 1350 relet them on leases of 40 and 60 years to Master Roger Belet, the butler to King Edward III's queen, Philippa, see WAMs 17635-7, 17652-3; and 17734, 17788 and 17798.  In the C16 a great mansion, by then built on the site, came into the hands of Lord Berners, the 'Deputy of Calais', and probably as a result of this French connection became known as 'Pety Caleys' or 'Petty Calais';  see p. 24 n.45, & *Survey of London*, X p.8 & XIII p. 259.

## B.  New people and places

Meanwhile, other residents had arrived or grown up in the town:

### 1.  The 'German mansion' – 'Almayne'

Richard, the brother of King Henry III, was only fifteen months younger than the king, and by 1232 Henry, who was aged twenty-five, had some grounds already for being on his guard as to the threat to his throne which Richard, who at this stage was his heir, might pose.  The brothers had already had two quarrels, and in several other ways Richard had shown dissatisfaction with his position, in spite of the fact that he had earlier been made the Earl of Cornwall and the Count of Poitou.[23]   So an intention to keep his brother well within sight and range may be the reason why Henry in about that year found room within the palace grounds in Westminster to give Richard a site, north of the palace itself, on which Richard could build a mansion for himself.

By April 1234 Earl Richard's building works were under way, and Henry was helping them along with a grant of thirty oak trees from the royal forest at Windsor, 'as timber for his houses in Westminster'.[24]  No doubt this was mainly for roof work, because at least the principal mansion was built of stone. The turretted building had a complex of other houses adjoining or nearby, and a garden or orchard.

Richard had earlier married, and in 1235 an heir, Henry, was born and survived, but the earl's wife died five years later.  His remarriage in 1243, to Sanchia a sister of Henry III's Queen Eleanor, was celebrated in great style at the abbey, with Richard granting her at the church door her dower of a third of all his lands, which were considerable.  Afterwards at his Westminster mansion an extravagant wedding feast was served, with 30,000 dishes, so earning the indignant scorn of Matthew Paris, the monk historian.[25]

In less than two years the king's operations for the great rebuilding of the abbey began.  One can infer that the town thereupon became less attractive a place of resort, and in any event Earl Richard of Cornwall had much to do elsewhere.  In what was (in effect) a quirky medieval auction, he bid for, and by 1257 had won, the throne of Germany – a place where he had never set foot before beginning the necessary electioneering. Thereupon his great house in Westminster began to be known as 'Almayne' (the *German place*), while he became 'the King of Almain', and his son and heir Henry, (who was cousin to prince Edward, the king's son and the future king, Edward I), became known as 'Henry of Almain'.

But in spite of the king's fears, the earl was conspicuously and unexpectedly loyal to his brother during the subsequent baronial disputes and the eventual civil war in the 1260s; so much so that his loyalty earned him both imprisonment by the barons and the destruction of his mansion and the rest of his Westminster complex.  In 1263 a mob of London citizens and residents, who supported the baronial cause and were also inflamed by recent disputes between the abbey of Westminster and the city of London about the abbey's claimed rights and privileges, invaded the town of Westminster and attacked the mansion in the earl's absence.  They toppled the turrets of the building and tore it down stone by stone, even uprooting the garden shrubs and orchard trees.[26]

23  See Denholm Young, *Richard of Cornwall*, p. 16 ff.   To keep Richard contented, the king had already made other generous grants, of wide estates and castles at Wallingford and Berkhampstead to his brother.
24  *Call. Cl. R.* 1231-34, p. 409.
25  See also p. 207 above.  For the dower, see Denholm Young, *Ric. of Cornwall*, p. 51.   Richard's new wife, renowned for her beauty, was one of the four daughters of the Count of Provence – who each became a queen.
26  Wykes, *Ann. Monast.*, R. S., iv. p. 141, printed in Rosser, *Med. Westminster*, pp. 25-26n; Denholm Young, *ibid.*, pp 126-7.  The mob had also marched to Isleworth further up the Thames and plundered that

So to his fury the earl's Westminster home was now reduced to ruins, and it seems that although (like his brother, the king) he survived until 1272, he had earlier handed the whole property over to his son Henry of Almain. Perhaps this happened soon after 1263, when the earl was himself captured by the barons at the battle of Lewes and in any case may have felt that he could not bear to continue to own such a heap of rubble or to start rebuilding the complex. Meanwhile after reprisals the citizens of London were ordered to pay him compensation of a thousand marks (£666) for the damage done at Westminster and other property at Isleworth and elsewhere, but this was trivial for a man as wealthy as Earl Richard had become by now.[27]

Almayne therefore, or at least its site, ended in the possession of Henry of Almain, but the remaining years of his life were taken up in the cause of the king and prince Edward, with events both abroad and at home arising from the civil war.[28] Finally he must have decided to transfer his 'whole tenement', including *'houses, garden, homages, reliefs, rents, escheats'*, to the abbey, as a charitable gift 'in soul alms'.[29] In this way, a large site which had originally been within the old palace precinct came into the hands of the monks, no doubt to their great satisfaction. The description of it in Henry of Almain's charter suggests some rebuilding, but the wording of it may be mere legal verbiage.

## 2. The Cantilupe family – residents and royal stewards

Between 1200 and 1252 two members of the Cantilupe family in successive generations served both King John and King Henry in turn, as stewards, and therefore heads, of the royal household, and for part of that half-century each of them occupied a house in Westminster just outside the abbey precinct. The stewards each bore the same name, William, and each became a close and trusted servant of his royal master(s), earning both respect and the resulting honours and wealth which such a relationship brought. The Cantilupe family grew to have other prominent members as well during King Henry's reign, but these had no direct connection with Westminster, other than inevitable attendances on the king at his palace or at other ceremonies in the town and abbey.[30]

We know only of the Cantilupe house in Westminster through chance references to it in later charters relating to other properties. The house is there described as 'the messuage once of William of Cantilupe'. It stood close to the abbey's western gate opposite Tothill Street and was part of the 'fee' of the Almonry which fronted onto that street. But its actual position near the gate was probably just outside the wall surrounding the abbey precinct, because an early holder of a house two doors away bore the name *Ludovicus atte walle*, or *extra muros* (Louis at, or outside, the wall(s)), and

---

manor of Earl Richard. Meanwhile the queen, trying to leave London by boat, was pelted with stones by the citizens. As to the disputes between the city of London and the abbey, see pp. 238 and 263 above.

27 Denholm-Young, *ibid*, p. 132. For the earl's wealth (in spite of the amount spent in acquiring his throne), see eg. Denholm-Young, *ibid*. pp. 157-170. In 1265, he was said to be in debt, and was even allowed to tax his tenants for an 'aid', *ibid*. p. 132 and *Cal. P. R.*, 1258-1266, p. 495. Yet he was 'the richest lay magnate in the country', and 'a famous fixer', Carpenter, *Reign of H. III*, pp. 353, 223.

28 See Prestwich, *Edward I*, pp. 27-8, 45-7, 68-9,

29 WAM 17360, a late 'soul alms' grant. This charter is usually attributed to 1270, but Master Alexander the Carpenter (see pp. 253 ff) who retired in about 1267 and died in 1269 was a witness. Later Henry of Almain was murdered by Simon de Montfort's sons in Sicily, in revenge for their father's death and disfigurement at the battle of Evesham.

30 For Walter, brother of William Cantilupe II, see text below. Thomas, son of William II, became Bishop of Hereford, highly influential and ultimately a saint.

another property close-by was said to lie 'outside the wall of the cemetery of Westminster'. So these houses probably had their backs to the abbey wall, fronting on to the road which ran from the end of 'King Street' towards the beginning of Tothill Street.[31]

William Cantilupe I had already served Count John during King Richard I's reign, at the time when John had been waiting in the wings to seize the chance of succeeding his brother. William's post was already as seneschal (steward, and therefore head) of John's household; as it also remained throughout John's subsequent reign as king, and for the next twenty-three years as well under Henry III. He served John loyally but as a result he and even his son earned a description as two of the king's 'evil counsellors'.[32] Whether that adjective was deserved or not is not clear, but he was close to the king over a protracted period; and had received a barony from him in 1205. William also stood by the king during the pope's interdict and did not join the other barons during John's disputes and war with them. Under Henry III he continued his faithful role, receiving many grants of lands and other privileges in return, before dying in 1239 after he had trained his son William (II) to succeed him in the same post.[33]

During William Cantilupe (II)'s time as steward of the royal household, the Cantilupe family waxed large, since his brother Walter had become bishop of Worcester and later figured very prominently among the magnates in dispute with the king. But William (II) remained loyal to King Henry, and received even greater

trust and standing in the additional confidential roles which he was given from time to time. Thus he had been made one of the regents of England appointed by the king for the period of his absence on his ill-fated military expedition to Poitou in 1242-3. The king's warm feelings for the Cantilupe family is best evidenced by his own words in a letter, where he referred to the first William as 'the beloved and faithful father of our William of Cantilupe'.[34] Like his father, William (II) also continued to receive many favours from King Henry, in the form of more grants of lands and privileges.[35] He died in February 1251.

There is little doubt that the second Cantilupe occupied the house outside the abbey's cemetery wall in Westminster. William (II)'s presence in the Westminster circle is also revealed by his appearing in the abbey court as witness to two of the more important of the charters which Odo the goldsmith was making in favour of the abbey in and after 1241.[36] On each occasion he appears in the list of witnesses as Sir William of Cantilupe, the king's seneschal, with other prominent names: such as Sir John, son of Geoffrey, the chief forester of England; Sir Jukel of St Germain, the (abbot's) steward of Westminster; Sir William of Medburne and Master Richard of Wyke, the king's Chamberlains at the Exchequer; and Richer of the Cross, the reeve of Westminster. When William Cantilupe (II) died, his son – another William – succeeded him but died within three years. In turn his sons were under age and became the wards of Prince Edward, later King Edward I.[37]

---

31 See WAMs 17553, 17362, 17550. Louis may have been the same man as Louis, clerk of the exchequer, see pp. 173-4 above. The roadway was the one which later became known as 'Thieving Lane' (about 1365?, see WAM 17680). Because of their royal duties as his steward, which required travelling with the king wherever he went, neither of the Cantilupes was likely to be in continuous residence in Westminster.

32 But the steward's post grew in dignity under John, Turner, *King John*, p. 75.

33 For the progressive advancement of the two Williams, see eg. *Cal. Ch. R.*, 1226-57, pp. 5, 66, 114, 115, 132, 225.

34 *Cal. Cl. R.*, 1237-42, p. 150.

35 eg. *Cal. Ch. R.*, 1226-57, pp. 253, 264, 276, 284.

36 WAMs 17333 and 17454. In 1252 Henry III bought the Cantilupe 'houses' and gave them to the sacrist of the abbey, see pp. 215 above.

37 His eldest son, another William, served the king as a soldier and courtier, not as steward, and died soon in 1254.

### 3. The 'house opposite Enedehithe': rising rents, as the house came home to the abbey

This is the story of one house whose progress can be traced over about sixty years from the late twelfth century to about 1250. It was a large house, described as a 'messuage', and it stood on the west side of 'King Street', with a broad frontage of 82 feet to the road. Its 'curtilage' included a garden and a 'marsh' or marshy area, standing probably behind the house on the edge of the present St. James's Park, where plenty of water still exists. Its location in 'King Street' was 'opposite Enedehithe' (Endiff), the lane running from the street towards the river Thames, and its history reveals the effects of continuing inflation on current prices and rents in central Westminster.

The first we know is that in about the 1190s it had belonged to William Creeton, the domestic chamberlain of Richard fitz Nigel, Henry II's first treasurer in the renewed exchequer.[38] Since the treasurer's own large house lay to the north of Endiff, overlooking the Thames, it was clearly convenient that his personal chamberlain should be quartered so near at hand, at the 'King Street' end of the lane.

From William Creeton the house was purchased, in probably the very early years of the new century, by Geoffrey of Hanley who in turn soon sold the tenancy on to Peter of Ely, for a price or premium (*gersum*) of four marks (£2. 13s. 4d), with an annual rent of one pound of cumin (aromatic seeds).[39] Peter of Ely was a long-standing and trustworthy serjeant of the new treasurer, William of Ely, and for many years spent his time escorting cartloads and shiploads of money or other forms of treasure around the country or abroad. He was almost certainly a protégé of the treasurer, who was himself a witness to the charter recording this sale to Peter, together with a number of other significant members of the new official class in Westminster.

Peter and his wife Agatha seem to have lived at the house for ten to twenty years until about the 1220s, and then sold it again (this time with a mention of its 'marsh' behind it), to a merchant of London appropriately called Richard Merchant (*Mercator*) of St. Pauls and his wife Sabine. This time the premium had risen by more than half, to six and a half marks (£4. 6s. 8d.), plus 1s. 6d. for Agatha.[40]

By about another twenty years later the London merchant (whose occupation had become his surname) had died, and his widow Sabine was selling the house on again, to another couple called Roger le Bere and Constance. Once again the total premium or *gersum* had risen by nearly another half in total: made up of six and a half marks (£4. 6s. 8d) for Sabine herself, *plus* two marks (£1. 6s. 8d) for Richolda, Sabine's own daughter and her husband Geoffrey *le fitur*, plus a tunic and a shirt for Edward, Sabine's son. So the lady had been able to procure something for both her daughter and her son, as well as recouping the original price she and her husband had had to pay. The rents of 2s. due to the bishop of Salisbury and one pound of cumin for Peter of Ely still stood, but Sabine was also able to ask and obtain an additional one penny pa. for herself. There were now three tiers of rent to pay by the purchasers, as well as the capital outlay by them.[41]

Roger and Constance seem to have enjoyed only a few years in their new house opposite Endiff lane, before they too moved again, and this time it led to a sale back to the abbey, specifically to the fund for St Mary's

---

38  See pp. 155-6 above (for fitz Nigel and Creeton), and also 110 ff. above (for fitz Nigel).
39  WAM 17443 (WAC 434; temp John), for both sales. The tenancy of the house also carried another tier of rent, 2s. pa., due to the bishop of Salisbury who must have held the property at an earlier stage. Another witness was Odo the goldsmith, *the reeve* of Westminster, which establishes Odo's first office, on behalf of the abbey.
40  WAM 17317.
41  WAM 17373.

altar in the church.[42] But this was no charitable gift by them, for Brother Ralph of Gloucester, the warden of the altar, had to pay 10 marks (£6. 13s. 4d) for the purchase, and there was no attempt to dress the sale up as a charitable one 'in soul alms' (as was sometimes done).[43] The premium agreed was slightly greater than the total which Roger and Constance had had to pay (ten marks, against eight and a half marks plus the value of a tunic and a shirt); but if rents had been and were still rising as previously, Roger and Constance may have been generous in their price, even if not seriously charitable, and they are not recorded as seeking or at least receiving another tier of rent for themselves.

So by about the middle of the thirteenth century the house had at last come home to the abbey, and was available for letting out by the warden of the new St. Mary's chapel. When towards the end of the century the abbot or the abbey's heads of departments began cautiously to grant formal leases of properties to tenants 'for life' and later for 'terms of years', the big house opposite Endiff lane was a potential, if not a prime, candidate for letting out on a formal lease. But unfortunately no charter has been identified as recording a lease or other letting of this particular house within the rest of the century. Indeed it was a hundred years before the house can be identified among the abbey's surviving charters, when in 1355 Abbot Simon of Langham, describing the house again as the 'messuage opposite the lane of Enedehithe',

with a garden included, leased it on behalf of St. Mary's chapel to John Penehalow, the royal gardener of King Edward III, on a long lease of 40 years at an annual rent of 10s.[44]

### 4. Another Westminster house restored to the abbey

Another property in the main street of Westminster which, like the previous one, passed through the hands of several occupiers before eventually reverting to the abbey's possession was the house which had been occupied by Richard of Dol, the abbot's steward. This house too shows the continued effects of inflation during the thirteenth century. As we have seen, Richard of Dol had served Abbot Ralph of Arundel in the first decade of the century, and may also have been steward of Abbot Postard in some of the concluding years of the previous century.[45] This house lay in 'King Street', and its later next-door neighbours were houses belonging to Odo the goldsmith and the exchequer clerk, Laurence of the Castle.[46]

From Richard of Dol the property had passed to a member of another prominent family in Westminster, Ralph Testard, the son of the manor reeve, Richard Testard.[47] Ralph appears to have occupied the house for more than twenty years at least. During that time he tried, by an unsuccessful legal action in 1231 before the king's court, to recover possession of three other houses in Westminster and a very large area of land (a whole 'hide') in the adjoining manor of Eye,

---

42 WAM 17379. For the fund for St. Mary's altar, see pp. 126 ff. By the late 1240s the fund for the 'altar' had been renamed the fund for the new 'chapel of St. Mary', but sometimes the old title was still used, as here. For the building and final integration of the chapel, see pp. 245 and 261 above.

43 eg. WAM 17542 (grant of a rent in soul alms, with 12d paid for it). The rent was for the land in WAM 17539.

44 WAM 17657. The lease reveals that, as one would expect, there had been an earlier letting, to one Thomas Pykard. The frontage is given as over 82 feet, but the depth of the plot and its marshy area is not given. Fifty years after the thirteenth century, such leases in Westminster contain most 'modern' terms such as an obligation to repair, a prohibition against any sale or other alienation, with rights of re-entry and distraint on non-payment of rent or breach of repair duties. Before 1300 such terms were only occasionally spelt out.

45 See p. 141 above.

46 For Odo's property, see WAM 17597 and p. 151 (house (a)), above; and for Laurence's, see pp. 183 and 269.

47 WAM 17316 (WAC 419). Ralph had to pay a small premium of 2s., and an annual rent of 3s.

all of which he asserted had belonged to his Testard forebears.[48]  At all events he appears to have decided in the late 1230s or early 1240s to move from his 'King Street' house and to sell the tenancy to another property-owning family, Robert the Winnower (*Vannator* or *Vannarius*) and his wife Cristiane.[49]  The purchase cost Robert and Cristiane 16s. as the price or premium, and as new 'sub-tenants' they also agreed to pay an extra annual rent of one penny to Ralph Testard, in addition to the existing annual rents of 2s. to the sacrist of the abbey (the chief lord) and 12d. to the heirs of Richard of Dol.[50]

Robert the Winnower was probably a servant of the abbey, because he was also known under the added title 'of Westminster', which usually was given to, and used by, those who held or had held significant posts at the abbey.  When in 1244-45 Robert decided to sell his interest in the house, he used this title 'of Westminster' in conveying that interest to John Barbarius, 'of the household of King Henry III' and to Alice his wife.[51]  Presumably John was the king's barber, a position which had to be one of considerable trust.  It was probably the old pattern of the abbey's man giving way to the king's man.

This time, the price or premium paid by the king's barber was the greatly increased sum of four marks (£2. 13s. 4d) and the cost of 'a green tunic' for Robert's wife; with an additional annual rent payable to Robert (and of course his heirs) of a pair of white gloves,

or their value, being one halfpenny.   This meant that there were now four tiers of rent payable each year by the new holder of the property : 2s. to the sacrist, 12d. to the heirs of Richard of Dol, 1d. to Ralph Testard, and the gloves or a halfpenny to Robert.

By reason of the recent sales, each of the previous vendors, Ralph Testard and Robert the Winnower, was now in separate receipt of a small rent from the house:  one penny for Ralph, and the pair of white gloves or a halfpenny for Robert.   Even by medieval values, these rents were hardly large sums, and each of them was subsequently donated by its owner to the abbey as a charitable gift: the former to the high altar, the latter to St. Mary's altar.[52]  The second of these gifts may have been one of the few occasions when the old campaign in favour of the cult of the Virgin was still being favoured with a donation, since with the start in 1245 of the new programme for the rebuilding of the whole abbey at King Henry III's expense, the cult, and indeed other local support for the abbey itself, had begun to wane, and after about 1250 few such charitable donations 'in soul alms' were made.[53]

But we left John the royal barber and Alice his wife in command of their new home in 'King Street', paying now their four separate rents, with two of them meanwhile assigned and therefore payable to the abbey.   But the barber then died, and the next we hear of the widow Alice is that she too has disposed very

48  See p. 145, nn. 38 and 40, above.  He failed on a technicality, and we do not know whether he succeeded on any later legal attempt in which the real merits of his case may have been tried.

49  For such occupational names in Westminster, eg. *Vannator*, which survived their origins, see App. E at pp. 410-11.

50  WAM 17597.  As so often happens in legal terminology, the charter describes the property as 'a plot of land' rather than a 'house', but another charter WAM 17429 (made by Ralph's son) shows that there was indeed a 'messuage' on the land when his father sold it, and that similarly there were messuages on the neighbouring 'lands' of Odo the goldsmith and Laurence of the Castle, as is also clear from other evidence.

51  WAM 17367.  Again the property was described as simply a 'plot of land', but this time, to make its character clearer, the words 'with its buildings and liberties' (rights) were added.

52  WAMs 17334 and 17386 (1250s).  It was Ralph's son Roger who made the gift of the 1d, after Ralph's death.

53  See pp. 126 ff. for the start and progress of the cult from about 1190, and Rosser, *Med. Westminster*, pp. 256-57, for the loss of local support for the cult and the abbey.  The result is a good lesson as to the effect which 'public' spending (in this case by the king) can have on private charity.

charitably of her whole house 'in soul alms to Abbot Richard and his monks', to pay for the cost of a lamp at St. Mary's altar.[54]

So the effect of the three last transactions relating to this house was that the abbey had benefitted to the tune of the house itself and also an annual penny and a halfpenny, which were now payable to the monks in respect of their repossessed interest in the house. The house itself which up to sixty to seventy years before had commanded a rent of 2s. could for the future command, by reason of the national inflation, a considerably higher rent for the benefit of the abbey. The Abbot Richard who had received this benefaction was either Richard of Crokesley (1246-1258), or perhaps his successor Richard of Ware (1258-1283); if the latter, this latest gift provided by the widow Alice may have been one of the last of such donations in favour of the monks' long-standing campaign on behalf of the cult of St. Mary.[55]

### 5. Houses round the palace gateway – and links with other families:
#### (a) the Levelonds – Richard Woolward

At the point where 'King Street' reached both the courtyard of the palace and the abbey's 'great cemetery' in its precinct, there was naturally an entrance to each of those enclosures, which stood fairly close to one another. Of course there was also a gate at each entrance,[56] and it seems that the original gateway into the palace courtyard had been built of timber and remained so until 1244-45, when it was dismantled by King Henry III and rebuilt in stone, with turrets.[57] Later a second 'great gateway' was built by Henry's son Edward I in 1278-79, outside his father's stone one, so that thereafter there was both an inner and an outer gate, each made of stone.

A cluster of houses had begun to grow up round the king's timber gate from before the beginning of the thirteenth century, and the families which had the main influence and property in this area of Westminster were, as one would expect, closely connected with the king and his service. Among these were the Levelond family, which held the office of hereditary keepers of the palace, possibly since the time of Domesday.[58] Shortly before 1200 Nathaniel of Levelond, the current keeper, presented a house 'at the gate of the king' as a marriage gift of to his daughter Juliana when she married Wlfward the carter, and over thirty years later Juliana, who by then had been widowed and had let the house at a rent of 2s., donated a charitable gift of that rent 'in soul alms' to the altar of St. Mary at the abbey and its current custodian Brother Ralph of Gloucester.[59] This house, or at least the entitlement to its rent, appears to have remained in the family, because about another ten years later Juliana's own daughter, Alice and her (Alice's) son Richard Woolward repeated the same gift of the rent to the altar and its custodian.[60] Although there had been male descendants of Nathaniel who had meanwhile inherited the office of keeper of the palace, in practice that office was later performed by Juliana's family, because in due course Alice's son Richard Woolward received

---

54  WAM 17353 (1250-60s).

55  For other late donations, see WAMs 17531 and 17532. For Crokesley, see pp. 209 ff.; and for Ware, see pp. 224 ff.

56  The gate into the abbey cemetery was the 'east' or sometimes the 'north' gate of the abbey, to distinguish it from the great West Gate and Gatehouse looking towards Tothill, cf. WAMs 17374 and 17426 (endorsement).

57  See Colvin, *King's Works*, i, p. 547; *Cal. Lib. R.* 1240-5, p. 267; and *ibid*, 1245-51, p. 89.

58  For the Levelonds, whose title to the office may have gone back to Domesday, see pp. 106-8 above.

59  WAMs 17375 and 17509. The specific object of the gift was to 'keep two lamps burning night and day before the altar'. For the cult of St. Mary, see pp. 126-9 above. Nathaniel had once performed his office of keeper by a deputy, Ailnoth, for whom see p. 107-9 above.

60  WAM 17509. In effect this was really a 'confirmation' of Juliana's gift, rather than itself a gift.

the office in 1286.[61] But this was probably a temporary arrangement, with Richard in the role of a deputy, or one of the guardians of Joan of Grendon, the under-age heiress of the hereditary office at that time.[62] As we shall see, Richard Woolward was also becoming a substantial holder of other properties near the king's gate.

### (b) the Marshals – Richard of the Cellar – Ralph the Vintner

Another family, the Marshals, also encircled the royal gateway during the course of the thirteenth century, and its members became entwined by marriage, or other relationship, with other families which each had close association with the king's service and owned houses at or near the gateway. It was clearly a privilege to be allowed to reside close to the palace entrance, which itself acted as an aid to the performance of not only the services which these families provided for the king and his court, but also the private commercial businesses which the families pursued.

Although the great William Marshal, Earl of Pembroke, who had been the principal regent during the first years of young King Henry III's reign, had himself owned property at Charing Cross, there is little to connect him with the other Marshal family which came to

live at the other end of 'King Street', by the palace gateway.[63] However even if the 'gateway Marshals' (as we can call them) could not claim kin with the line of the great Marshal, they established by the end of the century a net of relationships with members of other more ordinary families near the gateway.

The 'gateway Marshals' begin with John 'of Upton' who appears to have become a deputy of Henry III's marshal at Westminster palace before 1240; but like the deputies of other major offices, he too became known as 'the marshal of Westminster'. In 1240, having previously built a house for himself by the palace gate under royal licence to do so, John was confirmed by the king, as a gift, in his possession of the completed building.[64] Close by, he owned or built other smaller houses, and we can see that these formed a family enclave in due course. He apparently gave houses to each of his children: (a) one house and an adjoining shop as a wedding gift on his daughter Joan's marriage to a provision merchant called Richard of the Cellar (de celario); and (b) one or two houses to his eldest son Hugh; and (c) yet another house to his younger son Robert, each of them in the same enclave outside the king's gate.[65]

The first of these houses and its adjoining shop were already let to separate tenants, so

---

61  See Rosser, *Medieval Westminster*, pp. 23 & 25n; the Byerlys, *Records of the Wardrobe*, i. no. 1693; Clay, 'Keepership of the Palace', EHR. 59 (1944) pp. 10-11, & WAM 17475.  Rosser suggests the name 'Woolward' derives from Juliana's husband Wlfward the carter (presumably, a 'guardian against wolves', as a surname). Richard had earlier received the designation 'of Westminster'.

62  See Clay, *ibid.*, pp. 11 and 12.

63  For William Marshal, see pp. 29, 178-9, 186-7 above, & Dr. Crouch's biography of him, *William Marshal*. Equally Henry Marshal, who was the brother of the earl, and became Bishop of Exeter also held held property at Longditch in Westminster, (see pp. 139 and 161 above), but he too appears to have no discernible link with the Marshals who came to live at the palace gateway.

64  *Cal. Ch. R.*, 1226-57, p. 251, and see Rosser, *Med. Westminster*, p. 23. John of Upton was a royal serjeant and became the deputy marshal 'of the king's horses'; but he lost his sight in the king's service in 1254, and being much favoured, he got a daily pension of 6d. and annual robes from the king until he died in 1267. It must have been a close relationship, and when he died, his pension was assigned to the queen's 'beloved laundress'.

65  WAMs 17365 and 17382. The 'abutments' in the latter charter, and WAM 17470, show the sons' houses. Richard of the Cellar was a merchant (with a house in Tothill St.) who supplied many materials, mainly iron and sand, and carrying services for the new abbey and the palace, see Colvin, *Building A/cs*, index p. 447, and no doubt supplied the court with hardware & other provisions. Was 'class' marrying 'commerce'? Both Hugh and Robert were also known by the name Marshal (as a surname) or even 'the Marshal'.

they were not vacant at that time and may never have become occupied by Joan and Richard of the Cellar, but by reason of their location at the palace gate they were clearly valuable properties. Joan later let them both to another prominent resident and provisioner of Westminster, Ralph the vintner (le Vineter), for a large and, and as things turned out, probably excessive annual rent of 40s.[66]

Ralph's business as vintner was clearly an established one. His residence and, no doubt, his 'shop' near the royal gateway marked a good trade with the king, the country's best customer for wine, and probably also with members of the royal court and the public. His father had been William the vintner, with the approved title 'of Westminster', a title always identified as such whenever Ralph is mentioned as his son. With such a title, William had used Vinetarius, a Latin form, for his occupation; and there had also been an earlier 'Thomas Vinitor' in Westminster, who may have been a member of the same family. After William's death, his widow Edith, probably a daughter of Hugh Marshal, lived nearby, it seems, in Tothill Street.[67]

But Ralph was not the only son of William the vintner. There was also another younger son called John, and he too at some later stage

was set up in yet another house outside the king's gate.[68] With an apparently flourishing family business already in existence in the same locality, his name and his residence in the same quarter suggests that he too was involved in the same business, and he was certainly known as John le vineter like his brother.[69]

By the last quarter of the century Ralph the vintner was a substantial landowner in or near this part of Westminster. He had paid 20 marks to Hugh of Mohant for a nearby house which may have been a large property, lying between the wall of the king's courtyard and 'King Street'.[70]

Meanwhile Hugh Marshal, the eldest son of John 'the marshal of Westminster', was spinning his own web among the neighbours who lived close to him near the king's gateway. He had let another house by the gate to John of Cardoil (perhaps Carlisle), who already held one house in the enclave and almost certainly held some office in the king's service.[71] Hugh had also let another 'plot of land', this time in 'King Street' but probably close to the gateway area, to Richard Woolward. Since the annual rent for this plot was 10s., it is likely that the land already had a house on it.[72]

So we can already see some of the close-knit connections of the Levelonds, the

---

66  WAMs 17382 and 17473. If this rent was not excessive, Ralph and his wife must have become over-stretched by other debts, because there is a succession of later charters from 1292 to 1309 showing both waivers and payments of arrears of this 40s. rent, WAMs 17473, 17492, 17498 and 17559, and cf. 17475.

67  See WAM 17541. For Thomas Vinitor, see Index to Dr Mason's W.A. Charters and the 18 charters there to which he was a witness.

68  See WAM 15547.

69  See WAM 17426. Another neighbour was John of Cardoil who had property both here and elsewhere in Tothill Street and probably in Eye; and although his occupation has not been identified, it too almost certainly was connected with the palace or the abbey; see eg. WAMs 17470, 17382, 17518-19, 17526, 17654, etc.

70  WAMs 17513, 17377, 17594. Rosser, p. 24 says the price (17513?) was 90 marks, but query?. Ralph Vintner's family cast a long shadow after them, because after his death in the early 1300s his widow Joan survived for about forty years or more as 'Joan la Vinitière' and gathered further properties around her. For the 'consolidation' of such estates in the C14, see pp. 282 and 346 n 80, and App. F, on pp. 412 ff.

71  WAM 17470. This later charter, an arbitrators' award in 1287 about a wall between Ralph's and John of Cardoil's two adjoining properties, shows that already there was a detailed party-wall procedure in Westminster, anticipating the modern statutory procedure by more than 700 years.

72  WAM 17504. Hugh may have later disposed of his interest in this house, since he then empowered Richard to pay his rent (now given as 8s.) to another person, WAM 17543. There was certainly a tenement on the land at that time. In due course Richard Woolward appears to have become the landlord of this house too.

Woolwards, the Marshals, the 'Cellars' and the Vintners within an area in which a position in royal service or provisioning seems to have been almost an essential qualification. But there are even more strands of business and family affinity to be seen in this neighbourhood, both between members of the above groups and between them and other similar families who lived nearby.

For example Master Alexander the king's carpenter, who had been heavily involved in the programme for the abbey rebuilding, held much property, including (in addition to his own house nearby) at least two other adjoining houses and a shop on and behind 'King Street' in its southern quarter, and these his son Henry of Westminster inherited when his father died in about 1269.[73] Like his father, Henry of Westminster had also prospered as one of the king's clerks under King Henry, and was made keeper of the palace under Edward I.[74]

But we then find Henry of Westminster transacting what was probably some business deal with Ralph the Vintner, transferring these two other properties and the adjoining shop to Ralph; and subsequently having to take them back again. This reversal may have taken place because the legal title to the houses had been called in question as a result of adverse claims on them made by some third party – the usual reason at this time for such doubts about title to land.[75] But this was small fry: there was much more to the large estate which Henry of Westminster left when he later died – as we shall see later.

### (c) The Vintners and John of the Hyde

The Vintners had a further link with another family further afield in Westminster. It happened that Ralph the Vintner's wife Joan was the sister of John 'of the Hyde', the holder of a significant part of the land known even then as 'the Hyde' in the manor of Eye (which included some, perhaps much, of the present Hyde Park).[76] Although the two families were therefore connected with each other, or perhaps *because* they were connected, the Vintners appear to have had some sticky legal experiences with the Hyde family.

John of the Hyde had died in 1280-81, leaving a young son (also called John), and this boy had been made a ward of Ralph the Vintner (his uncle, 'in law'). As the boy's guardian, Ralph had also been entrusted with certain charters which presumably supported the Hyde family's entitlements in the northern sector of the manor of Eye. So during John's boyhood his uncle had been responsible for the administration of his estate and the custody of the charters.

Then shortly before 1298, by which time 'John son of John' must have reached the age of twenty-one, questions had arisen about the way in which the estate had been looked after by his uncle, and also about the custody of the charters. The young man made a claim against Ralph that he should be given an 'account' about all his 'lands and tenements' ever since the time when his wardship arose, and he pursued this claim as far as a legal action in the king's court. It looks as if there was then a

---

73  For Master Alexander, and his part in the abbey rebuilding, see pp. 253 ff. above.

74  See *Cal. Cl. R.* 1264-68, p. 181, and *ibid*, 1279-88, p. 483.

75  WAMs 17383 and 17468 (latter dated in 1286). But having originally received properties with doubtful titles from Henry himself, Ralph not unnaturally insisted that, contrary to the usual rule, he should not be obliged to 'warrant' (ie. to be obliged to uphold or underwrite) their titles back to Henry, if called on to do so. It may be that some loan and mortgage deal had originally been involved.

76  There can be no doubt that John was the holder of this 'estate' within the manor of Eye, because in the manor accounts for part of the year 1280-81 there is a reference to a ditch bordering 'the *curia* of John of the Hyde' (who had just died), see WAM 26854-5 and DS, *Eye A/cs*, pp. 33 and 25. The *curia* had been the administrative centre for his estate. John's father may have been Geoffrey of the Hyde who in mid-C13 held two large and expensive properties between the Strand (or Charing Street) and the river Thames, see WAMs 17157, 17159 and 17420. Or there was also another earlier 'John 'de Hida' who did at least hold some land in the Hyde area and may have been father of our John, see WAM 4881. The Hyde estate itself was not yet called a 'manor', as it was later by the monks in eg. 1358, see WAM 16265. See also the charters in note 49 on p. 36 above.

settlement of the action on terms which satisfied the young man, because we find that he made a charter in Westminster Hall, releasing his uncle from all claims about the 'account' and the custody of the charters.[77] So one action between them was disposed of, but this was not the end of legal problems between the families.

Before Easter 1305, Gillian the mother of Ralph Vintner's wife Joan (and presumably of Joan's brother, John of the Hyde) had apparently granted some properties in Westminster to her daughter, in circumstances which are not clear. The properties which Gillian had granted to Joan were *five tenements with houses built on them in the vill of Westminster'*. John of the Hyde was of course long dead, and his son 'John son of John' had inherited the Hyde lands and other lands in Westminster which his father had held when he died. Ralph Vintner had also meanwhile died, probably in the early 1300s, leaving Joan his widow but apparently no children; and his nephew John son of John now asserted a legal claim on Ralph's estate.

This took the form of a challenge to his great-aunt Gillian's grant to Joan, since he regarded the five houses as part of the property which he claimed under Ralph's estate. Again he resorted to law and brought another action, this time against Joan, his aunt, to recover the five houses from her. The case was due to be heard before the justices of the Bench in the Easter term 1305, but it seems that another compromise took place. The terms of the settlement are unknown, save that as part of it John son of John in effect conceded Joan's claim to the five houses.[78] Almost certainly he was paid something for them, depending on how strong his claim was thought to be.

Joan Vintner went on to be a great survivor, dying another forty or more years later. As the widow of Ralph, she became better known as 'La Vinitière' and probably continued to manage her former husband's business of wineselling. On the way, she accumulated other relationships and many properties to her name, and was a noticeable exemplar of those who contributed to the 'consolidation' of separate estates in Westminster during the first half of the fourteenth century.[79]

Although we hear of this 'Hyde' family in the second half of the thirteenth century, the manner in which they acquired their land, from presumably the abbey, in the present Hyde Park area has not been found. But we do learn of another family who in the same period obtained another adjoining swathe of land, probably in the present Mayfair district west of the Tyburn river.

During the abbacy of Richard of Ware (1258-1283) a tenant, Hugh of Kendal, had received from the abbot a grant (for Hugh's lifetime only) of two fields called Cresswellfield and Ossulston and other nearby land (pasture, meadow and arable), all or some of which lay in the present area of Mayfair, between the Park Lane roadway (then Tyburn lane) and the line of the river Tyburn. The charter by which this grant was made is lost, but we know of it from a later extant charter made by the next abbot, Walter of Wenlock and the convent in 1285.[80] By this later charter the abbey repeated the earlier letting to Hugh (now Sir Hugh), but not only as a lifetime grant because this time the charter included Sir Hugh's son (yet another John, so he was now known as 'John of Kendal') as one of the recipients of the grant.

---

77  WAM 17484A, and see also WAM 4873. There are a number of different possibilities about what may have happened in the negotiations between the litigants, but the above appears to me the most likely.
78  WAM 17496. John's action was by writ of *'mort d'ancestor'*, the form of action introduced by Henry II to resolve issues as to a disputed estate on the death of an 'ancestor', see p. 67 n. 20 above. He conceded Joan's claim by quit-claiming his own: but this conceals the other terms of the compromise.
79  See App. F, at p. 412 ff. Joan la Vinitière and Alice la Saucère (see pp. 280 n.70, and 346 n. 80 below) were two widows who each survived to save her husband's business and to inherit and/or build an empire of her own. But the Black Death, in mid-century, put an end to such empire-building.
80  WAM 4875. This makes it clear that at least part of the Mayfair area was included. Ossulston was a large south-west field in modern Mayfair (see map on Plate 23) and at least some of the land so let extended as far as the Tyburn (which was revealingly called the 'torrent', *torrens*, in the charter).

It looks as if the abbey was now satisfied with their original tenant Hugh, and was therefore prepared to extend the letting to include at least the next generation as well. This is hardly surprising since Sir Hugh was eminently suitable, having first become one of King Henry III's financial clerks, and being now one of Edward I's trusted advisers and also a canon of St. Paul's.[81]  In repeating the grant, Abbot Walter carefully ensured that the abbey was also given an express right to 'repair and cleanse the abbey's underground watercourse *(aqueduct)"* within the lands so let. This confirms that the abbey had a sophisticated pipe system for its water supply, but because of the geography it is not clear whether this came direct from the Tyburn, or from the 'springs' which helped to feed the Westbourne river in the present Paddington area, or perhaps both.[82]

The two families – of John of the Hyde, and Sir Hugh of Kendal – did not have a monopoly of the land in the present Hyde Park and Mayfair districts, because several other holders of lands in the area, such as 'William, son of John of Padington' (who had provided some of the land of the Kendals), 'Alexander the Carpenter' and others can also be identified.[83]  But there is little doubt that the Hydes and Kendals were the major holders, and Sir Hugh certainly increased his existing holdings by (so far as we know) at least another five acres. It may also be that he or

his son bought out the Hydes entirely in the early years of the 1300s, because later in 1315 when, after Sir Hugh's death, his son John of Kendal disposed of the family lands (by exchanging them wholesale for other lands in Harrow in Middlesex and Watford in Hertfordshire, supplied by their purchasers), his property was described as 'all his lands and tenements at La Hyde in Eye'.[84]  This was the first time they were described as being *'at La Hyde'* itself, rather than 'near La Hyde'. The new purchasers of the combined Kendal lands in Eye were another clerk, Master John of Pelham, and Denise of Wederhale who had three sons, although it is not certain who their father was.[85]  But that's another story, for the next century.

### (d) Richard Woolward – John the Convert and his wife Joan – Henry of Westminster

After Richard Woolward's death by 1293, some of his interests in houses in the enclave near the king's gate had been changing hands. Firstly in 1293, his son John at once sold to another prominent couple, John the Convert (*le Convers*) and his wife Joan, a rent of 20s. which his father had been receiving from Ralph the Vintner for a house which Woolward had let to Ralph.[86]  Secondly, Woolward had apparently in the past acquired (probably from Hugh Marshal) an interest in one of the Cardoils' houses and had been drawing a rent

---

81  See WAMs 16269 and 13880. Hugh had been busy on tax assessment for King Henry in 1271 before the king's death in the following year, see Powicke, *H. III and Ld. Edw.*, pp. 567-8.

82  See *The Westminster Corridor*, pp. 41-44. Since, in a contemporary document (see n. 80 above), the Tyburn was called a 'torrent', the doubts which have been expressed (by Barton, *Lost rivers of London*, p. 36) about the absence of any flow in that river may themselves be doubted.

83  WAMs 4834, 4874, 4881 and 4883. John of Padington had been a customary tenant of the manor of Eye, see DS, *Eye A/cs*, pp. 5, 11, 16.  Cf. the earlier 'Padington' family, at pp. 92 ff. above.

84  WAM 4883. So there were a house or houses and other buildings on the combined estate, including of course the farm buildings of the *curia* which had belonged to John of the Hyde before his death in 1280-81.

85  John of Pelham was the rector of St. Bride's (Fleet Street) & a citizen of London. Later charters in the C14 make it clear that the Pelhams did have the Hyde estate, including eg. a 'messuage called La Hyde near Knightsbridge', see eg. WAMs 16232 and 4767. The Pelhams & Kendals had made a clear 'swap' of their respective lands, but they provided also that the Pelhams (plus sons) were to have all the crops & chattels at La Hyde, as well as the corn in their grange at Pinner (Harrow) etc., see WAM 4871 and 4872. The sons or their survivors also had legal 'remainders' over the lands and tenements.

86  WAMs 17475 and 17547. John also became known as the *convers* 'of Westminster'.

of 8s. from it, but his son John now also sold that rent to the same Convert family. Thirdly, Woolward had also acquired a rental interest in a house by the king's gate which had been occupied by Thomas, the king's 'cofferer' or household treasurer, and either Woolward before his death, or his son John after it, sold this rental interest of 16s. pa, again to John the Convert and Joan.[87] It looks as if Richard Woolward had been following a deliberate policy of buying up all the local properties near the king's gate which he could.

John the Convert was probably one of the Jews whose conversion to Catholicism had been an active object of royal policy in the 1230s, when King Henry III had endowed and built a special home, the *Domus Conversorum* for converted Jews, in the Templars' 'New Street' (now Chancery Lane) on the site where the later (now 'old') Public Record Office was built. This road had recently been made when the Knights Templar moved their English headquarters from the Old Temple to the New Temple.[88]

If John was indeed a converted Jew, then by reason of his altered status he was no longer subject to the special taxations and other duress which King Henry was liable to inflict on the Jews whenever he was in financial straits, nor to the periodical pogroms which citizens in London and other towns carried out in troubled periods; still less to the later tallages and other discriminations under Edward I, which culminated in that king's edict of 1290 ordering the expulsion from England of all still-practising Jews.[89]

More significantly, John the Convert was himself employed in the king's service, as a royal serjeant.[90] On occasions he even acted as an envoy travelling to distant places on the king's business.[91] In the period around 1290 he was appointed as deputy of the underage keeper of the palace at Westminster by the king, and later in the early years of the 1300s was again given control of the palace as a deputy.[92]

Apart from his many Westminster properties, which included houses in the Strand near the old Stone Cross, John the Convert was also building up property interests in the manor of Knightsbridge and Westbourne, and for long had been a regular witness to Knightsbridge charters. For at least twenty years, from 1291 until 1310, he also held a significant area of land in the manor of Eye, let to him by the abbot, as a 'farm', for 7s. 6d. rent each year, plus two more small farms 'for life' in and after 1300.[93]

---

87   WAM 17547. So the total rents sold to the Converts amounted to 44s. John of Cardoil appears to have died by this time, and his son was reorganising his estate. His mother Juliana, probably as a widow, appeared later to be living in a house on the west side of 'King Street' in 1297 (see WAM 17482) and also to have had some interest in Eye in 1295-6, where she was subject to a distraint (see DS *Eye A/cs*, 97).

88   Later the king even procured the help of Abbot Crokesley in relation to his converted Jews, see *Cal. Cl. R*, 1247-51, pp. 238 and 260. One of the earliest 'keepers' of the House of Converts was a prominent resident in Charing Street, Stephen of the Strand, see pp. 40 n.75 above and 289-90 below. For the Templars' move, see pp. 42. Records from the old PRO in Chancery Lane have since been moved to the new one at Kew.

89   Eg. Henry III ordered a census of Jews in 1240, with huge forced tallages on them in that year and again in the later 1240s and early 1250s. Citizens of London killed and looted Jews in the civil war disturbances between 1263 and 1268. With their expulsion in 1290, Edward I could no longer rely on the Jews for money, and then had to depend on general taxation or to borrow money from Italian bankers. See Powicke, *H. III and Lord Edw*, pp. 310-313, and Prestwich, *Edw. I*, pp. 343-346.

90   He is so described in WAM 16202, and in *Cal. P. R.* 1266-72, p. 455.

91   One curious royal task he (and three others) were given was to excavate for treasure which the king had been told was buried at or near St. Martin's church at Charing, see *Cal. P. R*, 1292-1301, p. 479; the result is unknown.

92   See Clay, 'Keepership of the Palace', 59 EHR (1944), pp. 12-13.

93   See *Cal. P. R.* 1266-1272, p. 455 (for his houses in the Strand, which were all made free of livery, by the king's order in 1270); and eg. temp. Edw I, WAMs 16201, 16202, 16203, 17562, 17563 (for land in KNB); and 16261, 16246, 16191, 16280, 16269, 16364 (for some of his appearances as a witness in KNB and Westbourne). See also pp. 345-7 below, and DS, *Eye A/cs*, pp. 42, 63, 81, 109, 122, 132, 136, 150, 163, 186,

A further twist to the knots by which these families of Westminster were binding themselves together was that John the Convert and his wife Joan inherited all the property of Henry of Westminster, after Henry (the son of Master Alexander the king's carpenter) had died. It looks as if Henry, a royal clerk and later keeper of the palace, may have been Joan's father.[94] Henry had clearly acquired land and buildings for himself, and had previously inherited extensive properties from his father, the royal carpenter. Whatever the family connection was, the inheritance which John and Joan together received from him was so considerable that they appear to have decided to transfer some of it and also some of their own existing estates to their daughter, Alice who had married, or was about to marry 'William of Sandford, of Fulham'.

The charters by which the Convert parents conveyed these properties to their daughter Alice and her bridegroom reveal that Henry of Westminster's main establishment – his 'houses, gardens, roads and paths' – had been at or near Clousbridge, the bridge where the Clowson stream was crossed by 'King Street'. This large complex of property was now bestowed by John the Convert and his wife Joan on their daughter Alice and William of Sandford, together with some other lands in both Westminster and the adjoining manor of Chelsea, plus the annual income of 44s. from various rents in Westminster. These rents were all derived from the houses near the king's gate in which Richard Woolward had acquired interests, under his policy of making local

acquisitions, before their ultimate sale by his son to John the Convert and his wife.[95]

### 6. Sir John of Benstead, king's clerk, and his estate of Rosamund's

One of the closest advisers of King Edward I in the final fifteen years of his reign was John of Benstead, whom the king called 'our clerk who stays continually by our side'. He first served his time in the king's wardrobe, the royal secretarial and financial office, learning its practices and becoming its controller in 1295. Put in charge also of the privy seal as its keeper, he became 'one of the most active of all Edward's clerks'.[96] He served as the king's personal secretary, responsible, among other duties, for writing his letters as dictated, or himself drafting them as ordered and in effect 'signing' them with the king's privy seal. Apart from other financial rewards for all these services he received gifts of many benefices, other ecclesiastical preferments all over the country and considerable estates.[97]

When in Westminster, he had his own residence, the house with adjoining lands known by the name of 'Rosamunds' (sometimes, 'Rosemount'). It stood among the fields lying south east of the site on which Buckingham Palace now stands, probably on parts of the sites of the present Birdcage Walk and the Wellington Barracks. The house fronted towards the road which led from Tothill across the Eybridge towards the village of Eye, and it was at that point that one of the toll gates was located at which merchants and other visitors to the fairs of Westminster had to pay their entrance tolls.[98]

199, 214, 227, 240, 254, and WAM 4779 (1306) for his lands in Eye. There was a second, later John *le Convers*, nearer mid-C14; there may even have been three, see also p. 414.

94  See *Cal. Cl. R.*, 1279-88, p. 483, for Henry of Westminster's role as keeper of the palace. For Alexander, see pp. 253 ff.

95  See WAMs 17544, 17547 and 17475. The lands in Chelsea (see also VCH *Mdx* 12/107) included a house, at least ten acres of meadow and other land. It appears from the terms of WAM 17547 that there may also have been a tie of family relationship between the Woolwards and the Converts. But Wm. of Sandford died before May 1304, and Alice then restored one property to her father (in exchange for another), see WAM 17491. One Sandford family held the manor of Tyburn and a royal chamberlainship, see *The Westminster Corridor* p. 42.

96  *Cal. Cl. R.* 1296-1302, p. 602, and Prestwich, *Edward I*, p. 142.

97  *Cal. P. R.* 1292-130, pp. 57, 147, 223, 248, 249; Kingsford, 'Jo. de Benstede', in *Essays for Poole*, p. 332.

98  For this road and the Rosamund's estate, see pp. 49-51 above; and *Survey of London*, vol. XIII, p. 258; *Cal. P. R.*, 1307-13, p. 58. The road later became known as 'St. James's Street', then just 'James's Street'

Benstead must also have been granted a wider area of land, presumably near the site of Rosamunds, amounting apparently to 53 acres in Westminster, held from the abbey, and a further 45 acres in the manor of Eye, across the bed of the Tyburn, held from the king.[99]

Rosamunds had apparently become recognised as, in effect, a sub-manor of Westminster and included much supporting land, as well as the house with its own grounds. There, on those occasions when John Benstead was working with the king in Westminster, he could escape the hurly-burly of the town and find quietness closer to the fields of Eye and also to La Neyte, the country house to which the abbot could now habitually resort. In addition to the land held with his house, he had acquired other land in Eye, including a few half-acre strips in a nearby field which was appropriately called 'Shortespottes', and other arable land elsewhere. It seems that even this busy confidant of the king could become involved in small local matters as well.[105]

In the later years of King Edward's reign, we know that (as could be expected) John Benstead habitually enjoyed the abbot's generosity with gifts of produce from the manor of Eye. The clerk probably kept plenty of his own horses at Rosamunds, and in some years for which we have manorial accounts for Eye, Abbot Walter of Wenlock was giving him gifts of oats and hay for his horses, mown in the neighbouring field of Longemore which bordered the Tyburn.[101] In another year (1303-4), presumably in some unusual emergency, the abbot lent him four horses for a period of 21 days, and also gave him gifts of a bull and three cows.[102] We also know that in a previous year Benstead had been a guest at the abbot's table at La Neyte, a favour which was probably quite usual for him.[103]

But of course Abbot Walter was not a disinterested donor or host, since Benstead was a close adviser of King Edward, wielding influence at the palace and himself likely to become a royal justice. In accordance with accepted practices in the thirteenth century, he could be influenced favourably towards the abbey in administrative or legal matters, by such friendly gestures from the abbot.[104] In view of his associations with the abbey it was understandable that, after the deaths of both the old king and Abbot Walter in 1307, the new king Edward II when ordering a judicial inquiry about the recent and violent dissensions in the abbey should include John Benstead among the justices who were to investigate such scandals and the disarray and dilapidation at the abbey to which they had led.[105]

However Benstead's work had lain entirely with the king and often led him far from Westminster, accompanying the king or carrying out for him both continental and less distant missions in Scotland and elsewhere, or visiting his own estates in many of the home counties.

and is now 'Buckingham Gate'. Other toll gates for the fair were stationed at Tothill, Charing Cross, the palace wharf, see Rosser, *Med. Westminster*, pp. 104-5; and perhaps at Endiff wharf as well. There were at least seven gates or more in all, clearly designed to catch all comers. But not much toll was collected, it seems, at the Rosamunds gate. For the fairs, see pp. 204-5, 212 above and 308 below.

99	Kingsford, 'Jo. de Benestede', *ibid*, pp. 342-343.

100	WAMs 17560, 4826, 17610.

101	eg. DS, *Eye A/cs*, pp. 138, 141, 147, 165. In 1310, after Abbot Walter's death, even John Benstead had to buy his hay, *ibid.*, p. 256, and could not rely on further gifts.

102	*Ibid*, pp. 212 and 213.

103	WAM 24502. Benstead and John of Droxford, the keeper of the royal wardrobe, another beneficiary of the abbot's generosity, dined with him at La Neyte and were entertained by his minstrels. Like Benstead, Droxford received gifts of hay from the abbot, and also bought hay from Eye, eg. DS *Eye A/cs*, pp. 133, 165, 173, 174, 182, and p. 359 below. I am not certain if Droxford had a house in Westminster or Eye, but he probably did.

104	See eg. Harvey, *Walter de Wenlok*, pp. 30-33 for some of the justices who received regular 'annuities' or presents from the abbot at that time; and Pearce, *Walter de Wenlock*, pp. 90-5.

105	WAM 12777. For the dissensions and the abbot's death, see chapter 18, mainly at pp. 319 ff.

In 1305 Benstead was freed from his duties as controller in the king's wardrobe and was appointed to the office of chancellor at the exchequer. When the old king finally died, Benstead was still in that post. Early in Edward II's reign he abandoned his clerical orders and became a knight and a justice of the Bench, continuing also for many more years to enjoy royal favour and to be sent on national assignments abroad, to Gascony and elsewhere.

### 7. Sir John of Foxley, first an 'abbot's man' and then a 'king's man'

Unlike John Benstead who remained a steady 'king's man' throughout his career, John Foxley began his working life in the sole service of Abbot Walter of Wenlock, who had no doubt selected him for his good judgment and efficiency. While employed by Abbot Walter of Wenlock, Foxley had held the principal position in the abbot's service for at least twenty years, from 1286 (or before) until 1306, and as such had become known to the king. His post had been the abbot's 'steward of the lands', ie. of those manors which the abbot had retained under the agreements previously made between each of the three abbots named Richard and the convent during the middle of the century.[106] For this whole period John Foxley oversaw all the abbot's estates, acting as the abbot's factotum, and also had the task, with the help of the 'steward of the abbot's household', of seeing that every arrangement was made, and all necessary stores were available, for the abbot at whichever manor he might be visiting or residing.[107]

Foxley's main residence seems to have been at his own manor at Bray in Berkshire which he held from the king. However so much of his time, during his years of service,

must have been spent in liaison with the abbot himself that it is highly likely that he had accommodation provided for him at or near the abbot's country house, La Neyte, or in Eye, or elsewhere in Westminster. Only nine of his written instructions addressed to the reeves or other officials in the abbot's various manors have fortuitously survived for us to see; but of these, four such letters or 'writs' were sent from 'Westminster', one from Bray, and the other four from outlying manors where he happened to be on his journeys around the abbot's whole estate.[108] Over the twenty years of his service for the abbot, John Foxley must have issued vastly more than the nine written instructions which happen to have survived, and many of the missing ones must also have required his presence in Westminster. It would surely have been impossible for him to perform his duties in Westminster without having a residential base in that area.[109]

Moreover the manorial accounts for the manor of Eye confirm that John Foxley was often present in the area of Westminster and Eye, providing paid services of supervision within both manors on the abbot's behalf, or receiving gifts or purchases of hay, corn or animals. For example, in 1291-92 he received the sum of 12s. 4d. as 'expenses of his visits' in the administration of the manor of Eye. Or in 1300-01, in payment for some work done 'at the time of the (Westminster) fair', he and the steward of the abbot's household at La Neyte received one quarter and four bushels of wheat and six pigs from the stock of the manor of Eye. And in 1301-2 five cartloads of hay were provided exclusively 'for the use of John of Foxle' from the great demesne meadow called Market Mead in Eye.[110] Hay was the

---

106  For these agreements (usually called 'compositions') and their results, see pp. 195 ff. (Abbot Berking); 212-4 ff. (Abbot Crokesley); and 226-7 ff. (Abbot Ware). Foxley's fee for his stewardship was 20 marks pa. until 1299 when it was raised to £20; he was of course paid all the expenses of his work as well.
107  For the abbot's household arrangements when journeying, see pp. 300 ff. below.
108  Harvey, *Walter of Wenlok*, pp. 147-150, writs 326-334, spasmodically spread over a period of six years, 1292-98, with three years within that period not even represented once. Other writs which have not survived are referred to from time to time in the various financial accounts of the abbot's manors, eg. DS, *Eye A/cs*, p. 120.
109  Much later in life, Foxley (? his son, with the same name) had had a house in Tothill St, WAM 17650 (1349).
110  DS, *Eye A/cs*, pp. 47, 158, 162, 165. There are many similar examples in other accounts. On one later occasion (in 1310, after Abbot Walter's death), the roles were reversed as John Foxley was the provider of

subject of frequent gifts, and these suggest that John Foxley had his own residence and land either in the rural parts of Westminster, or in Eye nearer to his employer – unless these were to be carted all the way to Berkshire.

Apart from all the humdrum problems of his duties on the abbatial estates, the steward also performed other skilled tasks for his lord, such as masterminding a piece of litigation in the court of King's Bench to recover loans which the abbot had made earlier, through selling corn on credit. To recover his loans of 88 marks (£58 13s. 4d.) in the action, the abbot had to provide John Foxley on three occasions in 1295 with costs and fees amounting to a total of £26 8s. 4d., and even then, having procured a judgment from the court, the abbot still had to obtain execution against the main debtor's land and chattels in order to recover his money.[111] The steward also carried out tasks such as 'delivering the gaol' of Westminster, holding courts and entertaining members of the Westminster bench of justices or the exchequer on behalf of the abbot.[112]

In an earlier legal action in 1292 Foxley had had to appear himself as a defendant, together with the abbot and Philip the bailiff of Westminster, before the justices in eyre sitting at the Stone Cross in the Strand. A claim had been made against them by one of the abbey's serjeants, Richard atte Water or *de Aqua,* that he had been wrongfully ejected by the defendants from the gatehouse of the abbey and prevented from drawing his daily corrody of food, drink and hay and a yearly pension of six shillings. There was no dispute that the serjeant was entitled to all these benefits, provided he performed all his duties; but the real issue was whether or not he was also bound to keep the custody of those who

were imprisoned in the abbot's gaol within the gatehouse. Richard atte Water had maintained that he did not have to guard the prisoners as well, but only the gate. So John Foxley had been called on by the abbot to help the bailiff to eject Richard, on the grounds that his duties did include the custody of the prisoners as well as the gate. The court held that the serjeant's duties did include the custody of the prisoners, so that the ejection and prevention were justified. In the face of this, the serjeant had to agree to perform his twofold duties in order to keep his benefits.[113]

Well before Abbot Walter of Wenlock's death on Christmas eve in 1307, John Foxley was already known to the king, and had indeed been singled out by him for preferment and perhaps for later royal employment. He had been knighted before the 29th September of that year, when he was already being described as a *'miles'.* Indeed in the even earlier farm accounts for Eye in 1305-6 he had been given the title of *'dominus',* a title not previously used for him.[114]

Sure enough, as soon as the old abbot was dead, it was Sir John Foxley whom the new king Edward II appointed to the office of keeper of the abbot's temporal possessions during the vacancy, and Foxley remained in control of them for over two years while the former disputes between the old abbot and his prior were still being fought out. Finally on the 25 April 1310 Foxley was ordered by the king to restore control of the abbot's 'temporalities', his secular assets, to the new abbot.[115] Meanwhile however he had been made a baron of the exchequer in 1309, and thereafter remained at work both at the exchequer in the palace and on frequent royal assignments until shortly before he died in 1324.

     four horses, five foals and ten oxen, and the manor of Eye the recipient – the animals may have come from his own manor of Bray, DS *Eye A/cs,* p. 263A. For Market Mead, see pp. 336 and 356-9.

111   See Harvey, *W. of Wenlok,* pp. 68 and n.-70, writs 55, 57, 58 and 63. John Foxley has been described as 'one of the most successful of the Abbot's servants', Pearce, *Walter of Welock,* p. 86.

112   See Pearce, *W. of Wenlok,* p. 88. 'Delivering' the gaol meant dealing with all the cases of the prisoners in it.

113   Horwood (ed) *Year Books of reign of Edw. I,* Nos 21-22, pp. 576-586; WAD 92a-b.

114   For *'miles'* (a knight), see Pearce, *ibid.,* p. 86 and WAM 580. The *'dominus'* title was also used in the accounts for 1307-8, WAM 26848.

115   *Cal. P. R.,* 1307-13, p. 225; WAM 5435/C

Plate 17. This and the following Plate are rare pictures, shown here by permission of the Masters of the Bench of the Inner Temple, of medieval courts in action in Westminster Hall. They are dated to about 1460, much later than 1307, the end of the period of this book; but they can help to evoke the atmosphere of such courts at this earlier date. This court is the Court of the King's Bench, in which criminal cases were tried. The presence of a bench of justices (originally this had included the king himself); the clerks writing the records on parchment 'Rolls'; two serjeants in their white coifs (and, in 1460, green and blue robes) arguing at each other; the staff of the court with their rods of office; and the accused people (already in chains); all these would have been familiar, or at least becoming familiar, in court in the thirteenth century.

See pp. 67-69; and for members of the incipient legal profession, pp. 175, 289, 291 and 412, n.4.

Plate 18. See caption for Plate 17. This court was the Court of Common Pleas in 1460, in which civil actions between private individuals and/or public bodies or representative figures (eg. the abbey or the abbot) were heard. In the late twelfth and early thirteenth centuries it had first been known as the 'Bench' and was designed (and had then been ordered by Magna Carta) to sit in 'a fixed place' (Westminster), and therefore not 'to follow the king' when he was travelling the country. For an illustrious bench of named justices in one case in 1185, when the abbey recovered land in Paddington by compromise, see pp. 92-4.

Plate 19. Seen here is the base of the magnificent new shrine for St. Edward, pictured by David Gentleman. It had been decorated by the Cosmati workmen with their special stone patterning, and was topped by the shrine itself, which had been designed, built in wood and gold, and embellished with jewels, while the abbey was being built. The sick were brought and lodged in the niches of the base for healing.

Plate 20. The completion of the great tomb built by Edward I for his father Henry III. It has been decorated by new Cosmati workmen and is now being crowned with Henry's bronze-gilt effigy made by Torel the goldsmith. This was Henry's second and grander tomb, to which his body was moved by Edward. See also Plate 15(a), p. 258.

Plate 21.  A reading of scripture or a passage from the Benedictine 'Rule' takes place before the chapter of monks in the new Chapter House, with the central pillar, the lectern and the reader surrounded by a sea of tiles. Before the Chapter House was built the monks may have met in the refectory, and it was sometimes recorded that on solemn occasions the monks stood round with candles lit in their hands. See pp. 172, 174 and 227.

Plate 22. Almost all the early stained glass created during the rebuilding of the abbey was removed during the civil war in the seventeenth century, at a time when the abbey was abandoned. The only panels surviving are six small but beautiful medallions. Four of them are shown here: above, the Pentecost and the Ascension; below, the massacre of the Holy Innocents by Herod and the martyrdom of St. Alban. See p. 267 and cf. the local church of the Holy Innocents, at pp. 37-39.

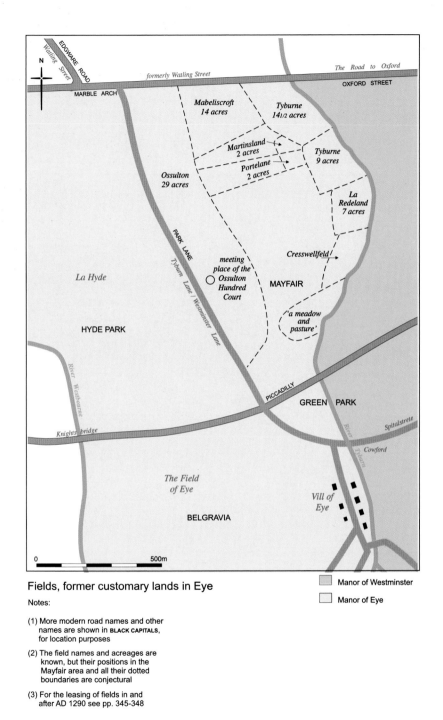

**Fields, former customary lands in Eye**

Notes:

(1) More modern road names and other
names are shown in **BLACK CAPITALS**,
for location purposes

(2) The field names and acreages are
known, but their positions in the
Mayfair area and all their dotted
boundaries are conjectural

(3) For the leasing of fields in and
after AD 1290 see pp. 345-348

Manor of Westminster

Manor of Eye

Plate 23. Map B. Fields and former customary lands in Eye

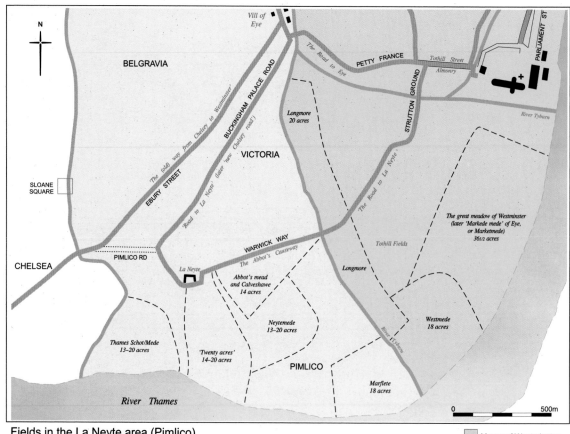

**Fields in the La Neyte area (Pimlico)**

Notes:

(1) More modern road names and other names are shown in **BLACK CAPITALS**, for location purposes

(2) Unlike the northern area of Eye (Mayfair), La Neyte provides little evidence of ever having held customary tenants

(3) The field names, and a variety of acreages for the fields, are known. Most of the fields' approximate positions can be inferred from evidence; but the lines and shapes of their boundaries are conjectural

Manor of Westminster

Manor of Eye

Plate 24.  Map C. Fields in the La Neyte area (Pimlico)

### 8. *Stephen de Stranda, and Gerin of St Giles*

In contrast with the king's and abbot's more conventional officers, who had regular posts and titles in eg. the exchequer or abbey departments, there were residents of Westminster who appear to have been more independent: on the one hand, prepared to work for king or abbot when their services were required but, on the other hand, having more outside interests and concerns of their own than the purely administrative members of Westminster society. One such person was Stephen of the Strand, whose milieu was, as his locative name shows, some distance from the core area of Westminster near the abbey and palace. Another was Gerin the linendraper, also a more distant resident of the neighbouring enclave and parish of St. Giles, who in the course of his work had much to do with the abbey and some of the convent's manors.

Stephen lived during the first half of the century and was a man of many colours. We do not hear of his father, but his mother was Alice la Blunde, perhaps a member of one of the great Blund families of London, and she too had lived on the Strand road leading from the city. In 1236 she sold a messuage there to the king's clerk, Henry of Westminster, who was starting to amass his own group of properties.[116] Stephen, who had his own house in the same road, was a clerk, with sufficient knowledge of the law and its practices to enable him both to act as an advocate and proctor for others in the courts, and also to take part successfully himself in property-

dealing and in actions in the king's court about his own empire of lands and houses.

Stephen's legal work was such that he has been named as a possible member of the earliest group of legal 'pleaders', or 'serjeants at law', who can be identified in the first half of the thirteenth century as emerging specialists in the oral pleading by which civil legal actions were 'opened' in court. This group of 'lawyers' were probably the first pioneers of a regular legal profession which by 1300 can be recognised as having come into being, together with 'professional attorneys' as another group.[117]

When we first meet him in 1219, his wife Matilda already held (in her own right, which was being disputed by a third party) a messuage 'in Stranda', and other houses and land in Aldewych.[118] Stephen was acting as attorney and in effect advocate for Matilda in that dispute, and in the same year was also acting for each of the Masters of the two leper Hospitals of St. James and St. Giles in two separate legal actions about land in the nearby small manor of Rugmere, just south of the present Primrose Hill area of Hampstead.[119] Thereafter his name appears, as himself a litigant this time, in at least five other legal cases about properties in Westminster and the other nearby manors of Hampstead, Hendon, Lilleston and Tiburn.[120]

Already he had been noticed by King Henry III, and in 1226 he was sent on a journey to Rome with Master Henry of Bisshopeston, as heralds on royal business at the court of Rome; and in the same year he was also sent

---

116  CP25(1) 146/10/140. For Henry of Westminster, son of Master Alexander, the royal carpenter, see above p. 285. Alice also held properties in Holborn and elsewhere, Williams, *Early Holborn*, §§ 399-400, 576.

117  Brand, *The making of the Common Law,* pp. 7, n. 21, and 11. The early serjeants formed an indistinct group in the early C13, some or all of whom were sometimes employed by the king when his own interests were in issue; and from the middle of the C14 the 'serjeants at law' remained a formal class of advocates from whom alone judges were appointed, until 1875 when no more serjeants were created. See p. 175 above.

118  CP25(1) 146/5/8. So although a clerk, Stephen had a wife; and she seems to have been a neighbour and heiress.

119  CP25(1) 146/5/9 and 12, (St. James's and St. Giles's Hospitals); For Rugmere, see *The Westminster Corridor,* pp. 107n. and 127 and Map A, after p. 96, (where it is marked only as 'R'). Not always successful, Stephen is recorded as being fined once by the court 'for his foolish talk' *(pro stultiloquio suo);* a useful remedy; and on another occasion he was sacked as attorney. A serjeant 'at law' (if he was one) could act also as an attorney.

120  CP25(1) 146/7/64 (Westminster); WAD 567 and CRR 12/130, para. 648 (Hampstead); CP25(1) 146/7/72 (Hendon); CRR 15/764 (Lilleston); CRR 15/127 and CP25(1)8/146/102 (Tiburn). For Hampstead, see also p. 374.

to Southampton and Portsmouth on other royal business, to arrest foreign merchants and their goods.[121] Later in about 1233, (together with 'Joscius, son of Peter', a citizen and, then or later, an alderman of the London ward of Newgate and Ludgate) Stephen accepted a post as one of two keepers of the 'House of Converts' which King Henry had just established in 'New Street' (now Chancery Lane), to house and help those former Jews who had been won over under the king's campaign to convert them to Christianity.[122] To begin with, Stephen could apparently still pursue his other interests as well, but he seems to have stopped acting at the House of Converts fairly soon in about 1234.

In the area immediately north of the Strand, Stephen held various pieces of land which he had bought from one of his neighbours, Christiana of the Godegrom family – a family whose members were also established residents in that location.[123] Two arable acres of these lands (with their crops included), which lay next to the 'great garden of the monks', were donated by Stephen 'in soul alms' to the new chapel of the Virgin Mary at the abbey in the 1240s. For her part, Christiana donated 'in soul alms' the 2d rent, which she was entitled to receive (now from the fund of that chapel) for these two acres, to the *'hospitaria of the monks of Westminster'*, meaning presumably the hospice at or near the church of the Holy Innocents on the Strand at that time.[124] Apparently Stephen also donated to St. Mary's altar at least one other acre of land in the same area, which he had also

bought from a Godegrom source.[125] His connections with the abbey ensured that he acted as a witness to a number of charters executed or registered in the abbot's courts, but clearly he was also taking an active part in other business and legal work in Westminster and Bloomsbury.

While Stephen of the Strand lived through much of the first half of the thirteenth century, Gerin the linendraper was a man of the second half. His father William had been a linendraper with a house and shop said to have stood on the curving high street of St Giles, and since Gerin was also known as 'le lynendraper' (and not just as 'Lynendraper', as a surname), it is possible that he too may have also practised for a while in the drapery business, even if he found more adventurous pursuits as 'Gerin of St. Giles' *(de Sancto Egidio)* in the acquisition of properties.

Like Stephen, Gerin was an educated man, a clerk who was capable of acting on his own in holding legal courts and inquiries in various nearby manors on behalf of the convent of monks at the abbey.[126] It was unfortunate for him that he eventually became notorious as being implicated in the great burglary of the king's treasure at the abbey in 1303, but well before that time he had been providing useful and responsible services for both the convent and the abbot. Such posts included even his despatch to the court of Rome on abbey business, and acting on behalf of the abbot in other legal business at Colchester and Feering (Essex) against the sheriff of Essex.[127] He also had been sent on various negotiating errands,

---

121 *Cal. P. R.*, 1225-32, p. 17, *Rot. Litt. Claus.* 1224-6, pp. 136b, 144b and 99.
122 *Cal. Cl. R.* 1231-34, p. 246, etc. For the *Domus Conversorum* and 'John the Convert', see p. 284 above. For Joscius as alderman, see *Cal. Cl. R.*, ibid, p. 494 and Williams, *Early Holborn*, §§ 693-4, et al.
123 WAM 17548 (20s paid by Stephen). Cf. WAM 17424, and pp. 38 and 40 above.
124 WAMs 17539 and 17542. (Cf. WAM 17145.) Although Christiana's donation was a charitable one 'in soul alms', she was in fact paid 12d. for it by Robert the 'chaplain of the Innocents', also called the *'hospitarius'*. This sequence of transactions had the unusual result that the chapel fund now had to pay 2d. pa. to another part of the abbey, namely the *'hospitaria'*. For the *hospitaria*, see p. 38 above.
125 WAM 17424.
126 He is called a clerk in WAM 26682 (re Ashford). For his other courts and inquiries on behalf of the abbey, at Aldenham, Kelvedon and Battersea, see WAMs 26038, 25601 and 27505.
127 WAM 25599.

together with a monk colleague, on other abbey business in distant places such as Scotland and York.[128] So that he would make himself available when required for such services, the abbey was paying him a retaining fee at the rate of 20s. pa. Meanwhile he had been picking up properties in Westminster and surrounding counties.

In 1286 Gerin had obtained a lease, for 14 years, of a large holding in the area later known as Belsize in the manor of Hampstead. It consisted of a messuage, about 40 acres of arable land and some woodland; and this holding was already in his possession, having been his father's before him under an earlier lease. Seven years later his title to all or part of this Hampstead land was challenged by a man called John Turpin, but Gerin successfully defended it. He was also able to acquire another lease of other land in the south-eastern part of Belsize.[129]

But Gerin's interest in land did not stop at Hampstead, and when he came in 1299 to dispose (for reasons which we do not know) of a large estate which he had by now accumulated, it included lands in Tiburn manor, Kentish Town, Westminster, and St Giles, as well as his Hampstead lands.[130] Earlier he had also sold to the Hospital of St. Giles a number of separate parcels of land around St. Giles, by exchanging them for two acres of other nearby land in 'La Pytancecroft' held by the Hospital.[131]

When the sensational burglary at the abbey took place in 1303, some of the 'jurymen' who gave evidence alleged that Gerin was an accomplice of the main villains and had carried a basket of stolen treasure valued at £200, first from the abbey to his own house at St. Giles and then to the fields of Kentish Town, at a place called Haggehedge, where he was said to have abandoned it – and that it was duly found there by a shepherd boy called Adam.[132] But another jury (the Middlesex jury) asserted that while Gerin was absent 'in a distant place', the basket of treasure had been taken to Gerin's house at St. Giles on the orders of two of the monks, in order to remove it from the vicinity of the abbey, and that when Gerin returned home a fortnight later, he found the treasure there and took it, or had it taken, to Haggehedge, wishing merely to avoid becoming implicated by the monks' action.[133] The exact truth is unascertainable. However Gerin suffered the same fate as the monks and was initially thrown into the Tower of London, but was later released, by royal grace rather than by acquittal.[134]

Again like Stephen of the Strand, Gerin has also been identified as one of the early professional lawyers, in his case as an attorney rather than a serjeant at law. In 1275, by the First Statute of Westminster, Edward I and his new parliament in that year had already started regulating the conduct of lawyers, by enacting that deception or collusion in a legal action by a professional serjeant at law, or 'anyone else', was an offence.[135] And by 1291 Gerin was at risk of imprisonment for just such an offence, presumably as a professional attorney caught by the 'anyone else' clause.[136]

---

128  WAMs 23631 ff. and 19838. In May 1298, Edward I (fighting the Scots) had moved the exchequer to York for over 6 years, to be conveniently closer to Scotland; Broome, in *Essays for Tout*, pp. 291 ff.
129  VCH *Mdx*. 9/95. See further p. 373 below.
130  WAD 119b-120, and CP25(1) 148/36/289. Gerin received 100 marks of silver for his estates. His former Belsize estate was acquired in due course by Sir Roger Brabazon the chief justice, see p. *ibid.* below.
131  WAM 17556.
132  Palgrave (ed), *Ancient Kalendars*, i. App., pp. 262, 266-7, 286, 292. For the burglary, which played such a part in the history of the abbey, see pp. 314 ff. below.
133  *Ibid*, pp. 279, 281-2.
134  See *ibid*, p. 269; and p. 317 n. 30 below. See further Pearce, *W. de Wenlok*, pp. 159-161.
135  Brand, *The making of the Common Law*, p. 13 and n. 48. For the statute, see p. 223 above.
136  cf. pp. 175 and 289 above, for similar early 'lawyers'.

# CHAPTER 17

# Abbot Walter of Wenlock
## 1283-1307

With the death of Abbot Richard of Ware in 1283, the abbacies of 'the three Richards' had come to an end. Their successor, Walter of Wenlock, fitted into a different pattern. Gone was the close personal and business liaison between the king and abbot which had marked the previous 61 years. Although Edward I, after his coronation in 1274, had retained the services of Abbot Ware as one of his personal envoys and had finally made him his treasurer, the same king now made no such demands on Ware's successor.[1] However the relationship between king and abbot remained cordial, though less intimate than it had been between the previous abbots and Henry III; and the abbey itself lost little from the change, with royal favour continuing to flow.

So Walter of Wenlock, was to spend less time on royal affairs and more on those of the abbey, and to play a significant part in modernising some aspects of administration in the abbey and its estates. But he proved to be one of those abbots whose 'proud and inflexible spirit' was matched only by the 'contumacy' of some of his monks,[2] and it was these two opposing forces which ultimately marked his last years and particularly 1307, the year of his death, in a turbulent period within the abbey, of accusations, counter-accusations, appeals to Rome, and even a flurry of imprisonments and excommunications.[3]

In spite of the pride and inflexibility which on some occasions the new abbot showed towards his convent in Westminster, his background was not an aristocratic one. He hailed from western parts, and his father Philip was a fairly prosperous apothecary in the Shropshire town of Wenlock. Both Philip and his wife Agnes were still alive when their son received the great honour of election as abbot at Westminster; but Philip had then died three years after Walter was elected. The abbot's mother lived for about another thirteen years, and probably carried on her husband's business, because she too became known as 'Agnes the apothecary'. The abbot's conduct towards his mother reveals none of the pride which he showed in his high ecclesiastical position. Throughout her widowhood, he looked after her constantly, sending small presents to her in Wenlock, visiting her when making progresses through his western manors and, in the autumn of 1289, even inviting her to visit him at his manors of Pyrford and Wandsworth in Surrey and finally to spend Christmas with him at Westminster, where she was able to view the new abbey and the high company which he had to keep.[4]

### The beginning of trouble
As a member of the Westminster convent, Walter of Wenlock had already served in a number of administrative positions in the abbey, although he had not had time to rise to the position of prior.[5] In December 1283 his election as abbot was completed quickly,

---

1   *Flete*, p. 116, asserts that, like Abbot Ware, Wenlock also became the royal treasurer, but the evidence suggests that this was not the case. He did become treasurer of Queen Eleanor's foundation, in Feb. 1286, see p. 305.
2   Miss Harvey, *WA Estates*, p. 99, has pointed out the 'inflexibility' and 'contumacy' which are evident from the dissensions between some of the abbots and their monks.
3   For this final explosion in the 'Days of Wrath', see pp. 319 ff. below.
4   For a colourful account of his relationship with his mother, see Pearce, *Walter of Wenlock*, pp. 49-59.
5   He had carried out work for the abbey in some of the nearer manors, including Knightsbridge; and this kind of work became an interest for him. See Pearce, *ibid.*, p. 3, and WAMs 26252-3, 25581, 26660, 16376.

scarcely three weeks after Abbot Richard of Ware had died.[6] During those three weeks, while he was still an ordinary monk, Wenlock must have been fully aware of what else was happening in the abbey. It had been an eventful period. In the absence of any abbot, the prior John of Coleworth and the rest of his monks had snatched the opportunity to formulate unilaterally and agree upon the terms of a long decree which they proposed to make, detailing the obligations which they required future abbots to comply with. Most of these obligations derived from the agreements already made between earlier abbots and their convents, but some of the articles in the decree were reformulations of those obligations and others were new.

Wenlock's election was made on the 31st December 1283. However, as an abbot elected but not yet confirmed by the pope, he so far had no official standing as 'the Abbot'. Two days later, in the new year, the proposed decree was formally executed 'in full chapter', in the recently-completed chapter house, by the prior and convent, with the convent's seal.[7] In accordance with its own terms, the decree was to be inscribed in the abbey's book of martyrology, and there read out each year, and all the monks were to swear an oath to observe all the agreements which had been made between the abbot and the convent, including the new decree. So before his election Walter of Wenlock probably took some part himself in the preceding negotiations within the convent about the terms of the decree, or at least he must have sworn on oath to abide by the decree (as was indeed later asserted in the recriminatory uproar at the end of his abbacy).[8] There is a certain irony in the fact

that he had, perhaps unwittingly, become involved in one way or the other in this new reformulation of 'duties' by which he himself would be bound, if and when he assumed a new formal identity as abbot.[9]

This unilateral decree which the convent had now made marked a clear shift in the relationships behind the extensive sharing-out of the abbey's possessions, upon which Abbot Richard of Berking had embarked in 1225. At that earlier time Abbot Richard had been freely conceding rights and assets, which had been *his* by Benedictine rule, to his deprived monks, and the monks were gratefully accepting his generosity and recording it. Now however the convent under Prior John of Coleworth had taken it upon themselves to redefine the abbot's 'duties' towards them under the division of assets, and were seeking to ensure that their interpretation of those duties would be binding upon future abbots, including their expected new one. The path leading towards this change had been becoming visible during the abbacies of the two intervening Richards, of Crokesley and of Ware, but a more serious shift in the relationship between abbot and monks had now become transparent.

It is hardly surprising, in view of the subsequent furore at the end of Walter of Wenlock's abbacy, that during the vacancy after *his* death in 1307 another opportunistic prior and a group of senior monks were to follow the example set 34 years before, in 1283/4, by Prior John of Coleworth and his convent. Early in 1308 a second and even more extensive unilateral decree, including other new provisions of their own making, was passed by them again defining the obligations which they conceived the abbot owed towards them.

6   *Flete*, pp. 115 and 116. He was elected unanimously, not by all the monks, but by 'compromission': by a group of seven monks chosen to make the decision, as a compromise between a number of equally favoured candidates.
7   No original document has survived, but the decree was copied later into the Westminster 'Domesday', WAD 638-639, printed in Harvey, *Wenlok*, pp. 229-33. To judge by its wording, the 'copy' does appear to be a copy of a genuine original.
8   See WAM 9497, and p. 322 below.
9   There are obviously fine legal points (which the abbot of course took in the later recriminations) about the 'capacity' in which he had or may have participated in the actual making of the decree or the binding procedures which it laid down.

There is no doubt that during the course of most of Wenlock's abbacy there were many individual disputes which arose between him and the convent as to whether he, or they, were infringing either one or more of the accepted terms, or some other additional right or rights which the convent laid claim to. And equally it is certain that each side was at fault on various occasions.

We can infer that on some of these occasions the abbot acted in a typically high-handed way, claiming rights which he regarded as belonging to him by virtue of the old Benedictine rule as to the primacy of the abbot. For example, it seems that without consulting or seeking the assent of the existing monks, he was in the habit of admitting new monks to profession; and appointing priests to vacant churches, without raising such matters in chapter; and would compromise legal actions about abbey property, without reference to the convent.[10]  Or again, he did not regard himself as bound by the rule laid down in the recent decree which he had sworn to abide by, that he should not employ any monk who was in charge of an abbey department to oversee the river walls which protected the abbey or other abbey property from floodings of the Thames.[11]  As regards all these and other similar situations, there were arguable legal issues which an 'inflexible spirit' such as his could rely on to justify his conduct, but neither the spirit nor such arguments promoted peace in a monastic house in which the monks now laid claim to enjoy extra rights.

But for their part, the monks also increased the underlying distrust by making additional claims for other rights which went well beyond those which had already been granted to them. After the abbot had promised to pay the sacrist £4 annually, to meet the special cost of spice for the convent, to be drawn from the rents of the fair at Westminster, he had to face a later claim from them, for half the profits of the fairs. The difference between the figures involved in this comparison was startling, since the receipts from the fair had reached nearly £90 or more, by about 1300, and were well over £100 shortly after Wenlock's death in 1307.[12]

Another cause of dissension arose after the abbey had received, in 1292, a munificent grant from King Edward of valuable lands from the estate of his beloved Queen Eleanor who had died in 1290. Ostensibly this endowment was to pay for the celebration of an 'anniversary' for Queen Eleanor, but for the king its munificence was to serve as a wider tribute to her memory. Subsequently the prior and convent claimed that after the costs of the 'anniversary' had been paid for, each year, it was they who were entitled to all the surplus income from the endowment, which should be divided (in money) among the monks themselves. This the abbot rejected, with good reason, until very shortly before his death, when he gave in to it, as we shall see.[13]

A further typically excessive demand which was being pressed by the convent against their abbot was a claim that when in 1299 he had successfully recovered, by

---

10 These are inferences from the fact that after his death the convent immediately insisted that for the future they should participate in such issues. See also Harvey, *W. of Wenlok*, p. 21.

11 The convent did not wish any of the river-wall costs to fall on them, since this was, and had always been, an obligation of the abbot, see p. 197 above.  But Wenlock did in fact employ monks as monk-wardens of the walls, see WAM 26868, Harvey, *ibid*, pp. 49 and 53, and p. 355 below.

12 Harvey, *ibid*, pp. 20, 98, 121, 169, 212; Rosser, *Med. Westminster*, pp. 101, 103-4. The claim by the convent for half the profits appears in the second unilateral decree made by the convent, ie. *after* Wenlock's death (Harvey, *ibid*, p. 239), but it seems probable that it had already been made against Wenlock during his last years, along with other extensive claims about properties, to some of which he eventually succumbed, see eg. *Flete*, pp. 116-7 and 118-9 and the later text below about the manor of Deerhurst, on p. 307.

13  For further details of this endowment, and the issues which it created between the abbot and the convent, see pp. 306 ff. below.   For the abbot's final concession on this issue, see p. 324 below.

purchase, possession of the valuable estate of Deerhurst (Gloucestershire) from the family who had been its long-sitting tenants since the twelfth century, he was obliged to assign it (for a rent of £60 pa.) to the convent, and even to agree to the sharing out of any surplus profits from it among the monks in the abbey. Having originally stood out against this claim, the abbot was apparently persuaded (by means unknown) to accede both to it, and also to their claims on Queen Eleanor's foundation, on the 18th December 1307. This was one week before he died, at a time when he was clearly ill and very near to his death which took place on Christmas night itself.[14] So again a still 'proud and inflexible spirit' was matched by an opposing 'contumacy', and in these instances was ultimately defeated by it. Whether the persuasion was lawful or not, it would be difficult to elucidate. However it so happened that in spite of Wenlock's surrender on this issue, and the inclusion of it in the convent's second unilateral decree, *after* his death, the convent's demand in relation to Deerhurst was in fact never implemented by him or his successors; and so in practice the convent went without.

### An abbot with a methodical and pragmatic turn of mind

An outstanding feature of Walter's abbacy was the more orderly discipline which he sought to impose upon abbey administration. This is particularly evident in those spheres of action in which as abbot he still had personal control. The monks, for their part, were by now comparatively independent within their own spheres, and this meant that

the abbot had less room to prescribe, though he might influence, their conduct and methods in those spheres.

But it can be no coincidence that a mass of documents have survived to show the efficiency which Abbot Walter sought to introduce into the administration both of those manors over which he still personally exercised complete control, and of his own household which was now principally based at his country house, his 'island' of La Neyte within his manor of Eye, next door to Westminster.[15] The survival itself of this evidence, however incomplete it may be, reflects the influence which his example must have had, because the documents are unique in their cumulative extent and in the methodical detail of medieval administration at the abbey which they disclose. Moreover the evidence reveals the personal character of the man.[16]

Foremost in this evidence is a collection of about 325 surviving brief 'writs', by which the abbot conveyed his orders not only to the officers (generally monks) whom he appointed to oversee his personal household and his finances, but also to his outlying officers, the lay reeves or bailiffs working in each of his manors, both in the home counties and in 'the western parts'. These were the two groups of officers with whom the abbot had to deal: his officers 'at home', and the more remote workers in the shires.

Abbot Walter was certainly not the first abbot of Westminster to employ the regular practice of sending written orders, since we know that at least his immediate predecessor, Richard of Ware, had earlier adopted a practice

---

14 *Flete*, pp. 118-9. Harvey, *ibid Walter of Wenlok*, pp. 19 and 239. The recovery of Deerhurst by Abbot Walter, together with Hardwicke and certain other hamlets, plus the half-hundred of Deerhurst in which the manor lay, is thought to have been the most beneficial recovery of property made by the abbey during the whole of the middle ages, see Harvey, *WA Estates*, pp. 167, 173-4, 197 and 416.

15 For Abbot Berking's acquisition of La Neyte, see p. 201 above.

16 Most of these documents are collected and printed in Harvey, *W. of Wenlok*, still in their Latin or old French, with other materials, together with invaluable notes and commentaries. The accounts of the farming of the manor of Eye, which the abbot influenced, are not there printed, but I have deposited a translation of them in the Muniment Room at the abbey. For a year's cycle based on the latter, see chapter 20 below, at pp. 350 ff.

of sending at least some of his orders in writ form.[17] But the new abbot, more free from exacting royal demands for his services, was able to devote more time to the administration of his own manors and, for that purpose, to use and develop the writ system more extensively. Such a system was an imitation of the royal practice of giving written orders, which by this time had had a long history. During this thirteenth century, that royal practice had also been much more widely copied by secular and other religious magnates in the administration of their estates, and by the king's sheriffs in the discharge of duties in their counties.[18]

One function of a 'writ' ('*breve*' in Latin) was the obvious one already mentioned, a reasonably reliable method of passing a written order to an absent officer, who might be as much as several days distance away from Westminster.[19] But it also had different and vital functions in accounting procedures. As we have seen, it was in this half century, 1250-1300, that 'professional' written advice became more readily available to describe not only what was required of those who managed the practical work on rural estates, but also the necessary steps to ensure that acceptable farm accounts could be both rendered and then checked by 'auditors'.[20]

When any officer, such as a treasurer, or a bailiff or reeve in charge of the work on a manor, received an order by written warrant, the document had to be kept by him, to serve as his proof, at the accounting or auditing stage, that the action which he then took was justified; with the consequence that the absence of the warrant might invalidate the action taken, so that he might find himself held liable for any financial effects. Indeed one of the available management treatises (the *Seneschausie*) even asserted that a reeve should not 'bake or brew, sell corn or stock...or entertain guests' *without* having a warrant from his lord or the lord's steward. Practice, however, did not often accord with this strict theory, and in the early farm accounts for the abbey's manors (and elsewhere), warrants are not often mentioned to justify an action taken by the officer concerned, such as a sale of corn.[21] A complementary purpose of a writ was to ensure that when the officer addressed had expended money as a result of the order given to him, the money spent was 'allowed' to him when auditing took place; and each writ gives a direction to that effect.

Apart from ordinary cases of sale or other disposal of corn or stock, the usual situations for which a local reeve or bailiff might need

---

17   Harvey, *W. of Wenlok*, p. 12. See also local evidence in eg. DS *Eye A/cs* 1/p.19 (WAM 26853, in 1280); including an auditor's specific rejection of a payment of grain: '*because without writ*'. It is likely that even earlier predecessors than Ware had used writs too. All recent abbots, and Abbot Ware in particular, must by now have been familiar with the use of writs and other written orders in royal and seignurial practice. For a 'head' of an abbot, perhaps Wenlock or Ware, see Plate 15 at p. 258.

18   'Probably all lords of any consequence were by this time conveying their orders to their manorial officers by writs', see Harvey, *W. of Wenlok*, p. 11; and Clanchy, *From Memory to Written Record*, pp. 90-91 and cf. 272-73. 349 writs of Abt. Wenlock exist, but these are only the survivors, Harvey, *ibid.* p. 49 ff. Royal orders had also been conveyed by various other formal methods, such as 'letters patent' (open letters) or 'letters close' (closed letters), but these were new varieties of instructions from the early years of the C13.

19   Runners (and payments of money to them) figure largely in the abbey documents, being one of the only means of carriage of such orders. Officials who brought a writ with them had often received special oral instructions as well from the sender, which they had to give by word of mouth to the reeve, or themselves had to carry out.

20   See pp. 216-18 above.

21   No copy of the *Seneschausie* was found among the abbey documents. It should be noted that a writ, being an advance order, did not establish the same fact or facts as a retrospective wooden 'tally' or a written 'acquittance' (which is often mentioned) would do. A writ could justify the *authority* for an action taken by the recipient; while a tally established a payment *made* and the amount; and an acquittance could establish the *discharge* or release of an obligation or the *surrender* of a right or a claim to a right.

the authority (and protection) of a written instruction were when he had to make decisions about taking on or managing workers, about building and repairing buildings in the manor, and about giving hospitality to persons arriving at his manor. In addition there were three special tasks during the farming year which needed special *supervision*, and when an officer from the abbot's household was appointed to be in attendance during the carrying out of any of these tasks, he had to be supplied with a writ authorising the reeve or bailiff to accept him and pay his wages. These three tasks, in chronological order during the year, were the shearing of the sheep (June-July), the harvesting of the corn (in theory beginning on Lammas day, the 1st August) and the autumnal threshing of the harvested corn.[22]

As the Latin name (*breve*) for a writ suggests, it was usually a short and succinct document, conveying the instruction or instructions. When addressed to an officer of the abbot's household (eg. a monk working as a steward of the household or an auditor), it was in Latin; and when sent to a reeve or bailiff of a manor or to the abbot's steward 'of the western parts' (the abbot's manors in the west), it was in old French, as the colloquial lay language.

But unfortunately these surviving writs of Abbot Walter are a far-from-complete record. Over the 24 years of his abbacy, the incidence of the survival of these documents has been very uneven: with, at one end of the scale, no writs during each of four individual years, and only one writ in each of seven other years; and at the other end of the scale, three annual clusters of 23, 36, and 28 writs in the years 1295-6-7; and another three clusters of 13, 78 and 28 in the abbot's final years of 1305-6-7.

The number of writs from those three final years which *were* preserved by the monks may perhaps reflect the fact that the dramas and furore which were enacted within that period made them memorable years, even if the practical steps which the abbot was still taking in the normal administration of his household and his manors might have little or no bearing on those dramas. In contrast, the large number preserved from the earlier period of 1295-7 may be connected with the fact that it was in October 1295 that the abbot remodelled his financial system.[23]

Up to 1295 the abbot had, in general, used the stewards who were in charge of his household as (also) his financial officers who received the revenues from his manors and elsewhere, and made all the payments necessary for the expenses of his manorial administration. But in the years 1295-96, following the national model, he created his own treasury, by appointing separate monk officers as 'receivers' of revenues and payers of expenses. His new system had a chequered history later and did not survive long in his successor's (fairly chaotic) abbacy.

Most (46 in all) of the surviving writs during 1295 and 1296 are addressed to the abbot's new treasurers ('receivers'), under his remodelled financial system, while only 14 sent to the local reeves or bailiffs working in the abbot's manors have survived. But in 1297 only one extant writ, out of 28, is addressed to the treasurers, with all the rest sent to the local officers. This suggests that the writs to the treasurers may have been preserved in 1295 and 1296 because of the change of regime starting in 1295, but were no longer preserved in 1297 because the new system was now established.[24]

A typical writ addressed by the abbot to his 'receivers' or treasurers on the 5th August 1296 ran like this (in Latin) :

*"Walter, by divine grace abbot of Westminster, to his beloved sons in Christ, brothers Richard of Fanelore and Alexander of Pershore, greeting. Pay to John Churchwine, our reeve of Eye, 16s. 8d from*

---

22   See Harvey, *W. of Wenlok*, pp. 11-12 and the evidences cited there. Gies, *Life in a med. village*, p. 147.
23   See Harvey, *ibid.*, pp. 13-15.
24   After 1297 the surviving writs are too infrequent to justify useful analysis, until 1306 is reached.

*our treasury, for him to make a certain purchase for our household in accordance with the written instructions we have given him. Also pay to Thomas the Young* [Thomas Jeofne – the reeve of Todenham, Glos.] *20s. for him to make a certain other purchase for our household. By this* [writ] *we order that this money is to be allowed to you over and above you own account. Given at Islip* [Oxon] *the Sunday next before the feast of St. Laurence* [5th August] *in the 24th year of the reign of King Edward* [1296]." [25]

### The course of the abbot's journeyings

So in August 1296, on one of his journeys through his manors, the abbot had been staying at his estate at Islip (close to Oxford), when he sent this order back to his treasurers in Westminster. He had also, it seems, sent separate written instructions (now lost) to his reeve in Eye. Earlier, in the middle of July, he had still been in Westminster, but by the 20th of that month he had come to Denham in Buckinghamshire, where he had one of his favoured houses.[26] He had already that year spent two long periods staying at Denham, but on this shorter visit he soon pushed on to Islip which he reached before the 5th August. There he had another of his houses, and he apparently now spent over a month there, just outside Oxford, before resuming his journey to Sutton-under-Brailes in Gloucestershire. Both at Islip and Sutton we know that he attended to other business, sending additional writs to his treasurers and to local officers in other western manors, before returning towards Westminster, again stopping off at Denham on the way and also at another of his manors, Laleham,

adjoining Staines in Middlesex. He was back in Westminster in time for the celebrations in the abbey of the feast of St. Edward on the 13th October, but even on that day he also found time to send two more writs to John Churchwyne, his reeve of Eye, who was now only a short distance away.[27]

This was a fairly typical journey which the abbot made among his estates.[28] We know only that he made this one journey to his distant western manors that year. But although 1296 is one of those years in which we have a large number (36) of surviving writs, it is very unlikely that (even for that year) all the writs which he had to send have survived. Moreover one can be certain that the sending of 36 (and more) writs in that year was only a small part of the abbot's involvement in the practical affairs of his manors, and that on each of his visits and longer stays he attended personally to much other business in the places wherever he stayed – viewing what had been done or not done since his last visit, interviewing local officers, learning and assessing the progress and gathering-in of crops and other agricultural practices, visiting nearby manors for similar purposes, and giving instructions orally, when needed (even if this precluded the supply of written 'proof' which a writ provided).

It is clear from the rather tortuous path which he took among his manors on some occasions that from time to time he was weaving backwards and forwards between the same places; and this only made sense if different business needs were arising at random and had to be attended to while he was still in the neighbourhood.[29]

---

25  Harvey, *ibid.*, p. 77, (§. 90).

26  Much earlier, Denham had been let heritably to a tenant family, subject to hospitality rights for the abbot (plus of course a fee-farm rent), but the hospitality had been commuted later for an extra £3 pa. rent; and more recently in 1292 possession of the manor had been restored to the abbot by Edward I in the name of his dead queen Eleanor and for her anniversary; see pp. 305 ff. below; for Denham, see text following, and pp. 197 above and Pearce, *W. de Wenlok*, pp. 71-73, and Harvey, *WA Estates*, pp. 338-9 and *Cal. Ch. R.*, 1257-1300, p. 411.

27  See Harvey, *W. de Wenlok*, p. 41. For more about John Churchwyne, now the local reeve in Eye, who had earlier been the reeve of Staines and then also one of the wardens of La Neyte, the abbot's 'island' house, see *ibid.*, pp. 155 and 57; and (in this book) pp. 334, 340, 343, 345-7 below.

28  The abbot travelled usually on horseback, on a special palfrey with his own groom. But his 'long-cart', designed to carry the abbatial luggage and special equipment, could take him too, when ill, tired or elderly.

29  Known journeys which the abbot made between 1284 and 1307 are listed in Harvey, *W. of Wenlok*, pp. 34-5.

It may be that the wear and tear on his house at Denham, which he visited at least five times during 1296, was excessive, because in the spring of the following year he had to begin sending a series of writs, ordering considerable repairs to it. Repairs were to be done 'in haste' on the chimney of his chamber; the walls and benches needed plastering and decorating; the room was to be raised and the foundations strengthened with good oak beams, covered with tiles; and *'all defects were to be put right, so that we find no defect on our coming'.*[30]

But both Denham and Islip also performed a special function in the agricultural round on which the abbey depended - as staging posts for the gathering and 'posting on' of abbey stock, both live and dead, on their way from the abbot's western manors to Westminster. It was of course a regular feature of medieval life that in the absence of transport, almost all live animals had to make a long slow trek on foot, often in great droves, across the country to any of the large urban areas, and also to their own nearby markets.

So we see the abbot instructing the bailiff and reeve of Islip to receive flocks of poultry and other animals, coming from the manors further west, and to send them on to Denham, making sure ('at your peril') that they are not overtired. At Denham they might need to be fattened up, before being sent on either to the abbey itself or to the London markets. Sometimes, as when a small flock of 36 capons were on their way from the west, it was at Islip that the fattening up had to be done, while the birds were waiting for another summons to be sent on, for the abbot's table. Like the animals, the wool crop from sheep in the rich pastures of the west had to be passed down the line, from the western manors to Islip, and thence

to Denham on its way to Westminster.[31] Wool sales were worth a gross income of about £70 pa. to Abbot Wenlock by his last years, and were one of his main sources of earned cash.[32]

Naturally most of the abbot's journeys tended to follow a course through his nearer estates in the home counties. As regards other visits to his more distant manors in the far west, the limited evidence suggests that from 1287 when he visited those 'western parts', it was usually for only one journey a year; and sometimes there may have been no visit at all (eg. in the years 1293- 5, 1298-1300, 1304-5 and his final year 1307).

But there were two exceptional years, in 1290 and 1292. In 1290 he made two journeys to the west, staying in mid-summer at various places in Worcestershire, Gloucestershire and Shropshire, for at least one month and a half in total (and possibly even for the whole of the autumn as well), with another visit of a fortnight, beginning just after Christmas. But 1292 was even more unusual, because we can see that he made no less than five journeys to the west in that one year, some for lengthy periods, staying there in various manors – for example, for nearly a month in April and May; another six weeks later in May through to July, again moving from one manor to another; and another three weeks in August and September, this time sleeping in even more beds.[33] So the abbot was much absent from Westminster and the home counties that year, and there was clearly a great deal of business to keep him both in his western manors and on the road, going backwards and forwards. At least these absences were not due to royal calls on his time, as his predecessors' had been, but to the demands made by the administrative methods which he was following.

---

30  *ibid*. pp. 84-5. See also Lathbury, *History of Denham*, pp. 91-3. Lathbury says a modernising was intended. And were the abbot's tiles to form a first recorded damp-proof course, similar to our old slate courses? For the writs, see Harvey, *W. de Wenlok*, pp. 84-6, §§ 111, 114, 118.

31  Harvey, *ibid.,* p. 86 (§121) and p, 142 (§305).

32  Harvey, *WA and Estates*, pp. 137 and 139.

33  Or did his 'long cart' (his transport carriage for the road) take his own bed for him? For references in the household accounts to the abbot's long cart, its journeys and its special driver, Thomas, see Harvey, *W. of Wenlok*, pp. 172, 185, 65, 168, 172, 185.

As for his closer journeys round nearby manors in Middlesex, it seems that he stayed in convent manors equally with abbatial ones. On the one hand, his own manor of Eye, whose *curia* (its court-yard or close, where the court building stood, or other administrative centre) was only a short distance from La Neyte, apparently could and did provide him with living quarters for a whole month, from the 23rd April to the 22nd May in 1290, with another week in June and yet another ten days in July of the same year, with the abbot paying fully for all his household expenses while he was there.[34] This suggests that for some unknown reason (such as building work?) his own house at La Neyte had become uninhabitable or otherwise intolerable. Equally his own manor of Paddington, again close by, became quite a frequent stop-over for him for a day and a night, often when he was on his way to some destination further afield; and also for two more extended stays, totalling eight whole days during February 1292.

On the other hand, the convent's manors of Knightsbridge and Hampstead were places where he was also sometimes received on his itineraries; the former as a stop-over for a day and night, for example on the 23rd May 1290 when the abbey cellarer provided hospitality there at his own department's expense for the abbot. But at Hampstead, where the abbot stayed apparently for five nights in May 1290, and again for perhaps three days and one night in March 1299, he had to pay for all his own household expenses incurred while he was there.[35] His longer stay there in May 1290 suggests (as his stay at Eye in the same month did) that he was dispossessed from La Neyte, and was being given shelter locally by the convent, but on the basis that he paid for it.[36]

### The abbot's household

When the abbot descended on you with his household retinue, it was no light thing. Many years before, Ivo the tenant of the abbey's manor of Deene (Northamptonshire) had already found that out, and had sought to reject the claim that he was obliged to provide annual hospitality at his own expense for the abbot. But in 1215 Ivo had had to concede before the king's court sitting in Westminster that the obligation existed, although by compromise with the then abbot he succeeded in obtaining a commutation of the entire duty at the cost of a further £2 pa., to be added to the existing annual rent of £16 for the manor. The compromise spelt out before the court on that occasion had revealed the strict and detailed regulation which had existed for the provision of hospitality by the tenant of Deene: with seven principal officers of the abbot's household – his steward, chamberlain, provisioner, butler, usher, cook and marshal – being given advance control of the various sections of the tenant's household, so that the abbot (at that time William of Humez) should receive his customary reception and treatment under the orders and surveillance of his own officers.[37]

---

34 One problem with 'Eye' is that, because the abbot's house La Neyte and its curtilage were an 'island of land' (and water) *within* the manor of Eye, we cannot be sure that every reference to 'Eye' relates to the surrounding manor itself or (confusingly) only to, or to include, La Neyte. See eg. the roll recording *'all expenses of the (abbot's) household, beginning at Eye on the [4 May 1290]'* until the 5 September that year (Harvey, *W. de W.*, p. 188) with later changes in the name from Eye to Eybury in the same roll. From the detail in the roll, it looks as if the abbot was genuinely staying in quarters in Eye manor itself, not at his own house, for some parts of the four months as identified in the roll, and throughout had to be paying his own regular suppliers of fish, poultry and other meat. See also n. 7 at Harvey, *ibid.*, p. 12.

35 See Harvey, *ibid*, pp. 37, 42, and 189 (for both Knightsbridge and Hampstead).

36 He was also being received at other convent manors, their 'principal ones', such as Aldenham, Wheathampstead, Feering etc. for other periods during the four months May to September 1290, but on the same financial basis, see *ibid.*, p. 189.

37 See pp. 136-7 above. By the compromise in that case, the tenant also benefitted by receiving a further grant of the manor *in perpetuity*. Many other strict rules set out in the compromise provided the detailed arrangements which were to define the relationship during the abbot's stay. A similar trade of hospitality rights, this time at the abbey's estate of Sudborough, also in Northamptonshire, was later

Eleven years later, in 1226, as a result of another court action, the hospitality which the abbot was entitled to receive (and in this instance continued to receive) at the manor of Hendon was defined in a wide-ranging compromise, on much the same basis as that which had been defined in relation to the manor of Deene. The same seven officers of the abbot at that time (Richard of Berking) were given control of the appropriate offices in the house at Hendon, ie. the hall, the chamber, the pantry, the buttery, the gate, the kitchen, and the 'marshalsea', on the occasion of the abbot's annual visit. However one surprising but prominent feature of that compromise was that the abbot was entitled to arrive at Hendon with 35 horses in his entourage; moreover it was expressed as *'only 35'*, as if it were a limitation on the number of the usual retinue which he might otherwise bring.[38]

### The household Ordinance

But thanks to Abbot Walter of Wenlock, the free hospitality which previous abbots had been entitled to receive at the manors of Hendon and Deene is not the only window through which we can view the organisation of the abbatial household. For at some point of time between about February 1295 and September 1298 Abbot Walter arranged for an 'Ordinance' to be drawn up, bringing together any existing regulations which already governed the duties and relationships of the different officers and their departments of his household. These were drawn up in old French, the language familiar to the gentry and to competent laymen, such as those members of the household who were directly affected by them. In this ordinance all the sections of the household and the principal officers in charge of them are depicted in considerable detail, and the interrelation of their duties is described.

The drawing up of a decree which contained all the responsibilities in the abbatial household was not an entirely original idea. Nearly twenty years before, in 1279, a similar decree had been drawn up for King Edward I, detailing the domestic arrangements for the sections or departments of the royal household. This too had been called an ordinance, the 'Ordinance of the King's Household', and it too had been in old French. In addition to the duties described, the officers were there named, and their wages and allowances were identified. In particular it detailed one essential procedure which was copied in practice in Abbot Wenlock's household and his own ordinance: namely, an accounting session which had to take place *every night* before the king's household steward, and other officers, who might include the treasurer and controller of his wardrobe, his chamberlain and a marshal, in order to check the records of the day from the kitchen, pantry and buttery against the amount of food and drink actually served.[39]

So Wenlock's household practices and his ordinance had earlier and greater models to follow. In his case, his most senior official was the 'steward of the lands', his paramount officer who oversaw all the abbot's estates and (with the assistance of the next-in-line, the 'steward of the household') had overall responsibility for seeing that all necessary

made by Abbot Richard of Berking in 1226, when in another court settlement he received £3 pa. as additional rent for the commutation of his rights; but on that occasion the rules governing the provision of hospitality at Sudborough were not included in the court documents; see pp. 202 above.

38 See WAD 121b - 122b; and CP25(1) 146/7/58. The figure of 35 horses contrasts with the limitation of 20 horses, and the 'usual' 10, as referred-to below on p. 303.

39 See Tout, *Chapters*, ii, 158; cf. *Fleta*, ii. cap. 14, ed. Richardson and Sayles, Selden Soc. vols. 72 (1953) and 99 (1983) pp. xii - xiv; and Prestwich, *Edward I*, p. 135. Even this ordinance had not been the first description of the royal household, because about 150 years before, in the 1130s, the *Constitutio Domus Regis* had been written to provide a less ambitious account of the king's domestic offices at that time; and other magnates had also copied these ideas for their own household administration, see Stenton, *English Feudalism*, pp. 69-72.

provisions and stores were available wherever the abbot might be staying among the manors. The 'steward of the lands' was also given authority to write 'letters' and give orders (in much the same way as the abbot did) to the bailiffs and reeves *'in all things which touch our honour or our profit'*, and the bailiffs and reeves were to give full heed to them. In fact a number of such orders given by the 'steward of the lands' (at those times, John of Foxley) by writ have survived, together with the collection of the abbot's own writs.[40] When this 'steward of the lands' visited the abbot's household, he had the privilege of being able to bring three horses of his own, his own clerk and three pages, and he was to be held in honour second only to the abbot.

But though *in* the household, the 'steward of the lands' was not really *of* it. It was one of the two 'stewards of the household' who in practice held the reins within the household itself, with all the responsibilities attached; he had full power there 'in all things within the household which can turn to our profit or our honour', and all members of the abbot's entourage were to obey him. Of the two stewards of the household, one was a monk-steward (a monk of the abbey) and the other a lay steward who was paid, and probably it was the latter who performed the day to day role. It was he who had to conduct the ceremony of a nightly accounting (as the king's steward did), to which all the principal officers had to come, and at which inquiries were to be made as to all faults and mistakes made during the day, with due corrections of them, or fitting

punishment meted out for the more serious. The abbot's rule was hard: all faults had to be *'put right for us'* by the steward of the household, so that *'we do not suffer by it'*.

It was the steward of the household's job to give orders to the bailiffs and reeves in the manors for the collection of all the wheat, oats, malt, wood and charcoal necessary for the maintenance of the abbot's household: and the bailiffs' and reeves' job to supply these. All wheat, oats and malt supplied from any manor to the household were to be valued at the market price in the neighbourhood, so that the manor could be credited with their value.[41] However more and more Abbot Walter's household came to rely later on cash purchases in the market for its supplies, rather than on produce from its demesne lands in its manors.[42]

The tasks of the principal officers of the abbot's household are described in some detail in the Ordinance, which reads like a series of modern 'job descriptions'. The theme throughout is, of course, service to the abbot, to be conducted with the highest standards of competence and propriety. The master cook must be clean, and must not allow anyone to approach the abbot's own dishes; the abbot's special bread must be made of wheat which is finer and whiter than that used in ordinary baking; the abbot and his clerks are to have only good unmixed beer; the marshal is to be of good address, courteous and prudent, he must be the earliest to rise and the last to go to bed, he must restrain the pages from mischief, and stop them and bad women consorting; the gatekeeper must be sober,

---

40  John Foxley served the abbot as his principal 'steward of the lands' for most of his abbacy, from about 1286 until 1306. For his few surviving writs (nine, over a period of 18 years), see Harvey, *W. of Wenlok*, pp. 147-150. For his house in Westminster and distinguished life in the abbot's and then the king's service, see pp. 287-8 above. In the far west, the 'steward of the western parts' also had the power to give such orders by writ, see *ibid.*, pp. 150-1, although that steward was strictly a subordinate, not an equal, of the 'steward of the lands', *ibid.*, p. 6.

41  The abbot's auditors by now had realised that when trying to assess the *profitability* of a manor, one had to allow for the value of all *produce* provided from the manor to the abbot's household. Wooden tallies were cut for these at the time of delivery, and for a time even the manor accounts had to show these supplies *as though* they were actually sold to the household at market prices, so that the correct credits to the manor were given in the account.

42  Harvey, *WA Estates*, pp. 134-5. Before Abbot Walter the surviving evidence about provisioning the abbot's household is scrappy or non-existent.

chaste and courteous to all, and must never leave the court of the place where the abbot is present, he must clear the court of *'boys, rude characters and women [sic], so that no unexpected damage occurs'*; and so on.

When the abbot set out on one of his journeys through the countryside, it is clear that his principal domestic officers accompanied him so that they could maintain their charge of the various departments at each of the places where he stopped, with whatever other staff was necessary for that purpose. He would always be attended by one or more of his own four chaplains, who were to be accorded an honorific standing *'second only to myself'* in the household so displacing (for this purpose only) even his 'steward of the lands'. Being clerks, they could act as the abbot's scribes whenever needed on the journey, if no other scribes had been brought, and one of them also often doubled up in the office of one of the two stewards of the household itself.[43]

The number and character of the rest of his entourage would depend on the scale of the journey and other contingent factors, such as perhaps the abbot's health at that time (he had his own doctor, a master physician), or special meetings to be attended by the abbot, such as the parliament which he attended at Bury St. Edmunds on the 3rd November 1296.[44] For such formal occasions as 'parliaments and assemblies with other great magnates', the abbot had ordered that his marshal should equip his retinue of esquires with fitting robes of a uniform kind, so as not to cause him shame before his equals.[45] Also among his entourage when he set out there might be his *legistre*, his legal officer, ranked as high as his lay steward of the

household, to deal with any legal problems of which the abbot had had notice. There would of course also be personal servants, such as his valet and pages.

Whatever the size of the required household when the abbot was jouneying, there was one practical limitation on its form of transport. Even before Abbot Richard of Berking had embarked on his wholesale division of the abbey's possessions in the first quarter of the century, the Benedictine monks' Provincial Chapter of Canterbury had ordained that an abbot's entourage should not usually exceed twenty horses, and this had been echoed in the requirement of the prior and convent under Abbot Crokesley that when the abbot visited any of their five principal manors, he could not expect free fodder for more than twenty horses.[46] The abbot's right to have as many as 35 horses when visiting Hendon was no doubt an ancient right, probably going back to the first half of the twelfth century, even though the first surviving record of it was Abbot Berking's agreement about Hendon in 1226.[47] But in practice Abbot Wenlock often had less than ten horses for his retinue, when on the road, so it looks as if there may often have been some doubling up of functions among the more practical members of the abbot's escort.[48] Certainly at times other than the abbot's excursions, some members of the household, like the abbot's valet or his grooms who looked after his special palfrey for him, must have become accustomed to being sent off on their own to perform other tasks at distant manors during busy periods.[49]

It is clear from all this that the lifestyle of an abbot of Westminster was becoming more and more secular for more of the time.

---

43 Harvey, *W. de Wenlok*, p. 25.
44 *ibid.*, p. 81n.
45 *ibid.*, p. 246. Wenlock might be employing as many as twenty esquires at a time, even if he was accompanied by far fewer, when visiting.
46 See also p. 213 n. 15 above.
47 See p. 198 above, for Abbot Berking's compromise. The records about Hendon in the C12 (see eg. pp. 79-81 above and refs. there) appear not to consider any right for the abbot at that time to bring a retinue of 35 horses. There was no legal case or debate about hospitality 'rules'. The Berking compromise is the first evidence.
48 Harvey, *ibid.*, p. 8.
49 *ibid.*, pp. 56, 61, 62, 83.

Although this abbot had not been called to follow his predecessors into a career as a royal intimate and envoy, he was similarly absent from the abbey for long periods in different parts of this country; his thoughts had to be directed more and more to all the practical and administrative problems of a country-wide estate, instead of to the life of devotion to which he had been originally called; and he was caught up in all the demands which the need to maintain favour with the king and with his royal and judicial officials in Westminster was making upon him.

Unlike Edward I's ordinance for the royal household, Abbot Wenlock's ordinance did not provide details of any officers' wages. But at the end of the document, there appears a list of the robes which the abbot had agreed to supply each year, either in free favour or payment or part-payment in kind to those who were members of his household and also to some others who were regarded as sufficiently close to deserve such favour. Here, significantly at the outset, one meets again the abbot's mother and sister, who were to have a robe each, with a hood; and all the familiar members of the household who are described once more, anonymously, by their occupation alone. Some, the great, received two robes each year; the lesser, one robe. For some, the robes were made of fur; for others, it was merely lambskin. Some robes were coloured, some were plain. Some members of the household received a horse as well; even two horses, for the steward of the 'western parts', who no doubt had much more riding to do; or half a mark.

Some recipients of robes, not being members of the household, were actually named, randomly it seems. We meet *Master Reginald of St. Alban's*, a powerful and ubiquitous proctor in both church and diplomatic affairs, who served great clients as an early 'professional attorney' at the Bench;[50] *Thomas Romein*, a London spice merchant (a 'pepperer') and alderman of the city who, with his wife Juliana, was often a creditor of the abbot, each having made loans to him. Romein was a rich Italian, owning much land outside and within the city, and when he died in 1312-13 he left 100 marks to the abbey;[51] *William of the Water* ('de Aqua') a former lay steward of the abbot's household, and once coroner of the abbey;[52] *John Churchwyne*, the reeve of Eye from about 1290 until 1302 and former reeve of the abbot's large semi-urban manor of Staines in Middlesex;[53] *Thomas le Jeofne*, the former reeve of Laleham (a regular visiting place for the abbot, near Staines), who had then been made serjeant of Todenham in the far west. But important officers such as the bailiffs of Westminster, Staines and Pershore, and other distant agents such as the woodward of Islip and the park-warden of Pershore, remained unnamed in the robe-list, but no doubt they did receive robes – for the bailiffs, two robes each, and for extra mobility for the bailiff of Westminster, a horse as well, which gave added status to an already significant person.

---

50  See Brand, *Making of Common Law*, p. 10 n. An experienced advocate and negotiator, he acted as proctor and envoy for Abbot Walter in Rome, and for the king and for each of the archbishops of Canterbury and York; he was rector of Chelsea, and pluralist holder of other benefices; a canon of St. Paul's and prebend of the small manor of Rugmere, on Hampstead's south boundary. He made gifts to the Lady Altar, including 200 marks at his death. His brother Joseph had a house or houses in Hampstead, with arable, meadow and pasture lands.

51  Pearce, *W. de Wenlok*, pp. 104, 120, Harvey, *ibid.*, pp. 246, and 179, 183, 194 et. al; Williams, *Med. London*, pp. 143-4, 259. For Romein, see also Nightingale, *The Grocers' Company*, pp. 94 and 123.

52  Harvey, *W. de Wenlok*, pp. 26 and 247. The 'de Aqua' family were closely associated with the abbey and its charters in both the thirteenth and fourteenth centuries. Richard de Aqua was janitor of both the gate and the prison in the gatehouse during Walter's abbacy, having lost an argument in court with the abbey in 1293 that (though conceding he was the gatekeeper) he had no duty as to the prison ; Horwood (ed), *Y.B., 21 and 22 Edw. I*, pp. 576 ff. To the abbey, he gave his land in Eye, on the 'Kingsway' (not the Abbotsway) to La Neyte, WAD 333.

53  See p. 298 n. 27, for John Churchwyne who appears in many of the abbot's writs, and many times in DS *Eye A/cs*. See also pp. 334, 340, 343, 345, 346, 347, etc, below.

## The abbey grows still further in wealth: Queen Eleanor's foundation

Two major increases in asset-wealth benefitted the abbey during Abbot Wenlock's time. The first of these, and the grandest, was the huge endowment of lands which the abbey received to pay for an 'anniversary' for Queen Eleanor of Castile, the revered wife of Edward I, who died in November 1290.[54] This anniversary had already been planned by the queen earlier during her lifetime. Like Henry III, her father-in-law, she was devoted to St. Edward (the Confessor), and once again it was the special relationship between royalty and the resident saint of Westminster which led directly to the enrichment of the abbey. At least four years before her death, the queen had supplied to the abbey large sums of money to enable the abbey to purchase lands to fund an anniversary after she died. By February 1286 the abbey already held more than £363 of the queen's money, and in that month Abbot Walter had become treasurer of the queen's foundation.[55] The queen herself had supervised this fund which she had provided, but only one major purchase, of the manor of Turweston in Buckinghamshire, was made as a prospective part of the foundation which was to endow her anniversary.[56]

However in 1292, after the queen had died, the king established the greater portion of her foundation, by granting to the abbey a clutch of manors (including actual possession of the already-purchased manor of Turweston, and also the restoration of the abbey's ancient manor of Denham), which were designed to be worth £200 pa. in total.[57] But three years later in 1295 he had to complete the story by restoring to the abbey the possession of a further group of lands within the manor of Hendon (forming, in effect, a 'sub-manor', called Hodford) to seek to make up a deficiency in the projected £200 value of the foundation.[58]

Not content with that, the king added at least four further ancillary subsidies to the abbey – freedom from all tallages (in effect, taxes) and freedom from all prises (royal requisitions of produce) on any of these lands which he had granted for Queen Eleanor's foundation; freedom from the burdens of military tenure for the manor of Denham; and for Hodford, all 'the liberties and free customs' which the abbey enjoyed already for its other lands.[59]

The establishment of this great endowment for the abbey owed more to good fortune than to deliberate policy and impetus on the part of the abbot. But even if the queen's personal favour towards the cult of St. Edward proved to be fortuitously beneficial to the abbey in leading to the making of this gift, Abbot Walter did at

54  For her death and burial, and the final 'Eleanor Cross' at Charing, see p. 30 above.
55  See WAM 23629, and Pearce, *Monks*, p. 15.
56  Turweston was bought from Simon, a royal servant, at a cost of £133. 6s. 8d., WAM 23628, and actual possession of it was given later to the abbey in 1292 by Edward I, *Cal. Ch. R.* 1257-1300, p. 461.
57  *ibid.*, pp. 411, 424-426; WAD 412b.
58  *Cal. Ch. R.*, 1257-1300, p. 461. Hodford (a part of Hendon) had been acquired by the king when Emma the widow of Nicholas 'de Insula' left the Hodford lands to him by will, almost certainly for the arranged purpose that the king could add them to the queen's foundation, see WAD 413a and the above ref. Nicholas and Emma had held Hodford from its principal tenants Sir Henry of Wymondeley and his wife Mabel.
    Very soon the monks were able to make use of the Hodford lands (after establishing a chapel in them, see WAM 17014 and WAD 440), by exchanging them (plus £100) in 1312 for their long-lost *main* manor of Hendon, which had been let to the Gunter and Gilbert family about 200 years before (see pp. 71-2, and p. 202 above) and had now been inherited and was currently held by Sir Richard le Rous ('the Red' - haired?), a military man. So in exchange for Hodford, Sir Richard gave up most of his interest in Hendon to the abbey; see *Cal. P. R.* 1307-13, p. 438. Nine years later, in 1321, the monks were able to carry out a large-scale survey of their restored manor of Hendon, similar to that carried out in 1312 for Hampstead, see p. 389 below.
59  WAD 412b and 413b; *Cal. Ch. R.*, 1257-1300., p. 411.

least contribute, on his part, a steady cultivation of good relations with the king and queen. Throughout his abbacy he sought to maintain the good will of not only the king and the queen, but also of other members of their families (such as the king's mother 'the old queen', *Edmund* the king's brother and, with an eye to the future, even young *Prince Edward*, the king's heir and future King Edward II) and, equally importantly, the good will of advisers and other officers close to the king and queen.

As a few examples of the 'stream of largesse' which flowed from the abbot's hand to all and sundry, there were personal presents for the king and queen, ranging from homely gifts of four dozen rabbits and eight peacocks at Christmas, and eight swans (bought on credit), to two silver bowls for the king; and hospitality and intimate suppers with the abbot at La Neyte for *John of Droxford* and *John of Benstead*, the keeper and the controller of the king's financial 'wardrobe'; and the use of the abbot's house at Denham, with hospitality and all 'courtesy' to be provided there, for the king's chamberlain, *John of Sudley*; and a flow of presents, a silver ewer, a silver goblet, a gilt cup and 24 capons for *Robert Burnell*, the king's chancellor whose love for silver and gold, even more than choice food, the abbot clearly knew.[60]

The long-term benefit which the Queen's endowment created for the abbey, and the short-term harm to which it also contributed, were enormous. The monks' personal gains from it, year by year, was the difference between the large income derived by the abbey from these new possessions and the smaller cost to the abbey of celebrating Queen Eleanor's anniversary on the 28th November each year. Apart from the prescribed solemn

masses, the burning of great candles and the tolling of bells, the anniversary required the payment of alms, of one penny to each of 140 poor people every week of the year, being 11s 8d. each week, plus a further 11s. 8d. on the eve of the anniversary, and an open-ended commitment to pay one penny to every poor person who appeared at the abbey to receive it on the day itself of the anniversary.[61] While the fixed payments amounted to less than £40 pa., after nearly ten years the open-ended obligation meant that more than 24,000 poor people were presenting themselves at the almonry entrance on the 28th November each year to receive the dole of one penny each. Added up, these amounted to an additional sum of just over £100, and so the total payments had become about £148 each year.[62]

Even with this large alms-giving from the Eleanor foundation, the income was such that by about 1300 there was a surplus of £28 each year, to benefit the monks. But this was in the early years of the foundation. A hundred years later the odds had moved still further in favour of the monks. While the income from the Eleanor estates had grown, expenditure on the poor had decreased because fewer poor were attending on the day of the anniversary; and the surplus was now about £185 each year. So the benefit from the thirteenth-century foundation had increased dramatically, and the monks had profited even further.[63]

But in the very short-term, these surplus moneys from the Eleanor estates fortuitously did more harm than good, because they became the focus of violent contention between Abbot Walter and his monks, which played a great part in their final show-down during the last years of the abbot's life. The king had expressly provided that the surplus moneys should belong to the prior and

---

60  Pearce, *W. of Wenlok,* pp. 116 (largesse); 55, 117 (king and queen); 89 (Droxford and Benstead); 71-2 (Sudley or Suthle or Sulle); 117 (Burnell). For Droxford, see also pp. 314 n. 14 and 359 below; for Benstead, see also pp. 285-7 above; and for Burnell, see also p. 269 above.

61  *Cal. Ch. R.,* 1257-1300, pp. 411 and 424-6. Remarkably the value of the 'one penny' was ordered to be index-linked in favour of the poor, thereby reducing the surplus moneys of the endowment.

62  Harvey, *Living and Dying,* p. 27, and Harvey, *WA and Estates,* Table 1, p. 34.

63  The main effect for the monks was that they were able to institute a 'wage' system for themselves.

convent, but specified that they were to pay for the grant of pittances (special additional dishes) for them. However, instead, the prior and convent had insisted to the abbot that any surplus residue should actually be divided between the monks in the form of money. This had led to a stalemate in which the abbot had rightly refused to agree to that demand, and there had been *'very many disputes'* between them on this subject. John Flete, the fifteenth-century historian of the abbey, seems to imply that this was the major factor in causing the ultimate show-down between the abbot and his monks. If that was so, there is considerable pathos in the fact that, only one week before his death, the now-ill abbot at last capitulated to the convent on this point (as a last resort?) and conceded to them that the surplus moneys should be assigned to them *'for your pittances or for division between you'*, as they had demanded.[64]  On any view this was a death-bed concession, and at the end of the same week he died, on Christmas night 1307, before its effect on the internecine conflict between them could be ascertained.

### *Another great acquisition – Deerhurst – made by the abbot*

The large and valuable estate of Deerhurst in Gloucestershire, which included not only that manor itself but also much surrounding land, forming separate but attached manors held by the same family, was restored to the possession of the abbey when Abbot Wenlock re-purchased it in 1299. Together they constituted the 'half-hundred' of Deerhurst, namely half of a whole 'hundred', one of the ancient territorial sub-divisions of each shire.[65]

From before the Norman Conquest the whole estate had belonged to the abbey, but it had been let to the Darneford family, on a hereditary basis, in the twelfth century by Abbot Gervase and had remained ever since in their possession. The restoration of the whole estate to the abbey under Abbot Walter has been described as 'the most valuable estate recovered [by the abbey] at any point in the Middle Ages'.[66]

The main feature of the re-purchase was that the abbot agreed to give the manor of Islip (Oxon) in exchange for the half-hundred of Deerhurst, granting Islip to William and Cecily Darneford for their joint and several lives, with a pension of £10 pa. and other cash sums amounting to £177 (which included the cost of the stock on the Deerhurst lands). Taking into account the value of the assets exchanged for Deerhurst, it has been calculated that the overall cost to the abbey of the purchase was as high as £1430, an enormous sum even if the property was a particularly valuable one.[67]

Like the Queen Eleanor estates, the Deerhurst purchase brought more dissension to the abbey and played its part in further fomenting the final cycle of bitterness between Abbot Walter and his prior's supporters among the convent monks. The claims made by the abbot's opponents among the monks, firstly that he had actually agreed to assign Deerhurst to the convent (in return for a rent of £60 pa.), and secondly that all surplus profits from it should be made available for the monks of the convent *to divide among themselves* or otherwise dispose of as they chose, led to a further death-bed capitulation on the part of the abbot on these issues.[68]

64  *Flete*, p. 118.

65  For the origins and meaning of 'hundreds' (particularly as relating to Mdx), see *The Westminster Corridor*, pp. 49-53 and coloured Map I. In Middlesex, for example, the area which became Edmonton was also once a 'half-hundred', see *ibid.*, p. 51, note 23. For Deerhurst's original 'sale' by Abbot Gervase in c. 1140, see p. 81, n. 54 above.

66  See Harvey, *WA Estates*, p. 167.

67  *ibid.*, p. 197

68  For the abbot's concession, see p. 324 below. There is no contemporary evidence proving the first of these claims by the convent, although the later unilateral composition made by the prior and convent *after* the abbot's death continued to assert it, see Harvey, *W. de Wenlok*, p. 239. For this subsequent unilateral composition, see p. 325 below. And the second claim is 'unsupportable', see Harvey, *ibid.*, p. 19.

## The Westminster fairs reorganised

The grants made by King Henry in the 1240s which had empowered the abbey to hold the two Westminster fairs in October and January each year had brought international markets to the town, and income to the abbey.[69] The original three days' duration for each of the fairs had then been extended to fifteen days for each, so increasing the benefits. But both fairs, linked as they were to events in the life of St. Edward the Confessor, had suffered from being autumnal and winter events, and also from the wear and tear of the rebuilding operations. Rain had made a quagmire of the abbey precinct, and this may have seemed the result of divine anger, since fairs in churchyards were forbidden by ecclesiastical decree. Although the main fair had then been ordered to be held on Tothill instead, there is no evidence that it was in fact ever removed to that even more soggy site.[70]

But at last, fifty years later, Abbot Walter apparently accepted that January was an even less auspicious season for a fair than October and so, well in advance of the main fair in October 1298, he requested King Edward to make a sensible change. As a result the king acceded to his request (acknowledging that it was the abbot and the convent who had initiated the move) and on the 12th August 1298 granted that the October fair should be extended to thirty-two days in all, and that the January fair should no longer be held at all.[71] Presumably fair, or less foul, weather during the 1298 and 1299 October fairs must have demonstrated the advantage of the change. And so on the 22nd October 1299 the king (apparently on his own initiative this time) repeated a previous order that all merchants coming to the fair during the newly extended period should be *quit of all king's prises* and should therefore be free from the demands of royal provisioning-officers to take whatever was deemed to be needed, without making immediate payment.[72] For the original two fairs, this had already been the position since King Henry's time, but now King Edward followed suit, so supplementing his new dispensation for a thirty-two day fair.

During his abbacy, Walter of Wenlock had also continued to extend the facilities for visiting merchants and other traders by buying nearby houses for them to use, and further stalls and booths were also provided for renting by the merchants and traders, just as Abbot Ware had made his 'long house' similarly available. The success of all the new orders is shown by a number of surviving records. By the early 1300s the annual income derived from the extended October fair was averaging well over £100, with the major part of this income coming from the rents. But it is not possible to say whether this was an increase on the annual income which had been made during the sixty years since the original two fairs had been granted to the abbey.[73]

## An abbot poor in the midst of wealth

It is ironic that someone as wealthy as the abbot should regularly have found himself short of ready money. Like some modern companies, he suffered from being asset-rich and often cash-poor; but also like them, he found it difficult to reduce his obligations or the expectations which were part of the medieval culture of 'financial encouragements', or to cut back on all the calls on his generosity. But, within these limitations, his own business skill managed to keep his head above water for most of the time.

Presents and 'pensions' seem to have played a major role in the recurrent shortage of ready money in the abbot's purse. The giving of presents was part of 'the stream of largesse', which was necessary in order to maintain

69  For the earlier grants of fairs, see pp. 204 and 212 above.
70  Rosser, *Med. Westminster*, pp. 98-99; *Cal. P. R.*, 1247-58, p. 76.
71  *Cal. Ch. R.*, 1257-1300, p. 471.
72  *ibid*, p. 479.
73  Rosser, *ibid.*, p. 103, Table 1, and pp. 104-6. For Abbot Ware's 'long house', see p. 239 above.

favour with the king and those around him.[74] But it extended to many others, both the exalted and the less exalted: to *Cardinals*, when they arrived on papal missions, and to their officers too; to *Piers Gaveston*, the young Prince Edward's favourite, who was already a figure in the politics of the last years of King Edward I; to *John of Botetourte,* a military and naval commander and a royal justice; to citizens of London, such as *Reginald of Toundesle*, the London draper, and his wife Margery; to familiar residents of Westminster and the neighbourhood, such as *Geoffrey de fonte, John the Tailor,* and *the wife of Hugh of Padington*, or to friends or relatives of the abbot in his home town of Wenlock. The presents ranged from expensive gilt or silver bowls or cups to decorated knives, purses, gifts of money, and simple presents of grain.

The 'pensions' paid by the abbot were more rarely for past services than for expected favours to come. This was a feature of medieval life which often clashes violently with modern ideas about conflicts of interest and corruption. Many of the 'annuitants' who received a yearly sum from the abbot were professional justices, sitting in Westminster itself on the (Common) Bench or in the court of King's Bench when the king was at home; others were competent men of affairs who were liable to be appointed regularly on royal commissions or inquiries or as itinerant justices; yet others were professional men regularly employed by the abbey as lawyers, clerks or on the lay side of abbey administration. This reflected a culture in which such payments were tolerated as 'encouragements to show favour', rather than open bribes.[75] The annual pensions usually ranged from one mark to ten marks, and were frequently paid belatedly, or in instalments, or both, because of the acknowledged lack of funds.

One of the obvious remedies for problems about cash-flow was, of course, to borrow money, and this Abbot Walter did from time to time. But borrowing money only meant more repayments, and we see the abbot having to struggle to keep up with his obligations to many lenders. The first half of the abbacy, the period up to the earlier 1290s, seem to have caused more problems than most, starting with great debts (over 1000 marks) incurred at the very start of the abbacy, when money was being borrowed in 1284 from Sienese merchants and bankers, the Bonsignori, to pay the costs of the abbot's election and journey to Rome for his confirmation and for other business there.[76]

Other debts to his Italian bankers clearly accumulated during the succeeding period, and we find Abbot Walter having to repay belated instalments to them over the years: in March 1287 he could afford to pay them £53; in 1288-89, he managed a repayment of £40, against a debt which had been quantified at £93; in 1289-90, £104 was discharged, and then another £46 against an 'old debt'.[77] But another loan of about £162 had had to be obtained on the 1st August 1289 *'for pressing affairs of the abbot and church'*.[78] So it went on. And in 1291 a huge further loan of 800 marks (£533) had then to be obtained from the Bonsignori, to pay for legal appeal proceedings which the abbey, in a sudden emergency, had to bring in the court of Rome,

---

74 For the 'stream of largesse', see p. 306 above
75 The dangers of a culture in which money could be given even to justices was clearly recognised (see eg. Prestwich, *Edward I*, pp. 290-1) and it was the widescale judicial acceptance of open 'fees' and bribes which led the king to purge and convict many of the judges in 1289, see *ibid.* pp. 292-4. But the practice of paying 'pensions' to men in public office continued, as is clear from Wenlock's own actions, see Harvey, *W. of Wenlok*, pp. 30-33, (where the apt term 'annuitants' is used, for the recipients of *pensiones* or *feodi*.)
76 Pearce, *Monks*, p. 60; WAMs 12879-83. See also n. 79 below.
77 Harvey, *ibid.*, pp. 50, 53, 167, 183. There may have been other repayments, but on any view the method of repayment was piecemeal – as and when funds became available.
78 See WAM 28843.

and so there were further agreed instalments of debt to be paid off; again belatedly.[79]

However the Italian bankers were not the only lenders who would oblige the abbot. He 'borrowed' freely, and sometimes on a large scale, from London merchants with whom his household also did frequent business, often on credit. On one occasion in 1287 (when he was repaying £53 to the Bonsignori) we see him also repaying debts to *Robert of Coleworth*, one of his London fishmongers (£20); to *Thomas Romein*, his regular 'pepperer' or spice dealer and rich financier in the city (£52); to *John of Sawbridgeworth*, his customary poulterer (£3); to *Nicholas of Suffolk*, one of his London wine-brokers (£6); to *Thomas of Ludlow*, a cordwainer in the city, who also did business in livestock, wine and fish, and was a partner with (another) *Walter of Wenlock*, a tailor and regular supplier of cloth to the abbey (£26); to *Thomas of Suffolk*, a London skinner (£6).[80]

It is sometimes difficult to tell whether the abbot's debts to merchants who were his suppliers were real loans, or simply the type of enforced 'loans' which any purchase on agreed credit, without interest, would create. But in other instances it is clear that the abbot

was not above asking for actual loans from his regular suppliers or from his own clerks, nor they in making such loans.[81]

In spite of the impression which such borrowings may initially give as to the competence of the abbot in the management of his share of the abbey's possessions, there can be little doubt that by the second half of his abbacy he had brought matters more under control.[82] Debts to the Italians disappeared, and although his officers' accounts continued, to the end, to be dominated by the expenses of his present-giving and his annuitants' pensions and fees, his indebtedness to other lenders was reduced.

### The last years

The more constructive measures which the abbot had introduced in the domestic administration of his estates and his household tend to be overshadowed by the sombre history of the abbey in the last nine years of his abbacy, and by the final parts played in that history by his own 'inflexibility' and the 'contumacy' of his monks. So overweening were these traits that they, and other disasters which befell the abbey, deserve the next chapter to themselves.

79  Harvey, *Wenlock*, p. 132. Contemporaneously, but on a much vaster scale, King Edward also was receiving loans from other Italian merchant bankers such as the Riccardi of Lucca and the Frescobaldi of Florence. The abbey's legal appeal arose because the abbey had given refuge to an apostate Franciscan friar, Wm. of Pershore, and the archbishop of Canterbury, himself a Franciscan, had excommunicated the abbey for doing so. The abbey's only recourse was to appeal to Rome: but the final outcome there was disastrous for the abbey and the abbot. For six months in 1291 Wenlok had even fled to France to seek peace and quiet, perhaps to avoid the Franciscan fracas or possibly creditors, see Pearce, *W. de Wenlok*, pp. 123-126 and Harvey, *ibid*, pp. 38-39.

80  Harvey, *ibid.*, p. 50. See also (eg.) *ibid.*, pp. 184 (Nicholas of Suffolk); 177, 178 and 187 (Thomas of Ludlow). Romein became the first grocer to be mayor of London; Nightingale, *Grocers Company*, 94-5, 123-7.

81  eg. Harvey, *ibid.*, p. 67 (£10 from Thomas Romein and his wife, Juliana; cf. p. 91); and p. 68 (£20 from Gerard of Standon, an abbatial clerk, who under Abbot Ware had been rewarded with the rectorships of both Mordon and Stevenage and had acted for Abbot Wenlock in legal matters in Rome, WAM 24493 (4)).

82  Harvey, *ibid.*, pp. 14-15. The contribution to this satisfactory result, made by eg. surplus moneys from Queen Eleanor's foundation, would be difficult to assess.

# CHAPTER 18

# The Days of Wrath
## 1298-1307

*Dies irae*   *The day of wrath,*
*dies illa*    *that (fateful) day*
*solvet saeclum*  *will close the century*
*in favilla*    *in ashes*

To us, looking back, the events of the last years of the thirteenth century and the first decade of the new one can appear to have reached an apocalyptic climax for the monks of Westminster. Nor would this be fanciful as an assessment of *contemporary* reactions as well, because the disasters which overtook the abbey during this period and the highly-charged documents about them which have come down to us reveal the sense of shock, anger and desperation which afflicted the monks, as events reached their apex.

This short period of nine years was followed by the deaths in 1307, within a few months of one another, of first the old king, Edward I, and then the old abbot, Walter of Wenlock. So the old order appeared to be changing; and it was as if an exclamation mark had been written, to accentuate the omens of the previous years. For the monks the events of this period had already blemished the ending of the old century, a sufficiently hectic century to stir medieval imaginations, and by 1307 it may have seemed to any superstitious monk that the hymn, *Dies irae*, which had been composed about fifty years before, with the theme of the day of the Last Judgment, might be about to be fulfilled.[1]

These nine years had witnessed three disasters at the abbey, rising to a crescendo:

**(a)** the extensive damage by fire, in 1298, of the main domestic buildings of the abbey, leaving intact the new abbey church itself and its equally new chapter house;

**(b)** the desecration of the abbey by the breaking open, in 1303, of the king's treasury which had been housed below the chapter house; the theft and dispersion of much of the treasure; and (worse still) the apparent and very public implication of some of the senior monks in this crime. This had resulted in the imprisonment in the Tower of London, for a time, of the whole complement of the abbey, including even the abbot himself, together with another group of lay persons some of whom were closely connected with the abbey;

**(c)** and, beginning in 1305, an impassioned conflict between Abbot Walter of Wenlock and his new prior, Reginald of Hadham, each supported by equally zealous adherents among the monks. This led first to the intemperate suspension and later the deposition of the prior, and the excommunication and even the imprisonment of various monks including the prior – all carried out by the abbot. But in turn his steps were countered by the prior and his supporters, with formal appeals to the king, to the court of Canterbury and finally to the pope, with a protest as well to the General Chapter of the Benedictine Order. It was a scandalous state

---

1 A late-C12 prayer used by the Benedictines, depicting the soul awaiting judgment, had been intensified into a hymn in mid-C13, probably by Thomas de Celano, a Franciscan. The opening words *Dies irae* came to mark the first passage of the Mass for the Dead: Cross and Livingstone, *Oxf. Dict. of the Christ. Church*, pp. 480-1.

of affairs for any religious house, let alone the abbey at Westminster, and it was only brought within sight of an end by the death of Abbot Walter on Christmas night, 1307.

Although the words *dies irae* became a familiar refrain in the liturgy for the dead, it is uncertain whether the Last Judgment hymn itself was known to the Westminster monks at the time, but if it was, its famous words might have appeared apt to anyone lamenting the fate of the abbey, particularly with its references to the anticipated end of an epoch, and to the ashes of a fire.

## The great fire, in 1298

Unlike the two subsequent disasters which overtook the abbey, the fire occurred through no fault on the part of its personnel. It overtook the abbey's domestic buildings after it had already blazed through parts of the royal palace next door.

In the middle of March King Edward had returned over the Channel after a six month's campaign in Flanders against the French, and by the 29th March he was expected to arrive at his palace in Westminster. It seems that a fire had been lit for him in the 'little hall' within the palace, and from it the chimney above caught alight and that hall was soon destroyed by a 'violent fire', together with some adjoining chambers in the palace.

But the wind also carried sparks onto the roofs of the abbey's infirmary next door to the palace, and the fire spread from there to the other domestic buildings within the abbey. Not only the infirmary but also the monks' nearby dormitory, their refectory, the cellarer's storerooms and the abbot's hall were extensively damaged. It apparently took two days and nights to bring the conflagration under control, and thanks were given by a Westminster chronicler to the bravery of those who fought the fire, and as well to the 'divine grace' which was said to have primarily stayed the flames. The mainly-stone abbey church and the stone chapter house were the main buildings saved intact, instead of being reduced to the 'charcoal and cinders' which remained of the rest.[2] It seems that two of the staff in the infirmary kitchens may even have lost their lives in the blaze, since their funeral costs are included among the expenses of the repairs.[3]

Because the fire had started in the palace, one might have expected that royal money would be contributed to pay for the resulting extensive repairs for the abbey buildings. But there is no evidence that the king (who had much else on his mind at the time, and was having great difficulties about raising money for himself in any case) gave anything for that purpose. It was apparently left to the abbey to carry out repairs at its own expense, but the full details are missing.

Some patchy works of repair to the infirmary were soon completed. From these, one can see the main necessities in that quarter, and their resolution. The sick and infirm patients had to be moved to a stone chamber, while their own burnt wooden 'houses' or sick quarters were repaired with newly purchased oak laths, timbers and plaster, and the roofs were re-shingled by a craftsman 'shingler' and his assistant, over a period of four and a half weeks.[4]

2   See Rackham, 'Building at WA: the great fire to the great plague, 1298-1348', Archaeol. Jo., vol 17 (2nd ser.), No. 3, pp. 259-78, and 'The Nave of WA', Procs of B. Acad. Vol 4, March 1909, pp. 1 ff.  St. Katherine's chapel, also mainly of stone, is neither mentioned as needing repair; nor as surviving intact, although it too was probably saved in its former state. For its use as an important meeting place for the king's council and other assemblies, see eg. p. 221.

3   There were two kitchens, and two members of staff whose funerals are included, I believe, among the other costs.

4   The nearby chamber to which the patients had had to be moved had previously been assigned to Robert Tiptoft, a fellow-crusader and close companion of King Edward (both when he had been prince and later as king), who had previously been granted a corrody of a chamber at the abbey, either as a pied-a-terre (as suggested in Harvey, *Living and Dying*, pp. 183 and 242), or as a permanent home for his lifetime as an old retainer – although in fact he died in May of the same year, 1298, (his death perhaps hastened?), see WAM 19318. The king could require monasteries to grant such corrodies to men chosen by him, Prestwich, *Edward I*, p. 156.

A new heating furnace had to be bought, for the patients' repaired sickrooms. The infirmary hall and another chamber had to be re-roofed by a tiler with 4000 new tiles. New doors and windows had to be made, and the carpentry work needed two carpenters working for thirteen and a half days.[5] That year 120 trees had to be cut down in Hampstead to supply materials for use at Westminster.[6]

Emergency work, we know, had to be carried out to the monks' huge dormitory, to clean out the dormitory drain and to repair and test the water conduit. But the records of the other damage and the works made necessary are missing. Perhaps the most intriguing fact known is that the abbey invested at once in a large purchase of 20,000 tiles, at a cost of 56s. 8d., but after the purchase the records are again silent, and it is not known whether these tiles were in fact used then and there.[7]

But eight years later, in 1306, further extensive repairs had to be planned and carried out, lasting from Easter to Christmas, to re-make and re-raise a whole new roof for the 'vast' refectory, a task which necessitated heavy purchases of 25 oak trees, 100 cut beams and other timbers. The convent had also provided another 80 beams from their woods at Hampstead in 1305, almost certainly for this purpose. So far as the known details go, at least £48 was spent on the refectory task alone,

and a master carpenter, Edmund with 16-19 other carpenters and five other workers as well, with Robert, a master mason, and a smith, had to be employed. It is not clear whether the tiles bought in 1298 were used on top of the new wooden refectory roof in 1306, or had been used immediately after the fire for a remaking of the roof of the dormitory (which was nearest to the advance of the fire from the infirmary), or for the abbot's hall.[8] It is certainly clear that the tiles had been bought because of the fire; and the dormitory was yet another 'vast' room, even longer than the refectory (173 feet against 130).[9]

Immediately after the fire, the monks had realised that they were faced with large costs, and resorted to a programme for meeting them, by resolving to appropriate for their own benefit, if they could, a number of valuable churches, namely those at Morden (Surrey), Sawbridgeworth (Herts), Kelvedon (Essex) and Longdon (Worcs).[10] They were successful in obtaining possession of Morden church three years later in 1301,[11] but forgot or ignored the need to obtain a consent from the king under the comparatively recent statute of Mortmain (1279); which cost them dear eighteen years later, when they were fined £40 by Edward II for failing to get his father's consent.[12]

The other three churches involved even longer-term efforts. It was only in 1333, thirty

---

5    Some details of employment terms are revealed. The carpenters were paid at a daily rate of 4d. each, but the more specialist tiler and probably the shingler were 'task' workers, who were paid sums agreed in advance (which conceal daily rates). The general workers, who cleared up the damage and/or repaired walls in the infirmary over the course of three weeks, were paid at a daily rate of $1\frac{1}{2}$d or 3d each, depending presumably on the complexity of the job or their respective skills or experience.
6    *Hampstead A/cs*, vol. 2/22B.
7    See Rackham, *ibid.*, pp. 261 and 268.
8    Miss Harvey in *Living and Dying*, pp. 88-89, has questioned the scale of the damage caused by the fire. But to my mind even such details as have survived indicate extensive damage, and clearly there are also missing details. The fact that the damage was not all repaired at once may reflect exactly the scale, and fear, of the cost which the monks foresaw by their plan for paying for repairs, and they must have had to live meanwhile with a ruined or patched-up refectory roof, and more work to the dormitory, their two main buildings.
9    *Ibid.*, pp. 41 and 130.
10   Harvey, *WA Estates*, p. 51.
11   They secured the appropriation of Morden church, by obtaining an order from the bishop of Winchester (in whose diocese it lay); but as this meant a transfer of property into the 'dead hand' of the church (to the damage of the crown) it needed royal consent (usually obtainable at a price) under Edward I's statute of Mortmain.
12   *Cal. P. R.*, 1317-21, p. 344.

five years later, that the monks were able to obtain the consent of the bishop of Worcester to the appropriation of Longdon church. As regards Sawbridgeworth and Kelvedon churches which were in the diocese of the bishop of London, the successive bishops proved difficult and it took papal orders and more than fifty years before the abbey was able to secure possession of those churches as well. By then of course the fire of 1298 was old history, but that does not detract from its contemporary impact, which must still have been present in the early years of the 1300s when the other two disasters were to add to the anguish of the monks.[13]

## The burglary of the treasury in 1303

The burglary was an extraordinary episode, mysterious in some of participants' motives and posing other unanswered questions, which survive only to tantalise. The crime was the subject of several judicial inquiries ordered by the king, and it is remarkably well documented. But even those records do not yield up all its basic secrets, particularly those about the involvement of the monks of the abbey. As a good story, it has naturally been embraced by historians with enthusiasm and even relish, but this lighter profile cannot conceal the distress which such an event and its consequences could give rise to in a religious house such as the abbey at Westminster.

The royal treasury which was maintained in a vault below the chapter house, on the east side of the abbey cloister, contained part of the treasure of the king's personal office, his 'wardrobe', most of it in the form of valuables

such as gold crowns, gold and silver plates, goblets, bowls, gold coins and jewels which might be used by the king for presents or on state occasions.[14] Apparently attempts had been made to break into this treasury a few years earlier, but the details are shadowy.[15]

By the early 1300s Westminster had temporarily ceased to be the seat of the exchequer. The king was working in the north, planning and executing campaigns against the Scots, and to facilitate this, he had been holding his councils in York and had moved the exchequer temporarily away from Westminster to that city. Another muster and campaign in Scotland had been planned for 1303, and by June of that year he was encamped at Linlithgow, his main base and castle in Scotland.

There bad news reached him, that in his absence a spectacular burglary had occurred at the abbey and that many valuable objects from his treasury had already been secretly circulating in London and the surrounding areas. Outraged, on the 6th June he ordered a commission of investigation by four justices, headed by Ralph of Sandwich, the Constable of the Tower of London.[16] They were to investigate in the usual way, by hearing 'juries' appointed by the wards of the City of London and from the Hundreds of the counties of Middlesex and Surrey.

These 'juries' were, in effect, local persons who were themselves to find out the facts and give 'evidence' as to their conclusions. They were not like modern juries whose task is to listen, passively and without prior knowledge, to evidence given in court by others. The 'evidence' of such medieval juries was itself to be collected from the inquiries which they

---

13 While the monks may have tended to exaggerate the effects of the fire, it is clear that powerful memories of its effects survived and their descriptions of those effects were accepted in 1301 by the bishop of Winchester who almost certainly had had occasion to witness them himself in the previous three years (see WAD 179b), and again more than thirty years later by the pope, see eg. WAM 21256.

14 On the 20th June, 1303, a full inventory of the valuables was taken by the king's keeper of his wardrobe, Sir John of Droxford, in the presence of three of the justices, the queen's cofferer, the mayor of London, the prior and seven other monks, see Cole, *Documents of the C13 and C14*, pp. 277 ff. For Droxford, see also pp. 286 n. 103 above and 359 below.

15 eg. Prestwich, *Edward I*, p. 536, records the imprisonment of 'the cellarer, another monk and thirty others' on an occasion in 1296, but I have not yet found the source of this information.

16 *Cal. P. R.*, 1301-7, p. 192.

were meant to make; and it often represented no more than matters of common opinion, reputation or belief, or even of rumour which members of the jury as local people had heard.[17] The clear modern distinctions between the evidence of facts, the evidence of expert opinion, and the findings expected of the court were blurred at this medieval time.

The case had now become a subject for continued public debate, enquiry and gossip, in addition to the shameful scandal for the abbey which such an episode gave rise to. And meanwhile valuable articles of gold and silver had been turning up at odd places in London and in Westminster, in the Thames (thrown in and hauled up by fishermen in their nets) and in various fields around the city. Gold plate and precious jewels from the treasury were being traded in the city among the goldsmiths, or were carried to such places as Northampton and Colchester for disposal there. All of London and Westminster were agog with the scandalous story.

Near the beginning of July, less than a month after their appointment, the justices had opened their inquiry, sitting at a number of places in the city of London, in Westminster and Surrey where they heard the 'evidence' from about forty juries.[18] Gradually the 'facts' began to emerge, and as ordered, the justices soon apprehended those who were most implicated by the evidence. At that stage, these included ten of the monks, the sacrist, the sub-prior, the cellarer and seven other monks, all of whom were named by the juries and were now arrested and lodged in the Tower. Six of the sacrist's lay assistants also joined him in the Tower.

The abbot, who (though named in the evidence) had not been blamed personally by anyone, was apparently 'bailed', so even at this early stage he too had been arrested as the person primarily responsible for the conduct of all abbey personnel. Fifteen lay people, some connected with the abbey or the king's palace, but including one well-known city goldsmith, were also arrested and imprisoned, eight in the Tower and seven in Newgate prison.

The two main culprits proved to be an enterprising merchant, named Richard of Pudlicott, and the deputy keeper of the king's palace, usually known as William of the Palace. Pudlicott made a startling public confession to the justices, boasting that he alone was responsible for the initiation and the whole execution of the whole enterprise. He was a strange character, who had once been a tonsured clerk, but was later a travelling merchant in wools, cheese and butter. In Flanders, he said, he had found himself arrested and made to pay, under compulsion as a hostage (though being himself 'entirely innocent', he said) certain debts which King Edward was said to have owed there. So Pudlicott had a grudge against the king and, in effect, carried out the theft of the royal treasure to get his own back.

His extraordinary story about the method used to effect the burglary itself was that he had gained access to the outside of the chapter house before Christmas 1302, and from then on, for four months until after Easter 1303, he had been working away to break through the walls of the vault below the chapter house with metal tools. On the 24th April he had at last broken through the thirteen-foot walls, and had spent the whole of the next day collecting valuables together, which he took away on the following nights – thirteen great pitchers full of gold and silver objects and jewels – some of which he dropped on his way through the cemetery. He said nothing of any accomplices, and his express boast was '*I alone*

---

17  Most of the 'evidence' relating to the burglary is collected in detail and published (in Latin and French) in Palgrave, *Ancient Kalendars*, i, Appendix., pp. 251 ff. Most of it is hear-say, or matters of belief or just rumour.

18  The justices sat first at the bishop of London's house in the City, then at the Leaden Hall, the Guildhall, the king's great Hall at Westminster, at Southwark and at the New Temple, all in the space of a few days in July.

*did it'*. At its best, the story was inadequate through its omissions, and some of it was just incredible.[19]

It was obvious that Pudlicott could not have done the deed without help, and that his easiest means of access had been through the palace. The acting keeper, William of the Palace, was no more than a servant of the king's real palace-keeper who, following the common medieval practice, was resident elsewhere and acted by deputy. But as the deputy, William (who was examined twice) had all the keys of the palace and was clearly an accomplice of Pudlicott, assisting the burglar by letting him have access into the abbey cemetery through a small gate in the wall between the palace and the abbey. Significantly William was also shown to have kept other members of the public out of the palace at the critical times when Pudlicott needed to work on the job.[20]

The nature of the 'evidence' from the various juries is revealing as to the undercurrents which underlay their assertions. Almost all were of course agreed that the primary culprits were the self-confessed Pudlicott, William of the Palace and some of their associates. But the twenty London juries (speaking for twenty six wards of the city) who gave such evidence were virtually unanimous in also alleging that Adam of Warfeld, the abbey sacrist (and, according to some wards, other monks or abbey servants as well) were aware of the breaking-in, as accessories. Some of the juries also asserted that the sacrist (who had clearly been collecting up various precious articles which were being found in the abbey precincts) had had some of the treasure in his possession. But it was left to the senior body of the city, the aldermen of London, to come out into the open and to put at the forefront of their 'evidence' the charge

that *'the sacrist of the abbey, Adam of Warfeld, and the monks Alexander of Pershore (the sub-prior) and Thomas of Dene were the originators and transactors of the burglary of the king's treasury'*.[21]

So the powerful men of the city were deliberately using the occasion to put the knife in, although they produced no hard facts other than that the sacrist (who in any case had collected up the scattered relics) had ended up in actual possession of some of the valuable articles. No doubt it was with some pleasure that they were able to record that the sheriff of London had already arrested 'the sacrist and others' (on the orders of the justices), and was 'keeping them safely'.

Historically the residents of London and Westminster were rivals and old enemies in various fields, such as the wrestling match and riots of 1222.[22] Furthermore there had been violent disputes and extreme ill-feeling between London and the abbey itself, during the years between about 1248 and 1280, when Richard of Crokesley and Richard of Ware were the abbots. On those occasions the monks had seen their recently-received right to hold fairs in Westminster extended by even more generous grants of improved rights from King Henry III, at the further expense of the citizens and other residents of London as well as of other fair-towns throughout the kingdom; and (conversely) during the king's later troubles and civil war with the barons, the monks had also seen their abbey being deprived of some of its established and traditional rights, which had been given to the city of London.[23]

In addition to the London juries, the juries from Westminster and elsewhere in Middlesex had also voiced milder suspicions about the connivance of the sacrist and other monks, but it was still the sacrist's possession of some of

19  An added feature (though strictly irrelevant) was that he had already broken in through the chapter house itself in the previous year, and had stolen a good number of silver articles belonging to the monks' refectory.
20  Apparently some members of the public had the right to enter the palace to collect water, or even to use the latrines.
21  Palgrave, *Ancient Kalendars*, i, p. 260.
22  See pp. 188-9 above.
23  See pp. 238, and 263 above.

the collected-up valuables which seemed to lie mainly behind their accusations. They did however add the fact that the sacrist had refused (so they said) to hand valuables over to Henry of Charing, the coroner of Westminster, and had forbidden him to hold an inquest on them (as 'treasure trove').[24]

It was clearly difficult for the justices to resolve some of the issues, particularly the part or parts played by the monks. Hard facts about these were not clear, and the well-known association between the crown and the abbey must also have posed certain delicate questions for the justices. They seem to have delayed, and in August the king, now at Brechin in Scotland, impatiently ordered them to proceed and report to him. But again nothing was forthcoming, and by October the king's patience was exhausted.

It seems that the justices had meanwhile ordered the re-arrest of the abbot and the arrest of thirty-eight other named monks (now making forty-eight in all in the Tower). But on October 10th the king (now at Kinloss in Scotland) addressed another commission, this time to his chief justice Roger Brabazon and four other justices (including two of those on the former commission), to hear petitions for bail from the abbot and all the forty eight monks, on the grounds that they were *falsely indicted for the breaking-into of the treasury at Westminster...'.*[25]   And at some point of time the abbot and all the monks – save ten – were bailed, on suitable sureties being found.[26]

Apart from the principal culprits

(Pudlicott and William of the Palace), at least eight other laymen were detained. These included the prominent clerk who acted as a lawyer and agent for the abbey, Gerin the linendraper, of St. Giles, who lived in a house in the main street of the nearby parish of St. Giles, near the leper hospital, and also had a large estate in Belsize in Hampstead.[27]

The next step was that a month later, on November 10th 1303, the king addressed yet another commission to the same five justices, who were to continue the investigation of the stolen treasure (now roundly assessed as worth £100,000). But again there were delays until January and March in the following year, 1304, when some of the justices sat at the Tower of London to hear a further session of evidence from some of the juries.[28] It was now more than nine months since the burglary had taken place, and much of this further evidence can be regarded as repetitive or stale.

But one of the most damaging facts now alleged against the abbey was earlier disorderly conduct on the part of nine named monks, including Alexander of Pershore the sub-prior, by consorting with William of the Palace and women 'of bad life' in the palace garden, 'playing, eating and drinking' there, for which (it was said) they had already been reprimanded by the prior.[29] It was also said that when an official search was being made for the missing treasure, two of the monks had taken some of it to Gerin's house in St Giles, so that it would be out of the way of the searchers.[30] This had followed earlier evidence

---

24  Palgrave, *Ancient Kalendars*, pp. 261, 261 and 263. Even this could be quite consistent with a genuine, if not necessarily lawful, claim of right by the sacrist on behalf of the true owner, the king. The coroner's jurisdiction had dated from Norman times.

25  *Cal. P. R.*, 1301-1307, pp. 194-5.

26  There are inconsistencies in the records as to the timing of some of these events, as the contradictions between the various historical accounts given by excited modern historians reveal.

27  See note 30 below, pp. 290-1 above and 373-4 below. Gerin often held courts in abbey manors, and travelled distantly on business for the abbot, see Pearce, *W. de Wenlock*, pp. 159-160; *ibid., Monks*, p. 70; WAM 23631-2. For his part in the burglary, see Palgrave, *Ancient Kalendars*, pp. 262, 266-7, 279, 281-2, 286, 292]

28  For sittings at the Tower, see Palgrave, *ibid.*, pp. 275, 278, 279; *Annales Lond.*, RS vol. 76, p. 132.

29  Palgrave, *ibid.*, p. 288.

30  *ibid.*, pp. 281, 286, 292; cf. p. 266-7. These may have been the valuable articles which the sacrist (innocently? or guiltily?) had been collecting as they were found from time to time in the cemetery. Gerin

(probably unreliable on its face, since it came from William of the Palace) that the same two monks and others had been seen, suggestively taking heavy covered baskets by boat from the king's quay at his palace in Westminster downstream to the city of London.[31]

Whatever truth there was in all this, it requires little imagination to envisage the impact which such events and such public allegations must have had upon the town and at least the quieter complement of monks at the abbey. In a religious house so closely connected with the crown and national administration, such a scandal was unique.

Historians have enthusiastically taken sides about the guilt of the monks, but it is impossible to resolve the issues reliably on the available evidence.[32] One can probably accept that by this time discipline among at least some of the monks at the abbey and their servants had become very lax, in spite of the stern attitude which the strict abbot adopted towards those who opposed his authority. But he too was getting old. Discipline in the convent rested in practice now with the prior, and at this period the prior was William of Huntingdon, an elderly man of about 63 in 1303, who was probably unable to curb excesses among his flock. He seems to have played little part in events at this time, although his name does appear in the list of the 48 monks who had been imprisoned (for a limited period) in the Tower. Since he probably died in 1305, he may well have been beyond the task of maintaining proper order and discipline among unruly members of the convent.

At all events the legal process and delays continued, and in due course in or after November 1304 Pudlicott and William of the Palace were hanged, together with four or five other lay men. When arraigned, the ten imprisoned monks had pleaded benefit of clergy and so avoided the jurisdiction of secular justices to try them.[33] From time to time both the abbot and those members of the convent who had been released continued to show their 'brotherly love' for the ten monks still incarcerated in the Tower, by openly sending them presents of both food and money.[34] And on at least one occasion in the earlier stages of the affair, Brother Alexander of Newport (who was one of the more suspect monks, but strangely was not one of the ten retained in the Tower) had ridden all the way to the king in Scotland to plead the case of those of his brothers who were in the Tower, and later rode to York several times again on their behalf.[35]

But at last with the capture of Stirling Castle in 1304 and the conquest of Scotland ostensibly completed, the king returned from Scotland. On the 25th March, 1305 he attended a ceremony held at the Abbey, in the presence of his magnates to celebrate his success, and *'the king gave thanks to God and St. Edward'*.[36] The coronation Stone of Scone, captured from Scotland nine years before, was already in its

was said to have then thrown them at first into his dove loft, but later to have taken them in a basket and (perhaps on his way to his Hampstead house?) to have thrown the basket into a hedge called Haggehedge in Kentish Town, where they were later found by a shepherd boy, called Adam.

31  Palgrave, *ibid.*, p. 268. There was other evidence not implicating the monks, but linking the Fleet gaol and the palace, which was consistent with the fact that the two places had the same 'keeper', see p. 116 above.

32  Contrast the main protagonists in this sport: anti-monks, Professor Tout, *A Medieval Burglary*, Bull. of Jo. Rylands Lib., 2 (1914-15) pp. 348-69, and pro-monks, Bishop Pearce, *W. de Wenlok*, pp. 146-166. I have contributed a more earthy version, using mainly original words taken from the recorded evidence, but (perforce) modern voices, and without any conclusive verdict (as I believe the evidence warrants), in a short BBC radio feature entitled *A Right Royal Burglary*. Another account is given in McCall, *The Medieval Underworld*, 153-7.

33  This did not prevent the justices continuing to keep them in prison, to the indignation of the monk chroniclers.

34  Pearce, *W. de Wenlok*, pp. 164, 166.

35  *ibid.*, p. 164; WAM 23638.

36  *Flores Historiae*, ed. Luard, RS 95, p. 95. However the king's troubles in Scotland were still not entirely over: William Wallace was still at large, and the rebellion of Robert Bruce was still to come.

place under the new Coronation Chair, which the king had had constructed to house it.[37] With his major problem over Scotland partly resolved and much of his treasure recovered, King Edward was apparently reluctant to push matters further against the monks, and gave orders for the release of the ten. So the scandal in which the monks had become embroiled and their continuing reminder of it evaporated, but the internal stresses which the great fire and the disaster of the burglary must have caused were shortly to redouble, for different but not entirely disconnected reasons.

Ten days after the king's celebration at the abbey, the old prior was dead, and it took four months for the new prior to be elected. When Brother Reginald of Hadham did become the new prior in August 1305, an unimaginable period of anguish and domestic strife lay ahead for the abbot, the prior himself and the rest of the monks. For over two years the House was to be split from top to bottom.

## The final explosion between the abbot and the prior

Already, long before the end of Abbot Walter's life, there had been a number of simmering disputes between the abbot and his monks, as we have seen.[38] Although such serious differences had been a feature of earlier abbacies as well during this eventful century, in one way or another those episodes had been contained or allayed, and there had been no public eruption sufficient to shake the abbey to its foundations. It is true that the unilateral decree which Prior Coleworth and his convent had passed after Abbot Ware's death was a sign of the pent-up earth-tremors which were at work below the surface.[39] But now the private affairs

of the house of Westminster were to become a public scandal yet again, surpassing even the disgrace and embarrassment to which the burglary of the king's treasury had given rise.[40]

As is often the case in such situations, the explosion which took place during the last year, and indeed during the last months, of the abbot's life had more to do with the personalities of some of those involved than with points of real principle. Two separate parties of monks can be identified as committed adherents of the two leaders respectively (with a third group of less-committed monks), but it was the abbot (principally) and the prior, together perhaps with two other monks called Roger of Aldenham and Alexander of Pershore, whose personalities gave rise to the final explosion. The abbot himself has already been correctly labelled as having 'a hasty authoritarian temper', and the monks in general as being 'contumacious', each party being determined not to compromise on any matter which *they* at any rate still regarded as a point of principle.[41]

When Brother Reginald of Hadham had been unanimously elected prior on the 2nd August 1305 without visible competition, one could have thought that all would be well between the abbot and him, even if there were still some official differences which had existed in the previous prior's time. Although during his past career Brother Reginald had acted in many of the convent's obedientiary offices, he had also had a long and close relationship with the abbot himself: –

(a) he had acted on behalf of both the abbot and the convent in business at Rome as early as 1286;

---

37  Stolen from the abbey in 1950 by Scottish nationalists, but recaptured and returned in 1951, the Stone has now been restored to Scotland since 1996, on condition that it is returned to the abbey for coronations.

38  See pp. 292-5 and 306-7 above.

39  See p. 294.

40  How far the *public* stigma of the burglary may have increased the tensions of the period for the abbey would be difficult to assess.

41  These descriptions of the abbot and his monks are given by Miss Harvey, *W. de Wenlok*, p. 23 and *WA Estates*, p. 99.

(b) in 1289, he had already been entrusted with the keys of the abbot's 'treasury', albeit on a temporary basis at that time;

(c) from 1292 to 1294 he had been the monk-warden of the abbot's country house, La Neyte and, at the same time, the abbot's bailiff for the surrounding manor of Eye;

(d) as recently as November 1304 until October 1305, he had been the senior of the abbot's two 'receivers' or treasurers, together (ominously) with Brother Roger of Aldenham who also played a significant part in the final outcome.[42]

However even this close relationship between the abbot and Brother Reginald did not prevent what happened next. Perhaps the truth may have been that it was this closer acquaintance with Abbot Walter's autocratic attitudes and methods which had regrettably begun to turn Brother Reginald more against him.[43]

This edges Brother Roger of Aldenham further into the story. He has rightly been described as a 'fighter'.[44] As a colleague who had already served in joint office with Brother Reginald, he had become the latter's stout champion and, as himself a leader of a faction among the monks, he threw himself, and no doubt his faction, enthusiastically into supporting Brother Reginald as the candidate for the vacant post of prior.

Although there is no official source to indicate that there had been any other candidate for the post, one personal document drafted by Brother Roger at the time of the election clearly intimated that a rival candidate was being manoevred into position, and that it was the abbot who was deviously promoting that other candidate.[45] His theme was that the abbot's intention was to subvert the position of Brother Reginald's supporters, and (through some sinister abbatial candidate) to undermine the convent's right to elect its own prior. As a firebrand, Brother Roger had no compunction in labelling that other candidate as 'criminosum, convictum seu infamem' – a criminal, a convict or a person of ill repute – and pugnaciously regarded even that candidate's promoters (ie. including the abbot) as criminosi also. Rhetorically he called upon the pope, the court of Canterbury and the king – 'the patron of the abbey' – to protect him and his adherents in their heroic fight for the convent's rights and the rightful candidate.[46]

So who was this other invisible candidate whom Brother Roger was fighting? There can be little doubt that it was the abbot's faithful ally, Brother Alexander of Pershore, who even more extensively than Brother Reginald had served the abbot, in many capacities and from the earliest days. Initially in 1284 he had accompanied the abbot-elect on his journey across the continent for confirmation as abbot by the pope, and had subsequently visited Rome on two further occasions on the abbot's business. Later in his career, in addition to

42 WAM 28821; Harvey, ibid., p. 159; ibid., pp. 28, 59, 62-3; ibid., pp. 27, 93-6. It should be noted that Reginald's position as monk-warden and bailiff meant that he was actually being employed by the abbot in those roles during the four months after the old prior's death and the 2nd August 1305 when he became the new prior.

43 As early as 1294-5, there were signs of possible conflict, when Brother Hadham protested publicly on behalf of the convent, at having to pay for support of papal cardinals who were visiting England, on the grounds that it was the abbot's duty to pay for such visiting dignitaries; WAM 9499A, Pearce, W. de Wenlok, p. 133.

44 Pearce, W. de Wenlok, p. 169

45 WAM 9508A. Although it purports to be a draft campaign promotion on behalf of the whole convent, it becomes more and more egocentric as it goes on, with the personal pronouns – I, me, my (adherents) – being used more than ten times, to denote the victim or victims, as Roger believed, of the abbot's subversive machinations.

46 One revealing fact is that Bro. Roger who refers often to his 'adherents' adds always that there were others who also 'wished to adhere' to him, but (by implication) did not dare to do so, in the face of an abbot who was sharp-eyed and quick to bite. At the end Bro. Reginald's supporters included some of the most senior monks who perhaps in the early days of the conflict did not wish to reveal their support for a firebrand like Bro. Roger.

holding convent posts such as almoner and sacrist, he had also served as the abbot's chaplain, the steward of his household, then his receiver or treasurer, his auditor, his constant agent and messenger, and the abbot's adviser and confidant; and in the abbot's final, and perhaps failing, months he later became one of his attorneys.[47]

But Brother Alexander had also been the sub-prior during the period of the burglary, and was personally implicated in the heaviest allegations made against the monks. Whether justifiably or not, he had been named on at least eight occasions, as a principal suspect, by juries from Westminster and Fleet Street, Middlesex and London (including the city aldermen) who gave 'evidence' before each of the judicial inquiries. Consequently, second only to the sacrist, he had been one of the ten monks who had been retained in the Tower when the rest were bailed.[48]

So in 1305 it must have been helpful for Brother Roger of Aldenham to detect a 'criminal and a convict' in the abbot's favourite assistant, even though Brother Alexander was released from the Tower in the spring or summer of 1305. Although the threatened candidature of Brother Alexander for the priorship had apparently not been pursued, or perhaps had been abandoned in the face of combative opposition from Brother Roger and his adherents, we can be certain that Brother Alexander was back at the side of the abbot before August 1305 and remained there until the end at Christmas, 1307.

Not content with his open attack on this 'criminal', Brother Roger the prior's appointed champion made an equally forthright attack on the abbot himself. While still observing the ironic niceties, in calling the abbot *Lord Walter, our reverend father and abbot by the grace of God'*, the monk accused him of having deliberately deviated or intending to deviate from the time-honoured customs of the convent in the election of its prior.

So with four of the main protagonists in place, the final period begins. We know that the earlier simmering disputes about the convent's claimed rights continued, as they had done under the old prior.[49] But whereas these issues seem to have hitherto been debated on their individual merits or demerits, under the new prior a subtle intensification of attitude may have finally taken place during the course of the year 1307.

Following the theme of Brother Roger's early draft war-cry, the individual disputes became generalised into a charge that the abbot wished to subvert the whole of the long-standing 'compositions' between the abbots and their convents, starting with the original one made between Abbot Richard of Berking and his monks – which had been, it was said, *'ordained by the illustrious King Henry III, the abbey's patron, with the advice of the magnates of the realm, and confirmed by the pope'*. That is how the prior's attitude was formulated, after the real legal battle had ultimately been joined.[50] But perhaps this change of approach should hardly be surprising to us, because we know that the person who drafted the prior's later legal documents was none other than Brother Roger himself.

However, before final battle was joined, it seems that even in the first half of 1307 any individual altercations were still being conducted formally in accordance with legal procedures, but had reached a point at which the prior and his supporters had realised that it might be necessary to have the outstanding issues decided by their final court of appeal, namely the court of Rome. They brought matters to a head, when in early July of that year the prior made a humble but formal

---

47 See Harvey, *W. de Wenlok*, passim, particularly pp. 16, 24-5, 27, and see also index at p. 273. Also Pearce, *W. de Wenlok*, passim, see index at p. 235.
48 See Palgrave, *Ancient Kalendars*, p. 269.
49 For discussion of the issues, see pp. 293-5 above and Harvey, *W. de Wenlok*, pp. 19-20.
50 WAM 9496.

request to the abbot not to violate the abbey's customs and the compositions. At this, the abbot appears to have lost his temper. Without warning, he suspended the prior from his office, and ordered the firebrand Brother Roger to be banished from Westminster, to serve his exile at Hurley Priory, the abbey's dependent cell in Berkshire. There was now little which the suspended prior and his supporters could do but make their appeals to Rome and also to the court of Canterbury. He and his party presented themselves in the chapter house at the abbey, and in the presence of the abbot, their advocate formally announced the appeals and spelt out their grounds.[51]

So now the fight was on. The abbot's rage had passed beyond boiling point, and his own group of monks were having to try to calm him. In answer to the entreaties of those whom he pointedly called 'our obedient monks', he issued a formal statement on the 16th August that he ratified and confirmed all the 'compositions' made between the previous abbots and their respective monks. That at least appeared to be a conciliatory pronouncement. But he added minatory footnotes, which must have confirmed the worst fears of the prior and his party. In promising, both for himself and his successors, to observe the compositions in good faith, the abbot added a significant reservation to his promise: *except in so far as I may give formal notice that I ought not to be bound or constrained by them during my lifetime'.* He had (so he openly claimed) *'prescriptive right and other lawful defences against the rigour of any legal obligation to observe the compositions'.*[52]

It was in these footnotes that Abbot Walter's true attitude was expressed, as his opponents correctly feared. A fortnight elapsed before the volcano finally burst. In those two weeks, the abbot's reservation to his promise was rejected by the prior and his party, and in refutation of it, some monks testified that many years before, on the occasion when he had been elected and blessed as abbot, he had himself sworn on oath, without any qualification, to observe the compositions.[53] The king had meanwhile known of these confrontations at the abbey and, just as he had done when the burglary of his treasury had taken place, he appointed four justices to investigate them.[54] For his part, the prior made arrangements for his case to be brought to the notice of the General Chapter of the Benedictine Order at its next meeting, which was to be held in September at Oxford. Ominously the presidents of that meeting were to be Abbot Wenlock himself and the Abbot of Malmesbury.[55] But it was Abbot Wenlock who struck first.

Without giving any notice, on the 1st September he caused a dramatic list of charges against the prior to be read out formally before all the monks assembled in the chapter house. The case had now been handed over to the 'lawyers', and it was the abbot's advocate, Master David of Northampton, who had the task, in the abbey's chapter house, of reading out eleven *'already notorious'* charges against the suspended prior. Some of these charges even alleged acts such as suspected embezzlements said to have been committed by the prior in various offices which he had previously held before he became prior. Others concerned acts of defiance committed by him after his suspension as prior, such as his order forbidding Brother Roger to leave the

51 WAMs 9499B and 9499E. The prior's main advocate was Master John of Deneby, rector of Launton (Oxon) and of a London church. He had worked for the abbot up to 1290, but since 1297 had become the prior's man.
52 WAM 5671, printed in Pearce, *W. de Wenlok,* p. 204. This is, I believe, the effect of his Latin, but see Pearce, *ibid,* at p. 173. By claiming this only 'during his own lifetime', he left open the question whether his successors could or would claim a similar right. This raises issues as to the personal nature of his claimed 'lawful defences', which were not otherwise explained by the abbot.
53 WAM 9497. See also pp. 293 above.
54 *Cal. P. R.* 1307-1313, p. 36.
55 WAM 9499D. This meant that he now had, in effect, three petitions on hand: to the Papal Court, the Court of Canterbury, and the General Chapter of the Black Monks.

abbey and so countermanding the monk's expulsion by the abbot.[56] Probably worst of all was the charge that the prior had earlier made *'false and malicious'* personal accusations against the abbot, *'wickedly slandering him'* in the matter of the burglary of the king's treasury, and causing him to be summoned before the king's court of the Exchequer.[57] The prior later recorded the personal hatred in the looks with which the abbot had eyed him, when these *'fabricated crimes'* were imputed to the prior by the abbot's advocate.

So these charges were all spelt out on the 1st September. Without proper notice being afforded to the prior, he was then and there ordered to 'purge' himself of the accusations on the very next day, at prime (the office at daybreak), 'with twenty-four hands', ie. with twenty four monks prepared to swear to his innocence. Unfortunately for the prior, his 'party' among the monks numbered only seventeen, as the abbot must have known, out of the total of about fifty monks at the abbey. So early next morning, at prime, all the prior could do was to appear in the chapter house, and appeal first on the grounds that the notice given to him was too short, secondly that only sixteen 'hands' were necessary for a canonical purgation, and thirdly that the abbot was well aware that an earlier appeal by the prior was already pending to the court of Rome, on which he (the prior) again rested.

But since Abbot Walter was not only the prosecutor but also the judge, Prior Hadham received short shrift. When he asked the abbot to supply him with a written copy of the charges, even this was refused to him. The abbot did defer the purgation but only very briefly, ordering it to take place at noon, that same day. At that hour the prior had to attend again in the chapter house, accompanied by only sixteen supporters. But since their number was insufficient to

match the number ordered, the abbot proceeded at once to pronounce his judgment against the prior, ordering him to be deprived of his office and to be imprisoned. When the prior expressed an added ground of appeal to Rome against these sentences, the abbot promptly excommunicated him, and for good measure he also excommunicated Brother Roger of Aldenham, then at Hurley Priory, and pronounced him to be an apostate from the Benedictine Order.

These tactics which Abbot Walter had employed were indefensible. But the opposing personalities were now at such cross-purposes that all reason had flown out of the window. Both sides had been acting provocatively, on an issue which had had its roots in the earliest days of Benedictine monks, namely the issue of the primacy of the abbot in his monastery. But life had changed dramatically since the sixth century, when St Benedict's Rule had handed that primacy to the abbot.

The monastery was now no longer a house of simple monks, devoted only to a life of religious seclusion. Here in Westminster it was already a social institution, surrounded by a sophisticated town and the apparatus of a national government; it had a complicated administration of its own, it held many estates, employed big staffs and enjoyed a large income. Even the detailed sharing agreements made earlier in the same century between the abbots and their monks had already led to dissensions. Rigid rules, whether upholding the old pre-eminence of the abbot or the new divisions of power in the monastery, were no longer exclusively apt for the needs of the times. Perhaps unconsciously Abbot Walter may have been right to look for some flexibility in favour of an abbot, so that when occasion really required it, he would be justified in departing from a too rigid division

---

56  In the abbot's eyes, the prior had made matters worse by later giving his own licence to Brother Roger to go to Hurley for a month, so substituting his own authority for that of the abbot.

57  I do not know the details behind this allegation, but it may have led to, or arisen out of, the undoubted fact that the abbot ended up by being sent to the Tower for a period.

of responsibilities. But meanwhile his own dictatorial manner of acting was still based on the old primacy of the abbot, after which, by personal temperament, he hankered.[58]

Naturally the matters in dispute could not end just with the peremptory deposition of the prior in September 1307. The personal temper of the times can be judged from the fact that the abbot's supporters were even being subjected to physical attacks and abuse from their opponents, and two of their leaders, Brothers Alexander of Pershore and William of Chalk, were being accused of incontinence with three named women; falsely, they claimed.[59]

Meanwhile the machinery of the Papal Court had been set in motion, and orders from Pope Clement V and his delegates were making arrangements in October and November for the sitting of commissioners to hear the disputes between the abbot and prior.[60] But the hearings were not to start until March of the following year, 1308, and in that interval the death of the abbot suddenly intervened. Taken ill abruptly in December, while staying at his manor of Pyrford in Surrey, he received medicines and attendances from two doctors,[61] but within a matter of weeks he was dead, dying in the middle of the second mass during Christmas night.

However one week before he died, there had occurred an event which (assuming that no undue influence had beeen brought to bear upon the ailing abbot) may have amounted to a genuine attempt at a last-minute reconciliation, on at least some of the divisive issues. The abbot made two concessions. On the 18th December by deed he agreed (a) that any surplus moneys

from Queen Eleanor's foundation should be assigned *either* for the convent's pittances (extra food for them: as King Edward, now also dead since July of that same year, had originally ordained) *or* for actual monetary division between the monks (as they had unjustifiably been demanding); and (b) that the valuable manor of Deerhurst should be assigned to the convent and that the surplus profits from it should be divided or disposed of as the monks wished (as they had also been demanding).[62] In effect these were death-bed concessions by Abbot Walter, now that his face-to-face and venomous clashes with the former prior had been brought to an end.

So the see-saw of events in the last years of Abbot Walter's life came to an end. His death, and the earlier death of the old king in the same year, marked, as it were, the death throes of the past eventful century, in which the abbey had seen great enhancement in its fortunes and had been substantially rebuilt. Through some of its abbots, it had been drawn ever closer to the world of national administration and to the expanding life of the commercial town; but the new century had now begun while the abbey was already falling to a low point in its reputation.

### The aftermath

These frenetic events of Abbot Walter's closing years cast their shadows over the succeeding period. First a new abbot had to be chosen, and although this was achieved in one month from the old abbot's death at Christmas, it renewed most of the bitterness which had marked the middle months of 1307. The prior, perhaps freed from imprisonment

---

58  Flete, *Hist. of WA*, p. 119, following *Flor. Hist.* iii, 140, calls Abbot Wenlock 'a supremely zealous supporter of the rule and order of St. Benedict'.
59  WAM 9499C. See Pearce, *W. de Wenlok*, p. 196.
60  WAMs 9499A and D, 9496, and 6679.
61  WAM 24260, see Harvey, *W. de Wenlok*, p. 212. Bro. Alexander was with him, and ordered these.
62  Flete, *ibid.*, pp. 117-119; WAD. 464. For Queen Eleanor's foundation, see pp. 305 ff. above. For Deerhurst manor, see p. 307 above. The abbot's deed was addressed to the 'sub-prior and convent'. The sub-prior was Bro. Henry Payn, who was also the abbot's faithful treasurer, and may even have urged a reconciliation. Hadham, no longer prior, may still have been in some form of imprisonment.

by the abbot's death, if not before, still had his party of supporters, and for their part the abbot's supporters were still strong. In the face of vociferous and unbridled opposition, notably from the intemperate Roger of Aldenham, the old abbot's supporters won the day with their candidate, Richard of Kedington, who was elected as abbot on the 26th January in the new year, 1308.[63] Although his reputation was bad, and has remained so, most of the criticisms of him have come from the prior's prejudiced supporters. But certainly his abbacy was undistinguished; and also mercifully limited in time, since as a result of the loud opposition to him which the prior and his adherents continued to express at the papal court at Avignon, he failed to secure final benediction as abbot for over two and a half years, and then died within five years after that.[64] It was a bad beginning, if there was to be any hope of wiping the slate clean.

While the old abbot's supporters were thus winning the day with their candidate for the vacant abbacy, the prior and his supporters, in the name of the whole convent, were settling old scores with Abbot Walter, in his absence.[65] On the 25th January 1308, the day before Kedington was elected, the 'prior' (who was still a deposed prior, even if he had an appeal pending) and 'the convent' passed a decree incorporating a very lengthy new 'composition', designed to be binding on future abbots in their relations with their monks.[66] In effect the prior was copying the example set by Prior John of Coleworth who had snatched the opportunity during the vacancy after Abbot Ware's death to put right (as he saw it) the wrongs which that abbot had imposed on the convent – with the difference

that Prior Coleworth had at least been an authentic prior.[67]

It is clear that Hadham and his associates must have been hard at work in constructing this decree either during the month since Wenlock's death, or perhaps even earlier during his lifetime, in anticipation of the situation after his death. It contained 40 or more 'articles', and was double the length of Prior Coleworth's earlier decree. It put right, in favour of the convent, those matters in which Wenlock had probably been in the wrong, and it also 'legitimated', again in favour of the convent, those matters in which the convent had probably been in the wrong. So it was a unilateral and biased pronouncement, although many other articles related to non-contentious matters. While Hadham and no doubt his adherents were almost certainly the prime movers behind it, many of the other monks as well may have been pleased to see their personal and financial interests advanced by the decree, and there is no hint of any dissensions.

As for the good name of the abbey, worse was to follow Kedington's election as abbot. There was still the hearing of the prior's appeal, now to be held in the city of London in the church of the Priory of the Holy Trinity, in the parish of Aldgate, beginning in March 1308. So in front of the appointed commissioners, the Prior and the Sacrist of that priory, the whole sorry history of the abbey's disputes and the final months of Wenlock's abbacy was rehearsed again by Master John of Deneby, the advocate acting on behalf of the prior. But no one appeared at any stage to represent the now dead abbot or his supporters, and so the commissioners had to listen to the prior's witnesses and to read his

---

63  Because the monks were divided, the election was by 'compromission'; see p. 293 n. 6 above, for its meaning.

64  He was not blessed as abbot until at least July 1310, and he died in April 1315.

65  The niceties continued to be observed in the new decree passed by Hadham and the convent, with Abbot Walter still being referred to as 'our abbot, of good memory'. But such niceties were probably the minimum required.

66  WAD 639-640.

67  See p. 293 again.

documents, without hearing any arguments or evidence on behalf of the abbot or his supporters. Finally on the 17th May 1308 the commissioners delivered judgment, revoking the abbot's sentences of suspension, excommunication and imprisonment of the prior, and restoring the latter to his full and original office and status.

For their part, the old abbot's supporters managed, it seems, to seek and perhaps obtain orders (from arbitrators) to protect themselves from the physical attacks and abuse to which they had been subjected by their opponents, and from any vindictive actions by the reinstated prior, and to clear their names from the 'malicious accusations' of incontinence.

Needless to say, Brother Roger of Aldenham the 'fighter' also returned to the fray, and on a further appeal to the papal court, which was again heard at the Priory of the Holy Trinity in London but was not concluded until the 5th February 1309, succeeded at last in obtaining a revocation of Abbot Walter's orders of excommunication and apostasy against him.[68]

So notorious had the continuing 'dissensions, controversies and discords' at the abbey become, that in the middle of 1308 even the new king, Edward II, had also registered his concern and had appointed five justices (including Roger Brabazon, the chief justice, and John Benstead) to investigate them and 'the dilapidations of the goods of the abbey'. Needless to say, four of the five appointed had already been closely connected with the abbey, receiving yearly fees or presents from the old abbot.[69]

At the same time the kingdom, like the abbey, had now also fallen into a trough of disquiet under its new king. The resoluteness and strength which the old king had shown was gone, and Westminster was now to face a period of instability and finally yet another civil war.

---

68  WAMs 9495, or 9494 (a copy).
69  *Cal. P. R.*, 1307-1313, p. 124; and WAM 12777. I have not found the outcome, but in any case by then this was past history and events had moved on. For the abbey's financial cultivation of prominent people, even judges, see p. 309 above. For Roger Brabazon, the kings' chief justice, see pp. 317 above and, as a later resident on a large estate in Hampstead, see p. 374 below. For John Benstead, see pp. 285-7 above.

# CHAPTER 19

# The abbot's manor and the village of Eye
## 1098-1307

In 1086, when the Domesday survey was being completed, the manor of Eye, lying immediately to the west of Westminster, was held by the Norman baron Geoffrey of Mandeville.[1]    In his eyes it was only a *maneriolum*, a 'little manor', since its extent was no more than ten 'hides', and that was small compared with some of his extensive lands elsewhere in Middlesex, Essex, Hertfordshire and other counties.[2]

However, though the manor of Eye may have seemed comparatively small to some of William the Conqueror's barons, it covered a large swathe of the present West End of London – namely the whole of Hyde Park, about half of the Mayfair area, part of modern Knightsbridge and Green Park, all Belgravia, the site of Buckingham Palace and its garden, part of the Victoria area and all Pimlico. Under its Latin name *Eia*, it was identified as a rural 'island', bounded by the three rivers, the Westbourne and the Tyburn to the west and east, and by the Thames in the south.[3] On the north, its only land-boundary was the line of the old Roman road (now Oxford Street) from its crossing with the Tyburn to the present Marble Arch and beyond, as far as the Westbourne river (at the present Lancaster Gate). The names 'Tyburn' and 'Westbourne' were each to survive not only as river names, but also more significantly as areas of *land*, each bordering a river and included in an estate held by Westminster Abbey.[4]

But Geoffrey of Mandeville, the holder of this rural area, had his mind on higher things. He had already been a supporter of the abbey at Westminster, and after the death of his first wife, Alice the mother of his sons, he had obtained a privilege for her to be buried within the abbey in the cloister.   Nearer the time of his own death he also obtained permission for himself to be buried near her, and maybe in gratitude for this further favour (which is mentioned in his ensuing grant) he donated his 'little manor of Eye' to 'St. Peter of Westminster' by early 1098.[5]

Unlike many documents which grandiloquently report such gifts, Geoffrey's

---

1  See DB *Mdx* 9/1, and *The Westminster Corridor*, p. 84.

2  In Middlesex, for example, his manor of Edmonton was 35 hides in size, and Enfield was 30: see coloured Map L in *The Westminster Corridor,* after p. 96.   On the  other hand Geoffrey (and other barons) also held many manors and other lands far smaller than ten hides in size.

3  See *The Westminster Corridor*, p. 59, and coloured Map H, after p. 96.   Confusingly a smaller part of Eye also became called the 'island' (*insula*), namely La Neyte the abbot's country house acquired by him in the C13.

4  For the *field* called 'Tyburne' within the manor of Eye, see p. 346 and Plate 23 below.  NB: confusingly there was also the quite separate *manor* of Tyburn, lying *north* of the Roman road and held by Barking Abbey, see *The Westminster Corridor*, Map A and pp. 73-4.)   For the *land* called Westeburne adjoining the river (part of the manor of Knightsbridge in the C13), see *ibid.*, p. 43. 'Westeburne' as a name for *land* had been used even earlier than for the *river*, which had been known as just the 'bourne' or (further north) the 'Kilbourne'.

5  WACs 436 and 52.  Geoffrey had held the manor for a short period, and according to DB had apparently not been paying King William his rent of £3 pa. for it.  In a ritual gesture, Geoffrey placed his charter on St Peter's altar.

charter which records this one is a model of factual clarity and brevity, running to only eleven lines.[6]  The scene of the baron's act of donation was played out, probably in the great refectory of the abbey, in the presence of the Norman abbot, Gilbert Crispin, and up to 80 of his monks and *'many of my and his men-at-arms'* (milites), ie. including some of the men-at-arms for whom the abbey had provided the *'25 houses'* for the abbot's *'men-at-arms and other men'* in Westminster which are specifically mentioned in Domesday Book.[7]

So now the abbey held this valuable adjoining land, and continued to hold it for nearly the next four and a half centuries.  Not only did the new manor have its own existing residents, but it became a source of easily-accessible tracts of rural land which, in the course of time, some of the residents of the developing town of Westminster were able to acquire, to use as smallholdings for the provision of agricultural produce for themselves or for the maintenance of necessary livestock such as their horses or sheep.  But apart from the information given by the Domesday Survey, we know no details of its much earlier history when it had lain under the control of Geoffrey of Mandeville; and the same silence over Eye continues for us for most of the next hundred years after 1100, since records were not made or, if made, have not survived.

### The manor of Eye in Domesday Book

In 1086 the Domesday Survey had already recorded, in its impersonal way, the presence of at least twenty-four families living in Eye, and more significantly had identified the real agricultural value of the land.  Since much of the manor lay on the well-watered river silt

bordering the Thames, its meadow land was sufficient, in its fertility and area, to sustain no less than eight plough-teams of oxen, and its annual hay crop alone was recorded as being worth a remarkable 60s., while the pasture which the manor also provided was valued at another 7s.[8]

Of the twenty-four known heads of families already living in Eye in 1086, four were identified as smallholders *(bordars)* and one as a cottager *(cottar)*, all undoubtedly serfs.  The rest were called 'villagers' *(villani)*, all probably at that stage *villeins* and therefore also unfree. So under the Norman dispensation, there were three categories of customary tenants present in the manor, all of them unfree, some of them owing no doubt onerous 'week-work' services to the abbey.  Nearly two hundred years were to elapse before systematic 'freeing' of most of this physical work burden was to take place, when tenants were finally allowed to commute their compulsory 'services' by, in effect, buying themselves out of them, each man paying an annual sum of money in exchange for his owed services or 'works', as each year came round.[9]

But the allocations of land to these Eye tenants show that the size of their holdings did not depend on their relative status within the three categories of the 'unfree'.  Each of the four *smallholders* in Eye, whose work duties were probably much heavier than those of the *villeins*, also had a holding of one virgate of his own – whereas fourteen of the *villeins* had no more than half a virgate each.  So there was no hard-and-fast relationship between land and duties within these classes of unfree tenants.  But no 'free' men were identified in Eye at the time of Domesday, even though one

6  Its style can be contrasted with another of Geoffrey's own charters (WAC 462), recording another major benefaction by him to the abbey, of the Berkshire vill of Hurley and of its church which, as a priory, then became a cell of the abbey.  That charter runs to 46 florid lines; and cf. Mason, *WA and its People*, p. 114.

7  DB. *Mdx.* 4/1. The twenty five houses were for the 'men-at-arms or other men', sworn to the abbot; see also *The Westminster Corridor*, p. 141.

8  DB, *Mdx.* 9/1. For the geology, see coloured Map D in *The Westminster Corridor*, after pp. 96, and p. 145 *ibid*.

9  See the sums paid by the tenants from 1291-2 onwards for their 'sale of works', at pp. 333-4 below.

of the *villeins* had as much as half a hide (about sixty acres) to himself.[10]

But in any case the distinction between 'unfree' and 'free' men was not a 'black-or-white' distinction. Many of those tenants who in later years won their freedom had to accept – in relation to their land – some residual obligations towards the abbey which were equivalent to some of the duties which serfs still owed by reason of their status. Indeed a raft of obligations might still have to be undertaken by a freed man (in effect, by 'contract', as a condition of getting his freedom or the grant of a tenancy), or by any free newcomer to the manor who took a tenancy from the abbey.

These duties could range from periodical ploughing or hay-mowing 'boons', to seasonal 'carrying' services (such as the carrying-in of the dried hay crop in mid-summer, or 'harvest works' in the autumn).[11] Even when a tenant had been freed, or when a free newcomer took a tenancy on demesne land, a 'relief' (an entry fee, normally the amount of one year's rent) usually continued as an impost to be paid to the abbey, when he took up the new tenancy, and/or when the tenancy passed to his heir or to a purchaser or other assignee.[12] And when a freed tenant died, a 'heriot' (the tenant's best beast or its value) might still have

to be handed over to the abbey under the terms on which he had continued to hold, just as was necessary when a customary tenant died. Any free man with a tenancy on demesne land would also usually continue to owe (in effect contractually) the duty of 'suit of court', an obligation to attend the lord's courts; and of course he would almost always be bound to pay a rent for his land, as any unfree man had to.[13]

The one duty which the freed man avoided was the heavy task of 'week-work', working several whole days, or even in some cases *every* working day, in each and every week or sometimes throughout certain seasons.[14] This was work which probably the early *bordars* in Eye would have had to perform, as also did most of the *villeins* to a lesser extent. We can see what practical difficulties this 'week-work' must have caused to the families which had over ten or twenty acres of their own to cultivate for their domestic needs. And the clash between a tenant's private needs and his servile obligations fell hardest on those who had the largest amount of land, in their own tenancies, to till or mow as well.

But with the exception of this badge of 'week-work' (where it can be detected in the evidence), there are usually few obvious clues

---

10 This half-hide tenancy may perhaps have been the seed of the later 'Hyde' tenancy and the abbey's eventual 'manor of Hyde', and then (with a little extra help from Henry VIII) of the present Hyde Park: see pp. 281-3 above. Or it could be that this half-hide *villein* in Eye in DB was an early holder of the land ('one hide') which in 1223 was bought back by Abbot Richard of Berking and became La Neyte, his country house & estate, see pp. 201 above and 330-1 below. Or it is possible that the unidentified 'Ralph' who (DB, *Mdx.* 9/2) held an estate of 1½ hides in Ossulston Hundred 'from Geoffrey' [de Mandeville] held this *as part of Eye* (G's main land in Ossulston); this may have been the origin of the later Hyde manor; cf. Harvey, *WA Ests.* p. 418.

11 For 'boons' and 'carrying services' in Eye, see also pp. 351-2 below.

12 One should remember that certain obligations of some 'free' people who, in relation to certain land, were 'copyholders' (the distant heirs of one-time serfs and later 'customary tenants') towards their surviving 'lords' persisted down many centuries, even into the C20. This was true of some of the land in Hampstead, where the land had to be freed from such duties ('enfranchised') by financial purchase in the C19 or C20.

13 See Harvey, *WA Estates*, pp. 107-108. This was the passage, over the course of centuries, from *servile status* giving rise to fixed obligations, to (in effect) *contract* which could give rise to similar or analogous obligations.

14 Such duties however would not apply when religious feast days gave exemption. For the 'sharing' of feast-days between a lord's and a tenant's entitlements, see Harvey, 'Work and *festa ferianda*', Jo. Ecc. H. 23 (1972) 289.

as to whether a later tenant in manors of the abbey was a free man or still a servile one (a customary tenant). But if we go to the other end of the period with which this book deals, we learn that by the early 1300s the acreage of the free tenancies within Eye had grown to equal or probably to surpass that of the remaining customary tenancies.[15] And certainly the personal status of many of the holders of land in Eye long before that date was so obviously that of free men and women. Thus when one finds Master Alexander, one of the main 'architects' of the new abbey and Henry III's trusted royal carpenter since 1234, holding land in Eye as well as Westminster, Knightsbridge and elsewhere, or Sir John Benstead, Edward I's adviser and right-hand man and the holder of the Westminster sub-manor of Rosamunds, holding also much other land in Eye, one does not have to ask whether such men were personally free or held their land in a free capacity, even if they had accepted (by, what we now would call 'contract') certain obligations to the abbey similar to those of customary tenants.

But much earlier – in the twelfth century – there were other known residents who held land and houses in Westminster, but themselves bore the personal locative designation, 'of Eye'. These deserve our attention as potentially still resident in Eye, and possibly as still (or once) customary tenants there, even though they had other 'free' interests in Westminster or elsewhere.

### The first known men 'of Eye' c. 1175 - 1220

Apart from a few scattered men 'of Eye' who acted as witnesses to Westminster charters in earlier years, the first three landholders who hailed from Eye and are known in any detail appear in records in the last twenty years of the twelfth century, between about 1180 and 2000, and they continue into the next century. This was exactly the period when the land market in Westminster properties had started to accelerate, following the arrival of administrative officials in the town which was now a seat of government.[16] Although labelled as men 'of Eye', these three are identified mainly as established holders of land in Westminster, so they had already migrated to the town.

The first two bore engagingly contrasting names: Richard the Tall (altus), and William the Little (parvus), each 'of Eye'. Richard already held a messuage in Westminster, probably in Tothill Street, and his 'landlord' was Adam of Westminster (the one who always liked to be called 'the nephew of the bishop', if he could).[17] Richard's tenancy in Westminster was a hereditary one, and already he held it in free tenure. The chances are that he was now a free man and that even if he still held land in Eye, he was no longer a customary tenant there. But he then disappears from the records, although his widow and two daughters can later be identified as still living in three different dwellings in Westminster, in the Tothill Street/Longditch area in 1234.[18]

But William (the) Little falls into a different category. It was his son, Laurence, a clerk who in the 1220s granted to Abbot Richard of Berking and the convent the valuable estate (known as the 'island') in Eye, part of which subsequently became the abbots' private house known as La Neyte.[19] Laurence's father William Little had also held this land (probably briefly), by buying it from a William of Hurley, before selling-on to the

---

15 Harvey, *WA Estates*, p. 122n.
16 See pp. 66-7 above. The increase in the number of surviving charters explains why some people connected with Eye begin to emerge a little more clearly at this time .
17 Mason, *Beau. Cart.*, Nos 184-6. For Adam, see pp. 180-1 above.
18 Mason, *ibid.*, No 201.
19 WAM 4772 and WAD 100-102b (the abbot's original acquisition). At a later date, 1236, the abbot also procured a 'fine', a court-recorded compromise with Laurence, in a legal action before the royal court (see CP25(1) 146/10/144), as a formal and permanent record of the deal, probably because of its importance for future abbots.

abbey.[20]  Laurence's charter recording his transfer to the abbey reveals that another previous holder of the 'island' estate in Eye had been Arnold of Hurley, a 'knight' who was the father of William of Hurley.[21]  At all events, Abbot Berking and the convent had had to agree at first to pay William of Hurley a large annual rent of £5, but they then obtained a release from this rent by assigning to William of Hurley some other land which they held in Hertfordshire, in exchange.[22]

Apart from any holdings in Eye, William Parvus also held at least two properties, probably more, in Westminster, and appeared as a regular witness to other owners' charters relating to Westminster land. One property was a hereditary plot of land, with probably a house on it, 'in the vill of Westminster' ('the king's street'?), and he sold his interest in that land shortly after 1200 to Alexander the clerk of the exchequer and his unmarried 'partner' Edith of the Bar, in a transaction conducted before the abbot's halimote court. Another house which William held lay at the 'head of Tothill Street', and this one was sold by him to an abbey servant called Thomas of the Infirmary.[23]

Apart from these two men 'of Eye' – Richard Tall and William Little – there was also a prominent 'Alexander of Eye' who held a quantity of land in or near Charing and had two brothers: one, a Tothill man, Ralph of Tothill, and the other, Salamon who was described as a priest.[24]  Alexander also had another connection with Eye, as his wife Alice was the grand-daughter of an earlier man 'of Eye', Thedric (a suitably English name for a former probably servile family), and together Alexander and Alice held (in Alice's right) land in Longditch in Westminster which they sold to the first William Mauduit after he had come to Westminster.[25]  It is probable that Alexander did hold property in Eye itself as well; and there is no doubt that later his son Alan clearly did have interests in two or three separate houses in the later village of Eye itself, and in at least four acres of agricultural land in nearby fields in the manor. These he later sold or gave to the Lady Altar at the abbey.[26]

The three brothers Alexander, Ralph and Salamon were the sons of William the chaplain, who was the vicar of St. Martin's church at Charing and himself later held land in Charing.[27]  And several other men 'of Eye', both before and after 1200, were now appearing as witnesses to Westminster transactions in the

---

20  William Little was called 'of Eye' in WAC 414 and elsewhere, He may be the 'William of Eye' (without the name *parvus*) in other early charters WAMs 17450, 17446, 17456, 17447, but all relating to lands in Westminster.

21  See WAD 470b for Arnold's title of *miles*. 'William son of Arnold' had been listed in 1166 as a military tenant in Middlesex, holding from Geoffrey Mandeville, second earl of Essex,, in the 'fee-lists' which Henry II had required (Inquest of Fees) from his tenants in chief; this fee was responsible for providing one knight for the 'feudal' army, Hall (ed), *Red Book of the Exchequer*, i. p. 346. It was listed as a 'new' fee, one granted since the time of Henry I.

22  See WAD 102a-b. Another William of Hurley had been the butler of Abbot Walter of Winchester and received abbey lands in Longditch (which he finally returned to the abbey), see pp. 147-8.

23  See WAC 413 (for the 'King Street' house). 'Alexander' is there called just 'the son of Henry', but WAC 414 shows that he was the exchequer clerk. There may be a connection with Hurley and La Neyte, because the charter reveals that William Little's 'landlord' for this Westminster house was Arnold's son, William of Hurley. For Alexander the exchequer clerk, known also as 'Alexander of Swerford', see pp. 170-2 above. See WAM 17388 (for the Tothill St. house, which Thomas later appears to have sold or donated to the Lady Altar). It is not clear at which end of Tothill Street the 'head' lay, but probably it was nearest to the abbey.

24  Mason, *Beau. Cart.*, No 195 and WAC 404. Alexander, as uncle to Ralph's son Geoffrey, was prepared to 'warrant' (underwrite) a deal (*ibid*, No. 194) between Geoffrey and the first William Mauduit, by pledging all his own Charing land in support of Geoffrey's liability under this deal.

25  Mason, *ibid.*, No 189. For William Mauduit, see pp. 113-4 above.

26  WAMs 4771 and 4821. These were probably in the 1240s, or possibly the 1250s.

27  Mason, *ibid*, Nos 189, 188 and 190. For William the chaplain's landholdings, see WAM's 17143B & 17144.

abbot's courts, even though their own rights to property in either Eye or in Westminster have not been identified in such records.[28]

Already therefore, on this limited surviving evidence, there was a tangle of relationships between people of Eye and residents of Westminster, and plenty of links also between Eye personnel and Westminster lands. In the succeeding years of the thirteenth century the traffic between the adjoining populations and progressively the two districts became closely reciprocal, with Westminster people acquiring more and more sectors of land within Eye, no doubt for the purpose of raising produce, either for themselves or for sale, or maintaining the livestock which could not be so easily accomodated within the shrinking available land in the developing town of Westminster.

However, what can this interplay between the two areas, which we can see had already begun in or before the decades round the turn of the twelfth and thirteenth centuries, tell us about the status of earlier categories of residents in or from Eye?

## The customary tenants – survival and mutation (Domesday to 1307)

The original classes of servile tenants described generally throughout the Domesday books had reflected certain differences of economic and social standing at that time. These classes (as they later developed) have been categorised in three more obvious and intelligible grades: a *primary* group, of wealthy and locally 'powerful' tenants; a *second* and larger group, of middling families with less wealth or land, but earning respect and occasional office in their own communities; and a *third* group of land-poor tenants who had to

rely on *either* their own paid agricultural labour for others, *or* on specialised skills such as blacksmithing, thatching or even tiling which they had to learn in order to make a living.[29]

It is highly probable that, well before 1200, men such as Richard Tall, William Little or Alexander – or more likely their forebears – had been or become members of the primary group of favoured tenants, and perhaps during the twelfth century had purchased or otherwise won their freedom from their original status as customary tenants. The monks already had incentives to grant freedom to some of their richer *villeins*, because it was profitable to do so: such tenants had to pay well for it.

Moreover the manor of Eye, when received from Geoffrey of Mandeville not so long after the Conquest, was probably still in a damaged condition, as had been recorded in Domesday Book.[30] As more land was improved or made newly cultivatable by assarting, the giving of freedom to servile tenants had probably been an important part of the bargaining necessary to ensure that new land was properly tenanted. Further since even free tenants might have to accept some duties (in effect, contractually) which had earlier been obligatory by status, the cessation of the previous mandatory services could often be arranged without serious loss to the abbey.[31]

There can be little doubt that there were also other tenants of Eye who had similarly been able to escape the bonds of their old status. And the proximity itself of Eye to Westminster, and the tenants' growing chance for supplying produce and other services to the expanding town, must have helped early Eye tenants to improve their social and financial position more quickly and to bring

28  eg. Edmund, Herbert, Ralph, John and Stephen (all 'of Eye'), see WACs 404, 440, 397; et. al. Alexander of Eye also was a witness to at least fifteen charters made in Westminster before and after 1200, WACs 311, 312, 413, 419, 440, 447, 448, and Mason, *ibid.*, Nos 187, 188, 190, 191, 192, 196, 197, 198.
29  See eg. Hanawalt, *The Ties that Bound*, p. 6 et. al.
30  Before the Conquest Eye was worth £12 pa. Its value was halved as a result of the Conquest, and it was still worth only £8 pa. at the time of Domesday, 1086, see DB. *Mdx* 9/1.
31  For the factors affecting the development of free tenure on abbey estates, see Harvey, *WA Estates*, pp. 107 ff. For the possible *contractual* arrangements, see text above and following pages.

influence to bear on the abbey to grant them their freedom – in exchange, of course, for the necessary price and any imposed obligations, at least analogous to old customary terms.

However, when we come to consider the later records of account for the farming of the demesne land in Eye, which began to be made in about the middle of the thirteenth century, we can see that there still remained an appreciable number of tenants whom we can now call 'customary' tenants, still bound by their long-standing status to serve the abbey in various ways.

The surviving accounts for Eye start spamodically, with only one year represented during the decade of the 1270s, and one other year during the decade of the 1280s. But from 1291 there is an almost complete run of consistent records for sixteen years, until 1307 – the year of the culmination of the 'Days of Wrath', ending with the death of Abbot Walter of Wenlock.[32] Before 1291 the rents and tax (tallage) collected from the customary tenants of Eye amounted to about 57s and 20s respectively each year. But by 1291, apparently coinciding with the beginning of the new accounting process, the totalled rents had been increased by about 14s. 6d, while the tax total fell by about 3s. 6d. So by 1291 the collected rents were about 71s. 6d., and the tax paid by the tenants was about 16s. 6d. With one increase of about one shilling in the tax in 1302-3 and after, these totals remained steady for the following years, and some of them provide a rough clue as to the number of customary tenants in Eye.

Although there may have been a differential between rents in Eye and rents in Hampstead, we know that in 1281 in Hampstead, up the hill

from Eye, there were 44 customary tenants paying about 77s. (in rents) and that, of these, about 32 tenants were together paying just over 20s in tax as well. By 1312 there were 41 customary tenants there, paying at least an extra 10s. in rents, say 87s in all; and much the same in tax as was being paid in 1281.[33] This affords a difficult comparison, but if one assumes that rents in Eye were probably rather higher than in Hampstead, one may hazard that by the end of the century there were still about 30-35 customary tenants in Eye.[34] This lower range is intended to reflect the fact that probably more of their class had gained their freedom, in a place of greater opportunities like Eye, and perhaps had moved on, into Westminster or elsewhere.

Another significant feature of the period in the 1290s, when Abbot Wenlock seems to have instituted in Eye a more regular system of accounting, was the practice which began in 1291 of the 'sale' of at least some of the obligatory 'works' owed by the customary tenants of Eye. At times when a growing population has created reserves of working men who have to compete for employment, rates of pay tend to be driven downwards. It then usually became sensible for a lord to allow his tenants to commute some or all of their work-duties, by making money payments to him, in lieu of their obligations, at rates fixed higher than those at which he could hire men to get the necessary work done on his manor.[35] So the landlord would benefit financially, and the tenants would get rid of some time-consuming obligations, for a price, and in the time saved would be able to follow their own interest to a greater extent. There is no doubt that the end of the century saw a growing population in Westminster and its

32 The earlier years were 1275-6 and 1280-1. But since Eye was one of the abbot's manors, it is most probable that the regular run of accounts, which were also broadly consistent in form from 1291, was attributable directly to his own administrative influence. A/cs *before* 1275 had been made, but are not extant, DS, *Eye A/cs* 1/1. (My translations are deposited at the abbey's Muniments Room.)

33 See VCH, *Mdx* 9/113 and 114. The 'extra 10s.' is an estimate of the value of certain livestock which forms part of the rents paid by some of the tenants, as listed in the VCH text on page 113.

34 This 'guestimate' also takes into account that Hampstead was a convent manor, whereas Eye was the abbot's, with the result that the tenants may have received more lenient terms than from the abbot.

35 See Miller and Hatcher, *Rural Soc. and Econ. Change*, pp. 238-9, et al.

neighbourhood (as also elsewhere), and no doubt Abbot Wenlock anticipated that with labour costs falling in the market he could pay less in hiring workers to do the work of the manor.

So for the rest of the abbot's lifetime regular agreements for the 'sale of works' between the customary tenants and the 'manor' took place every year. The result is shown in the demesne accounts from 1291 until the abbot died in 1307; and indeed the practice continued spasmodically thereafter into at least the early years of the dubious period of Abbot Wenlock's successor, Richard of Kedington.[36] Each year we can see extra income coming in from the sale, and also costs being incurred in hiring other men to do the usual work of mowing the hay, reaping the corn, carrying the various crops to the barns, ploughing and harrowing the land. The extra annual income ranged down and up, from about 33s pa. initially in 1291-2 and several years after, to a low point of about 17s in the years at the turn of the centuries, and then up again to about 28s towards the end of Wenlock's life.[37] But the accounts are not clear or detailed enough for me to assess confidently whether Wenlock made or lost money by his plan.

However the 'selling' of some work-obligations which we can see in Eye was a step in the slow emancipation of customary tenants. Even if they had to pay for it, the freedom from having to give unpaid hard work and other services to the manor meant that they could devote the saved time to labour on their own land, or to the cultivation of other skills and the promotion of other social or financial interests. This was a major impetus towards the development of a more free society in which individual skills and initiative could assist men to escape the social burden carried by their fathers. During the second half of the thirteenth century, this was already happening elsewhere in the country even in the minority of counties in which work services could still be really heavy.[38]

But in Eye one does not have only to generalise. Many of the customary or once-customary tenants appear personally in short 'snapshots' presented in the Accounts, even if it is often only in name. For example as early as 1275-6 (the date of the first surviving Account), there was John of Eye who received a special grant of an area of land in the manor, *'once held by Robert of Eye but placed at farm this year'*, for which John now had to pay a high rent of 16s.[39] In the same year John of Padington, a customary tenant in Eye, died and his son William had to pay a 'relief' of 7s. 6d to secure the transfer of his tenancy, and also had to hand over a young carthorse from his father's possessions as a 'heriot'. So John of Padington had probably still been a customary in Eye, or (if free) had accepted some obligations similar to those of a customary, by taking on a customary tenancy.[40] Or again,

---

36 Since there was a gap of ten years before 1291 in the surviving accounts, it is not certain whether the practice may have begun even earlier than 1291, but it certainly owed its origin to Abbot Wenlock and shows the way the labour market was moving towards the turn of the centuries.

37 For the calculation, the year was divided into two:– the two very busy harvest months of August and September (in which each work was charged at 1d), and the whole of the rest of the year (in which the charge was $\frac{1}{2}$d). Initially the income from the rest of the year was much the same as from the harvest period (eg. 18s, against 15s.); but later less harvest works were being sold so the gap widened; and then the trend reversed again.

38 Miller and Hatcher, *ibid.*, pp. 124, 223-4.

39 WAM 26850, and DS, *Eye A/cs*, p. 1. This could be a first mention of John Churchwyne who was also called John of Eye and became the reeve of Eye in or before 1291 He remained in that office for over ten years after 1291 and figured widely during Wenlock's abbacy (see Harvey, *W. Wenlock*, p. 257). But the name 'John' was very common, and 1275 may be too early for him. For Robert of Eye, see p. 338 below.

40 By 1309 William of Padington was selling a rent of 4d from one of the half-acre strips in Eye in the field called Shortspottes, see WAM 17560. The purchaser was a Joan Viel, perhaps Robert Viel's daughter. Robert and William Frankelein were witnesses to the charter, see text below. For another earlier family 'of Paddington', see pp. 92 ff.

whenever failures to pay rent or tax by particular tenants had to be recorded in the accounts, we usually see these other customaries being named, often with single names such as Alexander or Martin; or there was Gervase *'ate strande'*, who probably held land where Eye bordered on the shore at the bend of the river Thames. There Gervase had perhaps suffered from one or more of the annual floodings for which river defences such as palisades or earth walls had to be made periodically, and found now that he could not pay his tax.[41]

On one occasion all the 'fines' (*amercements*) which at least seventeen of the tenants had had to pay in the manor court during a short period of four and a half months in 1281 were listed individually in the accounts for that period, together with their names.[42] Many of these, such as Ralph le cherl, but not all, were probably customary tenants.[43] Others in the list, such as Margaret of the Hyde who had the largest fine of 2s. 6d, was probably a member of the free Hyde family on the Hyde lands in Eye, and owed her dues (on some customary tenancy) 'contractually'.[44] And yet others in the list such as Robert Viel and William Frankelein (families which became prosperous in Eye, and whose appellations were each, 'of Eye') may later have acquired their freedom and continued to owe their services to the abbey not because of an inherited binding status, but of their own choice or acceptance; again in

modern terms 'contractually'.[45]

These are a few illustrations of the customary tenants and their mutating successors which appear in the early Eye Accounts and continue throughout them into the 1300s. Many other similar illustrations can be culled from the later accounts. And as a result of the continuing process, by the end of the thirteenth century the balance between the acreage of the customary land in Eye and the acreage of the land held in free tenancies was such that already the latter had probably exceeded the former.[46]

## The village of Eye, and its residents (1240 -1307)

There are now good reasons for thinking that the village of Eye itself lay on the site of the modern Buckingham Palace and its garden.[47] There are many charters made during the later thirteenth century which relate to the village and identify some of its residents, but questions do arise as to when and how such a village had grown or been developed as a genuine settlement on its own, similar to but separate from the various settlements in Westminster.

There is some uncertainty whether, in the manor's early days as an estate of the abbey, it had been managed *in conjunction with* Westminster, in effect as a part of the abbey's home manor. Perhaps the most significant

---

41  WAM 26851. For the river floodings and walls, see pp. 197, 355. Five years later, probably with Gervase's tax still unpaid, his land 'was drawn into the demesne', so that instead of being 'tenant land', it became land which the abbey itself would cultivate for its own purposes, WAM 26855.

42  WAM 26855. During the year 1280-81, no less than four separate Accounts, each dealing with a period of months, were made. This WAM dealt with 19th May to 29th September, 1281. If any court rolls from Eye for this period had survived, much similar information would be available.

43  But Ralph was paid for (presumably extra) piece-work, as a reaper and carter of corn in 1281, DS, *Eye A/cs*, 38.

44  For the Hyde family, see pp. 281-3 above, and p. 345 below.

45  For Robert Viel and Edith his wife, and William Frankelein, see WAMs 4775, 4835 and 4782 (Viel); and 4764, 4777 and 4875 (Frankelein). The Frankelein land (only one acre at this time) lay in *La Brache*, a field almost certainly in the modern Green Park area, see 4764, while one of the Viel lands was in *La Brokforlong* nearby, a field adjoining both the Tyburn stream (the 'watercourse of King Edward the Confessor') and *'the road leading to Ossulton'*, ie. leading from the vill of Eye to the Eycross junction and thence to our modern Hyde Park Corner and Park Lane, see WAM 4835 and App. C, at p. 403 above.

46  See p. 330, n. 15 above.

47  See p. 49 and App. C, at pp. 400 ff.

piece of evidence on this is contained in the record of the great arbitration of 1222 as to the boundaries of the parish of St Margaret's church in Westminster.[48] One of the issues in that arbitration had been whether the three outlying north-western villages, of Knightsbridge, Westbourne and Paddington, 'pertained to' St. Margaret's parish, and the arbitrators held that they did so 'pertain', even though they lay well beyond the Tyburn stream which the arbitrators had also held to be the western limit of the parish of St. Margaret.

But no issue appears to have been raised, and certainly nothing was decided, about any village in Eye, although the area of Eye also lay beyond the Tyburn stream, and indeed much nearer to St. Margaret's church than any of the three other villages.

Having regard to its geographical position *between* Westminster and the three north-western villages, it is difficult to see how Eye could have been treated differently in this way from the other three villages (with their districts), unless it was still regarded and managed as part of Westminster itself at that time, and/or unless there was no real village in Eye comparable with those of the three more distant villages.

It is also noticeable that one of the earliest surviving charters which record a sale of identifiable land actually *in* Eye (the grant of the 'island', later La Neyte, to Abbot Berking in about 1223) refers to Eye with the rubric 'near Westminster', which may reflect a continuing close relationship and, in effect, a combination between Eye and Westminster at that time. In a number of other charters, references to Eye actually call it 'Eye in Westminster'. It is true that at least three later charters also contain the rubric, 'near Westminster', in their references to a plot and

a messuage in the 'vill of Eye'; but this may be no more than a lazy copying of legal descriptions which were accurate once but had become overtaken by later events.[49]

Moreover there appears to be no charter relating to property in the 'vill of Eye' itself until about the 1240-1250s, when Alan the son of Alexander of Eye gave up all claims on one messuage in the vill, in favour of St. Mary's Altar and Brother Ralph of Gloucester, the Altar's current warden. After that there follows a succession of similar records showing transactions relating to the purchase of plots or houses *in the vill of Eye*, many of them containing detailed measurements of their size, and most of them showing their location fronting onto the road which ran through the vill, with the 'brook' or 'ditch' at their back. These transactions, which collectively contain a lot of unusual detail, can be fairly safely dated to the period from about 1240 until about the end of Edward I's reign in 1307.

Another directly relevant factor is that it is probable that the largest meadow (Market Mead) which is treated as being part of Eye throughout the farm accounts of that manor probably lay *east* of the westernmost branch of the river Tyburn and therefore lay in Westminster. Moreover even in those accounts of Eye, this field was initially called 'the great meadow' – not 'of Eye' – but 'of Westminster'.[50]

All these factors suggest *firstly* that for farming purposes Eye was being managed in conjunction with Westminster until about 1240; *secondly* that until that time there was probably no established village in Eye, with a *curia* of its own, (even though there were separate dwellings of the tenants in the manor), and *thirdly* there was then a period in which a true village centre may have been in the throes of being developed, with an active

48 See pp. 36-7, and particularly App. B, at p. 399.

49 See WAMs 4772 (the La Neyte charter); and 4790, 4792 and 4821 (the three latter charters in Edw. I's reign).

50 See DS, *Eye A/cs*, pp. 35 and 36 (in 1281); and pp. 356-9 below. It should be noticed that this 'great meadow of Westminster' had exactly the same size (at its maximum) as Market Mead (36½ acres, see *ibid*. pp. 35 and 155), when in 1291-2 the name 'great meadow of Westminster' was dropped for ever in the A/cs and '*Markedemede*' began to be used, referring to a great meadow whose hay was reflected *in the Eye acccounts*.

market in the sale of plots and houses on the site which now happens to be occupied by Buckingham Palace and its garden.[51]

The probable architect of any plan for establishing a village in Eye, with a proper *curia* of its own, would have been Abbot Berking, whose reforming abbacy (1222-1246) had already marked the first systematic reorganisation of the abbot's relations with the convent of monks, together with a review and survey of at least some of the abbey's estates.[52] It would also have made sense for him to effect a formal separation of Eye from Westminster at this time, when administration within Westminster must have been drastically complicated by the onset of simultaneous plans by King Henry III to start rebuilding the whole abbey in the 1240s.

Another significant feature at this same time is the emergence of the first records to assert that lands in Eye lay within the *parish* of St. Martin's church which stood by the crossroads at Charing. The chapel, and later the church, of St. Martin had dated probably from the twelfth century in Henry II's reign, and both its parish and its chaplain or vicar had figured in records *from at least John's reign*.[53] Then in 1222 both the church and its cemetery had been specifically excluded by the arbitrators (in the dispute between the abbey and the bishop of London) from their delimitation of the parish of St. Margaret's of Westminster; but inexplicably no mention was made by them of any *parish* belonging to St. Martin's.[54]

But a few years later in about the 1230s, we find that *land in Eye* is first described as lying 'in [the parish of] St. Martin's in the Fields', and several other later charters also describe both lands and houses as lying in that parish.[55] So there can be no doubt that, within not many years after the arbitrators' award in 1222, Eye was regarded as lying in the existing parish of St. Martin's, with the consequent inference that the boundary of the parish of St. Martin (which already existed) must have been *extended* to include Eye around that time But with the vills of Knightsbridge, Westbourne and Paddington lying beyond Eye and therefore *further away from Westminster*, but held by the arbitrators to 'pertain' to the parish of St. Margaret's church, it was a very odd geographical situation which was created about the relationship between the two parishes.

The actual residents of the (perhaps new or relocated) village of Eye in the second half of the thirteenth century were closely connected in a network of proximity, with occasional new incomers from distant or neighbouring manors being introduced from time to time. We have surviving records of at least twelve transactions taking place over these years, and there may have been others at the same time, now unrecorded (or not found).[56]

51  It is worth remembering that the concept of planned developments had already been realised quite recently in two or three places in Westminster, see p. 271 above.

52  For Abbot Richard of Berking, see pp. 194 (his relations with his monks) and 199-201 (the *custumal*) above.

53  Two charters, datable to John's reign, refer specifically to the parish of St. Martin, WACs 398 and 399

54  For the arbitration see pp. 36 above and App. B, at pp. 396 ff. below.

55  WAM 4817 (grant by John Athelard, a mason who was a tenant of a house in the development of Tothill Street in about the 1230s, see Rosser, *Med. Westminster*, p. 152. This is dated to 'temp. John' in the WA 'Descriptions', but John is too early for that charter. For subsequent charters about the parish and Eye, see eg. WAMs 4787, 4819 and 4835 (each about temp. Edw. I) and 4883 (1315). None of this fits with the dating of the parish to the later C14, by both Saunders, 'Extent of Westminster', pp. 237-8 and Rutton, 'Manor of Eia', p. 40. Rosser, *ibid.*, pp. 230 and 253 attributes the creation of a *parish* for St. Martin to 'by c. 1300' and also 'by c. 1250', with a more limited boundary for St. Margaret's parish at a line "between the Tyburn and the Thames, passing through the ornamental waters of the later St. James's Park", but I cannot see the authority for this.

56  WAMs 4771, 4793, 4789, 4821, 4787, 4788, 4792, 4819, 4791, 4790, 4761, 4830. Of this total: eight provided precise measurements for the sites; five referred to the 'ditch' or 'brook' at the back of the sites on the east of the 'high street'; one referred to the *'campus'* behind the site, and this must have been on the

These charters reveal a merry-go-round of activity (perhaps not unlike the effects created by competing modern estate agents in a new development), and although it is difficult to work out exactly in what order the undated transactions took place, one might hope to summarise their effect as follows – admittedly without enormous confidence in the exact *sequence* of the chronology.

Foremost is Robert Brun [Brown] of Eye. He first appears in the 1240-50s as a buyer of a plot in the village from Walter the carter and his wife Alice, and he also buys another plot from Alan of London (*de Londres*). Alan of London also has another house, a 'tenement', next door to Robert Brun's first plot; but later his neighbour there changes because Robert Brun subsequently sells that first plot on, to Ralph of Corf, a 'marbler' (both a supplier and a cutter of marble) who has probably been taking part in the contemporaneous rebuilding operations for the new abbey.[57]    Robert Brun also has a messuage, probably his own house, perhaps built on his second plot, but he later sells this messuage to John Benyn of Aldeburgh (who also uses the simpler name, or nickname, of John 'Malot', ?*matelot*).    Then we find that John Malot's new messuage lies between the personal homes of Alan of London and Walter the carter. But John Malot also has another house which is next door to a plot which Agnes, the daughter of Alan of London (who is probably dead now), sells to Richard Wombe of Westminster, and Richard Wombe's new plot has Ralph of Corf's house next door to it, on the other side. Robert Brun meanwhile has even more 'land' in the village, or perhaps on its edge, and this land

is on the other side of the messuage which he has sold to Ralph of Corf.[58]

But the carousel turns again, this time with another prominent neighbour also called Alan, the son of the earlier resident in the manor, Alexander of Eye. Alan is also well-to-do and has interests in two or three houses in Eye village which he may have acquired for himself or inherited from his father. One of them is his own home, and another one he has let to a neighbour, Ralph the son of Gilbert *de Ponte*, who lives at the bridge at Knightsbridge. But he first donates his interest in this second tenanted house to the Lady Altar at the abbey; and later he also donates to the Lady Altar a rent of 3s. payable for presumably a third messuage in the village (which lay between the houses of Nicholas the carpenter of Eye and Alexander the tiler). But Alan also has an interest, it seems, in yet another house in the village next door to his own, and he sells this to the same Ralph of the Bridge for 10s. John Malot reappears when Matilda Witlock grants to Walter of Eye (possibly Walter the carter again) her messuage in the village, lying between John Malot's house and other land which he also holds.

This apparent barrage of activity in the second half of the thirteenth century, together with much factual information about the houses and plots in the vill of Eye at this time, needs to be explained. The only possibilities seem to be that (a) the village had already had a similar but earlier history as well, but neither any charters nor any other evidence whatsoever of it at that time have survived; or that (b) over the second half of this century

---

*west* of the 'high street'; and there were at least nineteen references to 'houses', including the stated 'abutments' (some references here overlapping); and six references to 'plots'.

57  For Ralph of Corf, see Colvin, *Building A/cs of H. III*, pp. 396, 408. Ralph had been shipping Purbeck marble from Corfe in Dorset all the way round the coast to Westminster, for use in Henry III's abbey works.

58  Robert Brun's wife was Margery, and his son was William, of the same name as the William Brun who became valet to King Edward I, see Harvey, *W. Wenlock*, pp. 32-33 and WAM 16240; but he may not be the same man. In the 1250-1260s Robert Brun also bought a house in 'King Street' (opposite Almaine) for 100s, and a rent in Westminster and held lands in Knightsbridge as well as in Eye, see eg. WAMs 17381, 17510, 16228 and 16271; and much later in 1341 a William Broun of Eye (possibly his son or grandson) was a party to large deals with nominees for the abbey, about his lands in Knightsbridge, Westbourne, Westminster and Eye, see WAMs 16226, 16206, 16231, 16264 and 5888.

the vill was being developed for the first time and in that place, or at least was being reconstructed there (together with its nearby *curia* equipped with all the farm buildings to which the accounts, starting in 1275, bear witness), after some more primitive and unrecorded existence either there or elsewhere.

Of these the latter possibility seems the more likely. With Westminster, as first a village and then a growing town, always situated on the doorstep of Eye, the area of Eye at first may not have needed any established village of its own: until, that is, the growing urbanisation of Westminster, the migration of Abbot Berking and his successors to La Neyte, their very presences and involvement in Eye, and meanwhile complicated plans for a large-scale abbey reconstruction in Westminster led – naturally or deliberately – to the separation of the two areas and the creation of a true vill in Eye from about the mid-thirteenth century.

## The 'ministers' accounts' for the manor – 1275-6; 1280-81; and 1291-1307

Some aspects of the Eye accounts have already been noticed above, in relation to the customary tenants of the manor, but they contain a wealth of other information about the management of the manor and about the life and activities of its inhabitants.

Although medieval accounts are naturally concerned with economics, they are in their effect a retrospective herald of human life during the agricultural year – almost, one could say, the belated newspapers of the time, even though their purpose was very different. Unlike the anonymous and charmless documents which pass for modern accounts, these early medieval records are stamped with the personalities of some of their makers and of the players in their story. Their accent is rough, and we can see their mistakes, and lament the omissions, but they speak in great detail of people, of their tools and labours, the fields where they worked, of their animals, and the continuous produce which the people and their animals provided together.

Less designed, during this period, to

display a true 'profit' to be made out of a manor, these accounts of receipts and expenses mainly reflected the obligations of the manor reeve (in conjunction with any 'serjeant' or 'bailiff' appointed by the abbey to supervise him) – obligations to be thorough, accurate and honest in managing the estate. Each year it was a reeve's task, subject to directions from any serjeant or bailiff, to recover all monies owed to the manor (arrears from the previous years, rents for customary holdings, and rents for land 'farmed-out'); to muster and oversee the physical works done throughout the year by both the 'in-house' employees (the *famuli*) and the customary tenants; to let out those fields which contained pasture to anyone who wanted to use it; to provide for the despatch of produce by cart, as needed, to the 'granger' at the abbey, or more often to the nearby hungry kitchen of the abbot at La Neyte; to sell or otherwise dispose of unneeded produce, and to plan and sow for the next year's crops; to buy whatever was necessary for other food required by the abbey or the abbot, or was needed for the *famuli* and for tenants hired for special activities in the manor; to record works of repair and servicing necessary for buildings, equipment and other annual tasks; to oversee the care of the manor livestock and to buy or procure new stock or to sell old stock as necessary; and so on.

Above all, the reeve's overriding duty was to be able to provide, at year-end or any other necessary point, details of an account (of in effect his own activities in discharge of his duties) for the year or other period, so that an abbey clerk could record them in brief on parchment, for the abbey's auditors to peruse and correct by allowing or disallowing items, and to hold the reeve to account for any failures or deceptions. But, without the initial details from the reeve, this whole process of accounting would of course be frustrated.

So how could the reeve himself keep a record of a complete year's details? It used to be believed that he was illiterate and had to rely on memory, and on records limited to the well-known medieval device, the cutting of wooden 'tally sticks', in which differing-sized notches were cut to record sums of money received or expended. Some tallies were certainly used, but the accounts for the abbey's manors are far more detailed than merely money entries and contain a mass of names, subject-matters and complicated 'histories'. For the money records alone, a warehouse of tallies would be required, and it is impossible to believe that even an unlettered memory would be adequate for all the other greater assortments of details, however much more efficient it may have been than a modern memory.[59]

This obvious practical problem has at last been sufficiently recognised. With 'the proliferation of documents' by the thirteenth century, it is certain that some if not all reeves could read at least sufficiently to understand and make simple records, in French at any rate.[60] For example John Churchwyne of Eye who acted as reeve of the manor for over ten years from 1291 to part of 1302, after serving in the 1280s as reeve of the important manor of Staines (Middlesex), could not have survived in such tasks without being able himself to follow the abbot's commands and to record events, let alone their financial consequences. And in this very case we also have many of the actual writs, written in French, which Abbot Walter of Wenlock regularly despatched to his reeves and other officers in different parts of the country, to convey his orders to them.[61]

# Policies and practices followed by Abbot Wenlock and his managers

## A. *Liaison and assistance between the abbot's manors*

One pronounced feature revealed by the Accounts is the degree of cooperation between the reeves of the abbey's nearby manors, and often distant manors as well, and the extent of the communications, the journeying and carrying between them which must have been entailed in this process. In every year the reeve of Eye had to buy or sell produce and/or livestock, and in most cases it was to his colleagues in the administrative circuit of manors which the abbot managed that the reeve turned. In the year 1301-2, for example (in which incidentally John Churchwyne who by then had been the reeve for ten years fell again under a cloud for misdeeds in this, his last full year as reeve),[62] he had to obtain the following amounts during the course of the year:-

78 quarters of oats from the reeves of Pyrford (Surrey), and Denham (Bucks)

21 quarters of wheat from the reeves of Denham, Laleham (Middlesex) and Pyrford

3 quarters of rye chaff from the reeve of Pyrford

6 bushels of white peas from the reeves of Laleham and Yeoveney (Middlesex)

1 ox from the reeve of Denham (to whom Churchwyne finally despatched 15 oxen)

323 sheep from the reeve of Bourton (Glos)[63]

---

59  It is well recognised that in more unlettered societies the memory can be trained to be a much more powerful tool, but by itself alone it could never be sufficient for the multifarious detail involved in this task.

60  For purely practical reasons, there must have been much more than memory and tallies. But in any event see eg. Clanchy, *From Memory to Written Record* 47, who points to the difficulty created for a reeve who received writs written in French, if he were entirely unlettered. Particularly in a monastic context, it is unthinkable that a reeve such as John Churchwyne could not read and write to some extent.

61  Harvey, *W. de Wenlok*, pp. 49-147, and see pp. 295-8 above.

62  For his 'fault .. in the ploughing .. at the time of sowing' JC was fined £5, but £4 was then pardoned, DS, *Eye A/cs*, p. 174. JC was reeve for only two months next year: for follow-up, see *ibid.*, 182, 195, 210, 223, 236. See also next note and p. 346 n. 82 below for other misdeeds. In 1281, Ralph Stub the reeve had been fined 66s. 8d. for the 'burning-down of the house', and another 40s, for some 'false tallies'.

63  JC said he had sold the 323 sheep to two named men, but because he did not produce 'a writ' to authorise such a sale, it was disallowed. But this led to him being charged in the A/cs with a *notional* sale of the sheep, for £16. 3s., because the sheep had apparently been disposed of. See DS, *ibid.*, pp. 178 and 167. This was a good illustration, both of the rule about the need for a writ, and of a notional sale *super compotum*.

57 pigs from the reeves of Denham, Laleham and Pyrford

43 geese, 4 capons and 103 chickens from the reeve of Denham.

So on the practical side the abbot's estates were, in one sense, being run as a circuit or collective, although their individual finances and liabilities towards each other had to be kept separate. As we shall see in relation to Hampstead, the same was true of the convent's circuit of estates, where a different group of manors were acting collectively in supplying one another when needs arose. And when necessary, a member of one of the two circuits would even help out a member of the other circuit, but this was less frequent.

Of course in making purchases or sales of produce or livestock during the course of a year, the reeve also had to make use of opportunities in the general 'market' in the neighbourhood. So all the purchases and sales of grain and animals recorded year by year in the accounts should reflect, one hopes, the 'best' prices which could be paid or obtained in the market in the relevant year. But there would be plenty of opportunity for fraud (by 'side-kicks'), unless the auditors were up-to-date in their knowledge of market prices. It is noticeable that there were a number of occasions on which the auditors did disallow a price paid or obtained in the draft accounts, and substituted a lower or a higher figure, to reflect the price which they thought the reeve should have paid or obtained; but equally most of the figures shown in the reeve's accounts passed without criticism.

B. *Changes made by the abbot: (i) his treasury; and (ii) the farm of the cows*

It seems that the years 1295-1296 and 1296-1297 marked a pivotal period in which a number of changes were introduced, both in the abbot's general administration of his manors, and in the way in which the individual manor of Eye was managed. To begin with, 1295-1296 had been the year in

which Abbot Walter of Wenlock had changed his financial system, by now employing new treasurers ('receivers') as his financial officers, instead of using for that purpose his main and stipendiary stewards who also managed his household at La Neyte.[64]  Having established this change, the abbot may then have turned his attention to more specific questions about the way in which the farming management was being conducted in particular manors. Eye was immediately next door to him; or more precisely the abbot's own house and grounds at La Neyte lay within Eye geographically, so it was the obvious place to start. At all events a big change was made in the management of Eye in the next year, 1296-1297. But it is not certain whether the change proved to be a good one.

Before 1295 the herd of cows belonging to the manor farm had always, so far as the account records go, been managed by the staff (the *famuli*, with or without assistance from the customary tenants). While the expenses of doing so had fallen on the manor, the manor had been able to take the benefits – the milk, butter, cheese, hides and meat, together with the new stock born each year, and the price of cows or calves sold – all of which were available for either use by the abbot and his household and the staff, or for disposal by sale in the 'market' or as gifts which could be donated to local or national figures, great and small, in and around Westminster, at the wish of the abbot or other monks in charge of the management. The number of cows kept in the 1270s and 1280s seems to have averaged about 50, varying between 38 and 66, but by the early 1290s, when the continuous run of surviving accounts begins, the number of cows had fallen to a figure of about 25-30 – where it remained over the next fifteen years.

Then in 1296-1297 the decision was made to put the 'issue and milk' of the cows out 'to farm', ie. to subcontract them to a 'farmer' for an annual price which would be fixed each year, depending on the number of cows and

---

64    See p. 297 above, and Harvey, *Walter of Wenlock*, pp. 13-15.

heifers available at that time. The 'issue' meant the calves born to the cows and heifers, and of course the 'milk' naturally included all the cheeses and butter which could be made from it. And so in place of the value of these benefits, the manor would receive simply the fixed price, but would be free of the costs of dealing with the calves, the milk and the making of large amounts of cheeses and a quantity of butter.[65] So was this a good decision for the abbot and monks? The various sums which the manor continued to receive annually in the next ten years from this 'farming out' of the 'issue and milk' of the cows ranged from £9 to £7. 4s. – say, an average of £8 pa.

The amount which the manor had received in the previous year (1295-1296) by selling its milk and milk products had been the much larger sum of £21. 2s. 10d.; its sale of 21 calves had brought in another £2. 1s. 8d; and four more calves had been swallowed up by the abbot's kitchen. But its 'dairy' expenses in relation to the calves and milk-products (as operations separate from the care of the flock itself) were small in comparison.[66] By that measure the new scheme would have been a disaster for the monks.

But *before* 1295-1296 their experience with the calves and milk products, while profitable, had not been so highly profitable as in 1295-96 (assuming that all benefits under the old arrangements were fully recorded – which may not be the case), and arguments can be made that a change to a regular, though lower, income would be a good idea. But it looks as if the excellent revenue received from the cows by the manor in 1295-1296 cannot have been regarded as reliably established before the

time when the change was made, because if it was thought to be reliable, second thoughts about a change must surely have prevailed. Unfortunately we cannot know what the profits for the farmers of the 'issue and milk' were in the subsequent years – profits which the manor lost. But there can be little doubt that the private exploitation of the calves and the milk continued to be a profitable operation to some extent, since the farmer or farmers apparently wished to continue to take the farm year by year for each of the next ten years – indeed until the surviving account documents unfortunately become ragged or missing after the time of the Days of Wrath and the death of Abbot Walter of Wenlock in 1307.

### C. *Yields obtained from the arable crops grown in Eye*

Also in 1296-1297 another administrative change came to completion, with good results, at least for our understanding of the scale and effectiveness of the cropping on the arable land in Eye. The change was the culmination of a useful process of investigation, presumably by the abbots, which had begun at least in or before the year 1275-1276 (the first year in which the manor farm accounts have survived). From at least that year such accounts as have survived announce the quantities of seed used for sowing the four main crops of wheat, rye, barley and oats grown in Eye, together with the three legume crops of beans, peas and vetch. One of the intentions behind this may have been to enable the 'yields' from the sowings to be calculated, by dividing the amount sown for each crop into the resulting amounts of grain or other crop delivered into the barns, after being harvested and threshed.[67]

---

65  This sounds like modern schemes in which particular operations (being parts of a greater undertaking, eg. in the railways) are 'privatised', by subcontracting them on terms. In 1296-7, the new scheme also meant that the manor still retained all the costs of managing the flock, and keeping it up to number by purchasing new stock, while retaining the benefits of sales of stock and hides. Some references for this abbreviated comparison are DS, *Eye A/cs*, pp. Bk. II / 63-66, 72, 80, 82-3, 87-8, 93, 96-7, 101-2, 111.

66  This assessment has to be generalised, because the contractual terms as to the separation of the *other* obligations as regards care of the herd are not clear, but most labour would not have incurred extra cost to the manor.

67  Of course the granger also needed a stock record of what came into and what went out of his barns, and the record of seed sown was one of the latter (unless it had been bought and used straight away).

So the policy of recording the amount of seed sown had been instituted from at least the time of the abbacy of Abbot Richard of Ware (1258-1283). In 1280-81, the year of the next surviving record, we can see that although the policy still stood, the accounts are unfortunately fragmented and present a less coherent picture. After a gap then in the records, the policy continued every year after 1291-1292 when John Churchwyne started his run of more than ten years as reeve of Eye, and it survived until the Days of Wrath and the death of Abbot Walter of Wenlock at Christmas 1307. But in the year of his death the policy began to crumble, with only the amounts of the wheat and rye sowings being recorded, and in the chaotic years which followed it then died altogether, like the abbot.

But meanwhile in the year 1295-1296 another policy had also been introduced, presumably on high from Abbot Walter (1283-1307). It was decided in that year that the records of seed sown should also include the acreage on which the seed of each crop was sown. This would reveal the amount of seed being sown on each acre, another factor which would have been useful for assessing and controlling the efficiency of the arable farming. But perhaps there was resistance to this idea from John Churchwyne the reeve, or perhaps he never got around to the job of measuring the relevant fields; but whatever the cause, none of the spaces left in the Account that year for the acreages were ever filled in. For example, the entry for the expected barley crop runs *'28 quarters and 5 bushels sown on ..* [blank].*. acres'.*

This was not good enough, and presumably on peremptory orders from on high it was corrected next year. So *uniquely* in 1296-1297 we can see that eg. 31 quarters and 3 bushels of barley seed were sown on 50 acres and one

'rood'. The wheat seed was sown on only 33 acres, the rye on 70 ½ acres, the oats on 47 acres, the peas on 16 acres and the vetch on 15 acres and one 'rod'. The acreage of the beans was not measured, as only four bushels were 'planted'. So if the records were accurate, we can calculate – and the Account for that year asserts – that the wheat, rye, peas and vetch were being sown at about the rate of 2 ½ bushels per acre, and the barley and oats at the denser rate of 5 bushels per acre.[68]

The irony is that the practice of actually recording the acreages sown, whose sizes must have varied each year, was then dropped. So in 1297-1298 the spaces in the Accounts for the acreages remain blank, and that remained the practice for the rest of Abbot Walter's time. Maybe the rates mentioned above were now hallowed, if not fixed, and were retained as such, but there is no record of anyone having used the new information or having varied the rate in order to experiment for a better yield by using, say, a denser rate. But the practice of keeping the incomplete formula *'sown on .... acres'* in the Accounts was still retained each year until the year of the abbot's death. So the result is that the year 1296-1297 was unique in showing both the amounts of the seed sown and the acreages sown. If one assumes that the *same* rates of seed per acre were 'customary' rates, one can work out what acreage was sown for each crop, each year; but this is to assume an absence of any experimentation with rates. This assumption may reflect what in fact happened, but we cannot know for certain.

However the practice of recording the quantities of seed sown, as well of course as the totals of the new crops stowed into the barns at the end of each year, enables us to see the yields actually being achieved for each crop within the period of seventeen years from

---

This was the main purpose of such an entry in the accounts. For a true comparison, one has to use the crop figures for the *next* year, because the crop harvested each Aug.-Sept is charged to the next reeve, not to the reeve of the year of sowing and harvesting; cf. Farr (ed.), *Stratton A/cs*, pp. xxxiv-xxxv.

68 But presumably the measurings were done in advance of the sowings, rather than retrospectively; and the hand-sowers would have been given the necessary amounts of seed in their baskets, for carrying out their sowing.

1292 to 1309 (with a few gaps here and there). Figures for Eye do contrast in some respects with a few of the lessons learnt from similar studies for other manors elsewhere.[69]

One of the new treatises in the thirteenth century about farm management had pointed out some basic economics of crop yields. 'If the sum content of thy barn do answer only three times so much as the seed was, thou gainest nothing by it, unless corn bear a good price.' So if prices are unreliable, you need a great deal more crop yield than 'three times the seed' to make the effort and expenditure worthwhile. Grain prices in the 1290s were up-and-down, with the inflationary trend surviving, if more slowly and with interruptions, into the first decades of the 1300s.[70] However another treatise over-optimistically looked for differential yields of four for oats, five for wheat, and eight for barley. How did the Eye crops measure against this ?

**Oats** in Eye had a mixed record in the 1290s and early 1300s. Of the eleven fairly consecutive years for which we can obtain yields, only in two years did the oats reach a yield of four-plus (ie. between 4.0 and 4.9); in three other years, it reached a yield of three-plus; in five years, its yield was two-plus; and in one year, the yield was even negative, ie. less crop than seed sown. The average yield for oats over these eleven years was 3.1, which in fact was higher than the average yield for oats (2.3) in the estates of the bishop of Winchester in the south of England during the second half of the thirteenth century.[71]

In the same period **barley** in Eye nowhere reached yields of even five, let alone eight. It reached a yield of four-plus in only four years (out of a total of thirteen); a yield of three-plus in six years; and a yield of two-plus in three years. But it never fell below 2.1, and its average was 3.4, almost exactly the same as in the Winchester estates.

**Wheat** was more erratic. In two years (out of fourteen), it reached a yield of five-plus; in three years, the yield was four-plus; in four years, the yield was two-plus; in three years, the yield was only one-plus; and in two years, the yield was negative in each, with less crop than the seed sown. The average yield over the fourteen years was only 2.8, whereas in the Winchester estates the average over the whole half-century was 3.8.

It was the rye crop (mainly used for feeding the Eye *famuli*) which reached the highest yield of six-plus, but this was only in three of the thirteen years for which we can calculate the yield. But in only one year, rye reached a yield of five-plus, and in one other year, four-plus. In four years, it reached a yield of three-plus; in three years, it reached a yield of two-plus; and in one year, the yield was 1.1, the crop virtually matching the seed sown. So even here, over half the years produced low yields, in only the ones, twos and threes. But at least there were no disastrous results, and the average was 4.0.

As to yields expressed in ratios of bushels of crop to the acre, it is clear that the Eye crops fell well below the ratios for wheat, oats and barley on the Winchester estates – namely 14 bushels per acre for wheat, 16 bushels for oats, and 28 bushels for barley. So even with an abbot who had a reputation for efficiency on his manors, Eye – his local manor – was not doing very well.[72] Of course many different factors can be responsible for poor results in

---

69  What follows in the text is not intended to be a full analysis of the effect of these figures for Eye. Many discussions of medieval yields range over long tracts of time, eg. Farmer, 'Grain yields on WA Manors', *Canadian Jo. Hist.* 18 (1983) pp. 331-348, with figures for 1271 to 1410, averaged over five periods of 25-30 years each, whereas this evidence for Eye deals with a short period and with figures for each year – with averaging as well. The summary about yields in Miller and Hatcher, *Medieval England*, pp. 215-17 is illuminating, and I gratefully have digested it and its Table.

70  Against the long-term rise of inflation with its slow increase in prices, one has to note, for example, the sharp fall in grain prices, from 8s. 2d. per quarter of wheat in 1294 to 4s. 10d. in 1296, right in the middle of the 1290s when Abbot Walter was facing the logic of low yields in demesne farming, Prestwich, *Edward I*, p. 409.

71  See Miller and Hatcher, *ibid.*, p. 216, Table 4.

72  Farmer, *ibid*, p. 347, in his wide-spanned article concludes that 'The Westminster abbey manors provide yet more evidence that medieval grain harvests were wretched'.

individual years – such as the weather, poor soil, exhaustion of even good soil, inbred seed, lack of proper rotation, etc. – and the lack of sufficient evidence of such medieval conditions makes it impossible to determine causation accurately.

### D. *The new policy to lease 'farms' in the northern region of Eye*

We have already seen that, by the second half of the thirteenth century, some lands in the northern part of the manor of Eye had been let to two prominent families: (a) some lands in part of the present Hyde Park, to the family which had become known as 'of the Hyde'; and (b) some lands in the present Mayfair area, between Park Lane (then Westminster Lane) and the line of the river Tyburn, to the Kendal family.[73] This was the district where the best land suitable for arable farming was to be found, on the gravel banks which lay above the silty region nearer the river Thames (which was more suited to hay).[74]

But the Hyde and Kendal estates did not comprise all the land within this northern region of the manor, for in that area there was both 'customary land' occupied by tied tenants, and other land which the abbot had kept in his own hand and through his own managers farmed as demesne land. But towards the end of the century his managers at Eye had started to follow, at no doubt his instigation, a much more extensive policy of 'farming out' parts of the land in this northern half of the manor, on profitable terms including new

market rents, when the land became available.

This policy was a progressive one, in the sense that it was bringing the previous management system to a close, whereby the abbey itself had farmed most of the manor, with the labour provided by the customary tenants.[75] Now it was for the new 'farmers' to make their own profits, but to pay the new rents. The policy was also progressive in the manner in which it was extended gradually to include more and more lettings by the abbey as the years went by, starting with short-term 'annual farms', and then including lifetime terms for many of the new tenants.

In 1275-6 (according to the first extant Eye Account), there was one large new 'farm' created that year, a re-letting to 'John of Eye' at what was clearly a new market rent of 16s., of land previously held by 'Robert of Eye', a customary tenant (whether or not he had been personally freed by that time). By 1291-2, fifteen years later, there were three 'farms' (none of them being the 1275 one), for market rents totalling 20s. 6d.[76] Significantly one of the new farmers was a man whom we have already met, John *le Convers*, perhaps a converted Jew who was also building up an estate of property in Westminster.[77] These three farms continued in force, with minor qualifications, for the next eight years until Michelmas 1299.

But during the ensuing year 1299-1300 another two large new farms were created, and two smaller ones. By these additions, the most significant changes were that two areas of the field *Tyburne*, which probably lay along the

---

73  For John of the Hyde and Sir Hugh of Kendal, see pp. 281-3 above.

74  For the geology, see *The Westminster Corridor*, pp. 25-27. For known 'farms' in what is now the Mayfair area, see Map B on coloured Plate 23, after p. 288. For the southern hay fields, see pp. 356-9 below.

75  This previous system was the system adopted in what has become known as 'the high-farming era', which some ecclesistical and lay 'lords' had started to embrace from near the end of the twelfth century, by recovering direct control, wherever they could, of their lands which had earlier been alienated. One of the main reasons for this policy of 'recovery' was the start of the great inflation in the second half of that century, which made the produce of land so much more valuable, see pp. 118-20 above and Miller and Hatcher, *Medieval England*, pp. 210 ff.

76  DS, *Eye A/cs*, p. 42. 'John of Eye' may have been the reeve John Churchwyne, see pp. 346-7. Robert of Eye was certainly Robert Brun (Brown), the prominent resident in the village of Eye, see p. 338 above. So far as we know, these four initial farms were on a yearly basis, not for longer terms.

77  See pp. 283 ff. above. John the Convert was having to pay 7s. 6d. rent pa. for this farm in Eye.

west bank of the river Tyburn in the present Mayfair area, had been leased to two married couples; and each of these four new farms was leased for the lifetime of the tenants, and at a market rent.[78] The two small farms are listed below.

First, 14½ acres of arable and pasture in Tyburne had been leased to Gilbert Woderove (probably an outside officer of the abbey, who had also had a lease of land near the Westbourne stream in the manor of Knightsbridge) and his wife, for the term of their lifetimes at an annual rent of 12s. 6d.[79] A second lease, of over 9 arable acres in Tyburne and over 7 arable acres in the field called La Redelonde (which with its reeds probably also bordered on the river Tyburn), had been granted to Master John *le Sauser* (the king's sauce-maker or 'salter') and his wife Alice, for their lifetimes at an annual rent of 15s. 3d.[80] A third (small) life tenancy of only one acre of unidentified land had also been granted to Geoffrey Bissop, at a rent of 1s. 6d.[81] And the fourth (small) lease was of two acres of pasture, called Martineslande, to the same Gilbert Woderove for life.[82]

At least two of these lands now leased 'at farm' had previously been held by a customary tenant. John *le Sauser's* new farm had once been 'the lands and tenements' of Ralph Stub, who had been the reeve of Eye for most of the year 1280-81, nearly twenty years before, and had died in 1298-99, the year before the re-letting. Geoffrey Bissop's acre had belonged to Robert le Messager, another customary who may have also died.[83] We do not know the previous holder of Gilbert Woderove's new lands in Tyburne or in Martineslande, but it is likely that each of them had also been a customary who had died or otherwise departed.

---

78  DS, *ibid*. pp. 136 and 138.

79  Woderove had received 8s. from the abbot at about Christmas 1293; ? for some service which may have been connected with the walls designed to keep the Thames at bay, see Harvey, *W. Wenlok*, I/40, p. 63. See WAM 6228 for his Knightsbridge lease. In 1304 he (or a son?) had trouble over an alleged breach of promise to marry, when he was summoned to appear at a London church: if he did not, 'she would have a licence to marry another'!

80  Like John the Convert, John *le sauser* was a big name in Westminster, with his position at court, the status of 'Master' and a house in Tothill Street opposite the almonry. A predecessor there, Master Ralph had been Edward I's previous sauce-maker (WAMs 17457 and 17467). Master John and Alice went on to purchase much property in Westminster and Eye. They lived in Tothill St., next door to 'Giffardeshall', where John Giffard (see p. 412) lived. After her husband's death before 1310, Alice (now *la Saucère*) inherited the estate and survived him for nearly 20 years. She became a landholder in her own right, and remarried another landholder. Eventually all this property became consolidated with other property held by Joan *la Vinitière*, another heiress and landholder, and came back to the abbey in c. 1360s. See also pp. 280 n. 70, 282 n. 79 and p. 412-3.

81  DS, *Eye A/cs*, p. 136. All these rents were market rents, although Geoffrey was probably also a customary tenant holding other land. The Sausers' tenancy must have started at about the end of March 1300, because they only had to pay half the above rent in that year. None of the lease-charters, nor the rolls of court which recorded some or all of these grants, have survived as documents, and only the A/cs report their effect.

82  DS, *ibid*., pp. 138, 152, 165. But this fourth lease, of Martineslande, was omitted by John Churchwyne the reeve, from his list headed 'farms' which had the three other new farms this year, and also in the next year; but in his last full year as reeve, 1301-02, his concealment of it – *and of its rent* – was discovered, and he had to pay arrears of the omitted rents, *ibid*., pp. 163, 136, 150, cf. 173. This was just one of several faults or frauds committed by John Churchwyne. Cf. the 'ploughing' fault, *ibid*., p.174, and p. 340 n. 62 above. By December 1302, he was in trouble & was sacked, & a new reeve was appointed for the last nine months of 1302-03, see *ibid*, pp. 173-4 & 186. Almost certainly Martinesland was also in the modern Mayfair area. It was probably the two acres, recorded at last as a 'farm' at 4s. rent in 1301-02, with arrears charged, DS, *Eye Acs*, p. 163. The previous holder of the close had been Richard le Faytour, another customary, see *ibid*., p. 179.

83  But no heriot for Robert le Messager has been traced in the accounts.

In the following year (1300-01) the same policy of creating leases for life was continued, and two more important ones were granted. Reginald *le porter*, probably a customary tenant of Eye who had done well for himself, and his wife (named later as Matilda) were granted a lease for life, at a rent of 26s. 7d., of 29 acres of land at Ossulston, the large field (or part of it) which also lay in the present Mayfair area, bordering Park Lane.[84] Secondly another small farm was also leased that year, of 2½ acres of unidentified land granted to John the Convert for his life at an annual market rent of 2s. 6d.[85] So John the Convert now had two farms for life in Eye, his earlier one probably being rather larger (location unknown), at a rent of 7s. 6d.[86]

In 1301-02, no new leases were granted, but in 1302-03 another farm of 16 arable acres was leased to Master John *le sauser* and Alice his wife, again for their lives at an annual rent of 13s. 4d.[87] The 16 acres consisted of 14 arable acres in Mabeliscroft (another field in the same area) and 2 arable acres 'at Pourtelane', presumably nearby too. This meant that the royal 'salter' and his wife now held 9 acres in Tyburne, 7 in La Redelonde, 14 in Mabeliscroft and 2 in Pourtelane, in addition of course to their urban holdings in Westminster. By this time most of the 'Mayfair area' in Eye must

have been leased out. That remained the position over the following years until 1311, when the extant Accounts in this period conclude. In 1327, when the next account survives, the rents of 'various farms' (which are not identified) are totalled at a figure of 92s. 11d. pa, which was nearly double the 1311 total (48s. 3d.); but it looks as if the same pattern existed.

So the conclusion must be that towards the end of the thirteenth century there was a clear decision by Abbot Walter, and then his successors, to lease all or a great deal of the land in the north-east corner of Eye on tenancies for life at market rents, as it became available. Some of the land seems to have become available for this purpose when deaths occurred of earlier tenants who had held their lands on customary terms (whether or not they themselves had become freemen by this time).

This policy to lease much available land in northern Eye for the new tenants' lives was a reflection of a wider practice upon which the abbey was embarking towards the end of the century, of now leasing houses or land in Westminster – at market rents; and usually for a life or lives; or later for fixed terms of years.[88] This practice was also echoed in the market of private transactions, made at about the same time or even a little earlier.[89]

---

84  See DS, *ibid*, p. 150. Ossulston field was probably the largest individual arable field in Eye (excluding the Hyde estate) and lay in the S-W and W of the present Mayfair area, and was named after the ancient (but surviving) Hundred and its court, see *The Westminster Corridor*, pp. 49 ff. and coloured Maps I and M. Land in Ossulston field had already been let in 1285 to the Kendals by Abbot Walter of Wenlock, but unless Ossulston was an extremely large field, that land must have come back to the abbey for it to be leased out again in 1300-01. Reginald had had to pay an additional 1d. rent for his other holding as a customary tenant, for a pledge (or mortgage) which he had received over 'Robert the Messenger's land', see *DS Eye Acs*, pp. 136 and 150.

85  DS, *ibid*., p. 150. These acres had previously been held by William Starling, probably another customary.

86  At about the end of the next year, 1303-04, John *le Convers* must somehow have stepped into the shoes of Gilbert Woderove as tenant of Martineslande. This is an irrelevance as to the present enquiry, since the tenancy was the same, whoever had it. There is conflicting evidence as to who was actually the tenant at the start, DS, *ibid*. pp. 163, 173, 186, 215. But John *le Convers* at least ended up with three farms in Eye. See Map B, on coloured Plate 23, after p. 288.

87  For 1301-02, see DS, *ibid*, p. 163. This was the year in which the fraud by John Churchwyne the reeve was uncovered, and the arrears made payable by him.

88  See WAMs 17159 (temp. Wenlock; for lives; 10s. pa.); 17512 (temp. Wenlock; for lives; 4s. pa); 17494 (1304; for lives; 4s. pa.); 17495 (1305; no term; 14s. pa.); 17497 (pre-1/11/1305; for life or lives; rent unknown); 17500 (1306; term not known; 13s. 4d, pa.); 17501 (1306; for lives; 10s pa.); 17573 (1319; for life; 7s. pa.); 17575 (1320; 20 years; 8s. pa.) Some of these leases contained sophisticated terms, eg.

### E. 'The Years of Crisis' and the threat from royal 'prises'

Medieval kings had long had the right to provision their royal household by making compulsory purchases, or 'prises', of foodstuffs and other necessary equipment. But in the 1290s the expenses which Edward I had incurred and still faced in his wars in Gascony, France, Wales and Scotland created a series of financial crises. These had reached a head in the years 1294 -1298, which have been called 'The Years of Crisis', and during them the right of 'prise' was in practice extended dramatically.[90]

The king needed to provision and equip his armies even more than his own household, and his demands for food and equipment grew accordingly. All over the country, landholders were liable to be subjected to seizures of their produce, livestock, farming instruments and even domestic goods, ostensibly as purchases but often with payment greatly delayed or denied. Equally merchants at fairs were usually subject to such seizures of their goods, even though in Westminster they had protections originally granted by Henry III. But the manor of Eye, being on the doorstep of the royal presence, was an easy source for the king's local requirements, and the manor accounts reveal frequent transactions and some of the steps which were taken by the abbot and his managers to avoid or minimise the demands made on them.

It was of course convenient for the manor to have a willing buyer when unneeded produce or other assets were available for sale, and many deals between the manor and the king's officers are recorded just as simple sales, with the manor receiving presumably proper prices. Earlier, in 1292-3, the royal household's requirements were still limited to its smaller needs, such as the cutting down of two elm trees in Eye in 1292-93 by the king's officers, probably for fire-wood or for timber for palace repairs, for which the king's 'purveyors' had to pay 5s. But by the middle of the Years of Crisis the needs had become greater. In 1296-97 many of the manor's carthorses and carts were being commandeered to transport unidentified royal equipment to several destinations, to Bury St Edmunds, to Canterbury, to Langley (probably the Langley in Bucks) and to 'the sea'. These were only temporary appropriations, but although the expenses incurred as a result by the manor (such as extra repairs to the carts, and charges for the keep of horses and men) are all itemised, there is no apparent evidence in the accounts that these extra expenses were in fact paid by the king's officers.[91] If they were not paid, then these royal requirements were met at the expense of the manor.

It was not only the king's own officers who descended on Eye to demand produce. In 1301-2, the manor sold (had to sell?) large quantities of oats to officers of Thomas earl of Lancaster, the king's nephew, and to officers of Edward the young prince of Wales (later Edward II). But it did well out of these no-doubt compulsory sales. The price was a reasonable one, and the reeve did not have to buy-in other oats, so the oats sold were apparently unneeded by the manor.[92]

But there is plenty of evidence, in the guarded language used in the accounts, that in many instances the manor was an unwilling seller. Many of the sales were of produce 'taken' or 'carried off' by the purveyors (even if some price was paid), rather than being

---

various rights of re-entry, etc. Another feature of these leases was that the rents were made payable to identified obedientaries (eg. the sacrist) or to wardens (eg. of St Mary's chapel). After Wenlock's death in 1307, the practice of similar leasings continued and accelerated, with many examples during the first half of the century.

89  See eg. WAM 17478 (1294; 10 years; rent unknown, but one mark was given as a price or premium).
90  Prestwich, *Edward I*, pp. 407-10. The prise system gave plenty of opportunity for corruption by officials, which the king had to investigate in 1298 and punish, see *ibid.*, pp. 431-2.
91  See eg. DS, *Eye A/cs*, pp. 113 and 117.
92  The price was 2s. per quarter, 2d. more than the price at which the manor bought in oats the previous year, though less than next year, see *ibid.*, pp. 157 and 194.

described as just sales, as they generally were when the manor was willing to sell. In 1298-99, 60 quarters of barley were quickly sold to someone else on the abbot's own order, 'because of fear of the king'; no doubt a low price from his officers was feared. Once when the royal officers had refused or threatened to postpone payment for straw which they were 'taking', a large reward of 12d. was later given to the abbot's employee, Nicholas of Reading and his assistants, for somehow *'obtaining payment'*.[93] The king's officers were also known for their roughness and willingness to break open the abbot's barns. Damage caused by the king's officers is sometimes mentioned in the manor accounts, and on one occasion it was more graphically recorded that the locks and key on the gate of a grange were broken and carried away by the officers, so that new ones had to be bought and *'fixed to the gate with nails'*. A goose was *'killed by the queen's officers'*; and another one was *'eaten by their hounds'*, so they even came with dogs to enforce their will.[94]

Conduct of this kind committed against the possessions of a great magnate – as the abbot of Westminster undoubtedly was, with courts of his own to punish such offenders; a magnate who himself might even have been present in Eye when the royal officers were behaving in this way – gives one a powerful impression of the still greater authority accorded in practice to even the minions of the king. Of course one did not argue with Edward I; nor apparently with even his minor officers. But it is only fair to add that the king, who was made well aware during the 1290s of recurrent complaints about such abuses on the part of his officers of prise, himself initiated earlier enquiries about them, and later acceded to a raft of legal measures which were passed at his Lenten parliament in Westminster in March 1303 and were designed to correct such conduct.[95]

---

93  DS, *Eye A/cs*, p. 246. At the end of one year, 1305-06, a crude attempt was made to assess a 'profit' for the year of £32. 6s. 2½d, subject to 'auditors' qualifications', including 'damage done by the king's officers and others'.
94  See *ibid.*, eg. pp. 130, 134, 147, 246, 239, 249 and 253.
95  See eg. *EHD* 3/490-492 and 496-498.

CHAPTER 20

# The cycle of the farming year in Eye
## 1291-1307

This is the 'record' of an imaginary year. But it is one derived entirely from real events – from day-to-day incidents, of which rural life in the abbot's manor of Eye was *typically* composed during a broken period of nineteen years, round the turn of the thirteenth and fourteenth centuries.[1] The details of events – collected assiduously by the manor reeve throughout each year; afterwards written out by a clerk in abbreviated form on vellum, at the reeve's dictation; with a final draft then corrected by shrewd auditors (who generally used fiercer black ink to cross out those items which they disallowed) – all these basic events were recorded in this way and form the elements from which this model of a typical year has been created. So the 'cycle' is an amalgam drawn from bare manor accounts over an extended period, and its content typifies both the daily round of life for those working in the manor and the passage of the circling seasons.

### The unending cycle of the years – told as a contemporary record

The timeless theme of the manor's accounts is the revolution of the seasons.[2] The feast of St. Michael on the 29th September, the traditional Michaelmas, customarily marks the turning point of the agricultural year. It comes at the end of the weeks of a strenuous harvest, which had begun shortly before the 1st

August, Lammas Day. But even before the end of August in this calendar year, the corn has already been reaped, and some of it is still waiting to be lifted and bound, before being carted from the fields into the Great Grange and the Corn Grange standing in the *curia* near the village.

Robert of Sende – the granger of Eye – and William of Wandsworth – a servant and factotum of the abbot, with a termly stipend – who have each acted as a 'leader of the reapers' for the last three weeks and a half, are now being paid-off from their work, which has cost the manor 1½ d. each per day.[3] Each 'leader' has himself wielded a scythe at the head of a team of reapers, directing the line and rate of their advance down the field. The total daily number of the reapers working under Robert and William's control has varied this year from 70 to 14. And when all the harvest work is finally done, the 'reap-goose' (*rip-gos*) or the 'autumn goose', the great harvest feast (with roast goose and beer) for the sixteen employed *famuli* of the manor will be held, probably in the hall at the *curia*, at a cost to the manor of another 1½ d. per head.

Unusually it has been a quick and easy harvest this year, mainly because earlier there was a 'great drought' (*magna siccitas*) which had thinned the crops; so the yield is not high, having fallen from the higher levels of recent years. In view of the unique importance of

---

1  The nineteen years were those for which we still have the original accounts, see pp. 339 above.
2  In view of the fusing of events and practices over many years, I have not tried to identify all the composite records relied on, but the text is based on the details of the accounts themselves. Translations of these accounts are lodged at the Muniment Room at WA and identified as 'DS, *Eye A/cs*'.
3  William was a regular leader of the reapers from 1297 to 1302; and Robert was their leader twice, as well as leading the threshers three times during this period. Another job for William was to act as 'keeper of the great horse', probably the largest cart-horse which led the team to pull the abbot's 'great cart' when he journeyed.

the harvest, Brothers Reginald of Hadham, acting here in the abbot's service but soon to be the prior and the abbot's bitter enemy, and John of Wenlock, the abbot's young nephew and now the warden of his house at La Neyte, have been overseeing the work and progress of the reapers, though not working with them in the field.[4]

For the carrying of the corn crops from the fields into the barns or for stacking, the manor has its own two carters, both members of the *famuli*, who have been working steadily at the job. So it has only been necessary this year for the reeve to order one 'boon', of one day's carting work, from those customary tenants who have their own carts and are liable to answer such demands for a carting boon. But for this boon, no less than twenty-eight carters are required for the task, and although they are not entitled to receive any pay (because these tenants are bound by their status and the customary terms of their tenancies) to obey this order, the manor has to provide one meal for them, and therefore to pay for twenty eight mid-morning 'dinners' at a cost of 3s. 11d. The dinner consists of beer and bread, improved by something to make the bread more palatable (*companagium*: 'to go with the bread'), with cows-milk or ewes-milk cheese made in Eye itself. On other boons, sometimes herrings or occasionally some meat may be provided.

In other years the crop, when carted, may prove to be too big for the granges to hold it all, and some of it may have to be stacked in temporary ricks by the stackers in or near the *curia* ; and then the thatchers will have to be called in to cover the ricks, to protect them against the weather until the crop can be placed under a proper roof. But this year there is no need for this.

Meanwhile a late crop of eight acres of vetch has also had to be 'mowed' in the field called la Redelonde, which borders the Tyburn stream (in the district known to us as Mayfair) and last year was pasture. Seven acres of peas

have also been mowed in the field called Kerswell, and fifteen acres of mixed vetch and peas in the Great Field opposite Kerswell. From this it is clear that even at the conservative abbey of Westminster the discoveries, learnt both from the past experience of farmers over endless years, and now recorded in the new treatises written in this century which describe good practices in farm-management, have been taken to heart.[5] The abbot and his managers have insisted on legumes being included in the sown crops every year, both to act as fodder for livestock and to restore a little fertility to the soil with a stimulus (known to us now as the fixing of nitrogen). But after its mowing, the legume crop this year takes the work of 44 man/days by hired workers to lift and collect, and then another 12 man/days on further 'boons', for customary tenants to cart the whole crop to the granges or the stacking ground.

Now all this lies behind them. The feast of Michaelmas is over and the circle of the year begins again. Ahead lies the late autumn, with the beginning of the threshing of the recent harvest. With the winter ploughing still to come, there will be some late pasturing on the remaining stubble (if the abbot does not take it all for his own horses); and after the ploughing, the sowings for next year's crops are still to come. The granger, Robert of Sende, is now on his home territory – the threshing – and after the 13th October (the great day at Westminster, celebrating the 'translation' of St. Edward) is over, he takes the lead again, this time as the 'leader of the threshers'. The work, for two to four threshers at a time, is a protracted operation. Half of the corn crops are brought to the threshing floor in the Great Grange, the flails start to fly, and thereafter the air is thick with flying chaff. The clacking of the flails and the stacking of the threshed corn lasts for no less than thirty seven weeks, until the 8th July next year, interrupted only by the change-over to the other half of the crop and by a holiday

---

4  For Brother John's particular expertise, in building and repair work, see pp. 354-5 below.
5  For the treatises, see p. 217 above. However the manor managers have not been successful in achieving good crop results, see pp. 342-5 above.

fortnight at Christmas and a week at Easter.[6] The hired threshers' pay is usually 3d. per 'quarter' of wheat and rye, 2d for barley and 1d. for oats, $2\frac{1}{2}$ d for the legumes; or sometimes they each take one bushel of rye chaff, peas and vetch mixed per week, without pay.

The winter ploughing also has to start, so that the ground will be ready for the sowing of the winter barley, and so a 'boon' for eight ploughs is called by the reeve. But it is then found that because the ground is so hard as a result of the earlier drought, the ploughs have become damaged, and there is delay while the smith has to do special repairs on them – from which there is then an extra expense for the manor.

The hiring out of this year's autumn pasture crop, on stubble or grass, has already been started. The pasture is usually sold in small areas, most of them in closes parcelled out within the larger fields in the northern parts of the manor; and some of them are for a defined number of animals and for a defined period. This year, for example, an area in the field of Tyburne (a field in the present Mayfair area which reaches as far as the great road, now Oxford Street) is hired out as pasture for eight of the plough oxen, for the period from Michaelmas to the feast of St Martin (10th November), at a charge of 6s. Other parcels sold are in Mabeliscrofte, in the 'field near Knightsbridge', in the field of Ossulston, in la Redelonde, les Halres and in Goosepool (*Gosepol*). Sometimes there is no pasture to sell (and therefore no income) in a field where you might expect it, but the ground has been designated as 'fallow this year', or the area has been laid down for arable in the coming year and is now 'already sown', or because the king or the abbot has 'required it for pasturing his own animals'.

Another great task for the winter is the collection of the dung which has accumulated in the pasture fields during the summer, for use as manure to be spread on the arable for the coming year, one of the advocated good practices now employed in the manor. Even the next-door fields of Westminster are a source for this, but because in Eye some of the pastured fields have been those nearer the Thames in the south, the manor has a small flat-bottomed 'dung boat' on the big river, into which the manure is loaded and so carried round to the mouth of the Tyburn, where the boat is hauled or punted up that tributary to points at which unloading can be more easily carried out on the fields which need manuring. But this year the dung boat is getting old and needs renewing, and so a new one is made at the considerable cost of 29s. 4d. Similarly carts are used to transport the dung, and in one (no-doubt protracted) episode 800 cartloads are collected and spread. Before the winter sowing can be carried out, the final feeding of the manure onto the fields takes seventeen days. Two 'boatmen' are generally included amongst the 16 or 17 *famuli* of the manor, and it is they who have to ply the boats needed for the purpose of carrying goods or people on the manor's business, and to man the dung boat as needed, since they share a good wage of 12s and yearly supplies of free rye or mixt.[7]

The sheepfold has to be repaired this year, and for this, 37 new hurdles have been bought at Staines further up the Thames. Staines has its own hazel woods and a hurdle-making business, and carriage from there to Eye is comparatively easy, by water down the river. So not only are the hurdles cheap, one penny each, but also the transport which avoids the slow and cumbersome journey by cart and road costs only 9d. Like Staines, Kingston even further up the

---

6   For this work Robert receives 6d per week, 18s. 6d in all. But having paid him, the reeve then finds that when his account is audited, this payment is at first disallowed (for a reason not given), but subsequently on a final reckoning to determine who owes what to whom on the whole year, the charge is allowed and restored, see DS *Eye A/cs*, pp. 116 and 118.

7   The abbot too has his own boatmen who carry him to London, Lambeth or Bermondsey and back, for a day's meeting; or they transport harness across the Thames to Battersea for him, or bear gifts to other great men; or even carry the abbot's servant bringing corn and wine to him at his manor of Pyrford in Surrey, via the Thames and the river Wey; see the abbot's household accounts, Harvey, *W. of Wenlok*, pp. 174, 175, 166. The abbot even hires his boat out to others, *ibid*, p. 161.

Thames is extremely well-wooded and is an even more common source for all kinds of timber for Eye, as it had been in earlier years for the king's great construction works on the abbey at Westminster.

Boats on the Thames are indeed one of the main means of transport for all manner of supplies coming to the manor of Eye, particularly from upstream. Purchases of peas and wheat come down river from Laleham; barley and rye from Staines, tiles and lime from Windsor, timber from Brentford, enough hay to fill nine 'cartloads', though not coming by cart, but under sail or being rowed or punted down the wide but shallow Thames from Laleham. Less usually, 1100 tiles are to be found and bought downstream in Woolwych, and are brought upstream, using the flood tide, for the repair of the buildings of Eye. In addition the 'ferryman of Chelsea' is always at hand for transport over the river, and his helpful availability is recognised each year with the free grant of four bushels of rye 'by custom'.

The winter is often a fertile time for the abbot's 'larder' or meat store to be restocked. This is located at his own *curia* just north of La Neyte, the site later known as Eybury farm. This year the livestock arriving at the *curia* to be slaughtered and salted for the larder have been prodigious. They have come from many of the abbot's manors around the provinces: -

26 oxen and cows from the reeves of
    Morton Foliot, Pershore and Todenham
    in the 'western parts' of Worcestershire
    and Gloucestershire, Islip near Oxford
    in middle England, and from Eye itself;
97 pigs from some of those places and
    Denham (Bucks) and Yeoveney
    (Middlesex);
202 geese similarly, with 23 coming from
    Eye;
148 capons from Laleham and Islip, and
109 cocks and hens.

All of these, save the chickens, have had, unbelievably, to walk the whole distance. Most of them are now handed over to Brother William of Chalk, the steward of the abbot's household, and John of Longford who is the lay or stipendiary steward in charge of the grisly winter operations of the slaughterhouse and salting.[8]

Since the winds and storms are at their worst as one year gives way to the next, the buildings in the *curia* of Eye suffer damage now and need urgent repairs from the carpenters, the tilers and the thatchers in the manor. One great wind has 'uncovered' the hall, the old grange, the granary and the dovecot, and the thatchers have had their work cut out. On another occasion in the previous March when the buildings suffered similar damage, the cost of repairs lasting a period of 24 days came to 13s. for a thatching team which had to be paid more than 6d. per day, because work 'before Easter' costs more than it does later.

But quite apart from damage by wind, the manor buildings, being of wood, need plenty of ordinary maintenance, and (subject to the weather) the whole of the winter period can be used for this. The structures for people are of course the 'houses' (*domi*, one of them a large one where most of the *famuli* sleep), with a separate one known as 'the carters' house'; and the big hall, where much business is done, including the holding of the abbot's court, sometimes as many as twelve times each year. The kitchen is a separate building, as is the dairyhouse where the dairymaid works and where the cowman, one of the *famuli*, makes the year's output of cheeses.[9] But many of the buildings are of course for the livestock: the oxshed with its fold, the pigsty, the cowshed, the stable for the horses, the sheepfold, the goose house, the henhouse, and the dovecot. A complete new grange has to be built, for

---

8  DS, *Eye A/cs*, II pp. 78-9. These did not include the many animals which were bought from Eye manor by the abbot's household during the course of the year, for more immediate kitchen use. In another year, fewer were slaughtered for the larder, 4 oxen, 16 cows, 51 geese and 43 pigs, *ibid*, p. 21.
9  But in 1296-97 the cows and milk were farmed out, so the cheese supply dried up, see pp. 341-2 below.

which 52 great beams have been brought from Greenford in Middlesex and (nearer at hand) from the old Westminster elms which stood near Spitalstrete, close to the leper Hospital of St James. There are now three granges in all, the 'old Grange (also called the Corn Grange), the newly built Great Grange, and the Hay Grange for the summer's hay. But the windmill stands outside the *curia*, with a ditch in between the two, and by the mill the 'old millpond' stands, perhaps a reminder still of some simple watermill once standing across the Tyburn stream.[10]

All these buildings are for ever being repaired, walls rebuilt, thatching constantly redone, the 'gate of Eye' restored, doors mended, while hinges and locks need refitting. Since a further great wind has broken the joisting of parts of the windmill and, as usual, the canvas fitted to its sails has been torn to shreds, the sails are now all being restored with new canvas (as they usually have to be each year), a beam has been bought for the fractured axle of its cogwheel, and the mill's broken timbers are being renewed or mended by a carpenter, at a total cost of nearly 32s.

The dovecot too is smashed, so much so that it will have to remain unrepaired, and the income from the sale of its doves and 'dovelets' to the abbot's kitchen at La Neyte, as delicacies for his guests, will be lost to the manor.

The essential man for all major repairs is Brother John of Wenlock who can both turn his own hand to anything mechanical or practical, and is also qualified to direct others in all repair work. As a kinsman of the abbot, he too came from Shropshire. His presence is required not only when Eye buildings have suffered real damage, but also when the

abbot's buildings in Westminster need serious repairs or when improvements have to be carried out to the abbot's buildings at La Neyte. He's a real working monk – just like the Cistercians.[11]

So it is Brother John who is given the task for the complete rebuilding of the windmill, after another wind has compounded the effects of years of wear and tear. The great post on which the mill building is supported, and on which it is turned round into the wind, is cracked and has to be replaced. A new one is sought at the abbot's manor of Denham in Buckinghamshire, where there are large woods. There a replacement is found and cut, but while it is being carried by slow wagon and cart to Eye, its weight breaks the axles of one of the wagons and one of the carts, which then have to be renewed on the road. On arrival the new post has to be shaped and fitted. The iron spindle too for the millstones, and other metal plates, also have to be mended or replaced, and after dismantling, most of the old timbers of the mill building itself are renewed. 'By the hands of Brother John' is the description of the main instruments for most of this work. The account this year has to be given a side-note, *'the mill was not working for half the year'*.

Another of the jobs for which Brother John's skills are needed is to reconstruct Eybridge, the bridge where the road from Tothill to the village of Eye crosses the river Tyburn, with two great beams bought for that purpose. It will certainly be he who, as the warden of La Neyte, is required to build a wall in the abbot's chamber in the house (presumably to make a private or separate space), and will be employed to make other things at that establishment, such as a new

---

10  Watermills, predating the Conquest, were much earlier than the windmills, which only 'arrived' here in the twelfth century.  There was a previous mill in Eye, since the ditch by 'the old mill' is referred to, see DS, *Eye A/cs*, p. 54. FitzStephen's merrily 'clacking' mills in about 1174 were watermills, see *The Westminster Corridor*, pp. 39 and 34.

11  The Cistercians arrived in England more than 150 years before this, and their buildings and farming further north were famous already.  For Brother John's work for 29 days on Queen Eleanor's foundation buildings, ordered by writs and costing £16. 18. 4d., and his repairs to 'buildings in Westminster' and in Eye, ordered by writ  and costing 77s. 6d., see DS *Eye A/cs* II / p. 89.

bridge, 'a third bridge', across the moat surrounding La Neyte.

So the winter is a busy time for all. In addition, there are all the other ordinary field works which need to be done, such as the endless digging out of new ditches and the older ditches and drains which criss-cross the manor. Among them, the existing long ditches which mark the boundaries round fields have to be scoured out: 780 yards between La Neyte and the Marsh, 660 yards round Longemore, 560 yards from the old millponds to the channel leading to the Abbotsbridge, and 484 yards elsewhere – nearly a mile and a half of ditches in those alone, and all to be done by hand.

And down by the river Thames the wallers seem always to be at work, building palisades to hold back the flooding river, mending the existing walls for 17 days at a time, while William the reeve of Pyrford (Surrey) has to be conscripted by the abbot to work on the walls of the Thames for five continuous weeks. For Abbot Walter, the Thames often spells trouble. He is already in dispute with his prior and monks, who have complained that he is not entitled to make use of one of the monks as a 'warden of the walls'. But the abbot has already done so, and now does so again – because, he says, it is not forbidden for him to do so.[12]

Brothers John of Wenlock, Thomas of Lenton, and later Ralph of Mordon have successively been ordered by the abbot to act as wardens of the walls. Some years ago Brother Ralph was actually *named* as 'warden of the walls' in an order made by Brother Reginald of Hadham himself; but in those days the latter was still acting as an officer of the abbot, well before he later became the prior and the abbot's arch-critic.[13] The palisade-and-earth wall against flooding has been built out beyond the marshy foreshore of the river, and a causeway from the firmer ground has had to be constructed over the foreshore to reach the wall. But all these works have no permanency, and areas of the riparian meadows continue to be regularly flooded.

Easter, like Christmas and Whitsun, is one of the great feasts of the medieval year, and a holiday of usually one week is allowed to the customary tenants. But at Westminster at least twelve days and sometimes more are usually allowed at Christmas, and special expenses on food and celebrations for the 16 *famuli* are incurred at Christmas and Easter, amounting to 4s., at 3d. per head. Easter is of course also the time when special rituals for the monks at the abbey on Maundy Thursday, to mark the Last Supper (the *Cena*), are laid down. Special alms-giving for the poor, (with contributory orders paid for in Eye, for up to 1000 herrings, wheat for bread, and beer), is usual at Easter and is probably performed in Westminster outside the west gate of the abbey. The qualification for such alms cannot be limited to the strictly 'urban poor', so even those who are prepared to admit to being 'rural poor' in Eye are qualified to partake of them.[14]

With Easter over, the new grass in the pasture fields and the lusher hay meadows is already beginning to grow, and in the arable fields the crops, some sown in the late months of the previous year and some sown this spring, are sprouting. The months which lie ahead are the seasons for the new pasture, the hay, and the corn and legume crops – in that order.

The main pasture fields are those mentioned above in the winter programme. But now a few new lettings have to be made

12  But his duty was to care for the walls *at his own cost*. After Abbot Walter's death at Christmas 1307, the prior and monks quickly passed a decree (see p. 325) which included a prohibition against the use of a monk for this purpose, stating that it was for the reeve of Eye or other secular officer to do so, Harvey, *W. de W.*, p. 235.
13  DS, *Eye A/cs*, p. 194. Bro. Ralph had also mended 'the causeway to the walls of the Thames' at Hadham's order, and received 30s. costs for so doing. He had also mended the manor boat at Hadham's order.
14  Queen Eleanor's charitable donations to the abbey towards the end of the C13 meant that the abbey's alms were catering for many of the London poor as well, Harvey, *Living and Dying*, p. 30, & pp. 306-7 above.

when previous ones have expired, and so we find a letting of pasture (in an unnamed close) 'for one foal and three oxen during the summer', costing the taker 4s. But there is no pasture income this year from Ossulston field (not yet let out as a farm) because it has been turned over to arable and 'is sown'; and no pasture at the 'Field near Knightsbridge', because the manor's own animals had been turned onto it, no doubt to enjoy the young grass as it grows, and perhaps because they have had a difficult winter.[15]

While the pasture in Eye is regarded as an important source for some income each year, the potential from the two hay crops each year in Eye is much greater. Indeed the hay is a real money-spinner, and long after the pasture and arable fields of the northern part of the manor have later been 'farmed out' on tenancies to individual farmers, the hay fields of the south are retained 'in hand' by the abbey.[16] From this southern area, the abbot's managers are able each year on his behalf to sell or donate individual parcels of the hay crop, sometimes already mown and sometimes still unmown (in this case, for the taker himself to deal with); usually for good money, but sometimes the grants are gifts from the abbot to powerful people in Westminster and sometimes even to less important people in Eye to whom he feels obliged.

The fields down in the south towards the Thames, between La Neyte and the river, are well-watered and rich, usually producing the large hay crop. Among them are Marketmead (*Markedemede*), at 36 acres more or less, the biggest of all the Eye fields; the 'Meadow of the Island' (*pratum de Insula*), also called 'Twenty acres', which probably used to be 20 acres in size, but has now been reduced to 14-15 acres; Longemore, the Long Marsh (a long narrow field of 20 acres, bordering the Tyburn stream; its name survived for many centuries after the Middle Ages); Westmead (*Westmede*, 18 acres); La Neytemead (*Eytemede*, 20 acres, or perhaps 13 more or less); Newmead (*Newemede*, 5 acres).[17]

Of these, Marketmead and Westmead are the two most interesting fields, because their treatment each year reflects certain collective agreements about work in them which have been made by the abbey (at no doubt the abbot's instigation) with various groups of customary tenants.

Westmead is the simplest, because the tenants involved are Eye tenants. At some point of time, an agreement has apparently been made that, instead of the manor having to require each of the individual tenants of Eye to carry out their separate duties in relation to the mowing of the hay crop in Westmead, the tenants should collectively be responsible as a group to carry out its mowing, when required. The manor will provide food on the day or days when the work is done. This arrangement has been in force from at least 1275 or before, and it has become established as a new 'custom'. It shifts the responsibility for raising the necessary work force for the job from the manor reeve to the tenants as a group; but it enables the tenants to make their own arrangements as to how, and by whom among their group, the job is done.[18] Such deals, which give a slightly greater degree of responsibility and independence to tenants who are still servile but now live in a changing world, are becoming commoner at this time.

---

15  Ossulston ceased to be a demesne field in 1300-01, and 29 acres of it were leased to Reginald le Porter & his wife, DS *Eye A/cs*, 150, see p. 347 above.

16  For the leasing of the lands in the northern half of the manor, including Ossulston, see pp. 345 ff. above.

17  Marflete (*Marleflete, Maresflete* ?, full size 18 acres) was also probably on the Thames bank, but was usually used for pasture or other crops, such as wheat, barley, oats or beans, so it was perhaps drier than the hay fields. For known fields in the La Neyte area, see Map C on Plate 24, after p. 288.

18  It is not clear when this deal was made, but it has the appearance of a C13 one, rather than an old 'custom'. It was in force before the arrangements under which the Eye tenants began to be allowed (from no later than 1291) to 'sell' their work obligations by paying a sum in exchange, see pp. 333-4 above and Harvey, *WA Estates*, pp. 225-9.

But the meadow of Marketmead is more complicated.  First, although by the 1290s this has been treated as an Eye meadow, it was not named at all in the 1275-76 accounts for Eye, and when it did appear in the next surviving accounts in 1280-81, it was actually described as 'the Great Meadow of Westminster'.  However it was treated as providing an Eye crop of hay, and that manor accounted for the proceeds.   The reason is presumably that it lies in the southern part of Tothill Fields, to the east of the river Tyburn's *western* branch and therefore strictly lies within the old manor of Westminster.   But it also lies west of the *eastern* branch of the Tyburn which runs towards the abbey and drives the abbey mill. This latter branch of the river is regarded, it seems, as the 'real' Tyburn, and so the meadow has now come to be treated as if it lies within Eye manor, and is managed by the officers of Eye.  In some year after 1280-81, its name as a 'Meadow of Westminster' has been dropped, and in effect now, by the 1290s, it has become an Eye meadow in name as well as by convention, under its new name, *Markedemede* or Marketmead.

Secondly, the customary tenants with whom the abbey has reached a collective agreement are not the Eye tenants, but two collective groups of 'foreign' tenants. The Eye accounts reveal that by the early 1290s 'the men of Staines and Laleham' (abbot's manors, in the south-west of Middlesex) have previously agreed with the abbot to come and mow the main hay crop annually in the meadow now to be known as Marketmead, when they are required to do so; but with the option on their part to pay 7s. (or 7s. 6d) to the manor of Eye in exchange for that obligation, if they cannot or do not wish to perform it.  But more than that, another group of tenants, 'the tenants of Westminster' have also agreed to continue to carry out their old task in what used to be a Westminster meadow – to 'lift' the mown hay there (ie. to raise and pitchfork it into carts) each year when required to do so, with the option on their part to pay the (much cheaper) annual sum of 3d. to the manor, to be free of the obligation.

We do not know whether there is any other benefit which these other 'foreign' tenants get from the deals made.  But for the men of Westminster, the task is comparatively light, since only a limited amount of work and travel is involved for them. So their option-cost is also light.   However, for the men of Staines and Laleham, the work of actually mowing up to 36 acres is more considerable. And an additional burden lies in the travel which their task of mowing in a distant part of Middlesex entails, even if (as we may guess) their journey by boat from Staines and Laleham to Eye along the highway of the Thames, armed with their scythes and other gear, may be novel and quite enjoyable.

But it is hardly surprising to find that within a few years after these arrangements were recorded, neither of the physical jobs is still being carried out.  For the men of Westminster, the abbot himself has acceded to objections from them, and has personally released them from their obligation altogether, when he met them on one of his 'itineraries of Middlesex'.  Although no such release has been given to the men of Staines and Laleham, they do have their own more limited remedy (in their own option), and we find that by the start of the next century and the later death of Abbot Walter of Wenlock in 1307, a steady sequence of no-doubt grudging but unbroken payments of 7s. each year frees them from their obligation to carry out this distant work.[19]

These agreements about Marketmead must surely indicate that, with the Great Meadow of Westminster now converted into an Eye meadow under a new name, it has been

---

19  See DS, *Eye A/cs*, pp. 133, 138 (re. Westminster); and pp. 166, 188, 202, 220, 229 (re. Staines etc.).  In all, the men of Staines and Laleham paid their 7s. (or 7s 6d) in 11 out of 15 recorded years.  The Westminster men paid certain option money in 1296-7 (2d) & 1297-8 (3d.), *ibid* pp. 111; & 124 (allegedly for 'harrowing'; or was this another similar obligation, under some different deal, with another option figure?).

found that there are too few customary tenants in Eye with the necessary work obligations to mow, lift and carry the hay crop in the meadow. The deals so made also fit into a pattern of similar deals which have been made with tenants in *other* 'foreign' manors, also managed by the abbot, during the thirteenth century.[20]  When the customary tenants of other manors do exercise such options given to them, the manor of Eye often has to pay considerably more to get the work done than the sums which it receives from the tenants; but this is not always the case.[21]

At all events the steps which will lead up to the mowing of the hay in all the Eye meadows are taken, one way or the other, during May and part of June. When there has been a summer drought *(de siccitate estivatis)* and the crop in a meadow proves to be unattractive to any buyer of hay, because the hay is 'weak' *(per debilitatem)*, the reeve may have to use the meadow for sale as pasture, if he can. But if a standing grass crop is not wanted even as pasture, he has to record 'nil, no buyers', and perhaps face the risk himself of resorting after all to an unpropitious mowing and then, he can only hope, to a sale of the mown hay, against the odds.

But if the crop (in Westmede, say) is good and there is a sufficient offer for the crop 'in gross' (ie. as it stands in the ground), we see then that it is sold *unmown* to a buyer such as

John of Halliford, who is probably a 'haymonger' or merchant;  and it is then the buyer who is left to deal with not only the mowing of the hay, but also its 'spreading', 'lifting', 'carting' and 'stacking', and with selling as much of the crop as he can, and storing any residue in his own barn for future use by him or for future sales. If however market terms are not good for such sales 'in gross', but the crop is still likely to sell well as mown hay, John Churchwyne the reeve of Eye has to carry out the mowing and lifting (either with the help of the men of Staines and Laleham, or the men of Westminster, or by hiring other men from Eye or elsewhere).[22] Then the reeve has to sell the mown crop in large or small parcels, as best he may;  or he may have to distribute some of it by cartload, as presents, if the abbot so wishes;  and eventually to make haystacks in or near the *curia*, with what remains, or to store it for a longer period inside the Hay Grange. And all these choices and decisions which he has to make for each of the meadows have to be carefully noted in his record-jottings and / or tallies which he will use when later he is confronted by the auditors of his account.

So this year the hay in the whole of Westmead is sold unmown to a buyer for £6. 13s 4d. The crop from 15 ½ acres in Le Longmore, also unmown, fetches more, at £8. 2s. 5d, while

---

20   For example, the hay in 'the Great Meadow *of Westminster*' in 1280-81 was previously due to be mowed by 'all the men of Teddington and Halliford' (abbot's estates in the southwest of Middlesex), as well as by 'Robert of Insula' (= Robert le Brun of Eye?, see p. 338 above), who all had similar options of buying themselves out and did so, see DS, *Eye A/cs*, pp. 35, 33 and 36. It is unclear how these duties fit with the Staines and Laleham obligations. See also Harvey, *WA Estates*, pp. 221-2, where certain (allied?) Teddington obligations as regards a so-called Westminster meadow can be seen to have been introduced by the early C14. The "¼ scythe" mentioned on *ibid*. p. 221 reveals a possible reduction of obligation for Teddington tenants, and thus an advantage to them of such a new collective agreement (if, say, there had been a prior obligation of a full scythe).

21   In 1303-4, for example the manor received 7s from the men of Staines and Laleham, but had to pay 10s. 2½ d to get even 27 acres of hay mown in Marketmead. And in 1281 the comparable figures had been 7s. 5d, and 15s. 3¾ d.  But in 1305-6, the contrast is between 7s and 3s 9d (for getting the mowing of only 11 acres done); so if that had been all, the manor was not in loss and was also able to use other parts of the field profitably by changing its ways of dealing with them. See DS, *Eye A/cs*, pp. 202, 205, 33, 35, 229, and 233, and Map C on Plate 24, after p. 288.

22   I have wondered whether in one year, the 13th June 1281, the elderly abbot (Ware) may himself have helped in the lifting of the hay, ('*auxilio domini abbatis*'; DS, *Eye A/cs*, p. I/35).  But Dr R. Mortimer suggests that the abbot had perhaps supplied some of the 11 workers needed for the job that day.

two more acres of that meadow are sold separately, also unmown, for 16s. to Richard the butcher of Westminster and Alice the milkseller (*la lekmongester*), who seem to be partners in a joint enterprise of meat and milk. But the whole of the smaller meadow of Priestsmead (*Prestesmede*) is sold for only 18s (its usual price for a sale 'in gross').

But all the crops of hay in other meadows, including Marketmead, have to be mown, and after a number of small sales of the mown hay, which bring in another £2. 3s. 6d., the rest is sold in larger but unidentified parcels for a total of £10. 1s. 0d. But then there is "no more, because Sir John of Droxford has had it". As there is no record in the Accounts of any sum paid by Sir John for whatever he has received, it can be assumed that the abbot, following his usual practice with this great keeper of the king's wardrobe, has chosen to give him a handsome present of hay for the horses which he keeps at Eye. Another year Sir John is treated favourably in a different way, by being allowed to pay only 14s. for all the hay from the meadow of Closham, and after the price there is added the revealing note "so little, at the lord's order".[23]

Other purchasers or recipients of the mown crops may receive their hay by the 'cartload', perhaps delivered still in the carts into which it has been loaded in the fields; or they may just purchase small 'parcels' of mown hay, and then no doubt they have to send their own cart to collect those parcels either from the stacks made in the meadow or in the *curia*. The smaller people like Philip Ediman, still a customary tenant but owning a number of small lands in the manor, William Bisouthe another customary of Eye, and William of Padington buy and fetch their own smaller parcels of hay, while John Foxley the

abbot's steward, has six cartloads delivered to him in payment of his 'expenses'. And Robert of Worstede the bailiff of Westminster, Robert Chamberlain of Reading and William Basing the clerk of Sir John of Berwick (himself a royal clerk), each receive one cartload. Robert Chamberlain gets his because the abbot orders it by writ, and William gets his at the steward's order; but in spite of appearances these special deliveries may be purchases, not gifts. At all events all these disposals of the mown hay raise another £5. 7s. 10d for the manor's account.

While all the meadows full of hay are being dealt with, the growing corn crops are suffering from unrelenting battalions of thistles, nettles and docks, against which there is no remedy except the hoe and bent backs. So all the work which involves this extra cost has to be methodically listed. Much of it is done by the *famuli* and so does not create additional cost, but other stretches of the corn are combed for weeds by hired men (and occasionally women) and this work all has to be detailed, with resulting expenses for the manor. Fourteen acres of barley in Eye's 'Field at Knightsbridge' have to be hoed, as does the rye near the *curia*, more rye in Tameseshote and the Twenty Acres (both these reaching down to the river Thames), the wheat and oats at Marflete, and even another crop of eight acres of oats which stand isolated in a separate 'field' within the great meadow Marketmead, among the other acres there of hay which have just been mown.[24]

So the wheel of the seasons is turning, and the final reckoning of the year again approaches, when the fields will come alive again with the reapers, lined up in their teams to scythe the long-stemmed corn, with their following 'rakers' and 'binders' and 'pitchers'. The weather must be favourable this year,

---

23  For John of Droxford, see also pp. 286 n. 103, 306 and 314 n. 14.

24  It is probably the absence of hedges and the more open aspect of medieval fields which result in the system whereby the bigger fields contain smaller fields or plots within them – some of which have separate names and uses while others remain unnamed. After later enclosures every smaller field began to get its own name and identity, so that the size of the original big field was either reduced or its name even lost.

because the men of Eye and all the extra hired men are already in the fields on the 27th July, (*'the Tuesday next after the feast of St James'*), even before the feast of St. Peter-in-Chains or 'Lammas Day', the 1st August, can announce the strict start of the harvest period.

Back in the early 1280s, before Wenlock became the abbot, the detailed record kept by the reeve or bailiff of how many reapers were mustered and paid each day used to be repeated in the formal account, day by day throughout the harvest period. On rare occasions more than 70-80 reapers used to be at work, each earning at that time a doubled daily wage of 2d, but usually the daily number of reapers has ranged from about 35 down to about 7. But now under Abbot Wenlock the system of accounting has been simplified (but, as so often, made more inscrutable), and this year we learn only that in the whole of the harvest period £8 6s 8d has been paid for the autumn reaping, carried out by 'diverse men', leaving even the wage rate unknown.[25]

So the autumn passes, and when the last reaping takes place, only 6 workers need to be present to finish things off after the busy weeks of scything. The annual 'boons' have been called by the reeve, to summon usually about 16 carts and more men (up to about 29) onto the fields for the loading of the corn, and so another busy period, with rakes and pitchforks, is still to follow the month of the scythes.

### The women at work

Although there is little differentiation between the sexes in the accounts, there are clues that the women certainly are present and can take part in the manor work, particularly in the harvesting season, in all those tasks which they can do. In this autumn period they come into their own. Presumably the 13 women who have to 'carry a stack of rye to the grange' are noted for their strong arms, while the 64 women who 'in shifts', after the reaping is over, have to cut and collect the stubble (and so must be able to bend a lot) are following the same discipline as the men and are therefore rewarded at the good daily rate of 13/4d, even if in this instance there is still a slight degree of differentiation from the men's harvesting rate of 2d.[26]

After the reaping is done, the women's work, in preparing materials for the re-thatching which is going to be needed during the winter, consists of severing the precious heads of corn, destined for the threshing to come, and collecting up bundles of the remaining 'long straw', ready for the thatchers. And later when the thatching itself has to be carried out, the thatcher may be assisted by a team of two, a man and a woman, apparently working equally but sharing in the daily rate of 6d which the thatcher receives; but we are not told what the shares are.

During the early spring the planting-out of bean seeds or plants, whether in the fields or in the abbot's garden at La Neyte, is a task in which the women are particularly employed, and their work recorded. So we can watch, in our mind's eye, the group of 40 'maids' who are hired for one day to sow fourteen bushels of bean seeds in the field of Marflete near the Thames. Their daily rate of pay, at 1¼d, is higher than the labourer's usual 1d, but lower than the 'stubbling' rate (1¾d)

25  In the 1270-80s the annual cost of the harvest did not exceed about £4. But by the 1290s it was at least more than £8 and sometimes £10 and more. So either the man/days of reaping, or the rate per day, had more than doubled. The rate could have increased a little (say by perhaps another halfpence), but doubling to 4d a day is almost inconceivable. Since payment had been per day and not related to productivity, many more hours and therefore days must have been worked. Had more acreage been put into production? What else could the abbot (or John Churchwyne?) have been doing? A movement towards payment *per acre* is just discernible. Could this have resulted in doubling of the cost?
26  Among these large numbers of harvest workers (both reapers and the later stubblers, men and women), there must have been workers drawn in from other communities, payable at the daily rates and glad to earn them.

which their sisters had received last autumn. On the other hand the three 'maids' who had been hired to 'select and clean' the rye for two days before the harvest have each been paid only the usual 1d. per day.[27] All their paid work is casual and cannot have been any reliable source of income.

But the most permanent female presence to be found is one of the *famuli* at the *curia*, the *'daie'*, the maid (sometimes called 'the maid of the house') who does everything which is needed in the dairy, day-in and day-out (apart from feast-day freedoms, if any) throughout the year. During the period up to 1295, one of her jobs has been to help the cowman in making the innumerable cheeses (212 in this year) which have been a staple produce of the farm, and apart from their value as a protein food, have formed a tremendous asset as a source for annual gifts for the abbot or his stewards to give to influential men whom they wished to cultivate. The maid's annual stipend, which is additional to her keep and share of other common benefits for the *famuli*, has varied between one and three shillings in the period up to about 1294, but after that it has settled at 1s 8d.[28] During the whole year she has precious little which she can buy, and even less to spend; one of the nearest people to a real serf left in the manor.

27 See DS, *Eye A/cs*, p. 7 for both these groups of 'maids'. Marflete (or *Maresflete*) was at or near the mouth of the western branch of the Tyburn river. It was separated from the land called Burgoyne by an area of sedge, *ibid*, p. 265. Although riparian (with wide river walls), it was used for pasture, not hay, and also surprisingly as arable for oats, barley and wheat, see *ibid.*, pp. 110, 155, 169, 205 etc.

28 In the later 1290s, the dairy maid regularly 'shared' a stipend of 5s. with the pigman; but there is one clue that her share of this (after her services in cheese-making were no longer necessary) was only 1s 8d, a good deal less than half, see *ibid*, p. 241.

# CHAPTER 21

# The manor of Hampstead: under foreign lords
## 1086-1257

The ancient ridge on which the village of Hampstead stood looked down over the valley where Westminster lay, and the adjacent lands of the manor fell quite sharply away on all sides from the top of the ridge.

One of the earliest estates of the abbey, the manor of Hampstead has already been described in *The Westminster Corridor*, from anglo-saxon times up to the time of the Norman Conquest and the later making of the Domesday Survey in 1086.[1]  By the time of Domesday the settlement at Hampstead held probably no more than fifty people. The population had been larger before the Normans landed, but the manor had then suffered losses at the hands of the invaders, both during their hostile encirclement of London and afterwards.[2]

Only seven families, of whom six were serfs and one was a slave, were counted in Hampstead by the Commissioners for the Domesday Survey. So the Survey had described a small and fairly primitive settlement, which like many of the other lands around London had suffered when the Normans took control of the city and its neighbourhood.

But already, within the twenty years after the time of the Conquest, something else of importance had happened in Hampstead.  A significant part of the manor had been taken out of the abbey's immediate control, and as subsequent events showed, this change foreshadowed the unusual future of this small estate for nearly the next two centuries. During most of that long period, much of the cultivatable land in Hampstead was no longer in the hands of the monks; and we know

nothing about the lives and fate of any of the ordinary tenants of the village.

The two centuries went by.  It was only in 1258 that the abbey again had control of the demesne lands of the manor, and once more could manage the farming of its own manor. It was only then that, for the rest of the thirteenth century, the people of the manor could begin to emerge from their obscurity – thanks to new and fashionable documents, such as 'rentals' and 'accounts', which the convent of Westminster monks had learnt to create in their restored role as managers of this, their own estate.  How had these far-reaching changes of fortune taken place?

### The absolute power of a Norman king
If it is difficult to appreciate fully the extent of the power wielded by an early medieval king, consider the position of the abbey at Westminster at the time of Domesday. Here was a powerful ecclesiastical church, which already owned many estates and, among them, enjoyed full rights over the land of Hampstead, granted to it by a king, Ethelred, nearly a century before.  By 1066 the abbey had already gained a special national status, having been rebuilt in stone by another king, Edward the Confessor, and chosen by him as the shrine for his burial; and during the course of that year it had also been selected, within a few months after the Conquest, by a third king, William the Conqueror, as his coronation seat. It now had a tough Norman abbot as its head. Against any other subject in the kingdom, the rights and status of the abbey, as a strong ecclesiastical institution able to deal as it liked

---

1   See *The Westminster Corridor*. pp. 99-111, 114-134, 169 and coloured Maps D, E, O and P in that book.
2   *ibid*, pp. 121-122.

with its own estates and people, were unassailable. Nevertheless, cutting right across these rights and the abbey's status, the Conqueror had imposed upon the abbey a new tenant for part of the estate of Hampstead.[3] This was the start of a destiny which, at royal hands, overtook Hampstead for nearly two hundred years, and during that period became even more pronounced.

A Norman baron, Ranulf Peverel, had been made the tenant of one 'hide' of the cultivatable land (perhaps 120 acres) in Hampstead – a holding of land whose previous role had been a special one, as 'land of the tenants' (in Domesday words), ie. a large area of land unusually laid aside for the sole use of customary tenants of the manor. But even more unusually, Ranulf Peverel had also been allowed a special paragraph of his own in Domesday Book, to record officially the present position which he now held as the new holder of this land.[4] This was a double intrusion – first upon the ancient rights of the abbey, and secondly upon the customary rights of existing Hampstead tenants, who were now subject to a more severe lay lord on their 'hide'; or, at worst, may even have lost the land which they had earlier enjoyed and no doubt depended on.

A further significance of this event is that within another fifty years its effect was

repeated, and indeed augmented. Before 1133 one of the Conqueror's sons, King Henry I, had granted all or a large part of the estate of Hampstead to a Norman man of his own choice, named Richard of Balta 'and his heirs' over the head of the abbey, for a rent of £2 payable to the abbey. On each of these two separate occasions the monks of the abbey no doubt had had to accept a situation which appeared inevitable, since their own rights were at the mercy of all-powerful kings who in practice could do what they wished, and even undo what they or their predecessors had done previously.[5]

So initially a part of the abbey's endowment estate had been appropriated for Ranulf Peverel; and fifty years later, more of the same estate was also taken compulsorily – even if the abbey was now to receive a rent for it.[6] Meanwhile customary tenants may have lost land which had been theirs to cultivate; or at the least had found themselves subjected to a new foreign lord.

In the long term, it was not until 1258, much more than a century after the transfer to Richard of Balta, that most of the manor of Hampstead was recovered for the abbey in legal proceedings, through the efforts of Abbot Crokesley.[7] So for most of that period the demesne lands of the manor were lost to the abbey, and the monks had had to be content

3   Some would argue that a justification in 'law' for this royal exercise of power was that the king remained the lord of all land at all times; that *occupiers* of it were merely his tenants or under-tenants; and that (in modern terms) one of the conditions on which such tenants held their lands was that the king could still do with it whatever he wished. Others may dispute such a contention. But I am concerned only with the practical outcome here.

4   See *The Westminster Corridor*, pp. 119-120 and Plate 8 (p. 86). Peverel's special mention in DB strengthens the view that this grant had been the doing of the Conqueror, not of the abbey – even if it may not have mattered much to the abbey, because it was the abbey's tenants who mainly suffered, by the change made to their 'hide'. From the abbey's standpoint, one did not argue with this king, whatever the merits; and so Peverel's rights were confirmed by DB. These were rights '*sub*' the abbot'; not '*de*' the abbot as a grantor.

5   Such exercise of royal autocracy, with or without justification, was far from unique, even in later times. But, as we have seen, the slow-growing influence of legal thought, of baronial and ecclesiastical opposition and of the growth of parliamentary consultation had begun by the C13 to exercise restraints upon royal powers.

6   It is not certain whether the whole estate or only a large part of it was granted by Henry I. For the former, see Harvey, *WA Estates*, p. 352, but cf. VCH, *Mdx* 9/92 where the issue is rightly raised. See n. 14 below.

7   For Crokesley's recovery of Hampstead, see p. 216 above, and 376 ff. below. He laid particular emphasis on his 'own efforts' in recovering the estate.

with the same rent of two pounds each year. This remained unchanged even during the onset of the great inflation, which had begun in the second half of the twelfth century and was still continuing in the next.[8]

During the long period of Hampstead's alienation from the abbey, we know a good deal about these foreign lords, and their successors, who held the lordship of the main estate, and about the other organisations (such as the order of the Knights Templars) which also obtained large and long-lasting holdings within the manor. But of the customary tenants during this period we know nothing. It is only after Abbot Crokesley's recovery of the manor and the contemporaneous start, in the middle of the thirteenth century, of the making and survival of manorial records at the abbey that we begin to learn about the ordinary people of Hampstead and their managers and their work.[9]

But meanwhile, who were these first new lords, Ranulf Peverel and then Richard of Balta? And why were they granted land in Hampstead?

### The start of the alienation of land in Hampstead

There has been much mythology about Ranulf Peverel. But some of the less contentious facts are that as a Norman he came over with the Conqueror and was rewarded with many East Anglian lands in Suffolk, Norfolk and Essex (including parts of what is now Greater London, such as West Ham). His whole estate in England became known as 'the honor of London', because it included properties and had its *caput*, or as we would say, its base in the city itself. Another title, 'Peverel of Hatfield Peverel' (now a small village in Essex) was also used for his son William who bestowed lands on a priory founded there. He and later his son also became benefactors of St. Paul's in London (where Ranulf was later buried) and of St Peter's abbey in Gloucester.

Some of the mythology about him centres on his 'marriage' and his lineage. He is variously reputed to have married Ingelrica, alleged to have been a former mistress of the Conqueror, or – as another story goes – the daughter of Ingelrica; but these stories are probably apocryphal.[10] Certainly he had a son called William, but that has given rise to more confused mythology, because another powerful William Peverel (himself alleged to be an illegitimate son of the Conqueror!) had taken part in the Norman invasion and had been similarly rewarded with even greater estates (in Nottingham, and elsewhere). This has led to confusions of the two Williams.[11]

Whatever his origins, Ranulf Peverel must have been introduced into the Hampstead scene through royal influence.[12] Although one of his known personal characteristics was that during the years *before* the Domesday Survey he was inclined to 'annex' lands which had *not* been granted to him, an illicit annexation of the abbey's Hampstead 'hide' would have been inconsistent with his formal paragraph

---

8  For the inflation, see pp. 118-121 above. Other smaller parts of the manor had also passed to other ecclesiastical institutions, see pp. 366-8; and 371-2 below.

9  For the start of written record-making in the abbey's demesnes, see pp. 216 ff. above; and Clanchy, as cited there.

10  From Dugdale, *Monast.*, 6/1794 and *Baronage* 1/436, onwards, to VCH *Essex* 2/105, etc.

11  The various Peverels need sorting out; though not here. Later the two main Peverel 'honors' reverted by separate escheats to the king during the C12 (thereby providing him with lands for doling out in grants).

12  For Hampstead as a convenient 'foothold' close to London, for barons and others, see p. 366 n. 21 below.

13  See text above and note 4. In Essex he annexed five different areas of land which had not granted to him. These were expressly recorded as 'annexations' in DB, and not given the status of legitimate holdings, see DB *Essex*, 90/10-14. Moreover an annexation against the rights of the Conqueror's coronation abbey was highly unlikely in itself; and if made, would not have been formally recognised in the way in which it was.

in the official record of the Domesday Survey.[13]

The 'hide' of land in Hampstead which Ranulf had been given was in the area now known as Belsize, and still retained its description as the 'hide' in 1258, in the first 'rental' of the Hampstead tenantry after the recovery of the manor by Abbot Crokesley.

The second Norman, **Richard of Balta**, was altogether different. He did not have the status of a baron, and at most was probably a knight. But more explicitly he also had royal influence behind him. 'Balta' was the name at that time for the modern Baupté, a small village in the Côtentin, the Norman peninsular on the northern end of which the port of Cherbourg lies. All that we know for certain about Richard's arrival in England derives from a charter of King Henry I, giving notice that he had 'conceded' to Richard and his heirs 'land of the fee of the abbot of Westminster in Hampstead' at an annual rent of £2.[14]

This charter was made after November 25th 1120 and possibly during the vacancy after Abbot Crispin's death;[15] and this, if correct, would make the date of the grant between about November 1120 and January 1121, when the vacancy ended. The charter declares that the abbey had already made a charter granting the land to Richard, but that act probably did not mean that this was a grant initiated by the abbey.[16] When dealing with the ruthless Henry I, as with his father before him, the abbey would have had to do what the king, or his managers, wanted. But there was also a special reason why the king should have wanted to reward Richard of Balta, and therefore the chances are that he had initiated the grant himself – as indeed the words of his own charter confirm.

The Côtentin (the Cherbourg peninsular) had been of vital importance to Henry since at least 1088. At that time, as the youngest son of the Conqueror, Henry had had no inheritance, since William Rufus (the middle son) was by then king in England, and his eldest brother Robert was and remained the Duke of Normandy. But Robert was always short of money, and in 1088 he 'sold' the Côtentin to Henry for 3000 pounds of silver. Henry then occupied the peninsular and *'recommended himself to all men'*, who therefore became loyal to him.[17] Although later he was temporarily driven out of that province by his two brothers, he recovered it after he had swiftly grabbed the English throne in 1100 (on Rufus's death by arrow in the New Forest) and had later inflicted a decisive defeat on Robert in Normandy. The throne of England and the imprisonment of Robert resulted in the re-combination of Normandy with England, after yet further fighting.

To those Normans who had supported and fought for him in, or from, the Côtentin, Henry was particularly indebted. Some of them received estates in Normandy; others were among the many Normans from that area and elsewhere, who later 'colonized' England from Normandy and received lands here, with some of them living and serving the king in England.[18] Although there is no direct evidence that Richard of Balta was a member of this group of Normans, the chances are strong that he too, as a knight who could be called on by the king himself or at least by the abbey for the king's army in

---

14  *Regesta R.A-N*, ii. 262, no. 1758; WAC 88. If the grant was made in the period 1130-1333, it might have come *after* the escheat of the former Ranulf Peverel estates (when RP's son died), and this might be relevant to the question whether Richard of Balta was being granted only the hide once held by Ranulf Peverel & his son; or some other greater estate, as appears more likely. See n. 6 above.

15  See note to WAC 88. But the date could have been later, up to 1133. For the vacancy, see pp. 72-4.

16  By writ Henry made clear his personal wish *(volo et precipio*, I wish and ordain) as to Richard's hereditary tenure.

17  Chibnall (ed), Orderic, *Eccles. History*, 5/295-7.

18  See Judith Green, *Government of England under H. I*, pp. 146-152; and *idem*, 'H. I and the aristocracy of Normandy', Actes de 111e congrès des soc. savantes, i. pp. 161-173, at p. 165. Bates, 'Normandy and England after 1066' *EHR* 413 (1989) 856 also refers to 'H. I's importation of favoured followers from the Côtentin'.

England, had been at least a supporter of Henry in Normandy and was now receiving a reward for both himself *and his heirs*.[19] Why else should we suddenly find a man from part of the Côtentin being given a hereditary estate in a manor belonging to the abbey, not far from Westminster where the king often was; and at exactly the right point of time?

So for a second period, which probably lasted until after the advent in 1154 of the Angevins with King Henry II, most of Hampstead lay under the practical control of another secular Norman lord; and throughout this time it may have seen nothing or little of the monks of the abbey. It was during this period that the abbacies of Herbert and Gervase went by, but significantly in 1136-7 King Stephen (whose natural son Abbot Gervase was) again confirmed the grant of the Hampstead land to Richard of Balta and his heirs.[20] This too is consistent with a continued royal interest in Richard of Balta, as no doubt a loyal supporter of the king or in his employ.

During this further period of secular lordship, which included the years of the disputes leading to and following the civil war between Stephen and Matilda, we have no indications at all as to how the ordinary tenants, whose servile services made any farming possible, or the farm itself of the manor fared. Presumably the new lord of Hampstead himself made use of his lands there, even if only as a 'foothold' for himself, when visiting the king in London – a function which Hampstead had performed, as earlier

noted, in anglo-saxon times as well.[21]

For the rest, only a small nunnery at Kilburn provides us with a small window-view as to what else was happening in one small corner of the manor of Hampstead.

### The hermitage and nunnery of Kilburn

All that we know about the rest of the manor, of which the abbey, as *chief* tenant, was still the principal holder from the king, is that even before the civil war period began, a small hermitage ('at Cuneburn') close to the great road Watling Street in Kilburn had been officially appropriated by the abbey. This may even have had its origins under Abbot Crispin, who perhaps granted a corrody to the original hermit.[22] But under Crispin's successor, Abbot Herbert, the hermitage was converted into a small nunnery of three maidens called Emma, Gunilda and Cristina, as a formal cell of the abbey.[23]

For this purpose the hermit Godwin had surrendered the building which he himself had erected, and in return he was appointed the warden of the new cell of nuns for his lifetime. The arrangement was that after his death the convent of the nuns was to elect, with the advice of the abbot of Westminster, a fitting senior person, a chaplain no doubt, to preside over their church.[24]

At the same time Abbot Herbert and the monks gave a first endowment of 30s. pa. to the nunnery ; and shortly afterwards they also granted a parcel of land (called 'the Gore', as it still is today) in a part of modern

---

19  This known group is of those who happened to be mentioned in the first extant Pipe Roll of 1130, see Green, *'Government'* (above) pp. 146 and 220 ff. But such a mention (or any absence of mention) is largely fortuitous.

20  *Regesta Regum A-N*, iii, 925; WAC 108. For Abbots Herbert and Gervase, see pp. 73-84 above.

21  See *The Westminster Corridor*, pp. 12-13, and Index there, p. 183, for 'foothold near London'.

22  See p. 73 n. 16 there, about the meaning of the 'corrody of Abbot Crispin' in WAC 264. There may also have been two 'hermits' at different stages, Godwin and Ailmar, since each was called a hermit at different times. Or Ailmar may have been an early chaplain, since he was also called 'the priest'.

23  The word 'nunnery', almost always used for this body, is not strictly correct, since the 'nuns' were anomalous and may not have been Benedictines, see Mason, *WA People*, p. 241. The original three were reputed to have been hand-maidens of Henry I's wife, Queen Matilda; or even 'canonesses', of perhaps St. Paul's.

24  This I believe is the effect of the Latin; not, as translated at WAC 249, that Godwin was to be followed by the 'senior nun'. There was to be an election of a suitable senior *male* person, as warden after Godwin. Nevertheless in the final event it was the senior nun, the 'prioress', who did preside over the nunnery.

Kensington, at that time a part of the manor of Knightsbridge, to the nuns and their successors. At that time their little Kilburn chapel or church was at first dedicated to St. John the Baptist, no doubt to commemorate its origin as a hermitage.[25]

This conversion of the hermitage to a nunnery as a cell of the abbey was said in the abbey's charter to have had the assent of the bishop of London, Gilbert known as 'the Universal'. Since this was the bishop who actually challenged the monks face-to-face in 1133 by suddenly appearing at the abbey and celebrating mass there, in order to assert control over them, it seems that relations between them went up and down.[26] Probably he was also the bishop who, having also first disputed the abbot's right to exert control over this Kilburn 'cell', later conceded the abbey's right to do so – and so assented to the above conversion.[27] However nearly a century later, in the 1220s, the same issue about the abbey's jurisdiction over the nuns was raised again by another bishop of London, but this time it was decided on terms, which included the right of the bishop at least to visit the nunnery formally whenever he wished to do so for canonical purposes, but leaving to the abbot all rights of regulation over the cell and its nuns, and of appointment or discharge of the prioress.[28]

For over 400 years from the 1120-30s the nuns of Kilburn continued to occupy their land in the south-west corner of the manor of Hampstead. The main part of the vill of 'Kilburn' lay on the other side of Watling Street, in the manor of Willesden which was territory of St. Paul's, and there it was managed by one of the cathedral's Canons. In Hampstead meanwhile the nuns' little chapel stood well back from the road itself, with no doubt a track for travellers to reach it, to seek shelter or to gather to say a prayer. The nunnery became known a little later as a priory, with a prioress at its head, and much later it was even called 'Kilburn Abbey', when abbeys no longer existed and had become romantic.[29] It was no doubt a helpful place for pilgrims and other travellers to halt before facing the long straight 'street' towards St. Alban's and any remaining woods which had survived around it.[30]

Other lands and assets also were given to the nuns by benefactors from the twelfth century onwards, so that by about 1307 they held a range of lands in London, Knightsbridge, Holborn, Southwark, Kent, Stanwell, Harrow and Hampstead. Shortly after its foundation, the nunnery had also received a 'perpetual' grant or confirmation of three 'corrodies' of food and drink from the abbey.[31] The priory, which retained its local function in connection with the great road, naturally did not became very wealthy and indeed fell into debt from time to time, but its gifted lands and the income from them feature extensively in records down the later centuries. We do not of course know what

---

25  WAC 250. Osbert of Clare played an important part and may have initiated the grants, see WACs 249 & 265.

26  See p. 75, above. On that occasion the abbey appealed to the pope, who re-granted it exemption from the bishop.

27  WAC 205. The bishop who made this charter was also called (simply) 'Gilbert', and so could have been another bishop, Gilbert Foliot, a little later in the C12; but I think the probabilities suggest it was 'Gilbert the Universal'. The same issue arose in the C13, with the same result in 1231, see ref. in the note to WAC 205.

28  See terms translated at Park, *Topog. of Hampstead*, pp. 168-170.

29  The first known prioress was Alice in 1207-8; her chapel was called 'of St. John of Kelebirne' at that time.

30  For the early woods and the wild beasts said to live in them, see *The Westminster Corridor*, pp. 37-38.

31  This was during Gervase's abbacy, WAC 264. One of the corrodies was 'the corrody of Abbot Gilbert', for which see p. 73 n. 16 above. Whether it was one given *to* or *by* or *in the name of* that abbot, it was apparently a double corrody. See also Harvey, *Living and Dying*, pp. 239-240.

offertory moneys they may have received from travellers who visited the priory. To judge by its value and possessions at the time of its eventual dissolution in 1536, the nuns should not have been on the bread line, even if they had had to give much hospitality to travellers.[32]

The main lands which the nuns held in Hampstead itself by the end of the thirteenth century were the priory grounds with the adjoining Kilburn Wood (36 acres or more), which fronted onto the lane (now known as West End Lane), which led from Watling Street to a clearing, or perhaps even a settlement, at the western end of the manor of Hampstead; and an area of about 14 acres or more of land which was called 'le Rudyng' (a 'clearing among woods'), at the point where the crossroads with Mill Lane at the modern West End lies. Of these, only le Rudyng carried a rent payable to the abbey at Westminster: a rent originally of 13s. annually, which increased later by another 4d, and lasted at that rate for the next three centuries until the dissolution of the nunnery by Henry VIII in 1536.[33]

Although in the twelfth century the new nunnery had become a component of the manor of Hampstead, its presence down in the south-west corner of the manor can have meant little to Richard of Balta, the new Norman holder of land in Hampstead.

### The Barentin family – the new Norman holders of the manor of Hampstead

Of Richard of Balta we know no more, save that in the civil war he obviously sided with King Stephen, who had renewed Richard's tenure in Hampstead. The anarchy of the war with the Empress Matilda took place without any record in Hampstead, but the swirling tides of fighting in and round London and Westminster and eventually the arrival of the Angevin era with the coronation of Henry II in 1154 may have caused a few ripples on the hills above. The next step in our knowledge of the new holders of the manor of Hampstead is that during the reign of Henry II, the king's butler **Alexander of Barentin**, yet another Norman from across the Channel, inherited or acquired the whole demesne manor, probably in or before the 1170s. Alexander has been described above in some detail.[34] It is not known how the manor came to him – whether through some descent from Richard of Balta, or by a grant from the new king whom Alexander served. Henry showed himself highly supportive of his butler in the acquisition of land and other properties in London and elsewhere, and may have insisted on a grant to him of the manor, yet another royal imposition.[35]

So one way or another, Alexander of Barentin became the new holder of the manor, and it was his family who, through two further generations, remained in command of the estate until finally Abbot Crokesley was able to recover it for the abbey by legal action in 1253-58.

During this whole period of the Barentins' lordship in Hampstead, from about the 1170s to 1258, the silence about the customary inhabitants of the manor and the use being made of the demesne land continued, because if any records were ever made at such a time, they have not survived. On the other hand we know that in about 1191 Alexander made

---

32 See Park, *Topog. of Hampstead*, pp. Appendices pp. xviii-xx; Text pp. 179-189.

33 See rentals of the manor, in 1258-59 and 1280-81 (rent 13s); 1371 (13s. 4d): WAMs 32360, 32361 and 32363. For the 1312 Extent, see translation and print of it in Kennedy, *Manor and Church of Hampstead*, § 15 at p. 119 (with one or two mistakes). The nuns still paid the 13s. 4d. in 1536, see Park, *Topog. of Hampstead*, p. 188. See also the map at VCH *Mdx* 9/94, and for later, Weindling & Colloms, *Kilburn and W. Hampstead*, pp. 8-10.

34 See pp. 115-6 above. Barentin was a town in Normandy on the lower reaches of the Seine, about 15 kilometeres below Rouen. It had no ostensible connection with Baupté (Balta) in the Côtentin, from which Richard of Balta had come, see p. 365 above.

35 For royal support of Alexander's landholding career, see WAMs 661, 660 and 662 (WACs 134, 135 and 139).

a charitable gift or bequest of a hide of land in 'Chalcots' (the south-east corner of the Hampstead manor) to the leper Hospital of St. James in Westminster.[36] So Chalcots was hived off from Hampstead and remained with the Hospital for centuries until, as part of the possessions of the hospital, it was transferred in 1449 by King Henry VI as an endowment to his new foundation of Eton College.

In due course we learn that in 1258 this property in Chalcots consisted of a house, a 'carucate' of arable land and 40 acres of woodland, when the abbey had to concede the property to the Hospital, in a legal action between them.[37] At this time the rent of £2 to the abbey for the Chalcots property was recorded.[38] Since much later the monks' great Survey of Hampstead in 1312 described this property as having 80 acres of land and wood, this means that (unless the size of the estate had been altered since 1258) the 'carucate' (or hide) of arable land in the 1258 charter was being treated as being only about 40 acres.

So Alexander the king's butler had earlier made his peace with God and the world by a gift to a worthy institution, but his death in 1203 may have been unexpected, because both his two sons, Richard and Thomas, were still under age when he died. As was the royal right, the king or his managers promptly 'sold' the wardship of the boys for 100 marks, and later when the elder of them, Richard, reached full age, he inherited the main Hampstead estate, among all the other lands, including property in Normandy, which Alexander had left.[39]

But Richard of Barentin was hardly a successful landowner, because in spite of his large inheritance, and other earlier gifts of property in London received from his 'uncle' the bishop of Winchester, Richard got into debt and when he died soon after 1210, his estates were in confusion.[40] Family lands in Normandy had been exchanged for other lands in Iveney (in Middlesex, near Staines, where Richard himself may have lived), but later after his death these Iveney lands had to be disposed of by his younger brother Thomas of Barentin, in order to pay off Richard's debts.[41] Thomas had paid a 'fine' to acquire his brother's lands, and may have become the guardian of Richard's daughter and heiress, Sibilla, who was also probably underage when her father died.

By this route the Hampstead lands had passed through the hands of Thomas, and then all or some of them (originally 'a messuage and three carucates') were inherited in due course by Sibilla, who later during Henry III's reign became a frequent if involuntary litigant (with her husband, Andrew of Grendon) in defence of their rights to these lands in Hampstead.

36  A grant confirmed in 1204 by King John, *Rot. Chart.* (Rec. Com.) i. 117b, and later reconfirmed by H. III in 1242, *Cal. Ch. R.*, 1226-57, p. 269. The hospital was personalised as 'the leprous maidens of St. James'.

37  CP 25 (1) 147/20/391. The reason why there was a legal action was that, five years before, the sheriff of London and Middlesex had in error dispossessed the Hospital of its Chalcots property, in mistake for the Hampstead lands held by Sibilla, Alexander's grand-daughter, and her husband, for which Abbot Crokesley was suing them. The sheriff had been ordered in 1253 to restore the land to the Hospital, *C. Cl. R.* 1251-3, p. 323.

38  This rent was paid to the abbey in 1258-9, 1280-1, and 1312, etc; WAMs 32360-1, and Kennedy, *ibid*, p. 119.

39  For the wardship sold to Wm. de Ste-Mère-Eglise, later Bp. of London, see Turner, *English Judiciary*, p. 115n.

40  VCH. *Mdx.* 9/92. For the gifts to Richard and Thomas from their 'uncle'/bishop, Richard of Ilchester, see WACs 139 and 144; and for the bishop himself, see App. A p. 392 below and other refs. in note 14. Richard of Barentin had served K. John in the feudal army in Ireland in 1210, which may have contributed to his failure.

41  See also Mason, *WA People,* p. 228 and 314, for these younger Barentins. It was probably through their link with Iveney that a holding of land in Hampstead came to be held by Constantine fitz Alulf of London, the hero/villain of the riots in Westminster in 1222, see pp. 188-9 above and VCH *Mdx* 9/92.

Andrew was a royal clerk from Grendon in Derbyshire. He was described as 'the king's serjeant' and was obviously a confidant of King Henry. Sometimes he was sent abroad on royal business, and was also posted in England 'in the service of the king'. On one occasion in 1231, when he and Sibilla were being sued, in the king's court, for possession of their lands in Hampstead, he was absent with the king at the stronghold of 'Matilda's Castle' (known also as 'Painscastle') in the Welsh marches, during one of Henry's wars with the Welsh. To assist Andrew in the Hampstead action, the king intervened and ordered an adjournment of the case.[42] As a clerk, Andrew also acted as an attorney on behalf of private clients in various parts of the country. His and his wife's Hampstead house and two (out of the three) carucates of arable land appear to have been their principal retained property, conveniently near to London and available for the performance of other duties towards the king in Westminster.[43]

### Recovery of Hampstead by the abbey

It is clear that much, or perhaps the whole, of Sibilla's inheritance was open to legal attack from a number of sides, but the reasons for this vulnerability are not clear. Between about 1220 and 1255 Andrew and Sibilla had to endure a series of legal actions brought by various claimants against Sibilla's rights of inheritance over the Hampstead lands – but

they survived them, until in a final action Abbot Crokesley sued them in about 1253 and five years later managed to recover from them the abbey's lands in Hampstead. So three hostile claims had been faced down, but the fourth succeeded.[44] The records of the four claims form an interesting illustration of how the vultures would gather when a title to property was thought to be weak, and also of how much more accessible the recourse to litigation about legal 'ownership' of land now was, due to Henry II's legal reforms in the twelfth century.[45]

So by the time that Abbot Crokesley girded himself to try to recover the Barentins' lands in Hampstead in 1253, part (latterly, the *main* part) of the manor had lain under the secular control of two or three Norman families since Domesday, a period of more than 170 years. We cannot be certain where towards the end of this period the 'messuage' of Sibilla and Andrew, the last holders of the Barentin estate, had lain. One possibility might be that it was at the place later identified as 'Belsize', itself a Norman name (meaning 'finely-sited') for a dominating position which looked down over Westminster and London – a site which might have appealed to powerful people like the Barentins.[46]

But if Belsize had been the site of the Barentin/Grendon house, it would leave serious doubts about what could have been happening at the other focal point of the

---

42 *Cal. Cl. R.*, 1227-31, pp. 334 and 559; see also Powicke, *H. III and Ld. Edw.*, vol. 2. pp. 624-5 and 628-9.
43 Sibilla and Andrew had got rid of one carucate, by selling it to a great aunt, Aubrey, see p. 372 n. 55.
44 These earlier claimants to the Hampstead lands included **1**. Geoffrey of Arbrier (undoubtedly related to the Arborarius kindred of Alexander of Barentin, see pp. 116 above); **2**. Gilbert of Hendon, see pp. 79-81 above and 372 n. 55 below); **3**. John of Be[i]rking and his wife 'Alice of Westminster'. The latter, a daughter of Stephen of Berking, was a free tenant of 50 acres in Hampstead in 1225, CRR 12/819; and, later when a widow, held a house near the Clowson sluice in Westminster: WAD 582). For other refs: see **1**. CRR 11/513, 12/674 and 1664 (for Geoffrey of Arbrier); **2**. *Cal. Cl. R.*, 1227-1231, pp. 334 & 559, and CP 25(1) 146/8/98 (for Gilbert of Hendon); **3**. *CRR*, 16/914 (for John of 'Birking' and Alice). For Stephen of Berking, see p. 178 above.
45 See pp. 49 n. 21 and 67 n. 20 above for Henry II's reforms which had replaced the old feudal trial-by-battle.
46 But the name Belsize has only survived from the C14/1. From at least 1260 there was a house at Belsize, later occupied by Roger Brabazon, Edward I's chief justice and trusted confidant, and the estate was bequeathed by him on his deathbed to the abbey in 1317. It was then assigned to the prior and, with other lands added, it remained a centre for the prior and his administration for the rest of the medieval period, VCH *Mdx* 9/96, et. al.

manor. The former 'manor place' had lain close to the chapel of St. Mary in Hampstead, where Frognal joined the lane to West End.[47] We can be sure that the original demesne fields lay in that area from the time of Domesday, and certainly it was from that junction at Frognal/West End Lane that the abbey began to exercise farming control of the demesne lands, after Abbot Crokesley had successfully won the Hampstead lands from Andrew and Sibilla. So it must be more likely that the Grendon house had been sited at or near this point.

### The Temple lands in Hampstead

Meanwhile – probably during Alexander of Barentin's lifetime – another exercise of royal autocracy had taken place. It was King Henry II, well-known for his patronage of the Knights Templar, who must have 'wished' the abbey and Alexander to grant a large free estate in the north-west of the manor of Hampstead to the Templars.[48] This extended from the boundary of the farm lands and original wood at the top of Child's Hill (the top being the present Telegraph Hill), westwards over to the line of Watling Street where it later had a frontage of well over 500 yards.

But about fifty years later the Templars also acquired another estate sited south-west of Hampstead in the manor of Lileston (Lisson), and this included an area apparently within the uncertain southern boundary of Hampstead.[49] This acquisition originally stemmed from a grant to them before 1237 of the Lileston manor by Otto, the current member of the fitz William family, descended from Otto fitz William 'the Conqueror's goldsmith', who had held the Lilleston manor after the Conquest in right of his serjeanty as the king's hereditary die-cutter for the London mint.[50] As defined by the boundaries of other known estates, this southern land of the Templars appears to have been a substantial area (perhaps as much as 100-140 acres), which they held with the Lileston manor estate received from the current Otto fitz William.[51]

The acquisition of these two estates in the north and south of Hampstead by the Templars meant that these one-time demesne lands were then administered by them for their own benefit, probably in conjunction with another Temple estate in Hendon, which gave rise to the modern name of Temple Fortune. But in the event the Templars held their extensive Hampstead lands for comparatively short periods: the northen estate for possibly 130 years, and the southern estate for perhaps 70. Finally the order of the Templars was dissolved in 1312 by papal order, for alleged heresy and corruption, and their lands were transferred to the Knights Hospitaller of St. John of Jerusalem, who thereby became the (irremoveable) tenants of the abbey.[52]

47  For the central demesne lands, see *The Westminster Corridor*, p. 123 ff. and coloured Map O (after p. 96). For the chapel, see *ibid.*, p. 99 and VCH *Mdx*, 9/145. The name 'West End' did not appear until the C16, but a hamlet was there much earlier, where the lane from near Kilburn Priory met the lane uphill to Hampstead, *ibid*, 9/42.

48  See VCH *Mdx* 9/102 for the connection. For some of Henry II's other acts of support for the Templars in London and Westminster, see p. 42, n. 90 above, and Williams, *Early Holborn*, § 1315 ff. For the Old and New Temple and the Templars, see also p.176 ff. above. This Temple estate probably formed a continuous block of land on Hampstead's northern border, with the Hampstead estate later called 'Flitcroft', see VCH *Mdx* 9/105 and the map at *ibid.*, p. 94.

49  The boundary between Hampstead and the northern area of Lileston (a heavily wooded area, known as St. John's Wood) was imprecise, and some part of Hampstead was (rightly or wrongly) included in the various grants, see VCH *Mdx* 9/102. For the conjectural original boundary before the Conquest, see *The Westminster Corridor*, pp. 107, 127 and coloured Maps O and P.

50  See *The Westminster Corridor*, pp. 73, 103-4. The 1237 grantor had the same name, Otto fitz William. Of course all serjeanties were excluded from his grant, CP (25) 146/12/184 and VCH *Mdx* 9/102.

51  As shown on the VCH *Mdx* map (at 9/94), this southern Temple estate may have been almost as big as the northern one, but clearly there were big disputes about where the boundary lay and who owned what (*ibid*, 9/102).

But meanwhile the two estates, called the 'Hampstead Temple', had continued as free land of the Knights Templar, outside the control of the abbey (even after Abbot Crokesley had recovered the main demesne lands), but still rendering an annual rent to it, of 20s starting in or before 1259.[53] When added to the lands already occupied by the Kilburn priory and the Chalcot land of the leper Hospital of St. James, these estates amounted to 900 acres or more, nearly half the manor still free from the abbey's reach. There was also one other small estate, a secular one, of 16 acres near the parish church which apparently had also become a freehold estate (for reasons not certain) before 1312 and belonged to the 'Kingswell' family of Hampstead.[54]

### Tidying up residual problems

In spite of Abbot Crokesley's success in recovering the main part of Hampstead, there were still problems in the manor for the abbey. To begin with, there was an additional 'carucate' of arable land in Hampstead which had originally been part of Sibilla's inheritance, but had been granted by her and Andrew to a couple who were related to Sibilla – Joscelin the archdeacon of Chichester and his wife Aubrey.[55] However this problem must have been subject to easy solution, because if Sibilla's right to inherit the house and

other lands in Hampstead was unjustified (as Abbot Crokesley's success showed), the title to the one carucate had been equally invalid. So the abbey must have recovered that too, probably by concession.

A greater problem was that there was still another landholder in Hampstead who (in spite of Abbot Crokesley's success against Sibilla and Andrew) was asserting a claim to be the true owner of the manor of Hampstead or part of it. This man was called Robert le Baud ('the bald', or 'the bold'), a powerful landowner from Lodington in Northamptonshire who was probably the *de facto* holder (and also the 'lord'; or he claimed to be the 'lord') of at least that area in Hampstead called the 'hide', which had once been held by Ranulf Peverel. We do not know what the basis of his claim was.[56] But we can see why he abandoned, before long, any claim which he may have had.

The period after 1258 (the year when Abbot Crokesley died) was the period when King Henry III was engaged in his disputes with many of the barons, and eventually in the civil war against them, culminating in the defeat of the king in 1264 at Lewes by Simon of Montford and finally the king's victory in 1265 at Evesham. But in that war Robert le Baud had been on the losing side, and after the final siege and capture of baronial forces

---

52   VCH *Mdx* 9/102. By chance, the Hospitallers by 1223 had already owned an (unidentified) house in Hampstead, where they had been attacked by a turbulent knight, fitly called Walter de Turbeville, *CRR* xi, pp. 109-110.

53   See WAMs 32360 and 32361. It was 20s still in 1312, Kennedy, *Hampstead*, p. 119. CRR, vol. 19 §1827 shows that the Templars had also held land in Hampstead from Sibilla and Andrew, for a term of 10 years.

54   Geoffrey of Kingswell had been one of the 'tenants of the hide' in 1280-81, and either he or his son Robert (who by 1312 was the tenant of the estate near the church) must have been granted that estate as a freehold by the abbey. This may have arisen out of Robert le Baud's claim on the 'hide' (see below); and Geoffrey of Kingswell (as 'Geoffrey s. of Agnes') may even have been one of the villeins whose services Robert le Baud released to the abbey.

55   Aubrey was probably Sibilla's great-aunt, see VCH *Mdx* 9/93 and *ibid. Sussex* 4/193 (Aubrey had inherited a Barentin estate in West Stoke in Sussex). In the 1220s Aubrey also must have received one Hampstead carucate *from* Sibilla and Andrew, because when Gilbert of Hendon launched an action in 1231 against Joscelin and Aubrey to claim this one carucate for himself, the latter (J and A) called on Sibilla and Andrew to 'warrant', ie. to establish the validity of her (Sibilla's) earlier grant to them (J. and A), see CP25(1) 146/8/98.

56   It is unlikely that any rights could have stemmed from Peverel; but Robert may have claimed from Richard of Balta (as VCH *Mdx* 9/93 suggests), or even a Barentin. In 1274 Robert was also claiming 140 acres of woodland from the Kts. Templar. His own forebears in Lodington dated from at least the C12, see VCH *Northants* 1/385a.

in Kennilworth Castle he suffered forfeiture of all his estates in Northamptonshire and was 'in mercy', in a state of submission to the king, and hoping to be able to redeem his lands in accordance with the 'Dictum of Kennilworth'.[57] So it was hardly the time for Robert le Baud to have a stand-up fight about part of a small manor in Middlesex, with the king's fine new abbey, however good Robert's claim was.

So this was the background to the ensuing relationship between Robert le Baud and the abbey at Westminster, in the period after 1258 when the main lands of the manor of Hampstead had already been re-acquired by Abbot Crokesley. As a result of the position in which Robert le Baud was now in, Abbot Richard of Ware was no doubt able to exert forcefully the abbey's right to free the manor of Hampstead from all such 'foreign' claims. It ended with a surrender by Robert of all his claims in Hampstead, on terms.

Initially he made two charitable grants to the abbey, probably in the early 1270s: first, of a wood and a garden in Hampstead, and secondly of the lands of six villeins in the manor, including their 'bodies and chattels' and their labour services to which he claimed to be entitled, together with other services from certain free tenants, including the Knights Templar in Hampstead.[58] These results were achieved by negotiation because the latter grant contained at least a small consensual rent of a garlic clove, payable annually by the abbey. And finally after 1275 Robert le Baud waived all his claims and rights in 'the manor and vill of Hampstead', in a formal quitclaim or surrender to Abbot Richard of Ware, this time for a more worthwhile down-payment of 20 silver marks (£13. 6s. 8d.)[59]

But to reflect the wild fluctuation of fortunes during this volatile period, it is worth noticing that within four more years the situation of Robert le Baud had completely changed. Like many of those 'disinherited' after the battle of Evesham and the later fall of Kennilworth Castle, he was soon back in royal favour, now of Edward I. By November 1279 the king made Robert sheriff of Northamptonshire and castellan of the castle and town of Northampton, which posts he retained for the next ten years, also serving often as a royal justice and commissioner.[60] His concession to the abbey on the Hampstead issue may even have helped to obtain the repair of his fortunes.

However before Robert le Baud leaves the Hampstead stage, we should look back to a letting which he had made of another substantial area of land in Hampstead, in the days before the disputed issues between the king and the barons had been resolved in battle. This property, in the area later known as Belsize, contained a house, 40 acres of arable land and some woodland, and Robert was, or claimed to be, the holder of its reversion, because in about 1260 he had let it to 'William the Lynendraper' at a rent of 6d. a year.[61]

William, a shopkeeper in the high street of St Giles, was the father of Gerin of St. Giles (or 'Gerin the linendraper'), the lay agent of the abbey who, in his capacity as a clerk, later acted professionally in the abbey's manorial and general service. Gerin was also the man who (whether he deserved it or not) later found himself implicated in the burglary of the king's treasure at the abbey in 1303, and ended up briefly in prison at the Tower of London, together with the monks.[62]

57  *Rot. sel. ex. archiv. in dom. capit. Westm.* (ed Hunter), p. 253. See also p. 225 above for Kennilworth.
58  WAM *Bk. II*, f. 115b. If the K.T.s were his tenants, their southern estate was the land so held. See n. 56.
59  *ibid*, f. 115a. So there was something in his claim. The first witness to this document was Master Robert of Beverley, Henry III's last senior mason in the rebuilding of the abbey, see p. 261 ff. above.
60  Bridges, *Northamptonshire*, vol 1, p. 5; *Cal. P. R.* 1272-81, pp. 474 and 81-92.
61  CP 25(1) 147/21/414, and VCH *Mdx.* 9/95. This letting resulted from a compromise in a legal action between William le Lyndraper and Robert le Baud, and the low rent may reflect legal doubts or the status of the holding.

The further significance of this property in southern Hampstead (later 'Belsize') is that, after Gerin had inherited it and had received a further lease for another 14 years from the abbey at a more realistic rent of 10s., the whole of his lands (including other land in that area, and many lands in other manors) passed by sale into different hands, when Gerin sold his entire estate. Finally the Hampstead lands in Belsize, on a further re-sale, were bought in 1311 by Sir Roger Brabazon, who had been Edward I's chief justice.[63] Sir Roger bought them for 100 marks and made them part of his estate, with other land which he also held in Belsize, and in 1317 later on his deathbed he restored the house and his estate to the abbey.[64] After a subsequent history as an administrative centre for the prior of the abbey at Westminster during the rest of the Middle Ages,[65] the priors' house (greatly enlarged in brick) became, after the dissolution of the monasteries, the forerunner of the later private and even more magnificent mansion-houses of Belsize, backed by the lands of the so-called and romanticised 'manor of Belsize', from the sixteenth century onwards.[66]

Like Gerin, another resident of Westminster and property-holder, Stephen of the Strand, had also dabbled in land in Hampstead, and this reflects the growing interest being shown by observant lay entrepreneurs from Westminster in land investment in surrounding manors, before and after the middle of the thirteenth century.[67]

### The alienation of Hampstead lands – a summary

So in the years since the Norman Conquest large swathes of the demesne lands of the manor had successively been placed by the kings in the hands of lay Normans and their successors – the Peverels, Richard of Balta, the Barentins, the Grendons and finally (whether by descent from one or other of these predecessors, or by some new grant or an unverified claim) Robert le Baud, of Lodington (Northants). By about 1280, two hundred years later, all these lands were back in the abbey's fold.[68]

Contemporaneously with these alienations to private lords, other substantial areas of the manor had been placed under the more permanent control of three ecclesiastical institutions: –

(a) the small nunnery in the south-west Kilburn corner of the estate, which from at least about 1130 held its own land surrounding a little priory chapel and the adjoining Kilburn woods, paying rent to the abbey only for the land 'Le Rudyng', which at some date it had also received in the heart of the settlement known later as 'West End';

(b) the leper Hospital of St James at Westminster, which from at least about 1190 had received from Alexander of Barentin the arable

---

62 See Pearce, *Monks*, pp. 159-161 for Gerin's extensive work as the abbey's agent; and pp. 290-1 and 317 above. Gerin also held at least one customary tenancy in Hampstead in 1280-81 at a rent of 6d, WAM 32361.

63 WAM Bk. II, f. 119b-120 (a formal cirograph by Abbot Wenlock in 1286), & Kennedy, *Hampstead*, p. 119. The property can finally be identified as the land which 'Gilbert canep' held in 1258, WAD 119b.

64 CP25(1) 149/41/71; VCH *Mdx* 9/96. See also n. 46 on p. 370 above.

65 See *Cal. P. R.* 1317-8, p. 220.

66 Kennedy, *Hampstead*, p. 119 and VCH *Mdx* 9/95-98. The house and estate were made over to the priors' use, and under them the house was improved in brick (as many as 400,000 bricks were contracted for at Belsize in 1496), even before the other private mansions of Belsize were later built. This was the same part of the *'hyda'* as the tenant 'Gilbert *canep'* had held when the first 'rental' of Hampstead was made in 1259 and most probably the original 'hide' held by Ranulf Peverel nearly 200 years before in the DB record.

67 See p. 289 above, WAD 567, CRR vol 12, p. 130 (§ 648).

68 1280 can be taken as about the date when Robert le Baud's claims on Hampstead were finally abandoned by him.

and woodland estate known later as Chalcots, in the south-east corner of the manor;

(c) the religious Order of the Knights Templar, which received two estates in the north-west and the south-west of the manor of Hampstead, with an interval of about half a century between these acquisitions. But by the final years of the thirteenth century that Order was already under threat in France, on suspicion of heresy. After the arrest and trials of many of its senior officials under the direction of the French king in and after 1307, the Order was formally dissolved in 1312 by Pope Clement V, under considerable military duress imposed on him, again by the French king.

Each of these four ecclesiastical estates in Hampstead must have originally been part of the original demesne of the manor.[69] But even after Abbots Crokesley and Ware had managed to recover most of the former demesne lands of Hampstead from their lay

holders in the second half of the thirteenth century, the four ecclesiastical estates remained in the hands of the three institutions which held them.[70]

But meanwhile, as soon as Abbot Crokesley had recovered Sibilla's lands, the convent of the abbey assumed control of the farming of the demesne lands. Since this coincided with Abbot Crokesley's drive towards the making and keeping of manorial accounts and other records, we soon begin for the first time to learn something of the customary tenants of Hampstead, their work and the conditions in the manor. Since the time of the Conquest, nearly 200 years had passed without information on any of these topics, and it took more than another fifty years before the monks were able to assess their new property satisfactorily. The process of this progressive enlightenment is discussed in the next chapter.

69  VCH *Mdx* 9/111.
70  Each of these estates survived the medieval period without physical recovery by the abbey, but two of them had meanwhile passed to new holders before the Dissolution: Chalcot's was granted by King Henry VI in 1448/9 to his new foundation, Eton College; and the Temple estate(s) in Hampstead had been granted by the pope to the Hospitaller Order of St. John of Jerusalem in 1312, after the Templars had been proscribed – in the same year coincidentally as the monks were now able to make their great survey of the manor of Hampstead.

# CHAPTER 22

# The manor of Hampstead: restored to the Convent
## 1258-1312

## The lighting of a lamp

The recovery of the main demesne lands of Hampstead by Abbot Crokesley acted, for the monks – and for us – like the lighting of a lamp in a darkened room. By its light the convent, to whom the manor had been entrusted, could now survey and begin to manage its estate.

The first step which the monks took was to carry out a 'rental' survey (a list of quarterly rents, and the names of all the tenants, both customary and free, who had to pay them) during the year 1258-9. This was a natural step for new managers to take, to identify their own people in the manor and to assess the income from their rents; and we can see that the convent repeated the same step just over twenty years later with a second rental, filling gaps in the earlier story and showing many changes among the tenants which had already taken place by 1281.[1]

In these first enlightenments we step into the more visible world of the working tenants, men whose names often described their occupation, or their place of origin, or the location of their dwelling-place in Hampstead – eg. John the reeve (who appropriately had to pay 6s. 8d pa., the highest of the ordinary rents in the village); Richard of Kilburn; John at the mews; Malekin of the mill; Walter *le herde;* Roger of the wood; Robert the smith; William and Walter, each a wood-warden

(*wodeward*); Asketin, Roger and Maud, each 'at the pond' (*atte-ponde*: possibly the pond which then lay at the bottom of the present Pond Street); Geoffrey *le werkeman;* Hereward of the east-wood; William of Aldenham; Laurence the forester; Geoffrey of Kingswell (a central part of the village still recorded by name); Thomas the carter; Laurence of Grendon (perhaps a working man who had followed a previous lord, Andrew of Grendon, to Hampstead); Nicholas the cowherd (*le kuherde*); Elias the shepherd; Robert of Westeburne (the river area near the present Paddington Station); John of Kingsbury (from the west of Watling Street); William of Beverley; John the fowler (*le ffoghler*); Thomas of Stevenage; and so on.

Significantly, a group of four special 'tenants of the hide' was identified in 1259. The 'hide' was probably the same hide of 'land of the tenants' which Ranulf Peverel had been given by William the Conqueror, in the area later known as Belsize. The largest of the four shares of the hide in 1259 was the land of 'Gilbert *canep*', a holding for which in 1280-81 the rent due was 10s: but before the latter date Gilbert himself may no longer have been in occupation and the land which he had held (or could still hold?) was simply described as the *'tenement kanep'.*[2]

Altogether there were 35 customary

---

1   WAMs 32360 and 32361. Since before the time (before c. 1220) when Abbot Humez had allocated 40s (the rent payable to the abbey for Hampstead) to the abbey's kitchener, Hampstead had been treated as a manor within the convent's share, although the convent had no control at that time over its management; see p. 135 above.

2   Curiously the rent recorded for Gilbert in 1259 was only 'one hen' (as it was for two of the other tenants), although the fourth tenant of the 'hide' in that year was paying 7s. (plus one hen) for his holding. Perhaps Gilbert's tenancy had also been 'freed' between 1259 and 1280, by purchase by Gilbert or some new tenant. I do not know what a *canep* was; no one else has tried to interpret it. I found one other *'canep'* in another local manor.

tenants in 1259, most of whom would have had families, so that the working population on the monks' restored demesne lands had now probably tripled since Domesday: from about 50 to about 150. But even this second figure may be an underestimate. A total estimate of all the people living within the *whole* area of the manor would have to include the additional people who would have been needed to service the separate (post-Domesday) estates such as Chalcots (given to the leper Hospital of St. James), the two Temple estates and the lands of the Kilburn priory, with some more in parts of the Belsize area.[3]  One can envisage a full total of at least 200, a quadrupling (or more) since Domesday up to 1259.[4]

It may be that even the figure for the number of the named tenants on the demesne lands in 1259 was itself depressed, because again by 1281 it had risen significantly from 35 to 44. It was still 41 in 1312 when the convent carried out a detailed survey of the whole manor – of all the people free and unfree, lands, work obligations, rents, the three main demesne fields, acreages of arable, meadow and pasture, and the enveloping woods.[5]  These increases of 25% or 17% (within only 20, and 50, years since 1259) may have been due to perhaps more lenient (or inefficient?) and therefore more attractive conditions introduced by the monks' regime, in place of the lay and perhaps more severe regime which had preceded the abbey's.[6]  In any case the estimates given above for the whole population of Hampstead would have to be increased again pro rata for the period of these later years, from 1259 until 1281, or until 1312.

*The main livestock in the manor*

If they did not know it already, the monks also learnt from their first survey in 1259 that at that time the main live source of produce in the manor was the sheep flock of 320 head, made up of 140 ewes, 80 wethers, 20 hogs and 80 lambs, able to produce large amounts of ewes-milk for cheese, one of the staple medieval foods, and plenty of fleeces or stripped wool – for sale or the making of clothes. In comparison the demesne's cattle herd stood at 18 cows, 9 calves and 1 bull (for milk and meat); with 8 oxen – which were still being used in the thirteenth century for the pulling of ploughs, though by now 2 great cart horses and 12 younger horses were also available for carting, and perhaps also for the ploughs when needed. But the surviving stock of domestic fowls was small (5 hens, 12 capons, 1 cock and 4 geese), no doubt because fowls were rapid 'currency', being generally bred or bought, and eaten or sold, all in one year. In any case this surviving stock of fowls tells us nothing about the 46 hens and 11 geese which would continue to be due annually *as rent* payable  by the tenants during the course of the year.

We will see below how these numbers of livestock changed over the next fifty years, but they were of course only the beasts and fowls which actually belonged to the demesne. With 35, or more, customary households in the manor and some free tenants, there were as well many other private stocks of animals within the manor. These, of course, belonged to the tenants and

---

3  Even if the services of some of the customary tenants had been 'sold' to the holders of these separate estates, some extra people would certainly have been needed there as well.

4  Whatever the final figure might be, the increase of population for this small area corresponds well with the estimates of growth in national population by the end of the C13 and the complementary expansion of cultivated land during the C12 and C13, see the admirable discussions in eg. Miller and Hatcher, *Med. England.*

5  CUL. Kk. V. 29, f. 31v.  Printed (with translation, but some mistakes) in Kennedy, *Hampstead*, pp. 114-140.

6  I have taken the figures of numbers of tenants from VCH *Mdx* 9/113, although my own differ slightly, without making any material difference in the final result.

were mainly used for the private purposes of each household and their tenanted land, but some of the animals also had to be available for the purposes of the services which individual tenants had to render to the abbey. As we have seen in the manor of Eye, so it was in Hampstead. Those who, by the terms of their customary tenancies, had to supply to the abbey and to use their own plough, or cart or harrow, had also to have the right animals (oxen, horses) to enable them to carry out their duties, including their obligations whenever they could be called upon to provide the extra service of a 'boon' for the abbey. Equally those who had to pay one or more fowls as their rent or part of their rent kept fowls for that purpose as well as for their own consumption or sale. So the convent and the community had some common interests in even the private animals, as well as in their tenancies.

The numbers of the livestock which might be held by individual tenants in the village can be illustrated by the sale in about the 1270s by Joseph of St. Albans of his (perhaps free) holding in Hampstead to Master John of Burton.[7] His holding was 9 acres of arable, with meadow land, pasture and 'buildings' as well, together with rights of common pasture for 60 sheep, 12 cattle, 16 pigs and 5 foals. Master Burton paid 40s, with a rent of 3s. to the abbey and 1d. to Joseph.

Although the first rental identified clearly the personnel of the manor, their rents and the livestock remaining at the end of 1258-59, there is no record of any other major assets. Apart from one or two domestic articles, such as 'a great bronze pot', it seems that any other equipment in whatever manor buildings there were had been stripped out by the previous managers – or perhaps even by some of the

tenants, taking advantage of any interlude in the lordship. But above all, no record of any remaining stock of grain has survived, still less of the recent history or methods of grain husbandry in the manor. Whether these issues were investigated at all, we do not know.

### The start of accounts in 1270

Having initially assessed some of the potential sources for their future income from the manor, the monks were equipping themselves to start keeping some form of accounts of the yearly farm work, but certainly no written accounts have survived from any year *before* 1270-71. Indeed there is no suggestion in the first accounts in 1270-71, that there had been any written accounts in any of the years since 1259, such as there had been before the first surviving accounts for Knightsbridge.[8]

A reason for the apparent delay, after the first rental in 1259, in starting written accounts in Hampstead may be that the monks decided to make initial trials of the farm, particularly of arable issues, and waited for about 11 years before embarking on written accounts. Or it may be that accounts made have not survived. The second rental survey made in 1280-81 may perhaps be seen as part of a check being made at that time of the fairly regular accounting which *had been* carried out during the 1270s, particularly in the light of the fact (which must have been obvious) that the number of tenants had been increasing appreciably since the previous rental survey.

### The reeve goes, and the serjeant stays

There is little doubt that from early on the convent was keeping a fairly careful watch on the efficiency of the farming management. This must be an inference from the administrative

---

7   WAD 118b-119. Joseph was the brother of Master Reginald of St Albans, Abbot Wenlock's capable proctor, see p. 304; his holding had surely once been a customary tenancy? It passed from John of Burton (a holder of clerkly benefices) to his cousin and heir, Reginald de Waleys, a royal serjeant-at-arms (Byerleys, *Records of Wardrobe* 1285-86, §§ 169, 501 et al.), by whom it was sold back to the abbot (Wenlock) and convent for 20s.

8   For Knightsbridge, see p. 217-18 above. Even the references in the first Hampstead a/cs to remaining ('*de rem*') stock of grain and animals do not predicate earlier *accounts*. Such stock could still be seen, weighed or counted. My translations of the Hampstead accounts are deposited at the abbey.

change made as early as April 1273. Between 1270 and 1273 a reeve had, as usual, been chosen from the villagers to organise the work and accounting – with some form of supervision from an external 'serjeant' (a *serviens*), who perhaps lived elsewhere and only visited the manor to supervise. But now there began the full-time employment of a serjeant *on his own*, from April 1273 onwards until well into the next century, and beyond. The reeve disappeared, and the serjeant must have become resident in the manor, because later he appears in the accounts as carrying out long periods of administrative and physical work in the fields. For this he eventually began to receive extensive wages, at 1s. 2d each week for 40-50 weeks during the year, as well as the regular stipend of 13s. 4d pa., with which he had started. He also earned various 'expenses' of food supplied to him while working in the fields. In effect he became the well-paid working manager, a factotum as well as the organiser of the work and accounting officer in place of the reeve.[9]

Moreover this post of 'serjeant' appears to have become a much more professional position than that of a possibly amateurish reeve (as it may have been in Hampstead). There was a marked tendency for the serjeant to be employed for periods of *successive* years at a time. It started with 'Robert' for three years; a little later, 'Geoffrey' for another three years; and immediately after him, 'Laurence' for a remarkable 11 years, from 1284 to 1295. With this sort of experience such men must have acquired a real knowledge and expertise in their job, in much the same way as John Churchwyne must have done as Abbot Wenlock's reeve at Eye for more than ten years.[10] Signs of this expertise appear in Laurence's accounts during the first half of the 1290s.

As the serjeant, Laurence was followed by William of Arkesdene (Essex) for at least four known years, and probably (since there are gaps of years in the surviving documents) for at least another four years as well. The only other noticeable point about him is that, overlapping with his tenure of the post of serjeant, one of the monks, Brother Walter of Arkesdene – surely his relative or fellow villager – became treasurer of the convent in 1299-1302, chamberlain in 1306-7 and a strong supporter of the prior, Reginald of Hadham, in his vitriolic disputes with Abbot Wenlock.[11] So probably there had been some influence at work from a senior monk in the original choice of William as serjeant in Hampstead.

### Visits by the Bailiff

Another feature which indicates the care with which the convent had approached the management of the demesne farm was the post of Bailiff for the manor, which every year was filled by a monk of the abbey, often for several consecutive years at a time. From the very first account in 1270, even when there were also a reeve and a serjeant at work in Hampstead, the bailiff was making one or two visits during the course of the year.

In these early years he made his journey by himself on horseback from Westminster to Hampstead, generally in the busy time of harvest. He then clearly liaised with the serjeant, giving orders for the sending of produce, as required or as available, to the abbey. He was paid his 'expenses' in the form of the food and drink supplied to him (it could be ale, meat and fish, all valued as an expense, for inclusion in the later farm account), and he also collected some of the tenants' rents and some of the other moneys in hand – for taking with him as he wended his way back to the abbey. Such moneys would have already been received by the reeve and

9   For his wages, ee DS, *H. A/cs*, eg. 1/34B, 32B, 39, 47, 51, 59; etc, in book II.
10  For eg. Laurence, see WAMs 32394, 32384, 32376, 32397, 32375, 32405, 32398, 32304, 32381, 32372, & 32374. For J. Churchwyne, see pp. 340 and 346 n. 82; but he knew the job too well, & cheated.
11  After the burglary of the royal treasure in 1303, Bro. Walter borrowed money and bought a silver cup which he gave to someone at the Tower of London to free the monks from fetters.

serjeant from many sources: the rent for the mill, which was farmed-out each year, court 'perquisites' (fines and 'reliefs', etc.), or sales already made of pasture, grain, hay, livestock, cheeses made from the ewes' milk, fleeces from the sheep, butter from the cows' milk, 'fagots' of wood made in the manor, etc.

Of course all such moneys received by the reeve and serjeant would have already been reduced by deductions of all expenses so far incurred in running the estate – on, for example, the repair and maintenance of ploughs, carts and buildings, the extra wages paid in the mowing of the hay, the reaping and threshing of the corn, the collection of wood from the woodlands and hedges and the making of fagots from it, the purchase of grain needed in the manor, including seed (from other soil) for the ensuing year, the cost of special food for the *famuli* (the fully employed servants in the manor) at Michaelmas, Christmas and Easter, the cost of food supplied to those who answered calls to 'boons', etc. In some years (such as 1296-97) the running expenses of the estate were apparently such that when the bailiff made his calls, there was no worthwhile balance of cash for him to collect that year.[12]

So each year, depending on the season, the weather, the requirements of the abbey, and the needs in the manor, the amount of the moneys still in hand varied greatly, and the collections made by the bailiff from the serjeant and reeve varied accordingly, taking into account as well the future costs which could be anticipated in the manor after the date of collection.

When in 1273 the reeve was banished and the serjeant became the sole manager, the pattern of the bailiff's visits changed slightly. He now made visits on more occasions, up to about four in the course of the year, and he

might be accompanied by other monks, who acted in effect as his agents, and any one of them might be named as the recipient of all or some of the moneys collected on such a visit. But sometimes the roles were reversed, with the bailiff or other monks actually bringing moneys to the manor, presumably as a result of cries for financial help urgently sent down the hill.

Sometimes (as in 1273-74) the bailiff, on one of his three visits, might be accompanied by yet other monks who *'came to convalesce or take the air, since some of them were sick'*; but they all had to be fed, and the 'expenses' of their food and drink had to appear later in the official accounts as a cost to the manor.[13]   It was the bailiff's habit to bring to Hampstead, or even to send separately, some colleagues from the convent to help in carrying out his supervisory work and to collect available cash during the 1290s, so that a succession of regular names of visiting fellow-monks come to be recognised.  There is little doubt that, since Hampstead (like Hendon) was accepted as a place of convalescence for sick personnel from the abbey, a day-out or more in the country, with quiet rides on horseback, must have been very welcome to other monks as well, even if it involved some work as well.[14]

In many of the years the monk who was acting as the bailiff is actually named, or his name can be inferred.  Thus in the first year 'Lord William', as he was called in the accounts, can be identified as the monk Brother William of Pharindon who had been appointed the precentor at the abbey, and was later the pittancer and finally the infirmarer. He remained the bailiff at Hampstead for probably about 8 years, and so must have become well acquainted with the manor and its ways. Later still in the 1280s the bailiff was Brother Richard of Waltham, whose period in

---

12 See DS, *H. A/cs*, p. 2/21. Yet that year was a profitable one, with income exceeding expenses by nearly £11.
13 See DS, *H. A/cs*, p. 1/22.
14 The old rules of St. Benedict and the *Regularis Concordia* about absence ('gadding about') from the monastery posed problems for monasteries with large estates; cf. *The Westminster Corridor*, p. 143, n. 37.

the office of bailiff was probably 7 years. His experience seems not to have been as an obedientiary at the abbey, but to have been mainly in bailiff-like posts on behalf of the convent, since he was later put in charge of an outlying manor, at Oakham in Rutland; and later still he was made an auditor of accounts in Queen Eleanor's foundation.[15] Like Brother Walter of Arkesdene, Richard of Waltham was another supporter of the prior Reginald of Hadham in the violent disputes with Abbot Wenlock.[16] And in the days before he became prior, Reginald of Hadham had not only figured among the monks who sometimes accompanied earlier bailiffs on their visits to Hampstead and made collections there of cash, but also in 1298-99 he had himself been the bailiff at Hampstead.[17]

### The manor centre

From the start the convent apparently adopted for their farming operations the same centre as had presumably been the place from which the managers of the previous lay owners had run the farm. This was at the junction where the lane later known as Frognal met a lane which led down to West End, adjacent to the wide spread of the three main demesne fields which sloped south-westerly towards Kilburn. Over the next fifty years of the farm accounts, we can see not a 'manor-house', but a 'manor-place', as it later came to be called, where a farm pond stood on the line of the Frognal lane, with nearby an extensive farm-yard with buildings on three sides, a hall with a solar above, a grange, granaries and other farm buildings such as a sheepcote, cowhouse, oxshed, henhouse, pighouse,

goosehouse and a kitchen, dairy, and a chamber, with other spaces roundabout and behind for the folding of animals, and an apple orchard behind.[18] Regularly each year a number of these buildings had to be changed, repaired, re-roofed, rebuilt or improved, and so they provided endless employment for the local carpenters, plasterers, thatchers, and fencers. Even 500 years later a hall on the same site was still 'very capacious', with the farm buildings grouped on three sides round a wide central yard.

Since there were regular visits by the bailiff and other monks and even on occasions by the prior and on other occasions by the abbot himself, there must have been facilities for them staying over. On one occasion, in May 1290, Abbot Wenlock spent five nights at Hampstead, and he must have had servants with him.[19] Probably the hall, which no doubt served for many different uses including the holding of manor court hearings, also acted in part as a dormitory for visiting monks; but, for the abbot, the 'chamber' (camera) or a solar no doubt served as his private bedchamber.

The manor windmill stood somewhere nearby, probably higher up the hill where it could catch the stronger winds, perhaps on the later 'Windmill Hill' near the top of the Frognal lane. It was farmed out at rents which varied up and down, at rates between 20s. and 30s, but the abbey was responsible for repairs and almost every year incurred cost in doing them. It was a post-mill, and in 1273 it suffered serious damage when somehow its foundations were weakened, a new oak post had to be bought and planted in a special clay

---

15  Pearce, *Monks*, p. 56.
16  Harvey, *W. of Wenlok*, p. 22n. For Walter of Arkesdene, see p. 379 above. For the disputes, see pp. 319 ff.
17  In eg. 1290-91, 1293-94 and 1294-95, see DS, *H. A/cs*, pp. 2/5, 14B and 17B. Since Reginald was also acting as the monk-warden of the abbot's country house La Neyte in 1292-94 and later as the abbot's receiver or treasurer, he had had experience of both 'camps' of those who took part in his later disputes with the abbot.
18  All these buildings appear frequently in the accounts for various purposes; and see VCH, *Mdx*, p. 9/95. The farmyard survived to the C18, see the 1762 manor map & Fieldbook of Hampstead, at Camden LS and Archives Centre.
19  Harvey, *W. de Wenlok*, p. 37.

bed, and heavy carpentry costs were incurred at a cost of over 39s.[20] Its cogwheel (*cogwule*) had to be repaired in 1289-90, and on 14th November 1293 the whole mill was blown down by the wind, so that another post and a beam had to be obtained from Hendon in 1294-95. But, from then on, neither rent nor repairs appear in any of the surviving accounts until 1303-04, so it must have been semi-permanently out of action.

### Fields and their crops

The three large fields of medieval Hampstead, 'Homefeld', 'Somerlese' and 'Pyrlegh', which formed the substance of the demesne lands stood to the south and south-west of the manor-place, on the downward slopes towards Kilburn which caught the maximum sun. We do not know how they had fared under the long years of secular lordship. After they were restored to the abbey, there were occasions on which one or more of them were casually named in the accounts, but their location on these slopes can only be identified with certainty from the names 'Summer Leys (Leas)' and 'Purloins (Purley)' on the great manor map made in 1762.[21]

In the convent's survey ('Extent') of 1312, Somerlese and Homefeld (the latter field was nearest to the manor-place) were at least 101 and 74 acres in extent, but divided into different functions, at least for that year.[22] At that time Purlegh (actually called a *campus)* was undoubtedly larger than the small total of 28 acres, of arable, meadow and pasture, ascribed to it.[23] All the arable in Somerlese (87 acres) and in Homefeld (61 acres) were in 'separate parcels', and this probably

indicates the residue of strip-farming from some previous period, or at least division into separate small crofts.[24] These three fields undoubtedly were and had been the largest fields, although there were other smaller named fields and crofts as well, the largest of which was Northfeld with at least 23 acres towards the top of the present Telegraph Hill.

The acreages of the grain crops varied considerably, as one could expect. Oats was the largest crop, providing the annual winter provender for the horses and oxen in the demesne, but about a quarter of the crop usually was taken down to the abbey with one or more of the monks. The average yield of oats from all the demesne fields was about 60 quarters (with a top figure of 130 quarters in 1291-2), compared with an average of 15 for wheat and even less for rye and barley. The rate of yield for all crops was remarkably low, sometimes (for wheat) barely exceeding the amount sown. Apart from the extra food which the *famuli* received on special occasions during the course of the year, these full-time employees of the farm received their pay in the form of a mix of some wheat (often wheat chaff) with other grains or legumes, such as rye, barley, beans or peas, as happened to be available, from the manor crops or bought-in from elsewhere – barely subsistence.[25]

In view of the vast extent of the labour expended throughout the year in the manuring, ploughing, harrowing, sowing, weeding, reaping, carting, threshing, storing and handling of the grain, one might think that the cultivation of land for arable crops was more an exercise in providing an occupation for tenants, rather than food. But even in the

---

20  DS, *H. A/cs,* p. 1/16. In 1280 the tenant miller was ejected (disseised) for some reason, *ibid,* p. 1/31.
21  See *The Westminster Corridor,* coloured Map O (after p. 96) and pp. 124-125. See also n. 18 above.
22  Kennedy, *Hampstead,* pp. 115-16 (but the Somerlese entry on p. 115 should read "In Somerlese, in separate parcels ... 87 acres 0 roods". Kennedy misunderstood the Latin numeration).
23  Even as late as 1762, the fields in the great manor map of that date which look as if they still constituted the old Purlegh *campus* (positioned at and between 'Upper Purloins' and 'Lower Purloins', the 1762 names) total more than 54 acres, see Camden Archives Centre, the 1762 man. map. and fieldbook.
24  I said 'scattered parcels' in *The Westminster Corridor,* p. 125, but 'separate' is more like the Latin 'diversis'. The VCH *Mdx* 9/112 holds out the possibility of a 3-field system way back. I think it more probable than that.
25  VCH, *Mdx* , 9/112, and DS, *H. Acs, passim.*

expansive thirteenth century a small amount of food could be a matter of life or death for both man and beast, and a yield of 'one for one' was better than 'none for one', while anything better than 'one for one' was a bonus.

From the abbey's point of view, the other forms of produce created in the manor were more beneficial financially, if less crucial than a basic amount of corn.

### The making of fagots

First and foremost was the production of wood for burning, and the output, year-in and year-out, of 'fagots' from the woods and hedges of Hampstead was enormous. Fagots were large cylindrical bundles of branches and twigs, collected laboriously from the six main woods of Hampstead and from the hedges too (which were often like small copses) and then bound round with one or two withies.[26] The great fires needed in the kitchens of the abbey and elsewhere for warmth devoured huge quantities of such bundles, which had to be carted throughout the year down to Westminster from the nearby wooded manors, such as Hampstead and Hendon. Some fagots, not many, were retained for use for fires in the farm kitchen, and a few in other buildings of the manor-place at Hampstead, and the rest could be sold very profitably.

The convent's 'jury' in 1312, when surveying and recording the structure and economy of the whole demesne farm in Hampstead, assessed at 8000 the number of fagots which *"can be sold"* annually, bringing-in an income of £6. 10s, (ie. at the rate of 16s. 3d, per 1000 fagots). However the figure of 8000 *sold* had never been reached in any of the previous recorded years: the average sold over the last seven recorded years leading to the end of the previous century was only 3000,

and it had not been exceeded since, so far as we know. But the figure of 8000 had often been reached, and indeed exceeded, *as the number sent annually to the abbey*. This tells us that apparently in 1312 the convent's valuers (looking at whatever problems the abbey had *at that time*) were considering how much extra income could be made, if the abbey's 'fuel requirements' were reduced dramatically and at least another, say, 5000 fagots diverted to being sold in the market.[27]

In practice, however, in the period from 1270 to the end of the century, the pattern of production was that in at least half the surviving accounts 10000 or more fagots were shown as being made annually, and in the last eleven years of the century the average annual number of fagots sent down to the abbey was 8300, with an average residue of up to about 3000 for sale.[28] Since in those eleven years the convent was generally making its fagots at a cost of about 3s. 9d or 4s. per 1000, and making a good profit by selling some of them on the market at a much larger price of 30s. per 1000, and providing more than 8000 for use in Westminster, the overall benefit for the abbey was great, even allowing for the costs to the convent of carting them down to the abbey.[29] Another benefit was that hurdles could be made as well from the branches collected from the woods and hedges, and either sold or used on the farm in place of bought hurdles, but this was small fry compared with the value of the profit on sales and the provision of fuel to the abbey.

Since making fagots was not part of the customary services owed by tenants, the manor had to pay those whom it employed to make the fagots. Some if not all of these would almost certainly have been tenants in Hampstead, and so (to the extent of their small

---

26  In addition to fagots, there were also 'bavins', smaller bundles bound with only one withy. For the six main woods of Hampstead, see *The Westminster Corridor*, coloured Map P and pp. 126-7.

27  This may reflect the state of finance in the abbey after the Days of Wrath (pp. 311 ff), the disputed election of a new & hopeless abbot, & the chaos or absence of accounts in Hampstead and elsewhere.

28  Details are from DS, *H. A/cs*, passim.

29  It is not clear whether, on any internal account, the convent received credit for the carting costs, but its members received the personal benefit of cooked food and some warmth.

pay) maybe many tenants and members of their families would have benefitted from this production and perhaps welcomed it, even if the work was long, exhausting and often very cold.[30]

### Sheep and cows

Another source of real benefit to the abbey were the sheep, at least for the period when they flourished in Hampstead. This was the initial spell from 1270, or perhaps earlier, until 1286 when (after one previous attack) the dreaded scab struck again, disastrously this time;[31] and after that the flock was kept at a much smaller total, and accordingly the benefit was reduced.[32] However by 1294-95 the scab struck again, and the convent then gave up the struggle entirely over sheep, and kept no more at Hampstead until well into the next century.[33] And by the new century the brave acccounting methods of the second half of the thirteenth century had gone by the board.

The main produce from the sheep had, of course, been their wool, and the ewes' milk from which large numbers of cheeses could be made, one of the principal sources of protein in medieval times. The wool was cut every year in about June-July when the washing and the shearing was carried out (a 'task' job, for an agreed cost, carried out presumably by specialist shearers in the usual way), and the resulting wool was counted as so many 'fleeces', which were then either used for despatch to the abbey or sold from Hampstead.

The numbers of fleeces sent to Westminster naturally varied according to the size of the flock, and therefore were much greater in the first period, up to 1286. In the first year, when the starting flock numbered 273, 27 sheep 'pelts' (the skin with short wool still on it) were first sold (for 4s.), and then 230 fleeces were sold (for 40s.) after the shearing. Although in that year 103 new lambs were born, 36 of them died and their pelts were sold, for only 1s. 4d. None were sent to the abbey that year, but in the following year 91 of the 110 fleeces obtained by shearing were sent down to the abbey. No doubt the bailiff had delivered an 'order' for an amount on a 'could-take' basis, either for sale by the abbey or for use by the chamberlain. As in the previous year, 47 pelts of old sheep and 31 lamb pelts were sold from Hampstead, both for small amounts.

In subsequent years, as the flock increased, the number of fleeces sent to Westminster soared to 195, 228 and 251.[34] Then they fell after the first attack of scab to 80 and 94, before falling further – after the disastrous attack in 1286 – to 49, and settling at a level each year between 39 and 59. Finally the fear of scab won in 1295, and this useful source of wool for the abbey dried up entirely for a long time after that year. It would be interesting to know how the monks found a substitute, or reduced their requirements.

Meanwhile copious supplies of cheeses had been made each year from the ewes' and cows' milk by the demesne maid (daie), sometimes with help from one of the famuli. These too were mainly used for profitable sales and for despatch to the abbey, as required. A few were also very useful as 'expenses' with meals which had to be provided, for supply

30  The rate of pay is never given, and we have not the data to calculate what it would have been. The rate of cost to the convent was only 3s. 4d per 1000 fagots from 1270 to 1297, & 3s. 9d – 4s. 2d in 1297-1303. 1d. per day?

31  The record reads pathetically: *Rams* 3 dead; *Wethers* 6 dead; *Ewes* 32 sterile, 29 dead; *Hogasts* 30 dead; *old Lambs* 93 dead; *new Lambs* 16 dead.

32  The numbers of the flock from 1270 (at the outset of each account; with new lambs that year in brackets) were: 273(+103), 284(+97), 251(+81), 295(+112), 412(+102), 97(+34), 116(+40), 114(+51), 206(+18); then 46(+16), 54(+16), 49(+17), 46(+19), 58(+17), 56(+21), 63(+20), 62(+0) in 1294-95.

33  The VCH *Mdx*, p. 9/112 refers to an a/c for 1314, but the a/c is ambiguously dated, and I think it is for the year 6-7 Ed. III, ie. 1333-34, not 6-7 Ed. II. Certainly there were still no sheep in the intervening a/c for 1321-2.

34  A tithe of one tenth of all these figures had always to be paid each year to the church.

to the *famuli*, to the men who cut the hay in summer, to those who provided services on 'boons', to the bailiff or other monks who visited Hampstead on duty or convalescence, or as gifts from the prior or other monks. The quantities of cheeses made were formidable. Between the years 1271 and 1295, the number made each year was never less than 146 and once reached as much as 209, which was the figure made in the year 1295, the last year before the managers gave up the sheep entirely and farmed out the cows to a contractor. As one might expect, the sizes varied greatly, and different weights were used, often confusingly with little known names, so that one cannot be sure how much *weight* of cheese was being used or distributed.

But sales were profitable, if varying. In the first year 1270-71, 100 cheeses were sold for 30s. 5d, while in the last year (1296) the price (or the weight) had varied, with the sale of 115 cheeses for 21s. In 1286-87, 149 cheeses had sold for over 41s, but in 1288-89, 91 cheeses brought in only 8s. 10d. and in the next year 136 cheeses fetched only 20s. 4d. The numbers sold were sometimes as low as 16, or as high as 190 in any one year. But the annual numbers sent to the abbey varied between, say, 21 and 58 in the period up to the year 1290, and then were increasing to a range of 72 to 121, before being cut off sharply when the milk vanished in 1295. We can also see that sometimes, instead of a large consignment of cheeses being officially 'sent to Westminster', a number of the cheeses were supplied to individual members of the visiting monks (those who came to do duty or to collect available cash), and presumably these cheeses had to be taken back to the abbey by those monks by pack-horse.[35]

Other farm produce initially enjoyed both at Hampstead and at the abbey included some of the milk from the herd of cows, and the butter which was made from it. But in 1296-97, the year in which the same change was made in the abbot's manor of Eye, the 'issue and milk' from the demesne cows were put out to farm, ie. contracted to a 'farmer' or privatised as we might call it, on a yearly letting for an annual sum. The price for the first year was £3. 10s., but thereafter £4. 1s. 8d. for each of the two next years (the only later ones for which we continue to have reliable accounts). It cannot be coincidence that both the abbot and the convent carried out this change at the same time: either it was a concerted plan, or at least the idea must have been mutually considered, with two separate decisions to the same effect.

Even after the privatisation, the stock of the herd remained the responsibility of the convent, and this meant that the managers could still continue to sell and buy cows – which they did. Trading in their livestock of all kinds had been a profitable source of income for the demesne over the years, to be balanced of course by the need to maintain sufficient stock for following years. In one year, such as 1278-79, 3 untrained or unwanted horses, 39 sheep and 5 calves were sold for over 75s., but no purchases were made. But in another year (1297-98) the sale of an old horse, an old sterile cow and 12 geese raised only a little over 14s., while the purchases of 2 horses, 4 calves and 5 pigs cost nearly 33s. But, for their livestock, the managers could also rely to a great extent on the natural births of calves, lambs, foals, chicks, and piglets, and noticeably over the years the balance was in favour of income over expense – quite apart from the produce used.

### Pasture and hay

Two other major sources of income, in Hampstead as in Eye, were the sales of pasture and of hay. Before the late 1280s the hay crop

---

35  See eg. DS, *H. A/cs*, p. 2/12c (1292-93) when 76 cheeses were supplied to Bro. Wm. of Watford, 27 to Bro. Alan of Leyton, and 6 to Bro. Ric. of Fanelor (not necessarily all at the same time). All three of these monks also had dealings with Abbot Wenlock, Fanelor as one of his receivers (1295-8), but that was in peaceful days before Fanelor supported Prior Reginald of Hadham in the 'Days of Wrath', Harvey, *W. of Wenlok*, pp. 22n and 23n.

had been volatile in Hampstead, but by the end of that decade it had reached a high plateau, and continued to produce 50s – 65s regularly each year during the 1290s. Equally the pasture sold each year was producing about 30s – 50s in the same period. The regular hay-source was to be found in each of the three great fields: 14 acres of meadow in Somerlese, 4½ in Purlegh and 4½ in Homefeld; and there were some other small patches, making 28 acres in all. Regularly 23-28 acres were mown each year, and it was valued at 4s. each acre in 1312.

And when one compares the accounts of the two manors of Eye and Hampstead during the 1290s, one has to infer that there was some common influence which was directing even the style in which these sales of pasture and hay and other 'issues of the manor' were then being recorded in each manor. But it is difficult to determine whether the cause was cooperation existing at this time between abbatial and conventual managers; or some simple copying, by one of the other; or perhaps firm directions from those who audited the accounts.

The 1290s, under the influence of both Abbot Wenlock and other competent monks in the convent, some of whom had been in his service, formed the high-water point for the newly-born Westminster accounts, before their lowest ebb in the first two decades of the fourteenth century. This makes the effect of the ultimate feud and total fracture between the two parties of monks the more poignant.

### The grant of leases in the 1290s

There were at least two other features of the Hampstead accounts which suggest that some influence at the abbey was creating not merely a common style of accounting, but also some common reactions in the management of both the abbot's manors and the convent's

manors. In the manor of Eye towards the end of the century the managers (which must include Abbot Wenlock) had adopted a policy of leasing-out, at new market rents, various 'farms' of lands in the northern sector of that manor; and the action of leasing presupposes that the lands in question had already been in, or had recently come into, the 'hand of the lord', eg. had been demesne land let to tenants and had been regained by the abbey and were therefore available for leasing.[36] The same policy can be seen in the manor of Hampstead, although rather later, as one might expect in a slightly more remote manor managed by the convent.

Before the year 1298-99 there were no farms of any land recorded in Hampstead, apart from the original farm of the mill which had begun in 1270, when the abbey's accounts start. But in 1298-99 two farms appear for the first time: *'Farm of lands of John Lyon and John of Kilburn, to the feast of Michaelmas – 13s. 11½ d'*, and *'Farm of Eastfields, to the same term – 3s. 9d'*. These were clearly new rents.

John Lyon was a customary tenant whose name had appeared twice in the 'rental' of 1280-81, holding one small tenancy at a rent of 1s. 6d, but also a second larger tenancy called 'Albyn', which later became known as 'Alwinesfield', containing 16 acres at a rent of 3s. 8d. But on the 20th March 1296, at the manor court held in Easter week, he surrendered this latter tenancy to the convent, *'because he cannot pay the rent and other services and taxes'*; and in that year and at least the following two years the monks kept Alwinesfield 'in hand', ie. treating it now as part of the demesne, and simply letting out the pasture in it each year for 4s. But then in 1298-99 this changed entirely. The whole 16 acres were now leased by the convent 'on farm' (with other land), for a good rent of 14s.[37]

---

36   For the policy, see pp. 345 ff. above. Such prior acquisition might come about because of a falling-in of an earlier tenancy, by surrender or the tenant's inability to pay the rent, or by the assarting of, say, wooded land.

37   WAMs 32359, 32374, 32403, 32373, 32401 (in chronological order). John Lyon also gave up other land as well; this land appears too in WAMs 32403 (1296-97) and 32373 (under the name 'John Leoni', a name by which he was known). As land 'in hand', it too was let for pasture. Or was it just a *second* let of the same land?

Unfortunately the accounts for the next four years have not survived, so we do not know whether this leasing policy survived or for how long. But in the following year after that, 1303-4, from which an account for half the year is extant, there is no record of any rent being received for such a farm. The climax of the 'Days of Wrath' was now looming, and after that climax, Alwinesfield by 1312 was definitely back 'in the lord's hand', according to the convent's survey of that date. No more accounts have survived until the year 1321-22, when Alwinesfield was still 'in hand' and part of the demesne, before being leased out again during that century and the next. But no matter what happened after 1299, this part of the demesne had certainly been leased for the first time in that year to a farmer at a high rent, just as several of the similar 'farms' in the manor of Eye were being leased to farmers at about the same time.[38]

The other property which was leased with Alwinesfield was land under another tenancy (probably a customary one) which had belonged to John of Kilburn, who held a house and 20 acres for a rent of 4s. 10d. Like John Lyon, and in the same year 1296 but at an earlier court in February, John of Kilburn also surrendered his tenancy to the abbey, but did so as a sale, for which he was paid 4 marks; and the monks at first kept the property 'in hand', selling the pasture and the hay from it. After two years, they then sold the 'old house' for 6s., and in 1299 leased the land 'on farm' with Alwinesfield, for nearly 14s. rent.[39]

The second farm leased in 1298-99, the farm of Eastfields, started differently. These fields lay on the *east* side of the road leading up the hill through Belsize towards Hampstead. Originally that sector of the manor had almost certainly been the site of the wood of Timberhurst, an oak and beech wood which had been one of the 'lord's' preserves and was not commonable.[40] In the thirteenth century, as in the previous one, the assarting (clearing) of woodland or scrub was a common method of acquiring fresh land for cultivation, at a time when population and demand was growing fast, as they now were in most of the country.

Some assarting of the land on the east of the road had begun much earlier in this area, probably before the abbey had cleared Robert le Baud's claims off the demesne, and there had been at least one customary tenancy of land near the road.[41] But at the latest by 1292-93 at least another field, called *Estfelde*, had been cleared and was now part of the demesne. Significantly in that year Eastfield was being 'weeded' at a cost of 1s., according to the accounts, and by 1294-95 the monks were letting out the pasture in it for 4s. By 1296-97 and 1297-98 Eastfield had now become 'two fields in Estfelde', and the pasture in them was let in each year for 4s. for each field. But then, as we have seen, during the course of 1298-99 a second farm – of 'Estfelds' – was made the subject of a lease, for a new rent of 3s. 9d.[42]

### The sale of works

At the same time as the managers of the Hampstead demesne were now granting leases in concert (in effect) with the managers of Eye, another development took place in Hampstead which mirrored events which had started a little earlier in the manor of Eye. This was the 'sale' or commutation of some of the customary 'works' which the tied tenants were meant to

---

38  WAMs 32385 and 32406.
39  WAM 32359, DS, *H. A/cs*, II/19, 22B, 25. Like Alwinesfield, J. of K.'s land was back in the lord's hand by 1312.
40  See *The Westminster Corridor*, p. 127 and n. 58; and coloured map P.
41  The land was Agadesfield, of 16 acres, which the tenant John *atte lofte* let for three years, in about 1295-96, to the abbey's clerk Gerin of St. Giles ('*le linendraper*'), who then had to defend his title in a legal action, see WAM 32359 and PRO Just/1/543. For this 16 acre holding in 1312, see also Kennedy, *Hampstead*, p. 127, § 39. For its previous history, see WAMs 32367, 32381, 32374, 32403, 32373; DS, *H. A/cs*, p. I/9.
42  DS, *ibid*, pp. II/12, 16, 19, 22B, and 25.

perform *'according to custom'*. In effect the tenants could buy themselves out of certain works, by paying at differing rates. This had begun in Eye, no doubt under the influence of Abbot Wenlock, in 1291 and had continued until at least 1307 when the abbot died.[43] It enabled the abbot to take advantage of falling rates of pay in the market, and the tenants to get rid of some of their obligations so as to free them for work in their own holdings or to pursue other activities which could be more beneficial for them.

In Hampstead this form of commutation started a good deal later than in Eye. The first occasion was in 1297, when 14s. 2¼d. income was received by the farm managers for boon-duties in autumn 'sold' by various tenants.[44] It was the same in each of the two following years, but in 1299 a number of other kinds of duties or 'works' were commuted as well – in ploughing, carting and threshing – and a further income of 12s. 8d. was received by the farm managers. So at least by the end of the century, the abbot's innovation in his manor of Eye had been reproduced in the convent's manor of Hampstead. But the Days of Wrath were about to smash the steady order of things at the abbey, and we lose the immediate sequel to the commutation story.[45]

When one lists the virtually simultaneous patterns of change in each of the manors of Eye and Hampstead, it is impossible to resist the conclusion that these were concerted policies between the abbot and the convent, not fortuitous. The farming out of the 'issues' from the cows; the common style of accounting adopted during most of the 1290s; the leasing of new farms; and the commutation of works – all these point to that conclusion.

### Liaison and assistance between the convent's manors

As was happening in the abbot's manor of Eye, so also the Hampstead accounts reveal that the managers kept in touch with the reeves in other estates within the convent's circuit, and supplied live and dead-stock and produce to each other, when need arose. In two patterns which can be seen, it looks as if either some managerial direction may have been guiding this liaison and assistance, or there may have been a personal relationship (eg. friendship, or antagonism) between the respective managers on either side which led to, or prevented, their exchange of help with one another.

Firstly between 1270 and 1286 there was steady traffic of help or commercial dealing between Hampstead and Knightsbridge, each the convent's manor, in almost every year – limited of course to the surviving accounts; but from 1287 onwards to the end of the century and well into the next, that traffic ceased abruptly, and a new pattern of liaison started between Hampstead and Hendon.

For example the first pattern began in 1270 -71 when the reeve of Knightsbridge supplied Hampstead with 2 bushels of barley which were needed as seed for the next year's crop, and the reeve of Hampstead lent or gave a cart in return. In 1278-79, Hampstead sold 39 older sheep to Knightsbridge, and 'sent' 30 young sheep as well (unaccounted for as any sale). In 1280 (a strange year for Hampstead, on any view) there were no less than 8 dealings between the two manors: cheeses, gloves, tallow and grease, ropes, metal repair patches, corn and 'mixt', reaping services, all these passed one way or the other. And so on, until 1286.

The second relationship began with Hendon, and Knightsbridge faded entirely from the picture. The exchanges were more intermittent and less 'helpful', but they went on. Hendon supplied one ox to Hampstead, without value given, but perhaps in order to recover some 'animals' which had been impounded by Hampstead. Hendon supplied,

---

43  See pp. 333-4 above.
44  The mathematics of the calculations are difficult to analyse with any certainty.
45  The half-year a/cs for 1303-4 have no mention of works-sold, but far-ahead in 1321-2 (the next surviving a/c) the sales of work reappear, bringing in nearly 21s. income. For the so-called 1313-14 a/cs, see n. 33 above.

on sale, big beams to Hampstead for repair of its mill. Hampstead kept 20 animals of Hendon in pasture for one week in Lent, for 3s. And in the next century the exchanges became more extensive.

Exchanges of produce or animals also took place with Haringey, Battersea, Chelsea, Paddington, Finchley, Wheathampstead and Ashford, but these were quite spasmodic, if not 'one-offs', and formed much less of any pattern.[46]

### The tenants again

Although the 'rentals' of 1259 and 1281 provided some valuable information, for both the monks and us, about both free and unfree tenants in Hampstead, no panoptic view of the manor appeared until 1312, when the convent carried out its great survey of the manor, with the aid of a jury of 14 of the customary tenants and one free tenant, Robert of Kingswell. Although by 1312 both King Edward I and Abbot Walter of Wenlock were dead, the details recorded by the jury were clearly not brand new in that year and can be taken as broadly representing an earlier position within our period, at say 1300. At that time the customary tenants were 41 in number, and the holdings were 51 because some tenants held more than one holding. The sizes of their holdings, including their houses (where there was one; and in some cases, more than one house was held by a tenant) are listed, together with their rents (including hens, geese or eggs) and the full work obligations which each owed.

There were only two 'week-workers', each of whom had to work for part of every working week; but even this was not too onerous in Hampstead, since it was limited to only one day a week, and of course none in Christmas, Easter and Pentecost weeks. One of these two tenants was appropriately known

as Geoffrey *le Werkeman;* and he had a house, but only 5 acres of land, paying no rent save a hen at Christmas and 5 eggs at Easter. In some other manors, with different lords, a few tenants still had to work two or even three days in every working week.

Of the rest, one man, Roger Adam, had the largest holding, with 24 acres; 14 other tenants had holdings of 10-20 acres each; and 13 had less than 10 acres – all of these had a house. There were 11 other tenants, with varying holdings: some with a house but no land, others with some land but no house (on that piece of land). A few tenants had two or even three holdings; and the houses are almost all described as 'messuages', of the larger kind. The amount of their money rents had little to do with the size of their holding: Roger Adam, with his house and 24 acres, paid only 3s. 9d, while the family 'Thomas Martyn, Sara and Johanna' who had a joint tenancy paid 6s. 8d. for a house and 10 acres.

Of the 41 tenants, only 19 by this date had work-obligations towards the abbey. So 22 tenants had no obligation save to pay their rents (including hens and eggs) on the four quarter-days; and for the rest of their time, they could work their own land, or practise new skills and seek paid work, as they chose.[47]

15 of the 19 'workers' each had the following duties during the course of the year : –

- to **plough** for **one** day at the winter sowings, and **one** day at the spring sowings, if they had a plough;
- to **harrow** for **one** day at the winter sowings, and **one** day at the spring sowings, with the monks to supply food;
- to **cart the lord's manure** for **one** day, with food supplied by the monks;
- to **hoe the lord's corn** for **two** days, with food supplied by the monks;
- to **make hay in the lord's meadow** for

46  DS, *H. A/cs,* passim.

47  Perhaps these were the rude forefathers of the later 'copyholders' of the manor who formed such a formidable group and defended their rights of common on the heath; even against their own lord of Hampstead in the C19.

**five** days, with the monks to supply one meal a day of 'bread, drink and cheese';

    - to **cart the hay** for **one** day, with food supplied by the monks;

    - to **reap the lord's corn** for **two** days in autumn, when called on to do so;

    - to **cart the corn in autumn** for **one** day, and **the oats** for **one** day, with food supplied by the monks.

    This meant 17 days work during the year for each 'working tenant', or 15 days work if he did not have a plough. One other tenant had to work double this number, and another tenant had to work half this number. And then there were the worst-off, the two 'week-work-ers', who each had to work one day in each of 49 weeks in the year. That accounts for the 19 'working tenants'.[48] Put in this perspective, the work burden of serfdom appears less than is usually thought. It was probably the other limitations of the status, such as the prohibition against emigration out of one's manor and the subservience imposed by compulsory attendance at manor courts and constant 'fines and reliefs' payable to the lord, which incensed or irritated the customary tenant.

    Many of these tenant families of the 1260-1280s can be traced over extended periods of Hampstead's subsequent history.[49] The descendant family of William of Aldenham, a tenant who was first sighted in the 1281 rental, survived for nearly 250 years in the manor, until 1529 shortly before the dissolution of the catholic monastery of Westminster Abbey. The *'atte ponde'* family or families, seen first in 1259 but later known as Pond or Ponder, were still visible in 1386. So too were a group of other early families, such as the Woodwards, the

Sturgises, the Browns and others who are also known to have survived for at least 125 years. But even in a structured society, such as a medieval manor was, the long-term survival of a family was a process which still depended on little more than the chances of good health, material success, fertility or fortunate accident.

    In most respects the endless cycle of work in Hampstead during the rural year in this period must have followed much the same pattern as that described above for the manor of Eye.[50] But the extensive woodland work and the making of fagots and hurdles in Hampstead did provide both a distinct difference between the two manors, and an exceptional opportunity for direct benefit to the abbey and a source of income both to the demesne farm and to the tenants.

    And there can be little doubt that as a hill-top manor, away from the sterner influences of abbey routines and duties, it came to be regarded with considerable affection by the monks and provided for many of them, and particularly for convalescents, a place for recreation or recuperation. The revealing latin word used to describe those monks who were permitted to visit it for a day or more, outside the calls of duty, was *spatiantes* – enjoying the space, roaming, 'taking the air'.

    From our standpoint, we could say light-heartedly that the crowds of people from London who after 1871 were first able to throng onto their newly-acquired public space of Hampstead Heath were in one respect following in the footsteps of early roaming monks of Westminster – even if these newcomers did not know it; and if they had known it, would with true Victorian and Protestant independence have stoutly disowned any such comparison.

---

48 Kennedy, *Hampstead*, pp. 121-127. There were also two additional major 'tenants', Richard Blacket and Richard Child, whose extensive lands lay across the northern boundary between Hendon and Hampstead, near the present Telegraph Hill. Their main land was in Hendon, but they each did have 30 acres in Hampstead. Their rents (each 3s. 10d) and some detailed work services 'should go [or are accounted for] in the Hendon account', Kennedy, *ibid*, p. 129 (though in fact they did not, in the parallel great survey of Hendon in 1321). 'Placket's Well' [sic] and 'Child's Hill' were later place names near the present Telegraph Hill, see also *The Westminster Corridor*, p. 92n.; and 'Child's Hill' survives strongly to this day for a whole area north of the border.
49 See VCH *Mdx*, p. 9/115.
50 See pp. 350 ff. above.

# Some named 'fees' in Westminster

The 'fee-holders'[1] named in the charters fall into several different categories: –

**(1) First there were abbey officers.**

Examples were: –

**(a)** *William of Hurley*, the usher of Abbot Walter of Winchester (1175-90). William and his wife Pavia were probably living in his 'fee' in the Longditch area in the 1180s, if not earlier, before restoring at least part of it to the abbey;[2]

**(b)** *Edward*, the abbey's reeve of Westminster, was in office under Abbot William Postard for a number of years before about 1197 and held a large 'fee' in the Tothill and Longditch area. The fee was inherited by his son John (always known as 'John son of Edward'), and at least some of the income from lands in the fee was restored to the abbey by way of gift to the Lady Altar;[3]

**(c)** *Adam of Sunbury*, the same abbot's chamberlain in the 1190s, and his widow *Juliana*, whose 'sub-fee', held from John son of Edward, lay on or near Tothill Street;[4]

**(d)** *Eadric the gardener*, who had one 'fee' in the early thirteenth century seemingly near Charing Street and appropriately close to the 'great garden' (now Covent Garden), where he probably was senior gardener; but he also had another sub-fee on Tothill Street, part of the fee of John, son of Edward;[5]

**(e)** *Walkelin*, serjeant of the almonry, who held a 'fee' in Longditch, conveniently close to his place of work near the abbey west gate;[6]

**(f)** *Stephen of Berking*, a clerk of the abbey, who also held a 'fee' in Longditch;[7]

**(g)** *Richer of the Cross*, who held a 'fee', probably in the 'King Street' area, in about the 1240s. He was the abbey's reeve of Westminster for part of that decade.[8]

**(2) Then there was a group of public figures and institutions.**[9]

**(a)** From 1128 by grant of Henry I the *Knights Templar* had held land in Holborn, on the east of the present Chancery Lane, where they built the 'Old Temple', with a round

---

1  See pp. 21-3 above. Very few of the *original* grants have survived; most 'fees' are fortuitously mentioned in later charters relating to other transactions or other parties. All the 'fees' listed here are referred to earlier in this book.

2  For William and Pavia, see pp. 96-7 and 147-8 above, and WAC 311 (1194 x 1200).

3  WACs 447, 449, 450. For Edward himself and his son John, see also pp. 142-5 above; and for the role of the reeves of Westminster, see pp. 103-6 above. For the campaign of charity towards the Lady Altar, at the changeover of the C12 and C13, see pp. 126-9 above.

4  WAC 449. cf. also WACs 446, 447, 448, 450. For Adam of Sunbury himself and his widow, Juliana, see pp. 148 and 163 above.

5  WAM 17453; cf. 17413, 17432, 17449. For Eadric himself, see pp. 149-50 above. For Eadric's sub-fee on Tothill Street (and similar sub-fees of William the Waller et. al.), see WACs 449 and 450, and p. 150 n. 66 above.

6  WAC 444 (temp. John). For 'serjeants' see pp. 99-101, and for Walkelin, see also pp. 100 and 148 above.

7  WAC 328 (1200 x 1203). For Stephen of Berking, see also p. 178 above.

8  WAMs 17510, 17511, 17419, 17340. See also Rosser, *Med. Westminster*, p. 328 and p. 28 n. 17 above.

9  The question whether (a) and (b) below are rightly included as 'fees' granted *within the boundaries of the abbey's jurisdiction* depends in part on the issue as to when that jurisdiction in the eastern end of the 'old' Westminster was reduced, see chapter 2 at pp. 36-7 and App B, at pp. 396 ff.

church, cemetery, garden and orchard.[10] But in 1161 they sold it to the bishop of Lincoln and acquired part of the land south of Fleet Street which the Earl of Leicester held (see (b) below). There they built the New Temple, with another round church (still surviving, with war-damage) and a great establishment.[11] It is likely that they also held a fee in the Charing, since they were entitled to a large rent of 40s. there;[12]

**(b)** *Robert of Beaumont, the second earl of Leicester* and *Henry II's justiciar* held a 'fee' of land on the bank of the Thames off Fleet Street, where the New Temple was later to stand;[13]

**(c)** *Richard of Ilchester*, the bishop of Winchester (1174-8), and after him his sons, Herbert le Poore and Richard, each the bishop of Salisbury in turn, held a large divided 'fee' (first acquired probably during the abbey's 'vacancy', in 1174): a great establishment (an 'inn') off Fleet Street, running down to the Thames (marked now by Salisbury Court and Square), and two houses in 'King Street';[14]

**(d)** *Roger Bigod, the fifth Earl of Norfolk*, or a predecessor, had apparently been granted a 'fee' which included four acres in the Tothill area. This fee is referred-to in a charter made after 1225, but the fee clearly predates that;[15]

**(e)** From before 1199, *William Marshal, the king's marshal who became Earl of Pembroke*, held a large property on the Thames bank at Charing, at the river bend where 'King Street' ran southwards from Charing. After his death in 1219, his son and heir, another William Marshal, granted the property in about 1230 to a Spanish Augustinian priory; and it became known as St. Mary's Hospital of Rounceval, principally to succour pilgrims going to the abbey;[16]

**(f)** The new leper *Hospital of St. James*, very soon after its foundation in Henry II's reign, held a 'fee' in Fleet Street, as well as other lands around the Hospital itself, and elsewhere;[17]

**(g)** From early in the thirteenth-century the *Mohun family* held a 'fee', described also as a 'soke', on or near Charing Street in the parish of St. Martin, partly between the street and the Thames;[18]

**(h)** The large property north of Endiff lane, held sucessively by two royal treasurers

10  Williams *Early Holborn*, § 1227, Burman, *Templars*, 33.

11  For the Templars, see pp. 42-3 and 176-7 above; and Williams, *ibid.*, § 1315.

12  WAM 17157 (1247 x 1258). See also p. 35, n. 47 above.

13  See also pp. 42-3 above.

14  Richard of Ilchester was a powerful royal official and confidant of Henry II, and held various successive roles. Herbert le Poore and Richard (II) were his illegitimate sons. Herbert le Poore, before becoming bishop of Salisbury, had done the abbey a favour, by restoring land in Staines which his father had misappropriated from the abbey, see WAM 16737 (WAC 457). Richard (II) succeeded Herbert as bishop in 1217, see Williams, *Early Holborn*, 1/775 and 756, and went on to establish the new cathedral in Salisbury. For their father Richard of Ilchester, see also pp. 43, 87, 111n. 97, and 117. For the 'King Street' part of the fee, see WAMs 17317, 17327-8 (WAC 421-2), 17373, 17430, 17443 (WAC 434) and 17448.

15  WAM 17319. The fifth earl succeeded in 1225. His fee lay next to land of the Mauduits, see para. (i) in text.

16  Crouch, *William Marshal*, pp. 146 and 168; Rosser *Medieval Westminster*, pp. 310-2. See further pp. 29 and 178-9 above.

17  WAM 13847 (WAC 392, temp. John). The hospital had been made subject to visitation and correction by the abbey, but it held its lands in its own right. These included a large area of land at Chalcots in Hampstead, see pp. 115 n. 114, and 369. There was a tradition that the hospital had been founded even before the Conquest by London citizens, see Stow, *Survey* (ed. Strype) vi/4, but no confirmation of this is known. See also *VCH London* 1/542. By the end of the C13, it held many other land and properties in the fields round the hospital; in the river Fleet area; in St. Andrew's parish in Holborn; and in the city of London; see Williams, *Early Holborn*, 121, 379, 383, 389, 390, 553, 708, 712, 733, 1045.

18  For the Mohun 'soke', see WAMs 17141, 17142, 17148, 17161, 17445; and 17420 ('soke'), and note to WAC 399 (= WAM 17142). The soke was recovered by Abbot Crokesley, by purchase in 1252, see p. 215 above, and Harvey, *WA Estates*. p. 415.

Richard fitz Nigel and William of Ely, and later by the justiciar Hubert de Burgh, before it became the palace or residence in Westminster of the Archbishops of York for the rest of the Middle Ages, was held as a 'fee'.[19]

(i) The properties in the Longditch/Tothill area, acquired after about the 1160s by the Mauduit family, the king's chamberlains, should also be counted as a 'fee'. In one charter in 1234 some of them were referred as a 'free tenement', though held from the abbot and sub-let to fourteen separate tenants.[20] In 1344, the main area of these lands was restored by sale to the abbey by the Earl of Warwick (a title which an earlier head of the Mauduit family had acquired in 1263).[21]

**(3) A number of lay men or women also appeared as holders of 'fees'**

(a) *Avice of Longditch* , who held a 'fee' in Tothill Street from the 1190s;[22]

(b) *Hamo of Hotot*, who in about 1200 held a 'fee, probably in the 'King Street' area, which he then sold to William of Hobregge (who in turn restored it to the abbey, by way of gift to the Lady Altar);[23]

(c) *Laurence, son of William Parvus, 'of Eye'*, who held a 'fee' on Tothill Street in about the 1220s;[24]

(d) *Brungar*, the duelling champion, who held a 'fee' in the proximity of the leper Hospital of St. James in the early thirteenth century, which was inherited by his daughter, Beatrix;[25]

(e) *Odo the Goldsmith*, who was said to hold a property in Westminster as a 'fee' (a sub-fee, in effect) from William of Leigh in King John's reign, and probably also held a 'fee' from the abbey of a large complex of buildings (his *'curia'*) north of the palace yard;[26]

(f) *Master Simon of London*, who had inherited or otherwise acquired a heritable 'fee' of apparently many lands and buildings in Westminster, which he restored to the abbey in King John's reign;[27]

(g) *William of Rockingham* (a protégé and deputy of Robert Mauduit, the royal chamberlain), who held a 'fee' in the Charing Street area in and before the 1240s. His father, Robert of Rockingham, probably had also held it;[28]

(h) *Hugh of the Fountain*, who before 1200 held a 'fee' in Charing (and claimed to be able to transfer the 'ownership' of a serf called William son of Herbert, with the tenement and land which William occupied in Westminster).[29]

---

19 See pp. 110-13 and 155-6 (for Richard fitz Nigel); & 156-7 and 159 (for William of Ely); 186 ff. (for Hubert de Burgh); 193 and 269 (for archbishops of York).

20 Mason, *Beau. Cart.*, No 201.

21 For the Mauduits, see pp. 113-4, 159-64 and 269-71 above.

22 WACs 446-8. The wife of John, son of Edward the reeve, was called Avice *(Avicia)*, and she inherited land from him in the Tothill/Longditch area, where John's inheritance also lay; see p. 143 ff. above. She survived him and took part in at least three legal actions in the king's court about her widow's one-third share, see CP 25(1) 146/5/2, 3 and 22. I do not know whether she had earlier figured as the 'Avice of Longditch', who appears in WACs 446-448.

23 WACs 428, 429 and 348 (WAM 17329). Hamo's occupation and status are not known to me, but the Hotot name was known later in the C13 in Peterborough; Harding, *England in the 13C*, 199.

24 WAM 17401. See further p. 22 n. 38 above. In addition to his fee in Tothill Street, Laurence appears to have been the holder of 'the island' in the manor of Eye which he restored in the 1220s to Abbot Richard of Berking, and which became thereafter known as La Neyte, the abbots' private country house; see further pp. 48, 201 and 330-1. For William's appellation, *'of Eye'*, see WAM 17416 (WAC 414, 1200 x 1210); he had probably held 'the island' before his son.

25 WAMs 17109, 17110, 17415, 17427, 17314. See also pp. 16, 30 n. 26, and 49 above.

26 WAM 17435 (WAC 426); and WAM 17333 (1241), which suggests that the latter had been a fee, as one would indeed expect, having regard to the importance of the property and the recipient.

27 WAM 17436 (WAC 431). This may have been a sub-fee of a larger fee, held of another lay man.

28 WAMs 17152, 17154, 17138. In 17138 he is also called 'Lord of the fief', as a witness. For both Robert of Rockingham and William, see pp. 174-5 above.

29 WAM 17320 (WAC 416), and see also WAM 17413 (WAC 418, early 13C)

**(4) A quite different category of recorded 'fees'**

A group of sub-estates, sometimes called 'fees', came to be held by some of the major obedentiary departments of the abbey itself, such as the almonry, the sacristy, the cellar, the infirmary, the office of the precentor, etc. A grant by the abbot, even without the convent's consent, to such a department would not break the rule against alienations, whether or not the monks resented it. Such dispositions were internal arrangements which in theory could cause no loss to the abbey overall, since they only involved the re-allocation of moneys and administrative obligations within the abbey itself.

*Note: It is clear that some of the individual holders identified above were not the original recipients of the 'fees' in question, but were later heirs or other successors in title.*

One important question is: *when* could such grants of 'fees' in Westminster have been made? The periods of the 'vacancies' when abbots died are obvious suspects.

There had been the early 'ruinous vacancy' in the abbacy in the years 1117-1121, before Abbot Herbert's period of office, when some alienations and irregular appropriations of abbey property had clearly taken place.[30] There appears to have been no ostensible allegation that any lands or houses within Westminster itself had also been improperly alienated. But full details are not available.

Equally, fees within Westminster itself are not included among the many faults of alienation of abbey properties which have been expressly attributed, either at the time or later, to Abbot Gervase (1138-57), who has been much criticised for other grants during and after the civil war.[31]

A further 'vacancy' of more than two years, after the death of Abbot Laurence, occurred between 1173 and 1175, and there is undoubted evidence that the abbey again suffered depredations at this time in the 'western parts', in Gloucestershire and Worcestershire.[32] But although we know of one large abbey property off Fleet Street (in present-day London) being granted at this time to Richard of Ilchester, the acquisitive bishop of Winchester, there is no record of complaints about illicit transfers of other abbey property occurring within the nearer parts of Westminster in these two years, before Abbot Walter of Winchester was appointed.[33]

Yet another period arose later between 1200 and 1214 when Abbot Ralph of Arundel was accused of alienating abbey possessions without the convent's consent; and for this he was actually deposed as abbot by the pope's legate, who had been sent from Rome to Westminster to investigate what was going on.[34] But again no property in Westminster itself is recorded as the subject of complaint made at the time or later.

Nevertheless in spite of the absence of contemporary complaints directed at the administration of *Westminster land* by royal managers during these vacancies at the abbey, the managers must remain under the strong suspicion that they created at least some of the alienations within Westminster. But other earlier disposals must have been carried out by abbots, probably without the agreement of all their fellow monks.

---

30  Harvey, *WA Estates*, 84, and see p. 19 n. 27 above. This first 'vacancy' occurred between the regimes of Abbots Crispin and Herbert, when the abbey was in the hands of Henry I's officers. See also Mason, *WA People*, 32-6, for a concise account of Herbert's subsequent success in recovering some of the lost properties, and of the cost to the abbey; but Westminster does not figure in the records.

31  See p. 78 above for the criticism of Abbot Gervase in relation to nearby Chelsea, but this was only one such criticism, Flete, *History of WA*, (ed. Robinson), p. 89. For Gervase's abbacy, see pp. 77 ff. above. He has been accused of many other wrongful alienations of land, but has received some stout if not complete defences, see Harvey, 'Abbot Gervase and Fee-farms', BIHR 40 (1967) p. 127, and Richardson and Sayles, *Governance of Med. England*, pp. 413-421.

32  For this 'vacancy' between Abbots Laurence and Walter, see p. 89 above.

33  The transfer of the Fleet Street property was probably carried out by royal managers then in charge of the abbey during this vacancy after Laurence, see p. 400 above. For Richard of Ilchester, see *ibid.* and other refs. given there; later abbots and monks apparently made no recorded objection to the alienation to him and repeated the transfer to his two sons in turn. For Abbots Laurence and Walter of Winchester, see pp. 84 ff. and 89 ff.

34  For Abbot Ralph's alienations without the consent of the convent, see pp. 132-3, above.

Based on the dates and the way in which the 'fees' are later referred-to, it seems that such estrangement of lands in Westminster must have been made gradually at many different times over perhaps the century since Domesday, both during the course of various abbacies and also during the above periods of 'vacancy' in the abbacy. If this is right, one cannot expect to find a single period, or even one or two periods, when a series of dramatic alienations took place. Rather the process must have been a 'drip by drip' one.[35] Compared with the abbey's larger and more lucrative rural manors to which the no-alienation rule was particularly relevant, the smaller value of a 'fee' in Westminster meant that it was less regarded – in spite of the fact that it meant, or might mean, the long-term loss of a property on the very doorstep of the abbey, and cumulatively with others could amount to a serious deprivation for the abbey.

It is not the mere fact of such lettings which is surprising. Particularly in any urban setting some forms of 'ordinary' grants (in effect lettings, in our terminology) had to be made, and frequently were made, by the abbey (as surviving charters of temporary effect demonstrate), in order to satisfy practical needs or to realise income from its urban – and rural – properties. What may be thought surprising is the *manner* in which 'fees' were created which would or might (and did) prove to be irrecoverable; and presumably some complaints were voiced later about such disposals of Westminster properties. But certainly few documents recording the granting of such 'fees' or reflecting the making of complaints were made or *kept*. Perhaps this merely reflects the early difficulties and dangers of any form of 'letting', at a time when 'records' were scarce anyway;[36] when the consequences of such lettings were uncertain, and when legal means of recovery were unpredictable or unreliable.

---

35  Rosser, *Med. Westminster*, 44, says that "as a result of grants made by the abbot during the previous two centuries [before 1200] a considerable part of the area had passed into the hands of lay landholders". On p. 16 Dr Rosser had ruled out any period *before* Domesday for any extensive parcelling-out of lands in Westminster, so the 'two centuries' may be overstretched. The problem is obviously difficult, and any answer must, to some extent, be speculative. But there are some unusual, if understandable, features of the monks' behaviour in, I believe, at some time or other suppressing or dealing carelessly with most of the direct evidence, whatever the stage when the alienations were actually made.

36  cf. Clanchy, *Memory to written record*, pp. 27-30, about the implications of missing documents at an even earlier period.

# The eastern boundary of Westminster

## 1.  The problem

At the time of the foundation of the abbey in the tenth century, the whole area between the roads which are now High Holborn, the Strand and Fleet Street, as far eastwards as the line of the river Fleet (the present Farringdon Street) had been included within the abbey's original estate of Westminster.[1] This meant that at that time the abbot had full jurisdiction over the whole district as far as the river Fleet, ie. secular power over the lands and the persons within that area, and ecclesiastical power over any church and priests within it at that time.[2]   But two inroads on these jurisdictions appear to have taken place in succeeding centuries.

First, on the *secular* front, the city of London at some date or dates asserted claims to jurisdiction over the east end of the Westminster estate, extending (visibly) as far as a defined point on each of the two main roads leading from the city — first, where the present Fleet Street meets the Strand at the point known as 'Temple Bar', and secondly, at the 'Holborn Bar' on the Holborn road, the present Staple Inn (the site of which, together with an old but later building on it, still exists), near the junction with the present Gray's Inn Road.

The circumstances in which these rights over the eastern sector of Westminster (within a boundary joining these two bars and extending down to the Thames) were successfully asserted, or perhaps simply appropriated, by the city of London are not certain.[3]  But the visible facts became eventually incontestable:  two physical barriers or gates were established at Temple Bar and Holborn Bar across the two roads leading into London, so marking the places to which the city's jurisdiction now extended.  In effect these were tollgates, where the necessary tolls for entry into the city by visitors and goods were payable.  The two tollgates were linked together by an irregular north-to-south boundary from Holborn Bar, which after passing Temple Bar then extended down to the Thames.[4]

The date or dates when this dramatic

1  See *The Westminster Corridor*, pp. 79-80 and 166, and Map M.  The 'London Fen', in the charter, cannot be anything but the marshes along the bed and mouth of the Fleet; cf. Barron, *Parish of St. Andrew*, p. 8.
2  The only church of which we know for certain at that time and in that area, was St. Andrew's, Holborn, mentioned in the charter of c. 971; but St. Bride's, St. Dunstan's in the West and St. Clement's Danes may have been there too or were founded within a century, see *The Westminster Corridor*, p. 55.  As far as we know, there were no others at that time, not even any parish church in central Westminster, such as St. Margaret's became in the C11, see *ibid.* p. 83.
3  It is not clear whether the upholding of the city's claims became legalised earlier (by, say. some form of official decision); or a *de facto* one, eg. by some form of creeping appropriation by the city, met eventually by reluctant acceptance on the part of the abbey; or by express agreement or agreements between the parties.  Even the voluble Williams in his *Early Holborn,* is reduced to asserting (§ 8) no more than 'a wordy conflict of long duration' between the abbot, city and bishop in the C12 about the extent of the abbot's ancient jurisdictions.
4  The abbey's loss of jurisdiction in the area west of the river Fleet did not mean that it lost any rights of actual possession of any lands which it already held within that eastern sector, or that it could not acquire such rights subsequently.  For example we know that before about 1174 the abbey held such rights in a substantial area of land between Fleet Street and the Thames, which it successively granted or confirmed to three generations of the same family (each a bishop; the first of Winchester; and the second and third, of Salisbury), and which later became known as the 'Inn' (as a London residence) of the bishops of Salisbury; see pp. 43 and 392 above, and Williams, *ibid.* § 775 and 756.

reduction of the abbey's secular lordship had occurred are uncertain. But one of the early records of the Temple Bar barrier appears in a charter at Westminster Abbey. In the ninth year of King Richard I's reign (September 1197 to September 1198), a certain Walter son of Cecily 'sold' to the abbey a package of rents worth 13s. pa., receivable from a group of properties 'behind the church of St. Clement [Danes] *beyond the bar*'.[5] So the original church of St. Clement's lay outside the city 'bar', where the tollgate already stood at the end of the twelfth century ; just as the more modern church still stands, islanded by traffic, a short way outside the Temple Bar today which still marks the boundary between Westminster (now itself a city) and the city of London. One of the earliest evidences for the similar 'bar' or tollgate on the Holborn road shows that it had been established at least before c. 1183.[6]

So it is probable that the abbey had lost its secular jurisdiction in this eastern end of its 'liberty' at some point in the twelfth century, either in its first half during the troubles in the civil war between King Stephen and the Empress Matilda, or later in its second half during the restructuring period of Henry II's reign. In any event one could expect that the two bars were established together at about the same time.[7] Another date which has

been suggested for the abbey's loss of this area is a date nearly 200 years before, in about 1000 AD, shortly after the abbey's foundation and well before the Norman Conquest. But this does not appear likely, on the evidence put forward for it.[8]

Although the abbey had therefore lost its secular jurisdiction over the further end of its old territory, the matter did not end there.

A similar dispute about the *ecclesiastical* jurisdiction over the churches, parishes and priests within the same eastern end of the territory must also have arisen at some time or times between the abbey and the bishop of London.[9] Along the line of Charing Street, the Strand and Fleet Street, the churches in issue included those of the Holy Innocents, St Clement Danes, St. Dunstan in the West, and St. Bride.

The course which such a dispute may have followed in its earlier stages is uncertain, but it too may have been accompanied (or perhaps initiated?) by a resurgence of the even older conflict between the abbey and the bishop, about the abbey's claim to be accountable only to the pope and to be 'exempt' from any rights of supervision by the bishop.[10] Eventually a bundle of such disputes, including other issues about the boundaries of the Westminster parish of St. Margaret's, was eventually referred to Pope Honorius III, and by

5 WAM 17080 (WAC 395, Sept 1197 x Sept 1198): it was a sale because the abbey paid a premium (*gersum*) of £5. 6s. 8d (a purchase-multiple of about 8). The reference in the charter to the 'bar' is 'extra barram'. In another St. Clement's charter, WAM 17077 (WAC 397, late 12C) one of the witnesses was Ansegod de Barra, 'of the Bar'; perhaps he was even the man who was in charge of the bar and took the tolls.
6 Harl. MSS 4015, f. 129b, printed at [Williams, *Early Holborn*, § 329 ].
7 But Williams, *ibid.* § 816, suggests that Temple Bar may have been set up in about 1161, when the Templars moved from the Old Temple on the east side of the northern end of Chancery Lane to the New Temple (the present Temple site). Moreover he also suggests that Holborn Bar(s) may have been in existence as early as 1128, when the Templars had set up their establishment at the Old Temple.
8 Honeybourne, *The Fleet*, LTR xix (1947) 13-87, at pp 16-18. This suggestion is based on what appears to be a mistaken interpretation of the second endowment charter of the abbey, namely the one granted by King Ethelred in c. 1002, only thirty years after its foundation; see *The Westminster Corridor*, pp. 166-7 and 80-83. If Miss Honeybourne's suggestion were right, it would mean that the Ethelred charter took away from the abbey more than it gave, and there are other considerations of interpretation of that charter which conflict with her view. But Brooke and Keir, *London*, p. 169, adopted her suggestion. Among other reasons for preferring a much later date, the twelfth century was the very period when the body of monks of WA became so dissatisfied with the abbey's losses to others, and although no documents have apparently survived about the loss of this particular area, one suspects that it was just such a loss as this, fairly close to the abbey, which may have underlain much of their feelings of deprivation during this century: see above pp. 73 and 120.
9 Such a dispute might have accelerated as a result of a grant by 'Master Gladwin' in Henry I's reign (1100-1135) of St. Andrew's church (which was 'in his patrimony') to St Paul's and its canons, see Williams, *ibid.*, 816 and 819. The bishop now had good reason to regard the large parish as deserving his embrace and supervision.
10 For some other occasions when this old dispute about the abbey's claim to such 'exemption' surfaced, see eg. pp. 36 n.54, 75, 87, 129 and 138.

him was submitted in or before 1222 to an arbitration by papal legates in England, presided over by Stephen Langton, the Archbishop of Canterbury.

The abbey won outright in its main claim to be exempt from the control of the bishop. But as regards the eastern end of Westminster, the arbitration Award in 1222 defined the ecclesiastical boundary between the abbey and the bishop, *neither* at the river Fleet *nor* even at the new secular barriers at Temple Bar and Holborn Bar, but even further westward at an irregular line which ran south-eastwards from the garden of the St. Giles enclave towards the Thames.

If this was the creation of a new boundary in place of the old one based on the river Fleet, the effect of the Award was to exclude from the abbey's ecclesiastical jurisdiction the parish of the Holy Innocents and all the further eastern parishes as far as the river Fleet, and meant that no longer was the diocese of the bishop of London to be restricted, in its junction with the 'liberty' of the abbey, to the old line of the Fleet river.[11]

On the other hand, if the Award was merely a restatement of an existing and recognised boundary, it meant that at some earlier and unknown point of time in the past the issue about the geographical limits of the abbey's ecclesiastical powers had *already* been resolved in favour of the bishop. In that event his diocese had already been enlarged at some earlier time to a boundary which the arbitrators were now merely restating to avoid future doubts.

But whatever the position had been before 1222, *after* that date there were now two new (and differing) limits to the eastern jurisdiction of the abbot of Westminster. His secular 'writ', as it were, ran as far as a boundary drawn (irregularly) from

Holborn Bar to Temple Bar and extended down to the Thames. But his ecclesiastical powers, as exercised throughout the parish of St Margaret's church, ran only as far as the boundary described by the papal arbitrators.[12] So after 1222 the Westminster over which the abbey had ecclesiastical jurisdiction ended just west of the parish of the Holy Innocents.

## 2.   So was it a new boundary, or just a restatement of an old one?

The view has been expressed that the arbitrators' Award created a new boundary between the abbey and the diocese of London, by effecting the exclusion of the whole of the eastern block of land.[13] However, although much evidence which might have been expected about such an issue is missing, on balance it seems that the only dispute about the eastern boundary of the parish of St. Margaret's, Westminster, was about certain details of the exact line of that boundary, *which was already accepted in other respects*, and that apparently there was no argument being put forward by the abbey to the effect that the boundary should be either on the river Fleet still or otherwise substantially different from that defined by the arbitrators.

The form and wording of the Award show that : -
(a)  the only substantial issue was whether the abbey and the parish of St. Margaret's (with all its chapels) were subject to the pope's authority, and 'exempt' from the powers of the bishop of London. On this, the arbitrators found wholly for the abbey;
(b)  the restatement of the *eastern* boundary of St. Margaret's parish was given 'in order to avoid future issues arising about it';[14]

11  Formally the issue, as no doubt argued before the arbitrators, was, What were the limits of the parish of St Margaret's church, the parish church of Westminster, which lay alongside the abbey and was subject to its control? So the arbitrators were, in form and substance, defining the boundary of that parish.

12  These contrasting boundaries left an ambiguous area, between the western boundary of the parish of the Holy Innocents (later St. Mary the Strand) and Temple Bar, which must have caused problems and may account for the disjointed appearance of the charters which the abbey still holds relating to the parishes along the Strand.

13  See Saunders, *Extent of Westminster*, Archaeologia 26 (1833) pp. 225-228 and 236. I used to take the same view, which I expressed in *The Westminster Corridor*, p. 83, but now that I have seen the further evidence, 'it does not appear to me now as it appears to have appeared to me then', as a judge once said. The secular 'bars' already established at the Temple and on Holborn are compelling, and it seems unlikely that a complete separation between the secular and ecclesiastical limits had taken place.

14  "*Ne vero super limitibus dicte parochie sancte Margarete questio possit suboriri*": 'so that no issue about the limits of the said parish of St. Margaret's can arise'.

(c) but one or two small questions about the exact line of that eastern boundary at a particular place or places were 'reserved' by the Award, so that they could be raised again;[15]

(d) the church of St. Martin's and its cemetery (though without any express reference to a parish) were excluded from the parish of St. Margaret's;

(e) the *western* and *northern* boundaries of the parish of St. Margaret's were respectively defined as the river Tyburn and the royal road (now Oxford Street, and Holborn as far as, but excluding, the St. Giles enclave);

(f) but 'outside' that western boundary, the vills of Knightsbridge, Westbourne and Paddington, with its chapel, were held to 'pertain to' the parish of St. Margaret's, and so to be subject to that church;

(g) however no mention was made of any part of the manor of Eia, although it too lay outside the boundary of the Tyburn river (and nearer to Westminster and St. Margaret's than even Knightsbridge).[16]

15 *"Salva questione monachorum Westm' ..... ."* The 'question' in issue was *either* 'concerning' the monks of Westminster present at a place or places along the boundary (Holy Innocents?), *or* (more likely) had been *raised by* the monks about the boundary at that place or places. This arose on either side of 'the house of Simon the weaver' on the irregular line of the boundary, but it is difficult to pin-point the exact position, or the problem.

16 The date of the Award being 1222, La Neyte had not yet become the private house of the abbot, so the omission of Eye from the Award had nothing to do with La Neyte (which in any case was only a *part* of the manor of Eye). In fact, after the Award, Eye was regarded as being in the parish of St. Martin's of Charing, not St. Margaret's: see pp. 337 above. If this was true also be*fore* the Award, it might explain the omission? But certainly 'the parish of St. Martin's' was being referred to between 1250 and 1300. It was an odd situation.

see pp. 49-50

# The location of the village of Eye

The position of the village of Eye has never been established satisfactorily.[1]    But it is clear from information supplied by some of the charters held by the abbey that the high street of the village lay a short distance from the Tyburn stream, the line of the boundary between the two estates of Eye and Westminster; and with a little investigative work, the more exact location of the medieval village can be discovered.

First, from simple compass directions (N.S.E.W.) given in some of the charters, it can be established that the main street of the village ran roughly south to north, and that the Tyburn flowed, north to south, roughly parallel to the street, behind the houses *on its eastern side*, at an average distance of about 195 feet.  Secondly, from various directional descriptions given in charters, it is clear that the village main street was the northerly continuation of the road, previously described, which had started by running westwards from Tothill and the rest of Westminster.[2]

In that gap between the main street and the river, there stood at least six properties with reliably recorded measurements of their sizes.   Each one fronted onto the street, and four of them extended to the 'brook' or 'ditch' at their rear.  They consisted of two built houses (each a 'messuage') with of course their own curtilages; and five other plots of 'land', probably with houses either then or later. Their lengths in feet were 165 and 175 for the two houses and their grounds; and 173, 206, 219 and 231 feet for the four 'plots'.  The smaller of these variations of length are probably explained by small curvings of the river or the street, but the three larger ones (206, 219 and 231, compared with those in the 165, 173 and 175 range) suggest that, instead of lying unnaturally parallel, the river and street were diverging in one direction (which of course means, converging in the other).[3]

The line of the river Tyburn is well-known.  It had passed through the present Mayfair district and the area of the modern Green Park, through (and later, under) the site of the present Buckingham Palace or its grounds, and then onwards in two beds to the Thames and the abbey.[4] So in order to pinpoint the position of the village of Eye, we need to locate the place at which at that time the stream and a known road lay fairly close to one another, with a divergence between them, each on a roughly north-south axis; and the road has to be the road (previously described) which had come from Westminster to Tothill and so reached the manor of Eye, after crossing the Tyburn by a bridge before arriving at the village.

1   Rutton, 'The manor of Eia', *Archaeologia*, 62 (1910) p. 42 asserts 'Buckingham Palace nearly occupies the situation' of the village, but gives no evidence for this, or for his earlier assertion that 'probably a small hamlet clustered round the Eye Cross, the 'Cuford' .......of Saxon times'.  Gatty, *Mary Davies and the Manor of Ebury*, p. 50 adds very little that is accurate.  With the evidence of the charters, I believe we can be more certain, with small but important corrections of these assertions.
2   See pp. 49-50 above.
3   *Houses*: WAMs 4819 and 4789 (each in Edw. I.'s reign).  *Plots of land*: WAMs 4793 (1250s), 4787, 4788, 4792,  (latter three in Edw. I.'s reign).  Of these six, one (4792) identifies the 'brook' at the rear;  four refer to the 'ditch' at the rear of the properties;  and one does not describe what was at the back. Several of these six charters relating to the east side are linked to one another, in having common owners or neighbours.  We have one other charter, which may be unreliably measured.   On the *west* side of the street, there is at least a record of one measured houseplot, whose charter (4830) refers to the *'campus'* at the rear of its site: this was the great Field, the *campus* of Eye, which lay on the west of the village and survived to the C17 as 'Croofeilde' or Crowfield (Eaton Square towards Grosvenor Place and Belgravia).  No doubt other charters have not survived.
4   See Barton, *Lost Rivers*, p. 36 and its Map (part-shown as Map H in *The Westminster Corridor*, after p. 96).

If we assume that topographical relationship, we can then search the course of the Tyburn for possible sites. Firstly, the final reach of the river - south of the site of the present Buckingham Palace, and running as far as the place where the stream flowed into the Thames, near the modern Vauxhall Bridge – can be ruled out. The road from Tothill and Westminster did not run along the west side of the stream but came from the east and only crossed the stream by its bridge virtually at the 'palace site'. Secondly, we can also eliminate the northern reach of the stream, from the present Oxford Street southwards through the Mayfair area to the Piccadilly roadway.[5]

Thirdly, the short stretch of the river from Piccadilly towards the palace grounds (ie. through the present Green Park), can also be ruled out, on the grounds that there is no evidence of any north-south road in Green Park. Moreover we already know that on the west side of the leper Hospital of St James the 'hospital road' (*Spitalstrete*, which passed the hospital on its *north* side, ie. where Pall Mall now lies) ran westwards, or north-westwards, through the Tyburn stream (at Cowford) and so on to the 'vill of Knightsbridge'. Even if there had been a now-unknown north-south road in Green Park, none of the charters which relate to the 'hospital road' give any mention of an existing 'vill of Eye' – which would, on this assumption, have figured at or near a cross-road on that very 'hospital road'. Further there may well have been a large pool in the bed of the Tyburn in the present Green Park area, but no pool receives any mention in any of the village's charters, and this also would have been odd if in fact the village had been located round such a pool.[6]

With these eliminations, the result is that it is only the central area round the site of the later Buckingham Palace, where there is a road and a stream running in roughly north-south directions. But (and this is a powerful 'but') in 1614, when a first early map of this part of Eye was made, it showed that *at that time* the then road from Tothill

did lie alongside the stream in the area of the later palace – but on the stream's *east* side, ie. on the wrong side to fit the evidence of the village charters.[7]

If no more could be said, this would disqualify the 'palace site' from being a place where the village could have lain. But there is more to be said. As already described, the charters show affirmatively that at that time the village high street lay on the *west* side of the stream (with an average of about 195 feet between them). So in the thirteenth century the original line of the village 'high street' *must* have lain *west* of the Tyburn stream, which we know ran through part of the 'palace site'. Moreover the road could not have been on the *east* of the boundary stream (as the 1614 map and all later maps show it, and as it remains today) because, if it had been on the east at that time, then the 'vill of Eye' would not have been in Eye at all, but within the manor of Westminster.

But can the road have been moved? The later history of the 'palace site' produces clues which afford a likely explanation – an explanation which has a resonance with the many other records of unwanted villages displaced.

## Kings, silkworms and the Mulberry Garden

Since the time when, before the dissolution of the abbey, King Henry VIII acquired the lands needed for his intended circle of hunting parks in London, the site now occupied by Buckingham Palace has had a royal and a patrician history. In the course of that history, we can see for certain that significant changes must have taken place in the layout of the adjoining roads and in the disposal of any relics of an old village. The land surrounding the site (in both Eye and Westminster) was certainly agricultural land in early medieval times, held by the abbey until its dissolution.

But in 1609 an unusual change in the use of part of the site of the present palace was planned. In that year, King James I arranged for the making of a royal 'mulberry garden' on four acres of the site, in order to 'wean his subjects from idleness' by

5   There was no appropriate road near the stream in either of these reaches, on its eastern or either side. The names used in the text are of course modern, to explain the location to present readers.
6   For the pool, see *The Westminster Corridor*, p. 41; and p. 30 n. 27 above. The geographical descriptions given in the Private Act (23 H. VIII, c. 33) by which H. VIII forced his purchase of the abbey's Westminster lands in December 1531 also tend to show that any vill, if it had survived, must have been south of Eycross.
7   City of Westminster Archives Centre 1049/12/115; as recreated on Plate 31 in Gatty, *Mary Davies and Ebury*. The C17 maps of London and Westminster, such as Faithorne's (1658) and Morden's (1682) confirm the compass relationship of the river and road as shown in the 1614 and 1663 Maps of 'Ebury' (ie. by then *conflicting* with the evidence from the medieval charters).

promoting his fixation with the silk trade and the need to encourage it with silkworms.[8] Subsequently a whole line of noblemen, ending with a new Duke of Buckingham, occupied the site and their successive houses built on it.[9] The final stage began in 1762 when George III made the site a royal one again, by buying 'Buckingham House', which contrary to his original purpose was later transformed into a monumental Palace, built at equally monumental cost by the egregious George IV and William IV.

So, in 1609 there was an obvious incentive for the king to make a change in the layout of the road, in order to give access to his mulberry orchard *at its frontage* towards St. James's Park (as shown five years later on the 1614 map of Eye), and to remove any relics of an old village (over 350 years old by then) which may or may not have still existed. Equally, if a removal of the old road took place before or after King James's obsessive interest in the silktrade, there was plenty of precedent in England for such a displacement of any awkward road or old houses which interfered with the actual or assumed rights of royal or noble landowners.[10]

## The new village

The conclusion from this story is that in the thirteenth century the village street, with its houses of the 'vill of Eye', had lain within the site of the present palace, and was probably displaced in one of the later centuries.

There is one other important feature which also shows that it was the present 'palace site' which must have been the location of the medieval village. A second map of Ebury was drawn in about 1663, a little less than 50 years after the 1614 map.[11] On this second map there is clear evidence that other significant changes in surrounding roads had been made even since 1614, for the very purpose of protecting the privacy of a site which was already a nobleman's house before becoming a royal palace. A road previously known as *'the way from Chelsey [to] Westminster'* (in effect, the way from Chelsea to London, via Westminster; with a 'stone bridge' of its own over the river Westbourne) is shown on both this 1663 map and the 1614 map as lined up so as to join the place where the village of Eye had originally stood, which by 1614 had become the site of the Mulberry Garden. But then on both maps, just before this old road from Chelsea reaches the Mulberry garden, it is shown as petering out in that direction and being deflected southwards.

One can also see that not only had this old main route to and from Chelsea been *prevented* from running to the site of the old village (by then, the Mulberry Garden, and later the palace), but also the road's previous role as the old Chelsea road had now been expressly given to a former local road (described as *'now the way from Chelsey'*) – on the line of the modern Buckingham Palace Road, parallel to 'the old way'. And in order for this former local road to go further and reach Chelsea, it had by 1663 been extended (*via* a new 'Pimlico Road'), so as to join the same 'stone bridge' over the Westbourne river which had previously served 'the old way'.[12]

On any footing, the 'Mulberry garden' as a royal site had certainly become a 'no go' area even

8   The 'mulberry garden' was clearly marked on the original 1614 map, made five years after 1609 – and while King James was still on the throne. But any importance of the garden for the silk-trade faded, and it became a place of public resort (as described by Evelyn, Pepys and Dryden). See Nash *Buck. Palace* pp. 10 ff; Horton Smith & C. Hussey, *Buck. Palace.*, pp. 11 ff. The 1614 map remains a chance contemporary record of King James's work.

9   The royal site climbed, as it were, through ascending ranks of noble owners – from Lord Goring to the Earl of Arlington; then to another earl who became the Duke of Buckingham – and finally, rounding-off its ascent to the summit, it regained its former royal status from 1760-1762 when George III bought Buckingham House for his queen.

10  King James is the earliest monarch known to me to have carried out works in connection with the site - by making the mulberry garden. Henry VIII's Private Act of acquisition of the St. James's Park area (23 H. VIII, c. 33; 23rd. Dec. 1531) does not refer to the *stream* or even its ditch, or to it as a boundary. Perhaps by the C16 the significance of the old river or its bed as a manor boundary had been reduced and the no-doubt well-used new road had a greater importance. The Act is printed in the *Survey of London*, vol. XIII, Appendix A, pp. 257.

11  See the Lond. Top. Soc's. publn. of the 1663 map, No. 39, at City of Westm. Archives, Nos. 1049/12/30 and 44.

12  The previous role of this 'local road' is described on the 1663 map as *'the old way from Westminster to Ebury Farme'*, before the map also gives its new role as *'now the way from Chelsey to Westminster'*. Ebury Farm was by 1663 the name for the former farm behind the abbot's house, La Neyte, which it had once served, but its date of origin as a farm is uncertain: probably later than the C13.

in 1614, as shown on the map of that date; and maybe its change to a 'no-go' area could have happened well before that. We can see that the abandonment or diversion of the old main road to and from Chelsea, and its replacement by the local road, had required serious road changes, both on the old road to and from Chelsea and on the former local road, *'now the way from Chelsey'*. Compared with works of that extent, the shifting of a short length of the former Eye village road, from one side of the bed of the old Tyburn stream to the other side, was less drastic.

Very appropriately, the historic route of the much older Chelsea road, leading directly towards the site of the vill of Eye at the Mulberry garden, can still easily be seen on the modern map and is well-known to this day, under the very appropriate name, 'Ebury Street'.[13] Heading straight, on the maps, as though to pass through the site of the palace, Ebury Street is of course *now* completely blocked off, by other modern road changes (*as well* as *by the obstruction of the palace and its predecessor, the mulberry garden)* from reaching that site. But originally by 1300 it had clearly joined the old Westminster-Eye road *on the site of the present palace,* where the comparatively new village of Eye by then lay.

To round off the village, it seems clear that just *north* of it, at a point which today is probably to be located in the southern edge of Green Park, the junction was made between the road which (a little further south) had acted as the village 'high street', and *Spitalstrete* the street running westwards from the leper hospital of St. James. The roads met near where the old 'cowford', or a later bridge over the stream or a culvert, lay. Although there is no evidence at all that *at that time* the junction between Spitalstrete and the road which had led out of the village was actually marked by a cross, it is certain that before the 1530s (nearly 300 years later) when the abbey's dissolution was looming, the junction had been marked by the 'Eycross'. This was an actual cross (*crux*) because it was so called, and was certainly made of stone.[14]

From that junction the conjoined road ran east and west; eastwards *via* Spitalstrete back towards Charing and London; and westwards through part of the present Green Park towards Hyde Park Corner, where it joined both the main west-bound highway (now Piccadilly, running towards Knightsbridge and the west) and Westminster Lane, running north on the old route past Ossulston, along the present Park Lane towards Marble Arch.

Immediately *south* of the old village another junction lay, where the road from Westminster coming from the south-east met the local road from La Neyte, and from that junction ran further northwards as the village high street, with the old 'Chelsey' road also joining it there. But to reach the *southern* junction, the road coming from Westminster itself had had to cross the river Tyburn by a bridge, the 'Eybridge' (which by the 1530s was certainly a bridge made of stone (*pons lapideus*).[15] It had probably been a bridge of stone since earlier times, since it became the main access from the Westminster side of the stream to the village of Eye, and beyond that to Knightsbridge and the main road to the west.[16]

So we have a picture of a village, the 'vill of Eye' in the thirteenth century, lying just outside the

13 The names 'Ebury' and 'Eye' (the older name, from the pre-Conquest *Eia)* appear to have once been synonymous for some purposes, but in the thirteenth century 'Ebury' began to be used to refer to the whole of Eye *apart from* the abbot's 'sub-manor' of La Neyte (Harvey *WA Estates* 350n). But later still, 'Ebury' was retained just for the central part of the manor (still excluding La Neyte), when a full 'Hyde manor' in the northern part of Eye was hived off as a separate letting. Was there some knowledge of the site of the old vill of Eye, in the later correct naming of the more modern 'Ebury Street' which is on the line of the *oldest* main road of all, through Eye, to and from 'Chelsey'?
14 WAM 17131: the survey report made by the abbey in June 1531 (p. 24 above) six months before Henry VIII's Act, about the abbey lands which were to be acquired by the king, refers to 'the highway from St James [ie. the hospital] to Eycross'.
15 See Henry VIII's private Act, 23 H. VIII, c. 33, and p. 49 above.
16 The Act also describes the road from the hospital 'turning and running south from the said Cross ....... as far as the stone bridge called Eybridge ...... and thence along the road leading to the vill of Westminster ....' (ie. towards the south-east, on about the line of the present Buckingham Gate (formerly the confusingly-named St. James's Street), and thence eastwards to the abbey. This bridge can be seen in both the Eye manor maps in 1614 (just visibly) and c.1663-70 (clearly).

boundary of Westminster, located where Buckingham Palace and its garden now stand; with road junctions not far from either end of its high street, connecting the village of Eye

   (a) with St. James's Hospital, via *Spitalstrete*, and thence, with Charing, and beyond with London;

   (b) with the centre of Westminster (via the 'vill of Tothill' itself and Tothill Street);

   (c) on the south-west side, with the abbot's own establishment at La Neyte, and the later 'Ebury Farm', by a local road;

   (d) also south-westwards, to Chelsea, via (at that time) the *old* 'Chelsey road';[17]

   (e) north-westerly, to join the main road to Knightsbridge and the west.

Most of the clues for this circle of roads are to be found in the thirteenth-century charters about the houses and plots in Eye, supported by the details contained (i) 300 years later, in the abbot's survey on the 15th June 1531 of the abbey's local lands, and in Henry VIII's ensuing Act of acquisition on the 23rd December of the same year – just in time to provide a good Christmas for him; and (ii) in the fortuitously informative maps of Eye in 1614 and 1663.

17   In some of the charters Eye is described as being 'near Westminster'. This may just have reflected the close proximity of the village of Eye to the Tyburn boundary; see also pp. 336 and 400-1above.

# The sizes and shapes of Westminster properties

Fortunately some of the early medieval buyers and sellers of houses and lands in Westminster required that the exact size of the properties being transferred should be precisely measured and recorded in their charters. About 60 such records of measurements in Westminster have survived, plus nearly another 20 from other nearby places, such as the village of Eye and the city of London. The exact total is made up of 37 houses (with their land) and 41 other properties described simply as 'lands' or 'plots', being in some cases, but not all, unbuilt-up. But even this not insubstantial total of 78 has to be contrasted with the hundreds of cases where such measurements were either not required or at least were not recorded in any surviving documents. However those figures which we do have provide a window onto several aspects of the town's structure and (in some places) the character of the houses.[1]

Since the sizes and locations of some of the houses and plots in the village of Eye and in the city of London afford good models for comparison with Westminster properties and also provide important topographical information, they too have been considered. In particular this is true of the measured properties in 'the vill of Eye', which stood near the Tyburn stream, only just outside the Westminster boundary.[2] In topographical terms, as we have seen, the Westminster road system at least in about the middle of the thirteenth century led to and included a village in Eye, on its various ways to Chelsea and to Knightsbridge and the west; and it may even be that the farming of the whole manor of Eye was managed earlier in conjunction with that of Westminster.[3]

## Units of measurement

Measurement in the early medieval period was hardly an exact science. The principal units used in and before the twelfth century for appraising the size of lands and houses were the two medieval latin words *ulna* and *pertica*. The *pertica* or 'perch' presents little difficulty, save in the application of its curious mathematics. It measured five and a half modern yards, or sixteen and a half feet – like the old unit of 'rod, pole or perch', probably based originally on the length of some wooden rod used for measuring land.

But the commonest latin word used, the *ulna*, is deceptive. Depending on the period, the latin word could mean the medieval 'ell', a medieval unit used for cloth; *or* it could mean the modern 'yard' of three feet. Though the cloth 'ell' could vary in size, the usual size attributed to it was 45 inches, ie. 3.75 feet. So the word *ulna* may mean either 3.75 feet, or 3 feet. And the period when it began to change from the former to the latter size was the twelfth and thirteenth centuries, the very period when we are faced by plot measurements in *ulnae* in some of the Westminster charters.

The leading Angevin king Henry II (1154-1189) was the first to adopt a fixed 'standard' for the unit called the *ulna*, in the form of an iron bar measuring a yard, or three 'feet'.[4] His sons followed suit, with their own standard metal bar. But there followed a transitional period until about 1300, and we cannot always be certain whether the *ulna* being used in any charter meant the old ell or the new yard. So if 'the iron *ulna* of the king' was actually referred to, one can be sure that the unit used by the measurer was a yard of three feet; but if during

---

1  The evidence here may be more widespread than I've been able to assess, and although I have given here my own thoughts in the form of conclusions, I have to confess some uncertainties – in what I think may be new ground.

2  See pp. 49-50 above and App. C at 400-404. Most of the relevant charters can be dated to the period 1250- 1307.

3  See pp. 336-7 above.

4  Even the medieval 'foot' and 'inch' had histories of variation, so the ground is shifting sand. Cf. the modern metal 'standard' for the yard and the foot, to be seen at the Guildhall in the city of London.

the transitional period the *iron ulna* was not referred to, there may be some uncertainty as to which unit was being used by the measurer.

Since most (but not all) measurers did refer expressly to 'the iron yard of the king', the ordinary unit of 3 feet for a yard has been employed by me in calculating the figures given here, unless it is clear, or seems likely, that the old 3.75 feet measure was being used.

The measurements of plot-size in Westminster which were recorded in some of the charters range over all parts of the town: from the parishes of St Clement Danes near the Temple to the church of the Holy Innocents along the Strand; from Charing Street to the east and west frontages of 'King Street'; from Longditch to Tothill Street, and to 'the vill of Tothill' itself and the purlieus of the Field of Tothill.[5]

## Plot sizes in 'King Street'

The main street of the emerging town of Westminster must of course occupy an important place in any survey. The known *lengths* of seven plots on the *east* side of the street (houses with land attached, rather than empty land, and all relating to the century 1200-1306) vary as follows: 160, 130, 113, 100, 87, 86 and 29 feet.[6] The reason for this degree of variation in length was probably the original shapes and sizes of the even larger and probably irregularly-shaped properties behind them (such as the house or houses of the treasurer Richard fitz Nigel), which had been the first to become established east of the road on the Thames bank, when that bank was still comparatively undeveloped and there was little incentive to conform to any pattern.

On the other hand, the known *widths* of six out of the eleven measured properties which fronted onto the *east* side of the street seem to show a limited pattern of street development, in the range 18-29 feet. However this pattern did not create any firm restriction on width, because two other plots on that eastern side of the road had larger frontages of 33 and 50 feet; and there were two plots with frontages of only 12.5 and 8 feet, probably each a shop.[7] Since there was probably little early 'terracing', the frontage may have mainly contained detached or set-back houses.

Unfortunately on the *west* side of 'King Street' the properties have no measured *lengths*. But at least eight known properties on that side of the road are uniformly described as running 'from the road to the ditch' at their rear (the ditch named as the 'common ditch' in seven of those cases).[8] This indicates that they were all of the same approximate length and may well have been developed in some concerted scheme, with a 'common ditch' to serve them.

But from the only two properties on that side of the road for which the *widths* were measured and recorded, we can see that the houses on that west side of the road may well have been more substantial than those fronting the east side of 'King Street'. The widths of these two properties on the west side were 48 and 66 feet, and some other houses on that side of the street also give the appearance of being larger than those on the *eastern* side.[9] In some instances there was appreciable land included with the house in question, presumably because there was more land on that western side of the road, where the properties backed onto a rural scene (now the area in and round the present St. James's Park), unlike the houses on the east side of the road.

Immediately behind one of these properties on the western side of 'King Street' there lay the 'smaller garden of the abbot'. This was possibly in

5    They also include the sizes of a number of properties in the city of London and in Ludgate, included among WACs 351-391.
6    WAMs 17441, 17371, 17368, 17367, 17451, 17486, and 17500. The 29' may be a small shop. There were three other identifiable houses on that side of the street, whose lengths were not given in a measured form, but each of them was described as running from the street to a 'private' ditch of another householder (different in each case) as its back boundary: WAMs 17416, 17376, and 17511.
7    The charters are as above (less WAM 17500 which is mutilated, and the plot width is indeterminate). NB: widths often varied along the lengths – increasing or reducing, sometimes extensively, from front to back.
8    WAMs 17482, 17499, 17589, 17602, 17609, 17657, 17670, 17671 (many of these were later records). For the 'common ditch', see pp. 53-5. I have had to try to work out which could be west of the road, and which east.
9    WAMs 17370 and 17657. For other properties on the west side (which appear larger but have no measurements to offer), see eg. the house with a long history which is identified as standing 'opposite Enedehithe', see pp. 155-6 and 275-6 above, and WAMs 17443, 17317, 17373, 17379.

the purlieus, say, of the present Horse Guards Parade. The 'smaller garden' contrasts with the 'great garden of the abbot', which later became the 'convent's garden', now Covent Garden'.[10] The abbot's 'smaller garden' had its own ditch, which served as the back boundary of the 'King Street' property in question, which lay between the ditch and the street.[11]

## Plot sizes in Tothill Street

As on part of the *west* frontage of 'King Street', so in Tothill Street it is clear that in at least parts of that road, on its northern side, there had been frontages of planned or concerted development, instead of haphazard or piecemeal building.

At least two different sections of the road were developed in group schemes. Each of these projects was built probably within the same period, between about 1220 and 1240 – a period of increasing building operations in Westminster, which also included much work ordered by Henry III on the palace buildings, and was followed shortly afterwards by the start in 1245 of the massive rebuilding of the whole abbey by the king.

**A.** One section of Tothill Street had probably been planned and developed in the 1220s by William Mauduit II.[12] At least fourteen houses were built, and of these, five properties had their measurements recorded during the period from about 1234 to 1265. It is noticeable that their lengths are all in the range 69-75 feet, and their *widths* were 20-24 feet (for four of them) and 42 feet (for the fifth).[13] These houses were close to one another, on the north side of the road opposite the abbey's almonry on the south side. It would be an odd coincidence if the only five properties in Tothill for which we have clear measurements during this period were of much the same *lengths* by pure chance: while their widths accorded with the ranges for 'King Street' .

We also know that some of these houses on the north side of Tothill Street had a 'common ditch' as their back boundary.[14] So it looks as if these properties had initially been built with a pattern of similar lengths, and acquired a 'common ditch' at their back either at that time, or later when ideas about sanitation had perhaps become more sophisticated. Even if it is too ambitious to infer an initial common pattern, the houses may well have been built sequentially on a 'follow-my-neighbours' principle, so enabling a 'common ditch' to be constructed subsequently to serve the whole range of the houses.

However, as on the west side of 'King Street', so in Tothill Street we have no measurements for the *lengths* of properties which backed onto the 'common ditch' behind. As in 'King Street', the bland formula used in these particular charters was on the lines, 'extending in length from the street to the common ditch'. The reason for this lack of such length-measurements was presumably that when a measurement was actually demanded, it had the very practical object of establishing a definite boundary line; whereas in the 'common ditch' cases a fixed back boundary already existed, namely the ditch itself; or in different cases, it might be a 'private' ditch, or a wall of an existing neighbour's building. It would therefore be unnecessary to measure and record the *length*; and this might be true even in those cases where the *width* did have to be measured and recorded because there was no fixed side-boundary, such as an earth-wall or fence between adjoining lands; or where a neighbour might be able to take advantage of a change of ownership and secretly move a boundary mark or a bit of fencing by night.

**B.** A second scheme of street development in another section of Tothill Street, further west, was carried out in probably the 1230s, as part of the campaign by the monks of Westminster to promote the building of a new chapel for the Virgin Mary. It gave rise to the creation of about a dozen new houses for important craftsmen involved in the large amount of construction work being conducted in Westminster at the time, and in particular the chapel.[15] The *lengths* of these new

10  For the convent garden, see pp. 33 and 199.
11  WAM 17370, and cf. WAM 17610.
12  For the date, before 1228, see Mason, *Beau. Cart.*, No. 201, and pp. 273. For Wm. Mauduit, see pp. 270 ff.
13  WAMs 17394, 17398, 17399, 17408 and 17409. It is clear that the first three properties stood close to each other, when one examines the description and abutments revealed in the charters; and for all one can tell, the fourth one also may have been a close neighbour, even if it did not share the same identical features.
14  WAMs 17569 (1316) and 17589 (1325). For common ditches, see also pp. 53-5 above. Other properties on Tothill St. extended to 'private' ditches, see WAMs 17400 (1260s) and 17638 (1344).
15  This was the 'Virgin Mary's new rent', see p. 47 above, and Rosser, *Med. Westminster*, pp. 152 and 48.

properties were 200 feet, with *widths* of only about 22-26 feet, and the 4s. rents were devoted to the new chapel.[16] So this bracket for widths conforms with the range ascertained for the east side of 'King Street.' But a length of 200 feet for these narrow sites was anomalous in Westminster.

## Plot sizes in Charing Street

Similar considerations arise in relation to Charing Street, although the evidence does not suggest a single scheme of development. That street, being the western section of the present Strand, lay south of and parallel to the long southern earth-wall enclosing the 'great garden of the abbot', which later became the 'convent's garden'. Therefore the properties which were built along the *northern* frontage of the street extended at their backs as far as that wall. But apparently no precise measurement for the length of any of the properties was recorded in extant charters, presumably because the end-boundary was already firmly fixed and obvious to the eye.

But in one charter there is fortunately a measurement of the *width* of a property lying *north* of Charing Street, between the road and the 'garden of the abbot' (ie. before the garden was transferred to the convent).[17] That measurement is 28 feet on the frontage, which conforms to the same range of ordinary widths as in 'King Street' and Tothill Street.[18] Other charters in the thirteenth century have also survived which relate to houses lying in the same position on the north side of Charing Street, but no other width-measurements were made in them.

In contrast, the houses and their lands lying on the *south* side of Charing Street appear from the earliest days to have been usually of a large size, as indeed the subsequent history of the great establishments along the river bank in later centuries confirms. These properties lay on the slope between the street and the river Thames, and they appear to have extended all or most of the way along the river bank from the Charing Cross area, as far as the Temple and beyond it eastwards as far as the river Fleet and its marsh. The measurements given in the charters of the twelfth and thirteenth centuries for some of these properties demonstrate the extent of their sizes and provide information about the distance from the line of the Charing Street/Strand road down to the Thames shore at that time.[19]

Details of five of these large properties have been described above,[20] and these show that the slope down to the river Thames from Charing Street was more than 100 yards long in places, and that some properties on that side of the road were of that length, while in width they could extend to 100 or more feet.

## Patterns of size

So, on the limited evidence, the measured *lengths* of properties in the main streets varied so considerably that it is impossible to see any broad pattern of size in them. But one can say that these variations probably reflected the wide range of personal wealth, ambitions and status which could be expected in any urban society. One can also identify those places – such as the Thamesbank east of 'King Street'; the area north of the frontage houses of Tothill Street; and more particularly along the Thames between the Charing crossroads and the Temple – where, as the years went by, there was still sufficient space in Westminster for the rich, the ambitious or the great to find sites grand enough for them.

But the *widths* of properties along all the streets do seem to present a consistent pattern over the centre of Westminster. Six measured properties on the eastern side of 'King Street' had a pattern of *width* in the range of 18-28 feet on the frontage; while on Tothill Street it seems that most of the plots of the Mauduit development conformed (with widths of about 20-24 feet) and the concerted properties in the 'New Rent' development also conformed (about 22-26 feet). The one width known on the north of Charing Street (28 feet) is

---

16  For the chapel, see p. 190 above.
17  WAM 17449 (1220s?).
18  While it was 28 feet at the frontage, the width tapered at the back, as widths often did. The only other width-measurements found by me for Charing Street are much later in succeeding centuries, WAMs 17167 (1360) and 17169 (1408); but at least they are not far removed from the above range, namely 14 and 27 feet.
19  Variations in the position of the shoreline of the Thames, particularly after embankment, are still shown by the site of the Buckingham Gate near the bottom of Villiers Street; see *The Westminster Corridor*, p. 82, n. 14.
20  See pp. 35-6 and 39-40 above

also consistent. So a frontage width of (say) 20-30 feet can be taken as a norm for these busier or more sought-after parts of the town.[21]

But of course exceptions to such norms existed. There was plenty of opportunity for the well-off or the more enterprising people in Westminster to find property in keeping with their status or aspirations. The best examples were the wide plots lying between the river Thames and Charing Street or on the great bend of the river at the Charing cross-road which are detailed above, with street frontages of 100 feet (and much grander *lengths* of 100 yards or more); and away from the river towards St. Giles there was at least one wide 'garden' plot of over 200 feet wide.[22]

At the other end of the scale there were the much narrower buildings or plots, ranging from only 7 feet (a 'chamber and shop', perhaps in Tothill Street), 14 feet (a messuage on Tothill Street, also probably used as a shop, with a length of only 16 feet), another 14 feet wide (a house, 16 feet long, with a shop added, in the cluster of houses just outside the gate of the king's palace), and about 13 feet (properties in both Longditch and Charing Street).[23] But exceptions such as these only serve to accentuate the norms shown by about two-thirds of the total number of measured properties .

But while the widths on a medieval street frontage may be able to give us a rough impression of the street's appearance, they cannot describe the shapes of houses or other buildings behind that frontage. Plots even on the main streets were far from regular and varied greatly in length and shape from the frontage to their rear. The symmetry of the modern urban terraced row or a modern suburban

estate is not for the medieval street. Thus the one measured property on the north side of Charing Street might have a frontage of 28 feet, but at its back it tapered off towards the earth wall of the 'great garden', down to a width of only 7 feet.[24] Conversely a plot on the east side of 'King Street' could have a frontage on the street of 20 feet, but increase in width to 48 feet at its rear, where it met the 'private' ditch of Master Odo the carpenter.[25] And on the west side of 'King Street' a site could be 48 feet wide at the street but tail off to 13 feet wide at its back boundary, where it met the ditch of the abbot's 'smaller garden'.[26]

Nowhere was this kind of variation in shape more evident than in Longditch, where the plots in this period conform to no regular patterns of urban-style building. There, the site of one 'house' had a width of nearly 14 feet, but a length of 102 feet.[27] Other plots there reveal little evidence of the usual shapes of urban properties, in which normal lengths usually exceed the widths by a considerable margin. Instead we often find 'plots' or 'lands' in Longditch which are much more compact and squarish: 36 feet by nearly 32; nearly 70 by 40; 33 by 21; even 24 by 24.[28] Since there were 'empty' lands there, without mention of 'messuages', 'houses' or 'tenements', and since Longditch ran along the edge of open agricultural land where St. James's Park now stands, even so-called 'plots' may have really been small crofts or fields, fitted-in among or around older properties which dated back to the twelfth century, such as the complex of land and buildings first collected by the Mauduits.[29] So Longditch was unique within the central district of Westminster.[30]

---

21  The properties in London and the vill of Eye are included and support the norm above, as much as the Westminster ones do. I stress that these figures are not averages, which can always be distorted by exceptional figures at one end of the range. They are patterns, chosen by eye and judgment. The properties in London are the subject of charters at WA : WACs 366, 367, 371, 372, 377, 378, 381, with WAC 356 acting as an obvious exception (a shop 8½ feet square). A shop in this context is likely to have been a small workshop, with perhaps a cobbler or tailor at work at a bench or table; not a 'display' shop.

22  WAC 309 and 314, and WAMs 17157, 17159 and 17378 (the wide Thames sites). WAM 17431 (a big garden site at Tockesgarden, from Aldewych to St. Martin's lane.

23  WAM 17633 (chamber and shop). WAMs 17503 and 17549B (messuage in Tothill St.). WAMs 17365 and 17382 (house by king's gate). WAMs 17515 and 17167 (buildings in Longditch and Charing St.).

24  WAM 17449 (1220-30s)

25  WAM 17511 (1250s)

26  WAM 17370 (1220s). Th abbot's garden must also be the garden referred to in WAM 17610 (1333).

27  WAM 17515 (1290-1300s). Cf. WAC 396 (late C12), a house and land in St Clement Danes parish, with a frontage of 25 feet (normal), but length 176 feet, perhaps another Thames-side property, if narrower.

28  WAMs 17514 (1290s); 17554 (1270-80s); 17599 (1290-1300s); 17566 (1316)

29  For the Mauduit family, the king's hereditary chamberlains, see pp. 113-4, 159-64 and 269-71.   For other 'old' sites in the Longditch-Tothill area, let by the abbey to senior servants, see pp. 20-1 above and refs given there.

30  Unlike 'King Street' and Tothill Street, Longditch (running with the Clowson ditch) was originally known as a rural 'lane' (*venella*), but did not survive as such and, like them, became an urban or semi-urban street (*vicus*).

# The occupational names of Westminster and its neighbourhood

Since Chapter 16 had to be selective in its record of representative residents and workers of Westminster, one cannot leave it without indicating the width of the evidence about the variety of occupations which Westminster contained. The general characteristics of the occupational activities of Westminster and the trends revealed by them have been summarised elsewhere by Dr Rosser. But in dealing with all the years 1200-1540 (ie. most of the medieval period), Dr Rosser had to cover a far greater span of time than the period up to about the end of the thirteenth century, with which this book is mainly concerned. This appendix seeks to capture here some of the evidence which the documents of the abbey provide about the occupations of Westminster residents during the shorter period which I have sought to cover.

In doing this, one has to remember that occupational names, such as 'William *faber* [or even *Faber]* (the smith), do not necessarily mean that William himself practised as a smith. By 1300 such a name may simply be evidence that a forebear of William had been a smith, and the name *faber* was (sometimes but not necessarily always) in course of becoming recognised as a 'proper name' or surname for William, although he himself may have had no knowledge of a smith's work.[1] In giving, below, an illustrative list of occupational names which are largely culled from the contemporary charters recording land transactions in Westminster in the twelfth and thirteenth centuries, I have avoided many

of the more ordinary royal or administrative servants, such as have been described in previous pages. However where there is appropriate evidence, I have exceptionally included the occupational names of several of the more unusual royal servants who are not often encountered.

The list reveals the preponderance of 'service' occupations, over what may be classed as manufacturing functions. Many of the names are drawn from the groups of those acting as witnesses to the charters, as well of course from the main parties directly figuring in the transfers of land interests or rents. I have aimed to give only one example below of any occupational second name, but for each such name there may often be several people who used the name – sometimes with the same first name, sometimes with a different one.

Moreover each occupational name appears frequently in different spellings or languages: eg. scissor, cissor, le tai*llur*, or *le taylur* (each meaning a 'tailor'); or *vannator, vannarius, le vannur* or *le fanner* (each meaning a 'fanner' or 'winnower'); or *cultellarius, le cutiller* or *le cuttilyer* (each meaning a 'cutler'). Again only one such version of an occupational name is included in the list below. Any genuine surname which may have subsequently evolved from such a named occupation may have been derived from any one or other of such varieties of spelling or language. I have not tried to assess whether any of these names had reached the stage of becoming a real surname.

1   See Rosser, *Medieval Westminster, 1200-1540,* chapter 5 ("Occupations") at p. 119 ff., and related evidence in his chapters 3, 4 and 6. In dealing with the *size* of the population, Dr Rosser concluded (at pp. 168-9) that the resident population of Westminster shortly after 1400 AD (when evidence was naturally becoming more extensive) was about 2000, but that this was probably *lower* than it had been a century before, at about 1300 AD. So the year 1300 represented the top of the hill, after the climb in population during the C13.

2   In one classic case (WAM 17314, = WAC 406) a purchaser, Ralph 'Clericus', was actually described in the charter in question as *"non officio ita vocatus sed cognomine"*, ie. 'so-called, not from his office, but from his surname'. But in the secondary evidence of the WA Domesday, f. 557, in a much later copy of a subsequent charter, his capital C became a small occupational c, without any reference to a surname. So the contemporary metamorphosis of the name had been lost in that record.

Robert agularius (hayward)
John le taillur (tailor)
Thomas sumetarius (packman)
Thomas fructuarius (fruiterer)
Robert aurifaber (goldsmith)
Richard de celario (storeman)
Robert le cutiller (cutler)
Wimund pistor (baker)
John le fundur (metal-founder)
John le saucer (salter) king's
William plumbarius (plumber)
Richard le criur (crier)
John vaccarius (cowherd)
William palmarius (palmer, pilgrim)
William le peinter (painter)
Eadric de gardino (gardener)
Hugh le mariner (sailor)
Hugh le coverur (roofer)
Elias le espigurnel (sealer of docs.)
Ralph cordwainer (shoemaker)
Simon le brewere (brewer)
John de granario (granger)
John pelliparius (skinner)
William cuvarius (cooper)
Richard furnatorius (baker, smelter)
Bartholomew faber (smith)
William le chapman (pedlar)
Richard ballivus (bailiff)
Hugh sutor (cobbler)
William le tapicer (weaver of cloth)
John le heyward (hayward)
Le ostremongere (goshawk-seller)
Ralph de la sertrie (tailor)
Robert molendarius (miller)
Nicholas summonitor (summonser)
John cancellarius (chancellor)
John carettarius (carter)
S. de la butillaria (buttery serjeant)
Geoffrey coopertor (roofer, thatcher)
Godfrey bedell (beadle)
Simon avenarius (oats seller)
Lambert le corder (ropemaker)
Hugh medeward (meadow-warden)
Robert le bokbyndere (bookbinder)
Walter le imavir (image-sculptor)
Richard clamator (court crier)
Henry marbeler (marble worker)
Elias chaufecire (wax-warmer, sealer)
Alan linendraper (linendraper)
John bucher (butcher)
Rose la custerere (seamstress)
Walter camerarius (chamberlain)
William le chandeler (candler)
Ralph janitor (gate-keeper)
Richer praepositus (reeve)
John barbarius (barber)
Robert cementarius (mason)
Willam tegulator (tiler)
Herward scriptor (writer, copyist)
Laurence [h]ostiarius (usher)
Gilbert cornmonger (corn-merchant)
William sawyer (sawyer)
Henry cocus (cook) convent's
Ralph allutarius (leather dresser)
Thomas le messager (messenger)

John le vacher (cowherd)
Thomas fisicus (physician)
Robert capellanus (chaplain)
Robert portarius (doorkeeper)
Robert porcarius (pigman)
George falconarius (falconer)
Stephen candelarius (candlemaker)
Walter de camera (chamberlain)
Richard le tueler (drainer, tiler?)
William le skynner (skinner)
Godfrey marescallus (marshal)
Stephen le kennelman (kennelman)
Robert hospitarius (hospice-keeper)
M. la heymongestre (hay-merchant)
John le brazur (maltster)
Elias le tannur (tanner)
William le verrur (glazier)
Ralph le taverner (inn-keeper)
Simon de bracina (brewer)
Ralph vinetarius (vintner)
Elias parmenter (trimmer, furrier)
Ansgod le corveser (leather-worker)
William le waller (waller)
Thomas le ferrour (ironmonger)
Robert de baignorio (bath attendant?)
William pincerna (butler) abbot's
Nicholas le peutrer (pewterer)
Robert le garlander (garland-maker)
John le fusor (melter) at the exchequer.
Sampson de refectorio (refectory serjeant)
William de locutorio (parlour serjeant)
Ralph diaconus (deacon) of Mdx
Robert aculator (sharpener)
Alan computator (teller)
Roger le herbergeour (billeting officer)
Wlvuna locrix (laundress)
Ate le draper (draper)
William stabularius (stable-man)
Thomas pisconarius (fishmonger)
William aquarius (ewerer) king's
Robert vannator (winnower)
J. C. le trumpour (trumpeter) king's
H. tymbere mongere (timber-seller)
Wm. Brun. le valet (valet) king's
Roger cheseman (cheese seller)
Odo le carpenter (carpenter)
Ralph janitor (gatekeeper)
William tector (thatcher)
John tixtor (weaver)
T. le coffrer (treasure-keeper) king's
Wm. de la barre (toll-gate keeper)
Ralph colpiator (wood-cutter)
Nicholas collarius (packman)
Gervase portator (carrier)
Nicholas de coquina (kitchener)
Hugh mercator (merchant)
William pictor (painter)
John le wayte (watchman)
Thomas seminarius (sower)
Ralph cordwainer (shoe-maker)
Hamo seisitor (giver of seisin)
Wm. le strawmonger (strawseller)
John de W. nuntius (messenger) king's
Robert. de juwels (jeweller?)
Alice la lekmongester (milkseller)

# The way ahead: consolidations of some estates, 1307 ff.

A 'furious activity' in the land market in Westminster had been taking place during the thirteenth century.[1] During this period the abbey's own re-possessory estate was being significantly increased, through pious donations and by commercial purchases made by the monks. On the other hand, private families and entrepeneurs were also creating small estates of their own, as more lands in Westminster became built up or existing houses became available for purchase.

However the fifty years after about 1300 are thought to have been marked by signs of decreasing activity in the land market, a trend revealed by traces of decay in land ownership.[2] But even if this is right, yet some of the people whom we have already seen taking part in the active land market also showed a similar activity in the same field over most of the next half-century. Two of these people were a pair of energetic women who were instrumental in a process which was leading to the consolidation of even sizeable estates into still larger units. But, as we shall see, it was the abbey which was ultimately able to scoop the final benefits.

## Alice la Saucère and Joan la Vinitière

The names of Alice la Saucère and Joan la Vinitière have already been mentioned in earlier chapters.[3] Alice had been the wife of Master John le Sauser, the 'sauce-maker' for King Edward I and other clients, and had joined her husband in various purchases and leases of property, including several in Tothill Street where their own house was, and in various lands in Eye.[4] They had no children, so when John died in the early years of the 1300s, Alice inherited his share of the estate which they had built up, and she probably continued his business, becoming known from that time as 'la Saucère'.

She also continued to deal in property on her own account, including another large house in Tothill Street and other lands.[5] In about 1323 she remarried. Her new husband was another property owner in Westminster, Richard of Reding who was an apothecary; but he died soon afterwards, apparently without other heirs, and Alice again became an heiress.[6] However she herself died late in the following year, and (for reasons which are not clear) Richard's brother, Henry of Reding, then granted all Richard and Alice's properties (which, according to him, 'ought to pass to me') to John Gyles 'of Westminster' and another heiress, Joan la Vinitière.[7] In this, John Gyles may have been acting as a trustee or other agent for Joan, a role in land-transactions which was to become well-known in Westminster and to be used extensively by the abbey later in the same century. But the

---

1   See Rosser *Medieval Westminster*, p. 45.
2   See Rosser, *ibid*, p. 54.
3   See pp. 346 n. 80, 280 n. 70 and 282 n. 79 above.
4   WAMs 17467, 17485, 17530, 17493, 17594. One of their Tothill houses was 'Giffardeshalle', which had once belonged to John Giffard, a '*narrator*', one of the early serjeants at law before the Bench, who sold it to a justice who later sold it to the Sausers, see Plates 17 and 18 showing serjeants in action (in 1460). For the Sausers' lands in Eye, see pp. 346-7 above; and also WAM 4826.
5   WAMs 17577, 17640, 17644, 17534, 17561. This house in Tothill Street was 'Elthammesmes', being probably 'Eltham's messuage', the former house of Master Richard of Eltham, a mason in the abbey-rebuilding.
6   WAMs 17528-9. Richard of Reding had acted for and was paid by Abbot Wenlock, Harvey, *Wenlok*, pp. 203, et al.; and acted professionally as apothecary/physician for the monks in 1309-10, Harvey, *Living and Dying*, 231.
7   WAMs 17582, 17584, 17585, and cf. 17583 and 17586. The terms of Joan's acquisitions from Henry are not known to me, but may emerge with further study.

name Gyles has a different resonance in the story to come.

Joan la Vinitière matched Alice la Saucère in many respects. With her husband Ralph Vintner, she had lived at their house outside the king's palace gate, where Ralph had practised his wine trade, with the king and other clients.[8] Like Master John le Sauser, Ralph had died in the early 1300s, leaving no children, so Joan had inherited the family properties and (to judge by her subsequent name) probably continued her husband's business after his death. In the course of her widowhood she became, as we have seen, the holder of Alice's accumulated empire of properties in 1324. Remarkably Joan la Vinitière then appears to have survived until about 1347-1348 – at about the time of the arrival of the Black Death in England.

Apart from the properties which she had inherited or otherwise acquired, Joan had also been an heiress in her own right, having been given five tenements in Westminster, 'with houses built on them', by her own mother Gillian (the widowed wife of, probably, Geoffrey of the Hyde). Later after the death of her husband, Joan (who was sister to John of the Hyde) managed to retain these houses, when young John of the Hyde, Joan's nephew, made a legal claim against her to acquire them for himself.[9]

The eventual destiny of Joan's empire was planned well before her death, when in 1334 she apparently chose to have 'all her lands in Westminster, Eye and Knightsbridge' settled jointly, in effect, on herself and an illegitimate daughter (also called Joan) of a property-owner well-known in Westminster, Thomas of Langford.[10] It seems that the purpose of this complicated operation was to make the illegitimate daughter the inheritor of all Joan la Vinitière's lands and other property when she died. Anyone reading this might well think that the illegitimate daughter must have been Joan la Vinitière's own child by Thomas, but we are told

that she was Thomas's child 'begotten on the body of Agnes Gyles', the same patronymic as John Gyles had had. Exactly what the circumstances in which all this was done, we may never know.

However both Joan la Vinitière and Thomas of Langford died, probably in about 1347-48. I suppose that his daughter Joan then became the owner of Joan la Vinitiere's former properties, and she certainly inherited her father's as well. As a rich heiress, she soon married Robert of Longdon, and when later he too died, at least all the former lands of Thomas of Langford were donated or sold by his daughter to nominees for the abbey.[11]

**Alice Lawes and Joan Lawes**

From this truncated history it is clear that much consolidation of estates was taking place in Westminster during the first half of the fourteenth century, and land-holders from the previous century had remained active into the next. Nor were these two women alone. Two sisters, Alice Lawes and Joan Lawes, were each married: the former to Geoffrey of Tyteburst, a landowner in Westminster, and the latter to John son of Richard de Aqua (*attewatere*), the abbey's serjeant of the gate and prison. Then like Alice la Saucère and Joan la Vinitière, Alice Tyteburst (formerly Lawes) was also widowed and considerable property interests accrued to her, before she eventually sold some of them to a man known as Richard of Sudbury, and after her death the rest were sold to the same man.[12]

But then in turn her sister Joan Lawes and her husband John de Aqua appear to have had a claim on the main group of five shops, two houses, other tenements in Westminster and land in Eye, which Geoffrey and Alice Tyteburst had previously received from various vendors, including Alice la Saucère; and so this claim of the Water family (the Aquas) had to be bought off by Richard of Sudbury.[13] But ultimately it seems that these

---

8   See pp. 279-82 above.
9   See pp. 281-2 above, and WAM 17496. The claim was by another writ of *mort d'ancestor*, see p. 67 n.20.
10  WAMs 17619, 16258, 17620; and cf. 17640. Thomas of Longford had been a steward of Abbot Wenlock in 1306-07 (see Harvey, *Wenlok*, p. 27) and had had a lease for life of a house in Tothill St. from the abbey in 1319 (WAM 17573). The complicated transactions made suggest he was acting as a trustee or agent for both Joans (and ? with distant thoughts for the abbey). A similar transaction was made 11 years later, as to Alice la Saucère's 'Giffardeshalle', 'Elthammesmes' and other properties; it is not clear why.
11  WAM 17668 (March 1362), and see 17672, 22937, 17676, 17677, 17684, 4781, 17646. The rest is not clear.
12  WAMs 17589, 17590, and 17588; see also 4826, 17487, 17484B, 17490, 17558, 17568, 17569, 17590, 17591A, 17595, 17615-7. There had even been Tyteburst transactions with Alice la Saucère.
13  WAM 17592.

properties must have returned to the possession of the abbey because the final reversionary interests in all of them had been granted to the abbot in 1325 by Geoffrey's brother William who must have inherited them after the life interest of the surviving Alice Tyteburst in them expired on her death.[14]

## John le Convers II

A further inquiry, again prompted by the evidence from the thirteenth century, relates to the personal and proprietorial history of 'another' later John le Convers, probably the son and heir of the John le Convers in Edward I's reign.[15] John (II)'s second wife in about 1346 was Denise Werdale, the widow of John Pelham of the La Hyde estate.[16] Denise as a widow had granted at least one lease of lands in Eye, presumably in the La Hyde area, but after her re-marriage to John le Convers (II), she and he together acquired the (whole?) La Hyde lands in May 1348. But then each of them died in the Black Death.[17]

John II's sister Cristine and her husband Peter of Alnemouth of Newcastle on Tyne then inherited John's large estate; and from it, in 1350-1 sold off 100 acres of land in Eye for £66. 13. 4d; and in 1352, 91 acres of lands in Knightsbridge, Kensington, Chelsea and Eye for the same price, in each case to nominees for the abbey.[18]

---

14  WAMs 17591A, and cf. 17616
15  See pp. 283-5 above.  The long period between the two episodes in which a John le Convers was involved suggests there were two with the same name.  And the first John le Convers was married to a Joan.
16  See p. 283. For the history of John (II) and Denise and their deaths, see WAM 16255 (NB. the memo on its back).  John (II) too had remarried Denise after a divorce (his first wife Amy is irrelevant to the present issues).
17  WAM 4767; WAM 16255.
18  For some of the abbey's acquisitions, see Harvey, *WA Estates*, 418-419.  For earlier transactions, see WAMs 4770, 4827, 4767, 4782*, 4765, 4882, 4780, 4882, 1571, 16209, 16210, 16232, 16255, 16270, 16272, 16283, 16283*.  The above summary of the situation is offered for what it is worth, without my chasing the issue still further.  There may well be other questions and answers.

# Select Bibliography

The main source of original material used has been the somewhat scattered collection of charters among the Westminster Abbey Muniments ('WAM'). The total number of these extant charters, over the *whole* medieval period, have been assessed at about two thousand. Many of these charters are grants or commands by a king or magnate, but many more are, in effect, contracts or other records of the transfer of lands in Westminster (or other dealings) between private indivduals, or between an individual and the abbey. It is the latter categories which have been of main value to me. Such charters made between 1066 and about 1214 were assembled and copied or calendared in 1988 by Dr Emma Mason in her *Westminster Abbey Charters* ('WAC'). In footnotes giving the grounds for what I have said, I have referred to many of these records (both before and, or course, after 1214, the terminal date in WAC), and the main ones so used come from the abbey's groups of WAMs 17300-99, 17400-99 and 17500-99, but others cited or consulted (but not cited) by me come randomly from the groups WAMs 17100s, or the 4000s, the 5000s, the 16000s, and indeed elsewhere.

## MAIN PRINTED SOURCES

*The Beauchamp Cartulary Charters 1100-1268*, ed. E. Mason (1980)
*Calendar of the Feet of Fines for London and Middlesex*, ed. W. Hardy and W. Page (1892)
*Calendar of Close Rolls* (HMSO, 1911-)
*Calendar of Liberate Rolls* (HMSO, 1916-)
*Calendar of Patent Rolls* (HMSO, 1901-)
*Curia Regis Rolls* (HMSO, 1922-)
*Customary of the Monasteries of St. Augustine, Canterbury & St. Peter, Westminster*, ed. EM Thompson
*Documents illustrating the Rule of Walter de Wenlok*, ed. B. Harvey (1965)
Flete, John, *The History of Westminster Abbey*, ed. JA Robinson (1909)
*Letters of Osbert de Clare, Prior of Westminster*, ed. EW Williamson (1929)
Matthew Paris, *Chronica Majora*, ed. H. Luard, RS (1872-84)
*Red Book of the Exchequer*, ed. H. Hall, RS (1896)
*Westminster Abbey Charters 1066-c.1214*, ed. E. Mason (1988)

## SECONDARY WORKS

| | |
|---|---|
| Barlow, F | *Edward the Confessor* (1970) |
| Barron, C | *The Parish of St. Andrew, Holborn* (1979) |
| Barton, N | *The Lost Rivers of London* (1992) |
| Bradbury, J | *Stephen and Matilda* (1998) |
| Brand, P | *The Making of the Common Law* (1992) |
| Brooke & Keir | *London 800-1216 : the shaping of a City* (1975) |
| Burman, E | *The Templars* (1986) |
| Carpenter, DA | *The Reign of Henry III* (1996) |
| Clanchy, MR | *From Memory to Written Word* (1993) |
| Clay, CT | 'Keepership of the old Palace of Westminster' *EHR* 59 (1944) 1 |
| Colvin, H | *The History of the King's Works*, vol. 1 (1963) |
| Crouch, D | *William Marshal: Court, Career and Chivalry* (1990) |
| Denham-Young, N | *Richard of Cornwall* (1947) |
| Duggan, C | 'Richard of Ilchester', *TRHS* (5th) 16 (1965) 1 |
| Dyer, C | *Everyday Life in Medieval England* (2000) |

| | |
|---|---|
| Farmer, A | *Hampstead Heath* (1984) |
| Foster, R | *Patterns of Thought* (1991) |
| Gatty, C | *Mary Davies and the Manor of Ebury* (1921) |
| Gelling, M | *Place-names in the Landscape* (1984) |
| Gem, RD | 'Romanesque Rebuilding of Westminster Abbey' *A-NS* 3 (1981) 33 |
| Green, JA | *The Government of England under Henry I* (1986) |
| Harding, A | *England in the Thirteenth Century* (1993) |
| Harvey, B | 'Abbot Gervase and the fee-farms of Westminster Abbey' *BIHR* 40/127 |
| Harvey, B | *Living and Dying in England. The Monastic Experience* (1993) |
| Harvey, B | *Westminster Abbey and its Estates in the Middle Ages* (1977) |
| Harvey, J | *English Medieval Architects* (1987) |
| Honeybourne, MB | 'The Fleet and its neighbourhood', *LTR* xix (1947) 13 |
| Honeybourne, MB | 'Leper Hospitals of the London area', *TLMAS* 21 (1963-7) 3 |
| James, MR | 'The Drawings of Matthew Paris', *Walpole Society* 14 (1925-26) 1 |
| Joliffe, J | 'The *'camera regis'* under Henry II' *EHR* 68 (1953) 337 |
| Kennedy, J | *The Manor and Parish Church of Hampstead* (1906) |
| Knowles, D | 'The Growth of Exemption', *Downside Review* 50 (1932) 201 and 396 |
| Knowles, D | *The Monastic Order in England 940-1216* (1963) |
| Lancaster, R Kent | 'Artisans, Suppliers and Clerks: patronage of Henry III' *Jo.W&CI* (1972) |
| Lees, B | *Records of the Templars in the Twelfth Century* (1935) |
| Lewis, S | *The Art of Matthew Paris in the Chronica Majora* (1987) |
| Mason, E | 'The Mauduits & their Chamberlainship' *BIHR* 49 (1976) 1 |
| Mason, E | *Westminster Abbey and its People c.* 1050-1216 (1996) |
| Miller E & Hatcher J | *Medieval England. Rural Society & Economic Change 1086-1348* (1980) |
| Mortimer, R | *Angevin England 1154-1258* (1994) |
| Parker, R | *The Common Stream* (1976) |
| Pearce, EH | *The Monks of Westminster* (1916) |
| Pearce, EH | *Walter de Wenlok, Abbot of Westminster* (1920) |
| Postan, MM | *The Medieval Economy and Society* (1975) |
| Powicke, FM | *King Henry III & the Lord Edward* (1947) |
| Powicke, FM | *The Thirteenth Century* (1953) |
| Prestwich, M | *Edward I* (1997) |
| Reynolds, S | *An Introduction to the History of English medieval towns* (1977) |
| Reynolds, S | *Fiefs and Vassals* (1994) |
| Richardson and Sayles | *The Governance of Medieval England* (1963) |
| Richardson, HG | 'William of Ely', *TRHS* (4th) 15 (1932) 45 |
| Robinson, JA | *Gilbert Crispin, Abbot of Westminster* (1911) |
| Rosser, G | *Medieval Westminster 1200-1540* (1989) |
| Round, JH | *Geoffrey de Mandeville* (1892) |
| Rutton, WL | 'The Manor of Eia', *Archaeologia* 62 (1910) 31 |
| Saunders, G | 'The situation and extent of Westminster', *Archaeologia* 26 (1836) 223 |
| Salzman, L | *Building in England, down to 1540* (1967) |
| Sayles, GO | *The King's Parliament of England* (1974) |
| Stacey, RC | *Politics, Policy and Finance under Henry III* (1987) |
| Stenton, FM | *The First Century of English Feudalism* 1066-1166 (1932) |
| Tout, TF | *Chapters in the Administrative History of Medieval England* (1920-33) |
| Turner, RA | *King John* (1994) |
| Turner, RA | *Men Raised from the Dust* (1988) |
| Warren, WL | *Henry II* (1973) |

# INDEX